D0934577

SYSTEMATIC THEOLOGY

Revised Edition

Edited By
Stanley M. Horton

LOGION PRESS

Springfield, Missouri

02–0319

4th Printing 2003

Logion Press books are published by Gospel Publishing House.

Library of Congress Cataloging-in-Publication Data

Systematic theology : / Stanley M. Horton,   general editor.
    p.   cm.
    Includes bibliographical references and indexes.
    ISBN 0–88243–319–9
    1. Theology, Doctrinal. 2. Pentecostal churches–Doctrines.
  I. Horton, Stanley M.
  BX8762.Z5S97   1994
230'.994–dc20   93–23568

Printed in the United States of America

Contents

List of Contributors

Benny C. Aker, Ph.D., Professor of New Testament and Exegesis at Assemblies of God Theological Seminary

Carolyn Denise Baker, M.Div., Instructor in Bible and Theology at American Indian Bible College and National Appointed Home Missionary

Michael L. Dusing, D.Min., Professor and Department Chair, Theology and Philosophy at Southeastern College of the Assemblies of God

John R. Higgins, Th.D., Educator, Missionary to India

Stanley M. Horton, Th.D., Distinguished Professor Emeritus of Bible and Theology at Assemblies of God Theological Seminary

Timothy P. Jenney, Ph.D., Associate Professor of Pastoral Ministries at North Central Bible College

Russell Joyner, MATS, Associate Pastor of West End Assembly of God, Richmond, Virginia

Byron D. Klaus, D.Min., Professor of Church Leadership at Southern California College

David Lim, D.Min., Senior Pastor of Grace Assembly of God in Singapore

Frank D. Macchia, Th.D., Associate Professor of Theology at Southeastern College of the Assemblies of God

Bruce R. Marino, Ph.D., Assistant Professor of Bible and Theology at Valley Forge Christian College

Gary B. McGee, Ph.D., Professor of Church History, Chair, Bible and Theology Department at Assemblies of God Theological Seminary

Mark D. McLean, Ph.D., Professor of Biblical Studies at Evangel College

Kerry D. McRoberts, M.A., M.C.S., Assistant Professor of Bible and Theology at Trinity Bible College

Timothy Munyon, M.A., Assistant Professor of Biblical Studies and Greek at Trinity Bible College

David R. Nichols, Ph.D., Associate Professor of Pastoral Studies at North Central Bible College

Daniel B. Pecota, D.Min., Professor of Theology, Greek, and Bible, Divisional Coordinator for Religious and Ministerial Studies at Northwest College of the Assemblies of God

Vernon Purdy, Ph.D. Candidate, Assistant Professor in Bible, Central Bible College

James H. Railey, Jr., Ph.D. Candidate, Associate Professor of Practical Theology at Assemblies of God Theological Seminary

John W. Wyckoff, Ph.D., Professor of Bible and Theology, Chair, Church Ministries Division at Southwestern Assemblies of God College

Preface

During the early centuries of the history of the Church, many stated their faith in letters, creeds, and confessions. These theological affirmations were used in the worship and in the defense of the faith. So it is to this day: The Church continues to affirm its faith in the revelation of God in Christ through the ongoing work of theological writing and dialogue.

This present volume comes from the Pentecostal community of faith and is the work of teachers of Bible and theology in the seminary and colleges of the Assemblies of God. It is a statement that the work of theology is valued and approached seriously and earnestly in the Pentecostal branch of the Church.

The first intended audience for this book is the students at the institutions represented by the authors. They deserve to read theology from the perspectives of teachers within the educational community in which they are studying. The clergy of the Assemblies of God and other Pentecostal fellowships, too, should have the privilege of a theological presentation that is in keeping with the faith they have received and are passing on to the congregations they serve. Local church members will also profit from reading this biblical affirmation of faith. Other churches and denominations can receive benefit as well, for most of the truths defended in this work are also held by all Bible believers.

I wish to thank Dr. G. Raymond Carlson, general superintendent of the Assemblies of God (1985–93); the Assemblies of God Theological Seminary; Central Bible College; Berean College; the Postsecondary Education Department of the Assemblies of God; the Division of Foreign Missions of the Assemblies of God; and others who have made this project possible. Special thanks are due to Dr. Edgar Lee, Dr. Elmer Kirsch, Dr. Zenas Bicket, and Rev. David Bundrick, who have read the manuscripts and made many helpful suggestions. Special thanks also are due to Glen Ellard and his editorial staff for their expert help.

In line with the usage of both the KJV and the NIV, Lord is used in capitals and small capitals where the Hebrew of the Old Testament has the personal, divine name of God, Yahweh (which was probably pronounced *ya-wā*).[1]

In quoted Scripture, words the authors wish to emphasize are in italics.

For easier reading, Hebrew, Aramaic, and Greek words are all transliterated with English letters.

These abbreviations have been used:

AV: Authorized Version
BDB: *New Brown-Driver-Briggs Gesenius Hebrew and English Lexicon*
DPCM: *Dictionary of Pentecostal and Charismatic Movements*
Ger.: German
Gk.: Greek
Heb.: Hebrew
KJV: King James Version
Lat.: Latin
NASB: *New American Standard Bible*
NCV: New Century Version
NEB: *The New English Bible*
NIV: New International Version
NKJV: New King James Version
NRS: New Revised Standard Version
RSV: Revised Standard Version

STANLEY M. HORTON
GENERAL EDITOR

---

[1]The Hebrew wrote only the consonants YHWH. Later traditions followed the New Latin JHVH and added vowels from the Hebrew for "Lord" to remind them to read *Lord* instead of the divine name. But this was never intended to be read "Jehovah."

CHAPTER ONE
Historical Background

Gary B. McGee

Someone once remarked that Pentecostalism is an experience looking for a theology, as if the movement lacked roots in biblical interpretation and Christian doctrine. Research on the historical and theological development of Pentecostal beliefs, however, has revealed a complex theological tradition. It bears strong commonalities with evangelical doctrines while testifying to long-neglected truths about the work of the Holy Spirit in the life and mission of the Church.

Beginning with the theological background of Pentecostalism, this chapter then focuses on the growth of Assemblies of God theology since the organization's founding in 1914. Factors considered include paramount concerns, influential personalities, significant literature, and various means employed to preserve doctrine.

THE CONTINUANCE OF THE CHARISMATA

Throughout the history of Christianity, there have always been individuals seeking for "something more" in their spiritual pilgrimage, occasionally prompting them to explore the meaning of Spirit baptism and spiritual gifts. Recent scholarship has shed new light on the history of charismatic movements, demonstrating that such interest in the work of the Holy Spirit has remained throughout the history of the Church.[1]

---

[1]According to Killian McDonnell and George T. Montague, *Christian Initiation and Baptism in the Holy Spirit* (Collegeville, Minn.: Liturgical Press, 1991), baptism in the Holy Spirit was an integral (normative) part of Christian initiation during the first eight centuries of the Church. For a related study on the second- and third-century North African church see

At least two revivals in the nineteenth century could be considered forerunners of modern Pentecostalism. The first occurred in England (beginning in 1830) during the ministry of Edward Irving and the second in the southern tip of India (beginning around 1860) through the influence of Plymouth Brethren theology and the leadership of the Indian churchman J. C. Aroolappen. Contemporaneous reports on both included references to speaking in tongues and prophecy.[2]

In part, the conclusions of this research correct the belief in some quarters that the *charismata* necessarily ceased with the Apostolic Era, a view most forcefully proposed by Benjamin B. Warfield in his *Counterfeit Miracles* (1918). Warfield contended that the objective, written authority of Scripture as inspired by the Holy Spirit would inevitably be undermined by those who taught a subjective concept of the Spirit.[3] In recent years, this perspective has steadily lost ground in evangelical circles.[4]

Cecil M. Robeck, Jr., *Prophecy in Carthage: Perpetua, Tertullian, and Cyprian* (Cleveland: Pilgrim Press, 1993). A survey of occurrences of charismatic gifts to the end of the third century is provided by Ronald A. N. Kydd in *Charismatic Gifts in the Early Church* (Peabody, Mass.: Hendrickson Publishers, 1984). Stanley M. Burgess furnishes a broader study of Latin, Greek, and Syrian spiritual writers to the end of the medieval period in *The Spirit and the Church: Antiquity* (Peabody, Mass.: Hendrickson Publishers, 1984) and *The Holy Spirit: Eastern Christian Traditions* (Peabody, Mass.: Hendrickson Publishers, 1989).

[2]For a helpful bibliography see David D. Bundy, "Irving, Edward," in *The Dictionary of Pentecostal and Charismatic Movements*, ed. Stanley M. Burgess, Gary B. McGee, and Patrick Alexander (Grand Rapids: Zondervan Publishing House, 1988), 470–71; hereinafter *DPCM*. For the thesis that Irving's doctrine of speaking in tongues served as the "standing sign" of Spirit baptism and parallels the later view of tongues as "initial evidence," see David W. Dorries, "Edward Irving and the 'Standing Sign' of Spirit Baptism," in *Initial Evidence: Historical and Biblical Perspectives on the Pentecostal Doctrine of Spirit Baptism*, ed. Gary B. McGee (Peabody, Mass.: Hendrickson Publishers, 1991), 41–56. For the revival in south India, see G. H. Lang, *The History and Diaries of an Indian Christian* (London: Thynne and Co., 1939); *Memoir of Anthony Norris Groves*, 3d ed. (London: James Nisbet and Co., 1869), 571–640.

[3]Warfield and other theologians of the "Old Princeton" school of theology represented antirevivalist sentiments in American Presbyterianism. See Mark A. Noll, ed. and comp., *The Princeton Theology: 1812–1921* (Grand Rapids: Baker Book House, 1983); Jon Ruthven, "On the Cessation of the Charismata: The Protestant Polemic of Benjamin B. Warfield," *Pneuma: The Journal of the Society for Pentecostal Studies* 12 (Spring 1990): 14–31.

[4]This is evident in Millard J. Erickson, *Christian Theology* (Grand Rapids: Baker Book House, 1985), 880–82.

With the coming of late seventeenth- and eighteenth-century revivalism in Europe and North America, Calvinist, Lutheran, and evangelical Arminian preachers emphasized repentance and piety in the Christian life.[5] Any study of Pentecostalism must pay close attention to the happenings of this period and particularly to the doctrine of Christian perfection taught by John Wesley, the father of Methodism, and his associate John Fletcher. Wesley's publication of *A Short Account of Christian Perfection* (1760) urged his followers to seek a new spiritual dimension in their lives. This second work of grace, distinct from conversion, would deliver one from the defect in one's moral nature that prompts sinful behavior.

CHAPTER

1

Historical Background

This teaching spread to America and inspired the growth of the Holiness movement.[6] With the focus on the sanctified life but without the mention of speaking in tongues, Pentecostal imagery from Scripture (e.g., "outpouring of the Spirit," "baptism in the Holy Spirit," "the tongue of fire") eventually became a hallmark of Holiness literature and hymnody. One of the foremost leaders in the Wesleyan wing of the movement, Phoebe Palmer, a Methodist, edited the *Guide to Holiness* and wrote, among other books, *The Promise of the Father* (1859). Another popular writer, William Arthur, authored the best-seller *Tongue of Fire* (1856).

Those who sought to receive the "second blessing" were taught that each Christian needed to "tarry" (Luke 24:49, KJV) for the promised baptism in the Holy Spirit; this would break the power of inbred sin and usher the believer into the Spirit-filled life. Furthermore, Joel had prophesied that as a result

---

[5]See F. E. Stoeffler, *The Rise of Evangelical Pietism* (Leiden: E. J. Brill, 1965), and *German Pietism During the Eighteenth Century* (Leiden: E. J. Brill, 1973); on the popular level see Dale W. Brown, *Understanding Pietism* (Grand Rapids: Wm. B. Eerdmans, 1978). For the Great Awakening in Britain and North America, see Robert G. Tuttle, Jr., *John Wesley: His Life and Theology* (Grand Rapids: Zondervan Publishing House, 1978); Jonathan Edwards, *Religious Affections* (1746); Darrett B. Rutman, ed., *The Great Awakening* (New York: John Wiley and Sons, 1970).

[6]See Donald W. Dayton, *Theological Roots of Pentecostalism* (Metuchen, N.J.: Scarecrow Press, 1987); and Melvin E. Dieter, *The Holiness Revival of the Nineteenth Century* (Metuchen, N.J.: Scarecrow Press, 1980). See also the "Higher Christian Life" series, a collection of Holiness and Pentecostal reprints issued by Garland Publishing, Inc.

of the outpouring of God's Spirit "your *sons and daughters* will prophesy" in the last days (Joel 2:28).[7]

Belief in a second work of grace was not confined to the Methodist circuit. For example, Charles G. Finney believed that Spirit baptism provided divine empowerment to achieve Christian perfection[8] at the same time that his theology refused to fit comfortably in either Wesleyan or Reformed categories. Although historic Reformed theology has identified Spirit baptism with conversion, some revivalists within that tradition entertained the notion of a second work for empowering believers, among them Dwight L. Moody and R. A. Torrey. Even with this enduement of power, however, sanctification retained its progressive nature.[9] Another pivotal figure and former Presbyterian, A. B. Simpson, founder of the Christian and Missionary Alliance, strongly emphasized Spirit baptism and had a major impact on the formation of Assemblies of God doctrine.[10]

Similarly, the Keswick conferences in Great Britain (begun in 1875) also influenced American Holiness thinking. Keswick's teachers believed that baptism in the Holy Spirit brought an ongoing victorious life (the "higher," or "deeper," life), characterized by the "fullness of the Spirit." This became the interpretation they preferred rather than the Wesleyan concept, which maintained that Spirit baptism brought "sinless" perfection.[11]

In the nineteenth century, medical science advanced slowly, offering little help to the seriously ill. Belief in the miraculous power of God for physical healing found a reception in a few circles. In nineteenth-century Germany, ministries that highlighted prayer for the sick (especially those of Dorothea Trudel, Johann Christoph Blumhardt, and Otto Stockmayer)

---

[7]Appeal to this promise effectively laid the foundation for women to preach, and serve in other ministries. For rationales for this interpretation see Donald W. Dayton, ed., *Holiness Tracts Defending the Ministry of Women* (New York: Garland Publishing, 1985); Joseph R. Flower, "Does God Deny Spiritual Manifestations and Ministry Gifts to Women?" 7 November 1979 (typewritten).

[8]John L. Gresham, Jr., *Charles G. Finney's Doctrine of the Baptism of the Holy Spirit* (Peabody, Mass.: Hendrickson Publishers, 1987).

[9]Edith L. Waldvogel (Blumhofer), "The 'Overcoming Life': A Study in the Reformed Evangelical Origins of Pentecostalism" (Ph.D. dissertation, Harvard University, 1977).

[10]Charles W. Nienkirchen, *A. B. Simpson and the Pentecostal Movement* (Peabody, Mass.: Hendrickson Publishers, 1992).

[11]Dayton, *Theological Roots,* 104–6.

gained attention in America. Holiness theology, with its belief in instantaneous purification from sin or spiritual empowerment, provided a warm environment for the teaching of immediate healing by faith.[12]

For many believers, Spirit baptism fully restored the spiritual relationship that Adam and Eve had with God in the Garden of Eden. Significantly, the higher life in Christ could also reverse the physical effects of the Fall, enabling believers to take authority over sickness. Healing advocates such as Charles C. Cullis, A. B. Simpson, A. J. Gordon, Carrie Judd Montgomery, Maria B. Woodworth-Etter, and John Alexander Dowie based much of their belief on Isaiah 53:4–5, as well as New Testament promises of healing. Since Christ was not only the "sin-bearer," but also the "sickness-bearer," those who lived by faith in God's promise (Exod. 15:26) no longer required medical assistance, clearly betraying a lack of faith if they did.

The increasingly "Pentecostal" complexion of the Holiness movement disposed adherents to a consideration of the gifts of the Spirit in the life of the Church. While most assumed that speaking in tongues had ended with the Early Church, the other gifts, including healing, were available to Christians.[13] Nothing but unbelief now could prevent the New Testament Church from being reestablished in holiness and power.

But when the radical Wesleyan Holiness preacher Benjamin Hardin Irwin began teaching three works of grace in 1895, trouble lay ahead. For Irwin, the second blessing initiated sanctification, but the third brought the "baptism of burning love" (i.e., baptism in the Holy Spirit). The mainstream of the Holiness movement condemned this "third blessing heresy" (which, among other things, created the problem of distinguishing evidence for the third from that of the second). Even so, Irwin's notion of a third work of grace for power in Chris-

---

[12]Paul G. Chappell, "The Divine Healing Movement in America" (Ph.D. dissertation, Drew University, 1983); for an abridged edition, see Paul G. Chappell, "Healing Movements," in *DPCM,* 353–74.

[13]W. B. Godbey, *Spiritual Gifts and Graces* (Cincinnati: God's Revivalist Office, 1895; reprinted in *Six Tracts by W. B. Godbey,* ed. D. William Faupel [New York: Garland Publishing, 1985]); S. A. Keen, *Pentecostal Papers; or the Gift of the Holy Ghost* (Cincinnati: By the author, 1895), 151–90.

tian service laid an important foundation for the Pentecostal movement.[14]

PENTECOSTAL THEOLOGY AND MISSIONS

Although nineteenth-century evangelicals generally adopted amillennial or postmillennial views, it was the latter that caught the spirit of the age. Writers of all kinds, from Charles Darwin to John Henry Newman to Charles Hodge, saw the positive values of progress in science, formation of doctrine, and eschatology, respectively. Others, however, concluded that the condition of humankind would get worse before the imminent return of the Lord.[15]

Premillennialists' gloomy assessment of the immediate future generated serious concerns among those committed to world evangelization. The larger part of the missions movement had spent considerable time and energy on civilizing the native populations—in preparation for their conversion—by building schools, orphanages, and clinics. Because of the secondary emphasis on coversionary evangelism, the actual number of converts proved to be alarmingly small.[16] Premillennial expositions of Daniel, Zechariah, and Revelation; the rise of the Zionist movement; the arms race of the 1890s; and the approaching end of a century caused many to wonder aloud how the unreached millions would hear the gospel message to save them from eternal destruction.

The blending of the themes of Christ as Savior, Baptizer (Sanctifier), Healer, and Coming King, described as the "full gospel" or the "fourfold gospel," reflected the desire to restore New Testament Christianity in the last days. The widespread interest in the Spirit's baptism and gifts convinced some that God would bestow the gift of tongues to outfit them with identifiable human languages *(xenolalia)* to preach

---

[14]H. Vinson Synan, "Irwin, Benjamin Hardin," in *DPCM,* 471–72; that Irwin later joined the Pentecostal movement has become evident from the research of David D. Bundy in his "Spiritual Advice to a Seeker: Letters to T. B. Barratt from Azusa Street, 1906," *Pneuma: The Journal of the Society for Pentecostal Studies* 14 (Fall 1992): 167–68.

[15]Timothy P. Weber, *Living in the Shadow of the Second Coming: American Premillennialism: 1875–1925* (New York: Oxford University Press, 1979), and George M. Marsden, *Fundamentalism and American Culture* (New York: Oxford University Press, 1980).

[16]Kenneth Scott Latourette, *Missions Tomorrow* (New York: Harper and Brothers, 1936), 94–96; also William R. Hutchison, *Errand to the World: American Protestant Thought and Foreign Missions* (Chicago: University of Chicago Press, 1987), 99–100.

the gospel in other countries, thereby expediting missionary evangelism.

In one instance, revival at the Topeka, Kansas, YMCA in 1889–1890 triggered the organization of the Kansas–Sudan Mission, whose members shortly left for missionary work in West Africa. Passing through New York City, they visited A. B. Simpson's headquarters, where they heard his views on healing and became confident that the simple faith life and the power of the Spirit would prepare them for whatever lay ahead. One observer reported that "two of their main principles were Faith-healing, and Pentecostal gifts of tongues; no medicines were to be taken, no grammars or dictionaries made use of; the party was attacked by malignant fever; two died, refusing quinine."[17] And though the expedition ended in tragedy, the ideal lived on.

In 1895, the widely read Holiness author and editor W. B. Godbey predicted that the "Gift of Language" was "destined to play a conspicuous part in the evangelization of the heathen world, amid the glorious prophetical fulfillment of the latter days. All missionaries in heathen lands should seek and expect this Gift to enable them to preach fluently in the vernacular tongue, at the same time not depreciating their own efforts."[18] Many others shared the same hope.

Another advocate of this missionary use of tongues was Frank W. Sandford, founder of the Holy Ghost and Us Bible School at Shiloh, Maine, in 1895. Through his teaching and mission endeavors (publicized in *Tongues of Fire*) Sandford also hoped to speedily evangelize the world. Not only did he pray to receive the gift of "power and eloquence" for evangelism, but others did as well.[19]

By the turn of the century, the Holiness movement had become preoccupied with the "Pentecostal reformation of Wesleyan doctrine" and the four themes of the full gospel. In fact, when the Pentecostal movement began a few years later, only the priority given to the gift of tongues distin-

---

[17]Robert Needham Cust, *Evangelization of the Non-Christian World* (London: Luzac and Co., 1894), 106–7. See also his *Gospel Message* (London: Luzac and Co., 1896), 146. For Simpson's perspective on the restoration of the gift of tongues, see Nienkirchen, *A. B. Simpson*, 74–76.

[18]Godbey, *Spiritual Gifts and Graces,* 43; cf., id. *Tongue Movement, Satanic* (Zarephath, N.J.: Pillar of Fire, 1918); reprinted in Faupel, *Six Tracts,* 5.

[19]William Charles Hiss, "Shiloh: Frank W. Sandford and the Kingdom, 1893–1948" (Ph.D. dissertation, Tufts University, 1978), 101–4; for others who sought, 163.

CHAPTER

1

Historical
Background

guished it theologically from Holiness beliefs.[20] Daniel W. Kerr, the most influential theological voice in the early years of the Assemblies of God, remarked in 1922:

During the past few years God has enabled us to discover and recover this wonderful truth concerning the Baptism in the Spirit as it was given at the beginning. Thus we have all that the others got [i.e., Luther, Wesley, Blumhardt, Trudel, and A. B. Simpson], and we got this too. We see all they see, but they don't see what we see.[21]

With little difficulty, Pentecostals continued reading Holiness literature and singing such favorite songs as "The Cleansing Wave," "The Comforter Has Come," "Beulah Land," and "Old Time Power": New wine had been poured into old wine-skins.[22]

Also hoping that they too would receive the power of the Spirit to quickly evangelize the world were the Kansas Holiness preacher Charles Fox Parham and his followers. Convinced by their own study of the Book of Acts, and influenced by Irwin and Sandford, Parham reported a remarkable revival at the Bethel Bible School in Topeka, Kansas, in January 1901.[23] Most of the students and Parham himself rejoiced at being baptized in the Spirit and speaking in tongues (i.e., *xenolalia*). Just as God had filled the 120 with the Holy Spirit on the Day of Pentecost, they too had received the promise (Acts 2:39). In fact, the "apostolic faith" of the New Testament Church had at last been *fully* restored. It followed then that Bennett Freeman Lawrence would name the first history of the Pentecostal movement *The Apostolic Faith Restored* (1916).

Parham's distinctive theological contribution to the movement lies in his insistence that tongues represents the vital "Bible evidence" of the third work of grace: the baptism in the Holy Spirit, clearly illustrated in the pattern of chapters 2, 10, and 19 in Acts. In his *Voice Crying in the Wilderness* (1902, 1910), Parham wrote that recipients were sealed as

---

[20]Dayton, *Theological Roots,* 173–79.

[21]D. W. Kerr, "The Basis for Our Distinctive Testimony," *Pentecostal Evangel,* 2 September 1922, 4.

[22]Charles Edwin Jones, "Holiness Movement," in *DPCM,* 406–9; id., *Perfectionist Persuasion* (Metuchen, N.J.: Scarecrow Press, 1974).

[23]James R. Goff, Jr., *Fields White Unto Harvest: Charles F. Parham and the Missionary Origins of Pentecostalism* (Fayetteville, Ark.: University of Arkansas Press, 1988).

the "bride of Christ" (2 Cor. 1:21–22; Rev. 7; 21). Sanctified and prepared now as an elite band of end-time missionaries, they alone would be taken by Christ at the (pre-Tribulation) rapture of the Church after they had completed their role in fulfilling the Great Commission. Other Christians would face the ordeal of survival during the seven years of tribulation to follow.[24] Despite the eventual relegation of this teaching to the fringes of the Pentecostal movement, it did raise an issue that still lingers: the uniqueness of the Spirit's work in those who have spoken in tongues as compared with those who have not.[25]

Topeka contributed to the later internationally significant Azusa Street revival in Los Angeles, California (1906–1909). Its foremost leader was the African-American William J. Seymour,[26] and news of the "latter rain" (of Joel 2:23) quickly spread overseas through Seymour's newspaper, the *Apostolic Faith,* and the efforts of many who traveled from the Azusa Street meetings across North America and abroad.

Although other important Pentecostal revivals occurred (e.g., Zion, Ill.; Toronto; Dunn, N.C.), the complexity and meaning of the Los Angeles revival still challenges historians. Its themes of eschatological expectancy and evangelistic power (Parham's legacy) mapped the path taken by white Pentecostals in their aggressive efforts to preach the gospel "unto the uttermost part of the earth" (Acts 1:8, KJV).[27] African-American Pentecostals, on the other hand, have drawn attention to the reconciliation of the races and the outpouring of power on the downtrodden at Azusa, evidenced by the uncommon interracial makeup of the services, catalyzed by

---

[24]Charles F. Parham, *A Voice Crying in the Wilderness* (Baxter Springs, Kan.: Apostolic Faith Bible College, reprint of 1910 ed.), 30–32; id., *The Everlasting Gospel* (Baxter Springs, Kan.: Apostolic Faith Bible College, reprint of 1911 ed.), 63–69; see also Goff, *Fields White,* 77–79.

[25]Gordon Anderson, "Pentecostal Hermeneutics," paper presented at the 22d annual meeting of the Society for Pentecostal Studies, Springfield, Missouri, November 1992, 12–14. See also, Gordon D. Fee, *Gospel and Spirit: Issues in New Testament Hermeneutics* (Peabody, Mass.: Hendrickson Publishers, 1991), 105–19.

[26]Cecil M. Robeck, Jr., "Azusa Street Revival" in *DPCM,* 31–36; also, Frank Bartleman, *What Really Happened at "Azusa Street?"* ed. John Walker (Northridge, Calif.: Voice Christian Publications, 1962; original printing, 1925); and Douglas J. Nelson, "For Such a Time as This: The Story of Bishop William J. Seymour and the Azusa Street Revival" (Ph.D. dissertation, Birmingham University, 1981).

[27]For Parham's legacy, see Goff, *Fields White;* also id., "Initial Tongues in the Theology of Charles Fox Parham," in *Initial Evidence,* 57–71.

the fruit of the Spirit (Seymour's legacy).[28] Both are vital parts of the story. Even though the burden for evangelism inspired global outreach, Pentecostals have much to learn from the message of reconciliation that also highlighted the revival.[29]

DIVISIONS OVER THEOLOGICAL DIFFERENCES

Theological differences did not evaporate in the excitement of announcing the coming of the latter rain. Three major controversies faced the new movement in the first sixteen years of its existence.

The first issue to divide Pentecostals arose in late 1906. It centered on the theological value of narrative literature (Acts and the longer ending of Mark 16) in building the case for the doctrine of tongues as the "initial evidence" of Spirit baptism. Those who followed in Parham's wake considered tongues evidential and the pattern in Acts authoritative, as much as any propositional passages. That is, tongues in Acts seemed to have the function of being evidence of the baptism; whereas tongues in 1 Corinthians had other functions: for the individual's prayer life (14:4,14,28) and (with interpretation) for the congregation's edification (14:5,27). But to those who scrutinized the Book of Acts from what they considered a Pauline point of view, the tongues in Acts was not different from the gift of tongues in Corinthians.[30]

Those who believe in tongues as initial evidence of Spirit baptism have followed the hermeneutical pattern of other restorationists: elevating factors in the life of the Church to doctrinal standing. After all, how could one possibly deny that the theme of Acts is the Spirit's work of sending the disciples to preach the gospel to the whole world, accompanied by "signs and wonders" (Acts 4:29–30)? In this doctrine, and in some circles the doctrine of footwashing, Trinitarian Pentecostals appealed to a doctrinal pattern in narrative literature.

During the years after 1906, more and more Pentecostals

---

[28]For Seymour's legacy, see Cecil M. Robeck, Jr., "William J. Seymour and 'the Bible Evidence,'" in *Initial Evidence,* 72–95; Leonard Lovett, "Black Holiness-Pentecostalism," in *DPCM,* 76–84; and Walter J. Hollenweger, *Pentecost Between Black and White* (Belfast: Christian Journals, 1974).

[29]Murray W. Dempster, "Pentecostal and Charismatic Scholars Call for End to Apartheid," *Transformation* (January/March 1992): 32–33.

[30]See Gary B. McGee, "Early Pentecostal Hermeneutics: Tongues as Evidence in the Book of Acts," in *Initial Evidence,* 96–118.

recognized that in most instances of tongues, believers were actually praying in unidentifiable rather than identifiable languages (i.e., *glossolalia* rather than *xenolalia*). Although Parham retained his view of the preaching nature of tongues, more and more Pentecostals concluded that tongues represented prayer in the Spirit, intercession, and praise.[31]

The second debate revolved around the second work of grace, sanctification: Was it instantaneous or progressive? Predictably, the lines were drawn between those Pentecostals with Wesleyan sympathies (three works of grace) and those with Reformed sympathies (two works). In the sermon "The Finished Work of Calvary" (preached in 1910 at the Pentecostal Convention at the Stone Church in Chicago, Illinois), Baptist-turned-Pentecostal William H. Durham declared that the problem of inbred sin had been dealt the fatal blow, having been crucified with Christ on the cross. By placing faith in the efficacy of that event, a person could continue to bear spiritual fruit from Christ's imputed righteousness.[32]

The third contention among Pentecostals resulted from the restorationist impulse and the heavy Christological emphasis of the full gospel. Questions about the nature of the Godhead manifested themselves at the international Pentecostal camp meeting at Arroyo Seco (near Los Angeles). During a baptismal sermon preached by R. E. McAlister, he observed that the apostles had baptized using the name of Jesus (Acts 2:38) instead of the Trinitarian formula (Matt. 28:19). Those who felt they had discovered more light on the restoration of the New Testament Church were rebaptized in the name of Jesus, following what they considered another pattern in the Book of Acts. Several people, including Frank J. Ewart, continued their study of water baptism and from this a new grouping of churches developed.[33]

---

[31]A. G. Garr, "Tongues, the Bible Evidence," *A Cloud of Witnesses to Pentecost in India* (September 1907): 42–44; Carrie Judd Montgomery, "The Promise of the Father," *Triumphs of Faith* (July 1908): 149. An insightful discussion on the meaning of Spirit Baptism to early Pentecostals can be found in Edith L. Blumhofer, *Pentecost in My Soul* (Springfield, Mo.: Gospel Publishing House, 1989), 17–38.

[32]D. William Faupel, "William H. Durham and the Finished Work of Calvary," in *Pentecost, Mission and Ecumenism,* ed. Jan A. B. Jongeneel (Frankfurt am Main: Peter Lang, 1992), 85–95.

[33]Frank J. Ewart, *The Phenomenon of Pentecost* (St. Louis: Pentecostal Publishing House, 1947). For a Oneness discourse on the Trinity see David K. Bernard, *The Oneness of God* (Hazelwood, Mo.: Word Aflame Press, 1983); for a Trinitarian response see Carl Brumback, *God in Three Persons* (Cleveland, Tenn.: Pathway Press, 1959); for a historical study see David A. Reed, "Origins and Development of the Theology of Oneness Pentecostalism in the United States" (Ph.D. dissertation, Boston University, 1978).

These believers emphasized the "oneness," or unity, of the Godhead in contrast to the orthodox Christian view of one God in three Persons.[34] In addition, Oneness theologians maintained that since Jesus Christ is the redemptive name of God, it is through that name that salvation and God's blessings are bestowed. Two camps have existed within the Oneness movement from the beginning: those who believe that conversion and water baptism in the name of Jesus are followed by a second experience of empowerment and those who maintain that the three elements of Acts 2:38 (repentance, baptism in Jesus' name, and receiving the Holy Spirit [speaking in tongues]) converge in one act of grace, the new birth.[35]

With the condemnation of the Oneness issue, the fathers and mothers of the Assemblies of God assumed that the restoration of the apostolic faith had been protected from error. In the years that followed, they concentrated on preserving the truths of the revival.

DEVELOPMENT OF ASSEMBLIES OF GOD THEOLOGY

When the General Council (an abbreviated title for the General Council of the Assemblies of God) came into being at Hot Springs, Arkansas, in April 1914, doctrinal consensus already existed among the participants, built on the historic truths of the faith and embellished by Wesleyan Holiness and Keswickian themes. When asked in 1919 what these Pentecostals believed, E. N. Bell, a member of the Executive Presbytery and the first general chairman (termed general superintendent later), began his response by saying:

These assemblies are opposed to all radical Higher Criticism of the Bible and against all modernism and infidelity in the Church, against people unsaved and full of sin and worldliness belonging to the church. They believe in all the real Bible truths held by all real Evangelical churches.[36]

However, the first General Council had not been convened to write a new creed or to lay the basis for a new denomination. Rather, the delegates simply adopted the proposed "Preamble and Resolution on Constitution," depicting their

---

[34]See chap. 5, pp. 171–76.

[35]David A. Reed, "Oneness Pentecostalism," in *DPCM,* 650–51.

[36]E. N. Bell, "Questions and Answers," *Pentecostal Evangel,* 27 December 1919, 5.

concerns and containing several important beliefs, chose officers, and approved incorporation.[37]

Like other Pentecostals, Assemblies of God members have been characterized by five implicit values: personal experience, oral communication (also reflected in testimonials in church magazines, booklets, Sunday school literature, pamphlets, and tracts), spontaneity, otherworldliness, and scriptural authority. All of them are observable in conceptions of leadership, life-style, worship, and church literature.[38] These values define much of the uniqueness of Pentecostalism and explain why little emphasis has been placed on the academic treatment of theology.

Editors and writers, therefore, have produced periodicals, books, booklets, tracts, and Sunday school curricula to aid in maturing believers. They have also illustrated the victorious life by recording thousands of testimonies of answered prayers, physical healings, exorcisms, and deliverances from chemical addictions. From the very beginning, the challenge to conserve the work of the Spirit has consumed substantial energies. For that reason, their literature has always exhibited a lay orientation, facilitated by many authors trained in Bible institutes and Bible colleges.

PRESERVATION OF DOCTRINE TO 1950

When the Oneness issue threatened to split the General Council at its gathering in 1916, church leaders willingly set aside the anticreedal sentiments of the Hot Springs meeting by drawing doctrinal boundaries to protect the integrity of the Church and welfare of the saints. Several leading ministers, led by Daniel W. Kerr, drafted the Statement of Fundamental Truths; it contained a long section upholding the orthodox view of the Trinity.

But even in taking this stand, the authors qualified it (and themselves):

---

[37]Edith L. Blumhofer, *The Assemblies of God: A Chapter in the Story of American Pentecostalism*, vol. 1 (Springfield, Mo.: Gospel Publishing House, 1989), 197–213.

[38]Russell P. Spittler, "Theological Style Among Pentecostals and Charismatics," in *Doing Theology in Today's World*, ed. John D. Woodbridge and Thomas E. McComiskey (Grand Rapids: Zondervan Publishing House, 1991), 291–318; Walter J. Hollenweger, "Charismatic Renewal in the Third World: Implications for Mission," *Occasional Bulletin of Missionary Research* [now *International Bulletin of Missionary Research*] 4 (April 1980): 68–75.

The Statement of Fundamental Truths is not intended as a creed for the Church, nor as a basis of fellowship among Christians, but only as a basis of unity for the ministry alone.... The human phraseology employed in such statement is not inspired nor contended for, but the truth set forth ... is held to be essential to a Full Gospel ministry. No claim is made that it contains all biblical truth, only that it covers our need as to these fundamental doctrines.[39]

Oneness ministers subsequently left the Council en masse.[40]

Apart from the lengthy explanation of the Trinity, other points (e.g., "Divine Healing," "Baptism in the Spirit") are remarkably succinct, despite their distinctive character. This corresponds to the impetus surrounding such documents: All creedal statements arise from controversy and usually highlight the particular teaching(s) under contention.[41]

The Statement of Fundamental Truths, therefore, serves as a framework of doctrine for growth in Christian living and ministry; it was not originally intended to be an outline for a cohesive systematic theology. For example, the section titled "The Fall of Man" naturally mentions that all humankind has fallen into sin; at the same time, however, it allows the reader some liberty to decide the meaning of original sin and the medium of its transmission from generation to generation.[42]

In the succeeding years, various approaches aided in the preservation of doctrine. Several reasons motivated these efforts. First, Christians must continue to advance in Spirit-filled living to enhance their effectiveness as witnesses for Christ. When the Executive Presbytery recognized the danger of the anti-Pentecostal annotations in the *Scofield Reference Bible,* they banned its advertisement in the *Pentecostal Evangel* for two years (1924–1926) before they were persuaded that the edifying commentary outweighed the unedifying.[43]

---

[39]General Council Minutes, 1916, 10–13. For a United Pentecostal Church perspective, see Arthur L. Clanton, *United We Stand: A History of Oneness Organizations* (Hazelwood, Mo.: Pentecostal Publishing House, 1970).

[40]General Council Minutes, 1916, 10. Significantly the document also mirrors the theology of A. B. Simpson and the Christian and Missionary Alliance; see Nienkirchen, *A. B. Simpson,* 41–50.

[41]Peter Toon, *The Development of Doctrine in the Church* (Grand Rapids: Wm. B. Eerdmans, 1979), ix-xi.

[42]General Council Minutes, 1916, 10.

[43]"A Great Move Forward," *Pentecostal Evangel,* 1 May 1926, 3. See also Gary B. McGee, *This Gospel Shall Be Preached: A History and Theology of the Assemblies of God Foreign Missions to 1959* (Springfield, Mo.: Gospel Publishing House, 1986), 169–71.

Not surprisingly, the denomination's Gospel Publishing House in Springfield, Missouri, produced a considerable variety of popular books with doctrinal themes in addition to Sunday school materials. Examples from this period include *The Phenomena of Pentecost* (1931) by Donald Gee, *Rivers of Living Water* (n.d.) by Stanley H. Frodsham, and *Healing from Heaven* (1926) by Lilian B. Yeomans. Alice Reynolds Flower, a founding mother of the Assemblies of God, began writing Sunday school lessons in the pages of the *Christian Evangel* (later the *Pentecostal Evangel*).[44] Over the course of time, the valuable training opportunities afforded by Sunday schools gained more attention. A textbook on the principles of biblical interpretation came in the translation by P. C. Nelson of Eric Lund's *Hermeneutics* (1938), produced by the Southwestern Press, an affiliate of an Assemblies of God Bible institute in Enid, Oklahoma.

For those unable to attend Bible institutes, the plan of redemption could also be studied through the ministry of itinerant evangelists bringing their large (sometimes thirty-foot) dispensational charts and hanging them across church platforms for teaching sessions. The evangelist, with pointer in hand, would then guide the audience across the seven dispensational periods of God's redemptive agenda, explaining biblical truth from the Age of Innocence in the Garden of Eden to the Millennium to come.[45] Among those who produced material for this kind of instruction, Finis Jennings Dake was probably the most well-known Pentecostal; in fact, his many publications, including printed lecture notes, books, and the later *Dake's Annotated Reference Bible* (1963), have continued to mold the theology of many Pentecostals.[46]

Anecdotal accounts of the spiritual life came from the pens of Elizabeth V. Baker, et al., *Chronicles of a Faith Life* (2d ed., ca. 1926); H. A. Baker, *Visions Beyond the Veil* (1938); Robert W. Cummings, *Gethsemane* (1944); and Alice Reynolds Flower, *Love Overflowing* (1928), to cite only a few. Poetry was also taken up as a medium for sharing spiritual

---

[44]Gary B. McGee, "Flower, Joseph James Roswell and Alice Reynolds," in *DPCM*, 311–13.

[45]J. G. Hall, "The Eternal Program of God of the Ages and Dispensations," color chart (n.d.); also Frank M. Boyd, *Ages and Dispensations* (Springfield, Mo.: Gospel Publishing House, 1955).

[46]Patrick H. Alexander, "Dake, Finis Jennings," in *DPCM*, 235–36; also, Jimmy Swaggart, "In Memory: Finis Jennings Dake, 1902–1987", *Evangelist* (September 1987): 44.

truths; among the best-known poets were Alice Reynolds Flower and John Wright Follette.

Not surprisingly, songwriters assisted in conveying doctrine. Along with old gospel favorites, congregations were blessed by the songs of Herbert Buffum, such as "The Loveliness of Christ" and "I'm Going Through."[47] The songs of African-American Oneness Pentecostals also found an audience, especially those of Thoro Harris (e.g., "All That Thrills My Soul Is Jesus," "More Abundantly," and "He's Coming Soon") and Bishop Garfield T. Haywood (e.g., "Jesus, the Son of God" and "I See a Crimson Stream of Blood").[48]

A second reason behind the preservation of doctrine is that believers require solid answers in the face of erroneous doctrine. When threats to the faith arose after 1916, the General Council moved quickly to resolve doctrinal questions. In 1917 it adapted Article 6 of the Statement of Fundamental Truths to refer to tongues as the "initial *physical* sign" (emphasis added).[49] When the hermeneutical issue over speaking in tongues as necessary evidence of Spirit baptism resurfaced in 1918, the General Council declared it to be "our distinctive testimony."[50] In the next few years, several cogent articles by Kerr appeared in the *Pentecostal Evangel,* among other published responses.[51]

Without amending the Statement, the Council passed bylaws as another way of addressing troublesome issues. In the category "Eschatological Errors," found in Article VIII in the Constitution and Bylaws, several condemned teachings are listed. For example, the doctrine of the "restitution of all things" originated outside the Assemblies of God. Charles Hamilton Pridgeon, a well-known minister in Pittsburgh, Pennsylvania, proposed in his book *Is Hell Eternal; or Will*

---

[47]Wayne Warner, "Herbert Buffum," *Assemblies of God Heritage* 6 (Fall 1986): 11–14, 16.

[48]Everett A. Wilson, "Harris, Thoro," in *DPCM,* 347–48; Cecil M. Robeck, Jr., "Haywood, Garfield Thomas," in *DPCM,* 349–50.

[49]General Council Minutes, 1917, 21.

[50]General Council Minutes, 1918, 10; see McGee, "Early Pentecostal Hermeneutics," in *Initial Evidence,* 103–10.

[51]D. W. Kerr, "Do All Speak in Tongues?" *Christian Evangel,* 11 January 1919, 7; id., "Paul's Interpretation of the Baptism in the Holy Spirit," *Christian Evangel,* 24 August 1918, 6; id., "The 'A' or 'An'—Which?" *Pentecostal Evangel,* 21 January 1922, 7; id., "Not Ashamed," *Pentecostal Evangel,* 2 April 1921, 5; id., "The Bible Evidence of the Baptism with the Holy Ghost," *Pentecostal Evangel,* 11 August 1923, 2–3. Other responses may be found in Gary B. McGee "Popular Expositions of Initial Evidence in Pentecostalism," in *Initial Evidence,* 119–130.

God's Plan Fail? (1918) that hell was of limited duration for the purging of sins, after which all humankind would experience the love of God. Pridgeon, a former Presbyterian and advocate of faith-healing, became Pentecostal in the early 1920s and continued teaching this form of universalism. The doctrine was sometimes referred to as the "reconciliation" of all things or simply "Pridgeonism." The General Council condemned it as heretical in 1925. While it is unknown how many Pentecostals accepted Pridgeon's universalism, the threat appeared to warrant official condemnation.[52]

Another issue had to do with the imminent return of Christ: Could a minister subscribe to a post-Tribulation Rapture? When Benjamin A. Baur applied to the Eastern District in the mid-1930s for credentials, the presbyters refused his application, saying that his view diminished the nearness of the Lord's return. According to his view, Christians would have to endure the entire seven years of the Tribulation Period, particularly the last three-and-a-half years, the time of the "Great Wrath," before Christ returned for His church. Although some of the district presbyters embraced a mid-Tribulation Rapture, Baur's view remained suspect despite his voluminous written defense of it. The 1937 General Council approved a motion noting its potential problems for Christian living in the present, since Christians might become complacent if told that Christ's return was not imminent. However, reflecting the interest of early Pentecostals in avoiding division and quibbling over fine points of doctrine, the new bylaw allowed ministers to believe in a post-Tribulation Rapture, but not to preach or teach it. (In the end, Baur did not receive credentials and remained outside the General Council.[53])

A third reason behind the preservation of doctrine is that Pentecostals have struggled to balance biblical teaching with their religious experience. Committed to the Reformation principle of biblical authority ("only Scripture") as the standard for faith and practice, they have nonetheless experienced the temptation to elevate personal revelations and other spiritual manifestations to the same level. This struggle is reflected in an early *Pentecostal Evangel* report, describing the expectations of Frank M. Boyd as an early Bible school educator and instructor at Central Bible Institute (College after 1965):

---

[52]Gary B. McGee, "Pridgeon, Charles Hamilton," in *DPCM,* 727.

[53]Interview with Joseph R. Flower, general secretary of the General Council of the Assemblies of God, Springfield, Missouri, 27 April 1988.

[H]e expected all the students to be more filled with fire and love and zeal and more filled with the Spirit when they left than when they came. He said that when men had the Word without the Spirit they were often dead and dull and dry; and when men had the Spirit without the Word there is always a tendency towards fanaticism. But where men had the Word and the Spirit, they would be equipped as the Master wants His ministers equipped.[54]

This challenge to instruct believers on how to have a mature Spirit-filled life helps to explain the high priority given to publishing.

Detailed doctrinal handbooks, however, did not appear until the 1920s and 1930s. One of the best known, *Knowing the Doctrines of the Bible* (1937), was compiled from the lecture notes of Myer Pearlman, an instructor at Central Bible Institute. Theologian Russell P. Spittler suggests that it is "the theological jewel of classical Pentecostalism's middle period."[55] Other books having similar agendas appeared, such as S. A. Jamieson's *Pillars of Truth* (1926), P. C. Nelson's *Bible Doctrines* (1934), and Ernest S. Williams' three-volume *Systematic Theology* (1953; although organized as a systematic theology, it is more accurately a doctrinal manual composed of the author's lecture notes delivered at Central Bible Institute from 1929–1949). Specialized studies on the Holy Spirit included *What Meaneth This?* (1947) by Carl Brumback and *The Spirit Himself* (1949) by Ralph M. Riggs. In a related development, Boyd prepared books of doctrinal instruction for correspondence courses, founding what is now Berean College of the Assemblies of God.

On another front, Alice E. Luce, a missionary to India and later to Hispanics in America, guided the General Council in articulating its theology and strategy of world missions. She was the first missiologist of stature in the Assemblies of God; her three articles on Paul's missionary methods in the *Pentecostal Evangel* in early 1921 prepared the way for the Assemblies of God's acceptance of a detailed commitment to indigenous church principles; this occurred officially that year at the General Council meeting in September. Luce, who received her theological training at Cheltenham Ladies' College (England), also wrote several books, numerous articles

---

[54]"Opening of the Central Bible Institute," *Pentecostal Evangel,* 25 October 1924, 8.

[55]Spittler, "Theological Style," in *Doing Theology,* 298.

in both Spanish and English, lecture notes, and Sunday school lessons.[56]

PRESERVATION OF DOCTRINE AFTER 1950

With the coming of a new generation and interest in improving the quality of training in the denomination's Bible and liberal arts colleges, teachers received encouragement to further their education. This began a gradual transition in Bible and theology department personnel: to instructors with graduate degrees in biblical studies, systematic theology, and church history and equipped with sharper skills in hermeneutics, Old Testament, New Testament, theology, and the historical development of doctrine and practice.[57]

Although many had long feared the intellectualizing of the faith, this new breed of teachers modeled the balance between Pentecostal spirituality and academic studies. One such professor, Stanley M. Horton, had received training in biblical languages and Old Testament at Gordon-Conwell Theological Seminary, Harvard Divinity School, and Central Baptist Theological Seminary.[58] Over the years, Horton has had a significant effect on the denomination through his teaching, books (e.g., *What the Bible Says About the Holy Spirit* [1976]), magazine and journal articles, and contributions to the adult Sunday school curriculum.

With increasing expertise, educators began to explore in greater depth the distinctive beliefs of the Assemblies of God. Many of them joined the Society for Pentecostal Studies, an academic society founded in 1970, and have contributed articles to its journal, *Pneuma. Paraclete* (begun in 1967), the denominational journal, has provided another opportunity for scholarly discussion, although until 1992 it was confined to pneumatology. A more short-lived source for theological opinion within the General Council appeared with the publication of *Agora* (1977–1981), an independent quarterly magazine.

Scholarly studies relevant to the person and work of the Holy Spirit include *Commentary on the First Epistle to the*

---

[56]Alice E. Luce, "Paul's Missionary Methods," *Pentecostal Evangel,* 8 January 1921, 6–7; 22 January 1921, 6, 11; 5 February 1921, 6–7. Gary B. McGee, "Luce, Alice Eveline," in *DPCM,* 543–44.

[57]Gary B. McGee, "The Indispensable Calling of the Pentecostal Scholar," *Assemblies of God Educator* 35 (July to September, 1990): 1, 3–5, 16.

[58]Gary B. McGee, "Horton, Stanley Monroe," in *DPCM,* 446–47.

Corinthians by Gordon D. Fee (1987), *The Book of Acts* (1981) by Stanley M. Horton, and *The Charismatic Theology of St. Luke* (1984) by Roger Stronstad (a minister in the Pentecostal Assemblies of Canada). Examinations of specific issues related to the Pentecostal heritage can be found in *The Spirit Helps Us Pray: A Biblical Theology of Prayer* (1993) by Robert L. Brandt and Zenas J. Bicket; *Called and Empowered: Global Mission in Pentecostal Perspective* (1991) by Murray Dempster, Byron D. Klaus, and Douglas Peterson, eds.; *Initial Evidence: Historical and Biblical Perspectives on the Pentecostal Doctrine of Spirit Baptism* (1991) by Gary B. McGee, ed.; *Power Encounter: A Pentecostal Perspective* (1989) by Opal L. Reddin, ed.; and *The Liberating Spirit: Toward an Hispanic American Pentecostal Social Ethic* (1992) by Eldin Villafañe.

Nonetheless, apart from the new line of collegiate textbooks offered by Logion Press (Gospel Publishing House), the denominational priority given to popularly written materials still prevails. The recently published *Bible Doctrines: A Pentecostal Perspective* (1993) by William W. Menzies and Stanley M. Horton represents a new survey of beliefs for adult Sunday school classes or undergraduate courses. The myriad of Assemblies of God publications produced by Gospel Publishing House and Life Publishers International still focus most of their attention on Bible study, discipleship, and practical studies for ministers. This is also true of ICI University and Berean College publications, both offering credit and noncredit programs by correspondence to laypersons as well as to candidates for professional ministry.

Other publications from various presses include another academic survey of doctrine, *An Introduction to Theology: A Classical Pentecostal Perspective* (1993) by John R. Higgins, Michael L. Dusing, and Frank D. Tallman; and the popularly written *Concerning Spiritual Gifts* (1928, rev. ed. 1972) and *Trophimus I Left Sick* (1952) by Donald Gee; two booklets titled *Living Your Christian Life NOW in the Light of Eternity* (1960) by H. B. Kelchner; *Divine Healing and the Problem of Suffering* (1976) by Jesse K. Moon; *Dunamis and the Church* (1968) by Henry H. Ness; and *The Spirit— God in Action* (1974) by Anthony D. Palma. Less didactic treatments on the spiritual life have been made available in books such as *Pentecost in My Soul* (1989) by Edith L. Blumhofer. Likewise, personal memoirs, such as *The Spirit Bade Me Go* (1961) by David J. du Plessis, *Grace for Grace* (1961) by Alice Reynolds Flower, and *Although the Fig Tree Shall*

Not Blossom (1976) by Daena Cargnel, have sparked interest due to their emphasis on the presence and leading of the Holy Spirit in the hearts of believers. Additional inspiration and teaching of this nature is provided by the weekly *Pentecostal Evangel* and by *Advance,* a monthly magazine for ministers.

Songwriters continued sharing their gifts for worship and instruction. One of the best known, Ira Stanphill, warmed the hearts of churchgoers with songs like "Mansion Over the Hilltop," "Room at the Cross," and "I Know Who Holds Tomorrow," designed to provide comfort and the assurance of God's grace.[59] So influential have composers been from the beginning of the Pentecostal movement that while most Pentecostals have never learned the Apostles' Creed or the Nicene Creed, they can sing an astonishing number of such songs and choruses from memory, obvious testimony that much Pentecostal theology has been transmitted orally.

By the 1970s, the Assemblies of God had become one of the major denominations in the United States—linked to even larger fraternal constituencies overseas. Facing new problems, church leaders chose the method of publishing position papers to address issues troubling the churches; in this way they continued to respond to issues, but without adding more bylaws to the constitution or amending the Statement of Fundamental Truths. Beginning in 1970, with the publication of "The Inerrancy of Scripture" (with its endorsement by the General Presbytery), over twenty such white papers have been issued. Topics have included divine healing, creation, transcendental meditation, divorce and remarriage, the initial physical evidence of Spirit baptism, abortion, the kingdom of God, and women in ministry.[60] In recent years, members of the denomination's Doctrinal Purity Commission, established in 1979 to monitor theological developments, have prepared the papers.

Obviously, the use of position papers has begun to broaden the confessional identity of the Assemblies of God. Resorting to position papers, however, has not been accomplished without some disagreement.[61] The authoritative weight of position

---

[59]Wayne E. Warner, "Stanphill, Ira," in *DPCM,* 810.

[60]The position papers through 1989 are bound together in *Where We Stand* (Springfield, Mo.: Gospel Publishing House, 1990). A recent paper on women in ministry is available separately and will be included in the next edition.

[61]Charles B. Nestor, "Position Papers," *Agora* (Winter 1979): 10–11.

papers in relation to that of the Statement of Fundamental Truths leaves room for discussion. Furthermore, at least one paper could be interpreted as a shift from an original understanding in the Statement when it mentions that some "have tried to set divine healing in opposition to or in competition with the medical profession. This need not be so. Physicians through their skills have brought help to many." Furthermore, Christians cannot reverse the physical effects of the Fall since "no matter what we do for this body, no matter how many times we are healed, if Jesus tarries we shall die."[62]

By the 1940s, many conservative evangelicals realized that theological agreements with Pentecostals outweighed differences and began to welcome their fellowship and cooperation. The Assemblies of God's accepting membership in the National Association of Evangelicals (NAE) at its founding in 1942 represented their entry into the mainstream of American church life (which was furthered by an upward social and economic mobility after World War II). The relationship became tenuous at times due to lingering suspicions about Assemblies of God pneumatology and the generally Arminian nature of its theological anthropology. Nevertheless, the impact of evangelicalism on the theology of Pentecostalism has been considerable.[63]

After the election of Thomas F. Zimmerman as president of the NAE (1960–1962), the General Council in 1961 made a few modifications of the Statement of Fundamental Truths. The most significant revision occurred in the section "The Scriptures Inspired." The 1916 version reads as follows: "The Bible is the inspired Word of God, a revelation from God to man, the infallible rule of faith and conduct, and is superior to conscience and reason, but not contrary to reason." The altered wording aligned more closely with that of evangelicals in the NAE: "The Scriptures, both the Old and New Testaments, are verbally inspired of God and are the revelation of God to man, the infallible, authoritative rule of faith and conduct." Constituents of the Assemblies of God have believed in the inspiration and inerrancy of Scripture since the found-

---

[62]"Divine healing: An Integral Part of the Gospel," *Where We Stand,* 53, 51. Cf., Lilian B. Yeomans, M.D., *Healing from Heaven* (Springfield, Mo.: Gospel Publishing House, 1926; rev. ed., 1973).

[63]Harold Lindsell, ed., *The Church's Worldwide Mission* (Waco, Tex.: Word Books, 1966), 8. For a discussion of the impact of the NAE on Pentecostals, see Cecil M. Robeck, Jr., "National Association of Evangelicals," in *DPCM,* 634–36.

ing of the General Council. Yet whether Pentecostals have a
unique contribution to make to the understanding of the
inspiration of Scripture as "God-breathed" (Gk. *theopneustos*) remains to be explored.[64]

The historic Reformed theology of most evangelicals, both
inside and outside the NAE, has continued to raise objections
to the Wesleyan and Keswickian understandings of a separate
work of grace following conversion—the theological foundation on which classical Pentecostals have built their doctrine of the baptism in the Holy Spirit.[65] This scholarly stand-
off, noted for its criticism of the exegetical basis for tongues
as initial evidence, has remained through the years. In response, two charismatic scholars have made important contributions to the classical Pentecostal doctrine of Spirit baptism: Howard Ervin (American Baptist), *Conversion-Initiation
and the Baptism in the Holy Spirit* (1984), and J. Rodman
Williams (Presbyterian), *Renewal Theology,* especially volume 2 (1990). Assemblies of God theologians have also produced important studies.[66]

Perhaps most substantially, evangelical scholars have influenced Pentecostal beliefs concerning the present and future
aspects of the kingdom of God, a concept only alluded to in
the Statement of Fundamental Truths. For many years, the
teaching about future events in the Assemblies of God had a

---

[64]General Council Minutes, 1916, 10. General Council Minutes, 1961,
92. For the significance of the change of wording in the statement on
Scripture, see Gerald T. Sheppard, "Scripture in the Pentecostal Tradition,"
(Part 1), *Agora* (Spring 1978): 4–5, 17–22; (Part 2) (Summer 1978): 14–
19.

[65]Frederick Dale Bruner, *A Theology of the Holy Spirit* (Grand Rapids:
Wm. B. Eerdmans, 1970).

[66]William W. Menzies, "The Methodology of Pentecostal Theology: An
Essay on Hermeneutics," in *Essays on Apostolic Themes,* ed. Paul Elbert
(Peabody, Mass.: Hendrickson Publishers, 1985), 1–22; Ben Aker, "New
Directions in Lucan Theology: Reflections on Luke 3:21–22 and Some
Implications," in *Faces of Renewal,* ed. Paul Elbert (Peabody, Mass.: Hen-
drickson Publishers, 1988), 108–27; Donald A. Johns, "Some New Direc-
tions in the Hermeneutics of Classical Pentecostalism's Doctrine of Initial
Evidence," in *Initial Evidence,* 145–56; William G. MacDonald, *Glossolalia
in the New Testament* (Springfield, Mo.: Gospel Publishing House, ca. 1964);
Fee, *Gospel and Spirit,* 83–119. For the current debate, see Roger Stronstad,
"The Biblical Precedent for Historical Precedent," paper presented to the
22d annual meeting of the Society for Pentecostal Studies, Springfield, Mo.,
November 1992, and the response of Gordon D. Fee at the same meeting,
"Response to Roger Stronstad," both published in *Paraclete* 27 (Summer
1993): 1–14.

strong dispensational orientation (i.e., a shared belief in seven dispensations, pre-Tribulation Rapture, and premillennial interpretation of Scripture, but setting aside a core teaching which separates the Church from Israel). This was popularized and reinforced by the writings of Riggs, Boyd, Dake, Brumback, John G. Hall, and T. J. Jones. New Testament references to the "kingdom of God" (briefly defined as the rule or reign of God) as a present reality in the hearts of the redeemed barely received notice, while its future millennial appearance received extensive consideration.[67]

According to historic dispensationalism, the promise of David's restored kingdom had been postponed to the Millennium because the Jews had rejected Jesus' offer of the Kingdom. This delayed the fulfillment of Joel's prophecy of the restoration of Israel and the outpouring of the Spirit until after the second coming of Christ. The events in Acts 2, therefore, represented only an initiatory blessing of power to the Early Church. Israel and the Church were logically kept separate; hence, the underlying anti-Pentecostal posture of this system of interpretation of Scripture.[68]

For Pentecostals, however, Joel's prophecy had been fulfilled on the Day of Pentecost, as evidenced by Peter's "This is that" (Acts 2:16, KJV). Unfortunately, Pentecostals' deference to dispensationalism bridled their pursuit of the implications of some references to the Kingdom and their claims of apostolic power in the last days (see Matthew 9:35; 24:14; Acts 8:12; and 1 Corinthians 4:20, among others).

Certain theologians, notably Ernest S. Williams and Stanley M. Horton, did clearly identify the kingdom of God with the Church ("spiritual Israel"), recognizing the vital connection

---

[67]John G. Hall, *Dispensations,* 2d ed. (Springfield, Mo.: Inland Printing Co., 1957); D. V. Hurst and T. J. Jones, *The Church Begins* (Springfield, Mo.: Gospel Publishing House, 1959); Carl Brumback, *What Meaneth This?* (Springfield, Mo.: Gospel Publishing House, 1947); cf. Gerald T. Sheppard, "Pentecostalism and the Hermeneutics of Dispensationalism: Anatomy of an Uneasy Relationship," *Pneuma* 6 (Fall 1984): 5–33.

[68]Dr. C. I. Scofield, *Rightly Dividing the Word of Truth* (Old Tappan, N.J.: Fleming H. Revell Co., 1896), 5–12; and the later Charles Caldwell Ryrie, *Dispensationalism Today* (Chicago: Moody Press, 1965). See also Vern S. Poythress, *Understanding Dispensationalists* (Grand Rapids: Zondervan Publishing House, 1987); French L. Arrington, "Hermeneutics, Historical Perspectives on Pentecostal and Charismatic," DPCM, 376–89.

to their belief about the Spirit's contemporary activity in the Church.[69]

After World War II, evangelicals renewed their study of theological and missiological implications of the kingdom of God, with Pentecostals' interest in the Kingdom gradually paralleling that of evangelicals. The well-known Assemblies of God missiologist Melvin L. Hodges recognized the importance of the Kingdom for understanding a New Testament theology of mission. Speaking at the Congress on the Church's Worldwide Mission at Wheaton College in April 1966, he declared the Church to be "the present manifestation of the kingdom of God in the earth, or at least, the agency that prepares the way for the future manifestation of the Kingdom. Its mission therefore is the extension of the Church throughout the world. ... It is the Holy Spirit that gives life to the Church and imparts gifts and ministries as well as power for their performance."[70] Although short of elaboration, Hodges' message indicated an important trend was afoot. The vital connection between the "signs and wonders" of the advancing Kingdom (power manifestations of the Spirit associated with the preaching of the gospel) awaited further exposition.

Some twenty years later, retired missionary Ruth A. Breusch laid out the implications for Pentecostal ministry in *Mountain Movers,* the foreign missions magazine of the Assemblies of God (again, showing the priority of discipling persons in the pew). In a series of ten articles under the theme "The Kingdom, the Power, and the Glory," Breusch, a graduate (B.A., M.A.) of Hartford Seminary Foundation, showed thoughtful New Testament interpretation and familiarity with missiological literature. She defined the Kingdom as the rule of God encompassing "the Church as the realm of God's blessings into which His people have entered. The Church is comprised of those who are rescued from the kingdom of darkness and brought into the kingdom of God's Son." Accordingly, "this Church is the *New Israel,* the people of God, under the new covenant. 'New' because Gentile believers are now included."

[69]Ernest S. Williams, *Systematic Theology,* vol. 3 (Springfield, Mo.: Gospel Publishing House, 1953), 95; id., "Thy Kingdom Come," *Pentecostal Evangel,* 31 July 1966, 8; Stanley M. Horton, *The Promise of His Coming* (Springfield, Mo.: Gospel Publishing House, 1967), 91; for a historical perspective, see Dwight Wilson, *Armageddon Now! The Premillenarian Response to Russia and Israel since 1917* (Grand Rapids: Baker Book House, 1977).

[70]Melvin L. Hodges, "Mission—And Church Growth," in *The Church's Worldwide Mission,* ed. Lindsell, 141, 145.

By God's choice, the Church is the vehicle for the extension of His kingdom throughout the earth. To Breusch, the advent of the Spirit reflects His redemptive nature by dynamically empowering the Church for the evangelization of the world.[71]

This attention to studying the biblical concept of the kingdom of God has contributed to a better understanding of the ethical teachings of the Gospels, the nature and mission of the Church, the meaning of signs and wonders in evangelism, and the role of the Christian in society.

Other writers on a more academic plane have hailed the importance of the kingdom of God in the study of Scripture. Peter Kuzmič, for example, noted in a recent publication,

> Pentecostals and charismatics are convinced ... that "the kingdom of God is not a matter of talk but of power" (1 Cor. 4:20), and expect that the preaching of the Word of God be accompanied by mighty acts of the Holy Spirit. ... For the followers of Jesus who believe the "whole/full gospel," the commission to preach the good news of the kingdom of God is linked with the equipping power of the Holy Spirit to overcome the forces of evil. ...
>
> ... In the age of rationalism, theological liberalism, religious pluralism, Pentecostals and charismatics believe that evidential supernatural activity of the Holy Spirit validates the Christian witness. As in the apostolic days, the Holy Spirit is the very life of the church and its mission, not replacing but always exalting Christ the Lord. This is the Spirit's primary mission and the way in which the kingdom of God is actualized in the believing community. Christ rules where the Spirit moves![72]

Furthermore, Kuzmič and Murray W. Dempster, among others, forthrightly speak to the implications of the Kingdom for Christian social ethics.[73]

---

[71]Ruth A. Breusch, "The Church and the Kingdom," *Mountain Movers,* July 1987, 9.

[72]"Kingdom of God" by Peter Kuzmič Taken from the book *The Dictionary of Pentecostal and Charismatic Movements* edited by Stanley M. Burgess, Gary B. McGee, and Patrick Alexander. Copyright ©1988 by Stanley M. Burgess, Gary B. McGee, and Patrick Alexander. Used by permission of Zondervan Publishing House.

[73]Peter Kuzmič, "History and Eschatology: Evangelical Views," in *In Word and Deed,* ed. Bruce J. Nicholls (Exeter, UK: Paternoster Press, 1985), 135–64; Murray W. Dempster, "Evangelism, Social Concern, and the Kingdom of God," in *Called and Empowered: Global Mission in Pentecostal Perspective,* ed. Murray Dempster, Byron D. Klaus, and Douglas Peterson (Peabody, Mass.: Hendrickson Publishers, 1991), 22–43. For a helpful study of Assemblies of God responses to key social issues, see Howard N. Kenyon, "An Analysis of Ethical Issues in the History of the Assemblies of God" (Ph.D. dissertation, Baylor University, 1988).

Recently, some Pentecostals and charismatics have advocated several forms of "Kingdom Now" theology, which in some quarters has represented a departure from the traditional pre-Tribulation Rapture view and/or premillennial interpretation of the Bible. Focusing on Christianizing society now and dismissing or minimizing the emphasis on the rapture of the Church (but not necessarily the second coming of Christ), this teaching has generated serious controversy.[74] The mere fact that these perspectives have developed demonstrates that contemporary Pentecostals are concerned about discovering their responsibilities as Christians in society.

Today, references to the kingdom of God abound in Assemblies of God publications. The values for the continuing study of cherished doctrines may be profound and far-reaching, reminding Pentecostals of the riches in God's Word.

CONCLUSION

Pentecostalism emerged out of the nineteenth-century Holiness movement. The formulation of the full gospel, concern for world evangelization in the closing days of history, and intense prayer for the outpouring of the Holy Spirit precipitated the revivals at Topeka, Los Angeles, and the many that followed.

The Pentecostal and charismatic movements in this century have indicated that something of unusual significance has occurred at this point in the history of the Church: God has been pouring out the Holy Spirit on Christians everywhere who are seeking a Spirit-filled life characterized by holiness and spiritual power. Spirit baptism's divine empowerment bestows insight into the Spirit's activity in the world, greater sensitivity to His promptings, a new dimension of prayer, and spiritual power to achieve their tasks in mission.

When independent Pentecostals organized the General Council in 1914, they did so to expedite their goal of winning the world for Christ. The urgency and problems of the hour dictated cooperation among the Spirit-baptized. Church leaders recognized the importance of Bible study and doctrine

---

[74]See *Where We Stand*, 185–94; William A. Griffin, "Kingdom Now: New Hope or New Heresy?" paper presented to the seventeenth annual meeting of the Society for Pentecostal Studies, Virginia Beach, Virginia, 14 November 1987; Gordon Anderson, "Kingdom Now Theology: A Look at Its Roots and Branches," *Paraclete* (Summer 1990): 1–12; and "Kingdom Now Doctrines Which Differ from Assemblies of God Teaching," *Paraclete* 24 (Summer 1990): 19–24.

to protect congregations from error, but more significantly to equip believers "for the work of the ministry" (Eph. 4:12, KJV).

The development of doctrine in the denomination has taken several forms: the Preamble, Statement of Fundamental Truths, bylaws, position papers, articles and editorials in magazines, tracts, books, Sunday school curricula, songs, and poetry. From Sunday school teachers to the song leader, pastor, and denominational officer—everyone is called to proclaim the good news of salvation, to share the compassion of Jesus Christ, and to disciple converts.

With the delay in the Lord's return and the changing cultural context bringing ever new challenges to the faith, scholarly responses to theological issues have gained greater appreciation. Correspondingly, the growing identification with evangelicalism has led to an increasing reflection on the distinctiveness of Pentecostal beliefs. Since World War II, evangelical interest in the biblical teaching on the kingdom of God has enriched the study of doctrine in the Assemblies of God.

The contemporary scene calls the Church to consider anew its faithfulness to God and its mission in the world. Prayerful and exacting study of the Scriptures, theology, missiology, and church history, therefore, constitutes an important gift of the risen Christ to His church.

STUDY QUESTIONS

1. Why must any study of modern Pentecostalism include the views of John Wesley on sanctification?

2. What did the Keswick movement and Reformed revivalists such as Dwight L. Moody and Reuben A. Torrey believe about the baptism in the Holy Spirit?

3. Why did belief in divine healing find such a warm reception in the Holiness movement?

4. Why did concern for world evangelism play such an important role in the emergence of the Pentecostal movement?

5. In what ways did early Pentecostals believe that the New Testament Church was being restored?

6. What were the legacies of Charles F. Parham and William J. Seymour? How did they affect the Pentecostal movement?

7. Discuss the first three issues to divide the Pentecostal movement.

8. Why has the Assemblies of God placed such a high priority on publishing popular-level materials?

9. After the approval of the Statement of Fundamental Truths in 1916, how did the General Council address questionable teachings?

10. What is the underlying argument against Pentecostalism in historic dispensationalism?

11. How has the growing identity with evangelicalism influenced Assemblies of God theology?

12. What service does the study of theology perform for the Assemblies of God at this point in its history?

CHAPTER TWO

Theological Foundations

James H. Railey, Jr.
Benny C. Aker

Good theology is written by those who are careful to allow their perspectives to be shaped by the biblical revelation. Therefore, throughout this book we shall keep in mind the following biblical assertions: God exists, He has revealed himself, and He has made that revelation available to humankind.[1]

In the Bible we see God coming down into the stream of human life and history to carry out His great plan of redemption. In other words, the Bible presents its truths in the midst of historical situations, rather than giving us a systematized list of what it teaches. Yet its teachings need to be systematized for greater understanding and for application to our lives.[2]

That systematizing must, however, be done very carefully, paying attention to both the context and content of the biblical material being used. The subtle temptation is for theologians to select only texts that agree with their positions, ignoring others that seem to disagree, and to use texts without proper concern for their context. The Bible must be allowed to speak with clarity, unclouded by the preconceptions and misconceptions of the individual.

Another biblical assertion guiding the development of the material in this book is that the Holy Spirit who inspired the writing of the Bible guides the mind and heart of the believer (John 16:13). The Holy Spirit's work in assisting the student to understand the Bible is, however, not to be feared as a work that will lead into bizarre interpretations previously

---

[1]See chap. 3, pp. 62–69.

[2]The beginnings of systematization can be seen in some books, especially in Romans.

unknown. In fact, "when the Spirit guides into all truth, it is actually a matter of bringing forth or eliciting what is already known." Moreover, "there can be no basic difference between the truth the Christian community knows through the indwelling of the Holy Spirit and what is set forth in Scripture."[3]

Pentecostals have a rich heritage in the realm of experience, and have had fervent convictions with respect to their faith, but have not been as ready to write down explanations of their experiences with the truths of the Bible. Now, however, there is a growing body of literature from the Pentecostal perspective which will continue the effort to expand understanding between the various groups within the Church. We trust this book will also provide further testimony to the items of faith dear to the experience of the faithful.

Again, we recognize that only the Bible has the final word in that it is the Word of God. All merely human words are at best tentative, being true only in so far as they align with the revelation of the Bible. We are not a cadre of superior believers who reach from their lofty heights to assist those of inferior development along the way. Rather, we are fellow travelers along the path of life who desire to share what we have learned about God and His dealings. The call is to those who read to come along and let us learn together about the riches of our Lord.

THE NATURE OF SYSTEMATIC THEOLOGY

THE CONCEPT OF RELIGION

The place to begin thinking about systematic theology is with an understanding of the concept of religion. Although religion can be defined in various ways, one of the simpler definitions is that religion is the search for the ultimate. Human beings almost universally acknowledge that there is something, or someone, beyond themselves and that in some way, or ways, they are responsible to that something or someone. The recognition that the human race is not alone in the universe and is dependent, at least to some extent, on the ultimate which is beyond is the starting place for religion.

Religion has taken many forms and expressions throughout human history—from philosophical speculation to the creation of gods in the form of material objects (see Rom. 1:21–

---

[3]J. Rodman Williams, *Renewal Theology,* vol. 1 (Grand Rapids: Zondervan Publishing House, 1988), 22–23.

23). The incessant longing after the ultimate has led to religious practices ranging from intellectual discussion to child sacrifice.

However, this longing of the individual, either alone or in society, should not be discounted or considered a negative factor. The church father Augustine (A.D. 354–430) confessed, "You have made us for yourself and our heart is restless until it finds its rest in you."[4] That is, the longing after the ultimate is the gift of God within persons so that they will be open to the revelation of God. He alone is the ultimate One who will be the full answer to the searching heart.

Religion as the human search for God, however, fails to provide anything or anyone truly ultimate. At best the searching ends with some lesser deity, or explanation for existence, which, because it is but the creation of the human mind, is not sufficient to answer all of the complexities of human existence. Religion ends in the frustration of not being able to conceive of a god who is big enough.

But this frustration is not the end of the story, for once people begin to sense futility, it can be the fertile soil in which reception of the revelation of God can grow. H. Orton Wiley, the late Nazarene theologian, notes that "religion furnishes the basic consciousness in man without which there could be no capacity in human nature to receive the revelation of God."[5] That is, the very fact people are seeking after something can provide the opportunity to present them with the good news. They can find what they are seeking in Jesus Christ. He not only brings salvation, but also reveals the majesty and immensity of God that more than satisfies the search for the ultimate. Most important, the seeker finds that God himself has been searching for His wandering creation all along!

TYPES OF RELIGIOUS AUTHORITY

When religion accepts the revelation of God in Christ, the issue of authority rises to prominence. What are the grounds for belief and practice? How does the revelation of God come to bear upon the individual? These questions direct our attention to the issue of authority.

---

[4]Augustine, *The Confessions of Saint Augustine,* vol. 18, translated by John K. Ryan (Garden City, N.Y.: Doubleday & Co., 1960), 43.

[5]H. Orton Wiley, *Christian Theology,* vol. 1 (Kansas City, Mo.: Beacon Hill Press, 1940), 17.

**CHAPTER
2**
———————
Theological
Foundations

The authority question, which really asks how the revelation of God bears on the way people live and conduct their lives, can be divided broadly into two categories: external and internal authority. Both categories take seriously the role of the Bible as the revelation of God, but differ dramatically in various ways.

External authority includes those authoritative sources that are outside of the individual: usually expressed as canonical, theological, and ecclesiastical.

Canonical Authority. Canonical authority holds that the biblical materials, as contained in the canon[6] of Scripture, are God's authoritative revelation. The Bible speaks to our beliefs and life-style with clarity and finality. The proponents of this view assert that (1) the Bible is authoritative because of its divine authorship and (2) the Bible is clear in the basic truths it presents. All questions of faith and conduct are subject to the scrutiny of the Bible, so that items of theological belief must have either explicit or implicit biblical support or be dismissed.[7]

An important consideration for proponents of the canonical view of authority is that the Bible must be properly interpreted. This issue faces the canonical view of authority and must be dealt with carefully.[8]

Theological Authority. The theological view of authority looks to the doctrinal confessions, or creeds, of the community at large as the source of faith and practice. From its beginning the Church has stated its beliefs in formulas and creeds. One of the earliest is the Apostles' Creed, so named because it claimed to summarize the teachings of the apostles. Throughout the history of the Church many other statements of faith have been adopted and used by believers to affirm the central tenets of their faith.

There is a value to the Church in these creedal statements because they serve to focus the attention of the worshiper upon crucial elements of belief. They allow the watching

———————

[6]The thirty-nine books of the Old Testament and the twenty-seven of the New Testament; see chap. 3, pp. 107–09, for more on the canon.

[7]Most cults have additional books they consider authoritative. We hold that the Bible alone is authoritative.

[8]See chap. 3.

world to hear a clear and united voice explaining the theology of the historic Christian Church.[9]

But the problem with the theological view of authority is that it tends to elevate creedal affirmations to an importance above that of the Bible. Also, even though they do show remarkable unity in key aspects of biblical truth, they may vary to a considerable extent in secondary matters of faith and practice. To the extent that they align with the Bible and serve to explain its truths, they are valuable. When they supplant the central place of biblical revelation they are a questionable authoritative source.

Ecclesiastical Authority. Ecclesiastical authority holds that the Church itself must be the final authority in all matters of faith and practice. Usually this understanding is held in conjunction with the canonical and theological views previously considered. The Bible is granted an important place, but it must be interpreted by those who are specially trained and chosen for that task. The interpretation, then, of the Church, usually promulgated in creedlike statements, becomes the authoritative one.

Often this ecclesiastical understanding of the authority is expressed through the earthly official head of a church, whether one person or a group of persons. Because they are in leadership positions within the community, it is assumed that they are in the proper relationship to God to communicate His truth to the Church.

Without in any way detracting from God-given leadership positions, it must be observed that this approach to authority is open to a good deal of corruption—the misuse of power for selfish or other sinful desires. Moreover, the interpretation of Scripture is usually done by only a few people on the behalf of the whole Church. This keeps the majority of believers from confronting the biblical claims for themselves.

The issue of the authoritative source for understanding the revelation of God can also be considered from the internal perspective—finding the authority source within the individual. Then, the external approaches which have been pre-

---

[9]The Assemblies of God has articulated a Statement of Fundamental Truths containing sixteen truths considered to be essential for establishing and maintaining fellowship within its membership. The Bible, however, is still considered the ultimate authority. For a full treatment see William W. Menzies, *Bible Doctrines: A Pentecostal Perspective,* ed. Stanley M. Horton (Springfield, Mo.: Logion Press, 1993).

natural
intuition

sented are considered at best secondary to factors at work in the individual person.

Experience as an Authority. The first internal authority source is that of experience. The individual relates to the revelation of God in the arena of the mind, the will, and the emotions. Considering the person as a unity, the effects in any of those areas are felt, or experienced, in the others either subsequently or simultaneously. In effect, the revelation of God comes to bear upon the totality of the human person.

Many, however, take this observation further, contending that experience is the real source of authority for faith and practice. They say only those truths that have been experienced as true by the individual can be accepted and proclaimed as true for others.

The contemporary elevation of experience to authority status began with the writings of Friedrich Schleiermacher (1768–1834).[10] Schleiermacher argued that the ground of Christianity was religious experience, an experience which became the authoritative determinant for theological truths. From his time to the present, experience has been accepted as the source of authority in some sectors of the Church.[11]

Although Schleiermacher and his followers treated the Bible as an ordinary human book and overemphasized experience, the value of experience in grasping the revelation of God must not be overlooked. This is especially true for Pentecostals, who place great emphasis upon the reality of a relationship with God that affects every aspect of the human being. Propositional truths take on vitality and force when they are confirmed and illustrated in the living experiences of devout disciples of Christ.

On the other hand, experiences vary and their causation is not always clearly discernible. A reliable authority source must be beyond the variables which mark experience, and must even be able to contradict and correct experience if

---

[10]For a good evaluation of the life and work of Schleiermacher see Richard R. Niebuhr, "Friedrich Schleiermacher," in *A Handbook of Christian Theologians,* ed. Martin E. Marty and Dean G. Peerman (Cleveland: World Publishing Company, 1965), 17–35. See also Friedrich Schleiermacher, *The Christian Faith* (New York: Harper, 1963).

[11]The philosophical school of existentialism (promoted especially by Søren Kierkegaard and Martin Heidegger) says the only way to truth is through our subjective experience of and participation in reality. This influenced neoorthodoxy and much of recent antisupernaturalism in theology (as in Rudolf Bultmann).

need be. Experience alone as an authoritative source mediating the revelation of God to people is not reliable.[12]

Human Reason as an Authority. With the Age of Enlightenment (from the late seventeenth century onward) many have made human reason the self-sufficient source of authority. This rationalism says it does not need divine revelation and, in fact, denies the reality of divine revelation. Colin Brown accurately notes that in "everyday language rationalism has come to mean the attempt to judge everything in the light of reason."[13] The results of the rise of rationalism have been felt in all areas of human endeavor, but especially in religion and theology.[14]

Our intellectual powers are a part of what it means to be created in the image and likeness of God. Therefore, to employ reason in the reception of the revelation of God is not in itself wrong. Tremendous advances have been made by the use of reason as it applies to many problem areas of human existence. Applying reason to biblical materials, researching ancient texts and documents, reconstructing the social and economic world of the Bible, and many other such efforts, have been helpful in carrying forward an understanding of the revelation of God.

Reason, then, is a good servant of the revelation of God, but it is not a good master over that revelation. When reason is assumed to be authoritative it stands above the revelation of God and judges which, if any, of it should be accepted. Usually rationalists make their own human reason the real authority.[15] It should be noted also that human reason that denies divine revelation has always come under the influence of sin and Satan ever since Adam's fall (Gen. 3).

Our belief, therefore, is that theology is done best when the Bible is acknowledged as the authority and the Holy Spirit

archaeology

---

[12]For a good treatment of the role of religious experience and how it influences theology see John Jefferson Davis, *Foundations of Evangelical Theology* (Grand Rapids: Baker Book House, 1984), 145–68.

[13]Colin Brown, *Philosophy and the Christian Faith* (Downers Grove, Ill.: InterVarsity Press, 1974), 48.

[14]For a discussion of rationalism see Colin Brown, *Christianity and Western Thought: A History of Philosophers, Ideas and Movements,* vol. 1, *From the Ancient World to the Age of Enlightenment* (Downers Grove, Ill.: InterVarsity Press, 1990), 173–96.

[15]Dr. Stanley M. Horton relates that one of his professors at Harvard University, Robert Pfeiffer, made a statement in class contradicting something stated in the Bible. When the students asked what was the authority for his statement, Pfeiffer pointed to his own head.

is allowed to mediate the revealed Word of God to us. Creedal affirmations and other statements of the Church are valuable aids in interpreting and applying the Bible. The experience of individuals, especially those which are prompted and directed by the Holy Spirit, and human reason, also, assist the believer in understanding the revelation. Nevertheless, the Bible alone is the sufficient rule for faith and practice. In it God spoke and speaks.

A DEFINITION OF THEOLOGY

Theology, simply defined, is a study of God and His relationship to all that He has created. We believe it must be derived from the revelation of God in the Bible, for in no other way could it be a reliable testimony for those who are searching after truth.

Not only does the biblical revelation direct the theologian to the items which must be believed, it also sets the outer limits of belief; theology must affirm as required belief only what the Bible either explicitly or implicitly teaches. Theology must also be vitally concerned about interpreting the Bible correctly and applying it properly.

While the source for theology is the biblical material, theology is also concerned about the community of faith from which that revelation comes and the community into which the message is going. Without understanding the ancient community, the message will not be heard clearly and accurately; without understanding the modern community, the message will not be applied properly. This dual concern may be brought out by defining theology as a discipline striving "to give a coherent statement" of the teachings of the Bible, "placed in the context of culture in general, worded in a contemporary idiom, and related to issues of life."[16] It has been further defined as "systematic reflection on scripture . . . and the mission of the Church in mutual relation, with scripture as the norm."[17] Theology is a living, dynamic discipline, not because its authoritative source changes, but because it is always striving to communicate the timeless truths to the ever-changing world.[18]

---

[16]Millard J. Erickson, *Christian Theology* (Grand Rapids: Baker Book House, 1985), 21.

[17]Davis, *Foundations,* 43.

[18]For a discussion of the way the meaning and usage of the term "theology" has changed since ancient Greece (and even conjectured future changes) see F. Whaling, "The Development of the Word 'Theology'," in *Scottish Journal of Theology* 34 (1981): 289–312.

Systematic theology is but one division within the larger field of theology, which also includes historical theology, biblical and exegetical theology, and practical theology. It will be helpful to look at each of the other divisions of theology and note how systematic theology relates to them.

Historical Theology. Historical theology is the study of the way in which the Church has sought down through history to clarify its affirmations about the revealed truths of Scripture. The Bible was written over a period of time as the Holy Spirit inspired various persons to write. Similarly, but without the inspiration which the Bible possesses, the Church, over time, has stated and restated what it believed. That historical development of doctrinal affirmations is the subject of historical theology. The study begins with the historical setting of the biblical books and continues through the history of the Church to the present.

Especially important to historical theology are the attempts to clarify and defend the teachings of the Bible. The Church was required by the pagan world in which it was born to explain what it believed in terms that could be understood. As attacks against those beliefs were mounted by antagonists, the Church was drawn into defending itself against accusations that ranged from the charge that believers were cannibals (because of the Lord's Supper) to the charge that they were revolutionaries (because they claimed but one Lord, and that was not Caesar). In these arenas the Church refined its statements of belief.

Biblical and Exegetical Theology. Biblical and exegetical theology are twin disciplines. They place great emphasis on employing the correct interpretive tools and techniques so as to hear accurately the message of the sacred texts. The overriding concern is to hear the same message of the Bible that the original hearers and readers heard. This drives this division of theology to studies in the biblical languages, the customs and culture of Bible times (especially what archaeology has discovered), etc.

Biblical theology does not try to organize the total teaching of the Bible under specific categories; rather, the goal is to isolate the teachings in given, and limited, biblical contexts, usually book by book, writer by writer, or in historical groupings. Exegetical theology, with the input of biblical theology "will seek to identify the single truth-intention of individual phrases, clauses, and sentences as they make up the thought of paragraphs, sections, and ultimately entire books."[19] Exegesis[20] (or exegetical theology) must be done in the light of the total context of the book as well as the immediate context of the passage.

Old Testament theology is the initial stage. It attempts to let the Old Testament stand on its own, speaking its own message for its own time to its own people.[21] Yet, in a progressive unfolding of God's plan, it has a forward look that points to the future.

New Testament theology must also be studied in its own right, looking for the message the writer had for the audience he was writing to, using good exegesis to determine his intended meaning.

Then it is important to see the unity of both Testaments, while at the same time recognizing the diversity of their different historical and cultural contexts. The divine Author, the Holy Spirit, inspired all the writers of the Bible and provided direction that brought unity to their writings. He caused the New Testament writers to use the Old Testament and project Jesus as its fulfillment, especially of God's plan of salvation. This unity of the Bible is important because it makes possible the application of biblical theology for different situations and in different cultures, as systematic theology attempts to do (taking biblical theology as its source).

Practical Theology. Practical theology is the division of theology that puts the truths of theological investigation into practice in the life of the community. Included in this division are preaching, evangelism, missions, pastoral care and counseling, pastoral administration, church education, and Christian ethics. The message of theology here takes on flesh and blood, so to speak, and ministers among the believers.

Systematic theology plays a vital role within theology in general. It makes use of the data discovered by historical,

---

[19]Walter C. Kaiser, Jr. *Toward an Exegetical Theology* (Grand Rapids: Baker Book House, 1981), 47, 138.

[20]For now, by "exegesis" we mean that the interpreter engages in a process that allows, or brings out, what the Spirit intended to say through the biblical author. Exegesis in no way diminishes the role of the Spirit, either in inspiration or in interpretation.

[21]Revelation given after the passage being studied should not be read into it (e.g., the New Testament is not to be read back into the Old Testament), though such revelation, as Kaiser says, "may (and should, in fact) be brought into our *conclusion* or *summaries after* we have firmly established on exegetical grounds precisely what the passage means." Kaiser, *Exegetical Theology,* 140.

biblical, and exegetical theology, organizing the results of those divisions into an easily transmitted form. As such, it is indebted to them for the truths it presents. Practical theology, then, makes use of the truths organized by systematic theology in its ministry to the body of Christ.

PROTESTANT THEOLOGICAL SYSTEMS

Within Protestantism are several theological systems. The examination of every such theological system would take more space than is available for this text. So we will survey two that have been prominent since the Reformation: Calvinism and Arminianism. Many other theological systems can be found in the present age. Three of them will be considered briefly: liberation theology, evangelicalism, and Pentecostalism. This selective approach is necessary both because of the space limitations and the relationship of these systems to the present text.

Calvinism. Calvinism owes its name and its beginning to the French theologian and reformer John Calvin (1509–64).[22] The central tenet of Calvinism is that God is sovereign of all of His creation.

One of the easier ways to gain a quick understanding of Calvinism is by the use of the acronym TULIP. Before explaining that acronym it must be admitted that any generalization about a theological system is subject to omissions and oversimplification. With that in mind, the acronym TULIP can identify five central beliefs in Calvinism: Total depravity, Unconditional election, Limited atonement, Irresistible grace, and Perseverance of the saints.[23] (T) The human race is so fallen as a result of sin that persons can do nothing either to improve or approve themselves before God. (U) The sovereign God in past eternity elected (chose) some of the race to be saved, without the prior condition of knowing who would accept His offer, out of grace and compassion for fallen humanity. (L) He sent His Son to provide atonement *only* for those whom He had elected. (I) Those elected cannot resist His gracious offer; they will be saved. (P) Once they have

---

[22]Calvinism has, of course, undergone some modification in the teachings of some of Calvin's successors.

[23]All five points of the TULIP are based on a specific view of God's sovereignty: It neglects the fact that God is sovereign over himself and is thereby able to limit himself in areas of His choice so that we might have true free will, able to choose to become His children, rather than bound to be His puppets.

been saved they will persevere to the end and receive the ultimate of salvation, eternal life.

Arminianism. The Dutch theologian Jacob Arminius (1560–1609) disagreed with the tenets of Calvinism, arguing that (1) they tended to make God the author of sin by His choice in past eternity of who would and who would not be saved and (2) they denied the free will of persons because they said no one can resist the grace of God.

The teachings of Arminius and his followers were codified in the five theses of the Articles of Remonstrance (1610): (1) Predestination is conditional on a person's response, being grounded in God's foreknowledge; (2) Christ died for each and every person but only believers are saved; (3) a person is unable to believe and needs the grace of God; but (4) this grace is resistible; (5) whether all the regenerate will persevere requires further investigation.[24]

The differences between Calvinism and Arminianism should be apparent. For Arminians, God knows beforehand those who will respond to His offer of grace, and it is those whom He predestines to share in His promises. In other words, God predestines that all who freely choose His salvation provided in Christ and continue to live for Him will share His promises. Jesus makes atonement potentially for all people, and effectually for those who respond to God's gracious offer of salvation, an offer that they can resist. If they respond with acceptance to God's grace, it is because of the initiation of grace and not of human will alone. Perseverance is conditional upon the continued living of the Christian faith, and falling away from that faith is possible, though God does not let anyone go easily.

Most Pentecostals tend toward the Arminian system of theology, seeing the necessity for response to the gospel and to the Holy Spirit on the part of the individual.[25]

Liberation Theology. Born in Latin America in the late 1960s, liberation theology is a "diffuse movement"[26] of various dissenting groups (e.g., blacks, feminists). Its main concern is the reinterpretation of the Christian faith from the perspective of the poor and the oppressed. Exponents claim

---

[24]R. W. A. Letham, "Arminianism," in *New Dictionary of Theology,* ed. Sinclair B. Ferguson, David F. Wright, and J. I. Packer (Downers Grove, Ill.: InterVarsity Press, 1988), 45–46.

[25]See chap. 10 for further discussion on Calvinism and Arminianism.

[26]H. M. Conn, "Liberation Theology," in *New Dictionary of Theology,* 387.

that the only gospel that properly addresses the needs of those groups of people is one that proclaims liberation from their poverty and oppression. The message of liberationists is judgment for the rich and the oppressor and liberation for the poor and the oppressed.

One of the central concerns of liberation theology is the concept of praxis: theology must be done, not just learned. That is to say, the commitment to the renovation of society so that the poor and oppressed are delivered from their circumstances is the essence of the theological endeavor. The commitment to such change often takes Scripture out of context and can (and often does) employ means that could be described as Marxist or revolutionary.[27]

Evangelicalism. The theological system known as evangelicalism has a widespread influence today. With the formation of the National Association of Evangelicals in 1942, new impetus was given to the proclamation of the tenets of this system, and they have been accepted by members of many Christian bodies. The name gives insight into one of the central concerns of the system, the communication of the gospel to the entire world, a communication that calls individuals to personal faith in Jesus Christ. The theological expressions of evangelicalism come from both Calvinist and Arminian camps. They claim that evangelicalism is nothing more than the same orthodox belief system that was first found in the Early Church. The social agenda of evangelicalism calls the faithful to work for justice in society as well as for the salvation of the people's souls.

Pentecostalism. For the most part, Pentecostal theology fits well within the bounds of the evangelical system. However, Pentecostals take seriously the working of the Holy Spirit to verify the truths as real and empower their proclamation. This often leads to the charge that Pentecostals are experience-based. The charge is not totally true, for the Pentecostal sees the experience brought by the working of the Holy Spirit to be secondary to the Bible in status of authority. The experience verifies, clarifies, emphasizes, or enforces the truths of

---

[27]For further study on liberation theology see Rubem Alves, *A Theology of Human Hope* (Washington: Corpus Books, 1969); Leonardo Boff, *Jesus Christ Liberator* (Maryknoll, N.Y.: Orbis Books, 1978); Gustavo Gutierrez, *A Theology of Liberation: History, Politics, and Salvation,* trans. and ed. Sister Caridad Inda and John Eagleson (Maryknoll, N.Y.: Orbis Books, 1973); Jose Miguez-Bonino, *Doing Theology in a Revolutionary Situation,* trans. John Drury (Philadelphia: Fortress Press, 1975); and, Juan Luis Segundo, *The Liberation of Theology* (Maryknoll: Orbis Books, 1976).

the Bible, and that function of the Spirit is important and crucial.

THEOLOGICAL METHOD

Since it is important that systematic theology be based on the Bible, in this section we will deal with theological method, especially as it interacts with exegesis and biblical theology.

EXEGESIS AND BIBLICAL THEOLOGY AS THE MATRIX

Several stages of development exist in this theological process in which one moves from the Bible to systematic theology: (1) exegesis and interpretation of individual texts, (2) synthesis of these interpretations, according to some system of biblical theology,[28] and (3) the presentation of these teachings in the systematician's own language and for his own needs and the needs of his people.[29]

In Western theology, some organizing principle is used to produce a coherent set of beliefs. Then the Bible's theology, without changing its meaning, is placed in the thought forms of the theologian's audience to communicate God's message

---

[28]For centuries, systematic theology in the West has been arranged according to a coherent system reflecting rational idealism (cf. theologians' quest for a unifying center). This arrangement has also controlled biblical theology, with few exceptions. This use of a single center, however, has limitations; for example, it does not allow for paradox, so prevalent in the ancient world. What is now becoming more acceptable to most theologians is to see some sort of system arranged around a number of centers. See Grant R. Osborne, *The Hermeneutical Spiral: A Comprehensive Introduction to Biblical Interpretation* (Downers Grove, Ill.: InterVarsity, 1991), 282–85; Gerhard Hasel, *New Testament Theology: Basic Issues in the Current Debate* (Grand Rapids: Wm. B. Eerdmans, 1978), especially 204–20; D. A. Carson, "Unity and Diversity in the New Testament: The Possibility of Systematic Theology," in *Scripture and Truth,* ed. D. A. Carson and John D. Woodbridge (Grand Rapids: Zondervan Publishing House, 1983), 65–95; Robert B. Sloan, "Unity in Diversity: A Clue to the Emergence of the New Testament as Sacred Literature," in *New Testament Criticism & Interpretation,* ed. David Alan Black and David S. Dockery (Grand Rapids: Zondervan Publishing House, 1991), 437–68.

[29]What we refer to here is systematic theology. This may even mean using a different system of arrangement. Many see an additional stage of development involving church history. See, for example, Osborne, *Hermeneutical Spiral,* 268–69. William Menzies argues against this stage when reviewing Gordon Fee's *Gospel and Spirit: Issues in New Testament Hermeneutics* (Peabody, Mass.: Hendrickson Publishers, 1991). See his review in *Paraclete* 27 (Winter 1993): 29–32.

in understandable language and help the listeners to solve their problems.

To maintain biblical authority in the process of systematic theology, it is imperative that the person doing the theology avoid deduction. By this we mean that theologians should not begin with a general theological statement and impose it on the biblical text to make the Bible mean what they want it to mean at the expense of the text's real intention. Rather, careful exegetical study of the biblical text should lead (inductively) to a theological statement.

THE NATURE AND FUNCTION OF EXEGESIS

The goal of exegesis is to let the Scripture say what the Spirit intended it to mean in its original context. The interpreter, then, for each text must analyze the social and historical context, the genre and other literary factors, and insights from the original language. Let us make some observations about each of these in order.

In regard to the social and historical context, a biblical writer presupposed his audience had a certain common culture and historical frame; much of this was assumed rather than stated. We must be careful not to assume naively that the biblical writer's cultural and historical frame is the same as ours. It is not. Between the interpreter and any biblical text vast cultural and historical differences exist.

Howard C. Kee makes the point that meaning can be determined only by looking at the social context of words. For example, by being sensitive to social and cultural factors, we can see that Matthew uses the term "righteousness" as "a quality of behavior ... demanded by God and to be fulfilled by his faithful servants," while Paul in a different framework uses it as an action where God sets things right.[30]

Furthermore, we need to be aware of the import of genre, the particular kind of document or literary form one is examining. Being aware of the nature of a document is one of the first principles of interpretation.[31] Unless we know how it is put together and for what reason, we will miss the meaning of the text.

[30]Howard C. Kee, *Knowing the Truth: A Sociological Approach to New Testament Interpretation* (Minneapolis: Fortress Press, 1989). See especially, 50–64. Bruce Malina makes the same point in *The Social World of Luke-Acts,* ed. Jerome H. Neyreys (Peabody, Mass.: Hendrickson Publishers, 1991), 3–23. These approaches are sociolinguistic.

[31]The use of genre is well-established in exegetical method.

Many different genres exist in Scripture: historical narrative (e.g., Genesis, Ruth, Chronicles, and Acts[32]), poetry (e.g., Psalms, Job, Proverbs), gospel (episodic narrative and sermon addressed to particular audiences), epistle (letter), apocalypse and prophecy (Revelation). By studying what the writer is using and why he is using that particular genre, one can more readily interpret the document.

Genre is of interest to the Pentecostal because of the theology of initial evidence, an interpretation that depends in part on the genre of Acts. Pentecostals and evangelicals have debated the genre, the latter often treating Acts as mere history. Pentecostals, on the other hand, argue that Acts is theological in nature,[33] much the same as the Gospel of Luke, since Luke wrote both. Therefore, we can use Acts as a source of doctrine.[34]

Another concern is the meaning of biblical words. Here we must avoid the root fallacy. Simply stated, the root fallacy occurs when a word's etymology (i.e., its root meaning) is applied to that word every time it appears. Or, as sometimes is done, the etymology is applied only to select appearances of the word to support the interpreter's viewpoint. However, usage, not derivation, determines meaning. (For example, "prevent" is from the Latin *praevenire,* "to come before." But it has an entirely different meaning in English today.) Consequently, context is extremely important. A word may have a variety of meanings, but in a particular context only one of them will apply.

BIBLICAL CRITICISM, INTERPRETATION, AND THEOLOGY

The whole area of criticism[35] has developed since the Reformation. The two major divisions of biblical criticism, formerly called higher and lower, are now usually called literary–historical and textual criticism, respectively. Conservatives

---

[32]In general, the hermeneutic applied to Acts must be the same as that applied to Luke, for both are narrative. Some differences do exist, though: The Gospel is episodic narrative; Acts is sustained narrative.

[33]That is, its purpose is to teach theological truth, not simply to satisfy historical curiosity. See I. Howard Marshall, *Luke: Historian and Theologian* (Grand Rapids: Zondervan Publishing House, 1970), 21–52; and Roger Stronstad, *The Charismatic Theology of St. Luke* (Peabody, Mass.: Hendrickson Publishers, 1984), 5–9.

[34]See chap. 13, pp. 432–37.

[35]By "criticism" we mean the art of investigating and analyzing. This has often been seen as negative, but should be understood as positive.

as well as liberals work in both areas, since both types of criticism are necessary in exegesis. Furthermore, both of these offer, and have offered, beneficial service to the Church at large. Historical criticism helps us to know more precisely the historical information of a biblical passage or book, enabling us to interpret it with more insight. Primary sources of historical information include the Bible itself, other ancient writings, and archaeological discoveries. Secondary sources include books written by interpreters, both ancient and modern.

Textual criticism is the science that examines ancient Hebrew, Aramaic, and Greek handwritten copies (manuscripts) of the Bible and seeks to recover what the original inspired writers actually wrote.[36] Thousands of ancient manuscripts of the Bible exist, and all of them have differences here and there in wording, in word order, and in the omission or addition of words.[37] Many of these are mistakes made by copyists. Others may have been deliberate changes or updating of the language. Textual criticism uses objective and scientific methods to sift through the various readings to discover the most probable one.[38]

On the one hand, some have applied to the biblical text fanciful historical reconstructions according to some modern theory of history (usually denying the supernatural in the process). On the other hand, we recognize that the proper frame of reference considers all Scripture to be inspired by God and to partake of a special character that deserves respect. When one engages in biblical criticism, then, ideally one does not attack the Bible (though many do). Rather, one attacks his or her understanding of the Bible so as to bring that interpretation into line with the original meaning of Scripture.[39]

---

[36]The original manuscripts themselves (autographs) were probably worn out by being copied again and again over many years.

[37]These differences are called textual variants. See chap. 3, pp. 106–07.

[38]Specialists use the word "probable" because we do not have the autographs. However, careful investigation shows we can be sure we have what the original writers wrote in all but about one-tenth of one percent of the variant readings, and most of the ones where we cannot be sure are minor variations, such as in spelling. None of these variants affect any of the great teachings of the Bible.

[39]Some of the current methods of literary–historical criticism are *source criticism* (which usually assumes Matthew and Luke used Mark and an unknown source [Q, for Ger. *quelle,* meaning "source"] for their material), *form criticism* (which usually denies the supernatural and breaks the Bible

For example, in its simplest form, **Pentecostal interpreters have for some time used what might be termed "narrative criticism."** Exponents of Spirit baptism have argued for a theology of initial evidence in Acts, believing that speaking in tongues is normative because the narrative frequently notes that this phenomenon occurs when the Spirit initially fills someone. The repetition in the narrative provides archetypical behavior and thereby expresses this theology. The nature of the narrative, then, provides the theology of initial evidence (i.e., an "oughtness"[40] is present in the narrative). That is, what Acts records was intended by Luke to show us that speaking in other tongues is not only the initial physical evidence, but also the convincing evidence that lets us know when a person has actually been baptized in the Holy Spirit.

The theological conservative believes the narrative to be rooted in actual history (i.e., history is the medium of revelation[41]). When the (biblical) writer wrote down the narrative, the Holy Spirit guided the selection of material that served His purpose and omitted that which did not.

Let us take Acts 2 and briefly demonstrate what we are saying. Acts 2 is one account within the larger narrative of

---

up into fragments supposedly pieced together by a collector), and *redaction criticism* (which considers the biblical writers as authors and theologians, but often ignores the great body of Jesus' teaching and the Holy Spirit's inspiration). Many Bible believers make some careful use of the first and third of these methods. D. W. Kerr, not knowing what it would later be called, actually utilized redaction criticism in "The Bible Evidence of the Baptism with the Holy Ghost," *Pentecostal Evangel,* 11 August 1923, in which he argued for the distinctiveness of Spirit baptism. For example, in referring to John 20:30 and 21:15 he wrote: "John made a *selection* of just such materials as served his purpose, and that is, to confirm believers in the faith concerning Jesus Christ the Son of God" (p. 2).

Other methods include *canon criticism* (which considers the present order of the books in the Bible to be important), *narrative criticism* (which pays attention to characters, plot, and climax), *social science criticism* (which uses sociological theories to set up a theoretical model to explain cultures, often from a secular, antisupernatural point of view), and *reader response criticism* (which ignores the world behind the Bible text and shifts the authority to the subjective response of the reader. (See Malina, *World of Luke-Acts,* 3–23, for reaction against reader response criticism).

[40]One of the significant features of theology is its "oughtness." By this I mean that there is some sort of compulsion about it, and in some points more so than others.

[41]Cf. Walter C. Kaiser's view, referred to, commented upon, and presented in Ben C. Ollenburger, Elmer A. Martens, and Gerhard F. Hasel, eds., *The Flowering of Old Testament Theology,* (Winona Lake, Ind.: Eisenbrauns, 1992), 233. In fact, in much of the approaches of biblical theology, history is significant, though in different ways.

Acts. We determine that it is a specific narrative because we
are able to distinguish its boundaries, within which we are
able to find the characters, plot, and climax. The chapter has
three parts: the Spirit's coming, the people's response, and
Peter's sermon.[42]

The heart of the narrative (Peter's message) explains the
theological function of tongues and the coming of the Spirit.
Tongues are the sign that the promised age of salvation and
the Spirit have arrived; tongues are the sign that the Spirit
has empowered the Church for inspired witness of Jesus.
Furthermore, the primary purpose of tongues is to witness
that the Hebrew Scriptures prophesied about this age of the
Spirit, that all of God's people would have the Spirit and speak
in tongues, and that these tongues would evidence that God
had raised Jesus from the dead and had exalted Him to heaven,
where He is now pouring out the Spirit. Also, people who
speak in tongues witness about the day of salvation and the
gospel of Jesus (cf. 1:8), the coming of the kingdom of God,
which now confronts the power of darkness in signs and
wonders. Luke, inspired by the Holy Spirit, selected the main
elements from the Day of Pentecost and placed them in this
brief narrative so as to convince the people that they should
seek the baptism in the Spirit.

The emphasis of the coming of the Spirit in power is a
major theme in Luke and Acts. This suggests that Luke's audience lacked the Spirit baptism and that he considered the
norm for the Early Church to be Spirit-baptized with the
evidence of speaking in tongues. His audience, then, should
receive this baptism with the sign of speaking in tongues. This
empowerment would thrust them out into their world as a
powerful witnessing community.

Narration was common in antiquity and still is in many
places, especially the Third World. It is also making a come-
back in the West. Narrative communicates indirectly: the nar-
rator makes his point(s) through such elements as dialogue
and behavior. Behavior in this way becomes archetypical, that
is, it is what the readers are expected to evaluate and emulate
(e.g., in Acts 2 receiving the Spirit with speaking in tongues
would be normative).

Narrative, and indirection, is contrasted to types of literature that communicate directly. In direct communication the
author makes his point in the first person, and it occurs in

---

[42]Actually, not a sermon in the ordinary sense of the word, but a manifestation of the Holy Spirit's gift of prophecy.

propositional form. An example of direction in Scripture is the letter form. The Bible contains theology in both narrative and propositional form.

PRESUPPOSITIONS OF THE INTERPRETER AND THEOLOGIAN

Finally, it is important that we discuss what we as interpreters bring to the text from our world (i.e., presuppositions). First, we should be committed to verbal, plenary inspiration.[43] The methods outlined above should affirm this view. We must pay attention to the whole counsel of God and avoid overworking any one theme or text. Otherwise, a canon within a canon emerges, another serious error. That is, in a practical way we draw a circle inside a larger circle (the entire Bible) and say in practice that this is more inspired than the rest. Or if we derive theology only from a select part of Scripture, the same thing happens.

It is important, therefore, that the Pentecostal have both a biblical and a Pentecostal base and frame of reference. First, the Pentecostal must believe in the supernatural world, especially in God who works in mighty ways and reveals himself in history. Miracles in the biblical sense are a common occurrence. In the Bible, "miracle" refers to any manifestation of God's power, not necessarily to a rare or unusual event.[44] Furthermore, other powers in that supernatural world, angelic (good) and demonic (evil), enter and operate in our world. The Pentecostal is not a materialist (believing that nothing exists except matter and its laws), nor a rationalist, but recognizes the reality of this supernatural realm.

Second, the Pentecostal's frame of reference must focus on

---

[43]See chap. 3, pp. 100–01. All evangelicals and Pentecostals should consider carefully Jeremy Begbie, "Who is this God?—Biblical Inspiration Revisited," in *Tyndale Bulletin* 43 (November 1992): 259–82. He points out significant weaknesses about the view of the Trinity and salvation manifested in B. B. Warfield's description of inspiration. Warfield's lack of biblical attention to the theology of the Spirit causes him to fall into these weaknesses. According to Begbie, James Barr falls into similar errors.

[44]This definition is against that of Norman L. Geisler in *Miracles and the Modern Mind: A Defense of Biblical Miracles* (Grand Rapids: Baker Book House, 1992), 14, who, after discussing definitions, concludes, "Natural law describes naturally caused regularities; a miracle is a supernaturally caused singularity." This approach to miracles is somewhat typical of the approach of the rational evangelical, who says miracles ceased after the New Testament was completed.

God's disclosure of himself.[45] The Pentecostal believes that
Scripture is the authoritative mode of revelation, which affirms, confirms, guides, and witnesses to God's activity in the
world, when properly interpreted. But a rational knowing or
simple memorizing of Scripture does not take the place of a
personal experience of regeneration and the baptism in the
Holy Spirit, with all the activities of witness and edification
that the Spirit opens up to us.

CHAPTER
2
Theological
Foundations

Pentecostals believe it is counterproductive to downplay
these experiences. John's Gospel clearly, purposefully, and
powerfully says that rebirth by the Spirit is the way to open
up knowledge of God. Without this experience, one cannot
know God. Another way to perceive this is to apply the term
"cognitive" to that which comes from studying Scripture (or
theology in the Western manner) and the term "affective" to
knowledge that comes from personal experience. We should
not play one against the other; both are essential. But personal
experience is important. How great regeneration and the baptism in the Spirit are! After both, we know God more fully
and, certainly, personally.

Furthermore, the Pentecostal believes God speaks to His
church through the gifts of the Holy Spirit to correct, edify,
or comfort. Although these are subordinate to and discerned
in light of Scripture, they should be encouraged.

With this in mind, theology (and education) need not
deaden spiritual fervor. Actually, it is not theology or education but the theological and educational frame of reference
that dampens the work of the Holy Spirit. It is important,
then, to interpret the Bible on its own terms and with the
appropriate frame of reference. That will give us an
experience-certified theology, a theology that through faith
and obedience becomes a Bible-based "experience-reality,"[46]
effective in our daily lives, rather than a theology that is
merely something to argue about.

STUDY QUESTIONS

1. What is religion and how does Christianity differ from
other religions?

---

[45]What we are suggesting here pertains to epistemology—ways of knowing and perceiving reality. Unfortunately, both conservative and liberal
Westerners hold to a primarily rational epistemology. This is inadequate
for the Pentecostal. The world of the Bible is not that of the rationalist,
for it recognizes the supernatural, and God-given supernatural experiences.

[46]Stronstad, *Charismatic Theology,* 81.

2. How do the various categories of authority differ in their methods and results?

3. Why is it important to understand the life and culture of Bible times?

4. What do historical and biblical theology contribute to systematic theology?

5. What are the strengths and weaknesses of Calvinism and Arminianism?

6. What is the goal of exegesis and what is involved in reaching that goal?

7. How have Pentecostals used narrative criticism and with what effect?

8. What is involved in having both a biblical and a Pentecostal base for our theology?

God's Inspired Word

John R. Higgins

Theology, in its attempt to know God and to make Him known, presupposes that knowledge about God has been revealed. This revelation is foundational to all theological affirmations and pronouncements. What has not been revealed cannot be known, studied, or explained.

Simply put, revelation is the act of making known something that was previously unknown. What was hidden is now disclosed. A mother reveals what is baking in the oven; the auto mechanic reveals what is causing the engine to stall; the little boy reveals what creature is jumping in his pocket. Each of the mysteries is ended.

Although revelation occurs in every area of life, the term is especially associated with matters of religion. "Wherever there is religion, there is the claim to revelation."[1] Questions of faith center on God's becoming known to human beings. Christianity is a revealed religion based on divine self-disclosure.

The Bible uses a number of Greek and Hebrew terms to express the concept of revelation.[2] The Hebrew verb *gālāh* means to reveal by uncovering or by stripping something away (Isa. 47:3). Frequently it is used of God's communication of himself to people. "Surely the Sovereign LORD does nothing without revealing his plan to his servants the proph-

---

[1]Emil Brunner, *Revelation and Reason* (Philadelphia: The Westminster Press, 1946), 20.

[2]Dewey M. Beegle, "The Biblical Concept of Revelation," in *The Authoritative Word,* ed. Donald K. McKim (Grand Rapids: Wm. B. Eerdmans, 1983), 95. Beegle suggests over thirty terms associated with the concept of revelation used in the Bible.

ets" (Amos 3:7). The Greek word *apokalupsis* (revelation) is associated with the making known of the Christian gospel. Paul said he did not receive the gospel from man's instruction, but he "received it by revelation from Jesus Christ" (Gal. 1:12). J. Oliver Buswell claims that *apokalupsis* may be used of persons or objects, but is usually used of some revealed truth.[3] On the other hand, it is God who manifests or shows (Gk. *phaneroō*) himself (1 Tim. 3:16).

In other words, revelation involves not only information about God, but also the presentation of God himself. This, however, does not mean that one must reject propositional revelation[4] in favor of existential revelation.[5] Rather, "revelation *about* God is crucial to the knowledge *of* God."[6] Through His words and acts God makes known His person, His ways, His values, His purposes, and His plan of salvation. The ultimate goal of divine revelation is that people will come to know God in a real and personal way.

Although divine revelation is often limited to God's self-disclosure, in original acts or words, it may also be understood as a larger chain of revelatory events. This broader understanding of divine revelation would include reflection and inscripturation (i.e., putting the revelation into written form) by inspired writers, the process of canonization of the inspired writings, and the illumination by the Holy Spirit of what God has revealed.

THE REVELATION OF GOD TO HUMANKIND

Inherent in the concept of a God who reveals himself is the reality of a God who is fully conscious of His own being. Cornelius Van Til describes God's knowledge of himself as analytical, meaning "knowledge that is not gained by reference to something that exists without the knower."[7] God's knowledge of himself did not come from comparing or contrasting himself with anything outside himself. "God had in himself all knowledge from all eternity. . . . Hence, all knowl-

---

[3]James Oliver Buswell, *A Systematic Theology of the Christian Religion,* vol. 1 (Grand Rapids: Zondervan Publishing House, 1962), 183.

[4]Statements that declare something about God.

[5]That is, knowledge that comes through one's own personal experience.

[6]Clark H. Pinnock, *Biblical Revelation—The Foundation of Christian Theology* (Chicago: Moody Press, 1971), 24.

[7]Cornelius Van Til, *The Defense of the Faith* (Philadelphia: The Presbyterian and Reformed Publishing Co., 1972), 37.

edge that any finite creature of God would ever have, whether of things that pertain directly to God or of things that pertain to objects in the created universe itself, would ... have to rest upon the revelation of God."[8]

The absolutely and eternally self-conscious God took the initiative to make himself known to His creation.

God's revelation of himself was a deliberate self-disclosure. No one forced God to unmask himself; no one discovered Him by accident. In a voluntary act God made himself known to those who otherwise could not know Him. Emil Brunner sees this self-revelation as an "incursion from another dimension," bringing knowledge "wholly inaccessible to man's natural faculties for research and discovery."[9]

Finite humanity is reminded that the infinite God cannot be found apart from His own invitation to know Him. J. Gresham Machen calls into question the gods of people's own making:

A divine being that could be discovered by my efforts, apart from His gracious will to reveal Himself ..., would be either a mere name for a certain aspect of man's own nature, a God that we could find within us, or else ... a mere passive thing that would be subject to investigation like the substances that are analyzed in a laboratory. ... I think we ought to be rather sure that we cannot know God unless God has been pleased to reveal Himself to us.[10]

In the Book of Job, the answer to Zophar's question, "Can you fathom the mysteries of God?" is a resounding no (Job 11:7). By one's own searching, apart from what God has revealed, nothing could be known about God and His will, not even His existence. Because the infinite cannot be uncovered by the finite, all human affirmations about God end up as questions rather than declarations. "The highest achievements of the human mind and spirit fall short of arriving at the knowledge of God."[11]

A person never progresses beyond the reality that what God has freely revealed sets the boundaries of all knowledge

---

[8]Cornelius Van Til, *An Introduction to Systematic Theology* (Phillipsburg, N.J.: Presbyterian and Reformed Publishing Co., 1978), 63.

[9]Brunner, *Revelation and Reason,* 23, 30.

[10]J. Gresham Machen, *The Christian Faith in the Modern World* (Grand Rapids: Wm. B. Eerdmans, 1936), 14–15.

[11]J. Rodman Williams, *Renewal Theology,* vol. 1 (Grand Rapids: Zondervan Publishing House, 1988), 31.

of Him. Divine revelation strips away all pretensions of human pride, autonomy, and self-sufficiency. The God of the universe has made himself known; the needed response to this initiative is, like Kepler's, to think God's thoughts after Him.

God not only initiated the revelation of himself, but also determined what that revelation would be, the form it would take, and the varied conditions and circumstances required for making himself known. His revelation of himself was a controlled self-disclosure. The communication of himself was exclusively determined by God.

God set the times of His revelation. He did not reveal himself all at once, but chose to make himself known gradually over many centuries. "In the past God spoke to our forefathers . . . at many times and in various ways" (Heb. 1:1). Even for God there is "a time to be silent and a time to speak" (Eccles. 3:7). He revealed himself when He was ready, when He wanted to declare His name and His ways (Exod. 3:14–15).

The manner in which God revealed himself—helping human beings to understand His nature, His ways, and His relationship to them—was also determined by Him. At times it was external, such as a voice, an event, a cloud, or an angel. On other occasions the revelation was internal, a dream or vision (Exod. 13:21–22; Num. 12:6; Dan. 9:21–22; Acts 9:3–4). But in either case, God did the revealing; He selected the manner in which His truth would be made known.

Likewise God determined the place and circumstance of His revelation. He made himself known in Eden's garden, in Midian's desert, and on Sinai's mountain (Gen. 2:15–17; Exod. 3:4–12; 19:9–19). In palaces, in pastures, and in prisons He made His person and ways known (Neh. 1:11; Luke 2:8–14; Acts 12:6–11). Human searching for God results only in finding God on His terms (Jer. 29:13). God determines even the recipients of His revelation, be they shepherd or king, fisherman or priest (See Dan. 5:5–24; Matt. 4:18–20; 26:63–64).

The content of divine revelation is what God wanted communicated—nothing more, nothing less. All talk about God is speculation apart from what He himself has revealed. Karl Barth describes God as the one "to whom there is no path nor bridge, concerning whom we could not say . . . a single word if He did not of His own initiative meet us."[12] From God's initial self-disclosure and throughout the eternal ages,

---

[12]Karl Barth, *Church Dogmatics,* vol. 1 (Edinburgh: T. & T. Clark, 1975), 321.

Carl F. H. Henry says, "the God of the Bible is wholly deter-
minative in respect to revelation."[13]

Revelation, initiated and determined by God, is therefore
personal communication. It originates in a personal God and
is received by a personal creation. God reveals himself, not
as some mere cosmic force or inanimate object, but as a
personal being who speaks, loves, and cares for His creation.
He scorns "other gods," who are only the work of a crafts-
man's hands (Isa. 40:12–28; 46:5–10), and reveals himself in
terms of personal relationships, identifying himself by such
terms as Father, Shepherd, Friend, Leader, and King. It is in
these kinds of personal relationships that human beings are
privileged to know Him.

Divine revelation is an expression of grace. God did not
have a need that compelled Him to reveal himself. Perfect
fellowship among Father, Son, and Holy Spirit required no
external supplement. Rather, God made himself known to
human beings for their benefit. Humankind's greatest privilege is to be able to know God and glorify and enjoy Him
forever.[14] Such privileged communication from the Creator
reflects God's love and goodness. Only because of God's gracious self-giving is a person able to come to know God truly.
Brunner finds it wonderfully amazing that "God Himself gives
Himself to me myself, and after that I can give myself to Him,
in that I accept His self-giving."[15]

Carl Henry draws attention to the "unto you, unto us"
character of divine revelation as God brings the priceless
good news that He calls the human race to fellowship with
Him.

God's purpose in revelation is that we may know him personally
as he is, may avail ourselves of his gracious forgiveness and offer
of new life, may escape the catastrophic judgment for our sins, and
venture personal fellowship with him. "I will . . . be your God, and
ye shall be my people" (Lev. 26:12, KJV), he declares.[16]

In mercy God continues to reveal himself to fallen human-

---

[13]Carl F. H. Henry, *God, Revelation and Authority,* vol. 2 (Waco, Tex.:
Word Books, 1976), 19.

[14]See "The Larger Catechism" in *The Westminster Standards* (Philadelphia: Board of Christian Education of the Presbyterian Church in the U.S.A.,
1925), Question and Answer 1.

[15]Brunner, *Revelation and Reason,* 42.

[16]Henry, *God, Revelation and Authority,* vol. 1, 31.

ity. To walk with Adam and Eve in the garden paradise is one thing, but to call wayward, rebellious sinners to forgiveness and reconciliation is another (Gen. 3:8; Heb. 3:15). One could understand had God's gracious revelation ended with Eden's flaming sword, Israel's golden calf, or Calvary's rugged cross. However, God's revelation is redemptive in character. "The invisible, hidden and transcendent God, whom no man has seen nor can see, has planted His Word in the human situation that sinners might be brought nigh unto God."[17]

An invitation to personal knowledge of himself is God's highest gift to the human race. Its attainment is the cry of the human heart. "Thou madest us for Thyself, and our heart is restless, until it repose in Thee."[18] To know God at all is to want to know Him more. "I consider everything a loss compared to the surpassing greatness of knowing Christ Jesus" (Phil. 3:8).

Clearly God's revelation of himself is for humankind's benefit. This does not mean, however, that divine revelation itself guarantees a positive response to God by the recipient of that revelation. "Precisely because divine revelation is for man's benefit we dare not obscure its informational content nor mistake God's disclosure as automatically saving. . . . Simply hearing God's revealed good news . . . does not redeem us automatically."[19]

God's revelation is a proclamation of life, but when rejected, a proclamation of death (Deut. 30:15; 2 Cor. 2:16).

God has graciously revealed himself and His ways to His creation. His self-disclosure spans the centuries, varies in form, and offers privileged communion with the Creator. This abundant revelation, however, has not exhausted the mystery of the eternal God. Some things about himself and His purpose He has chosen not to make known (Deut. 29:29; Job 36:26; Ps. 139:6; Rom. 11:33). This conscious withholding of information is a reminder that God transcends His own revelation. What God has withheld is beyond the need and possibility of persons to find out.

Revelation has both its basis and its limits in the will of God. . . . Human beings universally have no native resourcefulness for delineating God's nature and will. Not even gifted persons of special

---

[17]Pinnock, *Biblical Revelation,* 29.

[18]*The Confessions of St. Augustine,* trans. Edward B. Pusey (New York: P. F. Collier and Son Corporation,1937), 5.

[19]Henry, *God, Revelation and Authority,* vol. 1, 38.

capacity or notable religious endowment can by their own abilities divine the secrets of the Infinite. ... whereby they on their own power and initiative may clarify the mysteries of eternity.[20]

Libraries are full of explanations of God's self-revelation, but such explanations must not be understood as adding to that revelation. As John the Baptist, one is called "to testify concerning that light," not to create new light (John 1:7).

At all points God is fully in control of His own revelation. He is not imprisoned by the majesty of His person so that He cannot reveal himself, but neither is He incapable of selective revelation. Just as He determines the content and circumstances of His revelation, He likewise determines the extent of that revelation. God's conscious limiting of His revelation is reflective of the nature of His person. "While God is revealed in his creation, he nonetheless ontologically [in relation to His being or existence] transcends the universe as its Creator, and transcends man epistemologically [with respect to the nature and limits of human knowledge] as well."[21] The God of the Bible is not pantheistic but reveals himself as Creator to His creation—a separate and voluntary revelation of which He is totally in control.

Although human beings will never fully exhaust the knowledge of God, God's revelation is not incomplete with respect to humanity's needs. While not exhaustive, what God has made known is sufficient for salvation, for acceptability before God, and for instruction in righteousness. Through His revelation one can come to know God and to grow in that knowledge (Ps. 46:10; John 17:3; 2 Pet. 3:18; 1 John 5:19–20).

The inexhaustible God will continue to transcend His revelation, even though our knowledge of Him will be greater, or fuller, in heaven (1 Cor. 13:12). One of the joys of heaven will be the unfolding throughout all eternity of greater insights into God's person and His gracious dealings with the redeemed (Eph. 2:7). That we now know only "in part," however, does not alter the validity, importance, and dependability of His present divine revelation.

When it comes to divine revelation, the God of the Bible stands in stark contrast with the gods of polytheistic paganism.

---

[20]Ibid., 50.
[21]Ibid., 48.

He is no local deity competing for a voice in the affairs of a region with divided loyalties. He is not the dumb idol carved from wood or stone. Neither is He the projected voice of political leaders who cloak their ideas in religious mythology. Rather, He is the one true God who is Lord over the whole universe. The revelation of His will is law for all peoples. He is the Judge of all the earth (Gen. 18:25; Ps. 24:1; Rom. 2:12–16).

Walther Eichrodt notes the distinct linguistic possibility that the Hebrew *Sh{e}ma'* may be read, "Yahweh our God is one single God" (Deut. 6:4), indicating Yahweh is not a God who can be split into various divinities or powers like the Canaanite gods.[22] When He speaks, there is but one voice; there is no room for confusing or conflicting messages. Although God may choose to reveal himself through various means and to speak through many people, the message remains His and a continuity is evident. In divine revelation there are no dual or rival revelations, but a comprehensive unity flowing from the one and only God.

Consequently, there is an exclusiveness to true divine revelation. Henry suggests two prominent dangers that threaten this rightful exclusiveness. The first is the danger of seeing the human experience of the supernatural in non-Christian world religions as valid divine revelation. These religions do not speak with the voice of God but rather of Satan and his demons (see 1 Cor. 10:20). Some of them even deny the indispensable corollary of genuine divine revelation, the personal existence of God. The second is the tendency to acknowledge additional sources of independent revelation (such as human reason and experience) alongside God's own disclosure. While human reason enables one to know the truth of God, reason is not a new originating source of divine truth.[23] Similarly one may experience the truth of God, but one's experience does not create that truth. One's theology must not be built on subjective experience but on the objective Word of God. Our experience must be judged by the Word, and we must be like the Bereans who "received the message with great eagerness and examined the Scriptures every day to see if what Paul said was true" (Acts 17:11).

---

[22]Walther Eichrodt, *Theology of the Old Testament,* vol. 1 (Philadelphia: The Westminster Press, 1967), 226.

[23]Henry, *God, Revelation and Authority,* vol. 2, 72–73.

CATEGORIES OF DIVINE REVELATION

CHAPTER

3

God's
Inspired
Word

The two primary categories of divine revelation are general revelation and special revelation. General revelation involves God's self-disclosure through some mediate, natural mode. Special revelation is divine self-disclosure through an immediate, supernatural mode. Natural theology[24] and revealed theology are the theological understandings arrived at through human reason and reflection as one views general revelation and special revelation respectively. General revelation is usually understood as God's making himself known through history, natural environment, and human nature.

GENERAL REVELATION

Human History. God has revealed himself through the providential ordering of human history. As the divine Governor of His universe, He is at work in the oversight and direction of His creation. He guides the affairs of humanity as He moves toward the fulfillment of His purposes. In behalf of His people He acts forcefully and decisively. Israel delighted in rehearsing the mighty "acts of God" throughout their history (Ps. 136). He is the God who sets up kings and brings down kings (Dan. 2:21). The creeds of the Church recite God's redemptive acts in history. For example, the Apostles' Creed highlights the acts of creation; Christ's incarnation, crucifixion, resurrection, ascension, and second coming; and the judgment. The student of history may trace God's hand in the interactions of nations. As the God who is just and powerful, His dealings with humanity have continuity. "History has a theological character: all of it bears the imprint of God's activity."[25] All history unfolds under God's governing purpose as He controls, guides, and personally acts within it.

Nature. God also reveals himself through nature and through the universe. Creation, with its infinite variety, beauty, and order, reflects a God who is infinitely wise and powerful. The moon and countless stars in the heavens are the work of the fingers of the Lord; His name is majestic in all the earth, which He has created (Ps. 8).

---

[24]Natural theology develops its ideas using human reason apart from and often in a way critical of, or even rejecting, divine revelation. It often makes the individual's own reason the final authority.

[25]Williams, *Renewal Theology,* vol. 1, 34.

Psalm 19 provides important information about general revelation in nature.

> The heavens declare the glory of God; the skies proclaim the work of his hands. Day after day they pour forth speech; night after night they display knowledge. There is no speech or language where their voice is not heard. Their voice goes out into all the earth, their words to the ends of the world (Ps. 19:1–4).

This passage has been wrapped in controversy largely because of the more literal reading of verse three. "They have no speech, there are no words; no sound is heard from them" (v. 3, NIV, alternate translation). Four different interpretations of this passage suggest four views on general revelation in nature.

1. The universe is mute and there is no objective general revelation through nature.

2. There is an objective general revelation in nature, but it is not subjectively perceived because it falls on deaf ears and blind eyes adversely affected by sin.

3. There is no objective general revelation in nature. Rather, a subjective general revelation is read into nature by believers only. The one who already knows God through special revelation reads Him into the creation.

4. There is an objective general revelation, but it is not presented in a formal written or spoken language, nor is it propositional in form. Instead, it is embodied in the language of nature, which transcends all human language, has gone out to the ends of the earth, and is available to all humankind.

The fourth interpretation seems best to fit the context of Psalm 19 and the teaching of Scripture elsewhere on general revelation and nature. "The wordless message of God's glory extends to all the earth. The reflection of God in the vast array of heavenly bodies pulsating with light is viewed by a worldwide audience."[26] Other psalms, such as Psalms 29, 33, 93, and 104, celebrate God's majesty revealed in the realm of nature.

To the people of Lystra Paul speaks of a continuing witness the Creator God has left about His relationship to His world. "We are bringing you good news, telling you to turn . . . to the living God, who made heaven and earth and sea and everything in them. . . . He has shown kindness by giving you

---

[26]Bruce A. Demarest, *General Revelation: Historical Views and Contemporary Issues* (Grand Rapids: Zondervan Publishing House, 1982), 36.

rain from heaven and crops in their seasons; he provides you with plenty of food and fills your hearts with joy" (Acts 14:15,17).

In Paul's speech to the Athenians at the Areopagus (Acts 17), he appeals to what has already been revealed to them through general revelation—that God is Creator and is sovereign over His creation. He is self-sufficient, the source of life and all else needed by humankind, and is near and active in human affairs. Significantly Paul gives the reason for this self-disclosure of God in nature. "God did this so that men would seek him and perhaps reach out for him and find him" (Acts 17:27). This is the positive goal of general revelation.

Romans 1:18–21 has been called the locus classicus for God's self-disclosure in nature.[27] General revelation through nature is universally given and universally received. It brings truth about God to all human beings, including the sinner. Through nature the invisible qualities of God—"his eternal power and divine nature"—are made visible. This truth about God, mediated through nature, is "clearly seen, being understood from what has been made" (Rom. 1:20). Both the perception of the senses and the reflection of the mind are confronted by the phenomena of nature.

The revelation of nature is a revelation from God about God. "God's speech in nature is not to be confused with the notion of a talking cosmos, as by those who insist that nature speaks, and that we must therefore hear what nature says as if nature were the voice of God. 'Hear God!' is the biblical message, not 'Listen to Nature!' "[28]

God reveals himself in the created order of nature, yet He is not to be identified with the created universe as pantheism insists. The earth and the created universe are not god or gods. If they were, their destruction would be the destruction of God. On the other hand, God is involved in the ongoing processes of the universe He created, and He reveals himself in many ways.

Unfortunately, the rebellious sinner suppresses the truth from nature about God, incuring His wrath (Rom. 1:18) and sinking to further ungodliness (Rom. 1:21–32).

Human Nature. General revelation also includes God's self-disclosure through one's own human nature. The human race was created in the image of God (Gen. 1:26–27). The Fall

---

[27]Demarest, *General Revelation,* 238.

[28]Henry, *God, Revelation and Authority,* vol. 1, 98.

brought a break in the relationship with God. But the image of God in human beings was not annihilated by the Fall.

> Although man is a sinner through and through, the Bible acknowledges that he is a rational creature with whom God can communicate. ... Thus God's invitation ..., " 'Come now, let us reason together,' says the Lord." ... Moreover, New Testament texts such as Ephesians 4:24 and Colossians 3:10 assure us that a valid point of contact does exist at the epistemic level [that is, at a level of genuine knowledge] between God and man.[29]

After the Fall this image was marred and distorted but not utterly destroyed (Gen. 9:6; James 3:9). It is in need of renewal.

The moral and spiritual nature of humanity reflects, however inadequately, the moral character of the holy and perfect Creator. A universal, though distorted, awareness of a connection between humanity and God is affirmed repeatedly in Scripture and is the testimony of missionaries and anthropologists alike.[30] Romans 2 attests to the validity of God's revelation through human nature even apart from any special revelation from God (Rom. 2:11–15). Those who do not have the Mosaic law "do by nature things required by the law," because "the requirements of the law are written on their hearts" (Rom. 2:14–15). Even persons estranged from God because of sin are not bereft of a moral consciousness and moral impulses that reflect norms of conduct. God's gracious moral revelation to the human heart preserves sinful humankind from unchecked self-destruction.

The Jews had a written moral code in the Law. The Gentiles, on the other hand, had basic moral concepts, which were foundational to the law written on their hearts.[31] Paul's designation "requirements of the law" emphasizes that the Gentiles do not have a different law, but essentially the same law that confronts the Jews. This "heart law" is only less in detail and clarity. The unifying principle between the written Law and the heart law is the source of them both—God!

Many limit this mode of general revelation to a person's conscience. However, it seems preferable to include the whole of a person's moral nature, which would include the con-

---

[29]Demarest, *General Revelation,* 128.

[30]Ibid., 229, 243.

[31]The Jews had both the written Law and the heart law.

science. The conscience witnesses to God's "heart revelation" as a "second knowing"[32] alongside what has already been revealed. The "joint witness" of conscience judges whether one is living in obedience to the things of the law written on the heart. In addition, one's thoughts either accuse or excuse an individual on the basis of obedience or disobedience to the heart law (Rom. 2:15). Consequently, even without being confronted by any written law of God, unregenerate people experience countless mental conflicts every day as they are confronted by God's law within them.

General revelation brings cognitive knowledge of God to all humankind. This knowledge is true and clear and relentless. "The Creator God's testimony to himself . . . continues daily and hourly and moment by moment. Fallen man in his day-to-day life is never completely detached nor isolated from the revelation of God."[33] The person who declares there is no God is most foolish, for such a declaration denies what is known in the depths of one's being and what is displayed at every turn of life.

Bruce Demarest lists nineteen specific areas of knowledge about God that Scripture indicates come to humanity through general revelation.[34] He concludes that "God's glory (Ps. 19:1), divine nature (Rom. 1:20), and moral demands (Rom. 2:14–15) are to some extent known through general revelation!"[35] This revelation of himself is objective, rational, and valid regardless of human response to, or availability of, any special revelation from God. "General Revelation is not something read into nature by those who know God on other grounds; it is already present, by the creation and continuing providence of God."[36]

---

[32]Gk. *suneidēsis,* "co-knowing," "conscious, spiritual or moral awareness."

[33]Henry, *God, Revelation and Authority,* vol. 1, 85.

[34]"They include the facts that God exists (Ps. 19:1; Rom. 1:19) and He is uncreated (Acts 17:24); that He has standards (Rom. 2:15), requires persons to do good (Rom. 2:15), and judges evil (Rom. 2:15–16); that He is the Creator (Acts 14:15), Sustainer (Acts 14:17; 17:25), and Lord (Acts 17:24), and is self-sufficient (Acts 17:24), transcendent (Acts 17:24), immanent (Acts 17:26–27), eternal (Ps. 93:2), great (Ps. 8:3–4), majestic (Ps. 29:4), powerful (Ps. 29:4; Rom. 1:20), wise (Ps. 104:24), good (Acts 14:17), righteous (Rom. 1:32), sovereign (Acts 17:26), and to be worshiped (Acts 14:15; 17:23). Demarest, *General Revelation,* 243.

[35]Ibid.

[36]Millard J. Erickson, *Christian Theology* (Grand Rapids: Baker Book House, 1985), 170.

To affirm the validity of objective general revelation is not to deny the consequences of the Fall with regard to such revelation. The Bible clearly states that sin has adversely affected humankind's knowledge of God (Acts 17:23; Rom. 1:18–21; 2 Cor. 4:4). Sin obscures the objective knowledge of God that comes through general revelation to the point that it limits that knowledge to a cognitive understanding that God exists in majesty and power and executes moral judgment. Sin's effect on the intellect has influenced one's philosophical presuppositions and conclusions and has corrupted the will. "Unbelievers are not God's children, not because they have no knowledge of him, but because they lack spiritual commitment and vocational obedience."[37]

Sinful humanity willfully suppresses and rejects the knowledge of God. It manufactures truth substitutes, transgresses God's law that is stamped on the heart, and invents new gods. The knowledge of the true God through general revelation is perverted to become the source of the gods of many world religions.[38] God is made in the image of human beings, rather than human beings acknowledging they were made in the image of God.

Despite the popularity of a neo-universalism (see chap. 10) which accepts the truth of all religions, one must recognize these religions as serious distortions of God's true revelation. Persons seeking after God in false religions are not to be applauded as "good enough." The wrath of God is directed at them for their idolatry (Rom. 1:18,23–32).

Suppression of the truth of God in general revelation does not relieve one of the responsibility to appropriate that truth.

The revelation of God [cognitive] invades and penetrates the very mind and conscience of every man, despite the fact that in face of this very revelation, men do not *choose* to know God [existentially]. ... Man's situation is not one of natural agnosticism, nor is he called to trust in God in the absence of cognitive knowledge; rather, sinful man violates what he knows to be true and right.[39]

One can suppress only what one has first experienced. General revelation brings the knowledge of God to all persons

---

[37]Henry, *God, Revelation and Authority,* vol. 1, 129.

[38]See, for example, Raimundo Panikkar's scheme of religions in such writings as *The Unknown Christ of Hinduism* (London: Darton, Longman and Todd, 1964).

[39]Henry, *God, Revelation and Authority,* vol. 1, 130, 136.

and "though repressed, [it] is not destroyed. It remains intact, though deeply buried in the subconscious."[40] Since this knowledge of God comes to all, all are left "without excuse" before Him (Rom. 1:20).

While the Bible affirms the reality of objective general revelation, it denies the validity of a natural theology that is based on human reason alone. One cannot reflect on the truth revealed in general revelation and develop a theology that enables one to come to a saving knowledge of God. What Paul says in Romans 1 and 2 concerning general revelation must be understood in light of chapter 3, which emphasizes that all fall short of God's standard and therefore not a single one is righteous (Rom. 3:10,23). General revelation is not designed to allow one to develop additional knowledge of God from the truth it brings. Rather, the truth of general revelation "serves, as does the law [of Scripture], merely to make guilty, not to make righteous."[41] However, it does cause the believer to rejoice in the truth (Ps. 19:1) and may be used by the Spirit to cause one to seek the truth (Acts 17:27).

In response to the troubling question of God's justice in condemning those who have never heard the gospel in the formal sense, Millard J. Erickson states, "No one is completely without opportunity. All have known God; if they have not effectually perceived him, it is because they have suppressed the truth. Thus all are responsible."[42] It is important, however, to see general revelation not as the callousness of God but as the mercy of God (Rom. 11:32). "General cosmic-anthropological revelation is continuous with God's special revelation in Jesus Christ not only because both belong to the comprehensive revelation of the living God, but also because general revelation establishes and emphasizes the universal guilt of man whom God offers rescue in the special redemptive manifestation of his Son."[43]

As does the written Law, general revelation condemns sinners in order to point them to a Redeemer outside of themselves. Its intent is to lead them to special revelation. In fact, the insufficiency of general revelation to save fallen humanity necessitated a special revelation of Jesus Christ as the Truth who sets people free from the bondage of sin (John 8:36).

---

[40]James Montgomery Boice, *The Sovereign God* (Downers Grove, Ill.: InterVarsity Press, 1978), 34.

[41]Erickson, *Christian Theology*, 173.

[42]Ibid.

[43]Henry, *God, Revelation and Authority*, vol. 1, 86.

CHAPTER

3

God's
Inspired
Word

Because one cannot arrive at God's plan of redemption by a natural theology, a revealed theology is needed through a special revelation from God. For example, moral norms, commands, and prohibitions were established for Adam in Eden by special, not general, revelation. Even though it preceded the Fall, special revelation is primarily understood in terms of "redemptive purpose." Special revelation complements the self-disclosure of God in nature, history, and humanity and builds on the foundation of general revelation. But because general revelation cannot bring salvation, the added truth content of special revelation is essential (Rom. 10:14–17).

Personal. "Through Jesus Christ revealed in inspired Scripture, man comes to know God *personally* in a redemptive relationship. From knowing things *about* God (His existence, perfections, and moral demands), man gains practical knowledge of God *himself* in personal fellowship."[44] While neoorthodoxy views special revelation solely in the person of Christ[45] and sees the Scriptures as only a "witness" to this divine revelation, "evangelical Christianity acknowledges both the living Word and the written Word as revelation."[46]

The neoorthodox restriction of revelation to a nonpropositional personal encounter with God [who is "wholly other"] similarly fails to do justice to the full range of biblical teaching. Although the [Living] Word represents the highest form of the divine self-disclosure, Scripture scarcely limits God's revelation to this important modality.[47]

It is through the special revelation of Scripture that one comes to know Jesus Christ. "These are written that you may believe [*keep on believing*] that Jesus is the Christ, the Son of God" (John 20:31).

Understandable. In the special revelation of Scripture, God revealed himself in anthropic form, that is, in the character of human language at the time, using human categories of thought and action. Erickson has a helpful section dealing

---

[44]Demarest, *General Revelation,* 247.

[45]Neoorthodoxy does not mean the historic Christ, i.e. Jesus, but the Christ proclaimed in the church.

[46]Henry, *God, Revelation and Authority,* vol. 1, 80. See Barth, *Church Dogmatics,* vol. 1, chap. 1 for the viewpoint of neoorthodoxy.

[47]Demarest, *General Revelation,* 128.

with the language equivalence used in God's verbal communication. He distinguishes between the terms "univocal" (a word having only one meaning—e.g., tall) and "equivocal" (a word possessing completely different meanings—e.g., row in "row a boat" and "a row of corn plants") and suggests that Scripture uses analogical language (between univocal and equivocal—e.g., run in "running a race" and "a motor running").

In analogical usage, there is always at least some univocal element. ... Whenever God has revealed himself, he has selected elements which are univocal in his universe and ours. ... [U]sing the term *analogical,* we mean "qualitatively the same"; in other words, the difference is one of degree rather than of kind or genus.[48]

That is, when the Bible uses words such as "love," "give," "obey," or "trust," they convey the same basic meaning to us as they do to God (at the same time, His love, for example, is far greater than ours). In this way it is possible for God to communicate Scripture through verbally rational propositions.

What makes this analogical knowledge possible is that it is God who selects the components which he uses. ...

God ... knowing all things completely, therefore knows which elements of human knowledge and experience are sufficiently similar to the divine truth that they can be used to help construct a meaningful analogy.[49]

Since this analogical concept of communication cannot be verified by human reason alone, for we do not have all the facts, one embraces this presupposition as a matter of faith. However, it is rationally defendable in light of Scripture's own claim to be a divine revelation.

Humanity is dependent on God for special revelation. Because one knows only the human sphere of knowledge and experience (and that to a minimal degree) one is unable to develop any valid special revelation. Only God has knowledge of God and only God can make himself known. Since God has chosen to reveal himself analogically, we can apprehend God. However, because the finite cannot fully grasp the In-

---

[48]Erickson, *Christian Theology,* 179–80.
[49]Ibid., 180–81.

finite, we will never know God exhaustively. "God always remains *incomprehensible*. ... Although *what* we know of him is the same as his knowledge of himself, the degree of our knowledge is much less."[50] The knowledge of God through Scripture is limited—but true and sufficient.

Progressive. God did not reveal all the truth He wanted to convey about himself and His ways in Scripture all at one time, but over a period of about fifteen centuries (Heb. 1:1–2). Special revelation was progressive, not in the sense of a gradual evolutionary development, but in the sense of later revelation building upon earlier revelation. "This does not mean a movement in special revelation from untruth to truth but from a lesser to a fuller disclosure."[51] The very earliest revelation was true and accurately presented the message of God. Later revelation served to complement or supplement what God had disclosed before, but never to correct or contradict it. The whole of His revelation was to teach humankind who He is, how to be reconciled to Him, and how to live acceptably before Him.

Recorded. Certainly the modes of special revelation are not limited to the Scriptures. God has revealed himself in His mighty redemptive acts, through His prophets and apostles, and most dramatically through His Son (Heb. 1:1). One might wonder why God thought it necessary or important to have much of this revelation written down, creating the Scriptures as a unique special revelation of himself. What follows are three plausible reasons.

First, an objective standard by which to test the claims of religious belief and practice is needed. Subjective experience is too obscure and variable to provide assurance on the nature and will of God. Considering the eternal significance of God's message to humanity, what was needed was not an "uncertain sound" but a "more sure word" (1 Cor. 14:8; 2 Pet. 1:19, KJV). A written standard of revelation provides the certainty and confidence of "thus says the Lord."

Second, a written divine revelation ensures the completeness and continuity of God's self-disclosure. Since special revelation is progressive, with later building on earlier, it is important that each occasion of revelation be recorded for a fuller understanding of God's complete message. Generally speaking, the continuity of the Old Testament with the New

---

[50]Ibid., 180.

[51]Williams, *Renewal Theology,* vol. 1, 37.

Testament allows one to understand with greater clarity the message of redemption. Specifically, one would have a difficult time understanding the Letter to the Hebrews without knowing about the sacrificial system detailed in the Pentateuch. Therefore, by having the "whole" inscripturated, the "parts" are more meaningful.

Third, an inscripturated revelation best preserves the truth of God's message in integral form. Over long periods of time, memory and tradition tend toward decreasing trustworthiness. The crucial content of God's revelation must be accurately handed down to succeeding generations. The message one receives about God today must contain the same truth revealed to Moses or David or Paul. Books have been the best method of preserving and transmitting truth in its integrity from generation to generation.

Transmitted. By holding special revelation from God in a permanent form, the Bible is both a record and an interpreter of God and His ways. God's written revelation is confined to the sixty-six books of the Old and New Testaments. The whole of His revelation that He wanted preserved for the benefit of all humankind is stored in its integrity in the Bible. To search the Scriptures is to find God as He wants to be known (John 5:39; Acts 17:11). God's revelation is not a fleeting glimpse, but a permanent disclosure. He invites one to return again and again to Scripture and there to learn of Him.

God's revelatory acts and His self-disclosing words are brought together in the Scriptures. "The revelation of mighty deeds of God without revelation of the meaning of those deeds is like a television show without sound track; it throws man helplessly back upon his own human guesses as to the divine meaning of what God is doing."[52] The Bible faithfully records God's acts and enhances our understanding of them by providing God's own interpretation of those acts. "The deeds could not be understood unless accompanied by the divine word."[53] Revelation events along with their inspired interpretation are indivisibly unified in the Bible.

The Bible not only stores the revelation of God, but also brings that historical revelation to us in the present. Even Moses indicated the importance of writing down God's rev-

[52]Kenneth S. Kantzer, "The Christ-Revelation as Act and Interpretation" in *Jesus of Nazareth: Savior and Lord,* ed. Carl F. H. Henry (Grand Rapids: Wm. B. Eerdmans, 1966), 252.

[53]George E. Ladd, *The New Testament and Criticsm* (Grand Rapids: Wm. B. Eerdmans, 1967), 27.

elation so that it would benefit God's people on later occasions as well (Deut. 31:24–26). God has spoken in the past, and through the record in Scripture He continues to speak. " 'What Scripture says, God Says.' The divine Word is cast into permanent form in Scripture, which is the durable vehicle of special revelation and provides the conceptual framework in which we meet ... God."[54] What God said to others in the past, He now says to us through the Scriptures.

Debate often ensues over whether the Bible is the Word of God or merely contains the Word of God. Actually, both ideas are true, only from different perspectives. Revelation that preceded its inscripturation was later recorded as part of the Scripture message. Therefore the Bible record contains the Word of God that may have come to someone long before it was written down. For example, the Bible contains the record of God's speaking to Abraham or to Jacob (Gen. 12:1; 46:2). This fact, however, does not warrant the Barthian distinction between God's Word as divine and its record in Scripture as human.[55] Rather, the Bible is "a divine-human book in which every word is at once divine and human."[56] The whole of Scripture is the Word of God by virtue of the divine inspiration of its human authors. God's Word in the form of the Bible is an inspired record of events and truths of divine self-disclosure. Benjamin B. Warfield emphasizes that Scripture is not merely "the record of the redemptive acts by which God is saving the world, but [is] itself one of these redemptive acts, having its own part to play in the great work of establishing and building up the kingdom of God."[57]

A key issue in this debate is whether God can and has revealed himself in propositional form. Neoorthodoxy views God's revelation as "personal but nonpropositional," while Evangelicalism views it as personal, "cognitive and propositional."[58] How one defines revelation determines whether the Bible is coextensive with special revelation. If revelation is defined only as the act or process of revealing, then Scripture

---

[54]Pinnock, *Biblical Revelation,* 34.

[55]Barth, *Church Dogmatics,* vol. 1, 99ff.

[56]Benjamin B. Warfield, "The Divine and Human in the Bible" in *The Princeton Theology 1812–1921,* ed. Mark A. Noll (Grand Rapids: Baker Book House, 1983), 278.

[57]Benjamin B. Warfield, *The Inspiration and Authority of the Bible* (Philadelphia: The Presbyterian and Reformed Publishing Company, 1970), 161.

[58]Carl F. Henry, *God, Revelation and Authority,* vol. 3 (Waco, Tex.: Word Books, 1979), 455.

is not revelation, for revelation often occurred long before it was written down. If, however, revelation is defined also as the result, or product, of what God revealed, then Scripture as an accurate record of the original revelation is also entitled to be called special revelation.[59]

THE AUTHORITY OF SCRIPTURE

RIVALS OF SCRIPTURE

Historically, the Christian Church has acknowledged the authority of Scripture in matters of faith and practice. This does not mean there have not been, and continue to be, rivals to the Bible's claim of full authority. These rivals have tended to subordinate, qualify, or equal the authority of Scripture. The earliest rival was oral tradition. Alongside the written Word, religious stories and teachings circulated widely. However, oral transmission, regardless of the topic, is subject to alteration, development, change, and deviation. Scripture supplied a standard, a point of reference for the oral word. Therefore, where oral tradition accords with Scripture it reflects Scripture's authority; however, where it deviates from the written Word its authority vanishes.

A second claim to religious authority is the church. Roman Catholics hold to this because the Church was divinely established by Christ; it proclaimed the gospel before it was inscripturated. Roman Catholics also claim it was the institution that produced the New Testament Scriptures and in some sense it established the canon of Scripture. In practice the Catholic Church places itself above Scripture. Although originally it held to the supremacy of Scripture, by the time of the Reformation it had exalted its traditions to the level of Scripture. More significantly the Catholic Church insisted that the teachings of the Bible could rightly be mediated only through the church hierarchy. Subtly the Roman Church had usurped the authority of the Scriptures and vested it in their guarded teachings. Consequently, the rallying cry of the Protestant Reformers was *Sola Scriptura* ("Scripture alone")! The Bible given by God speaks with God's authority directly to the individual. It does "not need Popes or Councils to tell us, as from God, what it means; it can actually challenge Papal and conciliar pronouncements, convince them of being un-

---

[59]Erickson, *Christian Theology,* 196–97.

godly and untrue, and require the faithful to part company with them."[60]

Where the Church speaks biblically it speaks with authority; where it does not, individuals may reject and challenge any claim to authority it makes. Such is the case with any ecclesiastical voice of authority, not just that of the Roman Catholic Church.

Creeds, confessions, and other church standards have also at times, consciously or unconsciously, been allowed to rival the authority of Scripture. Throughout history, churches and church leaders properly have spoken out on important issues of life and doctrine. Godly persons, greatly gifted by God, have labored to set forth Christian standards designed to reflect the attitude and will of God. Over and over again these documents have been looked to for authoritative direction. However, the writers would no doubt be the first to acknowledge that their works are fallible and open to revision, though one easily recognizes the significant biblical scholarship behind those important writings. Further, all the great creeds of the church acknowledge the full authority of Scripture. These godly efforts should be appreciated. God has used them for His glory. However, they must be kept in their proper relationship to Scripture. To allow them to rival scriptural authority destroys their own normative value and debases the Word of God they desire to honor. The acknowledgment of the unique authority of Scripture establishes the value of these other standards.

The authority of Scripture has also been challenged by what some view as the authority of an individual's personal encounter with God. That is, the person's encounter with the Living Word, rather than with the written Word, is paramount. Those who hold this view say the Bible may be used to help bring about such an encounter; however, the Bible "does not have authority of itself, but rather by virtue of the God to whom it witnesses and who speaks in its pages."[61] This is subtly different from saying that the Bible is authoritative because it is inherently the Word of God. Existentialists be-

---

[60]J. I. Packer, " 'Sola Scriptura' in History and Today," in *God's Inerrant Word,* ed. John Warwick Montgomery (Minneapolis, Minn.: Bethany Fellowship, 1974), 45.

[61]John Bright, *The Authority of the Old Testament* (Nashville: Abingdon Press, 1967), 31.

lieve that through encounter with God "the Bible must become again and again His Word to us."[62]

It is true that the Christian's authority is more than paper and ink, but "God's propositional revelation ... cannot ... be distinguished from divine self-revelation."[63] No authoritative encounter with God supersedes the authority of His written Word. Otherwise the "experience of God" of the Hindu mystics or of one using mind-altering drugs could claim equal authority. The validity of one's encounter with God is determined by the authority of the Scriptures which disclose Him. All personal experiences must be checked and judged by Scripture.

Even the Holy Spirit has been viewed by some as a rival of biblical authority. D. Martyn Lloyd-Jones sees Pentecostalism and Roman Catholicism at opposite extremes in such areas as structure and hierarchy, yet very similar in their emphasis on authority. Catholicism emphasizes the authority of the Church, while some Pentecostals seem to emphasize the authority of the Spirit above that of the Word.[64] Erickson cites an interesting 1979 Gallup poll that showed that a greater number of eighteen- to twenty-nine-year-olds chose the Holy Spirit rather than the Bible as their main religious authority.[65] Some elevate a "direct impression" of the Holy Spirit or a manifestation of the Spirit, such as prophecy, above the written Word.[66] The Holy Spirit is the one who inspired the Word and who makes it authoritative. He will not say anything contrary to or beyond what the inspired Word declares.

These rival claims to religious authority are joined by a host of world religions and religious cults. Is Jesus to be believed over Sun Myung Moon? Is the Koran as authoritative as the Bible? Does a word of modern prophecy carry the authority of Scripture? These and other practical questions make it essential for one to consider seriously the evidences for biblical authority. Virtually all religions have their sacred scriptures. Although many of them may contain worthy moral

---

[62]Barth, *Church Dogmatics,* vol. 1, 110.

[63]Henry, *God, Revelation and Authority,* vol. 3, 462.

[64]David Martyn Lloyd-Jones, *Authority* (London: Inter-Varsity Fellowship, 1958), 7, 8. It should be noted, however, that the Statement of Fundamental Truths of the Assemblies of God puts the inspiration and authority of Scripture in first place.

[65]Erickson, *Christian Theology,* 244–45.

[66]In doing so they ignore the Bible's direction that "others should weigh carefully what is said" (1 Cor. 14:29).

CHAPTER

3

God's
Inspired
Word

teachings, Christianity has historically maintained that the Bible is uniquely and exclusively the Word of God.

EVIDENCES TO THE AUTHENTICITY OF SCRIPTURE

The following paragraphs present some of the evidences for identifying the Bible as God's Word.

Internal Support. It is legitimate to look for the source and character of a writing by examining the contents of the writing itself. The Bible provides convincing internal testimony to its unique authority as a message from God. "It is ... the positive internal evidence of a Divine origin which gives power and authority to the claims of the Bible."[67]

The Bible displays an amazing unity and consistency in its content considering the great diversity in its writing. It was written over a period of approximately fifteen centuries by more than forty authors from varied walks of life—politician, fisherman, farmer, doctor, king, soldier, rabbi, shepherd, and others. They wrote in different places (e.g., wilderness, palace, prison) and during varied circumstances (e.g., war, exile, travel). Some wrote history, some wrote law, and some wrote poetry. Literary genres range from allegory to biography to personal correspondence. All had their own backgrounds and experiences and their own strengths and weaknesses. They wrote on different continents, in three languages, and covered hundreds of topics. Yet their writings combine to form a consistent whole that beautifully unfolds the story of God's relationship to humanity. "It is not a superficial unity, but a profound unity.... The more deeply we study the more complete do we find the unity to be."[68]

Josh McDowell tells an interesting story comparing the Bible to the *Great Books of the Western World.* Although the set of books comprised many different authors, the sales representative admitted it offered no "unity" but was a "conglomeration."[69] "[T]he Bible is not simply an anthology; there is a unity which binds the whole together. An anthology is

---

[67]Charles Hodge, "The Scriptures Are the Word of God" in *The Princeton Theology 1812–1921,* ed. Mark A. Noll (Grand Rapids: Baker Book House, 1983), 133.

[68]Reuben A. Torrey, *The Bible and Its Christ* (New York: Fleming H. Revell, 1904), 26.

[69]Josh McDowell, *Evidence that Demands a Verdict: Historical Evidences for the Christian Faith* (San Bernadino, Calif.: Campus Crusade for Christ International, 1972), 19–20.

compiled by an anthologist, but no anthologist compiled the Bible."[70] Such extraordinary unity can be explained most plausibly as the result of the revelation by one God.[71]

The Bible, being correlated with the complex nature of the human person, addresses every essential area of one's life. As a person reads the Bible, the Bible in turn reads the person. Although written centuries ago, it speaks forcefully to the human needs of each generation. It is the voice of God penetrating to the very core of one's being, providing reasonable answers to the ultimate questions of life (Heb. 4:12–13). God's Word continually directs the reader toward God as the source of meaning and purpose for oneself and for one's world. For the one who embraces its message, the Word has a transforming power. It creates faith in the heart and brings that person into a dynamic encounter with the living God (Rom. 10:17).

Scripture sets forth an ethical standard that surpasses what would be expected of ordinary men and women. It calls one to a morality that exceeds one's own measure of righteousness. "Each of these writings ... has represented moral and religious ideas greatly in advance of the age in which it has appeared, and these ideas still lead the world."[72] The Bible deals frankly with human failure and the problem of sin. Its ethical system is comprehensive, including all areas of life. The concern of biblical ethics is not merely what one does but who one is. Adherence to an external code falls short of the Bible's demand for internal goodness (1 Sam. 16:7; Matt. 5; 15:8). Both one's moral failure and moral redemption are understood only in terms of one's relationship to a holy God. Through the Bible, God calls one not to reformation but to transformation by becoming a new creation in Christ (2 Cor. 5:17; Eph. 4:20–24).

Prophecies that speak of future events, many of them centuries in advance, pervade the Scriptures. The accuracy of these predictions, as demonstrated by their fulfillments, is absolutely remarkable. Scores of prophecies relate to Israel and the surrounding nations. For example, Jerusalem and its

___

[70]F. F. Bruce, *The Books and the Parchments,* rev. ed. (Westwood, N.J.: Fleming H. Revell, 1963), 88.

[71]One of the reasons some ancient books were not included in the canon of Scripture was because they did not fit in or contribute to the harmony of Scripture. See the discussion on the canon.

[72]Augustus H. Strong, *Systematic Theology* (London: Pickering & Inglis, 1907), 175.

temple were to be rebuilt (Isa. 44:28); and Judah, although rescued from the Assyrians, would fall into Babylon's hands (Isa. 39:6; Jer. 25:9–12). The restorer of Judah, Cyrus of Persia, is named more than a century before His birth (Isa 44:28).[73] The Bible contains hundreds of prophecies made hundreds of years before the actual events.[74] Included are predictions of Christ's virgin birth (Isa. 7:14; Matt. 1:23), the place of His birth (Mic. 5:2; Matt. 2:6), the manner of His death (Ps. 22:16; John 19:36), and the place of His burial (Isa. 53:9; Matt. 27:57–60).[75]

Some critics, in redating various Old Testament books, have tried to minimize the predictive miracle of biblical prophecy. However, even if one would agree with the later dating, the prophecies would still have been written hundreds of years before the birth of Christ. (Since the Septuagint [LXX] translation of the Hebrew Scriptures was completed by about 250 B.C., this would indicate that the prophecies contained in those writings had to have been made prior to this date.)

Some have suggested the prophecies did not predict Jesus' activity but that Jesus deliberately acted to fulfill what was said in the Old Testament. However, many of the specific predictions were beyond human control or manipulation. Nor were the fulfillments of the predictions just coincidences, considering the significant number of persons and events involved. Peter Stoner examined eight of the predictions about Jesus and concluded that in the life of one person the probability of even those eight being coincidental was 1 in 10^{17}(1 in 100,000,000,000,000,000).[76] The only rational explanation for so many accurate, specific, long-term predictions is that the omniscient God, who is sovereign over history, revealed such knowledge to the human writers.

External Support. The Bible also has areas of external support for its claim to be a divine revelation. Who would deny its tremendous influence on human society? It has been printed in part or in whole in nearly two thousand languages and

---

[73]Henry C. Thiessen, *Lectures in Systematic Theology,* rev. ed. (Grand Rapids: Wm. B. Eerdmans, 1979), 48.

[74]Floyd Hamilton, *The Basis of Christian Faith* (New York: Harper and Brothers, 1927), 297.

[75]McDowell, *Evidence,* chaps. 9 and 11. Josh McDowell provides ninety pages of analysis of biblical predictive prophecies and their fulfillments.

[76]Peter W. Stoner, *Science Speaks* (Chicago: Moody Press, 1963), 106.

read by more people than any other book in history.[77] Recognizing its wisdom and value, believer and nonbeliever quote it in support of their causes. Claim has been made that the Bible, if lost, could be reconstructed in all its principal parts from the quotations made in the books sitting on the shelves of public libraries. Its principles have served as the foundation for the laws of civilized nations and as the impetus for the great social reforms of history. "The Bible . . . has produced the highest results in all walks of life. It has led to the highest type of creations in the fields of art, architecture, literature, and music . . . . Where is there a book in all the world that even remotely compares with it in its beneficent influence upon mankind?"[78]

God is at work, impacting society through the lives changed by following the teachings of His Word (Ps. 33:12).

The accuracy of the Bible in all areas, including persons, places, customs, events, and science, has been substantiated through history and archaeology. At times the Bible was thought to be in error, but later discoveries time after time have attested to its truthfulness. For example, it was once thought that there was no writing until after the time of Moses. Now we know that writing goes back before 3000 B.C. Critics once denied the existence of Belshazzar. Excavations identify him by his Babylonian name, Bel-shar-usur. Critics said the Hittites, mentioned twenty-two times in the Bible, never existed. Now we know the Hittites were a major power in the Middle East.[79]

Biblical history is corroborated by the secular histories of the nations involved with Israel. Archaeological discoveries continue to support and help interpret the biblical text. McDowell shares an interesting quotation from a conversation between Earl Radmacher, president of Western Conservative Baptist Seminary, and Nelson Glueck, archaeologist and former president of a Jewish theological seminary:

I've been accused of teaching the verbal, plenary inspiration of the

---

[77]By 1992 the Scripture had been translated into many languages: 1,964 living languages had some Scripture; 276 languages had the whole Bible; 676 had the entire New Testament. Barbara F. Grimes, ed. *Ethnologue: Languages of the World,* 12th ed. (Dallas: Summer Institute of Linguistics, 1992), 931.

[78]Thiessen, *Systematic Theology,* 47.

[79]Keith N. Schoville, *Biblical Archaeology in Focus* (Grand Rapids: Baker Book House, 1978), 194.

scripture. . . . All I have ever said is that in all of my archaeological investigation I have never found one artifact of antiquity that contradicts any statement of the Word of God.[80]

The same judgment is rendered by renowned archaeologist William F. Albright.

The excessive skepticism shown toward the Bible by important historical schools of the eighteenth and nineteenth centuries . . . has been progressively discredited. Discovery after discovery has established the accuracy of innumerable details, and has brought increased recognition to the value of the Bible as a source of history.[81]

Even those religious scholars who deny total accuracy of the Bible on philosophical grounds (e.g., human authors demand human error) are hard pressed to substantiate their claim of inaccuracies in the biblical text. Kenneth Kantzer comments, "Though Barth continued to assert the presence of errors in Scripture, it is exceedingly difficult to locate any instances in his writing where he sets forth any particular error in Scripture."[82] Considering the multitude of details in the Bible, one would expect a considerable collection of errors. Its amazing accuracy points to revelation from the God who is true.

The remarkable survivability of the Bible also attests to its divine authority. Comparatively few books survive the ravages of time. How many thousand-year-old writings can one name? A book that survives a century is a rare book. Yet the Bible has not only survived, it has thrived. There are literally thousands of biblical manuscripts, more than for any ten pieces of classical literature combined.[83]

---

[80]McDowell, *Evidence*, 24.

[81]William F. Albright, *The Archaeology of Palestine*, revised ed. (New York: Pelican Books, 1960), 127–28.

[82]Kenneth S. Kantzer, "Biblical Authority: Where Both Fundamentalists and Neoevangelicals Are Right," *Christianity Today*, 7 October 1983, 12.

[83]The New Testament in the original Greek is found in 88 papyri, 257 uncial (capital letter) leather manuscripts, 2,795 minuscule (small letter) manuscripts, and over 2,200 lectionaries (manuscripts with New Testament portions arranged for daily or weekly readings). See Kurt Aland and Barbara Aland, *The Text of the New Testament: An Introduction to the Critical Editions and to the Theory and Practice of Modern Textual Criticism*, trans. Erroll F. Rhodes (Grand Rapids: Wm. B. Eerdmans, 1987), 102, 105, 128, 160. This compares with *Homer's Iliad*, which is preserved in 457 papyri, 2 uncial manuscripts, and 188 minuscule manuscripts. See Bruce M. Metzger, *The Text of the New Testament: Its Transmission, Corruption, and Restoration*, 3d ed. (Oxford: Oxford University Press, 1992), 34.

What makes this survival so remarkable is that the Bible has faced numerous periods of ecclesiastical restraint (e.g., during the Middle Ages) and governmental attempts to eliminate it. From Diocletian's edict in 303 to destroy every copy of the Bible to the present day, there have been organized efforts to suppress or exterminate the Bible. "Not only has the Bible received more veneration and adoration than any other book, but it has also been the object of more persecution and opposition."[84] Considering that in the early centuries of Christianity Scripture was copied by hand, the utter extinction of the Bible would not have been humanly impossible. The noted French deist Voltaire predicted that within one hundred years Christianity would fade away. Within fifty years of his death in 1778, the Geneva Bible Society used his press and house to produce stacks of Bibles![85] Only if the Bible is indeed God's redemptive message to humanity is its indestructibility not so amazing: God has kept His omnipotent hand on His Word.

Both the authenticity and historicity of the New Testament documents are solidly affirmed. Norman Geisler points out that the manuscript evidence for the New Testament is overwhelming and provides a solid basis for reconstructing the original Greek text.[86] Textual scholar Bruce Metzger says that in the third century B.C. Alexandrian scholars indicated that the copies of the Iliad they had were about 95 percent accurate. He also indicates that northern and southern texts of India's Mahābhārata differ in extent by twenty-six thousand lines.[87] This in contrast to "over 99.5 percent accuracy for the New Testament manuscript copies."[88] That final half percent consists mostly of copyists' errors in spelling, etc., where the original cannot be determined. No doctrine of the Bible depends on any of those texts.

JESUS' VIEW OF SCRIPTURES

The writing of the New Testament books was completed by the end of the first century at the latest, many of them

[84]Emery H. Bancroft, *Christian Theology* (Grand Rapids: Zondervan Publishing House, 1949), 360.

[85]Sidney Collett, *All About the Bible,* 20th ed. (New York: Fleming H. Revell Company, 1934), 63.

[86]Norman Geisler, *Christian Apologetics* (Grand Rapids: Baker Book House, 1976), 308.

[87]Bruce M. Metzger, *Chapters in the History of New Testament Textual Criticism* (Grand Rapids: Wm. B. Eerdmans, 1963), 148–51.

[88]Geisler, *Apologetics,* 308

within twenty to thirty years of Jesus' death. We have the assurance also that even the recounting of events by the writers was superintended by the Holy Spirit to prevent human error that might be caused by forgetfulness (John 14:26). The Gospels, detailing the life of Jesus, were written by contemporaries and eyewitnesses. These well-attested New Testament writings provide accurate, reliable information about Christ and His teachings. The authority of the written Word is anchored in the authority of Jesus. Since He is presented as God incarnate, His teachings are true and authoritative. Therefore, Jesus' teaching on Scripture determines its rightful claim to divine authority. Jesus gives consistent and emphatic testimony that it is the Word of God.

In particular, Jesus addressed His attention to the Old Testament. Whether speaking of Adam, Moses, Abraham, or Jonah, Jesus treated them as real persons in true historical narratives. At times He related current situations to an Old Testament historical event (Matt. 12:39–40). On other occasions He drew from an Old Testament happening to support or reinforce something He was teaching (Matt. 19:4–5). Jesus honored the Old Testament Scriptures, emphasizing that He did not come to abolish the Law and the Prophets but to fulfill them (Matt. 5:17). At times He castigated the religious leaders because they had wrongly elevated their own traditions to the level of Scripture (Matt. 15:3; 22:29).

In His own teaching Jesus himself cited at least fifteen Old Testament books and alluded to others. Both in tone and in specific statements He clearly demonstrated His regard for the Old Testament Scriptures as the Word of God. It was the word and commandment of God (Mark 7:6–13). Quoting Genesis 2:24 Jesus stated, " 'The Creator [not Moses] . . . said, "For this reason a man will leave his father and mother" ' " (Matt. 19:4–5). He spoke of David's making a declaration "speaking by the Holy Spirit" (Mark 12:36). Concerning a statement recorded in Exodus 3:6, He asked, " 'Have you not read what God said to you?' " (Matt. 22:31). Repeatedly Jesus claimed the authority of the Old Testament, citing the formula "It is written" (Luke 4:4). John W. Wenham asserts that Jesus understood this formula to be equivalent to "God says!"

"There is a grand and solid objectivity about the perfect tense *gegraptai,* 'it stands written': 'here is the permanent, unchangeable witness of the Eternal God, committed to writing for our instruction.' "[89] The decisiveness with which Jesus

---

[89]John W. Wenham, *Christ and the Bible* (Downers Grove, Ill.: InterVarsity Press, 1973), 22.

wielded this formula says something emphatic about how Jesus regarded the authority of the writings of Scripture. "The written Word, then, is the authority of God for settling all disputes of doctrine or practice. It is God's Word in man's words; it is divine truth in human terms."[90] Those who would claim that Jesus simply accommodated himself to the Jewish understanding of Scripture and went along with their false beliefs miss entirely His emphatic tone and emphasis of full acceptance and authority. Rather than accommodate himself to the views of His day, He corrected their errors and raised Scripture again to its rightful place. Further, accommodation to falsehood is not morally possible for the God who is absolutely true (Num. 23:19; Heb. 6:18).

Jesus claimed divine authority not only for the Old Testament Scriptures, but also for His own teachings. One who hears His sayings and does them is a wise person (Matt. 7:24) because His teachings are from God (John 7:15–17; 8:26–28; 12:48–50; 14:10). Jesus is the Sower, sowing the good seed of God's Word (Luke 8:1–13). His frequent expression "But I tell you" (Matt. 5:22), used side by side with an understanding of the Old Testament, demonstrated that "his words carry all the authority of God's words."[91] "Heaven and earth will pass away, but [His] words will never pass away" (Matt. 24:35).

Jesus also indicated that there would be a special divine character to the witness of His followers to Him. He had trained them by word and example and commissioned them to be His witnesses throughout the whole world, teaching people to observe whatever He had commanded them (Matt. 28:18–20). He instructed them to wait in Jerusalem for the coming of the Holy Spirit whom the Father would send in His name, so that they would have power to be witnesses unto Him (Luke 24:49; John 14:26; Acts 1:8). The Holy Spirit would remind the disciples of everything Jesus had said to them (John 14:26). The Spirit would teach them all things, testify about Christ, guide them into all truth, tell them what was yet to come, and take the things of Christ and make them known to the disciples (John 14:26; 15:26–27; 16:13–15).

Jesus' promises to His disciples were fulfilled. The Holy Spirit inspired some of them to write of their Lord. Consequently, in their writings, along with those of the Old Tes-

---

[90]Geisler, *Apologetics,* 362.
[91]Wenham, *Christ and the Bible,* 47.

tament, the Bible makes the express and direct claim to be special revelation from God.[92]

THE EXTENT OF BIBLICAL AUTHORITY

The Bible touches on a number of areas: economics, geography, culture, biology, politics, astronomy, and so forth; but it does not claim to be, nor should one regard it as, a textbook on all these subjects. Styles of dress, means of transportation, political structures, human custom, and the like are not intended to be followed simply because they are mentioned in the authoritative Scriptures. Although what is written in these areas is reliable, it is not necessarily normative or comprehensive. These areas lie outside scriptural authority except as they have theological or ethical implications. (For example, from the standpoint of Scripture it makes no difference if we ride a camel or a motorcycle, but it does make a difference whether we obtained either one honestly.)

The Bible's sixty-six books claim full and absolute authority in regard to God's self-revelation and all the implications for belief and practice that follow. Although the Bible's authority is historical because God has revealed himself in historical events, primarily its authority is theological. The Bible reveals God to humankind and sets forth His relationship to His creation. Because God is to be understood through this book, its words must be authoritative. The authority of the Word is absolute—God's own words about himself.

The Bible's ethical authority stems from its theological authority. It does not speak of all that should be done in every age or of all that was done in the times of its writing. However, the principles it sets forth, its standard of righteousness, its information about God, its message of redemption, and its lessons of life are authoritative for all ages.

Certain biblical passages are not binding on us today as far as conduct is concerned, but are authoritative in the sense that they reveal God in some relationship to humanity. For example, some of the Old Testament ceremonies have been fulfilled in Christ. "Where there is a relation of promise (or prefiguring) and fulfillment, the figure serves only a temporary purpose and ceases to have a binding status with the fulfill-

---

[92]See Inspiration of Scripture, pp. 93–97.

ment."[93] Even though Christ is the fulfillment, the ceremonies authoritatively present an aspect of God's redemptive work. The relationship of God to human beings and the relationship of human beings to God have implications for every aspect of life. Therefore the Word bears authoritatively upon these other spheres of life.

The scope of Scripture's authority is as extensive as God's own authority in relationship to all areas of human existence. God is over all areas of life and speaks to all areas of life through His Word. The authority of the written Word is the authority of God himself. The Bible is not merely a record of God's authority in the past, but is God's authority today. Through the written Word the Holy Spirit continues to confront men and women with the claims of God. It is still "Thus says the Lord!"

THE INSPIRATION OF SCRIPTURE

God has revealed himself to His creation. Inspiration refers to the recording, or writing down, of this divine revelation. Since the Bible was written by human authors, it must be asked, "In what sense, if any, can their writings be called the Word of God?" A related issue concerns the degree, or extent, to which their writings can be viewed as revelation from God.

THE BIBLICAL BASIS FOR INSPIRATION

Because any witness has the right of self-testimony, the claim of the biblical writers to divine inspiration will be examined first. Many of those who wrote the Scriptures were participants in or eyewitnesses of the events they wrote about.

That which was from the beginning, which we have heard, which we have seen with our eyes, which we have looked at and our hands have touched—this we proclaim concerning the Word of life. The life appeared; we have seen it and testify to it, and we proclaim to you the eternal life, which was with the Father and has appeared to us. We proclaim to you what we have seen and heard (1 John 1:1–3).

Whether Moses, David, Jeremiah, Matthew, John, Peter, or Paul, each wrote out of his own experiences as God revealed

---

[93]Geoffrey W. Bromiley, "The Inspiration and Authority of Scripture," *Eternity,* August 1970, 20.

himself in and through his life (Exod. 4:1–17; Ps. 32; Jer. 12; Acts 1:1–3; 1 Cor. 15:6–8; 2 Cor. 1:3–11; 2 Pet. 1:14–18). Yet their writings were more than the accounts of involved reporters. They claimed to write not only *about* God, but also *for* God. Their word was God's Word; their message was God's message.

Throughout the Old Testament one finds expressions such as "The LORD said to Moses, 'Tell . . .'" (Exod. 14:1); "This is the word that came to Jeremiah from the LORD" (Jer. 11:1); "'Son of man . . . say: "This is what the Sovereign LORD says . . ."'" (Ezek. 39:1); "The LORD said to me . . ." (Isa 8:1); or "This is what the LORD says . . ." (Amos 2:1). These statements are used more than thirty-eight hundred times and clearly demonstrate that the writers were conscious of delivering an authoritative message from God.[94]

The New Testament writers were no less certain that they too were communicating on behalf of God. Jesus not only commanded the disciples to preach, but also told them what to preach (Acts 10:41–43). Their words were not "words taught . . . by human wisdom but . . . words taught by the Spirit, expressing spiritual truths in spiritual words" (1 Cor. 2:13). They expected the people to acknowledge that what they were receiving was written as "the Lord's command" (cf. 1 Cor. 14:37). Paul could assure the Galatians "that what I am writing you is no lie" (Gal. 1:20), because he had received it from God (Gal. 1:6–20). The Thessalonians were commended for receiving their message "not as the word of men, but as it actually is, the word of God" (1 Thess. 2:13). Commands were written to the Church in the name of Jesus, and failure to obey them was reason for disassociation from the disobedient person (2 Thess. 3:6–14). Just as God had spoken in and through the holy prophets, now commands were given by the Lord to His apostles (2 Pet. 3:2). Receiving eternal life was connected with believing God's testimony concerning His Son, which the disciples recorded (1 John 5:10–12).

In these and similar passages it is evident that the New Testament writers were convinced that they were declaring the "whole will of God" in obedience to the command of Christ and under the direction of the Holy Spirit (Acts 20:27). The New Testament writers also acknowledged the absolute authority of the Old Testament Scriptures, because God "spoke

---

by the Holy Spirit" through the human authors (Acts 4:24–25; Heb. 3:7; 10:15–16).

Paul wrote to Timothy that the Scriptures were able to make him "wise for salvation through faith in Christ Jesus" (2 Tim. 3:15). The value of Scripture is derived from its source. Paul indicates that its value goes beyond the immediate human writer to God himself. He affirms, "All Scripture is given by inspiration of God" (2 Tim. 3:16, KJV). The term "inspiration" is derived from this verse and applied to the writing of the Scriptures. The Greek word used here is *theopneustos,* which literally means "God-breathed"; newer versions rightly read, "All Scripture is God-breathed" (2 Tim. 3:16, NIV). Paul is not saying that God breathed some divine characteristic into the human writings of Scripture or simply that all Scripture exudes or speaks of God. The Greek adjective *(theopneustos)* is clearly predicative and is used to identify the source of all Scripture.[95] God is the ultimate author. Therefore all Scripture is the voice of God, the Word of God (Acts 4:25; Heb. 1:5–13).

The context of 2 Timothy 3:16 has the Old Testament Scriptures in view; the explicit claim of Paul is that the whole Old Testament is an inspired revelation from God. The fact that the New Testament was just being written and was not yet complete prohibits such an internal explicit claim for it. However, some specific statements by the New Testament writers imply that the inspiration of Scripture extends to the whole Bible. For example, in 1 Timothy 5:18 Paul writes, "For the Scripture says, 'Do not muzzle the ox while it is treading out the grain,' and 'The worker deserves his wages.'" Paul is quoting from Deuteronomy 25:4 and Luke 10:7, and he regards both the Old and New Testament quotations "as Scripture." Also, Peter refers to all the letters of Paul which, though they write of God's salvation, "contain some things that are hard to understand." Therefore some people "distort [them], as they do the *other Scriptures,* to their own destruction" (2 Pet. 3:16, italics added). Notice that Peter puts all Paul's letters in the category of Scripture. To distort them is to distort the Word of God, resulting in destruction. The New Testament writers communicated "in words taught by the

---

[95]"Both Paul's usage and the Greek word order in 2 Tim. 3:16 call for the translation, 'All Scripture is inspired by God.'" The New Testament Greek-English Dictionary, Zeta-Kappa, vol. 13 in *The Complete Biblical Library* (Springfield, Mo.: The Complete Biblical Library, 1990), 87.

Spirit, expressing spiritual truths" (1 Cor. 2:13), even as Jesus had promised (John 14:26; 16:13–15).

In his second epistle Peter speaks of his impending death and his desire to assure his readers of the truth of what he had previously shared with them. He tells them he did not invent clever but false stories and reminds them he was an eyewitness—he was with Christ, he heard and saw for himself (2 Pet. 1:12–18). Peter then proceeds to write of an even "more certain" word than his eyewitness testimony (2 Pet. 1:19). Speaking of the Scriptures, he describes human authors as being "led along" *(pheromenoi)* by the Holy Spirit as they communicated the things of God. The result of the superintending of their activity by the Holy Spirit was a message not initiated by human design or produced by mere human reason and research (not that these were excluded). Peter says, "You must understand that no prophecy of Scripture came about by the prophet's own interpretation. For prophecy never had its origin in the will of man, but men spoke from God as they were carried along by the Holy Spirit" (2 Pet. 1:20–21).

Peter's use of the term "prophecy of Scripture" is a case of *pars pro tota:* in this case, a part standing for the whole of Scripture. For the whole of Scripture, "the impetus which led to the writing was from the Holy Spirit. For this reason Peter's readers are to pay heed ... for it is not simply men's word, but God's word."[96]

Because of the inspiration of the Holy Spirit, all Scripture is authoritative. Jesus spoke of even the least of the biblical commandments as important and binding.

I tell you the truth, until heaven and earth disappear, not the smallest letter, not the least stroke of a pen, will by any means disappear from the Law until everything is accomplished. Anyone who breaks one of the least of these commandments and teaches others to do the same will be called least in the kingdom of heaven, but whoever practices and teaches these commands will be called great in the kingdom of heaven (Matt. 5:18–19).

Reward or judgment is predicated on one's relationship to even the least of the commandments. Accused of blasphemy because of His claim to deity, Jesus appealed to the phrase "you are 'gods'" found in Psalm 82:6. He built His defense against their charge of blasphemy on the well-accepted truth

---

[96]Erickson, *Christian Theology,* 201.

that even a relatively obscure phrase of Scripture cannot be broken (John 10:34–35). The reason it could not be broken was that, as even a small portion of Scripture, it was still the authoritative Word of God.

MODES OF INSPIRATION

Once the self-testimony of the Scriptures is accepted, the inspiration of Scripture is clear. As the human authors wrote, in some sense God himself was involved in the communication of their message. Since in most cases, however, the Bible does not reveal the psychology of inspiration, various understandings of the mode of inspiration have arisen. Five basic views are briefly considered in this section.

Natural Intuition. Inspiration is merely a natural insight into spiritual matters exercised by gifted persons. Just as some may have an aptitude for math or science, the biblical writers had an aptitude for religious ideas. No special involvement of God is seen. One might just as naturally be inspired to write a poem or to compose a hymn.

Special Illumination. Inspiration is a divine intensification and exaltation of religious perceptions common to believers. The natural gifts of the biblical writers were in some way enhanced by the Holy Spirit, but without any special guidance or communication of divine truth.

Dynamic Guidance. Inspiration is a special guidance of the Holy Spirit given to the biblical writers to assure the communication of a message from God as it deals with matters of religious faith and godly living. Emphasis is on God's providing the writers with the thoughts or concepts He wanted communicated and allowing the human writers full, natural expression. The elements of religious faith and practice were directed, but so-called nonessential matters were wholly dependent on the human authors' own knowledge, experience, and choice.

Verbal Plenary. Inspiration is a combination of the writers' natural human expression and the Holy Spirit's special initiation and superintendence of their writings. However, the Holy Spirit not only directed the writers' thoughts or concepts, but also oversaw their selection of words for all that was written, not just for matters of faith and practice. The Holy Spirit guaranteed the accuracy and completeness of all that was written as being a revelation from God.

Divine Dictation. Inspiration is the infallible superintendence of the mechanical reproduction of divine words as the

Holy Spirit dictated them to the human writers. The Scripture writers were obedient stenographers writing under the Holy Spirit's special direction for content, words, and style.

FORMULATING A VIEW OF INSPIRATION

A view of inspiration must take into account everything necessary for God's revelation to be accurately communicated. A proper mode of inspiration must include all the elements that the Bible posits in both the act of inspiring and the effects of that act. It must also give proper place to God's activity and to human activity.

As one examines the data of Scripture, a number of elements involved in the act of inspiring are clearly presented. (1) "All Scripture is God-breathed"; it proceeds from the mouth of God (2 Tim. 3:16). (2) The writers of Scripture were "carried along [or 'led along'] by the Holy Spirit" (2 Pet. 1:21). (3) The writers did not speak from their own will, but from God's (2 Pet. 1:21). (4) Yet the writers did speak for themselves (Luke 20:42; John 12:39; Acts 3:22).

Likewise Scripture provides clear effects, or results, of the act of inspiring. (1) All Scripture is God-breathed and therefore all Scripture is the Word of God (1 Cor. 14:37; 2 Tim. 3:16). (2) All Scripture is profitable and is a complete and sufficient rule for faith and practice (2 Tim. 3:16–17). (3) Not a single line of Scripture may be set aside, nullified, or destroyed; the whole of Scripture is to be taken in its full integrity (John 10:35). (4) Scripture is more certain than even empirical observation (2 Pet. 1:12–19). (5) No Scripture is conditioned as to its truthfulness by any limitation of its human author (2 Pet. 1:20). Normal historical conditioning as well as humankind's sinfulness and finiteness are offset by the Holy Spirit's superintendence.

In light of the preceding observations drawn from Scripture, an evaluation of the five suggested modes of inspiration can be made. Those views that regard inspiration as only some natural gift of illumination do not give proper attention to God's "breathing out" the Scripture. The dynamic guidance view, which sees matters of faith and life as inspired apart from other more mundane content, leaves no sure method of determining what is inspired and what is not. Nor does it address the explicit biblical claim that all Scripture is inspired, even the most obscure verses.

The divine dictation view of inspiration does not give proper recognition to the human element—the peculiar styles, expressions, and emphases of the individual writers.

The verbal plenary view of inspiration avoids the pitfalls of emphasizing God's activity to the neglect of human participation, or of emphasizing the human contribution to the neglect of God's involvement. The whole of Scripture is inspired, as the writers wrote under the Holy Spirit's direction and guidance, while allowing for variety in literary style, grammar, vocabulary, and other human peculiarities. After all, some of the biblical writers had, in God's providence, gone through long years of unique experience and preparation, which God chose to use to communicate His message (e.g., Moses, Paul).

The dynamic guidance and verbal plenary views of inspiration are widely held, for these views recognize the work of the Holy Spirit as well as the obvious differences in the vocabularies and styles of the writers. A major difference between the two views involves the extent of inspiration. Acknowledging the Holy Spirit's guidance, how far did this guidance extend? With regard to the Scripture writings, proponents of various dynamic views would suggest the Spirit's guidance extended to mysteries unattainable by reason, or only to the message of salvation, or only to the words of Christ, or perhaps to certain materials (such as didactic or prophetic sections or maybe to all matters relating to Christian faith and practice). Verbal plenary inspiration maintains that the guidance of the Holy Spirit extended to every word of the original documents (i.e, the autographs).

With regard to the Spirit's guidance of the writer, the dynamic guidance view would suggest the Spirit's influence extended to only the initial impulse to write or to only the selection of topics, the subject matter, or to just the writer's thoughts and concepts—to be expressed as the writer saw fit. In verbal plenary inspiration the Spirit's guidance extended to even the words the writer chose to express his thoughts. The Holy Spirit did not dictate the words, but guided the writer so that he freely chose the words that truly expressed God's message. (For example, the writer may have chosen the word "house" or "building" according to his preference, but could not have chosen "field" since that would have changed the content of the message.)[97]

---

[97]The Bible indicates that God's guidance began from the point of conception (Jer. 1:5). The Holy Spirit led the writers along not only while they wrote, but also through all their experiences and development so that even their vocabulary was prepared to write the truth in the way the Holy Spirit wanted it to be recorded.

Any combination of the suggestions of the dynamic guidance view involves one in a relative stance on the subject of the extent of inspiration. This relative stance requires that some principle be employed to differentiate between inspired and noninspired (or lesser and greater inspired) portions of Scripture. Several principles have been suggested: whatever is reasonable, whatever is needful for salvation, whatever is valuable for faith and practice, whatever is Word-bearing (i.e, points to Christ), whatever is genuine kerygma, or whatever the Spirit bears special witness to. All such principles are essentially human-centered and subjective. Also, there is the problem of who shall employ the principle and actually make the determination. Church hierarchy, biblical scholars and theologians, and individual believers would all want to make the choice. In an ultimate sense the dynamic guidance view ends with the Bible's authority being derived from humanity rather than God. Only the verbal plenary view of inspiration avoids the quagmire of theological relativity while accounting for human variety by recognizing that inspiration extends to the whole of Scripture.

Verbal plenary inspiration essentially carries its definition in its name. It is the belief that the Bible is inspired even to the very words (verbal) that were chosen by the writers. It is plenary (full, all, every) inspiration in that all of the words in all of the autographs are inspired. A more technical definition of inspiration from a verbal plenary perspective might read something like this: Inspiration is a special superintending act of the Holy Spirit whereby the writers of the Scriptures were motivated to write, were guided in their writing even to their employment of words, and were kept from all error or omission.

At the same time, although every word is inspired by God, whether or not it is true depends on its context. That is, it may authoritatively record a lie; it is an inspired, true record of a lie. For example, when the serpent told Eve she would not die if she ate of the forbidden fruit, it was lying—she would die! (Gen. 3:4–5). However, because the whole of Scripture is inspired, the false words of the tempter are accurately recorded.

Verbal plenary inspiration was the view of the Early Church. During the first eight centuries of the Church no major church leader held to any other view, and it was the view of virtually all orthodox Christian churches until the eighteenth century.[98] Verbal plenary inspiration continues to be the view of Evangelicalism.

Verbal plenary inspiration elevates the concept of inspiration to full infallibility since all the words are ultimately God's words. Scripture is infallible because it is God's Word and God is infallible. In recent years some have attempted to support the concept of verbal plenary inspiration without the corollary of infallibility. In response, books have been written, conferences held, and organizations formed to try to shore up the historical understanding of inspiration. "Limited inerrancy" as opposed to "limited errancy" has been debated. A string of qualifiers has been added to "verbal plenary" until some would insist the view be called "verbal plenary, infallible, inerrant, unlimited inspiration." When one investigates what all these qualifiers mean, it is exactly what "verbal plenary inspiration" meant from the beginning!

BIBLICAL INERRANCY

One notable change in terminology resulting from all the discussion in the area of the inspiration of Scripture is the preference for the term "inerrancy" over "infallibility." This probably has to do with the insistence of some that one could have an infallible message but an errant biblical text.

"Infallibility" and "inerrancy" are terms used to speak of the truthfulness of Scripture. The Bible does not fail; it does not err; it is true in all that it affirms (Matt. 5:17–18; John 10:35). Although these terms may not have always been used, the early church fathers, the Roman Catholic theologians, the Protestant Reformers, modern evangelicals (and therefore "classical" Pentecostals), all have affirmed a Bible that is entirely true, without room for falsehood or error.[99] Clement of Rome, Clement of Alexandria, Gregory Naziansus, Justin Martyr, Iraneus, Tertullian, Origen, Ambrose, Jerome, Augustine, Martin Luther, John Calvin, and a host of other giants of church history acknowledge the Bible as breathed out by

---

[98]In the ninth century, Scholasticism began to assert reason over biblical authority through the School Men such as John Scotus. See "The Church Doctrine of Biblical Authority," Jack B. Rogers, *The Authoritative Word,* ed. Donald K. McKim (Grand Rapids: Wm. B. Eerdmans, 1983); Pinnock, *Biblical Revelation;* Robert D. Preus, "The View of the Bible Held by the Church: The Early Church Through Luther," in *Inerrancy,* Norman L. Geisler, ed. (Grand Rapids: Zondervan Publishing House, 1979).

[99]Pinnock, *Biblical Revelation,* 74, 154.

God and entirely true. Listen to the emphatic affirmation of a few of these notables:

Augustine: "I most firmly believe that the authors were completely free from error."[100]

Martin Luther: "The Scriptures never err."[101] ". . . where the Holy Scripture establishes something that must be believed, there we must not deviate from the words."[102]

John Calvin: "The sure and infallible record." "The certain and unerring rule." "Infallible Word of God." "Free from every stain or defect."[103]

Probably two of the most significant historical developments regarding the doctrine of infallibility and inerrancy have been the statement on Scripture in *The Lausanne Covenant* (1974) and the *Chicago Statement* (1978) of the International Council on Biblical Inerrancy. The Lausanne statement offers what some regard as too great a flexibility in its declaration that the Bible is "inerrant in all that it affirms." (That is, some things may not be "affirmed" in the Bible.) In response, the *Chicago Statement* affirmed: "Scripture in its entirety is inerrant, being free from all falsehood, fraud, or deceit. We deny that biblical infallibility and inerrancy are limited to spiritual, religious or redemptive themes, exclusive of assertions in the fields of history and science."[104]

The *Chicago Statement* was adopted by a gathering of nearly three hundred evangelical scholars in an effort to clarify and strengthen the evangelical position on the doctrine of inerrancy. It comprises nineteen Articles of Affirmation and Denial, with an extended closing exposition, designed to describe and explain inerrancy in a way that leaves absolutely no room for any errors of any kind in any part of the Bible.

While it may be questioned whether inerrancy is taught deductively in Scripture, it is the conclusion supported by inductive examination of the doctrine of Scripture taught by Jesus and the biblical writers. It should be made clear, how-

---

[100]Augustine, "The Confessions and Letters of St. Augustine, with a Sketch of His Life and Work," in *A Select Library of the Nicene and Post-Nicene Fathers of the Christian Church,* ed. Philip Schaff (Grand Rapids: Wm. B. Eerdmans, reprint 1988), letter 32.

[101]R. C. Sproul, *Knowing Scripture* (Downers Grove, Ill.: InterVarsity Press, 1978), 34.

[102]Geisler, *Inerrancy,* 373.

[103]Ibid. 391.

[104]Ibid. Kenneth Kantzer's doctoral dissertation is an excellent defense of Calvin's view on inerrancy.

ever, that the Bible's authority rests on the truth of the inspiration, not on a doctrine of inerrancy. Inerrancy is a natural inference that follows inspiration and is "drawn from the scriptural teaching and is fully supported by Jesus' own attitude."[105] Some have suggested that surrender of the doctrine of infallibility is the first step to surrender of biblical authority.

Inerrancy recognizes apparent contradictions or inconsistencies in the text not as actual errors, but as difficulties that can be resolved when all the relevant data are known. The possibility of harmonizing apparently contradictory passages has often been demonstrated by evangelical scholars who have patiently reviewed textual difficulties in light of new historical, archaeological, and linguistic discoveries. (One should, however, avoid forced or highly speculative harmonizations.)

The doctrine of inerrancy is derived more from the character of the Bible than merely from examining its phenomena. "If one believes the Scripture to be God's Word, he cannot fail to believe it inerrant."[106] God breathed out these words that were written down and God cannot lie. Scripture does not err because God does not lie. Consequently, inerrancy is an expected property of inspired Scripture. The critic who insists on errors in the Bible in difficult passages seems to have usurped for himself the infallibility he has denied the Scriptures. An erring standard provides no sure measurement of truth and error. The result of denying inerrancy is the loss of a trustworthy Bible. When errors are admitted, divine truthfulness is surrendered and certainty vanishes.

DEFINITION OF INERRANCY

Although the terms "infallibility" and "inerrancy" historically have been virtually synonymous for Christian doctrine, in recent years many evangelicals have preferred one term over the other. Some have preferred the term "inerrancy" to distinguish themselves from those who held that infallibility may refer to the truthful message of the Bible without necessarily meaning the Bible contains no errors. Others have preferred the term "infallibility" to avoid possible misunderstandings due to an overly restrictive definition of inerrancy. Presently the term "inerrancy" seems to be more in vogue

---

[105]Carl F. H. Henry, *God, Revelation and Authority,* vol. 4 (Waco, Tex.: Word Books, 1979), 164.

[106]Pinnock, *Biblical Revelation,* 74.

than "infallibility." Therefore, the following series of statements attempt to set bounds for a definition of verbal inerrancy that would be widely accepted in the evangelical community.

1. God's truth is accurately expressed without any error in the very words of Scripture as they are used to construct intelligible sentences.

2. God's truth is accurately expressed through all the words of the whole of Scripture, not just the words of religious or theological content.

3. God's truth is inerrantly expressed directly only in the autographs (original writings) and indirectly in the apographs (copies of the original writings).

4. Inerrancy allows for the "language of appearance," approximations, and varying noncontradictory descriptions from different perspectives. (For example, to say the sun rises is not an error but a recognized perceptive description.)

5. Inerrancy recognizes the use of symbolic, figurative language and a variety of literary forms to convey truth.

6. Inerrancy understands that New Testament quotations of Old Testament statements may be paraphrases and may not be intended to be word-for-word renderings.

7. Inerrancy considers the cultural and historical methods of reporting such things as genealogies, measurements, and statistics to be valid, rather than requiring today's modern methods of technological precision.

From these seven statements it is hoped that one can construct a view of inerrancy that avoids extremes while taking seriously the self-testimony of Scripture to its accuracy and truthfulness. However, our attempts to define inerrancy are not themselves inerrant. Therefore, while endeavoring to influence others to acknowledge the doctrine of inerrancy, it would be well to heed the wise, loving advice of respected inerrantist Kenneth Kantzer. "Conservative evangelicals, especially, must take great care, lest by too hasty a recourse to direct confrontation they edge into unorthodoxy the wavering scholar or student troubled either by problems in the biblical text or by some of the common connotations of the word *inerrant.*"[107]

Likewise, it should be understood that "scriptural inerrancy does not imply that evangelical orthodoxy follows as a nec-

---

[107]Kenneth S. Kantzer, "Evangelicals and the Doctrine of Inerrancy" in *The Foundations of Biblical Authority,* ed. James M. Boice (Grand Rapids: Zondervan Publishing House, 1978), 155.

essary consequence of accepting of this doctrine."[108] Right interpretation and spiritual commitment must follow.

PROPOSITIONAL REVELATION

A major philosophical issue related to the question of infallibility and inerrancy concerns whether God can reveal himself truly. Truth refers here to propositional statements, or assertions, that accurately correspond to the object or objects they refer to. Can God reveal truth about himself? Is He able to reveal propositionally something of who He actually is to humanity? If the answer is yes, but what He reveals is only generally trustworthy, then God's revelation contains error. If God has revealed himself through a mixture of truth and error, either He must have done so deliberately or He could not help doing so.

It is not likely that God deliberately revealed error. No firm evidence of any such revealed error is indicated in the Bible. Also, deliberately revealed error is antithetical to God's nature as the God of truth. God always acts according to His nature.

To say that God could not keep from revealing error in His self-disclosure calls into question both His omniscience and His omnipotence. To say what God can or cannot do, apart from divine revelation, is presumptuous. His revelation of himself truly is not one of the things the Bible says God cannot do (not an inability of power but of moral nature). If God, who created all things including the human mind, can communicate one truth to the human person, then there is no logical reason He cannot communicate any and all truth He desires.

After acknowledging that God is able to reveal himself truly, we may ask, Did He also cause His revelation to be inscripturated truly? To deny this reduces one to agnosticism or skepticism with regard to any absolute truth, awaiting empirical verification of each statement of Scripture (assuming all matters are capable of empirical verification). Instead, if one is to have confidence in the Bible as the Word of God, the witness of Scripture to itself must be taken as normative in defining the true doctrine of inspiration. As examined earlier in this chapter, Jesus and the biblical writers with one

---

[108]Henry, *God, Revelation, and Authority,* vol. 4, 204. Note that scientific language was not invented until modern times. The Bible uses everyday language; for example, it speaks of a sunset just like we do. However, when the Bible gives specific teachings in the area of science or history we hold that these teachings are inerrant.

voice proclaim that God's revelation of truth has inerrantly been inscripturated. It cannot be broken and will not pass away!

PRESERVATION OF THE TRUTH OF SCRIPTURE

Has God caused His revelation to be purely preserved? If "purely preserved" means "inerrantly preserved," the answer is no. As mentioned above, inerrancy adheres directly to the autographs only. In the many biblical manuscripts that have been preserved, there are thousands of variations. Most of these are so minor they are negligible (e.g., spelling, grammar, transposition of words, etc.). Not a single doctrine is based on a questionable manuscript reading.

If, however, "purely preserved" means the teachings of Scripture have been "uncorruptedly preserved," the answer is a resounding yes. Today the Church has several different modern versions of the Bible based on the many extant Hebrew and Greek manuscripts. These versions carefully compare the ancient manuscripts and early versions of the Bible. They provide the reader with the Scriptures in an up-to-date vocabulary and style while retaining the accuracy of meaning. These versions, in turn, have been translated into hundreds of languages.

Although today's Bibles are far removed from the autographs in time, they are not far removed in accuracy. A chain of witnesses exists going back to those who claim they saw the autographs (e.g., Polycarp, Clement of Rome). They had both the motive and opportunity to assure the reliability of copies made from the originals. There was a desire among believers to preserve the teachings of Scripture, and care went into its transmission from one generation to another. It is possible by the science of textual criticism to arrive at a biblical text that is an accurate representation of the autographs. Then, to the degree that we approximate the content and God's intended meaning of the Scripture through textual criticism, exegesis, and interpretation—to that degree we can say we are proclaiming the Word of God.

This can be true only if we can be sure the autographs were the Word of God, infallibly inscripturated by supernatural inspiration. Inerrancy is essential somewhere along the line if we are to know what is true. The value of inerrant autographs is that we are certain that what men wrote down was exactly what God wanted recorded. The autographs derive their value from the fact that, in essence, they are the Word of God rather than merely the words of human writers.

The apographs, on the other hand, derive their value from the fact that they so closely represent the autographs. The copies, versions, and translations cannot be said to have been inspired in their production, but surely they must in some derivative, mediate sense retain the quality of inspiration that was inherent in the autographs. Otherwise they would not be authoritative. The *act* of inspiration happened only once; the *quality* of inspiration was retained in the apographs. The original act of inspiration produced an inspired Word in *both* the autographs and the apographs.

THE CANON OF SCRIPTURE

All religious literature, even the most helpful and widely read, is not considered Scripture. This not only is true today, but also was true in the days of the writing of the Old and New Testaments. The Apocrypha, pseudepigrapha, and other religious writings were recognized as having varying degrees of value, but were not considered worthy to be called the Word of God. Only the sixty-six books contained in the Bible are referred to as the canon of Scripture.[109]

The term "canon" comes from the Greek *kanōn*, which denoted a carpenter's rule or some similar measuring rod. In the Greek world, canon came to mean "a standard or norm by which all things are judged or evaluated."[110] Canons developed for architecture, sculpture, literature, philosophy, and so forth. Christians began to use the term theologically to designate those writings that had met the standard to be considered holy Scripture. These canonical books alone are regarded as the authoritative and infallible revelation from God.

It is understandable that the Jewish and Christian believers would want to have an established canon as other fields of

---

[109]Roman Catholics and some other groups include, in addition, fourteen books of the Old Testament Apocrypha. These books were included in the LXX version. The Early Church as a whole considered them to be worth reading but not inspired. Some of the books, such as First Maccabees, contain good history. Others contain errors and doctrines contrary to the rest of the Bible. Jerome, the translator of the Latin Vulgate, did not consider them on the same level as the sixty-six books of the canon. All the Reformers rejected them.

[110]Lee Martin McDonald, *The Formation of the Christian Biblical Canon* (Nashville: Abingdon Press, 1988), 40.

learning had. Religious persecution, geographical expansion, and increasing circulation of a wide range of religious writings added to the impetus to gather such a canon. Tradition suggests that Ezra was largely responsible for gathering the Jewish sacred writings into a recognized canon. However, the recognition of a closed Old Testament canon is usually dated from a supposed Council of Jamnia about A.D. 90–100.[111] The oldest surviving Christian list of the Old Testament canon comes from about A.D. 170, compiled by Melito, bishop of Sardis.[112] In the early centuries of Christianity various canons of Scripture were proposed, from that of the heretic Marcion in 140 to the Muratorian Canon of 180 to the first complete New Testament Canon of Athanasius in 367. The New Testament canon as we now have it was officially recognized at the Third Council of Carthage in 397 and by the Eastern Church by 500.[113]

The establishment of the biblical canon was not the decision of the writers or religious leaders or a church council, however. Rather, the process of these particular books' being accepted as Scripture was the Holy Spirit's providential influence on the people of God. The canon was formed by consensus rather than decree. The Church did not decide which books should be in the biblical canon, but simply acknowledged those already recognized by God's people as His Word. Clearly, the Church was not the authority; it saw the authority in the inspired Word.

Various guiding principles, or criteria, for canonical writings, however, have been suggested. They include apostolicity, universality, church use, survivability, authority, age, content, authorship, authenticity, and dynamic qualities. Of primary concern was whether the writing was regarded as inspired. Only those writings breathed out by God fit the measure of the authoritative Word of God.

The biblical canon is closed. God's infallible self-revelation has been recorded. Today He continues to speak in and

---

[111]The Jewish Sanhedrin moved to Jamnia (Jabneel, Jabneh), south southwest of Jerusalem, after Jerusalem was destroyed. Little evidence exists of any official discussion or any "Council of Jamnia." However, during this period there was a general consensus, probably reached by common usage. See William LaSor, David Hubbard, Frederic Bush, *Old Testament Survey: The Message, Form, and Background of the Old Testament* (Grand Rapids: Wm. B. Eerdmans, 1982), 22.

[112]F. F. Bruce, "Tradition and the Canon of Scripture" in *The Authoritative Word,* ed. Donald K. McKim (Grand Rapids: Wm. B. Eerdmans, 1983), 65.

[113]Thiessen, *Lectures in Systematic Theology,* 60–61.

through that Word. Just as God revealed himself and inspired writers to record that revelation, He preserved those inspired writings and guided His people in the selection of them to ensure His truth would be known. Other writings are not to be added to, nor any writings taken from, the canonical Scriptures. The canon contains the historical roots of the Christian Church, and "the canon cannot be remade for the simple reason that history cannot be remade."[114]

The Holy Spirit and the Word

INSPIRATION

The Scriptures were breathed out by God as the Holy Spirit inspired men to write in behalf of God. Because of His initiation and superintendence, the writers' words were, in truth, the Word of God. At least in some instances the biblical writers were aware that their message was not merely human wisdom, but "in words taught by the Spirit" (1 Cor. 2:13).

Others were also aware of the Spirit-inspired quality of the writings of Scripture, as is shown by expressions such as the following: "David himself, speaking by the Holy Spirit, declared ..." (Mark 12:36); " 'The Spirit of the LORD spoke through me' " (2 Sam. 23:2); " 'Brothers, the Scripture had to be fulfilled which the Holy Spirit spoke long ago through the mouth of David' " (Acts 1:16); " 'The Holy Spirit spoke the truth to your forefathers when he said through Isaiah the prophet...' " (Acts 28:25); "So, as the Holy Spirit says: 'Today, if you hear his voice ...' " (Heb. 3:7); "The Holy Spirit also testifies to us about this. First he says: 'This is the covenant I will make' " (Heb. 10:15–16). Thus whoever the writers were—whether Moses, David, Luke, Paul, or unknown (to us)—they wrote "as they were carried along by the Holy Spirit" (2 Pet. 1:21).

Some have wrongly viewed this inspiration of the Spirit to be a mechanical dictation of Scripture, appealing to such a notable as John Calvin. Several times Calvin does use the term "dictation" in conjunction with the Spirit's inspiration. For example, "Whoever is the penman of the Psalm, the Holy Spirit seems by his mouth to have dictated a common form

---

[114]Bruce M. Metzger, *The Canon of the New Testament* (Oxford: Clarendon Press, 1987), 275.

of prayer for the Church in her affliction."[115] However, Calvin uses the term "dictation" in a less strict sense than is currently understood by the dictation view of inspiration. He was aware of the contribution of the human authors in areas such as style of writing. Note his observation of Ezekiel's style:

> Ezekiel is verbose in this narration. But in the beginning of the book we said, that because the teacher was sent to men very slow and stupid, he therefore used a rough style. . . . [H]e had acquired it partly from the region in which he dwelt.[116]

Calvin did believe, therefore, that God prepared the biblical writers through various experiences of life and that the Holy Spirit spoke according to the style of the writer needed for a particular occasion. Whether to reach the educated or uneducated, "the Holy Spirit so tempers his style as that the sublimity of the truths which he teaches is not hidden."[117]

The Holy Spirit, using the personalities, experiences, abilities, and styles of the human authors, superintended their writings to ensure that God's message was accurately and fully communicated. As Jesus had promised, the Spirit led them into truth, brought to them remembrances, and taught them all that was needed for God's divine revelation (John 14 through 16).

REGENERATION

The work of the Holy Spirit is complementary to the work of Christ in regeneration. Christ died on the cross to make it possible for the sinner to be made alive again to God. Through spiritual rebirth one enters the kingdom of God (John 3:3). The Holy Spirit applies the work of Christ's salvation to the heart of the individual. He works in the human heart to convict of sin and to produce faith in Christ's atoning sacrifice. This faith is responsible for regeneration through union with Christ.

This regenerating faith produced by the Holy Spirit, however, should not be considered abstractly. It does not exist in a vacuum, but arises in relation to the Word of God. Faith

---

[115]John Calvin, *Commentary on the Book of Psalms,* vol. 2, trans. James Anderson (Grand Rapids: Baker Book House, 1984), 205.

[116]John Calvin, *Commentaries on the Prophet Ezekiel,* vol. 1, trans. John Owen (Grand Rapids: Baker Book House, 1984), 392.

[117]Calvin, *Commentary on Psalms,* 229.

comes from hearing the Word of God (Rom. 10:17). Not only was the Holy Spirit responsible for recording the message of salvation found in the Scriptures, but He also witnesses to the truth of the Scriptures. If God has spoken to humankind in the Bible, then the Holy Spirit must convince persons of that fact. The Spirit convinces not just of a general truthfulness of Scripture, but of a powerfully personal application of that truth (John 16:8–11). Christ as personal Savior is the object of the faith produced in the heart by the Spirit. This faith is inseparably linked to God's promises of grace found throughout the Bible. "The Spirit and the Word are both needed. The Spirit takes the Word and applies it to the heart to bring repentance and faith, and through this, life."[118] For this reason the Bible speaks of regeneration both in terms of being "born of the Spirit" and of being "born again . . . through the living and enduring word of God" (1 Pet. 1:23; see also John 3:5).

CHAPTER 3

God's Inspired Word

ILLUMINATION

The doctrine of the *illumination* of the Spirit involves the Holy Spirit's work in a person's acceptance, understanding, and appropriation of the Word of God. Earlier we considered a number of internal and external evidences for the Bible's being the Word of God. However, more powerful and more convincing than all of them is the inward testimony of the Holy Spirit. While the evidences are important and the Spirit may use them, ultimately it is the Spirit's authoritative voice to the human heart that brings the conviction that indeed Scripture is the Word of God.[119]

Without the Spirit, humankind neither accepts nor understands the truths that come from the Spirit of God. The rejection of God's truth by unbelievers is linked to their lack of spiritual understanding. The things of God are seen as foolishness by them (1 Cor. 1:22–23; 2:14). Jesus described unbelievers as those who hear but do not understand (Matt. 13:13–15). Through sin "their thinking became futile and their foolish hearts darkened" (Rom. 1:21). "The god of this age has blinded the minds of unbelievers, so that they cannot see the light of the gospel" (2 Cor. 4:4). Their only hope for spiritual understanding (i.e., that they may perceive God's truth) is the illumination of the Spirit (Eph. 1:18; 1 John 5:20).

---

[118]Stanley M. Horton, *What the Bible Says About the Holy Spirit,* (Springfield, Mo.: Gospel Publishing House, 1976), 115.

[119]Calvin, *Institutes,* I, vii, 4, 5.

This initial spiritual perception results in regeneration but also opens the door to a new life of growing in the knowledge of God.

Although the promises of John 14 through 16 concerning the Spirit's guidance and teaching have special reference to the disciples of Jesus who would be used to write the New Testament Scriptures, there is a continuing sense in which this ministry of the Spirit relates to all believers. "The same Teacher also continues His teaching work in us, not by bringing new revelation, but by bringing new understanding, new comprehension, new illumination. But He does more than show us the truth. He brings us into the truth, helping us put it into action."[120]

It is important to keep the written Word of God and the illumination of the Spirit together: What the Spirit illumines is the truth of God's Word, not some mystical content hidden behind that revelation. The human mind is not bypassed but quickened as the Holy Spirit elucidates the truth. "Revelation is derived from the Bible, not from experience, nor from the Spirit as a second source alongside and independent of Scripture."[121] Even the gifts of utterance given by the Holy Spirit are in no way equal to the Scriptures and are to be judged by the Scriptures (1 Cor. 12:10; 14:29; 1 John 4:1). The Holy Spirit neither alters nor expands the truth of God's revelation given in Scripture. The Scriptures serve as the necessary and only objective standard through which the Holy Spirit's voice continues to be heard.

Illumination by the Spirit is not intended to be a shortcut to biblical knowledge or a replacement for sincere study of God's Word. Rather, as one studies the Scriptures the Holy Spirit gives spiritual understanding, which includes both belief and persuasion. "Philological and exegetical research is not rendered useless by His operation, for it is in the heart of the interpreter himself that He works, creating that inner receptivity by which the Word of God is really 'heard.' "[122] Causing the Word to be heard by the heart as well as by the head, the Spirit brings about a conviction concerning the truth that results in an eager appropriation (Rom. 10:17; Eph. 3:19; 1 Thess. 1:5; 2:13).

Neoorthodoxy tends to confuse inspiration and illumina-

[margin handwritten note: the study of literature or human speech]

---

[120]Horton, *What the Bible Says,* 121.

[121]Henry, *God, Revelation and Authority,* vol. 4, 284.

[122]Pinnock, *Biblical Revelation,* 215.

tion by viewing the Scriptures as "becoming" the Word of God when the Holy Spirit confronts a person through those human writings. According to neoorthodoxy, Scripture is revelation only when and where the Spirit speaks existentially. The biblical text has no definite objective meaning. "[S]ince there are no revealed truths, only truths of revelation, how one person interprets an encounter with God may be different from another person's understanding."[123]

Evangelicals, however, view Scripture as the objective written Word of God inspired by the Spirit at the time of its writing. True communication about God is present in propositional form whether or not one recognizes, rejects, or embraces that truth. The authority of Scripture is intrinsic due to inspiration and is not dependent on illumination. It is distinct from and antecedent to the testimony of the Spirit. The Holy Spirit illumines what He has already inspired and His illumination adheres only to that written Word.

THE WRITTEN WORD AND THE LIVING WORD

God's revelation of himself is centered on Jesus Christ. He is the *Logos* of God. He is the Living Word, the Word incarnate, revealing the eternal God in human terms. The title *Logos* is unique to the Johannine writings of Scripture, although the term's use was significant in Greek philosophy of the day. Some have tried to connect John's usage to that of the Stoics or early Gnostics, or to the writings of Philo. More recent scholarship suggests John was primarily influenced by his Old Testament and Christian background. However, he was probably aware of the wider connotations of the term and may have intentionally used it for the purpose of conveying additional, unique meaning.[124]

The *Logos* is identified with both God's creative Word and His authoritative Word (law for all humankind). John staggers the imagination as he introduces the eternal *Logos,* the Creator of all things, very God himself, as the Word made flesh to dwell among His creation (John 1:1–3,14). "No one has ever seen God, but God the One and Only, who is at the Father's side, *has made him known*" (John 1:18). This Living Word has been seen, heard, touched, and now proclaimed

---

[123]Erickson, *Christian Theology,* 253.

[124]Ruth B. Edwards, "Word" in *The International Standard Bible Encyclopedia,* vol. 5, ed. Geoffrey W. Bromiley (Grand Rapids: Wm. B. Eerdmans 1915), 3105.

through the written Word (1 John 1:1–3). The Bible ends with the living *Logos* of God, faithful and true, poised on heaven's balcony, ready to return as Kings of kings and Lord of lords (Rev. 19:11–16).

God's highest revelation is in His Son. For many centuries through the words of the Old Testament writers, God was progressively making himself known. Types, figures, and shadows gradually unfolded His plan for lost humanity's redemption (Col. 2:17). Then in the fullness of time God sent His Son to more perfectly reveal God and to execute that gracious plan through His death on the Cross (1 Cor. 1:17–25; Gal. 4:4). All Scripture revelation prior to and subsequent to Christ's incarnation center on Him. The many sources and means of previous revelation pointed to and foreshadowed His coming. All subsequent revelation magnify and explain why He came. God's revelation of himself began as cryptic and small, progressed through time, and climaxed in the incarnation of His Son. Jesus is the fullest revelation of God. All the inspired writings that follow do not add any greater revelation, but amplify the greatness of His appearance. "[The Spirit] will not speak on his own. . . . He will bring glory to me by taking from what is mine and making it known to you" (John 16:13–14).

In the person of Jesus Christ, the source and content of revelation coincide. He was not just a channel of God's revelation, as were the prophets and apostles. He himself is the "radiance of God's glory and the exact representation of his being" (Heb. 1:3). He is "the way and the truth and the life"; to know Him is to know the Father as well (John 14:6–7). The prophets said, "The Word of the Lord came unto me," but Jesus said, "I say unto you"! Jesus reversed the use of the "amen," beginning His statements with " 'Truly, truly, I say to you' " (John 3:3, NASB). By virtue of *His* saying it, truth was immediately and unquestionably declared.

Christ is the key that unlocks the meaning of the Scriptures (Luke 24:25–27; John 5:39–40; Acts 17:2–3; 28:23; 2 Tim. 3:15). They testify of Him and lead to the salvation He died to provide. The Scriptures' focus on Christ, however, does not warrant reckless abandonment of the biblical text in areas that seem to be devoid of overt Christological information. Clark H. Pinnock wisely reminds us that "Christ is the hermeneutical *Guide* to the meaning of Scripture, not its critical scalpel."[125] Christ's own attitude toward the whole of Scrip-

---

[125]Pinnock, *Biblical Revelation,* 37.

ture was one of total trust and full acceptance. Special revelation in Christ and in the Scriptures is consistent, concurrent, and conclusive. One finds Christ through the Scriptures and through the Scriptures finds Christ. "These are written that you may believe that Jesus is the Christ, the Son of God, and believing you may have life in his name" (John 20:31).

STUDY QUESTIONS

1. Animism usually involves the worship of aspects of nature. Reflect on how this would relate to general revelation. Could general revelation serve as a bridge to witnessing to animists? How?

2. The Bible affirms the value of general revelation. Yet sin has impacted general revelation in a negative way. How is general revelation to be understood prior to the fall of man, presently to sinful man, and presently to redeemed man?

3. The doctrine of the inspiration of Scripture does not require that the authors only mechanically transcribed what God wanted communicated. The writers retained their own particular literary style and form. Select two biblical authors and note some of their writing characteristics.

4. Both biblical prophecy and biblical archaeology have been appealed to as areas of evidence for the uniqueness of the Bible. Compile a list of biblical prophecies and their fulfillment and a list of archaeological discoveries that support biblical content.

5. The doctrine of biblical inerrancy refers to the biblical autographs. Since we do not have any of the autographs, how does inerrancy relate to the versions and translations of the Bible we use today?

6. Most non-Christian religions have their own holy book(s). In what ways is the Bible unique among such writings?

7. Choose two Scripture passages that seem to be contradictory or a passage that seems to contain an error. Suggest a possible solution.

8. How do spiritual gifts such as prophecy, tongues, and interpretation relate to the concept of a closed canon of Scripture?

CHAPTER FOUR

The One True God

Russell E. Joyner

Many systematic theologies of the past have succeeded in classifying the moral attributes of God and the nature of His being. However, God did not reveal himself in all the variety of biblical manifestations simply to give us theoretical knowledge about himself. Instead, we find God's self-disclosure is coupled with personal challenge, confrontation, and the opportunity to respond. This is evident when the Lord meets with Adam, Abraham, Jacob, Moses, Isaiah, Mary, Peter, Nathaniel, and Martha. Along with these witnesses and many others (see Heb. 12:1), we can testify that we study to know Him, not just to know about Him. "Shout for joy to the LORD, all the earth. Worship the LORD with gladness; come before him with joyful songs. Know that the LORD is God" (Ps. 100:1–2). Every Scripture passage that we examine should be studied with a heart toward worship, service, and obedience.

Our understanding of God must not be based on presumptions about Him or on what we want God to be like. Instead we must believe in the God who is and who has chosen to reveal himself to us in Scripture. Human beings tend to create fictitious gods that are easy to believe in, gods that conform to their own life-style and sinful nature (Rom. 1:21–25). This is one of the marks of false religion. Some Christians even fall into the trap of ignoring the self-revelation of God and begin to develop a concept of God that is more in line with their personal whims than with the Bible. The Bible is our true source. It lets us know that God exists and what He is like.

GOD'S EXISTENCE

The Bible does not attempt to prove God's existence.[1] Instead, it opens with His existence as a primary assumption: "In the beginning God" (Gen. 1:1). God is! He is the starting point. Throughout the Bible there is substantial evidence for His existence. While "the fool says in his heart, 'There is no God.' ...The heavens declare the glory of God; the skies proclaim the work of his hands" (Pss. 14:1; 19:1). God has made himself known through His creative and sustaining actions; giving life, breath (Acts 17:24–28), food, and joy (Acts 14:17). God accompanies those actions with words to interpret their meaning and significance, providing a record that explains His presence and purpose. God also reveals His existence by speaking and acting through prophets, priests, kings, and faithful servants. Ultimately, God has revealed himself clearly to us through His Son and through the indwelling Holy Spirit.

For those of us who believe that God has revealed himself in Scripture, our descriptions of the one true Deity are based on His self-disclosure. Yet we live in a world that generally does not share this view of the Bible as a primary source. Many people rely instead on human ingenuity and perception to arrive at a depiction of the divine. For us to follow the steps of the apostle Paul in leading them out of the darkness into the light, we need to be aware of the general categories of those human perceptions.

In the secular understanding of history, science, and religion, the theory of evolution has been accepted by many as reliable fact. According to that theory, as human beings evolved, so did their religious beliefs and expressions.[2] Religion is presented as a movement from simple to more complex practices and creeds. Followers of this scheme of the evolutionary theory say religion begins at the level of animism, in which natural objects are considered to be indwelt by supernatural powers or disembodied spirits. These spirits impact human life according to their own devious pleasure.

---

[1]Philosophers have attempted to do so. For a brief survey of the so-called rational proofs (ontological, cosmological, teleological, moral, and ethnological) for the existence of God, see L. Berkhof, *Systematic Theology,* 4th ed. (Grand Rapids: Wm. B. Eerdmans, 1941), 26–28. Some consider these as pointers rather than proofs.

[2]This theory is expressed with numerous variations and became a part of the antisupernatural philosophies and theologies of Wellhausen, Freud, and Nietzsche, as well as those of both Nazis and Communists.

Animism evolves into simple polytheism, in which certain of **CHAPTER** the supernatural powers are perceived as deities. The next **4** step, according to evolutionists, is henotheism, as one of the deities achieves supremacy over all the other spirits and is The One worshiped in preference to them. Monolatry follows when True God the people choose to worship only one of the gods, though not denying the existence of the others.

The logical conclusion of the theory is monotheism, which occurs only as the people evolve to the point of denying the existence of all other gods and worshiping only one deity. The research of anthropologists and missiologists in this century has shown clearly that this theory is not validated by the facts of history or by the careful study of contemporary "primitive" cultures.[3] When human beings shape a belief system according to their own design, it does not develop in the direction of monotheism, but rather toward more gods and more animism.[4] The tendency is toward syncretism, adding newly discovered deities to the set already worshiped.

In contrast to evolution is revelation. We serve a God who both acts and speaks. Monotheism is not the result of human evolutionary genius, but of divine self-disclosure. This divine self-disclosure is progressive in nature as God has continued to reveal more of himself throughout the Bible.[5] By the time of the first post-Resurrection Pentecost we learn that God does indeed manifest himself to His people in three distinct Persons.[6] But in Old Testament times it was necessary to establish the fact that there is one true God in contrast to the many gods served by Israel's neighbors in Canaan, Egypt, and Mesopotamia.

Through Moses, the teaching was asserted, "Hear, O Israel: The LORD our God, the LORD is one" (Deut. 6:4).[7] The Lord's existence and continuing activity were not dependent on His relationship with any other god or creature. Instead, our God

---

[3]See Don Richardson, *Eternity in Their Hearts* (Ventura, Calif.: Regal Books, 1961), 52–55.

[4]Cf. Rom. 1:21–23,25. Egyptian records confirm this. See Erik Hornung, *Conceptions of God in Ancient Egypt*, trans. by John Baines (Ithica, N.Y.: Cornell University Press, 1982), 98–99, 171. When the Aryans came to India they were already polytheists, but they worshiped only a few gods. Today in India many gods are worshiped and there is also more animism.

[5]See chap. 3, p. 78.

[6]See chap. 5 on the Trinity.

[7]"One" is the Heb. *'echad*, which can mean a compound or complex unity.

could simply "be," while choosing to call human beings to His side (not because He needed them, but because they needed Him).

GOD'S CONSTITUTIONAL ATTRIBUTES

" 'He is not served by human hands, as if he needed anything, because he himself gives all men life and breath and everything else' " (Acts 17:25). God is self-existent in the sense that He does not look to any other source for His meaning and being. His very name, Yahweh, is a statement that "He is and will continue to be."[8] God is not dependent on anyone to counsel or teach Him: "Who was it that taught him knowledge or showed him the path of understanding?" (Isa. 40:14). The Lord has not needed any other being to assist Him in creation and providence (Isa. 44:24). God wills to impart life to His people, and He stands apart as independent from all others. " 'The Father has life in himself' " (John 5:26). No created being can make that claim, so we creatures are left to declare in our worship: " 'You are worthy, our Lord and God, to receive glory and honor and power, for you created all things, and by your will they were created and have their being' " (Rev. 4:11).

SPIRIT

Jesus encountered a woman of Samaria at Jacob's well one day. Samaritans were regarded by first-century Jews as an aberrant cult, to be avoided. The Samaritans had been forced to give up idolatry, but they had modified the Pentateuch to limit the place of worship to Mount Gerizim, and they rejected the rest of the Old Testament. Jesus exposed the error of their worldview by declaring, " 'God is spirit, and his worshipers must worship in spirit and in truth' " (John 4:24). This worship would not be restricted by any physical site, since that reflects a false concept of the very nature of God. Worship must be in keeping with the spiritual nature of God.

The Bible does not define "spirit" for us, but it does offer descriptions. God as spirit is immortal, invisible, and eternal, worthy of our honor and glory forever (1 Tim. 1:17). As spirit, He lives in light that humans are unable to approach: "Whom no one has seen or can see" (1 Tim. 6:16). His spiritual nature is difficult for us to understand because we have not yet seen God as He is, and apart from faith we are unable to understand

---

[8]See the discussion on Yahweh, p. 134.

that which we have not experienced. Our sensory perception does not offer any assistance in discerning God's spiritual nature. God is not shackled by the bonds of physical matter. We worship One who is quite different from us, yet He desires to put within us the Holy Spirit as a foretaste of that day when we shall see Him as He is (1 John 3:2). Then we shall be able to approach the light, for we shall cast off mortality and take on glorified immortality (1 Cor. 15:51–54).

KNOWABLE

"No one has ever seen God" (John 1:18). The Almighty God cannot be fully comprehended by humanity (Job 11:7), yet He has shown himself at different times and in various ways, indicating that it is His will for us to know Him and to be in right relationship with Him (John 1:18; 5:20; 17:3; Acts 14:17; Rom. 1:18–20). This does not mean, however, that we can completely and exhaustively perceive all God's character and nature (Rom. 1:18–20; 2:14–15). As God reveals, He also conceals: "Truly you are a God who hides himself, O God and Savior of Israel" (Isa. 45:15).

Rather than detracting from His attributes, this concealing of himself is a confessional declaration of our limits and of God's infinitude. Because God determined to speak through His Son (Heb. 1:2) and to have His fullness dwell within His Son (Col. 1:19), we can expect to find the most focused manifestation of God's character in Jesus. Not only does Jesus make the Father known, He also reveals the meaning and significance of the Father.[9]

By means of numerous invitations God expresses His will that we know Him: " 'Be still, and know that I am God' " (Ps. 46:10). When the Hebrews submitted to the Lord, He promised that divine manifestations would show that He was their God and they were His people. " 'Then you will know that I am the LORD your God, who brought you out from under the yoke of the Egyptians' " (Exod. 6:7). The conquest of the Promised Land was also significant evidence of both the fact and knowability of the only true and living God (Josh. 3:10). The Canaanites and others who were to suffer God's divine judgment would be made to know that God existed and that He stood by Israel (1 Sam. 17:46; 1 Kings 20:28).

[9]John 1:18, *"exēgēsato."* Since no one has seen, or can fully comprehend, the Father, the *Logos* makes known, or "exegetes," Him for us, explaining by word and deed. See chap. 9, pp. 299–301.

Those who yielded to the Lord, however, could go beyond a mere knowledge of His existence to a knowledge of His person and purpose (1 Kings 18:37). One of the Old Testament benefits of being in a covenant relationship with God was that He would continue to reveal himself to those who obeyed the stipulations of that covenant (Ezek. 20:20; 28:26; 34:30; 39:22,28; Joel 2:27; 3:17).

Humans have searched for knowledge of the Deity since the beginning. Occurring in one of the earliest periods of biblical history, Zophar asked Job whether the search would yield any results: " 'Can you fathom the mysteries of God? Can you probe the limits of the Almighty?' " (Job 11:7). Elihu added, " 'How great is God—beyond our understanding! The number of his years is past finding out' " (Job 36:26). Whatever knowledge we have of God is because He has chosen to disclose himself to us. But even the admittedly limited knowledge we now have is glorious to behold and is a sufficient ground for our faith.

ETERNAL

We measure our existence by time: past, present, future. God is not limited by time, yet He has chosen to reveal himself to us within our framework of reference, so that we might see Him at work before and behind us. The terms "eternal," "everlasting," and "forever" are often used by English Bible translators to capture the Hebrew and Greek phrases that bring God into our perspective.[10] He existed before creation: "Before the mountains were born or you brought forth the earth and the world, from everlasting to everlasting you are God" (Ps. 90:2).

We must admit that because we experience time as a measurement with limitations, a full comprehension of eternity is beyond us. But we can meditate on the enduring and timeless aspect of God, which will lead us to worship Him as a personal Lord who has bridged a great gap between His infinite, unlimited vitality and our finite, limited mortalness. "He who lives forever, whose name is holy [says]: 'I live in a high and holy place, but also with him who is contrite and lowly in spirit, to revive the spirit of the lowly and to revive the heart of the contrite' " (Isa. 57:15).

Therefore, completely apart from trying to understand the relation of time and eternity, we can confess: "Now to the

---

[10]Deut. 33:27, "eternal God"; Ps. 102:12, "enthroned forever"; v. 27, "your years will never end."

King eternal, immortal, invisible, the only God, be honor and glory for ever and ever. Amen" (1 Tim. 1:17; cf. Num. 23:19; Pss. 33:11; 102:27; Isa. 57:15).

OMNIPOTENT

An ancient philosophical dilemma asks whether God is able to create a rock that is too large for Him to move. If He is not able to move it, then He is not all-powerful. If He is not able to create one that large, then that proves He is not all-powerful. This logical fallacy simply plays with words and overlooks the fact that God's power is intertwined with His purposes.

The more honest question would be, Is God powerful enough to do anything that He clearly intends to do and that fulfills His divine purpose? In the context of His purpose God shows that He is indeed able to accomplish whatever He wishes: "For the LORD Almighty has purposed, and who can thwart him? His hand is stretched out, and who can turn it back?" (Isa. 14:27). The unlimited power and might of the one true God cannot be withstood, thwarted, or turned back by humans (2 Chron. 20:6; Ps. 147:5; Isa. 43:13; Dan. 4:35).

God has shown that His primary concern is not with the size and weight of rocks (though He can make them give water [Exod. 17:6] or praise [Luke 19:40]), but with calling, shaping, and transforming a people for himself. This is seen in His bringing breath and life from the womb of Sarah when she was old—as God said, "Is anything too hard for the LORD?" (Gen. 18:14; cf. Jer. 32:17)—and from the womb of the young virgin, Mary (Matt. 1:20–25). God's highest purpose was found in bringing life from a tomb near Jerusalem as a demonstration of "his incomparably great power for us who believe. That power is like the working of his mighty strength, which he exerted in Christ when he raised him from the dead and seated him at his right hand in the heavenly realms" (Eph. 1:19–20).

Jesus' disciples pondered the impossibility of sending a camel through the eye of a literal sewing needle (Mark 10:25–27).[11] The real lesson here is that it is not possible for people to save themselves. However, that is not only possible for God, but also within His divine purpose. Therefore, the work of salvation is the exclusive domain of the Lord, who is al-

---

[11]Gk. *rhaphidos.* Luke 18:25 uses the more classical *belonēs*, usually used of a surgeon's needle.

mighty. We can exalt Him, not just because He is omnipotent and His power is greater than that of any other, but because His purposes are great and He applies His great power to accomplish His will.

OMNIPRESENT

The nations that surrounded ancient Israel served regional or national gods who were limited in their impact by locale and ritual. For the most part, these regional deities were considered by their devotees to have power only within the domain of the people who made offerings to them. Although the Lord did present himself to Israel as one who could focus His presence in the Holy of Holies of the tabernacle and temple, this was His concession to the limitations of human understanding. Solomon recognized this when he said, "Will God really dwell on earth? The heavens, even the highest heaven, cannot contain you. How much less this temple I have built!" (1 Kings 8:27).

We humans are presently limited to existence within the physical dimensions of this universe. There is absolutely nowhere that we can go to be out of the presence of God: "Where can I go from your Spirit? Where can I flee from your presence? If I go up to the heavens, you are there; if I make my bed in the depths, you are there. If I rise on the wings of the dawn, if I settle on the far side of the sea, even there your hand will guide me, your right hand will hold me fast" (Ps. 139:7–10; cf. Jer. 23:23–24). The spiritual nature of God allows Him to be omnipresent and yet very near to us (Acts 17:27–28).

OMNISCIENT

"Nothing in all creation is hidden from God's sight. Everything is uncovered and laid bare before the eyes of him to whom we must give account" (Heb. 4:13). God has the ability to know our thoughts and our intentions (Ps. 139:1–4), and He does not grow tired or weary in His activity of discerning them (Isa. 40:28). God's knowledge is not limited by our understanding of future time, since He can know the end of something from its very beginning (Isa. 46:10).

God's knowledge and wisdom are beyond our ability to penetrate (Rom. 11:33). That makes it difficult for us to fully comprehend how God has foreknowledge of events that are conditional upon our free will. This is one of those areas that place us in a healthy tension (not contradiction but paradox);

Scripture does not give enough information to adequately resolve the tension. It does, however, give us what we need—along with the help of the Holy Spirit—to make decisions that will please God.

WISE

In the ancient world, the concept of wisdom tended to belong to the realm of theory and debate. The Bible, however, presents wisdom in the realm of the practical, and again our model for this kind of wisdom is God. "Wisdom" (Heb. *chokhmah*) is the joining of the knowledge of truth with experience in life. Knowledge by itself may fill the head with facts without an understanding of their significance or application. Wisdom gives direction and meaning.

God's knowledge gives Him insight into all that is and can be. In view of the fact that God is self-existent, He has experience that we cannot even imagine and His understanding is unlimited (Ps. 147:5). He applies His knowledge wisely. All the works of His hands are made in His great wisdom (Ps. 104:24), allowing Him to set monarchs in position or to change the times and seasons as He wisely sees fit (Dan. 2:21).

God desires for us to partake of His wisdom and understanding so that we may know His plans for us and live in the center of His will (Col. 2:2–3).

GOD'S MORAL ATTRIBUTES

FAITHFUL

The religions of the ancient Near East were devoted to fickle, capricious deities. The grand exception to this was the God of Israel. He is dependable in His nature and actions. The Hebrew word *'amen*, "truly," is derived from one of the most outstanding Hebrew descriptions of God's character, reflecting His certainty and dependability: "I will exalt you and praise your name, for in *perfect faithfulness* [*'emunah 'omen*, literally 'faithfulness of reliability'] you have done marvelous things, things planned long ago" (Isa. 25:1).

While we use "amen" to express our assurance of God's ability to answer prayer, the biblical occurrences of the *'amen* family of words include an even broader range of manifestations of God's power and faithfulness. Abraham's chief servant attributed his successful search for a bride for young Isaac to the faithful nature of Yahweh (Gen. 24:27). The words "truth" and "faithfulness" (*'emeth* and *'emunah*) are, appropriately, extensions of the one Hebrew concept joined together in the nature of God.

The Lord evinces His faithfulness through keeping His promises: "Know therefore that the LORD your God is God; he is the faithful God, keeping his covenant of love to a thousand generations of those who love him and keep his commands" (Deut. 7:9). Joshua exclaimed at the end of his life that the Lord God had never failed him in even one promise (Josh. 23:14). The Psalmist confessed, "You established your faithfulness in heaven itself" (Ps. 89:2).

God shows himself to be constant in His intention to have fellowship with us, guiding and protecting us. Even the sin and wickedness of this world will not claim us if we submit to Him: "Because of the LORD's great love we are not consumed, for his compassions never fail. They are new every morning; great is your faithfulness" (Lam. 3:22–23).

Because God is faithful, it would be unheard of for Him to abandon His children when they suffer temptation or trial (1 Cor. 10:13). "God is not a man, that he should lie, nor a son of man, that he should change his mind. Does he speak and then not act? Does he promise and not fulfill?" (Num. 23:19). God remains stable in His nature, while exhibiting flexibility in His actions.[12] When God makes a covenant with people, His vow is a sufficient seal and profession of the unchanging nature of His person and purposes: "Because God wanted to make the unchanging nature of his purpose very clear to the heirs of what was promised, he confirmed it with an oath" (Heb. 6:17). If God were ever to stop upholding His promises, then He would be repudiating His own character.

Paul contrasts the human and the divine natures when He writes of the glory that follows the suffering of Christ: "If we are faithless, he will remain faithful, for he cannot disown himself" (2 Tim. 2:13). God's dependability is absolute because of what He is: faithful and true (Deut. 32:4; Ps. 89:8; 1 Thess. 5:23–24; Heb. 10:23; 1 John 1:9).

TRUTHFUL

"God is not a man, that he should lie" (Num. 23:19). The veracity of God is in contrast to the dishonesty of humans, but not just in relative measure. God is perfectly faithful to His word and His way (Pss. 33:4; 119:151), and His integrity is a permanent character trait that He exhibits (Ps. 119:160).

---

[12]Often classified as immutability; cf. Pss. 33:11; 102:27; James 1:17.

This stable and enduring truthfulness of the Lord is the vehicle through which we are sanctified, because the truth proclaimed has become truth incarnate: " 'Sanctify them by the truth; your word is truth' " (John 17:17). Our hope rests directly on the assurance that everything God has revealed to us is true, and all that He has done so far to fulfill His word gives us assurance that He will bring to completion what He has begun (John 14:6; Titus 1:1).

GOOD

God is, by His very nature, inclined to act with great generosity toward His creation. During the days of creation the Lord periodically examined His work and declared that it was good, in the sense of being pleasing and well-suited for His purposes (Gen. 1:4,10,12,18,21,25,31). The same adjective is used to describe God's moral character: "The LORD is good and his love endures forever" (Ps. 100:5). In this context, the expression carries the original idea of pleasing or fully suitable, but goes beyond to illustrate for us the grace that is essential to God's nature: "The LORD is gracious and compassionate, slow to anger and rich in love. The LORD is good to all; he has compassion on all he has made" (Ps. 145:8–9; see also Lam. 3:25). This facet of His nature is manifested in His willingness to provide our needs, whether they are material (rain and crops, Acts 14:17) or spiritual (joy, Acts 14:17; wisdom, James 1:5). This aspect is also in contrast to ancient beliefs, wherein all the other gods were unpredictable, vicious, and anything but good.

We can model ourselves after our generous and compassionate God, for "every good and perfect gift is from above, coming down from the Father of the heavenly lights, who does not change like shifting shadows" (James 1:17).

PATIENT

In a world full of retaliatory actions, often too hastily decided upon, our "LORD is slow to anger, abounding in love and forgiving sin and rebellion" (Num. 14:18). This "slowness" toward anger allows a window of opportunity for God to show compassion and grace (Ps. 86:15). The Lord's patience is for our benefit, so that we will realize that it should lead us to repentance (Rom. 2:4; 9:22–23).

We live in the tension of desiring Jesus to fulfill His promises by returning, yet wanting Him to wait until more people accept Him as Savior and Lord: "The Lord is not slow in keeping his promise, as some understand slowness. He is patient with you, not wanting anyone to perish, but everyone to come to repentance" (2 Pet. 3:9).

The Lord will punish the guilty for sin, yet for the present He will utilize His own standard of "slowness," since His patience means salvation (2 Pet. 3:15).

LOVE

Many of us began our early study of the Bible with memorization of John 3:16. As young Christians we recited it with vigor and enthusiasm, often with added emphasis upon " 'For God so loved the world.' " After further consideration, we find that the love of God in that passage is not being described as a quantity, but rather as a quality. It is not that God loved us so much that it motivated Him to give, but that He loved in such a sacrificial manner that He gave.[13]

God has revealed himself as a God who expresses a particular kind of love, a love that is displayed by sacrificial giving. As John defines it: "This is love: not that we loved God, but that he loved us and sent his Son as an atoning sacrifice for our sins" (1 John 4:10).

God also shows His love by providing rest and protection (Deut. 33:12), which our prayers of thanksgiving can focus on (Pss. 42:8; 63:3; Jer. 31:3). However, God's highest form and greatest demonstration of love for us are found in the cross of Christ (Rom. 5:8). He wants us to know that His character of love is integral to our life in Christ: "Because of his great love for us, God, who is rich in mercy, made us alive with Christ even when we were dead in transgressions—it is by grace you have been saved" (Eph. 2:4).

The most excellent path, the way of love, which we are charged to walk in, identifies the traits that God has modeled for us in His person and work (1 Cor. 12:31 through 13:13). If we follow His example, we will bear the spiritual fruit of love and will walk in a manner that will allow the gifts of the Spirit *(charismata)* to achieve the purposes of the grace *(charis)* of God.

GRACIOUS AND MERCIFUL

The terms "grace" and "mercy" represent two aspects of God's character and activity that are distinct but related. To

---

[13]Although the English particle "so" can signify quantity or quality, the Greek adverb *houtos* is used by John to mean "manner," "type," "in this way"; John 3:8; 21:1; 1 John 4:11.

experience the grace of God is to receive a gift that one cannot earn and does not deserve. To experience the mercy of God is to be preserved from punishment that one does in fact deserve. God is the royal judge who holds the power of ultimate and final punishment. When He forgives our sin and guilt, we are experiencing mercy. When we receive the gift of life, we are experiencing grace. God's mercy takes away the punishment, while His grace replaces the negative with a positive. We are deserving of punishment, but instead He gives us peace and restores us to wholeness (Isa. 53:5; Titus 2:11; 3:5).

"The Lord is compassionate and gracious, slow to anger, abounding in love" (Ps. 103:8). Since we have the need to be brought out of death into life, these aspects of God are often coupled in Scripture to show their interrelatedness (Eph. 2:4–5; cf. Neh. 9:17; Rom. 9:16; Eph. 1:6).

HOLY

" 'I am the Lord your God; consecrate yourselves and be holy, because I am holy' " (Lev. 11:44). We have been called to be different, because the Lord is different. God reveals himself as "holy," *qadosh* (Heb.), and the essential element of *qadosh* is separation from the mundane, profane, or normal and separation (or dedication) to His purposes. The commands given to Israel called for maintenance of the clear distinction between the spheres of the common and the sacred (Lev. 10:10). This distinction impacted time and space (Sabbath and sanctuary), but was most significantly directed at the individual. Because God is unlike any other being, all those submitted to Him must also be separated—in heart, intent, devotion, and character—to Him, who is truly holy (Exod. 15:11).

By His very nature, God is separated from sin and sinful humanity. The reason that we humans are unable to approach God in our fallen state is because we are not holy. The biblical issue of "uncleanness" is not dealing with hygiene, but with holiness (Isa. 6:5). The marks of uncleanness include brokenness (see Isa. 30:13–14), sin, violation of God's will, rebellion, and remaining in the state of being incomplete. Because God is whole and righteous, our consecration involves both separation from sin and obedience to Him.

Holiness is God's character and activity, as revealed in the title *Yahweh m^eqaddesh,* "the Lord, who makes you holy" (Lev. 20:8). The holiness of God should not become simply a point of meditation for us, but also an invitation (1 Pet. 1:15) to participate in His righteousness and to worship Him along with the multitudes. The living creatures in the Book of Revelation "never stop saying: 'Holy, holy, holy is the Lord God Almighty, who was, and is, and is to come' " (Rev. 4:8; cf. Ps. 22:3).

RIGHTEOUS AND JUST

The Holy God is distinct and set apart from sinful humanity. Yet, He is willing to allow us to enter into His presence. This willingness is balanced by the fact that He judges His people in righteousness and justice (Ps. 72:2). These two concepts are often combined to illustrate the standard of measurement that God presents.

Biblical righteousness is seen as conformity to an ethical or moral standard. The "rightness" (Heb. *ts^edaqah*)[14] of God is both His character and how He chooses to act. He is straight in ethical and moral character, and therefore serves as the norm for deciding where we stand in relation to Him.

Akin to that facet of God is His justice (Heb. *mishpat*), wherein He exercises all the processes of government. Many modern democratic systems of government separate duties of the state into various branches to balance and hold one another accountable (e.g., legislative to make and pass laws; executive to enforce them and maintain order; judicial to ensure legal consistency and penalize transgressors). The *mishpat* of God finds all of those functions within the character and domain of the one sovereign God (Ps. 89:14). The KJV often renders this Hebrew term as *judgment,* which emphasizes only one of the multiple aspects of justice (Isa. 61:8; Jer. 9:24; 10:24; Amos 5:24). The justice of God includes judgmental penalty, but subordinates that activity to the overall work of establishing loving justice (Deut. 7:9–10).[15]

The standard that God presents is perfect and upright (Deut. 32:4). Thus, we cannot, in and of ourselves, come up to the standard by which God measures us; we all come short (Rom. 3:23). And " 'he has set a day when he will judge the world with justice by the man he has appointed. He has given proof

---

[14]*Tsedeq,* R. Laird Harris, Gleason L. Archer, Jr. and Bruce K. Waltke, eds., *Theological Wordbook of the Old Testament,* vol. 2 (Chicago: Moody Press, 1980), 752–55.

[15]Millard J. Erickson, *Christian Theology* (Grand Rapids: Baker Book House, 1985), 288–98.

of this to all men by raising him from the dead' " (Acts 17:31). Yet God also seeks the preservation of His creatures now (Ps. 36:5–7), as well as offering them hope for the future. The incarnation of Christ included the qualities and activities of righteousness and justice. His substitutionary atonement then passed them to us (Rom. 3:25–26) so that we would be able to stand as righteous before the just Judge (2 Cor. 5:21; 2 Pet. 1:1).

CHAPTER

4

The One
True God

GOD'S NAMES

In our modern culture parents usually choose names for their children based on aesthetics or euphony. In biblical times, however, the giving of names was an occasion and ceremony of considerable significance. The name was an expression of the character, nature, or future of the individual (or at least a declaration by the namer of what was expected of the recipient of the name).[16] Throughout Scripture, God has shown that His name was not just a label to distinguish Him from the other deities of the surrounding cultures. Instead, each name that He uses and accepts discloses some facet of His character, nature, will, or authority.

Because the name represented God's person and presence, "calling upon the name of the LORD" became a means by which one could enter into an intimate relationship with God. This was a common theme in ancient Near Eastern religions. The surrounding religions, however, attempted to control their deities through manipulation of divine names, while the Israelites were commanded not to use the name of Yahweh their God in an empty and vain manner (Exod. 20:7). Instead, they were to enter into the relationship that was established by means of the name of the Lord and which brought with it providence and salvation.

OLD TESTAMENT NAMES

The primary word for deity found throughout the Semitic languages is *'El,* which possibly was derived from a term that meant power or preeminence. The actual derivation, how-

---

[16]For example, Elijah means "Yahweh is my God." The giving of a name could also be the parent's means of expressing great emotion: Rachel, in her final moments of life, named her last son Ben-Oni, "son of my trouble;" Jacob renamed the child Benjamin, "son of my right hand," that is, "son of blessing" (Gen. 35:18).

ever, is uncertain.[17] Since it was used commonly by several different religions and cultures, it can be classified as a generic term for "God" or "god" (depending on the context because the Hebrew Scriptures make no distinction between capital and lowercase letters).

For Israel, there was only one true God; therefore, the use of the generic name by other religions was vain and empty, for Israel was to believe in *'El 'Elohe Yisra'el*: "God, the God of Israel" (or, possibly, "Mighty is the God of Israel") —Gen. 33:20.

In the Bible this name is often made into a compound, using descriptive terms such as the following: *"'El* of glory" (Ps. 29:3), *"'El* of knowledge" (1 Sam. 2:3, KJV), *"'El* of salvation" (Isa. 12:2), *"'El* of vengeance" (Ps. 94:1, KJV), and *"'El,* the great and awesome" (Neh. 1:5; 4:14; 9:32; Dan. 9:4).

The plural form *'elohim* is found almost three thousand times in the Old Testament, and at least twenty-three hundred of those references are speaking of the God of Israel (Gen. 1:1; Ps. 68:1). The term *'elohim,* however, had a broad enough range of meaning to refer also to idols (Exod. 34:17), judges (Exod. 22:8), angels (Ps. 8:5, KJV), or the gods of the other nations (Isa. 36:18; Jer. 5:7). The plural form, when applied to the God of Israel, can be understood[18] as a way of expressing the thought that the fullness of deity is found within the one true God with all attributes, personhood, and powers.[19]

A synonym of *'Elohim* is its singular form *'Eloah,* which is also usually translated simply "God." An examination of the scriptural passages suggests that this name takes on a further meaning: reflecting God's ability to protect or destroy (depending on the particular context). It is used parallel to "rock" as a refuge (Deut. 32:15; Ps. 18:31; Isa. 44:8). Those who take refuge in Him find *'Eloah* to be a shield of protection (Prov. 30:5), but a terror for sinners: " 'Consider this, you who forget *'Eloah,* or I will tear you to pieces, with none to rescue' " (Ps. 50:22 see also 114:7; 139:19). Therefore, the name is a

---

[17]Geoffrey W. Bromiley, ed., *International Standard Bible Encyclopedia,* vol.1 (Grand Rapids: Wm. B. Eerdmans, 1979), 41–43.

[18]Jews and most liberal theologians understand it as an "intensive plural" or "plural of majesty"; however, there are no real grounds for this grammatically. The plural could be reflecting the Trinity. See chap. 5, p. 147.

[19]Eissfeldt, Otto, Trans. by H. H. Rowley and P. R. Weiss, "El and Yahweh," *Journal of Semitic Studies* 1:25–37; Jan. 1956. Harris, *Theological Wordbook,* vol. 1, 44–45.

comfort for those who humble themselves and seek shelter in Him, but a conveyance of fear to those who are not in right relationship with God.

The name stands as a challenge for people to decide which aspect of God they want to experience, because " 'blessed is the man whom *'Eloah* corrects' " (Job 5:17). Job ultimately chose to revere God in His majesty and repent before His power (37:23; 42:6).[20]

God often revealed something more of His character by providing descriptive phrases or clauses in conjunction with His various names. God first identified himself as *'El Shaddai* (Gen. 17:1)[21] when the time came to renew His covenant with Abram. Some of the biblical contexts suggest that *shaddai* conveys the image of one who has the power to devastate and destroy. In Psalm 68:14, the *Shaddai* "scattered the kings in the land," and a similar thought is spoken of by the prophet Isaiah: "Wail, for the day of the LORD is near; it will come like destruction from Shaddai" (Isa. 13:6). However, in other passages the emphasis seems to be upon God as the all-sufficient one: " *'El Shaddai* appeared to me at Luz in the land of Canaan, and there he blessed me and said to me, "I am going to make you fruitful" ' " (Gen. 48:3–4; see also 49:24). English translators have usually opted for "all-powerful" or "the Almighty" in recognition of the ability of *'El Shaddai* to bless or devastate as appropriate, since both these powers are within the character and power of that name.

Other descriptive appositions help to reveal the character of God. His exalted nature is displayed in *'El 'Elyon,* "God Most High"[22] (Gen. 14:22; Num. 24:16; Deut. 32:8). God's eternal nature is represented by the name *'El 'Olam,* with the descriptive term meaning "perpetual" or "everlasting;" when Abraham settled in Beersheba for a long time, "he called upon the name of the LORD, the Eternal God" (Gen. 21:33; cf. Ps. 90:2). All who live under the burden of sin and need deliverance can call upon *'Elohim yish'enu,* "God our Savior" (1 Chron. 16:35; Pss. 65:5; 68:19; 79:9).

The prophet Isaiah was used by the Lord in a powerful way to speak words of judgment and words of comfort to the

---

[20]Forty-one of the fifty-five verses that contain this term in the Old Testament are found in the Book of Job.

[21]*Shaddai* comes from an old word for "mountain." The New Testament translates it *pantokratōr,* "Almighty, omnipotent."

[22]*'Elyon* is a superlative adjective built from the verb meaning "go up," therefore carrying the idea of "uppermost," "most high," "exalted."

nations of his day. The words were not the result of speculation or demographic opinion-poll analysis. The prophet heard
from the God who revealed himself. His commission in Isaiah
6 can help to keep our study of God in perspective. There
God revealed himself exalted on a royal throne. The great
length of His garment confirmed His majesty. Seraphs declared His holiness[23] and pronounced the personal name of
God, Yahweh.

The name Yahweh appears 6,828 times in 5,790 verses in
the Old Testament[24] and is the most frequent designation of
God in the Bible. This name is probably derived from the
Hebrew verb that means "becoming," "happening," "being
present."[25] When Moses faced the dilemma of convincing the
Hebrew slaves to receive him as a messenger from God, he
sought out God's name. The form that the question takes is
really seeking a description of character rather than a title
(Exod. 3:11–15). Moses was not asking, "What shall I call
you?" but, "What is your character, or what are you like?"
God answered, "I AM WHO I AM" or "I WILL BE WHAT I WILL BE"
(v. 14). The Hebrew form *('ehyeh 'asher 'ehyeh)* indicates
being in action.[26]

In the next sentence, God identifies himself as the God of
Abraham, Isaac, and Jacob, who shall now be known as
YHWH.[27] This four-consonant Hebrew expression has been
known as the tetragrammaton and is usually translated in
English Bibles as LORD (in small capital letters). However,

---

[23]*Seraph* means "burning" or "fiery" and suggests that these heavenly
living creatures were either literally on fire, were purified by the fire of
God, or so reflected the glory of God that they seemed to be on fire. The
placement of their wings implies their experience of God: covering their
faces in reverence toward God, covering their feet as a gesture of modesty
in His presence, and flight as an expression of God's supernatural, royal
grant to accomplish His purposes. The threefold repetition of "holy" means
supremely holy. See p. 129 for the meaning of holy.

[24]Based on a computer text-based search using MacBible 2.4 Hebrew
Module from Zondervan Corp., 1991.

[25]Either *hawah* or *hayah.* For a full discussion of etymology and history
of interpretation see Harris, *Theological Wordbook,* vol. 1, 210–14.

[26]In Exod. 3:12, God said, "I will be with you" (Heb. *'Ehyeh 'inmakh*).
Thus the divine name involves purpose and action, not just being.

[27]In Old Testament times the Hebrew alphabet contained twenty-two
consonants and no vowels. Therefore the original text had *YHWH,* which
was probably pronounced "Yahweh," though the later Jews in Egypt pronounced it *Yahu.*

lordship is not really an essential aspect of this term.[28] Instead, it is a statement that God is a self-existent being (the I AM or I WILL BE) who causes all things to exist and has chosen to be faithfully present with a people that He has called unto himself.

In Old Testament times this name was pronounced freely by the Israelites. The Third Commandment (Exod. 20:7)— " 'You shall not misuse the name of *YHWH* your God,' " that is, use it in an empty manner or, like a name-dropper, for prestige or influence—originally would have had more to do with invoking the divine name in an oath formula than with using the name in a curse.

Over the centuries, however, scribes and rabbis developed a strategy for upholding this stipulation. Initially, the scribes wrote the Hebrew word *'adonai*, "master," "lord," in the margin of the scroll whenever *YHWH* appeared in the inspired text of Scripture. By means of written signals, whoever was reading the scroll publicly was to read *'adonai* from the marginal note instead of the holy name in the biblical passage. The theory was that one could not take the name in vain if one did not even say it. However, this device was not fail-safe and some readers inadvertently would utter the name during the public reading of the Bible in the synagogue. But the high reverence for the text prevented the scribes and rabbis from actually removing the Hebrew name *YHWH* and replacing it with the lesser term *'adonai*.[29]

Eventually the rabbis agreed to insert vowels in the Hebrew text (since the inspired text was originally only consonants). They took the vowels from *'adonai*, modified them to suit the grammatical requirements of the letters of *YHWH*, and inserted them between the consonants of that divine name, creating Y^eHoWaH. The vowels would then remind the reader to read *'Adonai*. Some Bibles transliterate this as "Jehovah," thereby perpetuating an expression that is a coined word, having, as it does, the consonants of a personal name and the vowels of a title.

By New Testament times the name had become shrouded

---

[28]The numerous verses that draw our attention to the "name" focus less on the lordship of God and more on His faithful presence and absolute existence (Deut. 28:58; Ps. 83:18; Isa. 42:8).

[29]This reverence was disregarded by the Septuagintal translators, who adopted the marginal reading and replaced the tetragrammaton with the Greek word *kurios*, which is basically equivalent to *'adonai* by meaning "master," "owner," "lord."

in secrecy, and the tradition of replacing the ineffable name with the substitute "Lord" was accepted by New Testament writers (which continues in many modern Bible translations, such as KJV, NIV, NKJV). This is acceptable. But we must teach and preach that the character of the "Lord/Yahweh/I Am/I Will Be" is active, faithful presence. "All the nations may walk in the name of their gods; we will walk in the name of [Yahweh] our God for ever and ever" (Mic. 4:5).

The seraphs in Isaiah's vision combine the personal name of the God of Israel with the descriptive noun *ts^eva'oth,* "armies" or "hosts."[30] This combination of *Yahweh* and *ts^eva'oth* (Sabaoth, KJV) occurs in 248 verses in the Bible (sixty-two times in Isaiah, seventy-seven in Jeremiah, fifty-three in Zechariah) and is usually translated "LORD Almighty" (Jer. 19:3; Zech. 3:9–10). This is the affirmation that Yahweh was the true leader of the armies of Israel as well as of the hosts of heaven, both angels and stars, ruling universally as the general chief of staff of the whole universe. Isaiah's use here (6:3) contradicts the position of the surrounding nations, that each regional god was the warrior god who held exclusive sway in that country. Even if Israel were defeated, it would not be because Yahweh was weaker than the next warrior god, but because Yahweh was using the armies of the surrounding countries (which He had created anyway) to judge His unrepentant people.

In the ancient Near East, the king was also the leader of all military operations. Therefore, this title *Yahweh Ts^eva'oth* is another way of exalting the royalty of God. "Lift up your heads, O you gates; lift them up, you ancient doors, that the King of glory may come in. Who is he, this King of glory? *Yahweh Ts^eva'oth*—he is the King of glory" (Ps. 24:9–10).

The seraphs in Isaiah's vision finally confess that "the whole earth is full of his glory." This glory (Heb. *kavodh*) carries the concept of heaviness, weightiness. The use of "glory" in this context is associated with one who is truly weighty not in measurement of pounds but in position, as recognized in society. In this sense, one would be called weighty if one was honorable, impressive, and worthy of respect.

God's self-disclosure is related to His intent to dwell among humans; He desires to have His reality and splendor known. But this is possible only when people take account of the stunning quality of His holiness (including the full weight of His attributes), and they set out in faith and obedience to let

_____

[30]Transliterated as Sabaoth (Rom. 9:29; James 5:4, KJV).

that character be manifested in them. Yahweh does not typically manifest His presence physically, yet many believers
can attest to that subjective and spiritual sensation that the
weighty presence of the Lord has descended. That is exactly
the image conveyed through Isaiah. God deserves the reputation of greatness, glory, kingdom, and power. But it is not
just His reputation that fills the earth, it is the very reality of
His presence, the full weight of His glory (cf. 2 Cor. 4:17,
KJV).

God's desire is that all persons gladly recognize His glory.
Progressively, God has dwelt in glory among people; first in
the pillar of fire and cloud, then in the tabernacle, then in
the temple in Jerusalem, then in the flesh as His Son, Jesus
of Nazareth, and now in us by His Holy Spirit. "We have seen
his glory, the glory of the One and Only, who came from the
Father, full of grace and truth" (John 1:14). Now we can know
that we all are the temple of Yahweh's most Holy Spirit (1 Cor.
3:16–17).

The name of the "I am/I will be" in conjunction with particular descriptive terms often serves as a confession of faith
that further reveals the nature of God. When Isaac asked his
father, "Here is the fire and the wood, but where is the lamb
for the burnt offering?" Abraham assured his son that God
would see to [yireh] it (Gen. 22:7–8). After sacrificing the
substitute ram that had been caught in the thicket, Abraham
called that place *Yahweh yireh*, "the LORD will provide" (v.
14).[31]

Abraham's faith went beyond a positive confession of God
as simply a material provider, however. His God was one who
was personally involved and willing to look into the problem
and bring about a resolution. The problem was resolved by
providing a substitute for Isaac as a pleasing sacrificial offering.
After the fact, we can testify that Yahweh really does provide.
But during the trek up the mountain, Abraham trusted God
to see to it, since he had assured the servants who were
waiting in the distance that both he and the boy would return
to them. Abraham's faith was total abandon to the ability of
God to look into any problem and take care of it according
to divine wisdom and plan, even if that meant obedient death
and then God raising the dead (see Heb. 11:17–19).

The tetragrammaton is used also in combination with a
number of other terms that serve to describe many facets of
the Lord's character, nature, promises, and activities. *Yahweh*

---

[31]Usually rendered in English "Jehovah Jireh."

Shammah, "the Lord is there," serves as a promise of Yahweh's presence and power in the city of Ezekiel's prophecy by placing His name there (Ezek. 48:35).

Yahweh 'osenu, "the Lord our Maker," is a declaration of His ability and willingness to take things that exist and fashion them into usefulness (Ps. 95:6).

The Hebrews in the wilderness experienced *Yahweh roph'ekha,* "the Lord your physician," or "the Lord who heals you," if they listened and obeyed His commands (Exod. 15:26).[32] In this way they were able to avoid the plagues and diseases of Egypt and be made whole. Our Lord by His nature is a healer for those who are submitted to His power and will.

When the Lord led Moses and Israel successfully against the Amalekites, Moses erected an altar dedicated to *Yahweh nissi,* "The Lord is my Banner" (Exod. 17:15). A banner was a flag that served as a rallying point throughout battle or any other common action.[33] This function of a raised banner appears typologically in the lifting of the bronze serpent on a pole and in the Savior who would serve as an ensign to the peoples as He was drawing all nations to himself (Num. 21:8–9; Isa. 62:10–11; John 3:14; Phil. 2:9).

When God spoke words of peace to Gideon, he built an altar to *Yahweh Shalom,* "The Lord is Peace" (Judg. 6:23). The essence of biblical *shalom* is completeness, wholeness, harmony, fulfillment, in the sense of taking that which is incomplete or shattered and making it complete by means of a sovereign act.[34] We can face difficult challenges, as Gideon did in confronting the Midianites, knowing that God grants us peace because that is one way He manifests His nature.

God's people need a protector and provider, so God has revealed himself as *Yahweh ro'i,* "the Lord is my shepherd" (Ps. 23:1). All the positive aspects of ancient Near Eastern shepherding can be found in the faithful Lord (leading, feeding, defending, caring, healing, training, correcting, and being willing to die in the process if necessary).

When Jeremiah prophesied of a king to come, the righteous

---

[32]The form *Jehovah rapha* is not in the Bible. *Rapha'* means "He healed" or "He used to heal." *Roph'ekha* combines *rophe',* a participle translated "physician" in Jer. 8:22 (KJV, NIV), and *Kha,* a pronoun meaning "your" or "you." *Kha* is singular and emphasizes that God is the physician for each of you individually.

[33]Harris, *Theological Wordbook,* vol. 2, 583.

[34]Ibid., 931.

branch of David that God would raise up, the name that this king would be known by was revealed as *Yahweh tsidkenu,* "The LORD Our Righteousness" (Jer. 23:6; see also 33:16). It is God's nature to act in justice and judgment as He works to place us in right standing with Him. He becomes the norm and standard by which we can measure our lives. Because God chose to make "him who had no sin to be sin for us" (2 Cor. 5:21), we can participate in the promise of God to declare us righteous ourselves. "It is because of him that you are in Christ Jesus, who has become for us wisdom from God—that is, our righteousness, holiness and redemption" (1 Cor. 1:30).

One way that God has shown His desire to have a personal relationship with His people is through the description of himself as "Father." This view of God as a father is much more developed in the New Testament than in the Old, occurring sixty-five times in the first three Gospels and over one hundred times in John's Gospel alone. The Old Testament identifies God as father only fifteen times (usually in relation to the nation or people of Israel).

The particular aspects of fatherhood that seem to be emphasized include creation (Deut. 32:6), redemption responsibility (Isa. 63:16), craftsmanship (Isa. 64:8), familial friendship (Jer. 3:4), passing along inheritance (Jer. 3:19), leadership (Jer. 31:9), being honorable (Mal. 1:6), and willing to punish transgression (Mal. 2:10,12). God is also noted as the Father of particular individuals, especially the monarchs David and Solomon. In relationship to them, God the Father is willing to punish error (2 Sam. 7:14), while being faithful in His love toward His children (1 Chron. 17:13). Above all, God the Father promises to be faithful forever, with a willingness to remain involved in the fathering process for eternity (1 Chron. 22:10).

NEW TESTAMENT NAMES

The New Testament gives a much clearer revelation of the triune God than the Old Testament. God is Father (John 8:54; 20:17), Son (Phil. 2:5–7; Heb. 1:8), and Holy Spirit (Acts 5:3–4; 1 Cor. 3:16). Since many of the names, titles, and attributes of God properly fit under the categories of "Trinity," "Christ," and "Holy Spirit," they are dealt with in greater depth in those chapters in this book. The following will focus on the names and titles that speak more directly about the one true God.

Our term "theology" is derived from the Greek word *theos.*

The translators of the Septuagint adopted it as the appropriate expression to convey the Hebrew *'elohim* and its related synonyms, and this understanding is continued in the New Testament. *Theos* was also the generic term for divine beings, such as when the Maltese said Paul was a god after he had survived the viper bite (Acts 28:6). The term can be translated "god," "gods," or "God," depending on the literary context, much as the Hebrew term *'El* (Matt. 1:23; 1 Cor. 8:5; Gal. 4:8). However, the use of this Greek word in no way makes concession to the existence of other gods, since literary context is not the same as spiritual context. Within spiritual reality, there is only one true Divine Being: "We know that an idol is nothing at all in the world and that there is no *theos* but one" (1 Cor. 8:4). God makes exclusive claim to this term as a further revelation of himself. The same can be said of the Greek expression *logos,* "Word" (John 1:1,14).[35]

The Old Testament introduces the image of God as Father; the New Testament displays how that relationship is to be fully experienced. Jesus speaks often of God in intimate terms. No Old Testament prayer addresses God as "Father." Yet, when Jesus trained His disciples in prayer He expected them to take the posture of children together and say, " 'Our Father in heaven, hallowed be your name' " (Matt. 6:9). Our God is the "Father" with all the power of heaven (Matt. 26:53; John 10:29), and He utilizes that power to keep, prune, sustain, call, love, preserve, provide, and glorify (John 6:32; 8:54; 12:26; 14:21,23; 15:1; 16:23).

The apostle Paul summarized his own theology by focusing on our need for unmerited favor and wholeness. He opens most of his epistles with this statement of invocation: "Grace and peace to you from God our Father and from the Lord Jesus Christ" (Rom. 1:7; see also 1 Cor. 1:3; 2 Cor. 1:2; Gal. 1:3; etc.).

In Greek philosophy, the divine beings were described as "unmoved movers," "the cause of all being," "pure being," "the world soul," and with other expressions of distant impersonality. Jesus stood firmly within the Old Testament revelation and taught that God is personal. Although Jesus spoke of the God of Abraham, Isaac, and Jacob (Mark 12:26); Lord (Mark 5:19; 12:29; Luke 20:37); Lord of heaven and earth (Matt. 11:25); Lord of the harvest (Matt. 9:38); the only God (John 5:44); Most High (Luke 6:35); King (Matt. 5:35)—His

---

[35]See chap. 9, pp. 299, 301.

favorite title for God was "Father,"[36] given in the Greek New Testament as *patēr* (from which we derive "patriarch" and "paternal"). An exception to this is found in Mark 14:36, where the original Aramaic term *'abba*, which Jesus actually used to address God, is retained.[37]

Paul designated God as *'abba* on two occasions: "Because you are sons, God sent the Spirit of His Son into our hearts, the Spirit who calls out, 'Abba, Father' " (Gk. *ho patēr*) (Gal. 4:6). "You did not receive a spirit that makes you a slave again to fear, but you received the Spirit of sonship. And by him we cry, 'Abba, Father.' The Spirit himself testifies with our spirit that we are God's children" (Rom. 8:15–16). That is, in the Early Church, Jewish believers would be calling on God, *'Abba*, "O Father!"[38] and Gentile believers would be crying out, *Ho Pater*, "O Father!" At the same time, the Spirit would be making it real to them that God really is our Father. The uniqueness of the term is in the fact that Jesus gave it a warmth and tenderness usually not found.[39] It characterized well not only His own relationship with God, but also the kind of relationship that He ultimately intended for His disciples.

GOD'S NATURE

The Almighty God cannot be fully comprehended by humanity, yet He has shown himself in various times and ways, that we might truly know Him. God is incomprehensible and His very existence cannot be proven by mere human logic. Rather than detracting from His attributes, this is a confessional declaration of our limits and God's infinitude. Our understanding of God can be built upon two primary presup-

---

[36]Sixty-five times in the Synoptics; over one hundred times in John.

[37]Occasionally the Greek manuscripts would continue to use the older Hebrew or Aramaic words to make a point or to retain the original flavor of the lesson or figure of speech. In Hebrew, God would be addressed as *Ha'av* and in the Aramaic used by Jews in New Testament times, *'Abba*, both meaning "The Father" or "O Father," both very respectful terms.

[38]Later Jews made *'Abba* a term of informal address: "An infant cannot say *'abba* (daddy) and *'imma* (mama) until it has tasted wheat [i.e., until it has been weaned]," Talmud Sanhedrin, 8:70B:VII:G. In New Testament times, however, it was a term of respect. See *The New Testament*, The Complete Biblical Library, vol. 11. *Greek English Dictionary Alpha-Gamma* (Springfield, Mo.: The Complete Biblical Library, 1990), 20–21.

[39]Marvin R. Wilson, *Our Father Abraham: The Jewish Roots of the Christian Faith* (Grand Rapids: Wm. B. Eerdmans, 1989), 56–57.

positions: (1) God exists and (2) He has revealed himself adequately to us through His inspired revelation.[40]

God is not to be explained, but believed and described. We can build our doctrine of God upon the preceding presuppositions and the evidences that He has given in Scripture. Some Scripture passages attribute qualities to the being of God that humans do not have, while other passages describe Him in terms of moral attributes that can be shared by humans in some limited measure.

God's constitutional nature is identified most often by those attributes that find no analogy in our human existence. God exists in and of himself, without dependence upon any other. He himself is the source of life, both in creation and sustenance. God is spirit; He is not confined to material existence and is imperceptible to the physical eye. His nature does not change, but stands firm. Since God himself is the ground of time, He cannot be bound by time. He is eternal, without beginning or end. God is thoroughly consistent within himself. Space is unable to limit or bound God, so He is omnipresent, and being able to do absolutely anything consistent with His nature and productive to His purposes, He is omnipotent. Furthermore, God is omniscient, knowledgeable concerning all truth—past, present, and future, possible and actual. In all of these attributes, the believer can find both comfort and confirmation of faith, while the unbeliever is served a warning and motivated toward belief.

The biblical evidences of God's moral attributes display characteristics that may also be found in humankind, but ours pale in the glory of the Lord's brilliant display. Of paramount importance in this group is God's holiness, His absolute purity and exaltation above all creatures. Included in this fundamental perfection are His righteousness, resulting in the establishment of laws, and His justice, resulting in the execution of His laws. The affection God has for His children is expressed by His sacrificial love. God's love is unselfish, self-initiated, righteous, and everlasting. Furthermore, God shows benevolence by feeling and manifesting affection for His creation in general. He shows mercy by directing goodness to those in misery and distress and by withholding deserved punishment. He also manifests grace as goodness given to the totally undeserving.

---

[40]Both the Scriptures (1 Thess. 2:13; Heb 4:12) and the Messiah (John 1:1; 1 John 1:1).

The wisdom of God is seen in the divine purposes and in the plans He uses to achieve those purposes. The primary example of God's wisdom, incarnate and in action, is in the person and work of Jesus. Other expressions of wisdom include patience, whereby God withholds His righteous judgment and wrath from rebellious sinners, and also truthfulness, wherein God stands by His Word as forerunner and foundation for our trust in His Word and action. Jesus, the Messiah of God, is the Truth in flesh. Finally, there is the moral perfection of faithfulness. God is absolutely reliable in covenant keeping, trustworthy in forgiving, and never failing in His promises, steadfastly providing a way for us. The image of a rock is often utilized to portray our Lord's firmness and protection.

CHAPTER

4

The One
True God

GOD'S ACTIVITIES

One other aspect requiring attention within the doctrine of God is that of His activities. This aspect can be divided into His decrees and His providence and preservation. The decrees of God are His eternal plan, and they have certain characteristics: They are all part of one plan, which is unchanging and everlasting (Eph. 3:11; James 1:17). They are free from and not conditioned by other beings (Ps. 135:6). They deal with God's actions and not His nature (Rom. 3:26). Within these decrees are those actions done by God for which He is sovereignly responsible, and then those actions allowed by God to happen but for which He is not responsible.[41] On the basis of this distinction we can see that God is neither the author of evil, even though He is the creator of all subordinates, nor is He the final cause of sin.

God is also actively sustaining the world He created. In preservation He works to uphold His laws and powers in creation (Acts 17:25). In providence He works continuously to control all things in the universe for the purpose of bringing about His wise and loving plan in ways consistent with the agency of His free creatures (Gen. 20:6; 50:20; Job 1:12; Rom. 1:24).

Recognizing this and delighting in the Lord, meditating upon His Word day and night, will bring every blessing of God, for we will understand who He is and how to worship and serve Him.

---

[41] For discussion of the matter of election from Calvinistic and Arminian viewpoints, see chap. 1, pp. 49–50 and chap. 10, pp. 352, 355–60.

The psalms are helpful in our worship. Many psalms open with the traditional Hebrew call to worship: Hallelujah! meaning "Praise the Lord!" (see Pss. 106; 111; 112; 113; 135; 146; 147; 148; 149; 150). In our modern experience this term often serves as a statement of exaltation. However, it began as a command to worship. The psalms that begin with this call to worship usually furnish information about Yahweh that focuses worship on Him and reveals features of His greatness that are worthy of praise.

Serving God begins by praying in His name. This means recognizing how distinct His nature is as revealed in the magnificent variety of His names, for He has revealed himself to us that we might glorify Him and do His will.

STUDY QUESTIONS

1. What obstacles will we face when we express our belief in the existence of God to those who do not share our worldview, and in what ways can we overcome those obstacles?

2. How does God reveal himself to us so that we might know Him?

3. How does our present experience of time affect our understanding of God's eternity?

4. How does the wisdom of God compare with the popular human concept of acquired wisdom?

5. What part does sacrifice play in the love that God has manifested?

6. In what specific ways have you experienced the grace and mercy of the Lord?

7. In what ways does the holiness of God, as reported in Scripture, help us to avoid the legalism that sometimes hinders some human expressions of holiness?

8. What do the names of God tell us about the personality and purposes of God?

9. In what ways has the theme of God as our Father in the Old Testament been further revealed in the New Testament?

10. What is the relationship between God's foreknowledge, predestination, and sovereignty?

The Holy Trinity

Kerry D. McRoberts

The Father uncreated, the Son uncreated: the Holy Spirit uncreated.

The Father immeasurable, the Son immeasurable: the Holy Spirit immeasurable.

The Father eternal, the Son eternal: the Holy spirit eternal.

And, nevertheless, not three eternals: but one eternal.[1]

The Trinity is a mystery. Reverent acknowledgment of that which is not revealed in Holy Scripture is necessary before entering the inner sanctum of the Holy One to inquire into His nature. The limitless glory of God should impress us with a sense of our own insignificance in contrast with Him, who is "high and exalted."

Does our acknowledgment of the mystery of the inner workings of God, particularly of the Trinity, then call for an abandonment of reason? Not at all. Mysteries do indeed exist in biblical Christianity, but "Christianity, as a 'revealed religion,' focuses on revelation—and revelation, by definition, makes manifest rather than concealing."[2]

Reason does discover a stumbling block when confronted with the paradoxical character of Trinitarian theology. "But," Martin Luther strenuously asserted, "since it is based on clear

---

[1] R. O. P. Taylor, *The Athanasian Creed in the Twentieth Century* (Edinburgh: T. & T. Clark, 1911), 57.

[2] John Warwick Montgomery, *Principalities and Powers: The World of the Occult* (Minneapolis: Pyramid Publications for Bethany Fellowship, Inc., 1975), 25.

Scripture, reason must be silent at this point and we must believe."[3]

Therefore, the role of reason is ministerial, never magisterial (i.e., rationalistic), in relation to Scripture and, specifically, to the formulation of the doctrine of the Trinity.[4] We are therefore not attempting to explain God, but rather to consider the historical evidence that establishes the identity of Jesus as both man and God (by virtue of His miraculous acts and divine character), and further, "to incorporate the truth which Jesus thereby validated as to His eternal relation with God the Father and with God the Holy Spirit."[5]

Historically, the Church formulated its doctrine of the Trinity following great debate concerning the Christological problem of the relationship of Jesus of Nazareth to the Father. Three distinct Persons—the Father, the Son, and the Holy Spirit—are manifest in Scripture as God, while at the same time the entirety of the Bible tenaciously holds to the Jewish *Sheʿma:* "Hear, O Israel: The LORD our God, the LORD is one" (Deut. 6:4).[6]

The conclusion derived from the biblical data is that the God of the Bible is (in the words of the Athanasian Creed) "one God in Trinity and Trinity in Unity." Does this sound irrational? Such a charge against the doctrine of the Trinity may very well itself be irrational: "[W]hat is irrational is to suppress the biblical evidence of the Trinity in favor of Unity, or the evidence for Unity in favor of Trinity."[7] "Our data must take precedence over our models—or, stating it better, our models must sensitively reflect the full range of data."[8] Therefore, our methodological sights must be scripturally focused with respect to the tenuous relationship between unity and

---

[3]Quoted in Paul Althaus, *The Theology of Martin Luther,* trans. Robert C. Schultz (Philadelphia: Fortress Press, 1966), 199.

[4]The word "trinity" does not appear in Scripture. But in the light of the biblical data, the Church is compelled to make use of words such as "trinity" for the purpose of systematizing the teaching of the Bible and exposing error in false teachers. The term "trinity" is therefore merely intended to express what the Bible clearly communicates concerning the nature of the one true God.

[5]Montgomery, *Principalities and Powers,* 45–46.

[6]"One" (Heb. *'echad*) can mean a compound or complex unity. The Hebrew has another word, *yachid,* which can mean "only one," but it is never used in passages relating to the nature of God.

[7]John Warwick Montgomery, *How Do We Know There Is a God?* (Minneapolis: Bethany House Publishers, 1973), 14.

[8]Ibid.

trinity, lest we polarize the doctrine of the Trinity into one
of two extremes: suppression of the evidence in favor of unity
(resulting in unitarianism, i.e., one solitary God) or misuse
of the evidence for triunity (resulting in tritheism, i.e., three
separate gods).

**CHAPTER
5**

The Holy
Trinity

An objective analysis of the biblical data concerning the
relationship of the Father, the Son, and the Holy Spirit reveals
that this great doctrine of the Church is not an abstract notion,
but is in fact a revelational truth. Therefore, before discussing
the historical development and formulation of Trinitarian theology, we will consider the biblical data for the doctrine.

BIBLICAL DATA FOR THE DOCTRINE

THE OLD TESTAMENT

God, in the Old Testament, is one God, revealing himself
by His names, His attributes, and His acts.[9] A shaft of light
breaks through the long shadow of the Old Testament, however, intimating plurality (a distinction of persons) in the
Godhead: "God said, 'Let us make man in *our* image, in *our*
likeness' " (Gen. 1:26).[10] That God could not have been con-
versing with angels or other unidentified beings is clearly
revealed in verse 27, which refers to the special creation of
man "in the image of God." The context indicates a divine
interpersonal communication requiring a unity of Persons in
the Godhead.

Other intimations of personal distinctions in the Godhead
are revealed in passages that make reference to "the angel of
the LORD" (Heb. *Yahweh*). This angel is distinguished from
other angels. He is personally identified with Yahweh and at
the same time distinguished from Him (Gen. 16:7–13; 18:1–
21; 19:1–28; 32:24–30—Jacob says, "I saw God face to face,"
with reference to the angel of the Lord). In Isaiah 48:16; 61:1;
and 63:9–10, the Messiah speaks. In one instance He identifies
himself with God and the Spirit in personal unity as the three
members of the Godhead. And yet, in another instance, the
Messiah continues (still speaking in first person) to distinguish himself from God and the Spirit.

Zechariah is most illuminating as he speaks for God about

---

[9]See chap. 4.

[10]Some, especially among the Jews, take the plurals here to be the plural
of majesty or something like an editor's "we," but there is no parallel for
this in the Bible.

the Messiah's crucifixion: " 'I will pour out on the house of David and the inhabitants of Jerusalem a spirit of grace and supplication. They will look on *me,* the one they have pierced, and they will mourn for *him* as one mourns for an only child, and grieve bitterly for *him* as one grieves for a *firstborn son*' " (Zech. 12:10). Clearly the one true God is speaking in the first person ("me") in reference to having been "pierced," and yet He himself makes the grammatical shift from the first person to the third person ("him") in referring to the Messiah's sufferings because of having been "pierced." The revelation of plurality in the Godhead is quite evident in this passage.

This leads us from the shadows of the Old Testament into the greater light of the New Testament's revelation.

THE NEW TESTAMENT

John commences the prologue of his Gospel with revelation of the Word[11]: "In the beginning was the Word, and the Word was with God, and the Word was God" (John 1:1). B. F. Westcott observes that here John carries our thought beyond the beginning of creation in time to eternity.[12] The verb "was" (Gk. *ēn,* the imperfect of *eimi,* "to be") appears three times in this verse, and by the use of this verse the apostle conveys the concept that neither God nor the *Logos* has a beginning; their existence together has been and is continuous.[13]

The second part of the verse continues, "And the Word was with God [*pros ton theon*]." The *Logos* has existed with God in perfect fellowship throughout all eternity. The word *pros* (with) reveals the intimate "face to face" relationship

---

[11]Gk. *Logos.* It is significant that John chose to identify Christ in His preincarnate state as the *Logos* instead of *Sophia* (wisdom). John avoids the contaminations of pre-Gnostic teachings that either denied the humanity of the Christ or separated the Christ from the man Jesus. The *Logos,* who is eternal, "became flesh" (*sarx egeneto,* v. 14).

[12]Quoted in Archibald Thomas Robertson, *Word Pictures in the New Testament,* vol. 5 (Nashville, Tenn.: Broadmen Press, 1932), 3. "In the beginning" *(en archei)* is similar to the Hebrew *(bᵉrēshith)* in Genesis 1:1. Neither *archei* nor *rēshith* has the definite article, but this does not bear any special meaning in the interpretation of the text unless it points us to the very beginning before all other beginnings.

[13]Robertson notes: "Quite a different verb (*egeneto,* 'became') appears in v. 14 for the beginning of the Incarnation of the Logos." Ibid.

the Father and the Son have always shared.[14] John's final phrase is a clear declaration of the deity of the Word: "And the Word was God."[15]

John continues to tell us, by revelation, that the Word entered the plane of history (1:14) as Jesus of Nazareth: himself "God the One and Only, who is at the Father's side" and who has made the Father known (1:18).[16] The New Testament further reveals that because He has shared in God's glory from all eternity (John 17:5), Jesus Christ is the object of worship reserved only for God: "At the name of Jesus every knee should bow, in heaven and on earth and under the earth, and every tongue confess that Jesus Christ is Lord, to the glory of God the Father" (Phil. 2:10–11; see also Exod. 20:3; Isa. 45:23; Heb. 1:8).

The eternal Word, Jesus Christ, is the one through whom God the Father created all things (John 1:3; Rev. 3:14).[17] Jesus

---

[14]Robertson observes: "*Pros* with the accusative presents a plane of equality and intimacy, face to face with each other. In 1 John 2:1 we have a like use of *pros:* 'We have a Paraclete with the Father' *(paraklēton echomen pros ton patera)*. See *prosōpon pros prosōpon* (face to face, 1 Cor. 13:12), a triple use of *pros.*" Ibid.

[15]Robertson comments: "By exact and careful language John denied Sabellianism by not saying *ho theos ēn ho logos.* That would mean that all of God was expressed in *ho logos* and the terms would be interchangeable, each having the article." *Ibid.*, 4. It should be noted also that in the New Testament God the Father is often referred to as *theos* without the article, and Jesus is called *ho theos* (John 20:28). Therefore, Jesus is just as fully divine, just as fully God, as the Father.

For further study, see: E. C. Colwell, "A Definite Rule for the Use of the Article in the Greek New Testament," *Journal of Biblical Literature* 70 (1933), 12–21. Cf. B. M. Metzger, "On the Translation of John i.1," *Expository Times* 73 (1951–52), 125–26, and C. F. D. Moule, "The Language of the New Testament," Inaugural Lecture, delivered at Cambridge University, 23 May 1952, 12–14.

[16]The KJV has "the only begotten Son" *(ho monogenēs huios).* However, some of the oldest Greek manuscripts (Aleph, B, C, L) read *monogenēs theos. Monogenēs* by New Testament times had lost the meaning of "only begotten" and had come to mean "only" in the sense of special, unique, one-of-a-kind, and was so used of Abraham's special and beloved son, Isaac (Heb. 11:17). That "God the One and Only" is a correct translation is supported by John 1:1, which clearly states that the *Logos* is deity *(theos),* and John 1:14 uses the term *monogenēs* as a description of the uniqueness of the Logos in His identification with the Father.

[17]The KJV of Rev. 3:14 reads, "the beginning of the creation of God." The NIV reads, "the ruler of God's creation." "Beginning" or "ruler" is *archē,* from which we derive the word "architect," which has to do with designing and building. This is what Jesus Christ is, the Designer and Architect of all creation. *Archē* is also translated "principality" (Eph. 1:21, KJV) or "rule" (Eph. 1:21, NIV, NASB margin); therefore, the NIV is also appropriate.

identifies himself as the sovereign "I am" (John 8:58; cf. Exod. 3:14).[18] We note in John 8:59 that the Jews were moved to pick up stones and kill Jesus because of this claim. They tried to do the same later, following His claim in John 10:30, " 'I and the Father are one.' " The Jews who heard Him considered Jesus a blasphemer, " 'You, a mere man, claim to be God' " (John 10:33; cf. John 5:18).

Paul identifies Jesus as the God of providence: "He is before all things, and in him all things hold together" (Col. 1:17). Jesus is the "Mighty God" who will reign as King on David's throne and make it eternal (Isa. 9:6–7). His knowledge is perfect and complete. Peter addressed our Lord: " 'Lord, you know all things' " (John 21:17). Christ himself said, " 'No one knows the Son except the Father, and no one knows the Father except the Son and those to whom the Son chooses to reveal him' " (Matt. 11:27; cf. John 10:15).[19]

Jesus is now everywhere present (Matt. 18:20) and unchanging (Heb. 13:8). He shares with the Father the title "the First and the Last," and He is "the Alpha and the Omega" (Rev. 1:17; 22:13). Jesus is our Redeemer and Savior (John 3:16–17; Heb. 9:28; 1 John 2:2), our Life and Light (John 1:4), our Shepherd (John 10:14; 1 Pet. 5:4), our Justifier, (Rom. 5:1) and the soon-coming "KING OF KINGS AND LORD OF LORDS" (Rev. 19:16). Jesus is Truth (John 14:6) and the Comforter whose comfort and help overflows into our lives (2 Cor. 1:5). Isaiah further calls Him our "Counselor" (Isa. 9:6), and He is the Rock (Rom. 9:33; 1 Cor. 10:4). He is holy (Luke 1:35), and He dwells within those who call upon His name (Rom. 10:9–10; Eph. 3:17).

All that can be said of God the Father, can be said of Jesus Christ. "In Christ all the fullness of the Deity lives in bodily form" (Col. 2:9); "God over all, forever praised!" (Rom. 9:5). Jesus spoke of His full equality with the Father: " 'Anyone who has seen me has seen the Father ... I am in the Father, and ... the Father in me' " (John 14:9–10).

Jesus claimed full deity for the Holy Spirit, " 'I will ask the

---

[18]The verb *eimi* ("I am") with the emphatic *egō* ("I") clearly means that Jesus is claiming to be a "timeless being," and therefore God. The context allows no other interpretation of the text.

[19]The fact that Jesus did not know the time of His return (Matt. 24:36) was undoubtedly a limitation He placed on himself while He was here on earth identifying himself with humankind. Cf. John Wenham, *Christ and the Bible* (Downers Grove, Ill.: InterVarsity Press, 1972), 45–46. He certainly has that knowledge now that He has returned to the glory He shares with the Father (John 17:5).

Father, and he will give you another Counselor to be with you forever' " (John 14:16).[20] By calling the Holy Spirit *allon paraklēton* ("another Helper of the same kind as himself "),[21] Jesus affirmed that everything that can be said about His nature can be said of the Holy Spirit. Therefore, the Bible testifies to the deity of the Holy Spirit as the Third Person of the Trinity.

Psalm 104:30 reveals the Holy Spirit as the Creator: "When you send your Spirit, they are created, and you renew the face of the earth." Peter refers to Him as God (Acts 5:3–4), and the author of Hebrews calls Him the "eternal Spirit" (Heb. 9:14).

As God, the Holy Spirit possesses the attributes of deity. He knows everything: "The Spirit searches all things, even the deep things of God. . . . No one knows the thoughts of God except the Spirit of God" (1 Cor. 2:10–11). He is everywhere present (Ps. 139:7–8). Although the Holy Spirit distributes gifts among believers, He himself remains "one and the same" (1 Cor. 12:11); He is constant in His nature. He is Truth (John 15:26; 16:13; 1 John 5:6). He is the Author of Life (John 3:3–6; Rom. 8:10) through rebirth and renewal (Titus 3:5), and He seals us for the day of redemption (Eph. 4:30).

The Father is our Sanctifier (1 Thess. 5:23), Jesus Christ is our Sanctifier (1 Cor. 1:2), and the Holy Spirit is our Sanctifier (Rom. 15:16). The Holy Spirit is our "Counselor" (John 14:16,26; 15:26), and He dwells within those who fear Him (John 14:17; 1 Cor. 3:16–17; 6:19; 2 Cor. 6:16). In Isaiah 6:8–10, Isaiah identifies the "Lord" as speaking, and Paul refers the same passage to the Holy Spirit (Acts 28:25–26). With regard to this, John Calvin observes: "Indeed, where the prophets usually say that the words they utter are those of the Lord of Hosts, Christ and the apostles refer them to the Holy Spirit [cf. 2 Peter 1:21]." Calvin then concludes, "It therefore follows that he who is pre-eminently the author of prophecies is truly Jehovah [*Yahweh*]."[22]

"The concept of the Triune God is found only in the Judeo-

---

[20]For further discussion of the personality of the Holy Spirit see chap. 11, pp. 377–78.

[21]*Allos* ("another of the same kind") is distinguished in the Greek from *heteros* ("another of a different kind"); cf. Gal. 1:6.

[22]John Calvin, *Calvin: Institutes of the Christian Religion*, vol. 1, John McNeill, ed. (Philadelphia: The Westminster Press, 1973), 140.

Christian tradition."[23] This concept has not come through the speculation of the wise men of this world, but through the step-by-step revelation given in God's Word. Everywhere in the writings of the apostles the Trinity is assumed and implicit (e.g., Eph. 1:1–14; 1 Pet. 1:2). Clearly, the Father, the Son, and the Holy Spirit eternally exist as three distinct Persons, and yet the Scriptures also reveal the unity[24] of the three members of the Godhead.[25]

The Persons of the Trinity have separate, though never conflicting, wills (Luke 22:42; 1 Cor. 12:11). The Father speaks to the Son using the second-person pronoun "you": " 'You are my Son, whom I love' " (Luke 3:22). Jesus offered himself to the Father through the Spirit (Heb. 9:14). Jesus states that He came " 'not to do *my will* but to do the *will of him who sent me*' " (John 6:38).

The virgin birth of Jesus Christ reveals the interrelationships of the three members of the Trinity. Luke's account says: "The angel answered, 'The *Holy Spirit* will come upon you, and the power of the *Most High* will overshadow you. So the holy one to be born will be called the *Son of God*' " (Luke 1:35).

The one God is revealed as a trinity at the baptism of Jesus Christ. The Son came up out of the water. The Holy Spirit descended as a dove. The Father spoke from heaven (Matt. 3:16–17). At creation, the Bible refers to the Spirit as being involved (Gen. 1:2); however, the author of Hebrews explicitly states that the Father is the Creator (Heb. 1:2), and John shows creation was accomplished "through"[26] the Son (John 1:3; Rev. 3:14). When the apostle Paul announces to the Athenians that God " 'made the world and everything in it' " (Acts 17:24), we can only reasonably conclude with Athanasius that God is "one God in Trinity and Trinity in Unity."

The resurrection of Jesus Christ from the dead is another outstanding example of the relationship of the triune God-

──────────

[23]James Oliver Buswell, *A Systematic Theology of the Christian Religion* (Grand Rapids: Zondervan Publishing House, 1962), 102.

[24]"Consubstantiality," i.e., the three Persons are of the same "substance" or "essence," and they are each therefore revealed as deity.

[25]Luther, following Augustine, inferred that the three "persons" cannot be theologically distinguished from each other by anything else than their respective relationships to one another as Father, Son, and Spirit. (Martin Luther, *The Smalcald Articles,* Part 1, Statement 1.)

[26]Gk. *dia,* used of secondary agency, as when God spoke "through" the prophets. Jesus was the one Mediator in creation.

head in redemption. Paul states that the Father of Jesus Christ raised our Lord from the dead (Rom. 1:4; cf. 2 Cor. 1:3). Jesus, however, emphatically claims that He would raise up His own body from the grave in resurrection glory (John 2:19–21). In another place, Paul declares that through the Holy Spirit God raised up Christ from the dead (Rom. 8:11; cf. Rom. 1:4). Luke places the theological capstone on Trinitarian orthodoxy by recording the apostle Paul's proclamation to the Athenians that the one God raised up Christ from the dead (Acts 17:30–31).

Jesus places the three members of the Godhead on the same divine plane in commanding His disciples to " 'go and make disciples of all nations, baptizing them in the name of the Father and of the Son and of the Holy Spirit' " (Matt. 28:19).

The apostle Paul, a monotheistic Jew trained under the great rabbinic scholar Gamaliel, "a Hebrew of Hebrews; in regard to the law, a Pharisee" (Phil. 3:5), was impressed with Trinitarian theology, as shown in his salutation to the church at Corinth: "May the grace of the Lord Jesus Christ, and the love of God, and the fellowship of the Holy Spirit be with you all" (2 Cor. 13:14).[27] The biblical data definitely brings us to the conclusion that within the nature of the one true God are three Persons, each of which is coeternal, coequal, and coexistent.

The orthodox theologian humbly subordinates his or her thinking on Trinitarian theology to the data revealed in the Word of God in much the same way the physicist does in formulating the paradoxical wave-particle theory:

Quantum physicists agree that subatomic entities are a mixture of wave properties (W), particle properties (P), and quantum properties (h). High-speed electrons, when shot through a nickel crystal or a metallic film (as fast cathode-rays or even B-rays), diffract like X-rays. In principle, the B-ray is just like the sunlight used in a double-slit or bi-prism experiment. Diffraction is a criterion of wave-like behaviour in substances; all classical wave theory rests on this. Besides this behaviour, however, electrons have long been thought of as electrically charged particles. A transverse magnetic field will deflect an electron beam and its diffraction pattern. Only particles

---

[27]Other texts that reveal the relations of the triune God include 1 Cor. 6:11; 12:4–5; 2 Cor. 1:21–22; Gal. 3:11–14; 1 Thess. 5:18–19; 1 Pet. 1:2. See J. N. D. Kelly, *Early Christian Creeds* (London: Longman's, 1950), 23, for a more complete list of texts relevant to the doctrine of the Trinity.

behave in this manner; all classical electromagnetic theory depends upon this. *To explain all the evidence electrons must be both particulate and undulatory* [emphasis added]. An electron is a PWh.[101]

———

[101]N. R. Hanson, *Patterns of Discovery: An Inquiry into the Conceptual Foundations of Science* (Cambridge: Cambridge University Press, 1958), 144.[28]

The analogy of the Trinity with PWh well illustrates the preliminary precautions of this chapter; that is, whereas the theologian must always strive for rationality in theological formulation, he must also choose revelation over the finite restrictions of human logic. Scripture alone is the touchstone for the theology of the Christian Church.

HISTORICAL FORMULATION OF THE DOCTRINE

Although Calvin was speaking of another doctrinal concern, his warning is equally applicable to Trinitarian formulation: "If anyone with carefree assurance breaks into this place, he will not succeed in satisfying his curiosity and he will enter a labyrinth from which he can find no exit."[29]

Indeed, the historical formulation of the doctrine of the Trinity is properly characterized as a terminological maze wherein many paths lead to heretical dead ends.[30]

The first four centuries of the Christian Church were dominated by a single motif, the Christological concept of *Logos.*[31] This concept is uniquely Johannine, found in both the prologue of the apostle's Gospel and his first epistle. The ecclesiastical controversy of the time focused on the question, "What does John mean by his use of *Logos?*" The controversy

———

[28]Quoted here by permission of Cambridge University Press. Quoted in John Warwick Montgomery, *The Suicide of Christian Theology* (Minneapolis: Bethany Fellowship Inc., 1970), 298.

[29]Quoted in Harold O. J. Brown, *Heresies: The Image of Christ in the Mirror of Heresy and Orthodoxy from the Apostles to the Present* (Garden City, N.Y.: Doubleday & Co., Inc., 1984), 154.

[30]Contemporary attempts to leap over the maze (e.g., the radical transcendentalism of Barth's neoorthodoxy) or the self-determined effort to tunnel under the maze in the "moment" (e.g., Bultmann's existentialism) are not options for the orthodox Christian. Rather, sound biblical theology is a "map," as J. I. Packer puts it, "to be used for the believer's route-finding in his personal pilgrimage of following his Lord." *Hot Tub Religion* (Wheaton, Ill.: Tyndale House Publishers, 1987), 14.

[31]See chap. 9, pp. 299–301.

reached its climax in the fourth century at the Council of Nicaea (A.D. 325).

In the second century the apostolic fathers displayed an undeveloped Christology. The relationship between the two natures in Christ, the human and the divine,[32] is not clearly articulated in their works. The doctrine of the Trinity is implied in their high Christology, but is not made explicit.

The great defenders of the faith in the Early Church (e.g., Irenaeus, Justin Martyr) referred to Christ as the eternal *Logos*. By their time, the concept of the *Logos* appears to have been understood as an eternal power or attribute of God that, in some inexplicable manner, dwells in Christ. An eternally personal *Logos*, in relationship to the Father, was yet without definition at this period.

IRENAEUS AGAINST THE GNOSTICS

We enter the ecclesiastical maze of the historical development of Trinitarian theology in the footsteps of Irenaeus. He was the bishop of Lyons, in Gaul, and a disciple of Polycarp, who himself was a disciple of the apostle John.[33] In Irenaeus, therefore, we have a direct tie to apostolic teaching.

Irenaeus entered the fray of theological debate in the last third of the second century. He is best known for his arguments against the Gnostics.[34] For centuries his great work *Against Heresies* has been a primary source of defense against the spiritually toxic influences of Gnosticism.

Irenaeus moved the Church in a positive direction by asserting the oneness of God, who is the Creator of heaven and earth. His commitment to monotheism protected the Church from taking a wrong turn in the maze and consequently arriving at a polytheistic dead end. Irenaeus also cautioned

---

[32]Later referred to as *hypostasis*, as defined at Chalcedon, 451.

[33]Jack N. Sparks, *Saint Irenaios' The Preaching of the Apostles* (Brookline, Mass.: Holy Cross Orthodox Press, 1987), 11.

[34]From Gk. *gnōsis*, "knowledge." The Gnostics used a dualistic approach to reality, wherein they believed that spirit is good and matter is evil. They taught that humanity has been enslaved because "the powers" have kept a tremendous cosmic secret from them. This secret knowledge was available through the Gnostic teachers. In the Gnostic viewpoint, the Creator God was defiled because He had corrupted himself by creating material things, such as the earth itself and human beings. Through *gnōsis* a human being could transcend the Creator God by moving through spiritual spheres called emanations, and thereby relate to the high God, who is far above the corruptions of matter.

against Gnostic speculation concerning the manner in which the Son was begotten by the Father.[35]

The Gnostics continually speculated about the nature of Christ and His relation to the Father. Some Gnostics ranked Christ with their pantheon of aeons (spiritual intermediaries between the Divine Mind and earth), and in this, they trivialized His deity. Others (Docetists)[36] denied the full humanity of Christ, insisting that He could not have been incarnate, but rather He only appeared to be a man and to suffer and die on the cross (cf. John 1:14; Heb. 2:14; 1 John 4:2–3).

Irenaeus passionately countered the teachings of the Gnostics with an impressively developed Christology, emphasizing both the full humanity and deity of Jesus Christ. In his defense of Christology, Irenaeus answered the Gnostics with two crucial sentences that would later emerge at Chalcedon:[37] *"Filius dei filius hominis factus,* 'The Son of God [has] become a son of man,' and *Jesus Christus vere homo, vere deus,* 'Jesus Christ, true man and true God.' "[38]

This necessitated a rudimentary concept of Trinitarianism. Otherwise, the alternative would have been ditheism (two gods) or polytheism (many gods). However, Irenaeus is said to have implied an "economic trinitarianism." In other words, "He only deals with the deity of the Son and the Spirit in the context of their revelation and saving activity, i.e., in the context of the 'economy' (plan) of salvation."[39]

TERTULLIAN AGAINST PRAXEAS

Tertullian, the "Pentecostal Bishop of Carthage" (160–ca. 230), made inestimable contributions to the development of Trinitarian orthodoxy. Adolph Harnack, for example, insists it was Tertullian who broke ground for the subsequent development of the orthodox Trinitarian doctrine.[40]

Tertullian's tract "Against Praxeas" is a brief fifty pages of

---

[35]Brown, *Heresies,* 84.

[36]From Gk. *dokeō,* "to seem or have the appearance of."

[37]In what is now northwest Turkey.

[38]Brown, *Heresies,* 84.

[39]Ibid.

[40]*Sitzungsberichte der koniglich preussischen akademie der Wissenschaften zu Berlin,* June, 1895, 595. In Benjamin Breckinridge Warfield, *Studies in Tertullian and Augustine* (Westport, Conn.: Greenwood Press, Publishers, reprint 1970), 5–6.

vigorous polemic against one Praxeas who is supposed to be the importer of the heresy of Monarchianism or Patripassianism into Rome.[41] Monarchianism teaches the existence of one solitary Monarch, God. By implication, the full deity of the Son and the Spirit are denied. However, to preserve the doctrines of salvation, the Monarchians concluded that the Father, as deity, was necessarily crucified for the sins of the world. This is the heresy called Patripassianism. Therefore, Tertullian said of Praxeas, "He had expelled prophecy and brought in heresy, had exiled the Paraclete and crucified the Father."[42]

As the heresy of Praxeas passed through the Church, Tertullian informs us that the people slept in their doctrinal simplicity.[43] Although he was determined to warn the Church of the dangers of Monarchianism, he entered the controversy at the eleventh hour, when the heresy was fast becoming dominant in the thinking of Christians.

It became Tertullian's task to dig an orthodox channel for the inherent implications of Trinitarian theology in the consciousness of the Church to flow into. Although Tertullian is accredited as the first to use the term "Trinity," it is not correct to say that he "invented" the doctrine, but rather that he mined the consciousness of the Church and exposed the inherent vein of Trinitarian thought already present. B. B. Warfield comments, "Tertullian had to . . . establish the true and complete deity of Jesus . . . without creating two Gods. . . And so far as Tertullian succeeded in it, he must be recognized as the father of the Church doctrine of the Trinity."[44]

Tertullian explicates the concept of an "economic Trinity" (similar to Irenaeus' concept, but with more explicit definition). He emphasizes God's unity, that is, there is only one divine substance, one divine power—without separation, division, dispersion, or diversity—and yet there is a distribution of functions, a distinction of persons.

---

[41]Praxeas was probably an earlier representative of the heresy that Tertullian, later, was so concerned about exposing and defeating.

[42]Benjamin B. Warfield, *Studies in Tertullian and Augustine* (Westport, Conn.: Greenwood Press, 1970), 7.

[43]Tertullian later joined the Montanists, some of whom were not as heretical as their opponents claimed. See, however, Brown, *Heresies,* 66–68.

[44]Warfield, *Studies in Tertullian,* 24.

CHAPTER

5

The Holy
Trinity

ORIGEN AND THE ALEXANDRIAN SCHOOL

In the second century B.C., Alexandria, Egypt, replaced Athens as the intellectual center of the Greco-Roman world. Christian academia later flourished at Alexandria. Some of the greatest scholars in the early history of the Church were of the Alexandrian School.

The Church progressed further through the theological maze of doctrinal formulation with the work of the celebrated Alexandrian theologian, Origen (ca. 185–254). The eternality of the personal *Logos* was explicated for the first time in Origen's thought.[45] With Origen, the orthodox doctrine of the Trinity began to emerge, though it was not crystallized in its formulation (progressing beyond Tertullian's "economic" concept) until the end of the fourth century at the Council of Nicaea (325).

In opposition to the Monarchians (also called Unitarians), Origen propounded his doctrine of the eternal generation of the Son (referred to as *filiation*). He attached this generating to the will of the Father, therefore implying the subordination of the Son to the Father. The doctrine of *filiation* was suggested to him, not only by the designations "Father" and "Son," but also by the fact that the Son is consistently called "the only begotten" (John 1:14,18; 3:16,18; 1 John 4:9).[46]

According to Origen, the Father eternally begets the Son and is therefore never without Him. The Son is God and yet He *subsists* (to use later theological language having to do with God's being) as a distinct Person from the Father. Origen's concept of eternal generation prepared the Church for its future understanding of the Trinity as *subsisting* in three Persons, rather than consisting of three parts.

Origen gave theological expression to the relation of the Son to the Father, later affirmed at the Council of Nicaea, as being *homoousios to patri*, "of one substance [or essence]

---

[45]Origen was a prolific writer who dealt with virtually every aspect of Christianity. Although he contributed significantly to the development of Trinitarian theology, he was given to eccentric extremes. Three centuries after his martyrdom, Origen was posthumously condemned as a heretic by the Fifth Ecumenical Council (553). See Brown, *Heresies*, 88.

[46]John refers to the *Logos* as the "One and Only" (John 1:14,18). The Greek word *monogenēs* was used of Isaac (Heb. 11:17), even though Abraham had other sons. Therefore, the scriptural meaning of the word is "only" in the sense of "unique," "special," "one-of-a-kind" and implies a special love (Gen. 22:2). It is used of Jesus to emphasize that He is by nature the Son of God in a unique, special sense that no one else is or can be.

with the Father."[47] The understanding of personhood, essential to the orthodox Trinitarian formula, was still lacking in precision. The Latin expression *persona,* meaning "role" or "actor," did not help in the theological struggle to understand the Father, Son, and Spirit as three Persons instead of merely different roles acted out by God. The theological concept of *hypostases,* that is, the distinction of Persons within the Godhead (in distinction to the unity of substance or nature within the Godhead, referred to as "consubstantiality" and relating to *homoousia*), allowed for the paradoxical formulation of Trinitarian theology.

Origen's doctrine of the eternal generation of the Son was a polemic against the notion that there was a time when the Son was not. His concept of "consubstantiality" stressed the equality of the Son with the Father. However, difficulties surfaced in Origen's thought because of the concept of subordination presented in the language of the New Testament and the idea of the submissive role of the Son to the Father while still maintaining the Son's full deity. Critical for our comprehension "is to understand the subordination in what we may call an economic sense," not in a sense that is related to the nature of God's being. Therefore, "The Son submits to the will of the Father and executes his plan *(oikonomia),* but he is not therefore inferior in nature to the Father."[48]

Origen was inconsistent in his formulation of the relationship between the Father and the Son, at times presenting the Son as a kind of second-order deity, distinguished from the Father as to person but inferior as to being. Origen essentially taught that the Son owed His existence to the will of the Father. This vacillation concerning the concept of subordinationism provoked a massive reaction from the Monarchians.

DYNAMIC MONARCHIANISM: THE FIRST WRONG TURN

The Monarchians sought to preserve the concept of the oneness of God, the monarchy of monotheism. They focused on the eternality of God, as the one Lord or Ruler, in relation to His creation.

Monarchianism appeared in two separate strains: Dynamic and Modalistic. Dynamic Monarchianism (also called Ebionite

[47]Origen probably proposed the word *homoousios,* for this term appears in the Latin text of Origen's *Commentary on Hebrews.* See J. N. D. Kelly, *Early Christian Creeds* 2d. ed. (London: Longmans, 1960), 215, 245.
[48] Brown, *Heresies,* 91.

Monarchianism, Unitarian Monarchianism, or Adoptionist Monarchianism) preceded Modalistic Monarchianism.

Dynamic Monarchianism denied any notion of an eternally personal Trinity. The Dynamic Monarchian School was represented by the Alogi,[49] men who rejected *Logos* Christology. The Alogi based their Christology on the Synoptic Gospels only, refusing to accept John's Christology because of their suspicions of Hellenistic intrusions in the prologue of his Gospel.

Dynamic Monarchians contended that Christ was not God from all eternity, but rather, He became God at a point in time. Although differences of opinion existed as to the particular time appointed for the deification of the Son, the widespread opinion was that the Son's exaltation took place at His baptism when He was anointed by the Spirit. Christ, then, through His obedience, became the divine Son of God. **Christ was considered the adopted Son of God, rather than the eternal Son of God.**

Dynamic Monarchianism also taught that Jesus was exalted progressively, or dynamically, to the status of Godhood. The relation of the Father to the Son was perceived not in terms of their nature and being but in moral terms. That is, the Son was not regarded as possessing equality of nature with the Father (*homoousios: homo* means "same" and *ousios* means "essence"). Dynamic Monarchians proposed that there is merely a moral relation between Jesus and the purposes of God.[50]

An early advocate of Dynamic Monarchianism was the third century bishop of Antioch, Samosata. A great debate developed between the Eastern Church and the Antiochan School on one side, and the Western Church and the Alexandrian School on the other. The focus of the debate was the relation between the *Logos* and the man Jesus.

Harold O. J. Brown observes that Dynamic Monarchianism's "adoptionism preserved the unity of the godhead by

---

[49]I.e., *a*—"without," *logi*—"word."

[50]Modern forms of Dynamic Monarchianism have been represented in the work of the nineteenth-century theologian Friedrich Schleiermacher, who thought of Jesus as the greatest example of God-consciousness. Albrecht Ritschl, in the same century, focused on the virtues of Jesus, defining His nature by the perfect sense of duty revealed in Jesus' life. In the twentieth century, the Anglican John A. T. Robinson asserted that Jesus was "the man for others," stressing that Christ was the most outstanding example of godly characteristics in history.

sacrificing the deity of Christ."[51] Dynamic Monarchianism is, therefore, a wrong turn in the doctrinal maze, ending in a heretical dead end.

Lucian followed Samosata as the champion of Dynamic Monarchianism. Lucian's prize pupil was Arius. He was behind the Arian controversy that resulted in the convening of bishops at Nicaea and the drafting of the great Trinitarian Creed (325). But before discussing Arianism, let us examine the second strain of Monarchianism: Modalism.

MODALISTIC MONARCHIANISM: THE SECOND WRONG TURN

The principal influences behind Modalistic Monarchianism were Gnosticism and Neoplatonism.[52] Modalistic Monarchians conceived of the universe as one organized whole, manifest in a hierarchy of modes. The modes (likened to concentric circles) were conceived of as various levels of manifestations of reality emanating from God, "The One" who exists in "pure being," as the Supreme Being at the top of the hierarchical scale. (This shows Neoplatonic influence.)

Modalistic Monarchians taught that reality decreases the farther an emanation is from The One. Therefore, the lowest order of being would be the physical matter of the universe. Although matter was still considered to be a part of The One from which it emanates, Modalists considered it to exist in a lower form. (This shows the Gnostic influence.) Conversely, reality was thought to increase as one progresses toward The One (also referred to as Divine Mind).

It is easy to see the pantheistic implications of this view of reality, since everything in existence is supposed to originate from the emanations (modes or levels of reality) from God's own essence. Some Modalists used an analogy of the sun and its rays. Sun rays are of the same essence as the sun, but they are not the sun. The Modalists supposed that the farther the rays are from the sun, the less they are pure sunlight, and that although the rays share the same essence as the sun, they are inferior to the sun, being mere projections of it.

The Christological application of this worldview identified Jesus as a first-order emanation from the Father, reducing Him

---

[51]Brown, *Heresies,* 99.

[52]Plotinus and others modified Plato's teachings and conceived of the world as an emanation from The One, with whom the soul could be reunited in some sort of trance or ecstasy.

to a level below the Father with respect to the nature of His being, or essence. Although Jesus was considered the highest order of being apart from The One, He was still inferior to The One and dependent for His existence on the Father, even though He was superior to angels and humankind.

Sabellius (third century) was the champion of Modalistic Monarchianism, responsible for its most formidable impression on the Church. He originated the above analogy of the sun and its rays, and denied that Jesus is deity in the eternal sense that the Father is. This idea led to the theological term *homoiousios.* The prefix, *homoi,* means "like" or "similar" and the root, *ousios,* means "essence." Therefore, Sabellius contended that the Son's nature was only like the Father's; it was not the same as the Father's.

Sabellius was condemned as a heretic in 268 at the Council of Antioch. The difference between *homo* ("same") and *homoi* ("similar") may appear trivial, but the *iota* ("i") is the difference between the pantheistic implications of Sabellianism (i.e., the confusing of God with His creation) and the full deity of Jesus Christ, apart from which, doctrines of salvation are gravely affected. Through this abandonment of the full deity and personhood of Christ and the Holy Spirit, Modalistic Monarchianism took a wrong turn in the doctrinal maze as well.

ARIANISM: THE THIRD WRONG TURN

Although a student of Lucian and, consequently, in the line of the Dynamic Monarchianism heralded by Paul of Samosata, Arius went beyond them in theological complexity. He was raised in Alexandria, where he was ordained a presbyter shortly after A.D. 311, even though he was a disciple of the Antiochan tradition. Around 318, he aroused the attention of Alexander, the new archbishop of Alexandria. Alexander excommunicated him in 321 for his heretical views concerning the person, nature, and work of Jesus Christ.

Arius was determined to be restored to the church, not in repentance, but to the end that his views of Christ might become the theology of the church. In his efforts to be restored to the church, he enlisted the aid of some of his more influential friends, including Eusebius of Nicomedia and the renowned church historian Eusebius of Caesarea, as well as several Asian bishops. He continued to teach without Alexander's approval, and his speculations stirred up considerable debate and confusion within the church.

Soon after Arius' excommunication, Constantine became sole emperor of the Roman Empire. Constantine discovered, to his great dismay, that the church was in such chaos over the Arian controversy that it was threatening the political and religious stability of the entire empire. He hastened to summon the First Ecumenical Council, the Nicaean Council, in 325.

CHAPTER 5

The Holy Trinity

Arius stressed that God the Father alone is the sole Monarch and therefore eternal. God is "unbegotten" and everything else, including Christ, is "begotten." Arius wrongly asserted that the idea of being "begotten" conveys the concept of having been created.[53] At the same time, he took pains to separate himself from the pantheistic implications of the Sabellian heresy by insisting that there was no internal necessity for God to create. He also said God created an independent substance (Lat. *substantia*), which He used to create all other things. This independent substance, first created by God above all other things, was the Son.

Arius proposed that the Son's uniqueness is limited to His having been the first and greatest creation of God. The incarnation of the Son is conceived, in Arian thought, as the union of the created substance (the *Logos*) with a human body. He taught that the *Logos* replaced the soul within the human body of Jesus of Nazareth.[54]

Harnack is correct in his observation that Arius "is a strict monotheist only with respect to cosmology; as a theologian, he is a polytheist."[55] Arius, in other words, acknowledged only one solitary Person as God; however, in practice he extended worship reserved for God alone to Christ, whom he otherwise said had a beginning.

Arius' Christology reduced Christ to a creature and, consequently, denied Christ's saving work. Arianism thereby took a wrong turn in the maze, down a heretical corridor from which there is no exit.

---

[53]See footnote 46.

[54]Apollinaris, the younger, of Laodicea (d. ca. 390) extended the idea that the *Logos* replaced the human soul in Jesus Christ. The problem with this view is that in replacing a human soul with a spiritual entity, the *Logos*, Christ is not true humanity. Apollinaris understood "flesh" (John 1:14) to mean "physical body" instead of "human nature," which is the common meaning in the New Testament.

[55]Quoted in Brown, *Heresies,* 115.

CHAPTER

5

The Holy
Trinity

TRINITARIAN ORTHODOXY: EXITING THE MAZE

Three hundred bishops from both the Western (Alexandrian) and the Eastern (Antiochan) Church convened in Nicaea[56] for the great ecumenical council that would attempt to bring theological precision to the doctrine of the Trinity. The council's concern was threefold: (1) to clarify terms used to articulate the Trinitarian doctrine; (2) to expose and condemn theological errors that were present in various parts of the Church; and (3) to draft a document that would adequately address the convictions identified in Holy Scripture and shared by the consensus of the Church.

Bishop Alexander was poised for battle with Arius. The Arians were confident that they would be victorious. Eusebius of Nicomedia prepared a document declaring the faith of the Arians, and it was proposed confidently at the very outset of the council. Because it boldly denied the deity of Christ, it provoked the indignation of the majority of those in attendance. They soundly rejected the document. Then Eusebius of Caesarea (who was not an Arian even though he was a representative of the Eastern Church) drafted a creed during the debate which later became the blueprint for the Nicene Creed.

Bishop Alexander (and the Alexandrians in general) was principally concerned with how Arius' views would affect one's personal salvation if Christ were not fully God in the same sense that the Father is. To bring man into reconciliation with God, contended Alexander, Christ must be God.

Bishop Alexander acknowledged the language of subordination in the New Testament, particularly the references to Jesus as being "begotten" of the Father. He indicated that the term "begotten" must be understood from a Jewish perspective, since Hebrews were the ones using the term in the Bible. The Hebrew usage of the term is for the purpose of setting forth the preeminence of Christ. (Paul speaks in these terms, using the word "firstborn," not in reference to Christ's origin but to the salvatory effects of His redemptive work [see Col. 1:15,18].)[57]

Alexander answered Arius by contending that the Son's begottenness is preceded in Scripture by the predicate *para* in John 1:14 (the Word is the only begotten *from* the Father), indicating a sharing of the same eternal nature as God (in

---

[56]Modern Nice in southeast France.
[57]See footnote 46.

line with Origen's "eternal generation" of the Son).[58] In the ears of the intractable Arius, this amounted to an admission of Christ's creation. He was desperately trying to rid theology of Modalistic implications which, to use the later words assigned to his archenemy, Athanasius, were guilty of "confusing the persons."[59] Therefore, it was crucial to distinguish Christ from the Father.

Bishop Alexander pressed on, claiming that Christ is "generated" by the Father, but not in the sense of emanation or creation. Theologically, the great challenge before the Western Church was the explanation of the concept of *homoousia* without falling into the error of Modalistic heresy.

Athanasius is generally credited with being the great defender of the faith at the Council of Nicaea. However, the weight of Athanasius' work actually followed that great ecumenical council.

The inflexible Athanasius, though deposed by the emperor on three occasions during his own ecclesiastical career, fearlessly contended for the concept of Christ's being of the same essence *(homoousios)* as the Father, not merely like the Father in essence *(homoiousios)*. During his career as bishop and defender of what emerged as orthodoxy, it was "Athanasius against the world."

The Alexandrian School finally triumphed over the Arians, and Arius was once again condemned and excommunicated. In the creedal formulation of the Trinity doctrine at Nicaea, Jesus Christ is "the only-begotten Son of God, begotten from the Father before all ages, light from light, true God from true God, begotten not made, of one substance with the Father."[60]

The Church would later use the term "procession" in place of "generation" or "begotten," for the purpose of expressing the Son's economic subordination to the Father: The Son *proceeds* from the Father. A kind of primacy is still assigned to the Father in relation to the Son, but that primacy is not a primacy of time; the Son has always existed as the Word.

---

[58]See Joseph Henry Thayer, *Greek-English Lexicon of the New Testament* (Grand Rapids: Zondervan Publishing House, reprint, 1976), 476–77, for an explanation of John's use of the predicate *para* with the genitive, indicative here of Christ's mutual possession of God's eternal nature.

[59]J. N. D. Kelly, *The Athanasian Creed* (London: Adam and Charles Black, 1964), 18.

[60]J. N. D. Kelly, *Early Christian Creeds* 2d ed. (London: Longmans, 1960), 315.

However, He has "generated" or "proceeded" from the Father, not the Father from the Son.

This procession of the Son (by the eighth century, referred to as "filiation") is understood theologically to be a necessary act of the Father's will, thereby making it impossible to conceive of the Son as not generating from the Father. Hence, the procession of the Son is an eternal present, an always continuing, never ending act. The Son is therefore immutable (not subject to change; Heb. 13:8) even as the Father is immutable (Mal. 3:6). The filiation of the Son is definitely not a generation of His divine essence, for the Father and the Son are both Deity and therefore of the "same" indivisible nature.[61] The Father and the Son (with the Spirit) exist together in personal subsistence (i.e., the Son and the Spirit are personally distinct from the Father in their eternal existence).

Although this exposition of the acute linguistic complexities of the Nicene Creed may be frustrating at a distance of sixteen centuries, it is important for us to consider again the crucial need to maintain the paradoxical formula of the Athanasian Creed, "One God in Trinity and Trinity in Unity." Theological precision is critical, for the terms *ousia, hupostasis, substantia,* and *subsistence* provide us with a conceptual understanding of what is meant by Trinitarian orthodoxy, as in the Athanasian Creed: "The Father is God, the Son is God, and the Holy Spirit is God. And yet they are not three Gods, but one God."

During the years 361–81, Trinitarian orthodoxy underwent further refinement, particularly concerning the third member of the Trinity, the Holy Spirit. In 381, at Constantinople, the bishops were summoned by Emperor Theodosius, and the statements of Nicene orthodoxy were reaffirmed. Also, there was explicit citation concerning the Holy Spirit. Hence, the Nico-Constantinopolitan Creed speaks of the Holy Spirit in terms of deity as "the Lord and life-giver, who proceeds[62] from the Father, who with the Father and the Son is coworshiped and coglorified, who spoke through the prophets."[63]

---

[61]That is, *homousios;* essence or substance; Lat. *substantia;* Gk. *hupostasis.* In contradistinction to *ousia,* however, Greek theological language uses *hupostasis* to mean "individual personal reality."

[62]The term *filioque* was used of the Spirit as analogous to the "filiation" of the Son.

[63]The Holy Spirit is referred to as the Spirit of the Father (Matt. 10:20) and also as the Spirit of the Son (Gal. 4:6). The sending of the Spirit (i.e., the Spirit's *filioque*) is ascribed to both the Father and the Son (John 14:16;

The title "Lord" (Gk. *kurios*), used in Scripture within certain outstanding contexts to ascribe deity, is assigned here (in the Niceno-Constantinopolitan Creed) to the Holy Spirit. Therefore, He who proceeds from the Father and the Son (John 15:26) personally subsists from eternity within the Godhead, without division or change as to His nature (i.e., He is essentially *homoousios* with the Father and the Son).

CHAPTER 5

The Holy Trinity

The personal properties (i.e., the inner workings of each Person within the Godhead) assigned each of the three members of the Trinity are then understood as follows: to the Father, ingenerateness; to the Son, begottenness; and to the Holy Spirit, procession. Insistence on these personal properties is not an attempt to explain the Trinity, but to distinguish Trinitarian orthodoxy from heretical Modalistic formulas.

The distinctions among the three members of the Godhead do not refer to their essence or substance, but to their relationships. In other words, the order of existence in the Trinity, with respect to God's essential being, is mirrored in the economic Trinity. "There are thus three, not in status, but in degree; not in substance, but in form; not in power, but in its manifestation."[64]

The enduring process of inquiry into the nature of the living God here gives way to worship. With the apostles, the church fathers, the martyrs, and the greatest of the theologians throughout the ages of church history, we must acknowledge that "all good theology ends with doxology" (cf. Rom. 11:33–36). Consider this classic hymn of Reginald Heber:

> Holy, holy, holy, Lord God Almighty!
> All Thy works shall praise Thy name
> In earth, and sky, and sea;

15:26; 16:7,13–14). The *filioque* was added to the Niceno-Constantinopolitan Creed by the Synod of Toledo in 589. However, the Eastern Church protested the *filioque* of the Spirit from both the Father and the Son (contending rather that the Spirit proceeded from the Father only) because the Western doctrine appeared to subordinate the Third Person of the Trinity to the concrete, historically revealed, incarnate Jesus. Further, the Western doctrine appeared to elevate the historical, objective Christ Jesus to a status comparable to the Father, making the Spirit inferior to both. By 1017, the *filioque* was officially established in the West. Photius of Constantinople had rejected the doctrine in the ninth century and the concerns of the East finally resulted in the rupture between the East and the West in 1054.

[64]Calvin, *Institutes,* vol. 1, 157.

Holy, holy, holy, merciful and mighty,
God in three Persons, blessed Trinity!

TRINITY AND THE DOCTRINE OF SALVATION

Non-Trinitarian views, such as Modalism and Arianism, reduce the doctrine of salvation to a divine charade. All of the basic Christian convictions centering on the work of the Cross presuppose the personal distinction of the three members of the Trinity. In reflection, one may ask whether it is necessary to believe in the doctrine of the Trinity to be saved. In response, historically and theologically, the Church has not usually required an explicit declaration of faith in the doctrine of the Trinity for salvation. Rather, the Church has expected an implicit faith in the triune God as essential to one's relating to the distinctive roles of each of the divine Persons in the Godhead in the redemptive work in behalf of humanity.

The doctrine of salvation (including reconciliation, propitiation, ransom, justification, and expiation) is contingent upon the cooperation of the distinctive members of the triune God (e.g., Eph. 1:3–14). Therefore, a conscious renouncing of the Trinity doctrine seriously jeopardizes the hope of one's personal salvation. Scripture indicts all humankind under the universal condemnation of sin (Rom. 3:23), and therefore, everyone is in "need of salvation; the doctrine of salvation requires an adequate Savior, i.e., an adequate Christology. A sound Christology requires a satisfactory concept of God, i.e., a sound special theology—which brings us back to the doctrine of the Trinity."[65]

The Modalistic view of the nature of God abolishes Christ's mediatorial work between God and people altogether. Reconciliation (2 Cor. 5:18–21) implies the setting aside of enmity or opposition. Whose enmity is set aside? The Scriptures reveal that God is at enmity with sinners (Rom. 5:9), and in their sin, people also are at enmity with God (Rom. 3:10–18; 5:10).

The triune God is explicitly revealed in the Bible in the redemption and reconciliation of sinners to God. God "sends" the Son into the world (John 3:16–17). In the shadow of Calvary, Jesus obediently submits to the will of the Father, " 'My Father, if it is possible, may this cup be taken from me. Yet not as *I will,* but as *you will*' " (Matt. 26:39). The subject-object relationship between the Father and the Son is clearly

---

[65]Brown, *Heresies,* 154.

evident here. The Son bears the shame of the cursed tree,[66] making peace (reconciliation) between God and humankind (Rom. 5:1; Eph. 2:13–16). As life quickly drains from His body, Jesus looks to the heavens from the cross and utters His final words, " 'Father, into your hands I commit my spirit' " (Luke 23:46). Unless two distinct persons are revealed here in the redemptive act of the Cross, then this event becomes merely the divine charade of one neurotic Christ.

In Modalism, the concept of Christ's death as an infinite satisfaction is lost. The blood of Christ is the sacrifice for our sins (1 John 2:2). The doctrine of propitiation connotes appeasement, the averting of wrath by means of an acceptable sacrifice.[67] Christ is God's sacrificial Lamb (John 1:29). Because of Christ, God's mercy is extended to us in place of the wrath we deserve as sinners. However, to suggest, as Modalism does, that God is one person and makes himself a sin offering to himself, being at the same time wrathful and merciful, makes Him seem capricious. In other words, the Cross would be a senseless act as far as the concept of a sin offering is concerned: Whose wrath would Christ be averting?

The apostle John identifies Jesus as our Paraclete (Helper or Counselor), "One who speaks to the Father in our defense" (1 John 2:1). This requires a Judge who is distinct from Jesus himself before He can fulfill such a role. Because Christ is our Paraclete, "He is the atoning sacrifice for our sins, and not only for ours but also for the sins of the whole world" (1 John 2:2). We therefore have full assurance of our salvation because Christ, our Helper, is also our Sin Offering.

Jesus came into the world not " 'to be served, but to serve, and give his life as a ransom for many' " (Mark 10:45). The concept of a ransom and its cognates in Scripture is used with reference to a payment that ensures the liberation of prisoners. To whom did Christ pay the ransom? If the orthodox doctrine of the Trinity is denied, disallowing a distinction of Persons in the Godhead (as is the case with Modalism), then Christ would have had to have paid the ransom either to people or to Satan. Since humanity is dead in transgressions and sins (Eph. 2:1), no human being is in a position to hold Christ for ransom. This would leave Satan as the cosmic extortioner. However, we owe Satan nothing, and the notion of Satan holding humanity for ransom is blasphemous because

---

[66]The Hebrew word for tree, *'ets,* also means wood, timber, or anything made of wood, and therefore includes the cross.

[67]See chap. 10, pp. 338, 344–46.

of its dualistic implications (i.e., the idea that Satan possesses power sufficient to extort from Christ His very life; see John 10:15–18).

The ransom was instead paid to the triune God in satisfaction of the full claims of divine justice against the fallen sinner. Because of Modalism's rejection of Trinitarianism this heresy correspondingly perverts the concept of justification. Although deserving of God's *justice,* we are justified by grace through faith in Jesus Christ alone (1 Cor. 6:11). Having been justified (i.e., having been pronounced not guilty before God) through the death and resurrection of Jesus, we are then declared righteous before God (Rom. 4:5,25). Christ declares the Spirit is "another" Person distinct from himself and yet of the "same kind" (*allon,* John 14:16). The Holy Spirit applies the work of the Son in rebirth (Titus 3:5), sanctifies the believer (1 Cor. 6:11), and gives us access (Eph. 2:18) through our Great High Priest, Jesus Christ (Heb. 4:14–16), to be received into the Father's presence (2 Cor. 5:17–21).

A God who changes through successive modes is contrary to the revelation of God's unchanging nature (Mal. 3:6). Such Modalism is deficient with regard to salvation, denying Jesus Christ's high priestly position. Scripture declares that Christ is our divine Intercessor at the right hand of God, our Father (Heb. 7:23 through 8:2).

Clearly, the essential doctrine of the substitutionary Atonement, in which Christ bears our sins in His death before the Father, is dependent on the Trinitarian concept. Modalism subverts the biblical concept of Christ's penal, substitutionary death in satisfaction of God's justice, ultimately making the Cross of no effect.

The defective Christology of the Arian heresy places Arianism also under the summary condemnation of Holy Scripture. The relationship between the Father, Son, and Holy Spirit is founded in their shared nature as deity, ultimately explained in terms of the Trinity. "No one who denies the Son," says John, "has the Father; whoever acknowledges the Son has the Father also" (1 John 2:23). Proper acknowledgment of the Son requires belief in His deity, as well as in His humanity. Christ, as God, is able to satisfy the Father's justice; as Man, He is able to fulfill humanity's moral responsibility toward God. In the work of the Cross, God's justice and grace are revealed to us.[68] The eternal perfection of God and the sinful

---

[68]This argument is derived from the classic argument of Anselm, the archbishop of Canterbury, in the eleventh century, as recorded in his brilliant treatise *Cur Deus Homo?* ("Why God [as] Man?"), 2.8–10.

imperfections of humanity are reconciled through the God-Man, Jesus Christ (Gal. 3:11–13). The Arian heresy, in its denial of the full deity of Christ, is without God the Father (1 John 2:23) and therefore without any hope of eternal life.

THE THEOPHILOSOPHICAL NECESSITY OF THE TRINITY

The eternal properties and absolute perfection of the triune God are critical to the Christian concept of God's sovereignty and creation. God, as Trinity, is complete in himself (i.e., sovereign), and, consequently, creation is a free act of God, not a necessary action of His being. For this reason, "before 'in the beginning' something other than a static situation existed."[69]

The Christian faith offers a clear, understandable revelation of God from outside the sphere of time, for God, as Trinity, has enjoyed eternal fellowship and communication among His three distinct Persons. The concept of a personal, communicative God from all eternity is rooted in Trinitarian theology. God did not exist in static silence only to one day choose to break the tranquility of that silence by speaking. Rather, the eternal communion within the Trinity is essential to the concept of revelation. (The alternative of a solitary divine Being who mutters to himself in His loneliness is a bit disquieting.) The triune God has revealed himself, personally and propositionally, to humankind in history.

The personality of God, as Trinity, is also the source and meaning of human personality. "Without such a source," observes Francis Schaeffer, "men are left with personality coming from the impersonal (plus time, plus chance)."[70]

Throughout eternity, the Father loved the Son, the Son loved the Father, and the Father and the Son loved the Spirit. "God is love" (1 John 4:16). Therefore, love is an eternal attribute. By definition, love is shared necessarily with another, and God's love is a self-giving love. Hence, the eternal love within the Trinity gives ultimate meaning to human love (1 John 4:17).

EXCURSUS: ONENESS PENTECOSTALISM

At the Arroyo Seco World Wide Camp Meeting, near Los Angeles, in 1913, a controversy arose. During a baptismal

---

[69]Francis Schaeffer, *The Complete Works of Francis Schaeffer*, vol. 2, *Genesis in Space and Time* (Wheaton, Ill.: Crossway Books, 1982), 8.

[70]Francis Schaeffer, *The Triology* (Wheaton, Ill.: Crossway Books, 1990), 283.

service, Canadian evangelist R. E. McAlister contended that the apostles did not invoke the triune Name—Father, Son, and Holy Spirit—in baptism, but rather they baptized in the name of Jesus *only.*

During the night, John G. Schaeppe, an immigrant from Danzig, Germany, had a vision of Jesus and woke up the camp shouting that the name of Jesus needed to be glorified. Thereafter, Frank J. Ewart began teaching that those who had been baptized using the Trinitarian formula needed to be rebaptized in the name of Jesus "only."[71] Others soon began spreading this "new issue."[72] Along with this came an acceptance of one Person in the Godhead, acting in different modes or offices. The Arroyo Seco revival had helped fire this new issue.

In October 1916, the General Council of the Assemblies of God convened in St. Louis for the purpose of digging a doctrinal fire line around Trinitarian orthodoxy. The Oneness constituency was confronted by a majority who demanded of them to accept the Trinitarian baptismal formula and the orthodox doctrine of Christ or leave the Fellowship. About one-fourth of the ministers did withdraw. But the Assemblies of God established itself in the doctrinal tradition of "the faith preached by the Apostles, attested by the Martyrs, embodied in the Creeds, expounded by the Fathers,"[73] by contending for Trinitarian orthodoxy.

Typically, Oneness Pentecostalism states, "We do not believe in three separate personalities in the Godhead, but we believe in three offices which are filled by one person."[74]

The Oneness (Modalistic) doctrine therefore conceives of God as one transcendent Monarch whose numerical unity is disrupted by three ongoing manifestations to humankind as Father, Son, and Holy Spirit. The three faces of the one Monarch are actually divine imitations of Jesus, the personal expression of God through His incarnation. The idea of personhood is understood by Oneness Pentecostals to require

---

[71]Many, including Myrle (Fisher) Horton, mother of the general editor, Dr. Stanley M. Horton, were told they would lose their salvation if they were not rebaptized.

[72]These included Andrew Urshan, T. Haywood, Glenn A. Cook, C. O. Opperman, George B. Studd, and Harvey Shearer.

[73]C. S. Lewis, *God in the Dock: Essays on Theology and Ethics* (Grand Rapids: Wm. B. Eerdmans, 1970), 90.

[74]Nathaniel A. Urshan, general superintendent of the United Pentecostal Church, International, quoted in *The "Jesus Only" or "Oneness" Pentecostal Movement* (San Juan Capistrano, Calif.: The Christian Research Institute, 1970).

corporeality, and for this reason, Trinitarians are accused of embracing tritheism.

Because Jesus is "the fulness of the Godhead bodily" (Col. 2:9, KJV), the Oneness Pentecostals contend that He is essentially the fullness of the undifferentiated Deity. In other words, they believe the threefold reality of God to be "three manifestations" of the one Spirit dwelling within the person of Jesus. They believe Jesus is the unipersonality of God whose "essence is revealed as Father *in* the Son and as Spirit *through* the Son."[75] They explain further that Jesus' divine pantomime is "Christocentric in that as a human being Jesus *is* the Son, and *as* Spirit (i.e., in his deity) he reveals—indeed *is* the Father—and sends—indeed *is* the Holy Spirit as the Spirit of Christ who indwells the believer."[76]

We have argued that the third-century Sabellianism is heretical. In its similar denial of the eternal distinctions of the three Persons in the Godhead, Oneness Pentecostalism unwarily becomes entrapped in the same heretical corner of the theological maze as classical Modalism.[77] It differs, as stated before, in that Oneness Pentecostals conceive of the "trimanifestation" of God as simultaneous instead of successive, as is the case with classical Modalism. They contend that, based on Colossians 2:9, the concept of God's personhood is reserved for the immanent and incarnate presence of Jesus only. Hence, Oneness Pentecostals generally argue that the Godhead is in Jesus, yet Jesus is not in the Godhead.[78]

Colossians 2:9 affirms, however, (as formulated at Chalcedon by the Church, 451) that Jesus is the "fullness of the revelation of God's nature" (*theotētos,* deity) through His incarnation. All of God's essence is embodied in Christ (He is full deity), though the three Persons are not simultaneously incarnate in Jesus.

Although Oneness Pentecostals confess the deity of Jesus Christ, they actually mean by this that as the Father, He is deity, and as the Son, He is humanity. In contending that the

---

[75]David A. Reed, "Oneness Pentecostalism" in *The Dictionary of Pentecostal and Charismatic Movements,* ed. Stanley M Burgess, Gary B. McGee, and Patrick Alexander (Grand Rapids: Zondervan Publishing House, 1988), 649.

[76]Ibid.

[77]See Calvin's condemnation of the unitarianism of his day in his *Institutes of the Christian Religion,* 127.

[78]Gordon Magee, *Is Jesus in the Godhead or Is the Godhead in Jesus?* (Pasadena, Tex.: Gordon Magee, n.d.).

term "Son" is to be understood as the human nature of Jesus and that the term "Father" is the designation of Christ's divine nature, they imitate their anti-Trinitarian predecessors in their grave compromising of the doctrines of salvation.

Jesus did state, " 'I and the Father are one' " (John 10:30). But this does not mean that Jesus and His Father are one Person, as contended by Oneness Pentecostals, for the Greek neuter *hen* ("one") is used by the apostle John instead of the masculine *heis*; therefore, essential unity is meant, not absolute identity.[79]

As has been stated, the subject-object distinction between the Father and the Son is revealed in bold scriptural relief as Jesus prays to the Father in His agony (Luke 22:42). Jesus also reveals and defends His identity by appealing to the Father's testimony (John 5:31–32). Jesus explicitly states, " 'There is another [Gk. *allos*] who testifies in my favor' " (v. 32). Here, the term *allos* again connotes a different person from the one who is speaking.[80] Also in John 8:16–18, Jesus says, " 'If I do judge, my decisions are right, because I am not alone. I stand with the Father, who sent me. In your own Law it is written that the testimony of two men is valid. I am one who testifies for myself; my other witness is the Father, who sent me.' " Jesus here quotes from the Old Testament law (Deut. 17:6; 19:15) for the purpose of again revealing His messianic identity (as subject) by appeal to His Father's witness (as object) to himself. To insist, as Oneness Pentecostals do, that the Father and the Son are numerically one would serve to discredit Jesus' witness of himself as Messiah.

Furthermore, Oneness Pentecostals teach that unless one is baptized "in the name of Jesus" only, then an individual is not truly saved.[81] Therefore, they imply that Trinitarians are not true Christians. In this they are actually guilty of adding works to God's revealed means of salvation by grace through faith alone (Eph. 2:8–9). Some sixty different references in the New Testament speak of salvation by grace through faith

---

[79] See R. C. H. Lenski, *The Interpretation of St. John's Gospel* (Minneapolis: Augsburg Publishing House, 1961), 759–61. Note that in John 17:21 Jesus prays concerning His disciples, " 'that all of them may be one' " [Gk. *hen*], which clearly does not mean His disciples were to lose their own personality and individuality.

[80] A different person of the same kind. William F. Arndt and F. Wilbur Gingrich, *A Greek English Lexicon of the New Testament and Other Early Christian Literature* (Chicago: University of Chicago Press, 1957), 39.

[81] Hank Hanegraaff, "Is The United Pentecostal Church a Christian Church?" (Perspective paper, Irvine, Calif.: The Christian Research Institute., n.d.)

alone apart from water baptism. If baptism is a necessary means to our salvation, then why isn't this point strongly emphasized in the New Testament? Instead, we find Paul saying, "Christ did not send me to baptize, but to preach the gospel—not with words of human wisdom, lest the cross of Christ be emptied of its power" (1 Cor. 1:17).

Additionally, it must be pointed out that the Book of Acts does not intend to prescribe a baptismal formula for the Church to use because the phrase "in the name of Jesus" does not occur exactly the same way twice in Acts.

In seeking to reconcile Jesus' command to baptize in "the name of the Father and of the Son and of the Holy Spirit" (Matt. 28:19) with Peter's statement " 'be baptized . . . in the name of Jesus Christ' " (Acts 2:38), we will consider three possible explanations.

1. Peter was disobedient to the clear commandment of his Lord. This, of course, is not an explanation at all and must be dismissed as ridiculous.

2. Jesus was speaking in cryptic terms, requiring some kind of mystical insight before one can clearly understand what He meant. In other words, He was really telling us to baptize only in the name of Jesus, though some fail to perceive this veiled intent of our Lord. However, there is simply no justification for drawing this conclusion. It is contrary to this particular genre of biblical literature (i.e., didactic–historical) and also, by implication at least, to the sinlessness of our Lord Jesus Christ.[82]

3. A better explanation is founded upon the apostolic authority in the Book of Acts, where the ministerial credentials of the apostles are concerned. When the phrase "in the name of Jesus Christ" is invoked by the apostles in Acts, it means "upon the authority of Jesus Christ" (cf. Matt. 28:18). For example, in Acts 3:6 the apostles heal by the authority of the name of Jesus Christ. In Acts 4, the apostles are summoned before the Sanhedrin to be interrogated concerning the mighty works they were doing: " 'By what power or what name did you do this?' " (v. 7). The apostle Peter, filled anew with the Holy Spirit, stepped forward and boldly announced: " 'By the

---

[82]Some say that the singular word "name" in Matt. 28:19 means that Jesus is the name of the Father, Son, and Holy Spirit. However, the word is distributive, just as it is in the Hebrew of Ruth 1:2, where the singular "name" (See KJV) refers to both Mahlon and Chilion and does not confuse them. If the plural "names" had been used, the Bible would have had to have given more than one name each.

name of Jesus Christ of Nazareth, whom you crucified but whom God raised from the dead, ... this man stands before you healed' " (v. 10). In Acts 16:18, the apostle Paul set a young woman free from demonic possession "in the name of Jesus Christ."

The apostles were baptizing, healing, performing deliverances, and preaching by the authority of Jesus Christ. As Paul said, "Whatever you do, whether in word or deed, do it all in the name of the Lord Jesus, giving thanks to God the Father through him" (Col. 3:17). Conclusively, the apostolic declaration "in the name of Jesus Christ" is then tantamount to saying "by the authority of Jesus Christ." Hence, there is no reason to believe that the apostles were disobedient to the Lord's imperative to baptize in the name of the Father, the Son, and the Holy Spirit (Matt. 28:19), or that Jesus was being cryptic. Rather, even in the Book of Acts, the apostles baptized by the authority of Jesus Christ in the name of the Father, the Son, and the Holy Spirit.[83]

The Trinity doctrine is the distinctive feature of God's revelation of himself in Holy Scripture. Let us then hold fast to our profession of one God, "eternally self-existent ... as Father, Son, and Holy Ghost."[84]

STUDY QUESTIONS

1. What does Christian theology mean when it speaks of mystery concerning the doctrine of the Trinity?

2. Discuss the tension between the concepts of unity and trinity in avoiding emphasizing one over the other in the doctrine of the Trinity?

3. What is the key to arriving at a truly biblical doctrine of the Trinity?

4. What is meant by an economic Trinity?

5. Discuss the significance of the massive conflict between the Eastern and Western Churches on the issue of the iota as distinguishing *homoousia* and *homoiousia.*

---

[83]A first-century document, the *Didachē* ("The Teaching of the Twelve Apostles"), supports this interpretation. The *Didachē* stresses that holy Communion is open only to those who have been baptized "into the name of the Lord." Under the subheading "Baptism," the *Didachē* then asserts, "But concerning baptism ... baptize *in the name of the Father and of the Son and of the Holy Spirit."* See J. B. Lightfoot, *The Apostolic Fathers* (Grand Rapids: Baker Book House, 1983), 126.

[84]See the second article of faith in the Statement of Fundamental Truths of the Assemblies of God, Article V of the Constitution and Bylaws.

6. What is the doctrine of *filioque* in relation to the Holy Spirit? (See footnotes 62 and 63.) Why did the Eastern Church oppose this doctrine?

7. In what ways is the orthodox doctrine of the Trinity essential to understanding our salvation?

8. How does Modalism corrupt the doctrines of salvation?

9. In what way is the doctrine of the Trinity critical to the concept of propositional revelation?

10. Is the insistence to baptize in the name of "Jesus only" by Oneness Pentecostals a significant issue? Why or why not?

CHAPTER SIX

Created Spirit Beings

Carolyn Denise Baker

ANGELS

Although angels are mentioned in many places in the Bible, more frequently in the New Testament than in the Old, many would agree with Tim Unsworth, "Angels, it seems, are hard to pin down."[1] Nevertheless, an examination of these created beings can bring spiritual benefit.

One reason angels are "hard to pin down" is that the theology of angels is incidental to and not the primary focus of Scripture. **Angelic contexts always have God or Christ as their focal point** (Isa. 6:1–3; Rev. 4:7–11). Most angelic appearances are fleeting and without provocation or prediction. Such manifestations underscore truth; they never embody it. "When they are mentioned, it is always in order to inform us further about God, what he does, and how he does it"[2]—as well as what He requires.

The Bible's primary emphasis then is the Savior, not the servers; the God of angels, not the angels of God. Angels may be chosen as an occasional method for revelation, but they never constitute the message. The study of angels, however, can challenge the heart as well as the head. Although angels are mentioned a number of times in both the Old and New Testaments, "they are, if we may speak abruptly, none of our business most of the time. Our business is to learn to love God and our neighbor. Charity. Sanctity. There is our whole work cut out for us."[3]

---

[1]Tim Unsworth, "Angels: A Short Visit with Our Heavenly Hosts," *U.S. Catholic* 55 (March 1990): 31.

[2]Millard J. Erickson, *Christian Theology* (Grand Rapids: Baker Book House, 1985), 434.

[3]Thomas Howard, "The Parts Angels Play," *Christianity Today* 24 (12 December 1980): 20.

CHAPTER
6

Created
Spirit
Beings

The old scholastic question which doubles as an exercise in logic, i.e., How many angels can dance on the head of a pin? is actually irrelevant, for it does not transform one's character.[4] But the study of angels can encourage Christian graces such as these:

1. Humility. Angels are beings near to God, yet they serve believers most often in unseen, sometimes unknown ways. They are pure examples of humble service, seeking only the glory of God and the good of others. They embody what the Christian's service can be.

2. Confidence, security, and a sense of calm. In times of desperation, God assigns these powerful beings to assist the weakest of believers. Because of this, tranquility and confidence can characterize our Christian living.

3. Christian responsibility. Both God and angels witness the Christian's most unholy actions (1 Cor. 4:9). What a cause for believers to behave in a worthy manner!

4. Healthy optimism. Defying the evil one himself, good angels chose—and still choose—to serve God's holy purpose. Consequently, their example makes devoted service to a perfect God in this imperfect universe plausible. In a future day angels will mediate the banishing of all who are evil (Matt. 13:41–42,49–50). This encourages healthy optimism in the midst of all life's situations.

5. A proper Christian self-concept. Men and women are created a "little lower than the heavenly beings" (Ps. 8:5). Yet, in Christ, redeemed humanity is elevated far above these magnificent servants of God and His people (Eph. 1:3–12).

6. A reverential awe. Men like Isaiah and Peter, and women like Hannah and Mary, all "recognized holiness when it appeared in angelic form, and their reaction was appropriate."[5]

7. Participation in salvation history. God used angels in sacred history, especially Michael and Gabriel, to prepare for the Messiah. Later, angels proclaimed and worshiped Christ in devoted service. A proper understanding of them will lead believers to do the same.

Where there is experience with angels today, however, the teaching of Scripture must interpret that experience. When

---

[4]Augustus H. Strong, *Systematic Theology* (Philadelphia: Judson Press, 1947), 443. Herbert Muschamp in "Angels," *Vogue* 179 (December 1989): 278, says this question may seem "the very symbol of scholastic absurdity," but to the scholastics it was a sincere question. Angels were "like protons and electrons [functioning] as a binding force of the universe."

[5]Howard, "Angels," 20.

the angel Gabriel appeared he brought a message that glorified God. But the claims of Joseph Smith with respect to the visitation of angels led directly into paths of error.[6]

The study of angels is a vital part of theology, having tangential value and implications for other teachings of the Bible: for example, the nature of God's inspired Word, since angels mediated the Law to Moses (Acts 7:38,53; Gal. 3:19; Heb.2:2);[7] the nature of God, since angels attend the holy God of the universe; and the nature of Christ and the end times,[8] since angels are included in the events of both Christ's first and second comings.

THE VIEW OF ANGELS THROUGH HISTORY

In pagan traditions (some of which influenced later Jews), angels were sometimes considered divine, sometimes natural phenomena. They were beings who did good deeds for people, or they were the people themselves who did good deeds. This confusion is reflected in the fact that both the Hebrew word *mal'akh* and the Greek word *angelos* have two meanings. The basic meaning of each is "messenger," but that messenger, depending on the context, can be an ordinary human messenger or a heavenly messenger, an angel.

Some, on the basis of evolutionary philosophy, date the idea of angels to the beginning of civilization. "The concept of angels may have evolved from prehistoric times when primitive humans emerged from the cave and started looking up to the sky ... God's voice was no longer the growl of the jungle but the roar of the sky."[9] This supposedly developed into a view of angels serving humanity as God's mediators. True knowledge of angels, however, came only through divine revelation.

Later, Assyrians and Greeks attached wings to some semi-divine beings. Hermes had wings on his heels. Eros, "the fast-

---

[6]See *The Book of Mormon; Doctrine and the Covenants; The Pearl of Great Price* (Salt Lake City: Church of Jesus Christ of the Latter Day Saints, 1986), 20:10; 27:16. Supposedly an angel named Moroni appeared to Mormonism's founder, Joseph Smith, and revealed the location of gold tablets (supposedly inscribed with the Book of Mormon) beneath the hill of Cumorah. Mormonism also erroneously advocates a special "gift given to behold angels and ministering spirits," *Doctrine and Covenants,* Index, 13.

[7]Probably a reference to the "holy ones" of Deut. 33:2.

[8]Robert P. Lightner, *Evangelical Theology: A Survey and Review* (Grand Rapids: Baker Book House, 1986), 129.

[9]Unsworth, "Angels," 30.

flying spirit of passionate love," had them affixed to his shoulders. Adding a playful notion, the Romans invented Cupid, the god of erotic love, pictured as a playful boy shooting invisible love arrows to encourage humanity's romances.[10] Plato (ca. 427–347 B.C.) also spoke of helpful guardian angels.

The Hebrew Scriptures give names to only two of the angels it mentions: Gabriel, who enlightened Daniel's understanding (Dan. 9:21–27), and the archangel Michael, the protector of Israel (Dan. 12:1).

Nonbiblical Jewish apocalyptic literature, such as Enoch (105–64 B.C.), also recognizes that angels assisted the giving of the Mosaic law. The apocryphal book Tobit (200–250 B.C.), however, fabricated an archangel named Raphael who repeatedly helped Tobit in difficult situations. Actually, there is only one archangel (chief angel), Michael (Jude 9). Still later, Philo (ca. 20 B.C. to ca. A.D. 42), the Jewish philosopher of Alexandria, Egypt, depicted angels as mediators between God and humanity. Angels, subordinate creatures, lodged in the air as "the servants of God's powers. [They were] incorporeal souls ... wholly intelligent throughout ... [having] pure thoughts."[11]

During the New Testament period Pharisees believed angels were supernatural beings who often communicated God's will (Acts 23:8). However, the Sadducees, influenced by Greek philosophy, said there was "neither resurrection, angel, nor spirit" (Acts 23:8, KJV). To them, angels were little more than "good thoughts and motions" of the human heart.[12]

During the first few centuries after Christ, church fathers said little about angels. Most of their attention was given to other subjects, especially to the nature of Christ. Still, all of them believed angels existed. Ignatius of Antioch, an early church father, believed angels' salvation depended on the blood of Christ. Origen (182–251) declared their sinlessness, saying that if it were possible for an angel to fall, then it might

[10]Ibid.

[11]James Drummond, *Philo Judaeus: Or the Jewish Alexandrian Philosophy in Its Development and Completion,* vol. 2 (Edinburgh: Williams and Norgate, 1888), 146. For bibliography on Philo's view of angels see Roberto Radice and David T. Runia, *Philo Judaeus: Or the Jewish Alexandrian Philosophy in Its Development and Completion* (New York: E. J. Brill, 1988); and William S. Babcock, "Angels" in *Encyclopedia of Early Christianity,* David M. Scholer, E. F. Ferguson, M. P. McHugh, eds. (New York: Garland Publishers, 1990), 38–42.

[12]Robert L. Dabney, *Lectures in Systematic Theology* (Grand Rapids: Zondervan Publishing House, 1878, 1972), 264.

be possible for a demon to be saved. The latter was ultimately rejected by church councils.[13]

By A.D. 400 Jerome (347–420) believed guardian angels were awarded to humans at birth. Later, Peter Lombard (ca. A.D. 1100–1160) added that a solitary angel could guard many people at one time.[14]

Dionysius the Areopagite (ca. A.D. 500) contributed this period's most notable discussion. He pictured an angel as "an image of God, a manifestation of the unmanifested light, a pure mirror, what is most clear, without flaw, undefiled, and unstained."[15] Like Irenaeus four hundred years previous (ca. 130–95), he also constructed hypotheses concerning an angelic hierarchy.[16] Then Gregory the Great (A.D. 540–604) awarded angels celestial bodies.

As the thirteenth century dawned, angels became the subject of much speculation. Most significant were questions asked by the Italian theologian Thomas Aquinas (A.D. 1225–74). Seven of his 118 conjectures probed such areas as the following: Of what is an angel's body composed? Is there more than one species of angels? When angels assume human form do they exercise vital body functions? Do angels know if it is morning or evening? Can they understand many thoughts at one time? Do they know our secret thoughts? Can they talk one to the other?[17]

Most descriptive, perhaps, were portrayals by Renaissance artists who painted angels as less than "manly figures . . . . childlike harpists and horn tooters [who were] a far cry from Michael the Archangel." Daubed as "chubby, high-cholesterol

---

[13]F. L. Cross and E. A. Livingston, "Angels" in *Oxford Dictionary of the Christian Church,* 2d ed. (London: Oxford University Press, 1974), 52–53.

[14]Unsworth, "Angels," 31. Scripture does not expressly endorse guardian angels as a special class. It speaks, rather, of angels who guard.

[15]Pseudo-Dionysius Areopagite, *The Divine Names and Mystical Theology,* trans. John D. Jones (Milwaukee: Marquette University Press, 1980), 153.

[16]Unsworth, "Angels," 31.

[17]Thomas Aquinas, *Great Books of the World: The Summa Theologica, Aquinas,* Robert Hutchinson, ed., vol. 19 (Chicago: Encyclopedia Britannica), 269–585. Aquinas finally loathed his theological method. After a "wonderful spiritual experience," Aquinas stopped writing forever, saying, "All I have written and taught seems but of small account to me." Alexander Whyte, *The Nature of Angels* (Grand Rapids: Baker Book House, 1976), 7. Johannes Duns Scotus (1265–1308), Albert the Great (1193–1280) and Francisco de Suarez (1548–1617) used an approach similar to that of Aquinas.

cherubs, dressed in a few wisps of strategically placed cloth"[18] these creatures were often used as decorative borders for many paintings.

Medieval Christianity assimilated the mass of speculations and consequently began including angel worship in its liturgies. This aberration continued to grow and Pope Clement X (who was pope in the years A.D. 1670–1676) declared a feast to honor angels.[19]

In spite of Roman Catholic excesses, Reformed Christianity continued to insist that angels help God's people. John Calvin (1509–64) believed that "angels are dispensers and administrators of God's beneficience towards us. ... [T]hey keep vigil for our safety, take upon themselves our defense, direct our ways, and take care that some harm may not befall us."[20]

Martin Luther (1483–1546) in *Tabletalk* spoke in similar terms. He remarked how these spiritual beings created by God served the Church and the *kingdom,* being very close to God and to the Christian. "They stand before the face of the Father, next to the sun, but without effort they [are able to] swiftly come to our aid."[21]

As the Age of Rationalism dawned (ca. 1800), the possibility of the supernatural was seriously doubted, and historically accepted teachings of the Church began to be questioned. Consequently, some skeptics began to label angels "impersonations of divine energies, or of good and bad principles, or of diseases and natural influences."[22]

By 1918 some Jewish scholars began echoing this liberal voice, saying angels were not valid because they are not necessary. "A world of law and process does not need a living ladder to lead from the earth beyond to God on high."[23]

---

[18]Unsworth, "Angels," 31. Muschamp, "Angels," 279, calls angels a "casualty of the Renaissance." For the historical presentation of angels in art and literature see Gustav Davidson, *The Dictionary of Angels, Including the Fallen* (New York: Free Press, 1971) and Theodora Ward, *Men and Angels* (New York: Viking Press, 1969).

[19]Unsworth, "Angels," 32.

[20]John Calvin, *Institutes of the Christian Religion,* John T. McNeill, ed., vol. 1 (Philadelphia: Westminster Press, 1967), 166.

[21]Martin Luther, "Protective Angels and Destructive Demons, Between November 24 and December 8, 1532, no. 2829." Luther's Works: *Tabletalk,* Helmut T. Lehman, ed. (Philadelphia: Fortress Press, 1967), 54:172.

[22]Dabney, *Lectures,* 264.

[23]Kaufmann Kohler, *Jewish Theology* (New York: Ktav Publishing House, Inc., 1968), 180.

This did not shake the faith of conservative Evangelicals. They have continued to endorse the validity of angels.[24]

THE CONSENSUS OF THE MODERN SCENE

Perhaps the liberal theologian Paul Tillich (1886–1965) posed the modern period's most radical view. He considered angels Platonic essences: emanations from God who desired to do more than reveal himself to humanity. He believed angels actually wanted to return to the divine essence from which they came and to again be equal with Him. Tillich's advice, then, was this: "To interpret the concept of angels in a meaningful way today, interpret them as the Platonic essences, as the powers of being, not as special beings. If you interpret them in the latter way, it all becomes crude mythology."[25]

Karl Barth (1886–1968) and Millard Erickson (1932–), however, encouraged an opposite approach of healthful caution. Barth, father of neoorthodoxy, tagged this subject "the most remarkable and difficult of all." He recognized the interpreter's conundrum: How was one to "advance without becoming rash"; to be "both open and cautious, critical and naive, perspicuous and modest?"[26]

Erickson, a conservative theologian, amended Barth's sentiment, adding how one might be tempted to omit or neglect the topic of angels, yet "if we are to be faithful students of the Bible, we have no choice but to speak of these beings."[27]

In popular writings about angels, however, there has been some extremism. Interest in angels has revived, but often with dubious or unscriptural ideas. One person, for example, claims to derive immense comfort from angels, saying, "I talk to my guardian angel often. It helps me to sort things out." Others report personal visitations and protection by angels, or describe them in a way that seems to make them butlers from

[24]Augustus H. Strong, Alexander Whyte, and Robert L. Dabney were some conservative scholars of this period.

[25]Paul Tillich, *A History of Christian Thought* (New York: Harper & Row, 1968), 94. See also James M. Wall, "Unlearning Skepticism: An Angelic Meditation," *The Christian Century,* 28 September 1988, 827.

[26]Karl Barth, "The Kingdom of Heaven, The Ambassadors of God and Their Opponents," *Church Dogmatics: Doctrines of Creation,* T. F. Torrance, and Geoffrey W. Bromiley, eds., vol. 3 (Edinburgh: T. & T. Clark, 1960), 369.

[27]Erickson, *Christian Theology,* 434.

heaven who serve the Christian's whims.[28] Some say angels "minister in accordance [with] the Word of God . . . . [and their only] limitation seems to be the deficiency of the Word in the mouth of the believers to whom they are ministering."[29]

BIBLICAL EVIDENCE

"There [is] only one way to demythologize popular fantasies about angels—get back to the biblical reality."[30]

Angels enjoy a reason for being that all volitional beings can experience. They worship God and render Him service. Their general purpose, reflected in the Hebrew and Greek words translated "angel" (*mal'akh and angelos,* "messenger"), is to carry the message of divine words and works.

Angels, then, primarily serve God. They also serve people as a direct result of serving God. While Scripture recognizes them as "ministering spirits sent to serve those who will inherit salvation" (Heb. 1:14), they are, nevertheless, "spirits sent" by God (Rev. 22:16).

That they are servants of God is implied also by the language of Scripture. They are designated "the angel of the

---

[28]Unsworth, "Angels," 32. Roland Buck, *Angels on Assignment* (Kingwood, Tex.: Hunter Books, 1979). Malcolm Godwin, *Angels: An Endangered Species* (New York: Simon & Schuster, 1990), describes how some believe angels disguise themselves as flying saucers. For conservative testimonies about angelic visits see W. Norman Day, "Guardian Angels," *The Pentecostal Testimony,* October 1986, 34–35; Carolyn Hittenberger, "Angel on the Fender," *Pentecostal Evangel,* 5 July 1987, 10; Melvin E. Jorgenson, "Angelic Escort," *Pentecostal Evangel,* 21 December 1980, 7–8; and Ann Wedgeworth, *Magnificent Strangers* (Springfield, Mo.: Gospel Publishing House, 1979). For evaluations of angelic visitations see B. Zerebesky, "What About All Those Angel Stories?" *Charisma* (December 1983), 76–78; J. Rodman Williams, *Renewal Theology* (Grand Rapids: Zondervan Publishing House, 1988), 195; and id., "Comprehensive Critique of *Angels on Assignment* Including a List of Five Tests for Angelic Visitations" (published by the author). Charles and Annette Capps, *Angels!* (Tulsa: Harrison House, 1984), encourage believers to command angels to assist them. Scripture, however, portrays angels commanding people (Matt. 1:24; 2:19–21; Acts 8:26; 10:3–5,22; 11:13; 12:7–8; Rev. 11:1).

[29]Marilyn Hickey, *Treading with Angels* (Denver: Layman's Library, 1980), 8. However, all benefits of salvation, including the protection of angels, are based on God's effort, not ours. Cf. Guy P. Duffield and Nathaniel M. Van Cleave, *Foundations of Pentecostal Theology* (Los Angeles: L.I.F.E. Bible College, 1983), 478, who add, "Nowhere are we instructed to pray to angels and request their help." See also Kenneth D. Barney, "Supernatural Bodyguards," *Pentecostal Evangel* (22 February 1981): 8–9.

[30]William Baker, "Angels: Our Chariots of Fire," *Moody Monthly,* 6 January 1986, 85.

Lord" (forty-nine times), "the angel of God" (eighteen times), and the angels of the Son of Man (seven times). God specifically calls them "my angels" (three times), and people referred to them as "His angels" (twelve times).[31] Finally, when the term "angels" occurs by itself the context normally indicates whose they are. They belong to God!

All angels were created at one time; that is, the Bible gives no indication of a schedule of incremental creation of angels (or anything else). They were formed by and for Christ when "He commanded and they were created" (Ps. 148:5; see also Col. 1:16–17; 1 Pet. 3:22). And since angels "neither marry nor [are] given in marriage" (Matt. 22:30), they are a complete company having no need for reproduction.

As created beings they are everlasting but not eternal. God alone has no beginning and no end (1 Tim. 6:16). Angels had a beginning but will know no end, for they are present in the eternal age and in the New Jerusalem (Heb. 12:22; Rev. 21:9,12).

Angels have unique natures; they are superior to humans (Ps. 8:5), but inferior to the incarnate Jesus (Heb. 1:6). The Bible brings out the following seven facts concerning them:

1. Angels are real but not always visible (Heb. 12:22). Although God occasionally gives them visible human form (Gen. 19:1–22), they are spirits (Ps. 104:4; Heb. 1:7,14). In Bible times people sometimes experienced the effects of an angel's presence but saw no one (Num. 22:21–35). Sometimes they did see the angel (Gen. 19:1–22; Judg. 2:1–4; 6:11–22; 13:3–21; Matt. 1:20–25; Mark 16:5; Luke 24:4–6; Acts 5:19–20).[32] In addition, angels might be seen but not recognized as angels (Heb. 13:2).

2. Angels worship but are not to be worshiped. "[T]hey are unique among the creatures, but they are nonetheless creatures."[33] They respond with worship and praise to God (Ps. 148:2; Isa. 6:1–3; Luke 2:13–15; Rev. 4:6–11; 5:1–14) and to Christ (Heb. 1:6). Consequently, Christians are not to exalt

---

[31]"My angels" occurs in Exod. 23:23; 32:34; Rev. 22:16. "His angels" in Gen. 24:40; Job 4:18; Pss. 91:11; 103:20; 148:2; Dan. 6:22; Luke 4:10; Acts 12:11; Rev. 3:5; 12:7; 22:6. The "Son of Man's" angels in Matt. 13:41; 16:27; 24:30–31; Mark 13:26–27).

[32]Allan K. Jenkins, "Young Man or Angel?" *The Expository Times* 94 (May 1983): 237–40. He doubts that the "young man" of Mark 16:5 was an angel. He connects the white robe with martyrdom.

[33]Erickson, *Christian Theology*, 439.

angels (Rev. 22:8–9); unwise Christians who do so forfeit their reward (Col. 2:18).

3. Angels serve but are not to be served. God sends them as agents to help people, especially His own (Exod. 14:19; 23:23; 32:34; 33:2–3; Num. 20:16; 22:22–35; Judg. 6:11–22; 1 Kings 19:5–8; Pss. 34:7; 91:11; Isa. 63:9; Dan. 3:28; Acts 12:7–12; 27:23–25; Heb. 13:2). Angels also mediate God's judgment (Gen. 19:22; see also 19:24; Ps. 35:6; Acts 12:23) or messages (Judg. 2:1–5; Matt. 1:20–24; Luke 1:11–38).[34] But angels are never to be served, for angels are like Christians in one very important way: They too are "fellow servants" (Rev. 22:9).

4. Angels accompany revelation but do not replace it in whole or in part. God uses them, but they are not the goal of God's revelation (Heb. 2:2ff.). In the first century, a heresy arose that required "false humility and the worship of angels" (Col. 2:18). It involved "harsh treatment of the body" but did nothing to restrain "sensual indulgence" (Col. 2:23). Its philosophy emphasized the false ideas that (a) Christians are inferior in their ability to personally approach God; (b) angels have a superior ability to do so; and (c) worship is due them because of their intervention in our behalf.[35] Paul responded with a hymn glorifying Christ who is the source of our future glory (Col. 3:1–4).

5. Angels know much but not everything. Their insight is imparted by God; it is not innate or infinite. Their wisdom may be vast (2 Sam. 14:20), but their knowledge is limited: They do not know the day of our Lord's second coming (Matt. 24:36) or the full magnitude of human salvation (1 Pet. 1:12).

6. Angelic power is superior but not supreme. God simply lends His power to angels as His agents. Angels are, therefore,

---

[34] Angels often mediate God's judgment (2 Sam. 24:16; 2 Kings 19:35; 1 Chron. 21:14–15; Ps. 78:49; Rev. 1:1–15; 5:2–11; 6:7–8; 8:2–13; 9:1–15; 10:1–10; 14:18–20; 15:1–8; 16:1–5,17; 17:1–17; 18:1,21; 19:17–18). They also declare God's message (Judg. 2:1–5; 3:3–22; 5:23; 2 Kings 1:3–15; Isa. 37:6; Zech. 1:9–14,19; 2:3–13; 3:1–10; 4:1–14; 5:5–11; 6:4–8; Matt. 28:5; Luke 2:9–21; John 20:12; Acts 7:53; 8:26; 10:3,7,22; 11:13; Heb. 2:2; Rev. 1:1).

[35] Most commentators believe very little evidence supports a universal cult of angel worship by the Jews. The heresy was merely a local Colossian problem. See E. K. Simpson and F. F. Bruce, *Commentary on the Epistles to the Ephesians and Colossians* (Grand Rapids: Wm. B. Eerdmans, 1957), 247–48. See also Peter T. O'Brien, *Word Biblical Commentary: Colossians, Philemon,* David Hubbard, Glenn W. Barker, eds., vol. 44 (Waco, Tex.: Word Books, 1982), 142–43.

"stronger and more powerful" than people (2 Pet. 2:11). As "mighty ones who do his bidding," (Ps. 103:20) "powerful angels" mediate God's final judgments on sin (2 Thess. 1:7; Rev. 5:2,11; 7:1–3; 8:2–13; 9:1–15; 10:1–11; 14:6–12, 15–20; 15:1–8; 16:1–12; 17:1–3,7; 18:1–2,21; 19:17–18). Angels are often used in mighty deliverance (Dan. 3:28; 6:22; Acts 12:7–11) and healings (John 5:4).[36] And an angel will single-handedly throw the Christian's chief and most powerful foe into the abyss and lock him in for a thousand years (Rev. 20:1–3).

7. Angels make decisions. The disobedience of one group implies an ability to choose and influence others with wickedness (1 Tim. 4:1). On the other hand, the good angel's refusal of John's worship (Rev. 22:8–9) implies an ability to choose and influence others with good.[37] Although good angels respond obediently to God's command, they are not automatons. Rather, they choose devoted obedience with intense ardor.

The number of angels is immense, "thousands upon thousands" (Heb. 12:22), "and ten thousand times ten thousand" (Rev. 5:11).[38] Jesus expressed the same idea when he said, "Do you think I cannot call on my Father, and he will at once put at my disposal more than twelve legions[39] of angels?" (Matt. 26:53).

Some interpreters see a five-stage hierarchy of angels with lower-ranking angels subject to those in higher positions: "thrones," "powers," "rulers," "authorities," and "dominion" (Rom. 8:38; Eph. 1:21; Col. 1:16; 2:15; 1 Pet. 3:22). Contextually, however, this is dubious. The plain emphasis of these passages is not the subjection of angels to one another, but

---

[36]Zane C. Hodges, "Problem Passages in the Gospel of John, Part 5: The Angel at Bethesda—John 5:4," *Bibliotheca Sacra* (January to March, 1979): 25–39. He cites strong manuscript evidence supporting the authenticity of John 5:4, thus allowing for the existence of the angel at Bethesda.

[37]Strong, *Systematic Theology,* 445.

[38]Duffield and Van Cleave, *Foundations,* 467, interpret Rev. 5:11 literally. Medieval scholars attempted to calculate what might be the minimum number of angels using biblical numerology, i.e., "calculating words into numbers and numbers into words." Based on this system fourteenth-century Cabalists posited the existence of 301,655,722 angels. See Gustav Davidson, *The Dictionary of Angels,* xxi.

[39]During the Republican conquest a Roman legion consisted of 4,200 foot soldiers and 300 calvary. *The Complete Biblical Library,* vol. 14 (Springfield, Mo.: 1986), 38.

the subjection of both angels and demons to Christ, the Lord of all (cf. Rom. 8:39; Eph. 1:22; Col. 1:16–18; 1 Pet. 3:22).[40]

Angels work for God in obedience to His dictates, never apart from them. "Are not all angels ministering spirits sent to serve those who will inherit salvation?" (Heb. 1:14). They are "sent." God commands their specific activities (Pss. 91:11; 103:20–21),[41] for they are His servants (Heb. 1:7).

Although angels are sent to serve us, that service (Gk. *diakonian*) is primarily spiritual help, relief, and support; however, it may include tangible acts of love as well. The corresponding verb *(diēkonoun)* is used of angels' supernaturally caring for Jesus after Satan tempted Him (Matt. 4:11). Other examples of God's sending angels for the help or relief of believers include the angels at the tomb (Matt. 28:2–7; Mark 16:5–7; Luke 24:4–7; John 20:11–13) and the angelic deliverances of apostles (Acts 5:18–20; 12:7–10; 27:23–26). An angel also gave directions to Philip because God saw the faith and desire of an Ethiopian eunuch and wanted him to become an heir of salvation (Acts 8:26). An angel brought God's message to Cornelius, too, that he might be saved (Acts 10:3–6). These were ministries sent in the providence of God.[42] In no case, however, is there any evidence that believers can demand angelic help or command angels. God alone can and does command them.

In addition to beings specifically designated as angels, the Old Testament speaks of similar beings often classed with angels: cherubs, seraphs, and messengers ("watchers," KJV).

Cherubs and seraphs respond to God's immediate presence. Cherubs (Heb. *keruvim*, related to an Akkadian verb meaning "to bless, praise, adore") are always affiliated with God's holiness and the adoration His immediate presence inspires (Exod. 25:20,22; 26:31; Num. 7:89; 2 Sam. 6:2; 1 Kings 6:29,32; 7:29; 2 Kings 19:15; 1 Chron. 13:6; Pss. 80:1; 99:1; Isa. 37:16; Ezek. 1:5–26; 9:3; 10:1–22; 11:22). Protecting God's

---

[40]Irenaeus (A.D. 130–200) and Dionysius (A.D. 500) speculated regarding angelic hierarchy. Scripture expresses a simple hierarchy—angels and a chief angel (the archangel Michael; 1 Thess. 4:16; Jude 9). Meyer reminds us that any attempt to precisely establish any order "belongs to the fanciful domain of theosophy." See Henry Alford, *The Greek Testament,* vol. 3 (Chicago: Moody Press, 1856), 205.

[41]Angels are sent by God's command (Gen. 24:7; 24:40; Exod. 23:20; 23:23; 32:34; 33:2; 2 Chron. 32:21; Dan. 6:22; Matt. 13:41; 24:31; Luke 1:26; 4:10; Acts 12:11; Rev. 22:6; 22:16).

[42]See Everitt M. Fjordbak, *An Exposition and Commentary on the Epistle to the Hebrews* (Dallas: Wisdom House Publishers, 1983), 39–42.

holiness is their great concern; they prevented Adam and Eve's reentry into the Garden (Gen. 3:24).[43] Carved figures of gold cherubs were fastened to the atonement cover ("mercy seat," KJV) of the ark of the covenant, where their wings were a "shelter" for the ark of the covenant and a support ("chariot") for God's invisible throne (1 Chron. 28:18).

In Ezekiel cherubs are highly symbolic creatures having human and animal characteristics, with two faces (Ezek. 41:18–20) or four (Ezek. 1:6; 10:14).[44] In Ezekiel's inaugural vision, God's throne is above the cherubs with their four faces. The face of the man is mentioned first as the highest of God's creation, with the face of the lion representing wild animals, that of the ox representing domestic animals, and that of the eagle representing birds; thus picturing the fact that God is over all His creation. The cherubs also have hooves (Ezek. 1:7), and the ox face is the actual face of the cherub (Ezek. 10:14). God is sometimes pictured as riding on them as "on the wings of the wind" (2 Sam. 22:11; Ps. 18:10).

The seraphs (from the Hebrew *saraph,* "to burn") are pictured in Isaiah's inaugural vision (Isa. 6:1–3) as so radiating the glory and brilliant purity of God that they seem to be on fire. They declare God's unique glory and supreme holiness.[45] Like cherubs, seraphs guard God's throne (Isa. 6:6–7).[46] Some scholars believe the "living creatures" (Rev. 4:6–9) to be synonymous with seraphs and cherubs; however, the cherubs

---

[43]The presence of cherubs before the death of any human being seems to be further evidence that human beings do not become angels after death.

Middle East excavations have revealed cherublike images possessing a human face and an animal body with four legs and two wings. Such figures appear repeatedly in Near Eastern mythology and architecture. See R. K. Harrison, "Cherubim," *The New Bible Dictionary,* 2d ed., J. D. Douglas, et al., eds. (Wheaton: Tyndale, 1982), 185–86; "Cherub," *The Theological Wordbook of the Old Testament,* R. Laird Harris, Gleason L. Archer, Jr. and Bruce K. Waltke, eds. vol. 1 (Chicago: Moody Press, 1980), 454–55.

[44]Ibid. Harris states these four faces represent "birds, tame animals, wild animals and men in attendance before God."

[45]The threefold repetition, "Holy, holy, holy," means God is "different," "unique," "set apart," and gives emphasis to God's holiness. Some see also an implication of the Trinity.

[46]The seraphs' covered faces depict an "awe that dared not gaze at the glory." Their covered feet illustrates "the lowliness of their glorious service." Their hovering posture portrays a readiness to do God's errands. See W. E. Vine, *Isaiah: Prophecies, Promises, Warnings* (Grand Rapids: Zondervan Publishing House, 1971), 29. See also Harris, "Cherub," 454–55.

in Ezekiel look alike and the "living creatures" in Revelation are different from each other.[47]

"Messengers" or "watchers" (Aram. *'irin,* related to the Heb. *'ur,* "be awake")[48] are mentioned only in Daniel 4:13,17,23. They are "holy ones" who are eager promoters of God's sovereign decrees and demonstrated God's sovereign lordship over Nebuchadnezzar.

Another special designation in the Old Testament is "*the* angel of the Lord" *(mal'akh YHWH).* In many of the sixty Old Testament occurrences of "the" angel of the Lord, he is identified with God himself (Gen. 16:11; cf. 16:13; 18:2; cf. 18:13–33; 22:11–18; 24:7; 31:11–13; 32:24–30; Exod. 3:2–6; Judg. 2:1; 6:11,14; 13:21–22). Yet this "angel of the Lord" is also distinguishable from God, for God speaks to this angel (2 Sam. 24:16; 1 Chron. 21:15), and this angel speaks to God (Zech. 1:12).[49] Thus, in the opinion of many, "the" angel of the Lord occupies a unique category. "He is not just a higher angel, or even the highest: He is the Lord appearing in angelic form." Since this angel is not mentioned in the New Testament, he probably was a manifestation of the Second Person of the Trinity.[50] Some object, saying that any preincarnate manifestation of Jesus would take away from the uniqueness of the Incarnation. However, in His incarnation, Jesus identified himself fully with humankind from birth to death and made possible our identification with Him in His death and resurrection. No temporary preincarnate manifestation could possibly detract from the uniqueness of that.

_____

[47]Henry Alford, *The Greek Testament,* vol. 4 (Cambridge: Deighton Bell and Co., 1866), 599, suggests that the living creatures are "forms compounded out of the most significant particulars of more than one Old Testament vision."

[48]A. D. "Watchers," in *The International Standard Bible Encyclopedia,* Geoffrey W. Bromiley, ed., vol. 4 (Grand Rapids: Wm. B. Eerdmans, 1979), 1023. Some believe "watchers" are a special class of angels affecting human history. See C. Fred Dickason, *Angels: Elect and Evil* (Chicago: Moody Press, 1975), 59. Others believe "watchers" was simply a descriptive phrase denoting the vigilance of angels. See John F. Walvoord, Daniel: *Key to Prophetic Revelation* (Chicago: Moody Press, 1971), 102.

[49]T. E. McComiskey, "Angel of the Lord," in *Dictionary of Theology,* Walter A. Ellwell, ed. (Grand Rapids: Baker Book House, 1984), 55.

[50]Williams, *Renewal Theology,* vol. 1, 181. Williams labels these theophanies "temporary visits by the Second Person of the Trinity prior to His coming in human flesh."

THE ROLE OF ANGELS

Angels work in Christ's life. In past eternity angels worshiped Christ (Heb. 1:6). They prophesied and announced His birth (Matt. 1:20–24; Luke 1:26–28; 2:8–20), protected Him in His infancy (Matt. 2:13–23), and witnessed His incarnate life (1 Tim. 3:16). They will also accompany Him in His visible return (Matt. 24:31; 25:31; Mark 8:38; 13:27; Luke 9:26; 2 Thess. 1:7).

During His life on earth Jesus sometimes desired angelic assistance. He welcomed the aid of angels after the wilderness temptation (Matt. 4:11) and during His struggle in Gethsemane (Luke 22:43). Both His resurrection (Matt. 28:2,5; Luke 24:23; John 20:12) and ascension (Acts 1:11) were accompanied by them. Yet sometimes He declined their help. During His wilderness temptation He said no to a potential misappropriation of their protective power (Matt. 4:6) and later refused their rescue from His impending trial and crucifixion (Matt. 26:53).[51]

Angels work in people's lives. Angels protect believers from harm, especially when such aid is necessary for the continued proclamation of the gospel (Acts 5:19–20; 12:7–17; 27:23–24; cf. 28:30–31). They assist but never replace the Holy Spirit's role in salvation and in the believer's proclamation of Christ (Acts 8:26; 10:1–8; cf. 10:44–48). Angels can help the believer's outward, physical necessities, while the Holy Spirit aids inward spiritual illumination.

Although angels escort the righteous to a place of reward (Luke 16:22), Christians, not angels, will share Christ's rule in the world to come (Heb. 2:5). Believers will also evaluate the performance of angels (1 Cor. 6:3). Until then, Christ's disciples must live and worship carefully so as not to offend these heavenly onlookers (1 Cor. 4:9; 11:10; 1 Tim. 5:21).

Angels work in the unbeliever's life. There is joy in the angels' presence when sinners repent (Luke 15:10); but the angels will soberly mediate God's final judgments upon humans refusing Christ (Matt. 13:39–43; Rev. 8:6–13; 9:1–21;

---

[51]Angels in the Gospels function like those in the Old Testament. However, "unlike the OT and other Jewish writings, the angelology of the Gospels is, like the Gospels as a whole, Christocentric." They bring direct revelation from God on two occasions only: Jesus' birth and resurrection. "In the interim he himself is the preeminent disclosure of God." M. J. Davidson "Angels," in *Dictionary of Jesus and the Gospels,* Joel B. Green, Scot McKnight, eds. (Downers Grove, Ill.: InterVarsity Press, 1992), 11.

14:6–20; 15:1,6–8; 16:1–21; 18:1–24; 19:1–21; cf. 20:2,10,14–15).

In times past, angels announced Christ's birth, altering human history forever. In the present, their protection gives us confidence. Their final exile of evil is part of our future victory. With the Father for us, Christ above us, the Spirit inside us, and angels beside us, we are encouraged to press on to the prize before us.

Frank D. Macchia

REPUDIATING THE ENEMY: SATAN AND DEMONS

In the small southern German village of Moettlingen, Pastor Johann Blumhardt found himself at sunrise on December 28, 1843, exhausted at the end of an all-night vigil of praying fervently for the deliverance of Gottlieben Dittus, a young woman severely tormented by evil spirits. Gottlieben had come to Pastor Blumhardt months earlier complaining of fainting spells and of hearing strange voices and noises in the night. He had attempted at first to help her through pastoral counseling. However, the more time he spent with her the more violent her symptoms and torment became. Investigation into Gottlieben's life revealed that at an early age she had been abused and dedicated to Satan by a wicked aunt, who had also involved her in occult worship.

Blumhardt could not tolerate watching the woman be tormented by dark forces. The burning question would not leave him, "Who is the Lord?" Blumhardt became preoccupied with the blatant contradiction between the reign of a sovereign God who sets the captives free and the needless suffering of Gottlieben Dittus. He could not merely accept this contradiction in passive resignation to the forces of darkness. Instead, he entered a "battle" (*kampf*) for Gottlieben's deliverance. After numerous prayer sessions at Gottlieben's home, she finally decided to come to Pastor Blumhardt's home for prayer, an obvious sign that she wanted deliverance for herself. Soon afterward, Pastor Blumhardt found himself at the close of the all-night prayer vigil mentioned above. Suddenly as the sun began to rise on that December morning on 1843, a demon cried out, "Jesus is Victor!" Gottlieben was completely set free.[52]

THE CALL FOR DISCERNMENT

In view of a Protestant liberalism's focus on inward experience, one must admire Blumhardt's courage in confronting the forces of darkness with the power of the kingdom of God to transform, not only the inward life of the believer, but the bodily and social dimensions of life as well. Such courage is sorely needed today. Evil is deeply felt in such massively destructive forces in our world as materialism, racism, sexism, and ideologies that deny both God and the value of human life. There are also destructive interpersonal relationships revealed in the mounting evils of wife and child abuse. Crime is on the rise in our urban streets, and countless homeless individuals, many of whom are mentally ill, roam our streets seeking sanctuary. The question that many have in their effort to combat such evil is why bring the devil into it? Does not demonology direct attention away from the human causes of and possible solutions to such widespread evil? As the late German biblical scholar Rudolf Bultmann maintained, does not demonology represent an escape into an outdated mythological worldview?[53] If social and moral problems are elevated to the realm of the church's struggle with the demonic, does the church not lose its capacity to engage in the kind of humble dialogue and wise analysis necessary for responsible moral action?

Demonology is indeed trivialized and problematic when confined to the realm of mythological fantasy involving dark and ugly little creatures with hooves and horns. Such fantasy creatures are easily dismissed by modern thinkers who share concerns such as those mentioned above. Such fantasy images of demons can also provide impetus for an unhealthy preoccupation with an abstract and self-made realm of horror far removed from the concrete evils that oppress people's lives and oppose the will of God for humanity. Consequently, C. S. Lewis was quite correct that demonology seems to provoke in a diversity of modern cultures either a simplistic rejection

---

[52]*Blumhardt's Battle: A Conflict with Satan,* translated by F. S. Boshold (New York: Thomas E. Lowe, 1970). Note Frank D. Macchia, *Spirituality and Social Liberation: The Message of the Blumhardts in the Light of Wuerttemberg Pietism* (Metuchen, N.J.: Scarecrow Press, 1993).

[53]R. Bultmann, *Jesus Christ and Mythology* (New York: Scribner, 1959), 65.

of the demonic or an unhealthy preoccupation with it.[54] Both errors remove believers from the real challenges of repudiating the forces of darkness where they are really confronted in the world. It is understandable that German Christians during World War II repudiated the devil and his works in their resistance of the Nazis. This repudiation was not a battle with mythological creatures abstracted from the real evils of life. It was a recognition of the fact that resistance to real evils in life has ultimate implications: God's eschatological victory over the forces of darkness, which lie at the root of all evil. Only in such a context does the battle against the devil make sense.

SATAN AND DEMONS IN THE OLD TESTAMENT

The Scriptures are not dominated by a concern with demonic forces. The accent of the Bible is on the sovereign reign of God, the gospel of salvation, and the demands of God's grace on the lives of the redeemed. Though the Scriptures do not ignore the forces of darkness, they emphasize the power of God to redeem and to heal. By way of contrast, the people of ancient societies during the development of the Scriptures tended to advocate a rather frightening view of the world. They believed that spirits and demigods, some more evil than others, were able to intrude at will into a person's everyday life. Elaborate incantations, spiritistic forms of communication, and magical rituals developed in various cultic settings to grant the common person a degree of control in this threatening world of spirit activity. Such a frightening worldview is still shared in parts of the world today.

In contrast to this chaotic and threatening view of the world stood the Old Testament witness to Jehovah (i.e., Yahweh), the Lord: This God and Creator of all is not only the Lord of Israel, but also the Lord of hosts, who reigns supreme over the entire universe. In life and in death one contends with the Lord and the Lord alone. God alone is to be loved, feared, and worshiped (Ps. 139; Isa. 43). In Israel the spirit beings that loomed so large in the religions of other ancient peoples receded into near oblivion in the light of the sovereign Lord and the divine Word to Israel. Therefore, no spiritistic communications or magical incantations or rituals

---

[54]C. S. Lewis. *Screwtape Letters* (Philadelphia: Fortress, 1980), introduction.

were to have any place in the faith of Israel (Isa. 8:19–22). Demonology plays no significant role in the Old Testament.

This is not to say, however, that there is no satanic adversary in the Old Testament. The term "Satan" in Christian theology comes from the word for "adversary." One does indeed find the presence of such an adversary in the Old Testament as early as the temptation of humanity's first parents, Adam and Eve, in the Garden of Eden (Gen. 1 through 3). Here the adversary, in the form of a reptile tempter, claims to speak on behalf of God, but ends up speaking falsely and tempting Adam and Eve to sin. But notice that this tempter is described as one creature among others, not as a god who can in any way compete with the Lord, the Creator of heaven and earth. Adam and Eve are not faced at the beginning with a struggle between two gods, one good and one evil. To the contrary, they are made to choose between the command of the one true God and the word of a creature-tempter who can thwart the will of God only through the disobedience of God's servants. In fact, the tempter actually seems to play a role in God's testing of Adam and Eve's faithfulness.

This adversary emerges again in another major Old Testament drama, in the prologue to the Book of Job. The adversary questions the Lord's assumption concerning Job's faithfulness. The adversary is then allowed to inflict suffering on Job within the boundaries set by the Lord. The entire Book of Job includes Job's search for God in the midst of his trials and ends with a dramatic appearance of the Lord to answer him (Job 38). Through a series of questions, the Lord leads Job to accept the mystery of divine sovereignty over the world and over all the affairs of life, no matter how perplexing they may seem. The adversary does not appear with the Lord. In fact, the adversary has no role to play in the Book of Job once the initial destruction depicted in the opening chapters has transpired. The Lord and His servant Job occupy center stage throughout the book. If Job wrestles, it is not with the adversary. Job wrestles with God.

Yet, Satan and his dark forces in the Old Testament do not function as tame pets in the heavenly court of the Lord or merely as tools of the Lord in the testing of humanity. In both Genesis 3 and the prologue to Job the adversary does present genuine opposition to the will of God for humanity. The Book of Daniel even depicts a battle between the "prince of the Persian kingdom" and an angelic messenger to Daniel (Dan. 10:13). Though Daniel had no part to play in the battle, the dark forces behind the Persian kingdom do provide genuine opposition to his reception of God's message. God is sovereign in the Old Testament but this sovereignty does not eliminate genuine opposition and conflict in the human obedience to the sovereign Word of God.

SATAN AND DEMONS IN THE NEW TESTAMENT

In contrast to the relatively scant attention paid to the defeat of the forces of darkness in the Old Testament, upon reading the Gospels one is struck by the increased attention paid to this matter. There was already an increased interest in demonology in Jewish intertestamental literature, leading some to speculate about the possible influence of Persian dualism.[55] But, theologically, the implication is that the increased attention to the defeat of demons in the Gospels is due to the prior revelation of the fullness of truth and grace in the coming of Jesus Christ (John 1:14). Indeed, the coming of the light into the world clarified the works of darkness (John 3:19–21). This means that the demise of darkness can be understood only in the light of God's grace and deliverance. One does not study the forces of darkness in order to discover the riches of God's grace. To the contrary, the focus is to be on the riches of God's grace, which will then expose just how deceptive the voices of darkness really are.

Jesus confronted His audiences with the astounding assertion that the kingdom of God had broken in to clarify the conflict with the forces of darkness and to bring it to a decisive turn. He stated: " 'If I drive out demons by the Spirit of God, then the kingdom of God has come upon you' " (Matt. 12:28). Jesus began His public ministry with a decisive victory over the tempter in the wilderness (Matt. 4:1–11). Satan tried to tempt Jesus to prove His messianic identity in ways that were disobedient to the will of the Father, but Jesus remained faithful. The numerous accounts of Jesus' casting out demons (Mark 1:23–28; 5:1–20; 7:24–30; 9:14–29), as well as the charge from Jesus' opposition that He cast out demons by the power of Satan (Matt. 12:27–28), give strong evidence that Jesus publicly defeated demonic spirits as an aspect of His ministry.[56] Just as Jesus commanded the stormy seas to

---

[55]W. Foerster, "DAIMON, DAIMONION," *Theological Dictionary of the New Testament,* ed. G. Kittel, trans. G. W. Bromiley, vol. 2 (Grand Rapids: Wm. B. Eerdmans Pub. Co., 1964), 1–10.

[56]J. Ramsey Michaels, "Jesus and the Unclean Spirits," in *Demon Possession, a Medical, Historical, Anthropological, and Theological Symposium,* ed. J. W. Montgomery (Minneapolis: Bethany Fellowship, 1976), 41–57.

be calm by His sovereign word in Mark 4:35–41, He commanded the legion of demons out of the Gerasene demoniac in the very next chapter (Mark 5:1–20).

Later, the apostolic proclamation made the death and resurrection of Jesus Christ the fulfillment of Jesus' victory over the forces of darkness (1 Cor. 2:6–8; Col. 2:14–15; Hebrews 2:14). The late Swedish Lutheran Gustav Aulen argued that God's sovereign victory over the forces of darkness represents the "classical" theory of the Atonement most basic to the proclamation of the New Testament.[57] By His death on the cross, Jesus destroyed "him who holds the power of death— that is, the devil—" and set "free those who all their lives were held in slavery by their fear of death" (Heb. 2:14–15). "Having disarmed the powers and authorities, he made a public spectacle of them, triumphing over them by the cross" (Col. 2:15). The Cross, where Satan did his worst, proved to be his downfall. When Jesus cried out, "It is finished!" He was declaring the completion of His passion for our redemption and of His decisive victory to be fulfilled in the resurrection over death and the forces of darkness headed by Satan.

By the fourth century, Christ's descent into hell at His death was added to the Apostles' Creed as part of the church's confession of faith. Indeed, the New Testament does speak of a descent of Christ at His death into *hadēs* (Acts 2:27) and the abyss (*abussos,* Rom. 10:7). These ancient terms were not just symbols of death per se, but of death in relation to the plight of the lost (e.g., Rev. 20:1–3,14). Hence, it would seem that Christ did descend into hell at His death to proclaim the victory of the Cross over the forces of darkness. It may be that Ephesians 4:9 and 1 Peter 3:18–20 refer to the same event.[58] But we must be cautious not to fantasize about battles

---

[57] G. Aulen, *Christus Victor, an Historical Study of the Three Main Types of the Idea of the Atonement,* trans. A. G. Hebert (New York: Macmillan, 1969).

[58] In favor of viewing Eph. 4:9 as implying Christ's descent into the demonic underworld is Donald Bloesch, "Descent into Hell," *Evangelical Dictionary of Theology,* ed. W. Elwell (Grand Rapids: Baker Book House, 1984), 313–15. Also supportive of this view is Markus Barth, *Ephesians 4–6, The Anchor Bible,* eds. W. F. Albright, D. N. Freedman (Garden City, N.Y.: Doubleday, 1960), 477. An example of an opposing view claiming that this text refers to the Incarnation is J. M. Robinson, "Descent into Hades," *Interpreter's Dictionary of the Bible,* ed. G. A. Buttrick, et. al., vol. 1 (Nashville: Abingdon, 1962), 826–28.

With regard to 1 Peter 3:18–20, note Bo Reicke's excellent discussion in *The Epistle of James, Peter, and Jude, The Anchor Bible* (Garden City, N.Y.: Doubleday, 1974), 109; 138, n. 37. According to Bo Reicke, Peter

between Jesus and demons in hell, since Christ completed His work of redemption on the cross.[59] We should also avoid claiming that Christ won the keys of hell and death from Satan, since Jesus received all authority from the Father (Matt. 28:18). Jesus' descent into hell to proclaim the victory of the Cross is meaningful as a sign to all that there is no dimension of evil or darkness outside of the reach of the Cross.

On the Day of Pentecost, the same Spirit of God by which Jesus defeated the forces of darkness was transferred to the Church. In the power of the Spirit, the Church could continue Jesus' ministry of "doing good and healing all who were under the power of the devil" (Acts 10:38). The Book of Acts contrasts the liberating power of the Spirit with the magical or superstitious acts that seek to control demonic power (e.g., 19:13–16). Discernment of spirits and healing were to be a part of the multiplicity of gifts in the body of Christ (1 Cor. 12:9–10) in anticipation of Christ's return (1 Cor. 1:7). Though Christ's death and resurrection dealt a fatal blow to Satan, he is still able to prowl like a lion looking for prey (1 Peter 5:8).

---

describes Christ's proclamation in the underworld to the evil rulers from the time of Noah as an example to the Church. If Christ proclaimed His victory even to the rebellious rulers of this the most wicked generation, how much more should the Church preach to ruling authorities of its day who may yet repent. The phrase "through whom" of 1 Peter 3:19 (*en hō*) should be translated "on which occasion," associating the preaching to the spirits in prison with the time of Christ's death. But there is no implication here that such a proclamation actually grants those in hell a chance to repent, leading to the possibility of universalism.

In the early centuries there was some disagreement as to whether *hadēs* into which Christ descended was the realm where lost souls were held captive by the forces of darkness or, on the basis of an interpretation of Luke 16, "Abraham's bosom" (KJV). Similarly, many Catholics formerly taught that Christ descended into the *limbus patrum,* a resting place for Old Testament saints, to proclaim His work of redemption. This view is no longer held by the Catholic Church. At any rate, *hadēs* and *abussos* imply connections with the realm of darkness as noted above. See J. B. Russell, *Satan, the Early Christian Tradition* (Ithaca, N.Y.: Cornell University Press, 1981), 117.

[59]Also to be avoided is the teaching of E. W. Kenyon, who took the fact that "God made him [Jesus] who had no sin to be sin for us" (2 Cor. 5:21) to mean Jesus became a sinner and had to be born again in hell to save us. But 2 Corinthians 5:21 surely refers to Christ's substitutionary death for us on the cross. Jesus, who knew no sin, became a sin offering for our redemption (the Hebrew word for sin may mean "sin offering"). Even Calvin's view that the descent into hell completed the work of Atonement must be rejected. Jesus' work of redemption on the cross was complete even without the descent into hell, which was only to proclaim the victory of the cross. Jesus died with the cry " 'It is finished!' " (John 19:30).

The devil hindered Paul's missionary work (2 Cor. 12:7; 1 Thess. 2:18). He blinds the minds of the unbelieving (2 Cor. 4:4) and throws "flaming arrows" against the redeemed in their efforts to serve God (Eph. 6:16).

CHAPTER 6

Created Spirit Beings

One's defense and victory is in submitting to God and resisting the deception of the enemy (James 2:19). Notice that the victory comes first by submitting to God or by focusing on the riches of God's grace and the demands of obedience that this grace implies. There can be no resistance to the enemy without this. In this way alone, God's people can be "strong in the Lord, and in the power of his might" (Eph. 6:10, KJV) and wear the whole armor of God (truth, righteousness, faith, salvation, prayer, and the Word of God), using the shield of faith to extinguish those "flaming arrows" (6:11–17). The empty tomb and the witness of the Holy Spirit are guarantees that final victory belongs to God. Though Satan will try to make a final stand against God, the attempt will be futile (2 Thess. 1:9–12; Rev. 19:7–10). The final victory belongs to God!

GOD'S SOVEREIGNTY AND DENYING THE ENEMY

How could God, as the sovereign Lord, permit such satanic opposition to exist? Why must the final defeat of satanic forces be delayed until God's sovereign lordship can conquer them through the triumph of Christ and a Church empowered by the Spirit? One cannot answer such questions by stating that God is powerless to do anything more than wait, as though God is caught in a dualistic battle with the god of evil and has no hope of victory without our help.[60] As noted above, this dualism would contradict what the Scriptures maintain about the absolute sovereignty of God. Neither can we answer such questions by stating that the satanic opposition and destruction are part of God's will for humanity, as though all of reality were a monism determined exclusively by God and without any sense of genuine conflict by opposing forces of

---

[60]Dualism came from Persian Zoroastrianism and was present in the east and the west through such heresies as Manichaeism. The latter influenced St. Augustine (354–430) early in life. He came to resist dualism, however, with an accent on the sovereignty of God and with the belief that evil is "privation," or the lack of good. Since evil is also a destructive force, St. Augustine went too far in merely making it the lack of good in his effort to avoid dualism.

evil.[61] This monism would contradict what has been noted about the genuine opposition between the forces of darkness and the sovereign Lord's love and redemptive purposes for humanity. Such questions have to do with "theodicy" (justifying God in the face of evil and suffering). It is not possible to introduce the complexities of this problem in the context of this chapter, but a few words of explanation are in order.[62]

Historically, the Church has stressed two related points relevant to a biblical orientation for dealing with the above questions. The first is the fact that God has created humanity with the freedom to rebel and become vulnerable to satanic opposition. God has allowed satanic opposition to exist to test humanity's free response to God. Second, God wills to triumph over satanic opposition, not only for believers, but also through them. Therefore, the triumph of God's grace has a history and a development. This triumph is not dependent primarily on human cooperation for its progress and accomplishment, but in its strategic fulfillment it does include the history of humanity's faithful response to God.

In the strategic accomplishment of redemption in history, God's allowance of satanic opposition is provisional and is not part of God's redemptive will for humanity. To the contrary, God's redemptive will is determined to triumph over all satanic opposition. God is not secretly behind the works of Satan, though God may use such to accomplish redemption. But there is no common ground between Satan and God. Satan has no continuity with God's redemptive will for humanity. God is clearly on the side of liberation and redemption from all that destroys and oppresses. This does not answer all questions about the how's and why's of evil and suffering in the world. The difficulty with philosophical solutions such as dualism and monism is that they seek to grant a final intellectual answer to the problem of evil. Ultimately, however, there is no such answer to the question of evil. But the gospel does grant a person hope and assurance of final redemption in Christ, and grants also the call to courageously battle by the grace of God toward its fulfillment.

_____

[61]Monism was held, for example, by the German philosopher Gottfried Wilhelm Leibnitz (1646–1716), who argued that all of reality is ultimately one: God. Evil is only shadows that accent God's artistic tapestry of creation, the mere consequence of the necessary limitation of finite reality.

[62]Note, J. Hick, *Evil and the God of Love* (New York: Collins World, Fount, 1977), and P. S. Shilling, *God and Human Anguish* (Nashville: Abingdon, 1977).

DEMONOLOGY AND HUMAN RESPONSIBILITY

CHAPTER

6

Created
Spirit
Beings

In a dualistic worldview, as noted above, God is not sovereign, nor is there any guarantee in such a philosophy that God will have the final victory. Such a worldview also eliminates human freedom and responsibility. This is so because, in a dualistic understanding, people become mere pawns in the battle between the gods of good and evil. Everything that happens in human life is due to one absolute power (good) or the other (evil) manipulating human events in their war with each other. Human decisions play no role in the fate of humanity. Hence, dualistic religions tend to be overly preoccupied with demonology.[63]

The sovereignty of God over the forces of evil actually serves to free humanity from such insignificance, so that people play a decisive role in human fate. In the Genesis account of the creation and fall (Genesis 1 through 3), the tempter could thwart God's will only to the degree that Adam and Eve freely chose to cooperate. This was so because God and not the tempter was the sovereign Lord. Hence, sin and death became the indirect result of Satan's work, but they were the direct result of human actions. Adam and Eve, not Satan, brought sin and death upon the world. Sin and death are aspects of human bondage, the human condition apart from God. It is human disobedience that has created this condition and it is human disobedience that maintains it. Satan is indeed the tempter (1 Thess. 3:5), but each person is tempted when, "by his own evil desires, he is dragged away and enticed" (James 1:14). Satan is the liar (John 8:44), the accuser (Rev. 12:10), the thief, and the murderer (John 10:10). Yet, he can fulfill none of these acts in creation without human participation, even initiative. A heavy accent on the role of demons in our view of what opposes God tends to evade human responsibility and to denigrate the sovereignty of God. One must correct this emphasis in order to give human responsibility the weight it should have in one's understanding of evil.

Note that the New Testament places sin and death as enemies in their own right alongside the forces of darkness (Rom. 8:1–2; 1 Cor. 15:24–28; Rev. 1:18). It is indeed interesting that Paul makes death, not Satan, the final enemy to be destroyed (1 Cor. 15:24–26). It is also worth noting that the Bible does not view the opposition to God solely in the con-

---

[63]This was the case, for example, with Persian Zoroastrianism.

text of demonology. Jesus claimed that the human opposition to His ministry fulfilled the works of the devil (John 8:44). Later, Paul would say that the "ruler of the kingdom of the air" is at work through "those who are disobedient" (Eph. 2:2). This does not mean that all disobedience to God is a response to direct demonic temptation. But it does mean that the kingdom of darkness is served, and its purposes are accomplished, through human disobedience. Hence, such disobedience and bondage to sin and death should receive proper attention in any discussion of what opposes God's will.

All of the above implies that there is an essentially human dimension to our personal and social ills and that human, scientific solutions must be allowed to play a legitimate role in the healing process. It must be admitted that the sciences have led to an understanding of the genuinely human dimension of individual and social problems, as well as the kinds of strategies that may be used to solve them. There is nothing necessarily contrary to the Scriptures in much of this, since the Bible, as we have noted, recognizes our fallen condition as a legitimately human condition apart from any consideration of direct demonic influence. In the Church one must be open to modern medical, psychiatric, and sociological insights in one's efforts to represent a healing and liberating force in the world. God heals and delivers through both extraordinary and ordinary means, or both miraculously and providentially. One dare not label all problems as demonic and advocate the illusion that they may all be solved by casting out demons!

Furthermore, many of the symptoms described by the Bible as demonic do parallel symptoms that have been isolated today as pathological and human. This makes distinguishing between demonic possession and pathological conditions among tormented individuals a delicate and complex task. But the Bible does distinguish between illness and demonic possession (Mark 3:10–12). So today, one must distinguish between psychiatric cases and possible demonic possession. This distinction is important, since, as Catholic theologian Karl Rahner pointed out, exorcisms of pathological patients may actually aggravate their delusions and make their condition more acute.[64] When possible, prayerful and scientific

---

[64]Rahner's view is discussed in J. P. Newport, "Satan and Demons: A Theological Perspective," in *Demon Possession, a Medical, Historical, Anthropological, and Theological Symposium,* ed. J. W. Montgomery (Minneapolis: Bethany Fellowship, 1976), 342.

discernment of the utmost care by qualified persons should be utilized in ministry to tormented individuals. Even cases that involve demonic influences may also require psychiatric attention.

The simplistic denial of the demonic as merely mythological, however, leaves one completely unable to explain or to cope with the depth of despair implied in human madness and evil, even where no direct demonic influence is involved. There is indeed a depth of despair implied in such distorted human behavior that transcends scientific or rational definitions. The scientific mind wishes that it can so neatly define this distortion that one can be done with it once and for all. But pathological behavior continues to plague humanity again and again, mystifying everyone. Even with the most descriptive disease categories, what more does one have but labels under which to cluster related symptoms? As helpful as these categories may be, do they solve the riddle of human existence that pathology seems to expose so forcefully? As the late German-American theologian Paul Tillich has noted, the category of the demonic serves to remind one of the depth and mystery involved in human distortion.[65]

Demonology in the light of the gospel of Christ Jesus can grant us the key to the mystery of evil mentioned above. As we noted above, the victory of Christ in His life, death, and resurrection clarified the conflict between God's redemptive will and the forces of darkness at the origin of evil. Yet Paul still used the term "mystery" to characterize the power of lawlessness at work in the world (2 Thess. 2:7). What is important to note is that the full disclosure of this depth of evil, termed "the demonic," is eschatological. Paul implies that the very last days of this age will include an increase in the disclosure of evil in the world through the appearance of "lawless one . . . whom the Lord will overthrow with the breath of his mouth and destroy by the splendor of his coming" (2 Thess. 2:8). This Antichrist figure will lead an emergence of evil in the latter days. God's final eschatological judgment over evil in the lake of fire will fully disclose the forces of darkness at the root of evil in the world (Rev. 20:10). At that time, the devil, death and *hadēs* will fall prey to the eschatological judgment of God (20:10,14). Though this lake of

---

[65]Though Tillich did not believe in demons as literal beings, he did understand the category of the demonic and its significance for theology. Note P. Tillich, *The Interpretation of History*, trans. R. A. Rasetzki, E. L. Talmey (New York: Scribner, 1936).

fire is understandably feared by people, it is actually meant by God to be a friend to humanity, i.e., the final destroyer of humankind's worst and ultimate enemies.

Only in God's final, eschatological judgment will the nature of the demonic and its connection with death and *hadēs* be fully disclosed. At that time, the mystery of iniquity will be revealed in the full depth of its resistance to God and God's redemptive will. Only then will the opposition and conflict be fully clarified. If the first coming of Christ brought the conflict with evil to clarity, it was only a penultimate clarity, for ultimate clarity must await His second coming. In this present age, to discern evil and suffering aright requires spiritual discernment in the light of the scriptural witness as well as careful scientific evaluation. At the final triumph of God over the devil, however, the ultimate root and nature of evil will be obvious, stripped naked of all of its disguises by the final judgment of God. This judgment has already been initiated by the cross and resurrection of Christ. It will be fulfilled in the final triumph of Christ in the *eschaton.*

The eschatological nature of the final disclosure and judgment of evil implies that the repudiation of Satan and his works is not a mythological "demonization" of human personal and social ills and a consequent flight from the careful discernment required to isolate and cure such problems. Eschatological, especially apocalyptic, movements that focus on the final judgment of God over the forces of darkness are tempted to reduce all present struggles with human evils to a struggle with the demonic. If complex and ambiguous human realities that seem threatening or alien to us are demonized in this way, then an arrogant ethical dualism is created, whereby we are in total light and others are in total darkness.

Demonology, properly conceived, will not cause one to deny the present human dimensions of evil and its effects, with all of their ambiguities and complexities. We will often be capable of discovering in ourselves elements of the evil that we resist, and we will often find elements of the desired good in others whom we are tempted to regard as enemies. We cannot simply reduce our struggle against human forces of evil and oppression to a struggle against demons. But our repudiation of Satan and his works in our struggles against godlessness and social oppression does set these struggles against the horizon of God's ultimate victory over the forces of darkness when the kingdom of God is fulfilled at the final end of all things. Repudiating the devil in our resistance to human evil and oppression implies that there is something deeper and more profound at stake than simply personal or social reform. At stake is the eschatological breaking in of the kingdom of God to undermine this present world's systems and to introduce by the Spirit of God a world-to-come patterned after the love of God revealed in Christ.

THE PLACE OF SATAN AND DEMONS IN CHRISTIAN THEOLOGY

Is there a legitimate place for demonology in Christian theology? Is there a legitimate basis for including a reference to the demonic in the Church's confessions of faith? Certainly to "believe in" the devil is not appropriate language for the Christian's creed. In the Christian creed, one's belief is in *God* and one's *repudiation* is of the devil and of all human forces of oppression that serve the cause of evil. But what kind of emphasis does one give this repudiation of Satan in Christian confession?

The poet Howard Nemerov stated, "I should be very chary in talking about the Devil, lest I be thought to be invoking him."[66] Karl Barth stated that he would give only a quick, sharp "glance" to the area of demonology. The glance must be "quick," lest he grant more weight and attention than is absolutely necessary to the demonic.[67] Theology for Barth was to be dominated by the grace of God revealed in Christ. But the glance must be "sharp," because the demonic is not to be taken lightly. Unfortunately, in Pentecostal and charismatic movements spiritual warfare and deliverance ministries abound, giving deliberate attention to the realm of the demonic. Many advocates of such ministries clearly transgress the legitimate place that the biblical message gives to the demonic. There seems to be a certain fascination with the realm of the demonic in such ministries, resulting in far more attention being paid to the demonic than the Bible supports.

Indeed, a certain glory and legitimacy are granted to the devil in such ministries. The devil is often referred to as the exclusive or, at least, dominant element in all opposition to

---

[66] Quoted in D. G. Kehl, "The Cosmocrats: The Diabolism in Modern Literature," in *Demon Possession, a Medical, Historical, Anthropological, and Theological Symposium,* ed. J. W. Montgomery (Minneapolis: Bethany Fellowship, 1976), 111.

[67] Note Barth's discussion in *Church Dogmatics,* 3:2: 599; 3:3: 519; 4:3: 168–71. The only difficulty is in his reference to the demonic as "nothingness," which seems contrary to his overall insistence that demonic forces represent genuine opposition to God's work of redemption.

God's redemptive purpose for humanity. God's whole redemptive activity is narrowed to destroying the devil, so that
soteriology, Christology, pneumatology, and all other areas
of theology, are discussed almost exclusively in the light of
fighting demons! Without the devil, such preaching and theologizing would be left an empty shell! In such a context, demonology competes quite well with God and all other areas
of theology, demanding and achieving equal or even greater
attention. R. Gruelich maintains that novelist Frank Peretti
has granted artistic support for such a theological distortion
by viewing the world and human destiny as dominated by
the results of warfare with demons.[68]

In such a context, demonology is granted a glory and theological significance beyond biblical boundaries. In such a
vision of reality, it is believed that the horizon of the Christian's world is filled with dangers of demonic attack and conquest at every turn. The grotesque form of this belief is found
in the assumption that demons can possess and dominate
Christians who are disobedient or in greater need of deliverance. To harmonize this assumption with the clear biblical
teaching that Christians belong to Christ and are directed in
life primarily by God's Spirit (e.g., Rom. 8:9–17), an unbiblical
dichotomy is made between body and soul, allowing God to
possess the soul, while demons control the body.[69] But the
Bible teaches that a loyalty so radically divided is an impossibility for the person of true faith (Matt. 7:15–20; 1 Cor.
10:21; James 3:11–12; 1 John 4:19–20).

The glorification of demons in the Christian world is paralleled by a similar tendency in culture. Humanity has always
had a certain fascination with the sinister and the demonic.
Maximilian Rudwin stated, for example, that the figure of
Satan "looms large in literature." He adds, "Sorry, indeed,
would the plight of literature be without the Devil."[70] The
history of occult practices has fed on the fascination of humanity with the realm of the demonic. Indeed, the rise of

---

[68]R. Guelich, "Spiritual Warfare: Jesus, Paul, and Peretti," *Pneuma,* 13:1
(Spring 1991): 33–64.

[69]Arguing that demons can possess the body of a Christian is, for example,
Derek Prince, *Expelling Demons* (Ft. Lauderdale, Fl.: Derek Prince Pub.,
n.d.). For an opposing view, note Opal Reddin, ed., *Power Encounter: A
Pentecostal Perspective* (Springfield, Mo.: Central Bible College Press, 1989),
269–77.

[70]M. Rudwin, *The Devil in Legend and Literature,* 272–73, cited in D.
G. Kehl, "The Cosmocrats," 109.

modern scientific thinking has had little effect on this fascination. The second half of the twentieth century has witnessed a resurgence of interest in the demonic and the occult.
The horror movie industry has grown even more outlandish
in its demonic imagery than in its financial profits. Movies
such as *The Exorcist, Poltergeist,* and *The Omen* series are
early examples of a number of films that have attempted to
reveal the inability of science and the Church to understand
or cope with evil spirits. They present stories in which the
demonic elements, often confused with the souls of departed
persons, dominate the flow of events. The grace of God is
absent or weak at best. Even the "happy" endings come as
more of a surprise than the demonic victories that preceded
them.

Surely such a fascination with the demonic is not healthy
or biblical. The fascination of Jesus' disciples with their authority over demons was countered by Jesus' admonition not
to rejoice in power over demons but to rejoice rather in
God's calling the disciples by name (Luke 10:17–20). The
opposition of Satan to the gospel can be understood only in
the prior light of that gospel itself. The real depth of evil can
be understood only in the light of the depth of God's grace
that evil opposes and seeks to destroy. The real tragedy of
darkness can be understood only in the context of the glories
of God's light. The accent of the New Testament is on the
glory of God and life with God, not on the attempts of the
enemy to oppose them.

Among Christians, the tendency to emphasize the role of
Satan has even led at times to a willingness to legitimize his
position and role over against God, as though Satan had a
rightful claim to persons and governments, as though his
position as "god of this age" should be respected by people,
even by God! Contrary to what some might think, there is in
Jude 9 no respect for Satan in the angelic hesitation to bring
a slanderous accusation against him. The angel Michael held
back any accusation based on his own authority in order to
say, "The Lord rebuke you!" This means that any rejection
of Satan's deceptive claims can come only from God's authority and God's grace, not from one's own self-generated
wisdom or authority.

Actually, a notion of satanic rights was supported by the
ransom theory of the Atonement advocated by certain early
and medieval Latin theologians of the West and by Origen in
the East. This theory assumed that Satan had a right to govern
and oppress humanity because of human rebellion against

**CHAPTER
6**

Created
Spirit
Beings

God. Christ was sent to pay Satan a ransom for the release of humanity. This ransom theory, however, eliminates from the beginning any real opposition between God and Satan. Assumed is God's acceptance of Satan's position and role and God's willingness to deal with Satan on Satan's terms. Satan is allowed to have his own legitimate place apart from God's redemptive purpose, a place that God must respect in God's effort to redeem humanity!

Over against this ransom theory is the biblical teaching that Satan's position and role are based on a lie (John 8:44). They have no legitimacy that God must recognize and to which God must conform! The triumph of God's grace over the forces of darkness grants no respectful and legitimate place to their role and claims. Satan, as "god of this age," has an illegitimate position granted to him by humanity's own spiritual blindness and rebellion (2 Cor. 4:4). A "payment" was indeed made by Christ on the cross, not to Satan, but to God on humanity's behalf.[71]

Our wisest response to the false, deceptive claims of Satan is to deny them, and to do so only through the quick, sharp "glance" that the theologian Karl Barth gave them in the greater light of God's truth and grace. But there seems to be a hidden assumption by many in the deliverance ministries that Satan is really defeated by those who know him best. In other words, the more mystery one can remove about demons, the more one can control and defeat them. Deliverance is understood here as the result of a secret knowledge (*gnōsis*) that others outside the deliverance movement do not share. Elaborate speculations are offered about the organization and characteristics of demons and how they relate to human governments and individual lives. Elaborate practices of "binding" the demonic powers are practiced once their true positions and functions in the world have been understood.

Yet, one is struck when reading the Bible by the total absence of such speculations and practices. The Bible encourages withstanding and resisting the deceptive forces of darkness, not studying and binding them.[72] There is no effort in the Bible to make us better acquainted with the devil. The

---

[71]A few who advocated the ransom theory even implied that God "tricked" the devil into accepting a ransom that would destroy him and his demons. In other words, the devil's right to the world is upheld while God wins the world back through a deceptive move! One might be amused by this theology, but it is hardly to be taken seriously from a biblical standpoint.

[72]Note R. Guelich, "Spiritual Warfare," 59.

sole focus is on getting better acquainted with God and the concomitant resistance to any of Satan's clamoring for our attention. Submitting to God and resisting the devil is the counsel from James (see James 4:7).

We are certainly not to ignore the devil. But any attention we grant to him must be in our denial of his claims and his works in the light of our focus on God's claims and God's works. The Bible does not speculate, or give much information, on Satan and demons. There is not much there to satisfy our curiosities. There are hints of a fall of Satan and demons from heaven (Jude 6; Rev. 12:7–9). Some have speculated that the Old Testament describes this fall in Isaiah 14:12–20, but the meaning of this passage is unclear, being perhaps no more than a poetic rebuke to the "king of Babylon" (14:4). The when and how of this fall are nowhere explicitly defined. The fact is that the Bible's purpose in dealing with Satan and demons is redemptive, not speculative. The focus is on affirming God's redemptive purpose and the power therefrom to deny the works and claims of Satan. The accent is not on gaining insight into Satan for the purpose of defeating him from the well of such knowledge!

Much discernment is needed in detecting what serves the kingdom of darkness and what does not, since Satan can mask himself as an angel of light (2 Cor. 11:14). His purposes are not only served where one expects (for example, in severe and utterly inexplicable cases of evil or torment), but often in what some may consider the most noble deeds and religious aspirations. Pride, idolatry, prejudice, and the most harmful phobias can surface in religiosity and patriotism and be defended by what may appear on the surface to be noble doctrines and practices. Slavery and racism, for example, have been defended by persons claiming to support the most noble religious and patriotic causes. Such sins only support the kingdom of darkness. Constant soul searching is necessary if the Church is to deny the works of the devil and affirm the renewal of the Spirit in and through the Church.

The scriptural witness provides us with definite sources of guidance for discerning the forces of evil and oppression. There is a Christological criterion and a basis in the Spirit of God for discerning evil. For example, if God created humanity in the divine image and laid claim to humanity in the birth, death, and resurrection of Christ, then any attempt to dehumanize anyone for any reason contradicts God's love for humanity and serves the forces of darkness. If the Spirit anointed Christ to preach good news to the poor, the blind, and the imprisoned (Luke 4:18), then those structures and forces that encourage poverty, sickness, and crime serve the forces of darkness. If Satan blinds the minds of the ungodly to the gospel (2 Cor. 4:4), then those things that discourage our gospel witness, both word and deed, to the needy also serve the forces of darkness.

The element of the demonic helps us to realize that human resistance to God has ultimate significance. Set against the horizon of the ultimate, eschatological victory of God's kingdom over the forces of darkness, present human obedience and disobedience to God are serious matters indeed. With each decision of the Christian life, believers must choose for God's kingdom and against the kingdom of darkness. Seeking first the kingdom of God and its righteousness constantly challenges the Christian. The choices may seem difficult and ambiguous at times. But the seriousness of the choice of obedience and the need for the comfort and forgiveness of God in all our choices must never be underestimated. The role the demonic plays in Christian theology and witness points to the seriousness of our choices.

STUDY QUESTIONS

1. Does demonology remove us from the real problems and evils of life? Explain how it could. Why is it meaningful to repudiate the devil and his works when resisting the forces of evil in life?

2. How is the Old Testament approach to demonology different from ancient pagan views of evil spirits? Discuss this in relation to God's sovereignty. In particular, does divine sovereignty mean that there is no real opposition between God and Satan in the Old Testament?

3. What truth can be found in the fact that the defeat of the forces of darkness was revealed in the New Testament only after the revelation of Christ as the incarnation of grace and truth?

4. Describe Christ's victory over the forces of darkness. Does this truth play any role in the apostolic proclamation of the gospel? Explain.

5. Describe the problems with philosophical dualism and monism. What is the biblical balance between God's sovereignty and the opposition of Satan to the purposes of God?

6. Does demonology eliminate human responsibility? Why or why not?

7. Can Christians be possessed by demons? Why or why not?

8. Are Satan's claims and accusations legitimate? Is he to be granted a legitimate right as god of this age? How has the ransom theory of the Atonement wrongly affirmed satanic claims and rights? What is wrong with such affirmations of satanic rights?

9. Do human and scientific insights into our problems have any legitimate place among believers? Why or why not?

10. Is there a certain fascination with the demonic in the Church and in culture? What is wrong with this? What is the real place of demonology in Christian theology?

CHAPTER

6

Created
Spirit
Beings

CHAPTER SEVEN

The Creation of the Universe and Humankind

Timothy Munyon

The Bible was written over a period of about fifteen hundred years by perhaps forty different writers. Yet God's saving activity, and humankind's response to it, seems to be a common thread woven through all of Scripture. Therefore, we will keep this motif in view as we approach the Bible's teaching on the creation of the universe and the nature of human beings.

THE CREATION OF THE UNIVERSE

The Scriptures clearly portray God as a purposeful Being. Proverbs 19:21 observes, "Many are the plans in a man's heart, but it is the LORD's purpose that prevails." God declares, "I make known the end from the beginning, from ancient times, what is still to come. I say: My purpose will stand, and I will do all that I please" (Isa. 46:10; cf. Eph. 3:10–11; Rev. 10:7).[1]

The study of creation must therefore seek to analyze God's purpose in creation (i.e., the universe is what it is because God is who He is[2]). And what is God's purpose in the creation of the universe? Paul explains, "He made known to us the mystery of his will according to his good pleasure, which he purposed in Christ, to be put into effect when the times will have reached their fulfillment—to bring all things in heaven

---

[1]Frank E. Gaebelein, ed., *The Expositor's Bible Commentary,* vol. 12 (Grand Rapids: Zondervan Publishing House, 1981), 497. He explains this mystery of Rev. 10:7 as God's "purposes for man and the world as revealed to both OT and NT prophets."

[2]H. Orton Wiley, *Christian Theology,* vol. 1 (Kansas City: Beacon Hill Press, 1940), 447.

CHAPTER
7
___

The
Creation
of the
Universe
and
Humankind

and on earth together under one head, even Christ" (Eph. 1:9–10).

Moreover, God's purpose for humanity is inseparable from His overall purposes for His creation (i.e., we human beings are what we are because God is who He is). The apostle Paul, in speaking of our future immortal existence with God, states, "It is God who has made us *for this very purpose* and has given us the Spirit as a deposit, guaranteeing what is to come" (2 Cor. 5:5).

There is an indissoluble unity, then, between the Bible's teachings about God, the creation of the universe, and the creation and nature of humankind. This unity stems from God's creative purpose. And God's purpose for His creation, and specifically for humanity, is captured by the familiar confession, "Man's chief end is to glorify God, and enjoy Him for ever."[3]

GOD AS THE CREATOR

The biblical writers unhesitatingly ascribe the creation of the universe to God. They deem it suitable, therefore, to reverently give Him glory and praise as the Creator.

Old Testament writers routinely attribute the creation of the physical universe to God with the word *bara'*, "he created." The opening verse of Scripture declares, "In the beginning God created the heavens and the earth" (Gen. 1:1). This succinct, summary statement anticipates the remainder of Genesis 1.[4] Introducing us to the subject of creation, Genesis 1:1 answers three questions: (1) When did creation take place? (2) Who is the subject of creation? (3) What is the object of creation?

Genesis 1:1 opens by emphasizing the fact of a real beginning, an idea avoided in most ancient and modern religions and philosophies. *"[B]ara'* . . . seems to carry the implication that the physical phenomena came into existence at that time and had no previous existence in the form in which they were created by divine fiat."[5] In other words, prior to this moment nothing at all existed, not even a hydrogen atom.

---

[3]See T. Vincent, *The Shorter Catechism Explained from Scripture* (Edinburgh: Banner of Truth Trust, 1980 from 1674), 13.

[4]Bruce K. Waltke "The Literary Genre of Genesis, Chapter One," *Crux* 27:4. (December 1991): 3.

[5]T. E. McComiskey, *" 'asa"* in *Theological Wordbook of the Old Testament,* vol. 2, R. Laird Harris, Gleason L. Archer, Jr. and Bruce K. Waltke, eds., (Chicago: Moody Press, 1980), 701.

Out of nothing (Latin *ex nihilo*), God created the heavens and the earth.

CHAPTER

7

The
Creation
of the
Universe
and
Humankind

According to Genesis 1:1, the subject of creation is "God." The word *bara'* in its most common Hebrew form is used only of God's activity, never of human "creative" activity.[6] Creation displays God's power (Isa. 40:26), majesty (Amos 4:13), orderliness (Isa. 45:18), and sovereignty (Ps. 89:11–13). As Creator, God should be recognized as omnipotent and sovereign. Anyone who abandons the biblical doctrine of creation diminishes the awe and reverence that are rightly due God for these attributes.

Genesis 1:1 informs us that God created "the heavens and the earth." In the Old Testament, "the heavens and the earth" comprise the entirety of the "orderly, harmonious universe."[7] Nothing exists that God did not create.

Old Testament writers also use the word *yatsar*, "form," "shape," to describe God's creative acts. For instance, this word aptly describes the "potter," someone who shapes, or forms, an object according to his will (Isa. 29:16). However, when used of divine agency,[8] the word appears to be employed in synonymous parallelism with *bara'*, indicating the same kind of divinely unique acts. Although we note that God "formed" the first man of the dust of the earth (i.e., He shaped the man from something that already existed), we would be taking this word beyond the Old Testament writer's intent to say *yatsar* opened the door to evolutionary processes.

Finally, Old Testament writers employ a third primary term when describing God's creative activity: *'asah*, "make." Like *yatsar* above, *'asah* generally has a much broader scope than the word *bara'*. However, when placed in a statement of creation parallel to *bara'* (Gen. 1:31; 2:2–3; 3:1; 5:1), there appears to be little difference in meaning between the two terms. Again, the term *'asah*, though at times broader in meaning than *bara'*, lacks sufficient flexibility to include the concept of evolution.

The New Testament writers were no less accustomed to

---

[6]Ibid., vol. 1, 127, *Bara'* everywhere ascribes creation to God (Gen. 1:27; 2:3; 5:1–2; Ps. 148:5; Isa. 42:5; 45:18) or calls Him Creator (Eccles. 12:1; Isa. 40:28).

[7]See Waltke, "Literary Genre," 3, where he indicates the Hebrew term "the heavens and the earth" is an example of what grammarians call a hendiadys, the use of two independent words connected by a conjunction to express one idea or concept (e.g., "old and gray" in 1 Sam. 12:2).

[8]Gen. 2:7,8,19; Ps. 95:5; Isa. 45:18; Jer. 33:2.

CHAPTER 7

The
Creation
of the
Universe
and
Humankind

ascribing creation to God than their Old Testament counterparts. We cannot disregard the Old Testament's teaching on creation (because of its supposed primitive scientific status) without at the same time doing violence to the New Testament teaching. In fact, the New Testament cites as authoritative the first eleven chapters of Genesis no less than sixty times.[9] Topics discussed in these passages include marriage, Jesus' lineage, human depravity, functional domestic roles, the Sabbath, our immortality, the future re-creation of the universe, and the removal of the curse in the eternal state. If the authority and facticity of Genesis' first eleven chapters fall, what are we to do with these doctrines in the New Testament?

It is evident that the New Testament writers viewed the Old Testament record as a reliable, factual account of what really happened. The primary New Testament term, *ktizō,* means "create," "produce," and occurs thirty-eight times when including derivatives. Colossians 1:16 affirms that by Christ all things were created, in heaven or on earth, visible or invisible. Revelation 4:11 finds the twenty-four elders laying their crowns before the Throne as an act of worship and ascribing creation to God. In Romans 1:25, Paul sadly observes that idolaters have "worshiped and served created things rather than the Creator—who is forever praised." Moreover, the New Testament, like the Old Testament, points to God's power as Creator as a source of comfort when we are suffering (1 Pet. 4:19); the same God still providentially superintends His creation.

Finally, the Bible proposes that God sustains, or maintains, the universe. The Levites, in ascribing praise to God, acknowledged that God gives life to everything (Neh. 9:6). In speaking of the starry host, Isaiah 40:26 states, "Because of his great power and mighty strength, not one of them is missing." The psalmist worships God because He preserves "both man and beast" (Ps. 36:6). Psalm 65:9–13 portrays God as governing the earth's meteorology and the production of grain.

In the New Testament, Paul states, "'In him we live and move and have our being'" (Acts 17:28). In Colossians 1:17 Paul affirms of Christ, "He is before all things, and in him all

---

[9]Matt. 19:4; 23:35; Mark 10:6; 13:19; Luke 3:38; 17:26; John 8:44; Acts 14:15; Rom. 5:12–19; 8:20–21; 1 Cor. 11:3,8–9; 15:21–22,45–49; 2 Cor. 11:3; Eph. 3:9; 5:31; Col. 1:16; Heb. 4:4; 11:4,7; James 3:9; 1 Pet. 3:10; 2 Pet. 3:6; 1 John 3:12; Rev. 22:3.

things hold together." Hebrews 1:3 declares that the Son is "sustaining all things by his powerful word." Numerous other Scripture passages point to God's direct superintendence and preservation of His creation.[10]

The triune God worked cooperatively in creation. Many Scripture passages attribute creation simply to God.[11] Other passages, however, specify Persons within the Godhead. Creation is attributed to the Son in John 1:3; Colossians 1:16–17; and Hebrews 1:10. Moreover, Genesis 1:2; Job 26:13; 33:4; Psalm 104:30; and Isaiah 40:12–13 include the Holy Spirit's participation in creation.

We may ask, Did the individual members of the Godhead perform specific roles during creation? Paul states, "There is but one God, the Father, from whom all things came and for whom we live; and there is but one Lord, Jesus Christ, through whom all things came and through whom we live" (1 Cor. 8:6). Millard J. Erickson, after a survey of creation passages, concludes, "Although the creation is *from* the Father, it is *through* the Son and by the Holy Spirit."[12] We would caution against accepting statements that are more specific than this.

The Scriptures are clear that God created everything that exists. As briefly mentioned earlier, the Bible employs the phrase "the heavens and the earth" to embrace all of creation, the entire universe. In fact, the "heavens" and the "earth" are sometimes set in parallel statements comprising all of creation. Finally, at times the word "heavens" is used by itself to refer to the entire universe.[13]

The New Testament writers use the term *kosmos,* "world," as a synonym of the Old Testament "heavens and earth," to embrace the entire universe. Paul seems to equate *kosmos* with "heaven and earth" in Acts 17:24. Many other New Testament passages refer to God's creation of the "world" and include the universe.[14]

Furthermore, the New Testament writers employed the term *ta panta,* "all things," to describe the scope of God's

---

[10]Pss. 104:30; 107:9; 145:15–16; 147:9; Matt. 5:45; 6:26; 10:29; John 5:17.

[11]Gen. 1:1; Ps. 96:5; Isa. 37:16; 44:24; 45:12; Jer. 10:11–12.

[12]Millard J. Erickson, *Christian Theology* (Grand Rapids: Baker Book House, 1985), 373.

[13]Gen. 1:1; 2:1,4; 2 Kings 19:15; 1 Chron. 16:26; Pss. 8:3; 19:1; 33:6; 96:5; 102:25; 113:6; 136:5–6; Prov. 3:19; Isa. 42:5; 45:12,18; 51:13,16; Jer. 10:11; 32:17; Acts 4:24; Heb. 1:10; 2 Pet. 3:10; etc.

[14]Matt. 25:34; Luke 11:50; John 17:5,24; Rom. 1:20; Eph. 1:4; Heb. 4:3; 1 Pet. 1:20; Rev. 13:8; 17:8.

CHAPTER
7

The
Creation
of the
Universe
and
Humankind

creative activity (not always with the definite article). John 1:3 emphatically declares "all things" were made through the living Word. Paul speaks of Jesus Christ, through whom "all things" came (1 Cor. 8:6; see also Col. 1:16). Hebrews 2:10 speaks of God, for whom and through whom "everything" exists. Then, in the Book of Revelation, the twenty-four elders render worship unto God because He created "all things" (4:11; see also Rom. 11:36).

Finally, the New Testament writers support the concept of creation *ex nihilo,* "out of nothing," with declarative propositions. In Romans 4:17 Paul speaks of the God who "gives life to the dead and calls things that are not as though they were." Also, Hebrews 11:3 declares, "By faith we understand that the universe was formed at God's command, so that what is seen was not made out of what was visible."

In summary, the Bible affirms that God created the entire universe. Everything "not-God" that exists owes its existence to the Creator. For this reason, the historic Church has upheld the doctrine of *ex nihilo* creation.

THE PURPOSE OF GOD'S CREATIVE ACTIVITY

Creation was an act of God's free will. He was free to create or not to create.[15] Creation communicated God's goodness in a gracious act. Genesis 1 indicates that all of God's creative acts led up to the creation of Adam and Eve. Genesis 1 shows correspondence between days 1 and 4, 2 and 5, and 3 and 6. Days 1 and 2 each describe one creative act, and day 3 describes two distinct acts. Days 4 and 5 describe what are actually one creative act each, while day 6 describes two distinct creative acts. Progress and climax can be seen leading to the creation of humankind. All this shows God created according to a plan, which He carried out to its completion. This encourages us to believe He will carry out His plan of redemption to its consummation in the return of Jesus Christ. A relationship existed between grace and nature in those created and God's providential order.

In other words, God had an eternal, saving plan for His creature, and creation progresses toward this ultimate purpose. Prior to the creation of the universe, God purposed to

---

[15]Miley opposes those who contend that since God is good, and since it is good to create, God had a moral obligation to create. See John Miley, *Systematice Theology,* vol. 1 (Peabody, Mass.: Hendrickson Publishers, 1989), 296–97; also see R. A. Muller, *God, Creation, and Providence in the Thought of Jacob Arminius* (Grand Rapids: Baker Book House, 1991), 230.

CHAPTER
7

The
Creation
of the
Universe
and
Humankind

have people fellowshipping with Him in a covenant relationship (2 Cor. 5:5; Eph. 1:4). Thomas Oden observes, "The real story concerning creation is about the creature/Creator relationship, not about creatures as such as if creation were to be considered an autonomous, independent, underived value in itself."[16]

God had a Kingdom prepared for those who would respond to Him since (or "before") the creation of the world (Matt. 25:34). God's eternal purpose for His creation was accomplished through the mediating work of Jesus Christ (Eph. 3:10–11), also planned before creation (Rev. 13:8). This divine, eternal purpose will be consummated "when the times will have reached their fulfillment" (Eph. 1:10). Then, everything will be under one head, Jesus Christ. This passage provides us with the true end, or purpose, of creation: "that God should be known."[17]

In reflecting on that moment when God's purpose for His creation is fulfilled, Paul writes, "I consider that our present sufferings are not worth comparing with the glory that will be revealed in us" (Rom. 8:18). He then points out how all creation groans, while waiting eagerly for that moment (8:19–22). In fact, despite the blessings believers have received, they too groan as they wait eagerly for that event (8:23–25). But in the meantime, "We know that in *all things*[18] God works for the good of those who love him, who have been called according to his purpose" (Rom. 8:28).

Since all of creation points to God's saving purpose, we would expect to find in that divine purpose a provision for a salvation sufficient for the whole of humankind, including a universal call to salvation. God's saving purposes also resulted in the creation of a creature with a free will.[19]

---

[16]Thomas C. Oden, *The Living God* (San Francisco: Harper & Row, Publishers, 1987), 198–99, 233. Also Walter C. Kaiser, Jr., *Toward an Old Testament Theology* (Grand Rapids: Zondervan Publishing House, 1978), 264–65.

[17]Charles Hodge, *Systematic Theology,* vol. 1 (New York: Charles Scribner's Sons, 1887), 568.

[18]Gk. *panta,* all things in heaven and earth. See pp. 215–16, 218.

[19]Muller, *Arminius,* 234, 257–58; *The Writings of James Arminius,* trans. J. Nichols and W. R. Bagnall, vol. 1 (Grand Rapids: Baker Book House, reprint 1977), 70, where Arminius says "the end of providence" points to, among other things, "the good of the whole." Also see p. 251, where providence is defined as God's evincing "a particular concern for all his [intelligent] creatures without any exception." See also vol. 2, 487.

CHAPTER
7
─────
The
Creation
of the
Universe
and
Humankind

As a natural corollary to God's "very good"[20] creative work, creation irresistibly brings glory to God (Pss. 8:1; 19:1).[21] The Scriptures also say that through the creation and establishment of the nation of Israel God would receive glory (Isa. 43:7; 60:21; 61:3). By extension, then, the New Testament affirms that all who avail themselves of God's plan will "be for the praise of his glory" (Eph. 1:12,14). Colossians 1:16 likewise affirms, "All things were created by him and for him." Furthermore, because of God's wondrous plan in creation, the twenty-four elders worship God and give Him the glory due His name (Rev. 4:11).

Finally, since God's purpose for His creation includes a time of consummation, we must bear in mind that this creation is transitory. Second Peter 3:10–13 describes a time when the heavens and the earth will dissolve, while Isaiah 65:17 and Revelation 21:1 speak of a new heaven and a new earth in fulfillment of God's plan.[22]

THE BIBLICAL COSMOGONY AND MODERN SCIENCE

Some Bible critics maintain that there is no way to reconcile the biblical cosmogony (the view of the origin and development of the universe) with what the scientific community acknowledges today. Some Bible scholars, taking numerous figures of speech in the Old Testament literally, contend that the Hebrews believed the universe comprised a flat earth supported by colossal "pillars" over a watery abyss, called "the deep." The "firmament" (sky)[23] above was a solid arch and held back the waters (which occasionally fell through "windows" in the arch) above the earth. Some posit that the Old Testament characters believed the sun, moon, and stars were all on the same plane in this arch over the earth.[24]

---

[20]"Good" meaning well-suited to what God intended. Compare this with the usage of "good" to describe when a basketball goes through a hoop. ("The throw was good.")

[21]See Donald G. Bloesch, *Essentials of Evangelical Theology* vol. 1 (New York: Harper & Row, Publishers, 1979), 38–40.

[22]See also Ps. 102:25–26; Isa. 13:10,13; 34:4; 51:6; Matt. 24:35; 2 Cor. 4:18; Rev. 20:11. See chap. 18, pp. 635–37.

[23]Actually, "firmament" translates the Hebrew *raqi'a,* which is better translated "expanse," and refers to the earth's atmosphere where the clouds float and the birds fly.

[24]W. White, "Astronomy," in *The Zondervan Pictorial Encyclopedia of the Bible,* M. Tenney, ed., vol. 1 (Grand Rapids: Zondervan Publishing Corporation, 1975), 395.

CHAPTER

7

The
Creation
of the
Universe
and
Humankind

H. J. Austel, reasoning against this overliteral interpretation of Old Testament passages, explains, "The use of such figurative language no more necessitates the adoption of a pagan cosmology than does the modern use of the term 'sunrise' imply astronomical ignorance. The imagery is often phenomenological, and is both convenient and vividly forceful."[25]

Even when figurative language is taken into account, however, some difficulties remain. Where do dinosaur fossils fit into the biblical cosmology? Is there any evidence for a global Flood just a few thousand years before Christ? Is the earth really 4.5 billion years old? Most evangelicals, convinced that God's world will agree with God's Word, seek answers to these and other penetrating questions.

Generally speaking, evangelical Christians follow one of four models that endeavor to provide a harmonization between God's special revelation (the Bible) and His general revelation (what we observe in the universe today). These views are (1) theistic evolution; (2) the gap theory, also called the ruin/reconstruction view; (3) fiat creationism, also called the young-earth theory; and (4) progressive creationism, also called the age-day theory.

We will briefly examine all of the above, except for theistic evolution. Studying theistic evolution serves no useful purpose here because its proponents basically accept everything secular evolution proposes with the proviso that God was superintending the whole process.[26] Proponents of theistic evolution typically deny that *yatsar* and *'asah* are used in parallel synonymity in creation accounts, but rather include the concept of evolution over aeons of time (see the discussion on p. 217).

Furthermore, in our discussion, certain generalizations are necessary. Even though one writer within a certain model does not accurately represent the consensus in every detail within that model, we may, for the sake of this survey, allow that writer to generally represent the whole. In truth, no single author agrees with all of the conclusions drawn by others who support the same general view. Finally, many authors do not specify the identity of their general model.

---

[25]H. J. Austel, *"shmh"* in *Theological Wordbook*, vol. 2, 935.

[26]For example, Oden argues, "Matter is created *ex nihilo* in a primary sense, radically given by God, but, as emergently developing through secondary causes . . . Once something is created out of nothing, then something else can be in due time created out of the prevailing and developing conditions," *The Living God* 265.

CHAPTER

7

———————

The
Creation
of the
Universe
and
Humankind

Theistic evolution aside for the moment, the other three views all agree that macroevolution, the transmutation of one type of organism into a more complex type of organism (i.e., evolution between species), has never taken place (such as a reptile changing into a bird, or a land mammal evolving into an aquatic mammal). However, all three views agree that microevolution, small changes within organisms (i.e., evolution within a species), has taken place (such as moths changing colors; the changing of beak lengths or plumage color in birds; or the variety we observe in human beings, all of whom descended from Adam and Eve). All three views agree that God should be worshiped as the Creator and that He supernaturally and without the interruption of any other cause or agency (by distinct, supernatural creative acts) created the genetic forebears of the major groups of plant and animal organisms we observe today. Finally, all three views agree that human beings derive their worth, or value, from being directly created in God's image. In the discussion that follows, the areas of agreement cited in this paragraph should be kept in the forefront.

The Gap Theory. Proponents of the gap theory contend that there was a "primitive creation" in the ageless past, referred to in Genesis 1:1. Isaiah 45:18 says, "This is what the LORD says—he who created the heavens, he is God; he who fashioned and made the earth, he founded it; he did not create it to be empty [Heb. *tohu*], but formed it to be inhabited." This verse, say gap theorists, proves that Genesis 1:2 cannot be taken to mean God's original creation was without form [Heb. *tohu*] and void, but was a good, created order containing uniformity, complexity, and life.[27]

Gap theorists propose that Satan, an archangel prior to his fall, ruled this pre-Adamic earth in what originally was a perfect reign.[28] Then Satan rebelled, together with the cities and nations of pre-Adamic people, at which time the earth (his domain) was cursed and destroyed by a flood (the remains of which are referred to in Genesis 1:2, "the face of the deep,"

---

[27]G. H. Pember, *Earth's Earliest Ages and Their Connection with Modern Spiritualism and Theosophy* (New York: Fleming H. Revell Co., 1876), 19–28. Also see F. J. Dake, *God's Plan for Man: The Key to the World's Storehouse of Wisdom* (Atlanta: Bible Research Foundation, 1949), 76. Other verses that gap theorists claim as support for a pre-Adamic period include Job 38; Pss. 8:3–8; 19:1–6; Prov. 8:22–31; John 1:3,10; Acts 17:24–26; Col. 1:15–18; Heb. 1:1–12; 11:3; Rev. 4:11.

[28]Isa. 14:12–14; Jer. 4:23–26; Ezek. 28:11–17; Luke 10:18; 2 Pet. 3:4–8. Pember, *Earth's Earliest Ages,* 36. Also see Dake, *God's Plan* 94, 118–24.

KJV). This verse points out that "the earth was without form, and void" (KJV). Arthur Custance contends that the phrase "without form and void" refers to a ruined, wasted void as a result of judgment and should therefore be rendered "a ruin and a desolation."[29]

Isaiah 24:1 and Jeremiah 4:23–26 are cited by gap theorists as evidence of this cataclysmic judgment of God (although these passages refer to future judgment). In the New Testament, Jesus' statement of Matthew 13:35, "from the foundation of the world" (KJV), is said to literally mean "from the overthrow of the world."[30] Second Peter 3:6–7 does not refer to Noah's flood (the context is said to be "the beginning of creation"), but refers to the first flood that destroyed the pre-Adamic world.[31]

Some proponents of the gap theory point to the Hebrew disjunctive accent *rebhia* introduced by medieval rabbis between Genesis 1:1 and 1:2 to indicate a subdivision.[32] Furthermore, the Hebrew conjunction *waw* can mean "and," "but," or "now." Gap theorists choose to read verse 2 as "The earth became without form and void," but they admit the Bible does not tell us how much time elapsed while the earth was in this chaotic state, or gap, between Genesis 1:1 and 1:2.[33] H. Thiessen says, "The first creative act occurred in the dateless past, and between it and the work of the six days there is ample room for all the geologic ages."[34]

The gap theorists claim, however, that eventually God began the creation process all over again in the neocreation, or reconstruction, of Genesis 1:3–31.[35] They also claim that the language of the "God created" passages allows for a re-creating or reshaping of the universe, and need not be restricted to a first-time event. Some gap theorists take the creative "days" as twenty-four-hour days. Others view the "days" of Genesis 1 as indefinitely long periods.

---

[29]Arthur C. Custance, *Without Form and Void: A Study of the Meaning of Genesis 1:2* (Brockville, Ontario: Doorway Publications, 1970), 116.

[30]Dake, *God's Plan,* 124. Actually, *katabolē* was used of sowing seed or making a down payment, as well as for "foundation" or "beginning." It is never used of overthrow. Usage, not derivation, determines meaning.

[31]Pember, *Earth's Earliest Ages,* 83.

[32]Custance, *Without Form,* 14.

[33]Ibid., 122, 124. Henry C. Thiessen, *Lectures in Systematic Theology* (Grand Rapids: Wm. B. Eerdmans, 1949), 164.

[34]Ibid.

[35]Pember, *Earth's Earliest Ages* 81. Dake, *God's Plan,* 134.

CHAPTER

7
_____

The
Creation
of the
Universe
and
Humankind

The wording of the KJV in Genesis 1:28, "Be fruitful, and multiply, and *replenish* the earth," is understood to suggest the earth had been full previously and now it required "re-filling."[36] Some point out that God employs the identical word when He commands Noah to "replenish" the earth in Genesis 9:1.

Moreover, the covenant in Genesis 9:13–15 (where God promises that "never again will the waters become a flood to destroy all life") could suggest that God had employed this form of judgment on more than one occasion.

Early human fossils, together with dinosaur fossils, are taken to be evidence of this pre-Adamic world. The note in Scofield's Bible explains, "Relegate fossils to the primitive creation, and no conflict of science with the Genesis cosmogony remains." G. H. Pember states:

Since, then, the fossil remains are those of creatures anterior to Adam, and yet show evident tokens of disease, death, and mutual destruction, they must have belonged to another world, and have a sin-stained history of their own, a history which ended in the ruin of themselves and their habitation.[37]

The gap theory has several weaknesses, however. The Hebrew language does not allow for a gap of millions or billions of years between Genesis 1:1 and 1:2. The language has a special form that indicates sequence and introduces that form beginning with 1:3. Nothing indicates sequence between 1:1 and 1:2. Therefore, 1:2 could well be translated, "Now [that is, at the time of the beginning] the earth was without form and empty of inhabitants."

Old Testament scholarship today generally recognizes that Genesis 1:1 functions as an introductory, summary statement of creation, upon which the rest of the chapter elaborates.[38] The verse does not describe a pre-Adamic world, but rather introduces the reader to the world that God created un-formed and unfilled. That is, God did not create the earth with its present form of continents and mountains, nor did He create it with people already on it. On days one through three, God gave form to His creation; on days four through

---

[36]Ibid., 118.

[37]C. I. Scofield, The Scofield Reference Bible: The Holy Bible (New York: Oxford University Press, 1909), 4, note 3. Pember, *Earth's Earliest Ages,* 35.

[38]Waltke, "Literary Genre," *Crux,* 3.

CHAPTER

7

The
Creation
of the
Universe
and
Humankind

six, God filled it. The rest of the Bible looks back on these days as creation, not re-creation.

Furthermore, the verbs *bara', yatsar,* and *'asah* are used in synonymous parallelism in various passages in Genesis and in other Bible books.[39] We must be cautious about assigning a vastly different meaning to any of these verbs simply because it better conforms to a certain harmonizing theory. Moreover, the KJV term "replenish" (1:28) does *not* mean "to refill" something that has already been filled previously; it simply means "to fill."[40] Also, the word "was" in verse 2 ("the earth was without form, and void") should not be translated "became" or "had become," as gap theorists contend.[41]

Finally, the gap theory is self-defeating. In relegating all fossil-bearing strata to the pre-Adamic world to harmonize Genesis 1 with the scientific data, there remains no evidence for a global, aqueous catastrophe in Noah's day. Custance, the most technical proponent of the gap theory in the second half of the twentieth century, noted this difficulty and opted for a local Flood in Mesopotamia and the surrounding vicinity.[42] However, Genesis 6:7,13,17; 7:19–23; 8:9,21; and 9:15–16 clearly say that the extent of the Flood was universal.

Fiat Creationism. Another viewpoint among evangelical Christians today is fiat creationism, also known as the young-earth theory. Proponents of fiat creationism contend that the Scriptures should be interpreted at face value whenever possible in order to arrive at the original author's truth-intention.[43] Therefore, fiat creationists maintain that a general calculation may be performed from the date of the building of the temple in 1 Kings 6:1 (966–67 B.C.) all the way back to the creation of Adam on day six of creation week. Even though the biblical writers may not have intended that a mathematical calculation of this nature be performed, because the Word of God is inerrant the results will be accurate nonetheless. These

---

[39]W. W. Fields, *Unformed and Unfilled* (Nutley, N.J.: Presbyterian and Reformed Publishing Co., 1976), 70–71.

[40]The KJV translates *male'* as "fill" about thirty-three times, including Gen. 1:22, and as "replenish" only twice.

[41]Fields, *Unformed,* 88–97. Verses cited by gap theorists to uphold the meaning "became" actually have a different Hebrew construction and context. Normally, when the word means "became," the Hebrew reads "was to" or uses an imperfect form.

[42]A. C. Custance, "The Flood: Local or Global?" *Doorway Papers No. 41* (Brookville, Ontario: Doorway Publications, 1989).

[43]J. C. Dillow, *The Waters Above: Earth's Pre-Flood Vapor Canopy,* 2d ed. (Chicago: Moody Press, 1981), 13.

CHAPTER

7

___

The
Creation
of the
Universe
and
Humankind

verses, then, seem to indicate the earth is no more than ten thousand years old at the most.[44]

Fiat creationists contend that God created the universe by divine fiat (a supernatural, immediate decree). He did not require millions or billions of years to accomplish His purpose. Proponents of this viewpoint say the creative days in Genesis 1 are to be taken as days in the commonly understood sense because that is the way the Hebrews understood the term. Exodus 20:11, explaining the rationale for keeping the Sabbath, states, "In six days the LORD made the heavens and the earth, the sea, and all that is in them, but he rested on the seventh day" (also see Mark 2:27). It is inconceivable, say fiat creationists, that God would have communicated this to Moses if, in fact, God's creative acts in Genesis 1 actually spanned billions of years.[45]

The vast ages arrived at through various forms of radiometric dating are challenged by fiat creationists on several grounds. First, the following assumptions of radiometric dating can never be proven: (1) that God did not create the earth with radioactive sites with daughter elements (elements that are also the product of radioactive decay) already present; (2) that the rate of radioactive decay has been constant for 4.5 billion years; and (3) that there has been no leaching of parent or daughter elements over 4.5 billion years. Second, recent work in the area of nuclear physics seems to put a question mark over Uranium-238 dating. And third, radiometric dating is unreliable because, depending on the method used, the earth can be "proven" to be anywhere from one hundred to millions of years old. Hence, the various methods are grossly incongruent with one another.[46]

Moreover, fiat creationists believe God created the entire biosphere in a mature, fully functioning state (with adult humans and animals; mature, fruit-producing trees; etc.), as well as the physical universe (the atmosphere, nutrient-rich

---

[44]Gen. 5:3–28; 6:1; 7:6; 11:10–26; 21:5; 25:26; 47:9; Exod. 12:40. Henry M. Morris, *The Biblical Basis of Modern Science* (Grand Rapids: Baker Book House, 1984), 260; J. C. Whitcomb and Henry M. Morris, *The Genesis Flood: The Biblical Record and Its Scientific Implications* (Philadelphia: Presbyterian and Reformed Publishing Co., 1961), 485.

[45]Morris, *Biblical Basis,* 117.

[46]Ibid., 261–62; Whitcomb, *Genesis Flood,* 334. R. V. Gentry, *Creation's Tiny Mystery,* (Knoxville: Earth Science Associates, 1986), 164. Morris, *Biblical Basis,* 477–80. Henry M. Morris and Gary E. Parker, *What Is Creation Science?* (San Diego, Calif.: Creation-Life Publishers, Inc., 1982), 252.

soil with dead organic matter in it, starlight already reaching the earth, etc.). Henry Morris calls this the state of "functioning completeness."[47] Therefore, even though fiat creationists concur that mutations (which are nearly always harmful) and horizontal variations (e.g., dog varieties) take place, they deny that macroevolution has ever occurred.

Finally, fiat creationists maintain that most or all of the fossil-bearing strata were deposited during and immediately following Noah's flood, while the waters were receding.[48] Noah's flood was a global, catastrophic event precipitated by the upsurging of subterranean water together with the collapse of a water-vapor canopy that at one time encircled the globe. Therefore, the fossil strata actually serve a theological purpose: (1) they are a silent testimony that God will not allow unrepentant sin to continue unchecked indefinitely, and (2) they testify that God has destroyed the entire world in an act of judgment in the past, and He certainly has the ability to do so in the future.[49]

The flood-deposition model requires that dinosaurs and modern humans walked the earth at the same time. However, human beings of that era may not have been aware of the existence of the dinosaurs (just as most people today have never seen a bear or a big cat in the wild). The dinosaurs were herbivorous prior to the Fall, as were all animals on the earth (Gen. 1:29–30; cf. 9:1–3). In God's ideal, future Kingdom, animals will not devour each other (Isa. 11:6–9; 65:25), possibly returning to their state prior to the Fall. Therefore, proponents of fiat creationism typically maintain that there was no death in God's "very good" creation prior to the fall of human beings in Genesis 3 (cf. Rom. 5:12–21; 1 Cor. 15:21–22).[50] Fiat creationists also point out that all old-earth models must explain the pre-Fall carnage of their model.

Fiat creationism, like all other views, has its share of problems. Some proponents of the young-earth theory, eager to

---

[47]Ibid., 274.

[48]Whitcomb, *Genesis Flood,* 116–17; 265, 291.

[49]The fossil distribution in the geological column is explained by three mechanisms: (1) pre-Flood ecological zonation (habitat elevation), (2) animal mobility, and (3) hydrodynamic sorting due to each organism's respective specific gravity. Morris, *Biblical Basis,* 361–62.

[50]Ibid., 123. Whitcomb, *Genesis Flood,* 455–56. Adam was given the task of taking care of the Garden (literally, "to work it and keep it"), which likely would have included trimming the vegetation; however, this would have resulted in cell death only, not human death.

CHAPTER
7
───────
The
Creation
of the
Universe
and
Humankind

buttress their argument with evidence, have a tendency to embrace findings uncritically. This was especially true a number of years ago. For instance, at one time fiat creationists publicized the so-called human footprints fossilized in the Paluxy riverbed in Texas. Later research by creationists called into question the identity of these footprints, and published materials about them were subsequently withdrawn.[51] Other similar examples have included some young-earth creationists' acceptance of a shrinking sun and a recent decaying of the velocity of the speed of light—by a factor of ten million.[52] In all fairness, much of the criticism and rejection of these purported young-earth evidences has come from within fiat creationism itself.

Another weakness of fiat creationism manifests itself in the tendency to employ an overly strict interpretation of Scripture. It does not recognize that Hebrew words can have more than one meaning, just as English words can. Nevertheless, some have used such methods to find support for young-earth tenets.[53] Another weakness, of course, is the marked disagreement with all forms of radiometric dating, as well as the rejection of nonradiometric data that seem to indicate an older earth.[54]

Progressive Creationism. The final model proposed by

───────

[51]These were featured in the film series *Origins: How the World Came to Be.* J. D. Morris, "Identification of Ichnofossils in the Glen Rose Limestone, Central Texas," in *Proceedings of the First International Conference on Creationism* (Pittsburgh: Creation Science Fellowship, 1986), 89–90.

[52]H. J. Van Till, D. A. Young, and C. Menninga, *Science Held Hostage: What's Wrong with Creation Science and Evolutionism* (Downers Grove, Ill.: InterVarsity Press, 1988), 47–48. Supported by T. Norman and B. Setterfield, "The Atomic Constants, Light, and Time," (Menlo Park, Calif.: SRI International, 1987). Denied by G. E. Aardsma, "Has the Speed of Light Decayed Recently?" *Creation Research Society Quarterly* 25 (June 1988): 40–41.

[53]For example, to produce evidence favorable to the pre-Flood coexistence of human beings and dinosaurs (a necessary tenet of fiat creationism), Henry Morris suggests the Hebrew word *tseph'oni* (which occurs in Prov. 23:32; Isa. 11:8; 59:5; Jer. 8:17 and is called *tsepha'* in Isa. 14:29) denotes a living fossil, perhaps a flying serpent (i.e., dinosaur?) of some kind. Morris, *Biblical Basis,* 359, 360. Hebrew scholars, on the other hand, consider *tsepha'* an onomatopoeic term (speaking the word makes a hissing sound not unlike that of a snake), appropriate to describe a snake, now identified as the Aegean viper *(Vipera xanthina).* William L. Holladay. *A Concise Hebrew and Aramaic Lexicon of the Old Testament* (Grand Rapids: Wm. B. Eerdmans, 1971), 310.

[54]Dan Wonderly, *God's Time-records in Ancient Sediments: Evidence of Long Time Spans in Earth's History* (Flint, Mich.: Crystal Press, 1977).

evangelicals is progressive creationism, or the age-day theory. Proponents of this model contend that the creative days of Genesis 1 connote overlapping periods of indeterminate time.[55] Progressive creationists typically point to passages in the Old Testament where "day" meant something broader than a literal, twenty-four-hour day. They note that the events of Genesis 2:7–23 included the naming of all the animals and birds, which took place on the latter part of the sixth "day." They believe God created various plant and animal prototypes during different, overlapping stages, from which the processes of microevolution have produced the variety of flora and fauna we observe today.

Typically, progressive creationists reject macroevolution and observe that scientists are increasingly questioning "the legitimacy of extrapolating microevolutionary observations to macroevolution." They recognize also that the genealogies of the Bible were not intended for the construction of an accurate chronology.[56]

Many take Genesis 1 as having been written from the viewpoint of a hypothetical observer on earth. Verse 1 simply emphasizes that there was a real beginning and that God is the Creator of all. Verse 2 describes the earth as being without form (such as continents and mountains) and without inhabitants. That is, God did not create the earth with people already on it. Verses 3–4 speak of the creation of light, without noting the source. Verse 5 indicates that the earth was rotating on its axis. Verses 6–8 describe the formation of the atmosphere, with a cloud blanket lifted above the primeval ocean. Verses 9–10 describe the formation of various ocean basins and the first land mass or continent. Verses 11–13, in an economy of expression, discuss the initial distinct acts of the creation of life on the planet. Verses 14–19 provide an account of God's creation of the sun, moon, and stars, which would have first become visible to the earth due to at least a partial breakup of the cloud cover. The rest of Genesis 1 reveals the final distinct creative acts of God's progressive creation, all of which possibly took place with the passing of time.[57]

---

[55]R. C. Newman and H. J. Eckelmann, Jr., *Genesis One and the Origin of the Earth* (Downers Grove, Ill.: InterVarsity Press, 1977).

[56]P. P. T. Pun, *Evolution: Nature and Scripture in Conflict?* (Grand Rapids: Zondervan Publishing House, 1982), 228, 256–59.

[57]Ramm explains his view of progressive creation: "God creating directly and sovereignly *outside* of Nature now brings to pass that creation through the Holy Spirit who is *inside* Nature." Bernard Ramm, *The Christian View of Science and Scripture* (Grand Rapids: Wm. B. Eerdmans, 1954), 78.

**CHAPTER
7**

The
Creation
of the
Universe
and
Humankind

Many progressive creationists believe that we are still living in the sixth creative day[58] and that God's Sabbath Day of rest will occur in the eternal state. Others believe we are in the seventh creative day because the word "rested" means "ceased," and no end is indicated for the seventh day in Genesis 2:3. Nothing in the Bible indicates that God is now creating new universes.

Progressive creationists say that because Christians are the stewards of God's creation (Gen. 1:28), and because "the heavens declare the glory of God" (Ps. 19:1), the pursuit of scientific knowledge should be "God-oriented," rather than "thing-oriented" or "knowledge-oriented." They reject the naturalistic, mechanistic, humanistic worldview that dominates contemporary science. While still rejecting those philosophies and speculations of naturalistic scientists, they are willing to reexamine the Scriptures if any previous interpretations of creation are based on theories that appear to be discredited by the data discovered by scientific research.[59]

Progressive creationists take the fossil record preserved in the geologic strata as a silent witness to rather long periods of time that have passed; yet they recognize that the fossils themselves descend in straight lines from the earliest times.[60] Concerning the young-earth theory, one progressive creationist says, "By its failure to deal with a wealth of relevant data, the recent creation-global flood model is unable ... to account for a wide diversity of geological phenomena."[61]

Progressive creationism has three major weaknesses. First, some of its proponents place too much stock in science's ability to recognize truth. For instance, Hugh Ross presents us with an alternative to the "single revelation view," in which the Bible is the only authoritative source of truth. Instead, he proposes "a dual revelation theology," in which the Bible (one form of revelation) is interpreted in the light of what science tells us (another equally authoritative form of revelation).[62] In short, progressive creationists who propose this approach tend to violate the Reformation's *sola scriptura*

---

[58]Newman, *Genesis One,* 85–86.

[59]Pun, *Evolution,* 238–39, 247.

[60]That is, an arrowworm in the Cambrian period was just as much an arrowworm as one now; an echinoderm in the Cambrian period was just as much an echinoderm as one now.

[61]Van Till, *Science Held Hostage,* 124.

[62]Hugh Ross, *The Fingerprint of God.* 2d ed. (Orange, Cal.: Promise Publishing Co., 1991), 144–45.

CHAPTER
7

The
Creation
of the
Universe
and
Humankind

principle. However, they do recognize that "Christian theism is in direct confrontation with the naturalistic monism of most evolutionists," and are also concerned about maintaining "the scriptural integrity of the Genesis account." Many progressive creationists reject the view of others within their camp who maintain that God's revelation in nature is just as authoritative as the Bible.[63]

The second weakness of progressive creationism is related to the first. When progressive creationists reject fiat creationism because it is based on what they view as obsolete science, there is a danger that the pendulum will swing too far the other way, resulting in an overdependence hermeneutically on present-day science. If that happens, it may produce a theological widow (i.e., a theological interpretation based on an abandoned scientific theory) in the succeeding generation.[64] Evangelical philosopher J. P. Moreland reminds us that science exists in a constant state of flux. What is viewed as true today may not be viewed in the same light fifty years from now. Moreland points out that science has changed so much in the past two hundred years that it is not accurate to speak of a *shift* in the way science looks at the world and provides solutions to its problems, but rather of the wholesale *abandonment* of old theories and old ways of seeing the world for completely new ones—even though the terminology remains unchanged. The same will happen to current theories.[65]

The third weakness of progressive creationism is that once the geologic strata are consigned to vast ages of gradual deposition, there remains no clear evidence for a universal Flood except in the Bible itself (Gen. 6:7,13, 17; 7:19–23; 8:9,21; 9:15–16). Many evangelical scientists who are progressive creationists hold to some kind of a local Flood explanation.[66]

Harmonizing the Views. If all current attempts to harmonize the Bible and science are plagued with difficulties, why consider them? First, some questions need answering,

---

[63]Pun, *Evolution,* 247, 299. For example, Ross, *Fingerprint,* 144–45; Davis Young, *Christianity and the Age of the Earth,* 154–55.

[64]Larkin did this when he incorporated the 1796 nebular hypothesis of La Place into his interpretation of creation. Clarence Larkin *Dispensational Truth,* rev. ed. (Philadelphia: Clarence Larkin, 1918), 20–22.

[65]J. P. Moreland, *Christianity and the Nature of Science* (Grand Rapids: Baker Book House, 1989), 195–98.

[66]Ramm, *The Christian View,* 162–168. Ramm depends too much on J. Laurence Kulp.

CHAPTER
7
_____
The
Creation
of the
Universe
and
Humankind

and we are convinced that because God is a consistent, truthful God (Num. 23:19; Titus 1:2; Heb. 6:18; 1 John 5:20; Rev. 6:10), His Word will agree with His world. Second, the Bible itself seems to call on evidence to support belief (Acts 1:3; 1 Cor. 15:5–8; 2 Pet. 1:16; 1 John 1:1–3); it seems to suggest that one ought to have something intelligent to say about science and the Bible if asked (Col. 4:5–6; Titus 1:9; 1 Pet. 3:15; Jude 3).

Even with difficulties, the above evangelical attempts at harmonization do much to answer the questions of saint and sinner alike.[67] In summary form, six primary tenets on which proponents of all views agree include the following:

1. The spontaneous generation of life from nonlife is impossible. Those who attempt to create life in a test tube unfairly "stack the deck"[68] in their favor.

2. Genetic variations appear to have limits; they do not occur in all directions, and mutations are almost always harmful.

3. Speciation can best be explained in terms of ecological isolation, not macroevolutionary processes.

4. The fossil record contains gaps between major forms of living organisms—gaps that fail to provide any missing links (which should be there by the thousands if evolution were true).

5. Homology (the similarities observed in living organisms) can best be explained in terms of intelligent design and the purposeful reuse of patterns, rather than by an alleged common ancestry.

6. When biochemists examine the structure of various organisms' protein and DNA, they find a random pattern in their chemical composition, not the incremental progression ascending with the organism's complexity implied by evolution.

Therefore, the creationist discussion has generated several significant answers to questions being asked. However, it would be helpful if proponents of all views would recognize

---

[67]See P. Davis and D. H. Kenyon, *Of Pandas and People: The Central Question of Biological Origins* (Dallas: Haughton Publishing Co., 1989); M. Denton, *Evolution: A Theory in Crisis* (London: Burnett Books Limited, 1985); C. Thaxton, W. L. Bradley, and R. L. Olsen, *The Mystery of Life's Origin: Reassessing Current Theories* (New York: Philosophical Library, 1984).

[68]I use this metaphor guardedly, here implying that truly random "chance" processes have been controlled so that the results will confirm the presuppositions.

that the Scriptures simply do not speak in support of their models with the degree of specificity they would like. We must be careful to give full recognition to humankind's finitude and fallenness (Jer. 17:9; 1 Cor. 2:14; Titus 1:15–16). Human thinking cannot be considered as a neutral, objective, and effective capacity in and of itself. As Eta Linnemann, a convert from the historical-critical interpretive method to saving faith, reminds us, "The necessary regulation of thought must occur through the Holy Scripture. It controls the thought process. Thought must subordinate itself to the Word of God. If difficulties crop up, it does not doubt God's Word but its own wisdom."[69]

CHAPTER 7

The Creation of the Universe and Humankind

THE CREATION AND NATURE OF HUMAN BEINGS

God's purposes cannot be separated from His creation. God created the universe with a view toward an everlasting relationship with humankind. The biblical writers, in unequivocal language, ascribe creation—everything "not-God" that exists—to the Triune God. Since God is Creator, He alone is worthy of our awe and worship. The fact that the same God presently sustains the universe provides us with confidence during the trials of life. Moreover, the biblical worldview (in light of creation) would affirm that the physical creation is basically orderly (making science possible) and beneficial to human existence. Furthermore, human beings themselves are "good" when they are in relationship to God. And finally, all of creation is moving toward the redemptive climax in Jesus Christ in the "new heavens and new earth."

THE BIBLICAL TERMINOLOGY FOR HUMANKIND

The Old Testament writers had numerous terms at their disposal when they described the human being. Perhaps the most important term, occurring 562 times, is *'adam.*[70] This word refers to humankind (including both men and women) as the image of God and the climax of creation (Gen. 1:26–28; 2:7). Humankind was created after special divine counsel

---

[69]E. Linnemann, *Historical Criticism of the Bible, Methodology or Ideology? Reflections of a Bultmannian Turned Evangelical,* trans. R. Yarbrough (Grand Rapids: Baker Book House, 1990), 111.

[70]Derived from *'adamah,* "ground," "soil," and *'edom,* "red-brown." Many take this to mean that Adam was created with a full set of inheritance factors (genes) that could separate into the various shades of skin color found today. See Walter Lang, *Five Minutes with the Bible and Science* (Grand Rapids: Baker Book House, 1972), 44.

CHAPTER
7

The
Creation
of the
Universe
and
Humankind

(v. 26)—after the divine type (vv. 26–27)—and was placed in an exalted position over the rest of creation (v. 28). The biblical writers employed the word *'adam* to connote "humankind" (as a noun) or "human" (as an adjective). Less frequently the word refers to the individual man, Adam.

Another generic term, found forty-two times in the Old Testament, is *'enosh,* a word that predominantly means "humankind" (Job 28:13; Ps. 90:3; Isa. 13:12). The word can, at times, refer to an individual, but only in the most general sense (Isa. 56:2). The term *'ish,* found 2,160 times in the Old Testament, is a more specialized term referring to a man as a male individual or husband, although at times the writer would use *'ish* to connote "humankind" generally, especially when distinguishing between God and humankind.[71] The Old Testament writers employed the term *gever* sixty-six times to depict youth and strength, sometimes using it even of women and children. A related word, *gibbor,* typically refers to mighty men, warriors, or heroes.

Turning to the New Testament, one finds the term *anthrōpos* generally means "humankind," distinguishing humans from animals (Matt. 12:12), angels (1 Cor. 4:9), Jesus Christ (Gal. 1:12; although He is *anthrōpos* in Phil. 2:7; 1 Tim. 2:5), and God (John 10:33; Acts 5:29). The word *anthrōpinos* also sets humanity apart from animals in God's created order (James 3:7), as well as occasionally distinguishing the human from God (Acts 17:24–25; 1 Cor. 4:3–4). At times, Paul uses *anthrōpinos,* connoting the human's inherent limitations (Rom. 6:19; 1 Cor. 2:13).[72]

Because of the generic use of terms such as *'adam, 'enosh,* and *anthrōpos,* believers must exercise caution when developing doctrines that distinguish between male and female roles. Often English versions fail to distinguish between the generic terms and gender-specific terms. Even when more specific gender-oriented words are used (such as *'ish* or *gever* in the Old Testament, and *anēr* in the New Testament), the teaching may not be limited to the gender being addressed, because many times the words overlap in meaning. For instance, even the word "brothers" *(adelphoi),* normally a gender-specific term, often implicitly includes "sisters" as well.[73]

---

[71]The feminine *'ishshah* means "woman" or "wife."

[72]*Anēr* is the term used for an individual man or husband; *gunē* means "woman" or "wife."

[73]Gordon D. Fee, *The First Epistle to the Corinthians* (Grand Rapids: Wm. B. Eerdmans, 1987), 52, n. 22.

CHAPTER

7

The
Creation
of the
Universe
and
Humankind

The biblical writers frequently describe humanity as sinful creatures in need of redemption. Indeed, we cannot study humanity in the Bible in an abstract sense because statements about humankind "are always partly theological pronouncements."[74] To sum up, the biblical writers fairly typically portray humanity as perverting the knowledge of God in rebellion against the law of God (Gen. 6:3,5; Rom. 1:18–32; 1 John 1:10). Therefore, Jesus extends a universal call to repentance (Matt. 9:13; Mark 1:15; Luke 15:7; John 3:15–18), as do other New Testament authors. Truly, "God has placed human beings at the focus of His attention, to redeem them for himself and to dwell with them forever."[75]

THE ORIGIN OF HUMANKIND

The biblical writers consistently maintain that God created human beings. Scripture passages that discuss the details more precisely indicate God created the first man directly out of the (moist) dust of the ground. There is no room here for the gradual development of simpler life forms into more complex ones, culminating in human beings.[76] In Mark 10:6 Jesus himself states, " 'At ["from" KJV] the beginning of creation God "made them male and female." ' " There can be no doubt that evolution is at odds with the biblical record. The Bible clearly indicates that the first man and woman were created in God's image, at the beginning of creation (Mark 10:6), not fashioned over millions of years of macroevolutionary processes.

In an intriguing passage, Genesis records God's special creation of woman: "Then the LORD God made a woman from the rib he had taken out of the man" (2:22). The original word "rib" here is *tsela'*, a term used of a human anatomical component only here in the Old Testament. Elsewhere, the word means a side of a hill, perhaps a ridge or terrace (2 Sam.

---

[74]H. Vorlander, *"anthrōpos"* in *The New International Dictionary of New Testament Theology,* Colin Brown, ed., vol. 2 (Grand Rapids: Zondervan Publishing House, 1978), 565.

[75]1 Tim. 2:3–6; 4:10; Titus 2:11; Heb. 2:9; 2 Pet. 3:9; 1 John 2:2; Rev. 22:17. H. Wayne House, "Creation and Redemption: A Study of Kingdom Interplay," *Journal of the Evangelical Theological Society* 35 (March 1992): 7.

[76]Gen. 1:26–27; 2:7; 3:19; 5:1; 6:7; Deut. 4:32; Pss. 90:3; 103:14; 104:30; Eccles. 3:20; 12:7; Isa. 45:12; 1 Cor. 11:9; 15:47. See J. Rankin, "The Corporeal Reality of Nephesh and the Status of the Unborn," *Journal of the Evangelical Theological Society* 31 (June 1988): 154–55.

CHAPTER
7
━━━━━
The
Creation
of the
Universe
and
Humankind

16:13), the sides of the ark of the covenant (Exod. 25:12,14), a side chamber of a building (1 Kings 6:5; Ezek. 41:6), and the leaves of a folding door (1 Kings 6:34). Therefore, the word could mean that God took part of Adam's side, including bone, flesh, arteries, veins, and nerves, since later the man says the woman is both " 'bone of my bones and flesh of my flesh' " (Gen. 2:23). The woman was made "of the same stuff" as the man (i.e., shared the same essence). Moreover, this passage (and others) makes it clear that the woman was the object of God's direct creative activity, just as the man was.

THE BASIC COMPONENTS OF HUMAN BEINGS

What are the basic components that make up the human being? The answer to this question usually includes a study of the terms "mind," "will," "body," "soul," and "spirit." In fact, the biblical writers employ a wide variety of terms to describe the elemental components of human beings.

The Bible speaks of the "heart," "mind," "kidneys," "loins," "liver," "inward parts," and even "bowels" as components of people that contribute to their distinctively human capacity to respond to certain situations. The Hebrew would use the word "heart" *(lev, levav)* to refer to the physical organ, but more often in the abstract sense to connote the inner nature, the inner mind or thoughts, the inner feelings or emotions, deep impulses, and even the will. In the New Testament, "heart" *(kardia)* also could refer to the physical organ, but it primarily means the inner life with its emotions, thoughts, and will, as well as the dwelling place of the Lord and the Holy Spirit.

Old Testament writers also employed the term *kilyah,* "kidneys" ("reins," KJV), to refer to the inner and secret aspects of personality. Jeremiah, for instance, laments to God concerning his insincere countrymen, "You are always on their lips but far from their kidneys" (Jer. 12:2, literal reading). In the New Testament, *nephroi,* "kidneys," is used only once (Rev. 2:23), when Jesus warns the angel of the church in Thyatira, "Then all the churches will know that I am he who searches kidneys and hearts" (literal).

At times the New Testament writers referred to a person's attitude with the word *splanchna,* "inward parts" ("bowels," 1 John 3:17, KJV). Jesus was "moved with compassion" toward the crowd (Mark 6:34, KJV; see also 8:2). The meaning in these passages seems to be "loving mercy." In one place,

**CHAPTER
7**
___

The
Creation
of the
Universe
and
Humankind

splanchna appears to be parallel to *kardia,* "heart" (2 Cor. 6:12); in another place, it occurs where we might expect the word *pneuma* ("spirit," 2 Cor. 7:15).

New Testament writers also frequently spoke of the "mind" *(nous, dianoia)* and "will" *(thelēma, boulēma, boulēsis).* The "mind" denotes the faculty of intellectual perception, as well as the ability to arrive at moral judgments. In certain occurrences in Greek thought, the "mind" seems to be parallel to the Old Testament term "heart," *lev.* In other places, the Greeks apparently distinguished between the two (see Mark 12:30). In considering the "will," the "human will or volition can be represented, on the one hand, as a mental act, directed towards a free choice. But, on the other hand, it can be motivated by desire pressing in from the unconscious."[77] Since the biblical writers use these terms in a variety of ways (just as we do in everyday language), it is difficult to determine from the Scriptures exactly where the "mind" ends and the "will" begins.

It should be apparent that many of the terms we have discussed are somewhat ambiguous and certainly overlap at times. Now the discussion turns to the terms "body," "soul," and "spirit." Is it possible to incorporate all of the previously mentioned terms into components such as "soul" and "spirit"? Or is such a division artificial, and the best we can hope for is a material/immaterial division?

The biblical writers had a wide variety of terms to choose from when referring to the "body." The Hebrews could speak of the "flesh" *(basar, sh^e'er);* "soul" *(nephesh),* referring to the body (Lev. 21:11; Num. 5:2, where the meaning appears to be "dead body"); and "strength" *(m^e'od),* meaning the "strength" of one's body (Deut. 6:5). The New Testament writers spoke of the "flesh" *(sarx,* at times meaning physical body), "strength" *(ischus)* of the body (Mark 12:30), or, most frequently, "body" *(sōma),* occurring 137 times.

When speaking of the soul, the Hebrews' primary term was *nephesh,* occurring 755 times in the Old Testament. Most often this all-encompassing word simply means "life," "self," "person" (Josh. 2:13; 1 Kings 19:3; Jer. 52:28). When used in this broad sense, *nephesh* describes what we are: We are souls, we are persons (in this sense, we do not "possess" souls or personhood).[78] At times *nephesh* could refer to a person's

___

[77]D. Müller, "Will, Purpose," in *New International Dictionary,* vol. 3, 1015.

[78]Rankin, "Corporeal Reality," 156.

CHAPTER

7

The
Creation
of the
Universe
and
Humankind

"will or desire" (Gen. 23:8; Deut. 21:14). Occasionally, however, it connotes that element in human beings which possesses various appetites or hunger. With this term, the Old Testament writers referred to physical hunger (Deut. 12:20), the sexual drive (Jer. 2:24), and a moral desire (Isa. 26:8–9). In Isaiah 10:18 *nephesh* occurs together with "flesh" *(basar)*, apparently denoting the whole person.[79]

The New Testament writers used *psuchē* to describe the soul of the human person 101 times. In Greek thought, the "soul" could refer to (1) the seat of life, or life itself (Mark 8:35); (2) the inward part of a human being, equivalent to the ego, person, or personality (the Septuagint translates the Hebrew *lev*, "heart," with *psuchē* twenty-five times); or (3) the soul in contrast to the body. The term *psuchē*, as a conceptual element of human beings, probably means "insight, will, disposition, sensations, moral powers"[80] (Matt. 22:37). However, it is not easy to draw hard-and-fast lines between the many meanings of this word.

When speaking of the spirit, the Hebrew would use *ruach*, a term found 387 times in the Old Testament. Although the basic meaning of this term is "air in motion," "wind," or "breath," *ruach* also denotes "the entire immaterial consciousness of man" (Prov. 16:32; Isa. 26:9). In Daniel 7:15, the *ruach* is contained in its bodily "sheath."[81] J. B. Payne points out that both the *nephesh* and the *ruach* can leave the body at death and yet exist in a state separate from it (Gen. 35:18; Ps. 86:13).[82]

Turning to the New Testament, the term *pneuma*, also basically meaning "wind," "breath," refers to the "spirit" of a man or woman. It is that power which people experience as relating them "to the spiritual realm, the realm of reality which lies beyond ordinary observation and human control." The spirit, then, links human beings to the spiritual realm and assists them in interacting with the spiritual realm. In other

---

[79]For a full analysis of *nephesh*, see R. L. Harris, *Man—God's Eternal Creation: Old Testament Teaching on Man and His Culture* (Chicago: Moody Press, 1971), 9–12; E. Brotzman, "Man and the Meaning of *Nephesh*," *Bibliotheca Sacra* 145 (October to December 1988) 400–409.

[80]Colin Brown, "Soul," in *New International Dictionary*, vol. 3, 677, 684.

[81]The Aramaic is literally "As for me, Daniel, my spirit was distressed in its sheath." The Septuagint, however, divides the words differently and reads "on account of this" instead of "in its sheath."

[82]J.B. Payne, *"ruach"* in *Theological Wordbook*, vol. 2, 836–37.

uses, however, when death occurs, the spirit departs and the body ceases to be the embodiment of the whole person (Matt. 27:50; Luke 23:46; Acts 7:59).[83]

After this brief survey of biblical terms, questions remain: What are the most basic constituent elements of human beings? Can all of the terms discussed be subsumed under body, soul, and spirit? Should we speak only of the material versus the immaterial? Or should we view human beings as a unity, and indivisible as such?

Trichotomism. Trichotomists hold that the constituent elements of the human individual are three: body, soul, and spirit. The physical makeup of human beings is the material part of their constitution that unites them with all living things, including both plants and animals. Plants, animals, and human beings all can be described in terms of their physical existence.

The "soul" is taken to be the principle of physical, or animal, life. Animals possess a basic, rudimentary soul, in that they give evidence of emotions, and are described with the term *psuchē* in Revelation 16:3 (see also Gen. 1:20, where they are described as *nephesh chayyah,* "living souls" in the sense of "living individuals" having a measure of personality). Human beings and animals are distinguished from plants, in part by their ability to express their individual personality.

The "spirit" is taken to be that higher power that establishes human beings in the realm of the spiritual and enables them to fellowship with God. The spirit can be distinguished from the soul, in that the spirit is "the seat of the spiritual qualities of the individual, whereas the personality traits reside in the soul." Although the spirit and the soul are distinguishable, they are not separable. Pearlman states, "The soul survives death because it is energized by the spirit, yet both soul and spirit are inseparable because spirit is woven into the very texture of soul. They are fused and welded into one substance."[84]

Passages that appear to support trichotomism include 1 Thessalonians 5:23, where Paul pronounces the benediction, "May your whole spirit, soul and body be kept blameless at the coming of our Lord Jesus Christ." In 1 Corinthians 2:14

---

[83]Colin Brown, "Spirit," in *New International Dictionary,* vol. 3, 693. Rom. 8:16; Gal. 6:18; Phil. 4:23; 2 Tim. 4:22; Philem. 25; Heb. 4:12; James 4:5. Brown, "Spirit," vol. 3, 694.

[84]Erickson, *Christian Theology,* 520. Myer Pearlman, *Knowing the Doctrines of the Bible* (Springfield, Mo.: Gospel Publishing House, 1981), 102.

CHAPTER
7
⎯⎯⎯
The
Creation
of the
Universe
and
Humankind

through 3:4, Paul speaks of human beings as *sarkikos* (literally, "fleshly," 3:1,3), *psuchikos* (literally, "soulish," 2:14), and *pneumatikos* (literally, "spiritual" 2:15). These two passages ostensibly speak of three elemental components. Several other passages appear to distinguish between the soul and spirit (1 Cor. 15:44; Heb. 4:12).

Trichotomism has been rather popular in conservative Protestant circles. However, H. O. Wiley points out that errors may occur when various components of trichotomism fall out of balance. The Gnostics, an early syncretic religious group that adopted elements of both paganism and Christianity, maintained that since the spirit emanated from God, it was incapable of sin. The Apollinarians, a fourth-century heretical group condemned by several church councils, thought that Christ possessed a body and a soul, but that the human spirit was replaced in Christ by the divine *Logos*. Placeus (1596–1655 or 1665), of the School of Samur in France, taught that the *pneuma* alone was directly created by God. The soul, Placeus thought, was mere animal life and perished with the body.[85]

Dichotomism. Dichotomists maintain that the constituent elements of human beings are two: material and immaterial. Proponents of this view point out that in both Testaments the words "soul" and "spirit" are used interchangeably at times. This seems to be the case with the parallel placement of "spirit" and "soul" in Luke 1:46–47, " 'My soul glorifies the Lord and my spirit rejoices in God my Savior' " (see also Job 27:3). Furthermore, many passages seem to imply a twofold division of human beings, with "soul" and "spirit" used synonymously. In Matthew 6:25 Jesus says, " 'Do not worry about your life *(psuchē),* what you will eat or drink; or about your body, what you will wear.' " In Matthew 10:28 Jesus again states, " 'Do not be afraid of those who kill the body but cannot kill the soul.' " However, in 1 Corinthians 5:3, Paul speaks of being "absent in body" (KJV; *sōma*) but "present in spirit" (KJV; *pneuma*), the two aspects apparently encompassing the whole person. Moreover, there are times when losing one's *pneuma* means death (Matt. 27:50; John 19:30), as surely as losing one's *psuchē* does (Matt. 2:20; Luke 9:24).

Dichotomism is "probably the most widely held view

---

[85]Wiley, *Christian Theology,* vol. 2, 18. Wiley gives other examples of historic errors due to an unbalanced treatment of elements within trichotomism.

through most of the history of Christian thought."[86] Proponents of this view, as with trichotomists, are capable of stating and defending their view without drifting into error. Pearlman states, "[B]oth views are correct when properly understood."[87] However, when components of dichotomism lose their balance, errors are possible.

The Gnostics adopted a cosmological dualism, which had a significant impact on their view of human beings. The universe was said to be divided by an immaterial, spirit side, which was intrinsically good, and a material, physical side, which was intrinsically evil. An unbridgeable gulf separated these two aspects of the universe. Paradoxically, human beings comprised both components. As a consequence of this innate dualistic nature, human beings could react in one of two ways: (1) sin at will because the good spirit would never be tainted with the evil body or (2) punish the body through ascetic disciplines because it was evil.

Moving to the modern era, Erickson cites errors within liberal theology, such as the following: (1) some liberals believe the body is *not* an essential part of human nature, i.e., the person can function quite well without it, and (2) other liberals go so far as to substitute the resurrection of the soul for the biblical doctrine of the resurrection of the body.[88]

Monism. Monism, as a worldview, dates back "to the pre-Socratic philosophers who appealed to a single unifying principle to explain all the diversity of observed experience."[89] However, monism may take a much narrower focus, and does so when applied to the study of human beings. Theological monists contend that the various components of human beings described in the Bible make up an indivisible, radical unity. In part, monism was a neoorthodox reaction against liberalism, which had proposed a resurrection of the soul, but not the body. But, as we shall see, monism, in rightly reacting against liberalism's error, has its own problems.

Monists point out that where the Old Testament employs the word "flesh" *(basar),* the New Testament writers apparently use both "flesh" *(sarx)* and "body" *(soma).* Any of these biblical terms can refer to the whole person because people in the biblical era viewed a person as a unified being. Ac-

---

[86] Erickson, *Christian Theology,* 521.

[87] Pearlman, *Knowing the Doctrines,* 101.

[88] Erickson, *Christian Theology,* 523–24.

[89] D. B. Fletcher, "Monism," in *Evangelical Dictionary of Theology,* Walter Elwell, ed. (Grand Rapids: Baker Book House, 1984), 730.

CHAPTER
7
—————
The
Creation
of the
Universe
and
Humankind

cording to monism then, we must view human beings as unified wholes, not as various components that can be individually identified in its own category. When the biblical writers speak of "body and soul. . . . It should be considered an exhaustive description of human personality. In the Old Testament conception," each individual person "is a psychophysical unity, flesh animated by soul."[90]

The difficulty with monism, of course, is that it leaves no room for an intermediate state between death and the physical resurrection in the future. This view is at odds with numerous Scripture passages.[91] Jesus also clearly spoke of the soul and body as divisible elements when He warned, " 'Do not be afraid of those who kill the body but cannot kill the soul' " (Matt. 10:28).

Having surveyed several views of the human being, and having observed possible errors within each position, we are ready to formulate a possible synthesis. The biblical writers appear to use terms in a variety of ways. "Soul" and "spirit" seem to be synonymous at times, while at other times they appear to be distinct. In fact, numerous biblical terms appear to describe the whole human person, or self, including "man," "flesh," "body," and "soul," as well as the compound "flesh and blood." The Old Testament, perhaps more obviously than the New, views the individual person as a unified being. Human beings are humans because of all that they are. They are part of the spiritual world and can relate to spiritual reality. They are emotional, willful, moral creatures. Humans are part of the physical world and therefore can be identified as "flesh and blood" (Gal. 1:16, KJV; Eph. 6:12; Heb. 2:14). The physical body, created by God, is not inherently evil, as the Gnostics contended (and as some Christians seem to believe).

The Bible's teaching concerning the sinful nature of fallen human beings affects all of what a human is, not just one component.[92] Moreover, human beings—as we know them, and as the Bible identifies them—cannot inherit the kingdom of God (1 Cor. 15:50). An essential change must take place first. Furthermore, when the immaterial component of a human departs at death, neither separated element can be described as a human being. What remains in the ground is a corpse, and what has departed to be with Christ is a disem-

---

[90]Erickson, *Christian Theology,* 526.

[91]Luke 22:43; 2 Cor. 5:6,8; Phil. 1:21–24. See also chap. 18, pp. 606–11.

[92]See chap. 8, pp. 277–78.

bodied, immaterial being, or spirit (which is a personal conscious existence, but not a "fully human" existence). At the resurrection of the body, the spirit will be reunited with a resurrected, changed, immortal body (1 Thess. 4:13–17), but still will never again be considered human in the same sense as we are now (1 Cor. 15:50).

Viewing the human being as a conditional unity has several implications. First, what affects one element of the human being affects the whole person. The Bible sees the person as a whole being, "and whatever touches one part affects the whole." In other words, a person with a chronic illness in the body may expect that the emotions, the mind, and the ability to relate to God as usual may all be affected. Erickson observes, "The Christian who desires to be spiritually healthy will give attention to such matters as diet, rest, and exercise."[93] In a similar vein, a person undergoing certain mental stresses may manifest physical symptoms or even physical illnesses.

Second, the biblical view of salvation and sanctification is not to be thought of as bringing the evil body under the control of the good spirit. When the New Testament writers spoke of the "flesh" in a negative sense (Rom. 7:18; 8:4; 2 Cor. 10:2–3; 2 Pet. 2:10), they were referring to the sinful nature, not specifically to the physical body. In the process of sanctification, the Holy Spirit renews the whole person. Indeed, we are a whole "new creation" in Christ Jesus (2 Cor. 5:17).

THE ORIGIN OF THE SOUL

No one in the medical or biological field quarrels over the origin of the human being's physical body. At conception, when the male sperm cell unites with the female ovum, the DNA molecule in each respective cell unravels and unites with the DNA from the other, forming an entirely new cell (a zygote). This new living cell is so different that after it attaches to the uterine wall the mother's body responds by sending antibodies to eliminate the unrecognized intruder. Only special, innate protective features in the new organism safeguard it from destruction.[94]

Therefore, it is improper for female proponents of abortion

---

[93]J. S. Wright, "Man," in *New International Dictionary,* 567. Erickson, *Christian Theology,* 539.

[94]See Dr. Liley in J. C. Willke, *Abortion: Questions and Answers,* rv. ed. (Cincinnati: Hayes Publishing Co., Inc., 1990), 51–52.

CHAPTER
7
───────
The
Creation
of the
Universe
and
Humankind

to speak of the embryo or fetus—at any stage—as "my body." The developing organism within the mother's womb is, in fact, a discrete, individual body. From conception on, this distinct body will produce more cells, all of which will retain the unique chromosome pattern of the original zygote. It is clear, therefore, that the human body finds its origin in the act of conception.

The origin of the soul is more difficult to determine. For the purpose of the following discussion, we will define the soul as the entire immaterial nature of the human being (encompassing the biblical terms: "heart," "kidneys," "bowels," "mind," "soul," "spirit," etc.). The biblically oriented theories[95] of the soul's origin are three: preexistence, creationism (God directly creates each soul), and traducianism (each soul is derived from the soul of the parents).

Preexistence Theory. According to the preexistence theory, a soul created by God at some time in the past enters the human body at some point in the early development of the fetus. More specifically, the souls of all people had a conscious, personal existence in a previous state. These souls sin to varying degrees in this preexistent state, condemning them to be "born into this world in a state of sin and in connection with a material body." The most important Christian proponent of this view was Origen, the Alexandrian theologian (ca. 185–ca. 254). He maintained that the present state of being we observe now (the soul/body individual) is only one stage in the existence of the human soul. Hodge elaborates on Origen's view of the soul: "It has passed through innumerable other epochs and forms of existence in the past, and is to go through other innumerable such epochs in the future."[96]

Because of its insuperable difficulties, the preexistence theory has never won many supporters. (1) It is based on the pagan notion that the body is inherently evil and therefore the embodiment of the soul is tantamount to punishment. (2) The Bible never speaks of the creation of human beings prior to Adam, or of any apostasy of humanity prior to the Fall in Genesis 3. (3) The Bible never attributes our present sinful condition to any source higher than the sin of our first parent, Adam (Rom. 5:12–21; 1 Cor. 15:22).

───────

[95]We will not survey pagan theories, such as reincarnation, which is contrary to the Bible's linear view of history.

[96]Charles Hodge, *Systematic Theology,* vol. 2 (New York: Scribner, Armstrong, and Co., 1877), 66.

CHAPTER
7
The
Creation
of the
Universe
and
Humankind

Creationism Theory. According to the creationism theory, "Each individual soul is to be regarded as an immediate creation of God, owing its origin to a direct creative act."[97] The precise timing of the soul's creation, and its uniting with the body, is simply not addressed by the Scriptures. (For this reason, analyses by both proponents and antagonists are somewhat vague on this point.) Supporters of this view include Ambrose, Jerome, Pelagius, Anselm, Aquinas, and most of the Roman Catholic and Reformed theologians. Biblical evidence used to buttress the creationism theory tends toward those Scripture passages that ascribe the creation of the "soul" or "spirit" to God (Num. 16:22; Eccles. 12:7; Isa. 57:16; Zech. 12:1; Heb. 12:9).

Some who reject the creationism theory point out that the Scriptures also assert that God created the body (Ps. 139:13–14; Jer. 1:5). "Yet," Augustus Strong remarks, "we do not hesitate to interpret these latter passages as expressive of mediate, not immediate creatorship."[98] Furthermore, this theory does not account for the tendency of all people to sin.

Traducianism. Strong cites Tertullian, the African theologian (ca. 160–ca. 230), Gregory of Nyssa (330–ca. 395), and Augustine (354–430) as making comments that support traducianism,[99] although none of them provides a full explanation of the view. More recently, the Lutheran reformers generally accepted traducianism. The term "traducian" stems from the Latin *traducere,* "to bring or carry over, to transport, transfer." The theory maintains that "the human race was immediately created in Adam, with respect to the soul as well as the body, and that both are propagated from him by natural generation."[100] In other words, God provided in Adam and Eve the means by which they (and all humans) would have offspring in their own image, comprising the totality of the material-immaterial person.

Genesis 5:1 records, "When God created man, he made him in the likeness of God." In contrast, Genesis 5:3 states, "When Adam had lived 130 years, he had a son in *his* own likeness, in *his* own image." God empowered Adam and Eve to bear children who were like themselves in composition. Furthermore, when David said he was "sinful from the time

---

[97]Louis Berkhof, *Systematic Theology,* 4th ed. (Grand Rapids: Wm. B. Eerdmans, 1941), 199.

[98]Strong, *Systematic,* 491–92.

[99]Ibid., 493–94.

[100]Thiessen, *Lectures,* 165.

CHAPTER
7

The
Creation
of the
Universe
and
Humankind

my mother conceived me" (Ps. 51:5), we find evidence that David inherited from his parents, at conception, a soul with tendencies to sin. Finally, in Acts 17:26 Paul states, "From one man he made every nation," implying that all that constitutes "humanity" came from Adam. For the proponent of traducianism, abortion at any stage in the development of the zygote, embryo, or fetus constitutes the termination of someone who was fully human.

Opponents of traducianism object that in contending for the parental generation of a soul as well as a body in the offspring, the soul has been reduced to a material substance. Traducianists would reply that this conclusion is not necessary. The Bible itself does not specify the precise procreative process that generates the soul. It must, therefore, remain a mystery. Opponents also object that traducianism requires Christ to have partaken of the sinful nature when He was born of Mary. Traducianists would reply that the Holy Spirit sanctified what Jesus received from Mary and protected Him from any taint of human sinful tendencies.[101]

THE UNITY OF HUMANITY

The doctrine of the unity of humanity contends that both male and female human beings of all races originated through Adam and Eve (Gen. 1:27–28; 2:7,22; 3:20; 9:19; Acts 17:26). That both male and female humans are in the image of God is clear from Genesis 1:27, "Male and female he created them" (see also Gen. 5:1–2). The point is that all human beings of both sexes, in all races, economic classes, and age-groups, equally bear the image of God and therefore are all equally valuable in God's sight.

Since the Bible presents both sexes of the human race as being made in the image of God, there is no room for males' viewing females as somehow inferior, or as second-class members of the human race. The word "helper" (Gen. 2:18) is often used of God (Exod. 18:4) and does not indicate a lower status.[102] Moreover, when the New Testament places wives in a role of functional subordination to their husbands (Eph. 5:24; Col. 3:18; Titus 2:5; 1 Pet. 3:1), it does not necessarily

---

[101]Luke 1:35; John 14:30; Rom. 8:3; 2 Cor. 5:21; Heb. 4:15; 7:26; 1 Pet. 1:19; 2:22.

[102]For interaction with Aquinas and others who said male and female were equally image-bearers in a primary sense, but unequal in a secondary sense, see H. Lazenby, "The Image of God: Masculine, Feminine, or Neuter?" *Journal of the Evangelical Theological Society* 30 (March 1987): 63–64.

follow that females are inferior to males, or even that females should be functionally subordinate to males generally (the New Testament pattern is that wives are subordinate to their own[103] husbands).

The verb "submit" (Gk. *hupotassō*), used in the four submission passages above, is also employed in 1 Corinthians 15:28, where Paul states that the Son will be "subject" to the Father.[104] Yet all believers generally understand that an administrative subjection is intended—the Son is in no way inferior to the Father. The same may be said of the wife and husband passages. Although God has ordained different functional roles for various members of a family, the family members in subordinate roles do not have less personal value than their administrative leader. Indeed, the apostle Paul teaches that in Christ there is neither male nor female (Gal. 3:28). All the blessings, promises, and provisions of the kingdom of God are equally available to all.

Additionally, racism cannot be sustained in the face of the human race's origin in Adam and Eve. Instead, the Bible focuses on other distinctions. For instance, the Old Testament writers mention "seed," "descendant" *(zera‘);* "family," "clan," "kindred" *(mishpachah);* "tribe" *(matteh, shavet)* for general divisions by biological lineage; and "tongue" *(lashon)* for divisions by language. Following a similar pattern, the New Testament writers refer to "descendant," "family," "nationality" *(genos);* "nation" *(ethnos);* and "tribe" *(phulē).*

The biblical writers simply were not concerned with race as a distinction between human beings based on hair color and texture, skin and eye color, stature, bodily proportions, and the like. M. K. Mayers concludes, "The Bible does not refer to the term 'race'; nor is there a concept of race developed in the Bible." Therefore, the racial myths that Cain's curse brought the black race into the world, or that Ham's curse was dark skin, must be rejected.[105] Instead Genesis 3:20

---

[103]The Greek specifies that wives are to submit to their "own" *(idiois)* husbands (1 Pet. 3:1).

[104]Note that citizens are to submit to the government (Rom. 13:1); the church to its leader (1 Cor. 16:16); and the younger to the older (1 Pet. 5:5).

[105]M. K. Mayers, "Race," in *The Zondervan Pictorial Encyclopedia of the Bible,* Merrill C. Tenney, ed. vol. 5 (Grand Rapids: Zondervan Publishing House, 1975), 22. Note that all Cain's descendants died in the Flood. Also, Noah's curse was only on Canaan, the ancestor of the Canaanites, not on the African descendants of Ham. Noah's family undoubtedly had inheritance factors that would settle out into the races of people that we have today.

CHAPTER
7

The
Creation
of the
Universe
and
Humankind

simply declares, "Adam named his wife Eve, because she would become the mother of *all the living.*"

In the New Testament, the gospel of Christ invalidated all distinctions between human beings that were, during the first century, quite significant. They included the divisions that existed between Jews and Samaritans (Luke 10:30–35); between Jews and Gentiles (Acts 10:34–35; Rom. 10:12); between Jews and the uncircumcised, barbarians, and Scythians (Col. 3:11); between males and females (Gal. 3:28); and between slaves and free people (Gal. 3:28; Col. 3:11). In Acts 17:26 Paul states, "From one man he [God] made every nation of men, that they should inhabit the whole earth." In the next verse Paul indicates God's purpose in this creative act: "God did this so that men would seek him and perhaps reach out for him and find him" (17:27). In light of passages such as these, it would be hopeless to try to sustain a racist view based on some supposed support from the Bible.

Finally, there can be no ranking of human worth based on economic station or age. God's purpose for humankind is for us to know, love, and serve Him. God made us "able to know Him and respond to Him. This is the fundamental distinguishing characteristic ... shared by all humanity."[106] Therefore, any ranking or classification of the intrinsic value of any group of human beings must be rejected as artificial and unscriptural.

THE IMAGE OF GOD IN HUMAN BEINGS

The Bible affirms that human beings were created in God's image. Genesis 1:26 records God saying, " 'Let us make man ['*adam,* "humankind"] in our image, in our likeness' " (see also 5:1). Other Scripture passsages clearly show that human beings even though descended from fallen Adam and Eve (rather than being objects of God's immediate creation) are still image-bearers (Gen. 9:6; 1 Cor. 11:7; James 3:9).

The Hebrew terms in Genesis 1:26 are *tselem* and *d^emuth.* The word *tselem,* used sixteen times in the Old Testament, basically refers to an image or working model. The word *d^emuth,* used twenty-six times, refers variously to visual, audible, and structural similarities in a pattern, shape, or form. These terms seem to be explained in the rest of 1:26–28 as humanity having the opportunity to subdue the earth (that is, bring it under control by learning about it and using it

---

[106]Erickson, *Christian Theology,* 541.

properly) and to rule (in a beneficent way) over the rest of earth's creatures (see also Ps. 8:5–8).

The New Testament uses the words *eikōn* (1 Cor. 11:7) and *homoiōsis* (James 3:9). The word *eikōn* generally means "image," "likeness," "form," "appearance" throughout its range of uses. The word *homoiōsis* means "likeness," "resemblance," "correspondence." Since both Old and New Testament terms appear to be broad and interchangeable, we must look beyond lexical studies to determine the nature of the image of God.

Before we affirm what the image of God is, we will briefly explain what it is not. The image of God is not a physical likeness, as per the Mormon and Swedenborgian views. The Bible clearly says that God, who is an omnipresent Spirit, cannot be limited to a corporeal body (John 1:18; 4:24; Rom. 1:20; Col. 1:15; 1 Tim. 1:17; 6:16). The Old Testament does use terms such as "the finger" or "the arm of God" to express His power. It also speaks of His "wings" and "feathers" to express His protecting care (Ps. 91:4). But these terms are anthropomorphisms, figures of speech used to give a picture of some aspect of God's nature or love.[107] God warned Israel not to make an image to worship, for when God spoke to them at Horeb (Mount Sinai), they "saw no form of any kind" (Deut. 4:15). That is, any physical form would be contrary to what God is really like.

Another error, perhaps a modern version of the serpent's lie in Genesis 3:5, is that the image of God makes humans "little gods."[108] Certainly, "[s]ound exegesis and hermeneutics are and always will be the only effective antidote to [these and other] 'new' doctrines, most of which are just old heresies."[109]

Having identified positions to avoid, we now direct our attention to the biblical view of the image of God. Several New Testament passages provide us with the foundation for our definition of the image of God in the human person. In Ephesians 4:23–24 Paul reminds the Ephesians that they were taught "to be made new in the attitude of [their] minds; and to put on the new self, created to be like God in true righ-

CHAPTER 7

The Creation of the Universe and Humankind

---

[107]See W. Kaiser, *Hard Sayings of the Old Testament* (Downers Grove, Ill.: InterVarsity Press, 1988), 78–84.

[108]This error has found supporters among the so-called Word of Faith speakers.

[109]Gordon Anderson, "Kingdom Now Theology: A Look at Its Roots and Branches," *Paraclete* 24 (Summer 1990): 8–11.

CHAPTER
7
—————
The
Creation
of the
Universe
and
Humankind

teousness and holiness." In another place, Paul says the reason we make proper moral choices is because we "have put on the new self, which is being renewed in knowledge in the image of its Creator" (Col. 3:10).

These verses indicate that the image of God pertains to our moral-intellectual-spiritual nature. To elaborate, the image of God in the human person is something we are, not something we have or do. This view is in perfect accord with what we have already established as God's divine purpose in the creation of humankind. First, God created us to know, love, and serve Him. Second, we relate to other human beings and have the opportunity to exercise proper dominion over God's creation. The image of God assists us in doing precisely these things.

Turning our attention to the specific nature of the image of God, Wiley distinguishes between the natural, or essential, image of God in the human and the moral, or incidental, image of God in the human.[110] By the natural image of God we mean that which makes humans human and therefore distinguishes them from animals. This includes spirituality, or the ability to sense and have fellowship with God. Moreover, Colossians 3:10 indicates that the image of God includes knowledge, or the intellect. Because of our God-given intellect, we have the unique capacity to communicate intelligently with God and with each other on an order quite unknown in the animal world.[111]

Furthermore, human beings alone in God's creation have the capacity for immortality. Even when God's fellowship with humankind was broken at the Fall, in Genesis 3, the cross of Christ ushered in the means that provided for fellowship with God forever. Finally, according to the context of Genesis 1:26–28, the image of God undoubtedly includes a provisional dominion (with responsibility for proper care) over the creatures of the earth.

Concerning the moral image of God in humans, "God made mankind upright" (Eccles. 7:29). Even pagans who have no knowledge of the written law of God nevertheless have an unwritten moral law imprinted by God upon their hearts (Rom. 2:14–15). In other words, human beings alone possess the ability to sense right and wrong and have the intellect and will with the capacity to choose between them. For this

---

[110]Wiley, *Christian Theology,* vol. 2, 32–39.

[111]See M. Cosgrove, *The Amazing Body Human: God's Design for Personhood* (Grand Rapids: Baker Book House, 1987), 163–64.

reason, human beings are often called free moral agents, or are said to possess self-determination. Ephesians 4:22–24 appears to indicate that the moral image of God, though not completely eradicated at the Fall, has been negatively affected to some extent. To have the moral image restored "in true righteousness and holiness," the sinner must accept Christ and become a new creation.

One final word is in order on the volitional freedom humans enjoy. Fallen humans, even with volitional freedom, are incapable of choosing God.[112] God, therefore, munificently equips people with a measure of grace, enabling and preparing them to respond to the gospel (John 1:9; Titus 2:11). God purposed that He would fellowship with people who of their own free will decided to respond to His universal call to salvation. In keeping with this divine purpose, God endowed human beings with the capacity to accept or reject Him. The human will has been freed sufficiently to, as the Scriptures implore, "turn to God," "repent," and "believe."[113] Hence, when we cooperate with the Spirit's wooing and accept Christ, that cooperation is not the means to renewal, but is instead the result of renewal. For Bible-believing Christians of all persuasions, salvation is 100 percent external (an unmerited gift from a gracious God). God has graciously given us what we need to fulfill His purpose for our lives: knowing, loving, and serving Him.

STUDY QUESTIONS

1. What does the phrase "creation *ex nihilo*" mean, and what biblical evidence is there for the doctrine?

2. Why should Christians be involved in attempts to harmonize the biblical data with the scientific data?

3. What good has resulted from the ongoing debate between proponents of the various creationist models?

4. What are the advantages of a conditional-unity view of the constitution of human beings over trichotomism and dichotomism?

5. What constitutes the image of God in human beings?

---

[112]*Writings of James Arminius,* vol. 1, 526; see also vol. 2, 472–73.

[113]1 Kings 8:47; 2 Chron. 20:20; Prov. 1:23; Isa. 31:6; 43:10; Ezek. 14:6; 18:32; Joel 2:13–14; Matt. 3:2; 18:3; Mark 1:15; Luke 13:3,5; John 6:29; 14:1; Acts 2:38; 3:19; 16:31; 17:30; Phil. 1:29; 1 John 3:23.

The Origin, Nature, and Consequences of Sin

Bruce R. Marino

The Bible's teaching about sin[1] presents a profound, and profoundly bifurcated, vista: the plunging depravity of humanity and the surpassing glory of God. Sin shades every aspect of human existence, enticing us from the outside as an enemy and compelling us from the inside as a part of our fallen human nature. In this life sin is known intimately, yet it remains alien and mysterious. It promises freedom but enslaves, producing desires that cannot be satisfied. The more we struggle to escape its grasp, the more inextricably it binds us. Understanding sin assists us in the knowledge of God, yet it is that which distorts knowledge of even the self. But if the light of divine illumination can penetrate its darkness, not only that darkness, but also the light itself, can be better appreciated.

The practical importance of the study of sin is seen in its seriousness: Sin is contrary to God. It affects all creation, including humanity. Even the least sin can bring eternal judgment. The remedy for sin is nothing less than Christ's death on the cross. The results of sin embrace all the terror of suffering and death. Finally, the darkness of sin displays the glory of God in a stark and terrible contrast.[2]

The importance of the study of the nature of sin may be

---

[1]The technical term for the study of sin is "hamartiology," derived from Greek *hamartia,* "sin."

[2]See Lewis Sperry Chafer, *Systematic Theology,* vol. 2 (Dallas: Dallas Theological Seminary Press, 1947), 227–28, 252–53.

understood in its relation to other doctrines. Sin distorts and casts doubt upon all knowledge. In defending the Christian faith, one struggles with the ethical dilemma of how evil can exist in a world governed by an all-good, all-powerful God.

The study of the nature of God must consider God's providential control over a sin-cursed world. The study of the universe must describe a universe that was created good but that now groans for redemption. The study of humankind must deal with a human nature that has become grotesquely inhuman and unnatural. The doctrine of Christ faces the question of how the fully human nature of the virgin-born Son of God can be fully sinless. The study of salvation must state not only *to* what but also *from* what humanity is saved. The doctrine of the Holy Spirit must consider conviction and sanctification in light of a sinful flesh. The doctrine of the Church must shape ministry to a humanity that is distorted by sin outside and inside the Church. The study of the end times must describe, and to some extent defend, God's judgment upon sinners while proclaiming sin's end. Finally, practical theology must seek to evangelize, counsel, educate, govern the Church, affect society, and encourage holiness in spite of sin.

The study of sin, however, is difficult. It is revolting, focusing on the gross ugliness of widespread, open sin and the subtle deception of secret, personal sin. Today's post-Christian society reduces sin to feelings or to acts, ignoring or wholly rejecting supernatural evil. Most insidiously, the study of sin is frustrated by the irrational nature of evil itself.

The number of nonscriptural views of sin is legion. Despite their being nonscriptural, studying them is important for the following reasons: to think more clearly and scripturally about Christianity; to defend more accurately the faith and to critique other systems; to evaluate more critically new psychotherapies, political programs, educational approaches, and the like; and to minister more effectively to believers and nonbelievers who may hold these or similar nonscriptural views.[3]

Building on Søren Kierkegaard's existentialism, many theories argue that humans are caught in a dilemma when their limited abilities are inadequate to meet the virtually limitless possibilities and choices of their perceptions and imaginations. This situation produces tension or anxiety. Sin is the

_____

[3]For a summary of many of these views, see Millard J. Erickson, *Christian Theology* (Grand Rapids: Baker Book House, 1985), 581–95.

futile attempt to resolve this tension through inappropriate means instead of pessimistically accepting it or, in Christian versions, turning to God.[4]

In a more radical development, some argue that individual existence is a sinful state because people are alienated from the basis of reality (often defined as "god") and from each other. This theme can be found in an early form in the ancient Jewish philosopher Philo. It is currently expressed by liberal theologians such as Paul Tillich and within many forms of Eastern religion and New Age thought.[5]

Some believe sin and evil are not real but merely illusions that may be overcome by right perception. Christian Science, Hinduism, Buddhism, the positive thinking of some popular Christianity, much psychology, and aspects of the New Age movement resonate with this view.[6]

Sin also has been understood as the unevolved remnants of primal animal characteristics, such as aggression. Advocates of this view say the story of Eden is really a myth about the development of moral awareness and conscience, not a fall.[7]

Liberation theology sees sin as the oppression of one societal group by another. Often combining the economic theories of Karl Marx (which speak of the class struggle of the ultimately victorious proletariat against the bourgeoisie) with biblical themes (such as Israel's victory over Egyptian slavery), liberation theologians identify the oppressed in economic, racial, gender, and other terms. Sin is eliminated by removing the social conditions that cause the oppression. Extremists advocate violent overthrow of unredeemable op-

---

[4]On Christian existentialism, Søren Kierkegaard, *The Concept of Dread,* 2d ed., Walter Lowrie, trans. (Princeton: Princeton University Press, 1957); id., *Fear and Trembling* and *The Sickness unto Death,* Walter Lowrie, trans. (Princeton: Princeton University Press, 1954). For a fully developed theory: Reinhold Niebuhr, *The Nature and Destiny of Man: A Christian Interpretation,* vol. 1 *Human Nature* (New York: Charles Scribner's Sons, 1964), 178–86.

[5]Paul Tillich, *Systematic Theology,* vol. 2 (Chicago: University of Chicago, 1957), 19–78. J. Isamu Yamamoto, *Beyond Buddhism: A Basic Introduction to the Buddhist Tradition* (Downers Grove, Ill.: InterVarsity, 1982). Wendy Doniger O'Flaherty, *The Origins of Evil in Hindu Mythology* (Berkeley: University of California Press, 1976). Karen Hoyt, *The New Age Rage* (Old Tappan, N.J.: Fleming H. Revell, 1987).

[6]Mary Baker Eddy, *Science and Health with a Key to the Scriptures* (Boston: First Church of Christ, Scientist, 1934), 480.

[7]Frederick R. Tennant, *The Origin and Propagation of Sin* (London: Cambridge University Press, 1902).

pressors, while moderates emphasize change through social action and education.[8]

Among the most ancient views of sin is dualism, the belief that there is a struggle between (virtually or actually) preexistent and equal forces, or gods of good and evil. These cosmic forces and their battle cause sinfulness in the temporal sphere. Often, evil matter (especially flesh) either carries or actually is sin that must be conquered. This idea appears in ancient Near Eastern religions such as Gnosticism, Manichaeism, and Zoroastrianism. In many versions of Hinduism and Buddhism, and their New Age offspring, evil is reduced to an amoral necessity.[9]

Some modern theology sees "god" as finite and even morally evolving. Until the dark side of the divine nature is controlled, the world will suffer evil. This is typical of process theology's blending of physics and Eastern mysticism.[10]

Much popular thought, uninformed Christianity, Islam, and many moralistic systems hold that sin consists only in willful actions. Morally free people simply make free choices; there is no such thing as a sin nature, only actual events of sin. Salvation is simply being better and doing good.[11]

Atheism holds that evil is merely the random chance of a godless cosmos. Sin is rejected, ethics is merely preference, and salvation is humanistic self-advancement.[12]

Although many of these theories may appear to contain some insight, none takes the Bible as fully inspired revelation. Scripture teaches that sin is real and personal; it originated in the fall of Satan, who is personal, wicked, and active; and through Adam's fall sin spread to a humanity created good by an all-good God.

---

[8]Alfred T. Hennelly, ed., *Liberation Theology: A Documentary History* (New York: Orbis, 1990), an anthology of primary sources.

[9]R.C. Zaehner, *The Teachings of the Magi, A Compendium of Zoroastrian Beliefs* (New York: Oxford University Press, 1956).

[10]Royce Gordon Gruenler, *The Inexhaustible God* (Grand Rapids: Baker Book House, 1983), a general critique of process.

[11]Fazlur Rahman, *Major Themes of the Qur'an* (Minneapolis: Bibliotheca Islamica, 1980).

[12]Paul Kurtz, ed., *Humanist Manifestos I and II* (Buffalo, N.Y.: Prometheus Books, 1973), 15–16.

THE BEGINNINGS OF SIN

The Bible refers to an event in the darkest recesses of time, beyond human experience, when sin became reality.[13] An extraordinary creature, the serpent, was already confirmed in wickedness before "sin entered the world" through Adam (Rom. 5:12; see Gen. 3).[14] This ancient serpent is met elsewhere as the great dragon, Satan, and the devil (Rev. 12:9; 20:2). He has been sinning and murdering from the beginning (John 8:44; 1 John 3:8). Pride (1 Tim. 3:6) and a fall of angels (Jude 6; Rev. 12:7–9) also are associated with this cosmic catastrophe.[15]

Scripture also teaches of another Fall: Adam and Eve were created "good" and placed in an idyllic garden in Eden, enjoying close communion with God (Gen. 1:26 through 2:25). Because they were not divine and were capable of sinning, their continuing dependence on God was necessary. Similarly, they required regular partaking of the tree of life.[16] This is indicated by God's invitation to eat of every tree, including the tree of life, before the Fall (2:16), and His strong prohibition afterward (3:22–23). Had they obeyed, they may have been blissfully fruitful, developing forever (1:28–30). Alternatively, after a period of probation, they may have achieved a more permanent state of immortality either by translation into heaven (Gen. 5:21–24; 2 Kings 2:1–12) or by a resurrection body on earth (cf. believers, 1 Cor. 15:35–54).

God permitted Eden to be invaded by Satan, who craftily tempted Eve (Gen. 3:1–5). Ignoring God's Word, Eve gave in to her desire for beauty and wisdom, took the forbidden fruit, offered it to her husband, and they ate together (3:6). Eve was deceived by the serpent, but Adam seems to have sinned knowingly (2 Cor. 11:3; 1 Tim. 2:14; God's tacit agreement in Gen. 3:13–19). It may be that while Adam heard the command not to eat of the tree directly from God, Eve heard it only through her husband (Gen. 2:17; cf. 2:22). Hence, Adam was more responsible before God, and Eve was more

---

[13]It is crucial to the present argument that the narratives of the creation and, by extension, the Fall are factual and historical. *Where We Stand* (Springfield, Mo,: Gospel Publishing House, 1990), 105.

[14]See chap. 6, p. 196.

[15]See chap. 6, p. 210.

[16]Pelagianism denies Adamic immortality. "Contingent" immortality first appears in Theophilus of Antioch (115–68–81): "To Autolycus," 2.24.

CHAPTER
8
━━━━━━
The Origin,
Nature, and
Consequences
of Sin

susceptible to Satan (cf. John 20:29). This may explain Scripture's emphasis on Adam's sin (Rom. 5:12–21; 1 Cor. 15:21–22) when actually Eve sinned first. Finally, it is crucial to observe that their sin began in free moral choices, not temptations (which they could have resisted: 1 Cor. 10:13; James 4:7). That is, although temptation provided the incentive to sin, the serpent did not pick the fruit or force them to eat it. They chose to do so.

Humanity's first sin embraced all other sins: effrontery and disobedience to God, pride, unbelief, wrong desires, leading astray of others, mass killing of posterity, and voluntary submission to the devil. The immediate consequences were numerous, severe, extensive, and ironic (note carefully Gen. 1:26 through 3:24): The divine–human relationship of open communion, love, trust, and security was exchanged for isolation, defensiveness, blame, and banishment. Adam and Eve and their relationship degenerated. Intimacy and innocence were replaced by accusation (as they shifted the blame). Their rebellious desire for independence resulted in pain in childbirth, toil, and death. Their eyes were truly opened, knowing good and evil (through a shortcut), but it was a burdensome knowledge unbalanced by other divine attributes (e.g., love, wisdom, knowledge). Creation, entrusted to and cared for by Adam, was cursed, groaning for deliverance from the results of his faithlessness (Rom. 8:20–22). Satan, who had offered Eve the heights of divinity and promised that the man and woman would not die, was cursed above all creatures and condemned to eternal destruction by her offspring (see Matt. 25:41). Finally, the first man and woman brought death to all their children (Rom. 5:12–21; 1 Cor. 15:20–28).

The Jewish Midrash takes God's warning that death would come when (literally, "in the day") they ate of the tree (Gen. 2:17) as a reference to Adam's physical death (Gen. 3:19; 5:5) since a day, in God's sight, is as a thousand years (Ps. 90:4) and Adam lived only 930 years (Gen. 5:5). Others see it as a necessary consequence of being cut off from the tree of life. Many Jewish rabbis noted that Adam was never immortal and that his death would have come immediately if God had not delayed it out of mercy. Most hold that spiritual death or separation from God occurred that day.[17]

───────────

[17]Meir Zlotowitz, *Bereishis, Genesis,* vol. 1 (New York: Mesorah Publications, 1977), 102–3. U. Cassuto, *A Commentary on the Book of Genesis* Part 1 (Jerusalem: The Magnes Press, 1972), 125. Some, in this connection,

Yet, even in judgment God graciously made Adam and Eve coverings of skins, apparently to replace their self-made coverings of leaves (Gen. 3:7,21).[18]

ORIGINAL SIN: A BIBLICAL ANALYSIS

Scripture teaches that Adam's sin affected more than just himself (Rom. 5:12–21; 1 Cor. 15:21–22). This issue is called original sin. It poses three questions: to what extent, by what means, and on what basis is Adam's sin transmitted to the rest of humanity? Any theory of original sin must answer these three questions and meet the following biblical criteria:

Solidarity. All humanity, in some sense, is united or bound to Adam as a single entity (because of him, all people are outside the blessedness of Eden; Rom. 5:12–21; 1 Cor. 15:21–22).

Corruption. Because human nature was so damaged by the Fall no person is capable of doing spiritual good without God's gracious assistance. This is called total corruption, or depravity, of nature. It does not mean that people can do no apparent good, but only that they can do nothing to merit salvation. Nor is this teaching exclusively Calvinistic. Even Arminius (although not all his followers) described the "Free Will of man towards the True Good" as "imprisoned, destroyed, and lost ... it has no powers whatever except such as are excited by Divine Grace." Arminius' intent, like Wesley's after him, was not to retain human freedom in spite of

---

say that that meant Adam and Eve "became mortal." But the Bible is very clear that God alone has immortality (1 Tim. 6:16). "You will surely die" occurs twelve other times in the Old Testament and always refers to punishment for sin or untimely death as punishment. Cf. Victor P. Hamilton, *The Book of Genesis, Chapters 1–17: New International Commentary of the Old Testament* (Grand Rapids: Wm. B. Eerdmans, 1990), 173–74. J. H. Hertz, ed. *The Pentateuch and Haftorahs,* 2d ed. (London: Soncino Press, 1978), 8. H. C. Leupold, *Exposition of Genesis* vol. 1 (Grand Rapids: Baker Book House, 1782), 128. He points out, "The contention that the Old Testament does not know spiritual death, because it does not happen to use that very expression, is a rationalizing and shallow one, which misconstrues the whole tenor of the Old Testament."

[18]Note the possible symbolism of the God-given coverings, which necessitated the spilling of blood, suggesting atonement (cf. Gen. 4:2–5; Heb. 9:22).

the Fall, but to maintain divine grace as greater than even the destruction of the Fall.[19]

Such corruption is recognized in the Bible: Psalm 51:5 speaks of David's being conceived in sin; that is, his own sin goes back to the time of his conception. Romans 7:7–24 suggests that sin, although dead, was in Paul from the first. Most crucially, Ephesians 2:3 states that all are "by nature objects [literally, 'children'] of wrath." "Nature," *phusis*, speaks of the fundamental reality or source of a thing. Hence, the very "stuff" of all people is corrupt.[20] Since the Bible teaches that all adults are corrupt and that like comes from like (Job 14:4; Matt. 7:17–18; Luke 6:43), humans must produce corrupt children. Corrupt nature producing corrupt offspring is the best explanation of the universality of sinfulness. While several Gospel passages refer to the humility and spiritual openness of children (Matt. 10:42; 11:25–26; 18:1–7; 19:13–15; Mark 9:33–37,41–42; 10:13–16; Luke 9:46–48; 10:21; 18:15–17), none teach that children are uncorrupted. In fact, some children are even demonized (Matt. 15:22; 17:18; Mark 7:25; 9:17).

Sinfulness of All. Romans 5:12 says "all sinned." Romans 5:18 says that through one sin all were condemned, implying all have sinned. Romans 5:19 says that through one man's sin all were made sinners. Passages that speak of universal sinfulness make no exception for infants. Sinless children would be saved without Christ, which is unscriptural (John 14:6; Acts 4:12). Liability to punishment also indicates sin.

Liability to Punishment. All people, even infants, are subject to punishment. "Children of wrath" (Eph. 2:3, KJV) is a Semitism indicating divine punishment (cf. 2 Pet. 2:14).[21] The biblical imprecations against children (Ps. 137:9) indicate this. And Romans 5:12 says physical death (cf. 5:6–8,10,14,17)

---

[19]Arminians would not define the acceptance of God's offer of salvation as a meritorious act. H. Orton Wiley, *Christian Theology,* vol. 2 (Kansas City: Beacon Hill, 1940), 138. Arminius (1560–1609), "Public Disputations" in *The Writings of James Arminius,* vol. 3, trans. W. R. Bagnall (Grand Rapids: Baker Book House, 1986), 375. See also Carl Bangs, *Arminius, A Study in the Dutch Reformation* (Nashville: Abingdon, 1971), 343. John Wesley, "Sermon LXII.—On the Fall of Man," *Sermons on Several Occasions,* vol. 2 (New York: Carlton & Porter, n.d.), 34–37.

[20]Andrew T. Lincoln, *Ephesians,* Word Biblical Commentary, vol. 42 (Dallas: Word Books, 1990), 99.

[21]Ibid., also G. Braumann's treatment of *teknon* in "Child" in *New International Dictionary of New Testament Theology,* Colin Brown, ed., vol. 1 (Grand Rapids: Zondervan Publishing House, 1975), 286.

comes on all, apparently even infants, because all have sinned. Children, prior to moral accountability or consent (the chronological age probably varies with the individual), are not personally guilty. Children are without a knowledge of good or evil (Deut. 1:39; cf. Gen. 2:17). Romans 7:9–11 states Paul was "alive" until the Mosaic law (cf. 7:1) came, causing sin "to spring to life" (cf. NIV), which deceived and killed him spiritually.

Childhood Salvation. Although infants are considered sinners and therefore liable to hell, this does not mean any are actually sent there. Various doctrines indicate several mechanisms for saving some or all: unconditional election within Calvinism; paedobaptism within sacramentalism; preconscious faith; God's foreknowledge of how a child would have lived; God's peculiar graciousness to children; the implicit covenant of a believing family (perhaps including the "law of the heart," Rom. 2:14–15), superseding the Adamic covenant; prevenient grace (from Latin: the grace "which comes before" salvation), extending the Atonement to all under the age of accountability. In all events, one may rest assured that the "Judge of all the earth" does right (Gen. 18:25).

The Adam–Christ Parallel. Romans 5:12–21 and, to a lesser extent, 1 Corinthians 15:21–22 emphasize a strong parallel between Adam and Christ. Romans 5:19 is especially significant: "As through the disobedience of the one man [Adam] the many were made [Gk. *kathistēmi*] sinners, so also through the obedience of the one man [Christ] the many will be made [*kathistēmi*] righteous." In the New Testament, *kathistēmi* typically refers to one appointing another to a position. No actual act is required to attain the position. Hence, people who had not actually sinned could be made sinners by Adam. In a mirror image of Christ, Adam can make people sinners by a forensic, or legal, act not requiring actual sin on their part. (That a person must "accept Christ" to be saved cannot be part of the parallel, since infants who cannot consciously accept Christ may be saved; 2 Sam. 12:23.)

Not All Like Adam. Some people clearly did not sin in the same manner as Adam, yet they did sin and they did die (Rom. 5:14).[22]

---

[22]Because Paul stipulates the period between Adam and Moses, he must be primarily thinking about adults disobeying a direct command of God with a death penalty attached, as did Adam in Eden and Israel after the Mosaic law. That is, since Adam's sin brought death, God was just in decreeing that their sins should bring death. This can refer to infants (as some think), but only by extension.

One Man's One Sin. In Romans 5:12–21, Paul repeatedly says that one man's one sin brought condemnation and death (see also 1 Cor. 15:21–22) on all people.

The Cursed Ground. Some basis must be identified for God's cursing the ground (Gen. 3:17–18).

Christ's Sinlessness. Christ must be allowed a complete human nature and also safeguard His complete sinlessness.

God's Justice. God's justice in allowing Adam's sin to pass to others must be preserved.

ORIGINAL SIN: A THEOLOGICAL ANALYSIS

Many attempts have been made to construct a theological model or theory to fit these complex parameters. Some of the more significant are discussed here.[23]

Jewish Conceptions. Three main motifs are found in Judaism. The dominant theory is that of the two natures, the good, *yetser tov,* and evil, *yetser ra'* (cf. Gen. 6:5; 8:21). The rabbis debated the age at which these impulses manifest themselves and whether the evil impulse is true moral evil or only natural instinct. In all events, wicked people are controlled by the evil impulse while good people control it. A second theory concerns the "watchers" (Gen. 6:1–4), angels who were to oversee humanity but sinned with human females. Finally, there are ideas of original sin that anticipate Christianity. Most dramatically, the Midrash (commentary) on Deuteronomy explains the death of the righteous Moses by analogy to a child who inquires of the king as to why he is in prison. The king replies that it is because of the sin of the boy's mother. Similarly, Moses died because of the first man who brought death into the world. In summary, original sin

---

[23]Space precludes subtleties such as the precise nature of corruption and dozens of other positions, such as the philosophical realism of Odo and the Arbitrary Divine Constitution and Approval of Edwards. More complete, if still biased, summaries include Henri Rondet, *Original Sin, the Patristic and Theological Background,* trans. C. Finegan (Staten Island, N.Y.: Alba House, 1972); F. R. Tennant, *The Sources of the Doctrine of the Fall and Original Sin* (London: Cambridge University Press, 1903); Norman P. Williams, *The Ideas of the Fall and Original Sin: A Historical and Critical Study* (London: Longmans, Green and Co. Ltd., 1927).

is not a Pauline innovation, but Paul, by the Spirit, developed it in accordance with progressive revelation.[24]

Agnosticism. Some hold that there is insufficient biblical evidence to form a detailed theory of original sin. Any statement beyond a connection between Adam and the human race in the matter of sinfulness is deemed philosophical speculation.[25] Although it is true that doctrine ought not to be based on extra-scriptural speculation, deduction from Scripture is valid.

Pelagianism. Pelagianism strongly emphasizes personal responsibility in opposition to moral laxness. Pelagius (A.D ca. 361–ca. 420) taught that God's justice would not permit the transfer of Adam's sin to others, so all people are born sinless and with a totally free will. Sin is spread only through bad example. Hence, sinless lives are possible and are found within and outside the Bible. Yet, all this is unscriptural. It also makes the biblical connections of Adam to humanity meaningless. Jesus' death becomes only good example. Salvation is merely good works. New life in Christ is really old discipline. While rightly emphasizing personal responsibility, holiness, and that some sins are learned, Pelagianism has correctly been judged a heresy.[26]

Semipelagianism. Semipelagianism holds that although humanity is weakened with Adam's nature, sufficient free will remains for people to initiate faith in God, to which He then responds. The weakened nature is transmitted naturally from

---

[24]E.g., Talmud: Berakoth 61a and Nedarim 32b; Genesis Rabbah 9:10; Testament of Asher 1:5. A. Cohen, *Everyman's Talmud* (New York: Schocken, 1949), 88–93. Baruch 56:11–16; 1 [Ethiopic] Enoch 1:5; 10:8–15; 12:2–4; 13:10; 14:1–3; 15:9; 39:12–13; 40:2; and Jubilees 4:15,22; 7:21; 8:3; Testament of Reubin 5:6; Damascus Document (Zadokite Fragment) 2:17–19; Genesis Apocryphon (1QapGen) 2:1. In Talmud: Shabbath 88b, 104a; Pesahim 54a; Behoraoth 55b; Tamid 32b. In Apocrypha and Pseudepigrapha: Apocalypse of Moses (The Greek Life of Adam and Eve) 14, 32; 2 Baruch 17:2–3; 23:4; 48:42–43; 54:15–19; 56:5–10; Ecclesiasticus or The Wisdom of Jesus Son of Sirach 14:17; 25:24; 2 Enoch 30:14–31:8; 4 Ezra 3:7,21–22; 4:30–32; 7.116–18; Life of Adam and Eve 44; Wisdom of Solomon 2:23–24, cf. 10:1–4. Rabbah 9:8, cf. Aboth 5:18.

[25]Supporters include Peter Lombard (ca. 1100–1160), Sentences II 30.5; The Councils of Trent (1545–63), and Vatican II (1962); G. W. Bromiley, "Sin" in *The International Standard Bible Encyclopedia,* ed. Geoffrey W. Bromiley, vol. 4 (Grand Rapids: Wm. B. Eerdmans, 1988), 519–20.

[26]Pelagius (ca. 360–ca. 420), Celestius (fl. 411), Rufinus Tyrannius (ca. 355–ca. 410), Julian of Eclanum (born 380–died between 425 and 455), and many modern theological liberals hold the position.

CHAPTER
8
⎯⎯⎯⎯
The Origin,
Nature, and
Consequences
of Sin

Adam.[27] Yet, how God's justice is maintained in allowing innocent people to receive even a tainted nature and how Christ's sinlessness is protected are not well explained. Most important, in some formulations, semipelagianism teaches that though human nature is so weakened by the Fall that it is inevitable that people sin, yet they have enough inherent goodness to initiate actual faith.

Natural or Genetic Transmission. This theory holds that transmission of the corrupt nature is based on the law of inheritance. It assumes that spiritual traits are transmitted in the same manner as natural ones. Typically such theories speak of the transmission of corruption but not guilt. Yet, there seems to be no adequate basis for God to inflict corrupt natures on good souls. Nor is it clear how Christ can have a fully human nature that is free from sin.[28]

Mediate Imputation. Mediate imputation understands God as charging or imputing guilt to Adam's descendants through an indirect, or mediate, means. Adam's sin made him guilty and, as a judgment, God corrupted Adam's nature. Because none of his posterity was part of his act, none are guilty. However, they receive his nature as a natural consequence of their descent from him (not as a judgment). Yet, before committing any actual or personal sin (which their corrupted nature necessitates), God judges them guilty for possessing that corrupted nature.[29] Unfortunately, this attempt to protect God from unfairly inflicting "alien guilt" from Adam upon humanity results in afflicting God with even greater unfairness, as He allows sin-causing corruption to vitiate parties who are devoid of guilt and then judges them guilty because of this corruption.

Realism. Realism and federalism (see below) are the two most important theories. Realism holds that the "soul stuff" of all people was really and personally in Adam ("seminally present," according to the traducian view of the origin of the soul),[30] actually participating in his sin. Each person is guilty because, in reality, each sinned. Everyone's nature is then

---

[27]Key supporters include Johannes Cassianus (ca. 360–ca. 435), Hilary of Arles (ca. 401–ca. 450), Vincent of Lerins (flourished ca. 450), some later Arminians, and the New School Presbyterians (nineteenth century).

[28]E.g., John Miley, *Systematic Theology,* vol. 1 (Peabody, Mass.: Hendrickson, 1989), 505–9.

[29]Key supporters are Placaeus (1596–1655 or 1665) and the School of Saumur.

[30]See chap. 7, pp. 247–48.

corrupted by God as a judgment on that sin. There is no transmission, or conveyance, of sin, but complete racial participation in the first sin. Augustine (354–430) elaborated on the theory by saying corruption passed through the sexual act. This allowed him to keep Christ free of original sin through the Virgin Birth.[31] W. G. T. Shedd (1820–94) added a more sophisticated underpinning. He argued that beneath the will of everyday choices is the deep will, the "will proper," which shapes the ultimate direction of the person. It is this deep will of each person that actually sinned in Adam.[32]

Realism has great strengths. It does not have the problem of alien guilt, the solidarity of Adam and the race in Adam's sin is taken seriously, and the "all sinned" of Romans 5:12 appears well handled.

However, there are problems: Realism has all the weaknesses of extreme traducianism. The kind of personal presence necessary in Adam and Eve strains even Hebrews 7:9–10 (cf. Gen. 46:26), the classic traducianistic passage. The "One might even say" (Heb. 7:9) in Greek suggests that what follows is to be taken figuratively.[33] Concepts like a "deep will" tend to require and presuppose a deterministic, Calvinistic view of salvation. Realism by itself cannot explain why, or on what basis, God curses the ground.

Therefore, something like the covenant is required. For His humanity to be sinless, Jesus must have committed the first sin in Adam and was subsequently purified, or He was not present at all, or He was present but did not sin and was conveyed sinless through all succeeding generations. Each of these presents difficulties. (An alternative is suggested below.) That all personally sinned seems inconsistent with one man's one sin making all sinners (Rom. 5:12,15–19). Since all sinned in, with, and as Adam, all appear to have sinned in Adam's pattern, contrary to 5:14.

Federalism. The federal theory of transmission holds that corruption and guilt come upon all humanity because Adam

---

[31]E.g., *On Marriage and Concupiscence* vol. 1, 27, in *A Select Library of the Nicene and Post-Nicene Fathers of the Christian Church,* ed. Philip Schaff, trans. Peter Holmes and R. E. Wallis (Grand Rapids: Wm. B. Eerdmans, reprinted 1971), vol. 5, 274–75.

[32]William G. T. Shedd, *Theological Essays,* reprint (Minneapolis: Klock & Klock, 1981), 209–64. Realism began with Tertullian (fl. 200) and has been held by many theologians since.

[33]See Ronald Williamson, *Philo and the Epistle to the Hebrews* (Leiden: E. J. Brill, 1970), 103–9. Heb. 7:9–10 may support a generic traducianism.

was the head of the race in a representative, governmental, or federal sense when he sinned. Everyone is subject to the covenant between Adam and God (the Adamic covenant, or covenant of works, in contrast to the covenant of grace). Analogy is made to a nation that declares war. Its citizens suffer whether or not they agree with or participate in the decision. Adam's descendants are not personally guilty until they actually commit sin, but they are in a guilty state and liable to hell by the imputation of Adam's sin to them under the covenant. Because of this state, God punishes them with corruption. Many federalists therefore distinguish between inherited sin (corruption) and imputed sin (guilt) from Adam. Most federalists are creationists concerning the origin of the soul, but federalism is not incompatible with traducianism.[34] Adam's covenant included his stewardship over creation and is the just basis of God's curse on the ground. Christ, as the head of a new covenant and race, is exempt from the judgment of corruption and so is sinless.

Federalism has many strengths. The covenant, as a biblical basis for the transmission of sin, is in reasonable agreement with Romans 5:12–21 and provides mechanisms for cursing the ground and protecting Christ from sin. However, federalism also has weaknesses. Romans 7 must describe only Paul's realization of his sinful nature, not the actual experience of sin killing him. More important, the transmission of "alien guilt" from Adam is often seen as unjust.[35]

An Integrated Theory. Several of the above theories may be combined in an integrated approach. This theory distinguishes between the individual person and the sin nature of flesh. When Adam sinned he separated himself from God, which produced corruption (including death) in him as an individual and in his nature. Because he contained all generic nature, it was all corrupted. This generic nature is transmitted naturally to the individual aspect of the person, the "I" (as

---

[34]See chap. 7, pp. 247–48.

[35]Little-appreciated foreshadowings of federalism are first found in Irenaeus (ca. 130–ca. 200; *Against Heresies:* Adam and Christ: III.22.3–4; Adam and the race: II.19.6, 21.2, 21.33, 23.8, 33.7; IV.22.1; V.16.2; 17.1, 26.2; Adam's effect on the race: III.22:10, 23:8, IV.22.1; guilt: V.34.2). Many of the Reformed held this view (Hodge, *in extremis*), as did Arminius ("Public Disputations" XXXI.9; but cf. VII.16's realist emphasis), but not all of his followers. Wesley's key materials are cautiously federalist (*Notes on the New Testament,* Rom. 5:12–21; *Doctrine of Original Sin,* sec. VI–VII), as are many of his followers (Wiley). Wesleyans tend toward traducianism.

in Rom. 7).[36] The Adamic covenant is the just basis of this transmission and also of the curse on the ground. The "I" is not corrupted or made guilty by the generic nature, but the generic nature does prevent the "I" from pleasing God (John 14:21; 1 John 5:3). Upon reaching personal accountability, the "I," struggling with the nature, either responds to God's prevenient grace in salvation or actually sins by ignoring it, and so the "I" itself is separated from God and becomes guilty and corrupt. God continues to reach out to the "I" through prevenient grace, and it may respond to salvation.

Therefore, Romans 5:12 can say "all sinned" and all can be corrupt and in need of salvation, but guilt is not inflicted upon those who have not yet actually sinned. This is consistent with the struggle of Romans 7. Not all people sin like Adam (Rom. 5:14), but one man's one sin does bring death and make all sinners; it does so by the Adamic covenant, a mechanism parallel to Christ's making sinners righteous (Rom. 5:12–21). Extreme semipelagianism is avoided since the "I" can only acknowledge its need but cannot act in faith because of the generic human nature (James 2:26). Since separation from God is the cause of corruption, Christ's union with His part of the generic nature restores it to holiness. Because the Spirit came to Mary in the conception of the human "I" of Christ it was preresponsible and therefore sinless. This arrangement is just, because Christ is the Head of a new covenant. Similarly, the Spirit's union with the believer in salvation is regenerating.[37]

Although Scripture does not explicitly affirm the covenant as the basis for transmission, there is much evidence in favor of it. Covenants are a fundamental part of God's plan (Gen. 6:18; 9:9–17; 15:18; 17:2–21; Exod. 34:27–28; Jer. 31:31; Heb. 8:6,13; 12:24). There was a covenant between God and Adam. Hosea 6:7, "Like Adam, they have broken the covenant," most likely refers to this covenant since the alternative translation of "men" (NIV margin) is tautological. Hebrews 8:7, which calls the covenant with Israel "first," does not preclude the Adamic covenant because the context indicates that it refers only to the first covenant of God with Israel (not all humanity)

---

[36]This theory is compatible with either dichotomy or trichotomy and with either creationism or a moderate traducianism in which personhood emerges in human conception.

[37]It is of no small moment that Adam and Eve passed the sentence of separation from God upon themselves by fearing and hiding prior to God's passing the sentence upon them.

and there is an explicit, earlier covenant with Noah (Gen. 6:18; 9:9–17). Biblical covenants are binding over future generations for good (Noah, Gen. 6:18; 9:9–17) or ill (Joshua and the Gibeonites, Josh. 9:15). Covenants are often the only observable basis for judgment (the Israelites who died at Ai because of Achan's sin at Jericho [Josh. 7]; the suffering of the people due to David's numbering them [2 Sam. 24]). Covenantal circumcision could bring even alien children into Israel (Gen. 17:9–14).

Some object that any theory that transmits any consequence of Adam's sin to others is inherently unfair because it imputes his sin gratuitously, that is, without basis. (Only Pelagianism fully avoids this by making everyone personally responsible. Realism's preconscious sin retains most of the difficulties.) Covenants are, however, a just basis for such transmission for the following reasons: Adam's descendants would have been as blessed by his good behavior as they were cursed by his evil work. The covenant is certainly more fair than mere genetic transmission. The guilt and consequences transmitted by the covenant are similar to sins of ignorance (Gen. 20).

Some object that Deuteronomy 24:16 and Ezekiel 18:20 prohibit transgenerational judgment. But other passages speak of such judgment (the firstborn of Egypt; Moab; Exod. 20:5; 34:6–7; Jer. 32:18). It is just possible, however, to see the former passages as referring to biological headship as an insufficient ground for transmitting judgment and the latter passages as referring to a covenantal basis, which is adequate for passing on judgment. Alternatively, in the integrated theory, since the corrupt nature is not a positive judgment of God, the issue of punishment for the father's sin does not really occur. Finally, who, even without corruption and in the perfect Garden, would do better than Adam at obeying God's commandments? And surely what some call the "unfairness" of imputed sin is more than overcome by the graciousness of freely offered salvation in Christ!

Although speculative, and not without its difficulties, this integrated theory utilizing the covenant appears to account for much of the scriptural data and may suggest a third alternative to the dominant theories of realism and federalism.

THE EXISTENCE AND DEFINITION OF SIN

How can evil exist if God is all good and all powerful?[38] This question, and the related one concerning the source of

---

[38]This is the key question of theodicy.

evil, is the specter that haunts all attempts to understand sin. Before proceeding further, several kinds of evil must be distinguished. Moral evil, or sin, is lawlessness committed by volitional creatures. Natural evil is the disorder and decay of the universe (natural disasters, some sickness, etc.). It is connected to God's curse on the ground (Gen. 3:17–18). Metaphysical evil is unintentional evil resulting from creaturely finitude (mental and physical inability, etc.).

The Bible affirms God's moral perfection (Ps. 100:5; Mark 10:18) and power (Jer. 32:17; Matt. 19:26). He alone created (Gen. 1:1–2; John 1:1–3), and all He created was good (Gen. 1; Eccles. 7:29). He did not create evil, which He hates (Ps. 7:11; Rom. 1:18). He neither tempts nor is tempted (James 1:13). Yet, two apparently contradictory passages must be considered: First, in Isaiah 45:7, the KJV says God creates evil. But *ra'*, "evil," also has a nonmoral sense (e.g., Gen. 47:9, KJV), as in the NIV's "disaster." This best contrasts with "peace" (cf. Amos 6:3) and is the preferred translation. Hence, God brings moral judgment, not immoral evil.

Second, God's hardening or blinding of people also raises questions. This can be a passive "giving over" in which God simply leaves people to their own devices (Ps. 81:12; Rom. 1:18–28; 1 Tim. 4:1–2) or an active imposition of hardening in people who have irrevocably committed themselves to evil (Exod. 1:8 through 15:21; Deut. 2:30; Josh. 11:20; Isa. 6:9–10; 2 Cor. 3:14–15; Eph. 4:17–19; 2 Thess. 2:9–12).

Note the example of Pharaoh (Exod. 1:8 through 15:21). Pharaoh was not created for the purpose of being hardened, as a superficial reading of Romans 9:17 ("I raised you up") might suggest. The Hebrew *'amad* and its counterpart in the Septuagint (LXX), *diatēreō* (Exod. 9:16), refer to status or position, not creation, which is within the semantic range of *exegeirō* (Rom. 9:17). Pharaoh deserved God's judgment when he first rejected Moses' plea (Exod. 5:2). But God preserved Pharaoh so He might be glorified through him. Initially, God only predicted His hardening of Pharaoh's heart (4:21, Heb. *'achazzeq*, "I will make strong"; 7:3, Heb. *'aqsheh*, "I will make heavy," i.e., hard to move). Before God acted, however, Pharaoh hardened his own heart (implicitly, 1:8–22; 5:2; and explicitly, 7:13–14). Pharaoh's heart "became hard" (literally, "became strong"), apparently in response to the gracious miracle that removed the plague, and God said Pharaoh's heart was "unyielding" (Heb. *kavedh*, "is heavy"[39] 7:22–23;

---

[39]The Hebrew does not indicate any action by God in this.

8:15,32; 9:7). Pharaoh then continued the process (9:34–35)
with God's assistance (9:12; 10:1,20,27; 11:10; 14:4,8,17).

This pattern is explicit in or compatible with the other
cases and with God's holy justice (Rom. 1:18). Therefore,
God can accelerate self-confirmed sinfulness for His purposes
(Ps. 105:25), but sinners remain responsible (Rom. 1:20).[40]

Since God did not create evil yet did create all that exists,
evil cannot have a unique existence. Evil is an absence or
disordering of the good. This may be illustrated by common
table salt, a compound, or tightly bound mixture, of two
chemicals, sodium and chloride. When not bound together,
both elements are highly lethal. Sodium bursts into flame
upon contact with water, and chlorine is a deadly poison.[41]
Like disordered salt, God's perfect creation is deadly when
thrown out of balance by sin.[42] Through the falls of Satan and
Adam all evil arises. Therefore, natural evil stems from moral
evil. All sickness is ultimately from sin, but not necessarily
the sin of the one who is sick (John 9:1–3), although it may
be (Ps. 107:17; Isa. 3:17; Acts 12:23). The great irony of
Genesis 1 through 3 is that both God and Satan use language:
one creatively to bring reality and order *ex nihilo,* the other
imitatively to bring deception and disorder. Evil is dependent
on the good and Satan's work is only imitation.

Because God was capable of stopping evil (by isolating the
tree, for instance) and yet did not, and because He certainly
knew what would happen, it seems He allowed evil to occur.
(This is far different from causing it.) It follows that the Holy
God saw a greater good in allowing evil. Some of the suggestions of the exact nature of this good follow: (1) that
humanity would mature through suffering (cf. Heb. 5:7–9);[43]
(2) that people would be able to freely and truly love God
since such love requires the possibility of hate and sin;[44] (3)
that God could express himself in ways that would otherwise
be impossible (such as His hatred of evil, Rom. 9:22, and

---

[40]William Hendriksen, *Exposition of Paul's Epistle to the Romans,* New
Testament Commentary (Grand Rapids: Baker Book House, 1981) 325–
26.

[41]Household bleach is only about 2 percent chlorine.

[42]Augustine thought this disordering resulted when a creature sought
other than the highest good (*City of God,* 12.6–8); cf. Rom. 1:25.

[43]Held by Irenaeus and many of the Eastern fathers.

[44]Held by Augustine and many of the Western fathers.

gracious love of sinners, Eph. 2:7).[45] All these understandings have some validity.[46]

Describing sin is a difficult task. This may result from its parasitic nature, in that it has no separate existence but is conditioned by that which it attaches to. Yet, an image of sin's chameleonic, derivative existence does appear in Scripture.

There have been many suggestions of the essence of sin: unbelief, pride, selfishness, rebellion, moral corruption, a struggle of flesh and spirit, idolatry, and combinations of the preceding.[47] While all these ideas are informative, none characterizes every sin, for example, sins of ignorance, and none adequately explains sin as a nature. Most significantly, all these ideas define sin in terms of sinners, who are many, varied, and imperfect. It seems preferable to define sin with reference to God. He alone is one, consistent, and absolute, and against His holiness the contrariness of sin is displayed.

Perhaps the best definition of sin is found in 1 John 3:4— "Sin is lawlessness." Whatever else sin is, at its heart, it is a breach of God's law. And since "all wrongdoing is sin" (1 John 5:17), all wrongdoing breaks God's law.[48] So David confesses, "Against you, you only, have I sinned" (Ps. 51:4; cf. Luke 15:18,21). Furthermore, transgression forces separation from the God of Life and Holiness, which necessarily results in the corruption (including death) of finite, dependent human nature. Therefore, this definition of sin is biblical, precise, and embraces every type of sin; it accounts for sin's effects on nature and is referenced to God, not humanity. That is, we see its true nature by observing its contrast to God, not by comparing its effects among human beings.

Although believers are not under the Mosaic law, objective standards still exist and can be broken (John 4:21; 1 John 5:3; the many regulations in the Epistles). Because of the human inability to fulfill law, only a relationship with Christ can

---

[45]See Lewis Sperry Chafer, *Systematic Theology,* vol. 2 (Dallas: Dallas Theological Seminary Press, 1974), 229–34.

[46]Good introductions include Norman Geisler, *Philosophy of Religion* (Grand Rapids: Zondervan Publishing House, 1974), 311–403, and the liberal John Hick, *Evil and the God of Love* (New York: Harper and Row, 1966).

[47]For a good summary see Erickson, *Christian Theology,* 577–80; on idolatry, see Tertullian, *On Idolatry,* 1.

[48]The Westminster Divines are notably concise: "Sin is any want of conformity unto, or transgression of, the law of God" (Answer 14, *The Shorter Catechism*).

provide atonement to cover sin and power to live a godly life. The believer who sins must still confess and, where possible, make restitution, not for absolution, but to reaffirm his or her relationship with Christ. It is this faith that has always been contrary to "works righteousness" (Hab. 2:4; Rom. 1:17; Gal. 3:11; Heb. 10:38), so that whatever is not of faith is sin (Rom. 14:23; cf. Titus 1:15; Heb. 11:6). Therefore, sin—in believers or unbelievers, before or after the Crucifixion—is always lawlessness, and the only solution is faith in Christ.

Sin is not defined by feelings or philosophy,[49] but only by God in His law, desire, and will. This is discovered most concretely through Scripture. Although optimally the believer's heart (broadly defined) can sense sin (Rom. 2:13–15; 1 John 3:21), its spiritual sensitivity to good and evil requires development (Heb. 5:14). The heart has been deeply wicked (Jer. 17:9) and can be seared (1 Tim. 4:2); it also feel false guilt (1 John 3:20).[50] For this reason, subjective feelings must never be placed above God's objective, written Word. Yet, one must be spiritually sensitive.

The idea of sin as breaking law is imbedded in the very language of Scripture. The *chatta'th* word group, the most important in Hebrew for "sin," carries the basic idea of "missing the mark" (Judg. 20:16; Prov. 19:2). With this idea of an objective mark or standard, it can refer to willful sins (Exod. 10:17; Deut. 9:18; Ps. 25:7), an external reality of sin (Gen. 4:7), a pattern of sin (Gen. 18:20; 1 Kings 8:36), errors (Lev. 4:2), and the offerings required for them (Lev. 4:8). *'Awon,* "iniquity," from the idea of "crooked" or "twisted," speaks of serious sins, often being paralleled with *chatta'th* (Isa. 43:24). The verb *'avar* speaks of the crossing of a boundary, and so, metaphorically of transgression (Num. 14:41; Deut. 17:2). *Resha'* can mean wrong (Prov. 11:10) or injustice (Prov. 28:3–4).

In Greek, the *hamartia* word group carries the generic concept of sin in the New Testament. With the basic meaning of "missing the mark" (as in *chatta'th*), it is a broad term originally without moral connotation. In the New Testament,

---

[49]On moral philosophy see, for instance, Emmanuel Kant, *Groundwork of the Metaphysics of Morals and Critique of Practical Reason.* Ironically, "conscience," such a relativized term in today's society, derives from the Latin, *conscientia,* "with knowledge," or "shared knowledge."

[50]"Seared" may mean "branded." Habitual criminals were branded. Therefore a seared conscience is one that acts like a criminal's conscience and excuses sin.

however, it refers to specific sins (Mark 1:5; Acts 2:38; Gal. 1:4; Heb. 10:12) and to sin as a force (Rom. 6:6,12; Heb. 12:1). *Anomia* (Gk. *nomos,* "law," plus the negating *a*), "without law," "lawlessness," "iniquity," and its related terms represent perhaps the strongest language of sin. The adjective and adverb may refer to those without the Torah (Rom. 2:12; 1 Cor. 9:21), but the word usually identifies anyone who has broken any divine law (Matt. 7:23; 1 John 3:4). It is also the "lawlessness" of 2 Thessalonians 2:7–12.

Another term for sin, *adikia,* is most literally translated "unrighteousness" and ranges from a mere mistake to gross violations of law. It is great wickedness (Rom. 1:29; 2 Pet. 2:13–15) and is contrasted with righteousness (Rom. 6:13). *Parabasis,* "overstepping," "transgression," and its derivatives indicate breaking a standard. The word describes the Fall (Rom. 5:14; cf. 1 Tim. 2:14), the transgression of law as sin (James 2:9,11), and Judas' loss of his apostleship (Acts 1:25). *Asebeia,* "ungodliness" (the negating *a* added to *sebomai* ["to show reverence," "to worship," etc.]), suggests a spiritual insensitivity that results in gross sin (Jude 4), producing great condemnation (1 Pet. 4:18; 2 Pet. 2:5; 3:7).

The idea of sin as lawbreaking or disorder stands in stark contrast to the personal God who spoke into existence an ordered and good world. The very idea of personness (whether human or divine) demands order; its absence gives rise to the common and technical term "personality disorder."[51]

Characteristics of Sin

Many of the facets of sin are reflected in the following characteristics drawn from the biblical record.

Sin as unbelief or lack of faith is seen in the Fall, in humanity's rejection of general revelation (Rom. 1:18 through 2:2), and in those condemned to the second death (Rev. 21:8). It is closely connected with Israel's disobedience in the desert (Heb. 3:18–19). The Greek *apistia,* "unbelief" (Acts 28:24), combines the negating *a* with *pistis,* "faith," "trust," "faithfulness." Whatever is not of faith is sin (Rom. 14:23; Heb. 11:6). Unbelief is the opposite of saving faith (Acts 13:39; Rom. 10:9), ending in eternal judgment (John 3:16; Heb. 4:6,11).

---

[51]*Diagnostic and Statistical Manual of Mental Disorders,* 3d ed. rev. (Washington, D.C.: American Psychiatric Association, 1987), 335–58, lists some eleven types of personality disorders.

Pride is self-exaltation. Ironically, it is both the desire to be like God (as in Satan's temptation of Eve) and the rejection of God (Ps. 10:4). Despite its terrible price, it is worthless before God (Isa. 2:11) and is hated by Him (Amos 6:8). It deceives (Obad. 3) and leads to destruction (Prov. 16:18; Obad. 4; Zech. 10:11). It helped make the unbelief of Capernaum worse than the depravity of Sodom (Matt. 11:23; Luke 10:15) and stands as the antithesis of Jesus' humility (Matt. 11:29; 20:28; cf. Phil. 2:3–8). In the final judgment, the proud will be humbled and the humble exalted (Matt. 23:1–12; Luke 14:7–14). Although having a positive side, the Hebrew *ga'on* (Amos 6:8) and the Greek *huperēphanos* (James 4:6) typically denote a deep and abiding arrogance.

Closely related to pride, unhealthy or misdirected desire and its self-centeredness are sin and a motivator to sin (1 John 2:15–17). *Epithumia*, "desire" (James 4:2), used in a bad sense, leads to murder and war, and *pleonexia*, an impassioned "greed" or "desire to have more," is equated with idolatry. Consequently, all wicked desire is condemned (Rom. 6:12).

Whether Adam's disobedience or the believer's lovelessness (John 14:15,21; 15:10), all conscious sin is rebellion against God. The Hebrew *pesha'* involves deliberate, premeditated "rebellion" (Isa. 59:13; Jer. 5:6). Rebellion is also reflected in *marah* ("be refractory, obstinate"; Deut. 9:7) and *sarar* ("be stubborn"; Ps. 78:8), and in the Greek *apeitheia* ("disobedience"; Eph. 2:2), *apostasia* ("apostasy" or "rebellious abandonment, defection"; 2 Thess. 2:3), and *parakoē* ("refusal to hear," "disobedience"; Rom. 5:19; 2 Cor. 10:6). And so, rebellion is equated with the sin of divination, which seeks guidance from sources other than God and His Word (1 Sam. 15:23).

Sin, the product of the "father of lies" (John 8:44), is the antithesis of God's truth (Ps. 31:5; John 14:6; 1 John 5:20). From the first, it has deceived in what it promised and incited those deceived to further prevarication (John 3:20; 2 Tim. 3:13). It can give dramatic, but only temporary, pleasure (Heb. 11:25). The Hebrew *ma'al*, "unfaithfulness," "deceit" (Lev. 26:40), and the Greek *paraptōma*, "false step," "transgression" (Heb. 6:6), can both signify betrayal due to unbelief.

The objective side of the lie of sin is the real distortion of the good. "Iniquity," *'awon*, from the idea of twisted or perverted, conveys this (Gen. 19:15, KJV; Ps. 31:10, KJV; Zech. 3:9, KJV). Several compounds of *strephō*, "turn" (*apo-*, Luke 23:14; *dia-*, Acts 20:30; *meta-*, Gal. 1:7; *ek-*, Titus 3:11), do the same in Greek, as does *skolios,* "crooked," "unscrupulous" (Acts 2:40).

In general, the biblical concept of evil encompasses both sin and its result. The Hebrew *ra'* has a wide range of uses: animals inadequate for sacrifice (Lev. 27:10), life's difficulties (Gen. 47:9), the evil aspect of the tree of Eden (Gen. 2:17), the imaginations of the heart (Gen. 6:5), evil acts (Exod. 23:2), wicked people (Gen. 38:7), retribution (Gen. 31:29), and God's righteous judgment (Jer. 6:19). In Greek, *kakos* typically designates bad or unpleasant things (Acts 28:5). However, *kakos* and its compounds can have a wider, moral meaning, designating thoughts (Mark 7:21), actions (2 Cor. 5:10), persons (Titus 1:12), and evil as force (Rom. 7:21; 12:21). *Ponēria* and its word group develop strongly ethical connotations in the New Testament, including Satan as the "evil one" (Matt. 13:19; see also Mark 4:15; Luke 8:12; cf. 1 John 2:13) and corporate evil (Gal. 1:4).

Sins that are especially repugnant to God are designated as detestable ("abominations," KJV). *To'evah,* "something abominable, detestable, offensive," can refer to the unjust (Prov. 29:27), transvestism (Deut. 22:5), homosexuality (Lev. 18:22), idolatry (Deut. 7:25–26), child sacrifice (Deut. 12:31), and other grievous sins (Prov. 6:16–19). The corresponding Greek word *bdelugma* speaks of great hypocrisy (Luke 16:15), the ultimate desecration of the Holy Place (Matt. 24:15; Mark 13:14), and the contents of the cup held by the prostitute Babylon (Rev. 17:4).

THE FORCE AND EXTENT OF SIN

As indicated throughout this chapter and in the study of Satan (chap. 6), a real, personal, and evil force is operating in the universe against God and His people. This suggests the crucial importance of exorcism, spiritual warfare, and the like, but without the ungodly hysteria that so often accompanies these efforts.

Sin is not only isolated actions, but also a reality or nature within the person (see Eph. 2:3). Sin as nature indicates the "seat," or "location," of sin within the person as the immediate source of sin. Negatively, it is seen in the requirement for regeneration, the giving of a new nature to replace the old sinful one (John 3:3–7; Acts 3:19; 1 Pet. 1:23). This is emphasized by the idea that regeneration is something that can happen only from outside the person (Jer. 24:7; Ezek. 11:19; 36:26–27; 37:1–14; 1 Pet. 1:3).

CHAPTER 8

The Origin, Nature, and Consequences of Sin

The New Testament relates the sin nature to the *sarx,* or "flesh." While originally referring to the material body, Paul innovatively equates it with the sinful nature (Rom. 7:5 through 8:13; Gal. 5:13,19). In this sense, *sarx* is the seat of wrong desire (Rom. 13:14; Gal. 5:16,24; Eph. 2:3; 1 Pet. 4:2; 2 Pet. 2:10; 1 John 2:16). Sin and passions arise from the flesh (Rom. 7:5; Gal. 5:17–21), nothing good dwells in it (Rom. 7:18), and gross sinners within the Church are handed over to Satan for the destruction of the flesh, possibly sickness that will cause them to repent (1 Cor. 5:5; cf. 1 Tim. 1:20). *Sōma,* "body," is only occasionally used in a similar way (Rom. 6:6; 7:24; 8:13; Col. 2:11). The physical body is not looked on as evil in itself.[52]

The Hebrew *lev* or *levav,* "heart," "mind," or "understanding," indicates the essence of the person. It can be sinful (Gen. 6:5; Deut. 15:9; Isa. 29:13) above all things (Jer. 17:9). Hence, it needs renewal (Ps. 51:10; Jer. 31:33; Ezek. 11:19). Evil intention flows from it (Jer. 3:17; 7:24), and all its inclinations are evil (Gen. 6:5). The Greek *kardia,* "heart," also indicates the inner life and self. Evil as well as good comes from it (Matt. 12:33–35; 15:18; Luke 6:43–45). It may signify the essential person (Matt. 15:19; Acts 15:9; Heb. 3:12). The *kardia* can be hard (Mark 3:5; 6:52; 8:17; John 12:40; Rom. 1:21; Heb. 3:8). Like the *sarx,* the *kardia* can be the source of wrong desires (Rom. 1:24). Similarly, the mind, *nous,* can be evil in its workings (Rom. 1:28; Eph. 4:17; Col. 2:18; 1 Tim. 6:5; 2 Tim. 3:8; Titus 1:15), requiring renewal (Rom. 12:2).

Sin struggles against the Spirit. The sin nature is utterly contrary to the Spirit and beyond the control of the person (Gal. 5:17; cf. Rom. 7:7–25). It is death to the human (Rom. 8:6,13) and an offense to God (Rom. 8:7–8; 1 Cor. 15:50). From it comes the *epithumia,* the entire range of unholy desires (Rom 1:24; 7:8; Titus 2:12; 1 John 2:16). Sin even dwells within the person (Rom. 7:17–24; 8:5–8) as a principle or law (Rom. 7:21,23,25).

Actual sins begin in the sinful nature often as the result of worldly or supernatural temptation (James 1:14–15; 1 John 2:16). One of sin's most insidious characteristics is that it gives rise to more sin. Sin, like the malignancy it is, grows of itself to fatal proportions in both extent and intensity unless dealt with by the cleansing of Christ's blood. Sin's self-reproduction may be seen in the Fall (Gen. 3:1–13), in Cain's

---

[52]See chap. 7, p. 244.

descent from jealousy to homicide (Gen. 4:1–15), and in David's lust giving birth to adultery, murder, and generations of suffering (2 Sam. 11 through 12). Romans 1:18–32 recounts humanity's downward course from the rejection of revelation to complete abandon and proselytization. Similarly, the "seven deadly sins" (an ancient catalog of vices contrasted with parallel virtues) have been viewed not only as root sins, but also as a descending sequence of sin.[53]

This process of sin's feeding on sin is realized through many mechanisms. The ambitious author of wickedness, Satan, is the archantagonist of this evil drama. As the ruler of this present age (John 12:31; 14:30; 16:11; 2 Cor. 4:4; Eph. 2:2), he constantly seeks to deceive, tempt, sift, and devour (Luke 22:31–34; 2 Cor. 11:14; 1 Thess. 3:5; 1 Pet. 5:8), even inciting the heart directly (1 Chron. 21:1). The natural inclination of the flesh, still awaiting full redemption, also plays a part. The temptations of the world beckon the heart (James 1:2–4; 1 John 2:16). Sin often requires more sin to reach its elusive goal, as in Cain's attempt to hide his crime from God (Gen. 4:9). The pleasure of sin (Heb. 11:25–26) may be self-reinforcing. Sinners provoke their victims to respond in sin (note the contrary exhortations: Prov. 20:22; Matt. 5:38–48; 1 Thess. 5:15; 1 Pet. 3:9). Sinners entice others into sin (Gen. 3:1–6; Exod. 32:1; 1 Kings 21:25; Prov. 1:10–14; Matt. 4:1–11; 5:19; Mark 1:12–13; Luke 4:1–13; 2 Tim. 3:6–9; 2 Pet. 2:18–19; 3:17; 1 John 2:26). [54] Sinners encourage other sinners in sin (Ps. 64:5; Rom. 1:19–32).[55] Individuals harden their hearts against God and try to avoid the mental distress of sin (1 Sam. 6:6; Ps. 95:8; Prov. 28:14; Rom. 1:24,26,28; 2:5; Heb. 3:7–19; 4:7). Finally, the hardening of the heart by God can facilitate this process.

Temptation must never be confused with sin. Jesus suffered the greatest of temptations (Matt. 4:1–11; Mark 1:12–13; Luke 4:1–13; Heb. 2:18; 4:15) and was without sin (2 Cor. 5:21; Heb. 4:15; 7:26–28; 1 Pet. 1:19; 2:22; 1 John 3:5; and the

---

[53]The classic formulation is pride, greed, lust, envy, gluttony, anger, and sloth. Relevant literature includes John Cassian, *Conference* 5; Gregory the Great, *Moralia on Job* 31.45; and especially Aquinas, *Summa Theologica* 2.2.

[54]Many rabbis considered murder less grave than enticing another to sin, because the former only removes one from this world while the latter keeps one from heaven (Sifr Deut. sec. 252; 120a; Sanhedrin 55a, 99b). Cohen, *Everyman's Talmud,* 102.

[55]Note the Hebrew *resha',* "wickedness" or "troubling" (Job 3:17; Isa. 57:20–21), in relation to the general idea of sinners stirring up trouble.

proofs of deity). Furthermore, if temptation were sin, God would not provide help to endure it (1 Cor. 10:13). Although God does test and prove His people (Gen. 22:1–14; John 6:6) and obviously allows temptation (Gen. 3), He himself does not tempt (James 1:13). Practically, the Bible admonishes about the danger of temptation and the need to avoid and be delivered from temptation (Matt. 6:13; Luke 11:4; 22:46; 1 Cor. 10:13; 1 Tim. 6:6–12; Heb. 3:8; 2 Pet. 2:9).

The Bible is abundantly supplied with descriptions of sinful acts and warnings against them, including catalogs of vices (typically: Rom. 1:29–31; 13:13; 1 Cor. 5:10–11; 6:9–10; 2 Cor. 12:20–21; Gal. 5:19–21; Eph 4:31; 5:3–5; Col. 3:5,8; Rev. 21:8; 22:15). Such accountings show the seriousness of sin and display its incredible variety; however, they also carry the danger of inciting morbid despair over past or future sins. Even more seriously, they can reduce sin to mere actions, ignoring the profundity of sin as law, nature, and a force within the person and the universe, leading the person ultimately to see only the symptoms while ignoring the disease.

Scripture describes many categories relating to sin. Sins may be committed by unbelievers or believers, both of whom are injured by it and require grace. Sins may be committed against God, others, self, or some combination. Ultimately, however, all sin is against God (Ps. 51:4; cf. Luke 15:18,21). Sin may be confessed and forgiven; if unforgiven, sin will still exercise its sway over the person. The Bible teaches that an attitude can be as sinful as an act. For exmple, anger is as sinful as murder, and a lustful look is as sinful as adultery (Matt. 5:21–22,27–28; James 3:14–16). An attitude of sin defeats prayer (Ps. 66:18). Sin can be either active or passive, that is, doing evil and neglecting good (Luke 10:30–37; James 4:17). Bodily sexual sins are very grievous for Christians because they misuse the body of the Lord in the person of the believer and because the body is the temple of the Holy Spirit (1 Cor. 6:12–20).

Sins can be done in ignorance (Gen. 20; Lev. 5:17–19; Num. 35:22–24; Luke 12:47–48; 23:34).[56] The Psalmist wisely asks

---

[56]The KJV's "ignorance" and the NIV's "unintentionally" (e.g., Lev. 4:1 through 5:13) are imprecise. They are better rendered "to err" (*shagag* and *shagah*), as the NIV does elsewhere. Clearly, some of these sins were committed knowingly, but out of human weakness rather than rebellion (e.g., 5:1). The contrast seems to be with "defiant" sins or, literally, sins done with a "high hand" (Num. 15:22–31). R. Laird Harris, "Leviticus" in *Expositor's Bible Commentary,* Frank E. Gaebelein, ed., vol. 1 (Grand Rapids: Zondervan Publishing House, 1990), 547–48.

help in discerning them (Ps. 19:12). It seems those who have only the law of nature (Rom. 2:13–15) commit sins of ignorance (Acts 17:30). All people are to some degree responsible and without excuse (Rom. 1:20), and willful ignorance, like that of Pharaoh, from continuing self-hardening is vigorously condemned. Secret sin is as wicked as sin done in public (Eph. 5:11–13). This is especially true of hypocrisy, a form of secret sin in which outward appearance belies inward reality (Matt. 23:1–33; note v. 5). Sins done openly, however, tend to presumption and subversion of the community (Titus 1:9–11; 2 Pet. 2:1–2). Many rabbis believed that secret sin also effectively denied God's omnipresence.[57]

A person commits sins of infirmity because of a divided desire, usually after a struggle against temptation (Matt. 26:36–46; Mark 14:32–42; Luke 22:31–34,54–62; perhaps Rom. 7:14–25). Presumptuous sins are done with deeply wicked intent or with "a high hand" (Num. 15:30). Sins of weakness are of less affront to God than presumptuous sins, as indicated by the severity with which Scripture regards presumptuous sins (Exod. 21:12–14; Ps. 19:13; Isa. 5:18–25; 2 Pet. 2:10) and the absence of atonement for them in the Mosaic law (although not in the gospel). However, this distinction of weakness and presumption must never be used unbiblically as an excuse for taking any sin lightly.

Roman Catholic theology distinguishes between venial (Latin *venia,* "favor," "pardon," "kindness") and mortal sins. In venial sins (as in sins of weakness) the will, though assenting or agreeing to the act of sin, refuses to alter its fundamental godly identity. Venial sins can lead to mortal sins. Mortal sins, however, involve a radical reorienting of the person to a state of rebellion against God and a forfeiture of salvation, though forgiveness remains possible. The real distinction between these sins, however, seems to be not in the nature of sin but in the nature of salvation. Catholicism believes that sins are not inherently venial, but that believers have a righteousness which largely mitigates the effect of lesser sins, making them venial. As such they are not a direct detriment to the believer's relationship with God and technically do not require confession.[58] This is not scriptural (James 5:16; 1 John 1:9).

---

[57]Higagah 16a.

[58]See G. C. Berkouwer, *Sin,* trans. Philip C. Holtrop (Grand Rapids: Wm. B. Eerdmans, 1971), 302–14. Loraine Boettner, *Roman Catholicism,* Phillipsburg, N.J.: Presbyterian and Reformed, 1956.

Beyond all other sins, Jesus himself taught that there is a sin without pardon (Matt. 12:22–37; Mark 3:20–30; Luke 12:1–12; cf. 11:14–26). There has been much debate over the nature of this "unforgivable sin" or "blasphemy against the Holy Spirit." The texts suggest several criteria that any analysis must take into account.

The sin must have reference to the Holy Spirit (Matt. 12:31; Mark 3:29; Luke 12:10). Yet, blasphemy against God or other members of the Trinity (Matt. 12:31–32; Mark 3:28; Luke 12:10; Acts 26:11; Col. 3:8; 1 Tim. 1:13,20) is forgivable. It cannot be a sin that the Bible lists as forgiven. Such sins include those committed prior to a knowledge of God—demon possession (Luke 8:2–3), crucifying the Lord (23:34), nearly lifelong ungodliness (23:39–43), blaspheming (1 Tim. 1:13), compelling believers to blaspheme (Acts 26:11)—and sins committed after a knowledge of God. In addition, the unpardonable sin does not include denying the God of miracles (Exod. 32), returning to idolatry in spite of great miracles (Exod. 32), murder (2 Sam. 11 through 12), gross immorality (1 Cor. 5:1–5), denial of Jesus (Matt. 26:69–75), seeing Jesus' miracles yet thinking Him "out of his mind" (Mark 3:21, just before His teaching on blasphemy), and turning to law after knowing grace (Gal. 2:11–21).

The sin must be blasphemy (Gk. *blasphēmia),* the vilest slander against God. In the LXX, *blasphēmia* often describes the denying of God's power and glory, which is consistent with the Jewish leaders' ascribing Jesus' miracles to the devil.[59] The sin must be comparable to the Jewish leaders' charge that Jesus had an evil spirit (Mark 3:30). The sin cannot be merely denying the witness of miracles, because Peter denied Christ (Matt. 26:69–75) and Thomas doubted Him (John 20:24–29) after seeing many miracles, and they were forgiven.

Since Jesus explicitly says all other sins may be forgiven (Matt. 12:31; Mark 3:28), the sin against the Holy Spirit must be compared with Hebrews 6:4–8; 10:26–31; 2 Peter 2:20–22; and 1 John 5:16–17, which also describe unforgivable sin. Notably, Hebrews 10:29 connects unforgivable sin with in-

---

[59]Hermann Wolfang Beyer, *"Blasphemia,"* in *Theological Dictionary of the New Testament,* Gerhard Kittel, ed., Geoffrey W. Bromiley, trans., vol.1 (Grand Rapids: Wm. B. Eerdmans, 1964), 621–25. For a fascinating parallel see the Dead Sea Scrolls, "The Damascus Document," section 5, which focuses on the lack of discernment among the people.

sulting the Spirit.[60] It also appears that irrevocable hardening of the heart and presumption could be included (e.g., 2 Thess. 2:11–12). As a corollary, neither the incarnate Jesus nor the apostles need to be present for this sin to be committed, since they were seen neither by anyone in the Old Testament nor (most likely) by those addressed in Hebrews, 2 Peter, and 1 John. Hence, the unpardonable sin cannot be a failure to respond to miraculous manifestations of the incarnate Jesus or of the apostles.[61] Nor can it be a temporary denial of the faith,[62] since Scripture considers this forgivable.

The unpardonable sin is best defined as the final, willful rejection of the Holy Spirit's special work (John 16:7–11) of direct testimony to the heart concerning Jesus as Lord and Savior, resulting in absolute refusal to believe.[63] Therefore, blasphemy of the Holy Spirit is not a momentary indiscretion but an ultimate disposition of will, although Jesus' statements do suggest that it may be manifested in a specific act.[64] This is consistent with John's assessment that believers cannot commit continuing sin (1 John 3:6,9). True heartfelt concern indicates the unpardonable sin has not occurred. Such concern, however, is not measured in emotions or even suicidal depression (Matt. 27:3–5; perhaps Heb. 12:16–17), but rather in a renewed seeking after God in faith and dependence upon

---

[60]That these epistolary passages speak of unforgivable sin that causes forfeiture of salvation is in harmony with the position of the Assemblies of God, *Where We Stand*, 108.

[61]The opposite position is often attributed to Jerome (Letter 42) and Chrysostom ("Homilies on Matthew," 49; Matt. 12:25–26, sec. 5). Yet it seems, especially for Chrysostom, that a rejection refers to the Spirit's inner witness in any period. The latter may be seen in John A. Broadus, *Commentary on the Gospel of Matthew* (Philadelphia: American Baptist Publication Society, 1886), 271–73.

[62]So held the rigorist Bishop Novation (fl. mid-third century) concerning the *"lapsi"* (Lat. "those who have fallen or failed"; applied to Christians who worshiped false gods to escape the persecution of Decius, A.D. 249–51). Jerome's *Epistle 42* contains both description and rebuttal.

[63]This view, in essence, was held by Augustine, by many Lutherans, and by most Arminian theologians. For a good analysis see Stanley M. Horton, *What the Bible Says about the Holy Spirit* (Springfield, Mo.: Gospel Publishing House, 1976). 96–102.

[64]Often blasphemy against the Holy Spirit has been distinguished from final impenitence or consistent disregard for the witness of the Spirit that leads to salvation. However, especially in an Arminian soteriology, continued rejection (complete obduracy) of the Holy Spirit's offer of salvation results in a hardness of heart that prevents any possibility of repentance, reducing the distinction to one of appearance only.

Him. The passages in Hebrews exemplify this firm, yet sensitive, pastoral balance.[65]

The Bible admits degrees of sin. This is demonstrated in several of the categories of sin (above) and differing divine judgments (Matt. 11:24; Mark 12:38–40; Luke 10:12; 12:47–48; John 19:11). Yet, Scripture also teaches that to sin at all makes one fully a sinner (Deut. 27:26 through 28:1; Gal. 3:10; James 2:10).[66] The apparent discrepancy is resolved by the fact that both the most insignificant sin and the most heinous sin are sufficient to bring eternal condemnation. However, more serious sin usually does have more significant implications not only for those sinned against, but also for the sinner as he or she moves farther from God's presence.

---

[65]In passing, Jesus' statement concerning the impossibility of forgiveness "in the age to come" (Matt. 12:32) does not imply post-death forgiveness or purgatory (cf. Mark 10:30). It is probably a peremptory denial of the rabbinic hope that blasphemy can be forgiven in death. See John Lightfoot, *A Commentary on the New Testament from the Talmud and Hebraica*, vol. 2 (Peabody, Mass.: Hendrickson Publishers, 1979), 206–7. His argument is strengthened by Talmud, Yoma 86b's use of Isa. 22:14.

This discussion evokes a progression of provocative corollaries. In some sense, it may be said that all those eternally damned have committed the unpardonable sin. Their final and willful rejection of God brings ultimate separation from Him. This separation of the dependent being from its source necessarily brings ultimate impairment. This impairment certainly extends to the *imago dei* (the image of God), which seems to be a locus of sensitivity to the wooing, direct testimony of the Spirit within the person. Because the rejection of and separation from God in the Garden profoundly distorted human nature and because sin typically separates one from God, further damaging the person, this final rejection and separation may result in the total loss of the image. It seems that the loss of the image is what constitutes the rejection of and separation from God as irrevocable. For the person bereft of the image of God, the call of God would not merely cease to resonate but would be distorted by senseless ears into repellent, cacophonous silence. The unpardonable sinner's choice to refuse to accept God is also an ultimate acceptance to refuse choice.

Such a conception also provides an elegant solution to the problems of how God can command the killing of humans while forbidding murder because of the presence of the image within the person (Gen. 9:6, cf. Jas. 3:9) and of how God can condemn people to eternal damnation without at the same time damning His image eternally. Here also emerges a clue to theodicy reminiscent of supralapsarian formulations, but without their difficulties concerning the reprobate, being birthed in their wickedness from the perfect, divine will. The damned receive what they deserve as they become what they desire: godless.

[66]Although Deut. 27:26 does not contain the word "all," there are several good reasons for accepting it as implied: (1) It is required by the context of Deut. 28:1. (2) It is translated so in the LXX. (3) Paul includes it in his citation in Gal. 3:10. (4) Although the Mosaic law is in view, clearly Paul sees this and the "law of nature" (Rom. 2:13–15) as closely connected.

The Bible teaches that only God and unfallen spiritual beings (such as angels) are unstained by sin. The idea that ancient people lived a simple, quiet life is belied by modern anthropology, which reveals the dark side in all human societies.[67] Even liberal theology's evolutionary explanations of sin admit sin's universality.

CHAPTER 8

The Origin, Nature, and Consequences of Sin

Sin contaminates the spirit world. Satan's fall (Job 1:6 through 2:6), Satan's fall from heaven (Luke 10:18 and Rev. 12:8–9; however interpreted), "war" in heaven (Dan. 10:13; Rev. 12:7), and references to evil or unclean spirits (2 Cor. 12:7; Eph. 6:10–18; James 4:7) all attest to this. Sin has infected the universe to an extent well beyond the scope of physical science.

Scripture also teaches that every individual is sinful, in some sense. Since Eden, sin has also occurred within groups. Sin is clearly encouraged through group functioning. Contemporary society is a breeding ground for bias based on ability (in the case of the fetus), gender, race, ethnic background, religion, sexual preference,[68] and even political stands.

As in Israel, sin is found in the Church. Jesus anticipated it (Matt. 18:15–20) and the Epistles testify to its presence (1 Cor. 1:11; 5:1–2; Gal. 1:6; 3:1; Jude 4–19). A Church without spot or wrinkle will not be a reality until Jesus returns (Eph. 5:27; Rev. 21:27).

Scripture teaches that the effects of sin are found even in nonhuman creation. The curse of Genesis 3:17–18 marks the beginning of this evil and Romans 8:19–22 proclaims nature's disordered state. The creation groans awaiting the consummation.[69] The Greek *mataiotēs,* "frustration," "emptiness" (Rom. 8:20), describes the uselessness of a thing when divorced from its original intent, epitomizing the futility of the present state of the universe itself. The divine thought here may range from plants and animals to quarks and galaxies.

---

[67]E.g., Melvin Konner, *The Tangled Wing: Biological Constraints on the Human Spirit* (New York: Holt, Reinhart and Winston, 1982).

[68]This is not to condone homosexual behavior but to condemn anti-homosexual violence.

[69]This passage does not refer to persons. (1) Believers are mentioned separately (Rom. 8:18,21–25). (2) Sinners would not eagerly expect "the sons of God" (8:19,21). (3) It would imply universal salvation. (4) Paul uses *ktisis* to mean "creation" elsewhere (cf. Rom. 1:20). (5) It is consistent with God's curse on the ground (Gen. 3:17). (6) It is consistent with the eschatology (2 Pet. 3:13; Rev. 21:1–2). For a defense, see William Hendriksen, *Exposition of Paul's Epistle to the Romans,* New Testament Commentary (Grand Rapids: Baker Book House, 1981), 266–69.

The extent of sin is circumscribed chronologically. Prior to creation, and for an unspecified period after, sin did not exist and all was good. Yet not only Christian memory, but also Christian hope knows a future when sin and death will no longer exist (Matt. 25:41; 1 Cor. 15:25–26,51–56; Rev. 20:10,14–15).

THE CONSEQUENCES OF SIN

Sin, by its nature, is destructive. Hence, much of its effect already has been described. Yet a brief summation is required.

Discussion of the results of sin must consider guilt and punishment. There are several types of guilt (Heb. *'asham,* Gen. 26:10; Gk. *enochos,* James 2:10). Individual or personal guilt may be distinguished from the communal guilt of societies. Objective guilt refers to actual transgression whether realized by the guilty party or not. Subjective guilt refers to the sensation of guilt in a person. Subjective guilt may be sincere, leading to repentance (Ps. 51; Acts 2:40–47; cf. John 16:7–11). It may also be insincere, appearing outwardly sincere, but either ignoring the reality of the sin (responding instead to being caught, shamed, penalized, etc.) or evidencing only a temporary, external change without a real, lasting, internal reorientation (e.g., Pharaoh). Subjective guilt also may be purely psychological in origin, causing real distress but not based on any actual sin (1 John 3:19–20).

Penalty or punishment is the just result of sin inflicted by an authority on sinners predicated on their guilt. Natural punishment refers to the natural evil (indirectly from God) incurred by sinful acts (such as the venereal disease brought on by sexual sin and the physical and mental deterioration brought on by substance abuse). Positive punishment refers to the direct supernatural infliction of God: The sinner is struck dead, etc.

The possible purposes for punishment follow: (1) Retribution or vengeance belongs to God alone (Ps. 94:1; Rom. 12:19). (2) Expiation brings restoration of the guilty party. (This was accomplished for us in Christ's atonement.[70]) (3) Judgment makes the guilty party become willing to replace what was taken or destroyed, which can be a witness of God's work in a life (Exod. 22:1; Luke 19:8). (4) Remediation in-

---

[70]Some see this in Isa. 10:20–21 and 1 Cor. 5:5, but such an interpretation seems contrary to the Atonement. On Isa. 10:20–21, see Erickson, *Christian Theology,* 610.

fluences the guilty party not to sin in the future. This is an expression of God's love (Ps. 94:12; Heb. 12:5–17). (5) Deterrence uses the punishment of the guilty party to dissuade others from behaving similarly, which may often be seen in divine warnings (Ps. 95:8–11; 1 Cor. 10:11).[71]

The results of sin are many and complex. They may be considered in terms of who and what they affect.

Sin affects God. While His justice and omnipotence are not compromised, Scripture testifies of His hatred for sin (Ps. 11:5; Rom. 1:18), patience toward sinners (Exod. 34:6; 2 Pet. 3:9), seeking of lost humanity (Isa. 1:18; 1 John 4:9–10,19), brokenheartedness over sin (Hos. 11:8), lament over the lost (Matt. 23:37; Luke 13:34), and sacrifice for humanity's salvation (Rom. 5:8; 1 John 4:14; Rev. 13:8). Of all the biblical insights concerning sin, these may be the most humbling.

All the interactions of a once pure human society are perverted by sin. Scripture repeatedly decries the injustice done to the "innocent" by sinners (Prov. 4:16; social, James 2:9; economic, James 5:1–4; physical, Ps. 11:5; etc.).

The natural world also suffers from the effects of sin. The natural decay of sin contributes to health and environmental problems.

The most varied effects of sin may be noted in God's most complex creation, the human person. Ironically, sin has apparent benefits. Sin can even produce a transient happiness (Ps. 10:1–11; Heb. 11:25–26). Sin also spawns delusional thinking in which evil appears good; consequently, people lie and distort the truth (Gen. 4:9; Isa. 5:20; Matt. 7:3–5), denying personal sin (Isa. 29:13; Luke 11:39–52) and even God (Rom. 1:20; Titus 1:16). Ultimately, the deception of apparent good is revealed as evil. Guilt, insecurity, turmoil, fear of judgment, and the like accompany wickedness (Ps. 38:3–4; Isa. 57:20–21; Rom. 2:8–9; 8:15; Heb. 2:15; 10:27).

Sin is futility. The Hebrew *'awen* ("harm," "trouble," "deceit," "nothingness") summons the image of sin's fruitlessness. It is the trouble reaped by one who sows wickedness (Prov. 22:8) and is the current uselessness of Bethel's (derogatorily, *Beth 'Awen,* "house of nothing") once great heritage (Hos. 4:15; 5:8; 10:5,8; Amos 5:5; cf. Gen. 28:10–22). *Hevel* ("nothingness," "emptiness") is the recurrent "vanity" (KJV), or "meaningless," of Ecclesiastes and the cold comfort of idols (Zech. 10:2). Its counterpart, the Greek *mataiotēs,*

---

[71]Louis Berkhof, *Systematic Theology,* 4th ed. (Grand Rapids: Wm. B. Eerdmans, 1941) 255–61, is useful on penalty and punishment.

depicts the emptiness or futility of sin-cursed creation (Rom. 8:20) and the puffed-up words of false teachers (2 Pet. 2:18). In Ephesians 4:17, unbelievers are caught "in the futility of their thinking" because of their darkened understanding and separation from God due to their hardened hearts.

Sin envelops the sinner in a demanding dependency (John 8:34; Rom. 6:12–23; 2 Pet. 2:12–19), becoming a wicked law within (Rom. 7:23,25; 8:2). From Adam to Antichrist, sin is characterized by rebellion. This can take the form of testing God (1 Cor. 10:9) or of hostility toward God (Rom. 8:7; James 4:4). Sin brings separation from God (Gen. 2:17, cf. 3:22–24; Ps. 78:58–60; Matt. 7:21–23; 25:31–46; Eph. 2:12–19; 4:18). This may result in not only God's wrath, but also His silence (Ps. 66:18; Prov. 1:28; Mic. 3:4–7; John 9:31).

Death (Heb. *maweth*, Gk. *thanatos*) originated in sin and is sin's final result (Gen. 2:17; Rom. 5:12–21; 6:16,23; 1 Cor. 15:21–22,56; James 1:15). Physical and spiritual death may be distinguished (Matt. 10:28; Luke 12:4).[72] Physical death is a penalty of sin (Gen. 2:17; 3:19; Ezek. 18:4,20; Rom. 5:12–17; 1 Cor. 15:21–22) and can come as a specific judgment (Gen. 6:7,11–13; 1 Chron. 10:13–14; Acts 12:23). However, for believers (who are dead to sin, Rom. 6:2; Col. 3:3; in Christ, Rom. 6:3–4; 2 Tim. 2:11) it becomes a restoration by Christ's blood (Job 19:25–27; 1 Cor. 15:21–22) because God has triumphed over death (Isa. 25:8; 1 Cor. 15:26,55–57; 2 Tim. 1:10; Heb. 2:14–15; Rev. 20:14).

The unsaved live in spiritual death (John 6:50–53; Rom. 7:11; Eph. 2:1–6; 5:14; Col. 2:13; 1 Tim. 5:6; James 5:20; 1 Pet. 2:24; 1 John 5:12). This spiritual death is the ultimate expression of the soul's alienation from God. Sinning believers even experience a partial separation from God (Ps. 66:18), but God is always ready to forgive (Ps. 32:1–6; James 5:16; 1 John 1:8–9).

Spiritual death and physical death are combined and become most fully realized after the final judgment (Rev. 20:12–14).[73] Although ordained by God (Gen. 2:17; Matt. 10:28; Luke 12:4), the fate of the sinful is not pleasurable to Him (Ezek. 18:23; 33:11; 1 Tim. 2:4; 2 Pet. 3:9).

The only way to deal with sin is to love God first, then become a channel of His love to others through divine grace. Only love can oppose that which is opposed to all (Rom.

––––––––
[72]Ibid., 258–59. He seems extreme in stating, "The Bible does not know the distinction."

[73]See chap. 18, pp. 634–35.

13:10; 1 John 4:7–8). Only love can cover sin (Prov. 10:12; 1 Pet. 4:8) and ultimately remedy sin (1 John 4:10). And only "God is love" (1 John 4:8). In relation to sin, love may express itself in specific ways.

Knowledge of sin should engender holiness in the life of the individual and an emphasis on holiness in the church's preaching and teaching.

The Church must reaffirm her identity as a community of God-saved sinners ministering in confession, forgiveness, and healing. Humility should characterize every Christian relationship as believers realize not only the terrible life and fate from which they are saved, but also the more terrible price of that salvation. When each person is saved from the same sinful nature, no amount of giftedness, ministry, or authority can support the elevation of one above another; rather, each must place the other above himself or herself (Phil. 2:3).

The universal breadth and supernatural depth of sin should cause the Church to respond, with an every-member commitment and a miraculous Holy Spirit power, to the imperative of the Great Commission (Matt. 28:18–20).

Understanding the nature of sin ought to renew sensitivity to environmental issues, reclaiming the original mandate of caring for God's world from those who would worship the creation rather than its Creator.

Issues of social justice and human need should be championed by the Church as a testimony of the truth of love against the lie of sin. Such testimony, however, must always point to the God of justice and love who sent His Son to die for us. Only salvation, not legislation, not a social gospel that ignores the Cross, and certainly not violent or military action, can cure the problem and its symptoms.

Finally, life is to be lived in the certain hope of a future beyond sin and death (Rev. 21 through 22). Then, cleansed and regenerate, believers will see the face of Him who remembers their sin no more (Jer. 31:34; Heb. 10:17).

STUDY QUESTIONS

1. Why is the study of sin important and what difficulties does it encounter?

2. Identify, describe, and critique the major nonscriptural views of sin and evil.

3. What was the nature and significance of the fall of Adam?

4. What are the biblical issues relevant to the study of original sin?

5. What are the strengths and weaknesses of each of the major theories of original sin?

6. How can evil exist since God is both good and powerful?

7. What is the essence of sin? Give scriptural support.

8. What are the major characteristics of sin? Identify and discuss them.

9. What are some major categories of sin? Briefly discuss them.

10. Discuss the problem of the unpardonable sin. Suggest pastoral concerns and how you would deal with them.

11. Discuss the extent of sin. Give scriptural support.

12. Describe the results of sin. Give special attention to the issue of death.

CHAPTER NINE

The Lord Jesus Christ

David R. Nichols

The Lord Jesus Christ is the central figure of all Christian reality; therefore, the truths about Him are central to Christianity.[1] Any theology that deemphasizes Christ by placing humankind in the center cannot ultimately disclose to us the fullness of what the Bible teaches.[2] Jesus is the fulfillment of many Old Testament prophecies, and He is the author of the teaching of the New Testament. He is understood by Christians to be the Lamb slain from the foundation of the world, as well as the coming King (Rev. 13:8 and 19:11–16).

KNOWLEDGE OF JESUS

We must begin by recognizing that knowledge about Jesus Christ is at once the same as and different from knowledge about other subjects. As the spiritual leader of Christianity, Jesus is both the object of knowledge and of faith. He also produces spiritual knowledge through the Holy Spirit in us. Christians universally believe that Jesus is alive now, hundreds of years after His life and death on earth, and that He is in the presence of God the Father in heaven. But this persuasion is certainly a product of what is called saving faith, whereby

---

[1] The scriptural study of Christ is normally called Christology, from the Greek *Christos* ("Messiah," "Christ," "Anointed One") and *logos* ("word," "discourse").

[2] The Assemblies of God Statement of Fundamental Truths reinforces this emphasis by its careful delineation of the relationship between the Father and the Son in Statement 2, "The One True God." The centrality of Christ is further indicated by Statement 3, "The Deity of the Lord Jesus Christ." See William W. Menzies and Stanley M. Horton, *Bible Doctrines: A Pentecostal Perspective* (Springfield, Mo.: Logion Press, 1993), 42–72.

a person encounters Jesus Christ and, through repentance and faith, is regenerated, becoming a new creation. Knowledge of Jesus as Savior then leads, through experience, to a spiritual apprehension of Jesus' personal existence in the present. In this way, knowledge of Jesus is different from knowledge of other historical figures.

The New Testament writers were committed Christians and wrote from this perspective. This fact was not missed by nineteenth-century liberal theologians, who asserted that the New Testament books could not teach history about Jesus because they were not objective in the modern sense.[3] However, much recent work in hermeneutics has shown that no one writes anything from a neutral or totally objective standpoint.[4] What better perspective could there be than that of Christians writing about Someone they had known in the flesh, who also continued in a resurrected state after His life on earth? This leads, of course, to the issue of historical knowledge of Jesus.

If our inquiry is to be valid, it must also address the historical side of Jesus' existence. In the nineteenth century, a search for the historical Jesus was mounted in an attempt—under severe antisupernaturalistic, higher critical presuppositions—to distill facts liberal scholars felt they could accept and thereby compile a picture of Jesus that could be relevant and understandable to modern persons. These endeavors drove a wedge between the Jesus of history, who supposedly could be known only by means of rationalistic,[5] historical criticism of the Gospels, and the Christ of faith. The latter was viewed as being much larger than the historical Jesus because faith in Him caused the Gospel writers to base their

---

[3]Carl E. Braaten "Revelation, History, and Faith in Martin Kähler," in *The So-Called Historical Jesus* by Martin Kähler, translated and edited by Carl E. Braaten (Philadelphia: Fortress Press, 1964), 23. See also Werner G. Kümmel, *The New Testament: The History of the Investigation of Its Problems,* trans. by S. M. Gilmour and H. C. Kee (Nashville: Abingdon Press, 1970), 203.

[4]Anthony Thistleton, *The Two Horizons: New Testament Hermeneutics and Philosophical Description with Special Reference to Heidegger, Bultmann, Gadamer, and Wittgenstein* (Grand Rapids: Wm. B. Eerdmans, 1980) 3–47, 283–92.

[5]By "rationalistic criticism" they meant methods that reject the supernatural and have their authority in the scholar's own human reason. Some referred to this as "scientific."

presentation of Jesus on what was preached (the kerygma[6]), rather than on the so called historical facts.[7]

Widely accepted among liberal scholars, this view set the stage for the form-criticism approach, led by Martin Dibelius and Rudolf Bultmann. These critics believed that by working backward through the "forms" the Church used to describe Jesus in the kerygma,[8] they could at least attempt to discover the historical Jesus. They said the Synoptic Gospels could not be trusted to present the historical Jesus, for they believed He had been blurred by the presentation of the "Christ" Jesus in the kerygma.

Bultmann broke up the Synoptic Gospels into individual units, attempting to show that they took shape gradually, "out of quite definite conditions and wants of life from which grows up a quite definite style and quite specific forms and categories."[9] In his view, the Early Church created concepts of Jesus' nature and work that were foreign to His own understanding. Bultmann suggested that the evangelists "superimposed upon the traditional material their own belief in the messiahship of Jesus."[10] Hence, he believed that working from the twentieth century with rationalistic, historical tools, he was able to separate the historical Jesus from the Christ of the Church's proclamation.[11] The deficiencies of this approach began to be pointed out by some of Bultmann's own students, Ernst Käsemann and Gunther Bornkamm.

Ernst Käsemann is usually viewed as the initiator of the "new quest of the historical Jesus," advanced by a group of scholars known as post-Bultmannians. He argued that the New

---

[6]The English word "kerygma" is a direct cognate of the Greek *kērugma,* "proclamation," "preaching." Here the term has the more technical meaning of the preaching of the Early Church during the first thirty to forty years after Jesus' resurrection.

[7]Albert Schweitzer summarized the eighteenth- and nineteenth-century approaches to the problem of the historical Jesus. His own answer was that Jesus was an apocalyptic visionary whose eschatology was consistent with that of His times. See Albert Schweitzer, *The Quest of the Historical Jesus: A Critical Study of its Progress from Reimarus to Wrede,* trans. J. M. Robinson (New York: Macmillan Publishing, 1968).

[8]Rudolf Bultmann, *The History of the Synoptic Tradition,* trans. J. Marsh (New York: Harper & Row, 1963), 3–4.

[9]Ibid., 4.

[10]Rudolf Bultmann, *Theology of the New Testament,* trans. Kendrick Grobel, vol. 1 (New York: Charles Scribner's Sons, 1951), 26.

[11]Actually, he was unsuccessful, for he ended up believing he could not know anything about the historical Jesus.

Testament writers themselves attributed the message they were preaching to the historical Jesus, investing Him "unmistakably with pre-eminent authority."[12]

Another representative of this school of thought, Gunther Bornkamm,[13] wrote that Jesus had no messianic consciousness and that the Christological titles were applied to Him by Christians after the Resurrection. Variations of this theme have followed: Gerhard Ebeling[14] has stated that Jesus was known as Son of God before the Resurrection. Ernst Fuchs[15] has taken up the question of the theological legitimacy of the quest. He contends that the solution to the problem lies in seeing Jesus as the example of faith in God. When the Christian follows His example, the Christ of faith is the historical Jesus.

Several other scholars have had more confidence in the relationship between the Jesus of history and the Christ of faith. Nils Dahl[16] has advanced the argument that the historical investigation of Jesus has theological legitimacy and can yield understanding of Jesus, particularly in the face of the tendencies of the church to create Him in its own image. Charles H. Dodd has argued that the Christological titles are actually from the earthly ministry of Jesus and that Jesus understood himself to be the Messiah at His trial.[17] Finally, Joachim Jeremias has argued for the necessity of basing Christianity on the teaching of Jesus as reported in the Gospels, which he believes are reliable. He further shows that one of the dangers of the form-criticism approach is that it bases Christianity on an abstraction of Christ, not the historical reality which it promises.[18]

---

[12]Ernst Käsemann, "The Problem of the Historical Jesus," *Essays on New Testament Themes* (Philadelphia: Fortress Press, 1982), 15–47.

[13]Günther Bornkamm, *Jesus of Nazareth,* trans. F. Mcluskey with J. M. Robinson (New York: Harper, 1960).

[14]Gerhard Ebeling, "The Question of the Historical Jesus and the Problem of Christology" in *Word and Faith,* trans. J. W. Leitch (London: SCM Press, 1963) 288–304.

[15]Ernest Fuchs, "The Quest of the Historical Jesus" in *Studies of the Historical Jesus,* trans. A. Scobie (London: SCM Press, 1964), 11–31.

[16]Nils Alstrup Dahl, "The Problem of the Historical Jesus," *The Crucified Messiah and Other Essays* (Minneapolis: Augsburg Publishing, 1974) 48–89.

[17]Charles H. Dodd, *The Founder of Christianity* (New York: Macmillan Publishing, 1970), 101–2.

[18]Joachim Jeremias, *The Problem of the Historical Jesus,* trans. N. Perrin (Philadelphia: Fortress Press, 1964), 11–24. Joachim Jeremias *New Testament Theology: The Proclamation of Jesus,* trans. J. Bowden (New York: Charles Scribner's Sons, 1971).

CHAPTER

9

The Lord
Jesus
Christ

In any responsible study, the methodologies used to analyze the data and produce the conclusions must come under scrutiny. Methods that have been subjected to scrutiny will produce stronger studies than those that have not. The study of Christology suggests at least the following areas as frontier zones for methodology.

The couplet "doing versus being" raises the issues of functional versus ontological[19] Christology. A Christology that primarily defines Jesus by *what He did* is a functional Christology. A Christology that primarily defines Jesus by *who He is* is an ontological Christology. Traditionally, these two approaches have been aligned with two different kinds of theology. Functional Christology[20] has largely been advanced by biblical theologians and exegetes, and ontological Christology[21] has largely been advanced by systematic theologians. Since functional Christologies stress Jesus' action on the earth as a man, they tend to emphasize Jesus' humanity at the expense of His deity.[22] Ontological Christologies stress the eternal existence of God the Son and tend to emphasize Jesus' deity at the expense of His humanity. Notice that these are tendencies, not absolute positions. Through careful balance of the statements of the Word of God, either approach could present an orthodox position.

One of the most profound mysteries of the Christian faith is the union of the divine and the human in Jesus Christ. No subject excited more controversy than this one in the time of the church fathers. The Christological heresies that were tested and condemned in the third through fifth centuries are described later in this chapter.

Our study of Christology would not be complete unless we considered the relationship that exists in the New Testament among Christology, salvation, and the prophesied

---

[19]Ontology deals with the nature of being.

[20]A good example of this kind of Christology may be found in James Dunn, *Christology in the Making: A New Testament Inquiry into the Origins of the Doctrine of the Incarnation* (Philadelphia: Westminster Press, 1980).

[21]A good example of this kind of Christology may be found in Millard J. Erickson, *The Word Became Flesh* (Grand Rapids: Baker Book House, 1991).

[22]Other authors have attempted to strike a balance between the two approaches. See, for example, Oscar Cullmann, *The Christology of the New Testament,* trans. S. Guthrie and C. Hall (Philadelphia: Westminster Press, 1959).

kingdom of God. For the New Testament writers, Christology does not stand alone as an abstract category of knowledge. Their primary concern is God's salvation of humankind through the one Mediator, the Lord Jesus Christ (Matt. 28:19–20; Acts 2:38; Rom. 1:16). Therefore, from the exegetical point of view, the existence of God's salvation on the earth creates a need for understanding the One who brought it. Once this fact is acknowledged, it is possible to take the theological point of view, wherein Christology is a discrete subject, worthy of investigation in its own right. Then, because salvation is the starting point of the New Testament's message, the cross of Christ should be taken as the central defining element, since, according to the New Testament writers, that is where our salvation was accomplished. The Cross therefore defines the organic relationship that exists between the doctrine of salvation and Christology, at least at the exegetical level.

There is also the issue of the prophesied kingdom of God in its relationship to Christology and salvation. When Jesus is called Christ (Messiah, "Anointed One") we immediately are in the realm of prophecy. This title carried an enormous load of prophetic meaning for the Jews, both from the Old Testament canonical books and from intertestamental apocalyptic writings. The fulfillments of many Old Testament prophecies[23] in the incarnation, life, death, and resurrection of Jesus show the inbreaking of the kingdom of God.

The importance of acknowledging prophecy's role here is that it helps us understand how Christianity differs from Judaism. While Judaism expected the Messiah to play a key role in the political deliverance of the nation, Christianity teaches that Jesus is truly God's Messiah, even though He declined political rulership in His first coming. In Christian theology this leads to the necessity of the Second Coming as future reality. Both of these truths are based, of course, on the teachings of Jesus reported in the New Testament. The two comings of Christ are two poles of God's plan, each necessary to the total picture of God's Messiah, Jesus. This split in prophecy is not possible in the theology of Judaism and remains one of the great barriers between these two religious systems.

---

[23]See, for example, Matt. 1 through 2, where the following Old Testament passages are reported to be fulfilled:

Matt. 1:23—Isa. 7:14;

Matt. 2:6—Mic. 5:2;

Matt. 2:15—Hos. 11:1;

Matt. 2:18—Jer. 31:15.

A New Testament Understanding of Jesus

The titles given Jesus in the New Testament help us understand Him in terms that were meaningful in the ancient world He lived in. They also help us understand His uniqueness.[24]

LORD AND CHRIST

What kind of Christology do we have in Acts 2:22–36? Peter starts out by reminding the Jews of the miracle-working power of Jesus that they all knew about. This was important. Paul's characterization, "Jews demand miraculous signs and Greeks look for wisdom" (1 Cor. 1:22), is accurate for both peoples. But as in any responsible proclamation of Jesus, Peter quickly begins talking about the death of Jesus—He was crucified,[25] but God raised Him from the dead! Peter and many others were witnesses to that fact. Then Peter gives a lengthy explanation of the Resurrection and some Old Testament passages that prophesied it. Using responsible hermeneutics, he proves Psalm 16 cannot be applied only to David, but also surely applies to Jesus (Acts 2:29,31).

Jesus, now exalted to the right hand of God, has, together with the Father, poured out the Holy Spirit (Acts 2:33). This explains the speaking in tongues and the proclaiming of the good things of God heard by the Jews from fifteen different nations who were gathered from the Dispersion for the Feast of Pentecost in Jerusalem. It was indeed a miraculous sign.

Next, Peter attests to the truth of the Ascension by using Psalm 110:1 (see Acts 2:34–35): "The Lord said to my Lord: 'Sit at my right hand until I make your enemies a footstool for your feet.' " This adequately explains the Lord Jesus Christ

---

[24]See Cullmann, *Christology,* 5–6.

[25]The scholarly debate over the speeches in the Book of Acts has seen the rise of two main positions: (1) that the speeches are accurate reports of what Peter, Paul, and others said; (2) that Luke created the speeches to fit his purposes in writing the Book of Acts. The latter view attributes more to the creativity of Luke than has traditionally been accepted.

Some works that favor the first view are George Ladd, "The Christology of Acts," *Foundations* 11 (1968) 27–41; O. J. Lafferty, "Acts 2,14–36: A Study in Christology," *Dunwoodie Review* 6 (1966): 235–53; William Ramsey, *The Christ of the Earliest Christians* (Richmond: John Knox Press, 1959). Some works that favor the second view are Donald Jones, "The Title *Christos* in Luke-Acts," *Catholic Biblical Quarterly* 32 (1970): 69–76; Jacques M. Menard, "*Pais Theou* as Messianic Title in the Book of Acts," *Catholic Biblical Quarterly* 19 (1957): 83–92.

CHAPTER 9

The Lord
Jesus
Christ

who was here in the flesh on the earth and then ascended into heaven where He received His present status.

Acts 2:36 clearly declares what we must believe in order to receive the salvation of God's Messiah. " 'Therefore let all Israel be assured of this: God has made this Jesus, whom you crucified, both *Lord* and *Christ*.' " Notice the continuity expressed here. This exalted Jesus is the same Jesus who was crucified. The two titles "Lord" and "Christ" are the prime terms in Peter's sermon on the Day of Pentecost. The tie to Jesus' earthly ministry is significant here, for God the Father's making Jesus Lord and Christ is the ultimate stamp of approval on His life and ministry—His miracles, His signs and wonders, His teaching, His death, His resurrection.

SERVANT AND PROPHET

The context of Acts 3:12–26 is the healing of the man at the Beautiful Gate. On the occasion of this miracle, a crowd gathered and Peter preached to them. He began with the fact that God glorified "his servant Jesus" (v. 13) after the Jerusalem Jews killed Him. They killed Jesus even though He is "the author of life" (v. 15). What a paradox! How do you kill the Author[26] of life? That ought not to have happened and yet it did.

"Servant" (v. 13) is another important title of Jesus. Some versions of the Bible translate "servant" (Gk. *pais*) in this passage as "child." *Pais* can mean "child," but it should not be rendered that way in Acts 3 and 4. The child Jesus did not die on the cross; the man Jesus died, bearing the sins of the world. The context here demands the meaning "servant," for in Acts 3 a servant Christology begins to emerge. Starting with verse 18, notice how the Old Testament prophecies vindicate Jesus as the Messiah in ways that for the Jews were very unexpected. The Jews expected the Christ to rule, not suffer.

Furthermore, Peter states that Jesus will return (vv. 20–21)—which is not mentioned in chapter 2. Then, after the Second Coming, God will restore everything that was prophesied in the Old Testament. Please notice that we are not now in the time of the restoration of all things. The text here clearly puts that in the future. When it is time for God to restore everything, Jesus will come back in His second coming. The Millennium will begin and the whole reality of the

---

[26]Gk. *archēgos,* "leader," "ruler," "prince," "originator."

age to come that is shown to us in several books of the Bible will be initiated.[27]

Next, Peter presents Jesus as the Prophet like Moses (vv. 22–23). Moses declared, "The LORD your God will raise up for you a *prophet* like me from among your own brothers. You must listen to him" (Deut. 18:15). Naturally, one would say that Joshua fulfilled this. Joshua, the follower of Moses, did come after him and was a great deliverer in his own time. But another Joshua came (in the Hebrew language the names Joshua and Jesus are the same).[28] The early Christians recognized Jesus as the final fulfillment of Moses' prophecy.

Then, at the end of this passage (Acts 3:25–26), Peter reminds his audience of the covenant with Abraham, which is very important in understanding Christ. " 'You are heirs of the prophets and of the covenant God made with your fathers. He said to Abraham, "Through your offspring all peoples on earth will be blessed." When God raised up his servant, he sent him first to you to bless you by turning each of you from your wicked ways.' " Clearly, Jesus now brings the promised blessing and is the fulfillment of the Abrahamic Covenant, not just the fulfillment of the Law given through Moses.

LOGOS

John 1:1 presents Christ by means of the term *logos.* This Greek term means "word," "statement," "message," "declaration," or "the act of speech." But Oscar Cullman shows the importance of recognizing that in John 1 *logos* has a specialized meaning; it is described as a *hupostasis* (Heb. 1:3): a distinct, personal existence of an actual, real being.[29] John 1:1 shows that "the Word was *with God,* and the Word *was God* " are both true at the same time.[30] This means that there has never been a time when the *Logos* did not exist with the Father.[31]

---

[27]See chap. 18, pp. 629–30.

[28]Joshua (Heb. *Yᵉhoshu'a*), "The LORD is salvation," has a later form, *Yeshu'a,* which was transliterated into Greek as *Iēsous* and comes into the English as "Jesus."

[29]Cullmann, *Christology,* 251–52.

[30]Some argue that "was God" means was a god, because the Greek *theos* does not have the article *ho,* "the," in this phrase. However, *theos* without the article occurs in John 1:18, where it clearly refers to God the Father. And in Thomas' confession, "My Lord and my God," "My God" is *ho theos mou* and does have the article. Therefore, in John 1:1, "was God" needs the capital "G."

[31]See chap. 5, p. 148–49.

John then shows that the Word has agency in creation. Genesis 1:1 teaches us that God created the world. John 1:3 lets us know specifically that the Lord Jesus Christ in His preincarnate state actually did the work of creation, carrying out the will and purpose of the Father.

We find also that the Word is where life is found. John 1:4 says, "In him was life, and that life was the light of men." Because Jesus is the location of life; He is the only place where it may be obtained. A quality of life is being described here, eternal life. This kind of life is available from God with His life-giving power through the Living Word. We have eternal life only as Christ's life is in us.

The world's misunderstanding of the *Logos* is hinted at in John 1:5. "The light shines in the darkness, but the darkness has not understood it." The passage continues by saying that John the Baptist came as witness to that Light. "The true light that gives light to every man was coming into the world. He was in the world, and though the world was made through him, the world did *not recognize him*" (1:9–10). We want to focus our attention on this point. The Creator of the world, the Second Person of the Trinity, God the Son, was here in the world, but the world did not recognize Him. The next verse gets more specific. "He came to that which was his own [His own place, this earth He had created], but his own [His own people, Israel] did not receive him" (1:11).

The heirs of the covenant, the physical descendants of Abraham, did not receive Him. Here we see a very prominent theme that runs through the Gospel of John: the rejection of Jesus. When Jesus preached, some Jews mocked. When Jesus said, "Your Father Abraham rejoiced at the thought of seeing my day; he saw it and was glad," the Jews in unbelief said, "You are not yet fifty years old ... and you have seen Abraham!" Then Jesus declared, "Before Abraham was born, I am!" (John 8:57–58). The present tense of the verb "I am" (Gk. *eimi*) indicates linear being. Before Abraham was, the Son *is.*

Although many rejected the message, some were born of God. In John 1:12 we read, "Yet to all who received him, to those who believed in his name, he gave the right to become children of God." In other words, Jesus was redefining the whole reality of becoming a child of God. Up to that time, one had to be born into or join the specific, called, covenant people, Israel, to have that opportunity. But John emphasizes here that the spiritual message, the powerful gospel, had come and people had received Jesus, the *Logos.* Receiving Him meant receiving the right or the authority to become children of God. Some of those who received Him were Jews and some were Gentiles. Jesus broke down the dividing wall and opened up salvation to all who would come and receive Him by faith (1:13).

The essential truth about the *Logos* who is being described here is in John 1:14. "The Word *became flesh* and made his dwelling among us." Here we see that the term *logos* is being pressed into the service of describing Jesus Christ, but that the reality of His person is more than the secular meaning of the concept is able to bear. To the ancient philosophic Greeks, a fleshly *logos* would be an impossibility. However, to those who will believe in the Son of God, a fleshly *logos* is the key to understanding the Incarnation. In fact, this is exactly what the Incarnation means: The preexistent *Logos* took on human flesh and walked among us.

SON OF MAN

Of all His titles, "Son of Man" is the one that Jesus preferred to use of himself. And the writers of the Synoptics used it sixty-nine times. The term "son of man" has two main possible meanings. The first meaning is simply a member of humanity. And in that sense, everybody is a son of man. That meaning does carry down to Jesus' own day from at least as far back as the Book of Ezekiel, where the Hebrew phraseology *ben 'adam* is used, with a nearly identical meaning.[32] In fact, this phrase can function simply as a synonym for the first person personal pronoun, "I" (cf. Matt. 16:13).[33]

However, the term is also used of the prophesied figure in Daniel and in the later Jewish apocalyptic literature. This person appears at the end of time to intervene dramatically and bring God's righteousness and God's kingdom and judgment to this world. Daniel 7:13–14 is the source for this apocalyptic[34] concept:

"In my vision at night I looked, and there before me was one like a son of man, coming with the clouds of heaven. He approached

---

[32]In the case of both Ezekiel and Jesus it may carry the connotation of a representative man.

[33]Geza Vermes, "The Use of *bar 'enash/bar 'enasha* in Jewish Aramaic," *Post-Biblical Jewish Studies* (Leiden: E. J. Brill, 1975): 147–65.

[34]From the Greek, *apokalupsis,* "revelation," "unveiling," used of language rich in symbolism that relates to the coming kingdom of God.

the Ancient of Days and was led into his presence. He was given authority, glory and sovereign power; all peoples, nations and men of every language worshiped him. His dominion is an everlasting dominion that will not pass away, and his kingdom is one that will never be destroyed."

The appearance of this manlike figure before the Ancient of Days, as reported in the Book of Daniel, gave rise to much speculation, writing, and interpretation in the intertestamental period.

In the Book of Daniel itself, however, a question concerning the identity of the Son of Man arises from the passage starting in 7:15. The saints of the Most High battle against evil, against the horn, etc. But is the Son of Man an individual or is the Son of Man collectively the saints of the Most High?[35] The latter view was not popular in ancient times. In fact, as the Son of Man concept began to be connected more and more to glory and power and coming with clouds, which Daniel wrote about, the interpretation of the figure began to move in the direction of the Son of Man's being an individual: God's agent to bring about His day.[36]

The apocalyptic book 1 Enoch, which claims to be written by Enoch but was actually written in the first century B.C., is not inspired Scripture. Yet, historically, it is helpful for our understanding of the development of apocalyptic thought. Chapter 46 says:

And there I saw one who had a head of days, and his head was white like wool, and with him was another being whose countenance had the appearance of a man. And his face was full of graciousness like one of the holy angels. And I asked the angel who went with me and showed me all the hidden things concerning that Son of Man, who He was, whence He was, and why He went with the head of Days.[37]

---

[35]The collective view was promoted by Ibn Ezra (A.D. 1092–1167), but did not become popular until the twentieth century. See Arthur J. Ferch. *The Son of Man in Daniel Seven* (Berrien Springs, Mich.: Andrews University Press, 1979), 20–27.

[36]Barnabas Lindars, "Re-Enter the Apocalyptic Son of Man," *New Testament Studies* 22 (October 1975): 52–72. Also John J. Collins, "The Son of Man and the Saints of the Most High in the Book of Daniel," *Journal of Biblical Literature* 93 (1974): 50–66.

[37]R. H. Charles, *Apocrypha and Pseudepigrapha of the Old Testament,* vol. 2 *Pseudepigrapha* (London: Oxford Univ. Press, 1913), 214–15.

This passage clearly develops themes found in Daniel 7. The "head of days" is the Ancient of Days from Daniel 7, and the one who had "the appearance of a man" is the Son of Man of Daniel 7. First Enoch continues: "He answered and said unto me, 'This is the Son of Man who has *righteousness.*' The Lord of Spirits has chosen him and . . . this Son of Man whom you have seen shall raise up the kings . . . and break the teeth of the sinners. He shall put down the kings from their thrones and kingdoms because they do not extol and praise him."

Notice the subtle shift that takes place here. In Daniel, the Lord God, the Ancient of Days, does the judging; the Son of Man simply appears before Him. Here the Son of Man becomes the agent. He breaks the teeth of the sinners and tears kings from their thrones. In other words, in the centuries between the Old and New Testaments, Jews gave the apocalyptic Son of Man a much more active role in bringing about God's judgment and His kingdom.[38]

When we see the phrase "Son of Man" in the Gospels, we need to ask whether it means a member of humanity or Daniel's triumphant Son of Man. Jesus seemed to choose this title because it had mystery, intrigue, and a certain hidden character to it. For Jesus, it concealed what needed to be concealed and made known what needed to be made known.

Although the title "Son of Man" has two main definitions, it has three possible New Testament contextual applications. The first of these applications is the Son of Man in His earthly ministry. The second application is in reference to His future suffering (e.g., Mark 8:31). This gave new meaning to an existing terminology within Judaism. The third application is the Son of Man in His future glory (see Mark 13:24, which draws directly on the whole prophetic stream that came forth from the Book of Daniel).

Jesus, however, was not limited to the categories that existed. Certainly the apocalyptic categories were there, but He taught new and unique things about them. Then at Jesus' trial, in His response to the high priest, we find another reference

---

[38]Matthew Black, "Aramaic *Barnasha* and the 'Son of Man' " *Expository Times* 95 (1984): 200–206. Another apocalyptic book that deals with this is IV Ezra. See Howard C. Kee, " 'The Man' in Fourth Ezra: Growth of a Tradition," *Society of Biblical Literature 1981 Seminar Papers,* ed. K. Richards (Chico, Calif.: Scholars Press, 1981), 199–208. See also Joachim Jeremias, *New Testament Theology: The Proclamation of Jesus,* trans. J. Bowden (London: SCM Press, 1971), 257–76.

to the Son of Man in His future glory. Mark 14:62 says, " 'You will see the Son of Man sitting at the right hand of the Mighty One and coming on the clouds of heaven.' " Jesus here identified himself with Daniel's Son of Man. This helps us understand the divisibility of the term. The Son of Man had come and was present on the earth *and* He is yet to come with power and glory.

This divisibility is unique. Jesus came to earth, referred to himself as the Son of Man, and then did things like the healing of the paralytic and talked about His future suffering and death. But this understanding of the Son of Man is divided from His coming in power and glory and dominion, judging sinners and taking control. Therefore, Jesus is the Son of Man—past, present, and future.

That the Son of Man is a real man is also unique. From the Jewish apocalyptic writings, we would expect Him to be a superangelic being or a powerful associate of the Ancient of Days. That the Son of Man turns out to be Jesus on earth taking His place as truly man is remarkable.

MESSIAH

The title "messiah" is at the center of the New Testament understanding of Jesus and became a name for Him. Its importance, then, can hardly be overestimated.

The Greek term *Christos,* "Anointed One," translated the Hebrew *mashiach,* which is rendered in our English Bibles as "Messiah"[39] or, more commonly, "Christ." From its basic meaning of anointing with olive oil, it referred to the anointing of kings, priests, and prophets for the ministry God had called them to. Later, it came to mean a specific Davidic descendant who was expected to rule the Jews and to give them victory over the Gentiles, their oppressors.[40] To many Jews, Jesus was not their kind of Messiah.[41]

Knowing that Jesus was not the only one who claimed to be the Messiah in ancient Judaism can aid our understanding of the use of the term "Messiah" (or Christ). When the Council arrested Peter and John and was considering what to do

---

[39]Cullmann, *Christology,* 113–14.

[40]Ibid., 114–16; also Reginald H. Fuller, *The Foundations of New Testament Christology* (New York: Collins, 1965), 23–31, 158–62, 191–92.

[41]Some critical scholars have tried to demonstrate that Jesus himself rejected this title, but they have been unsuccessful. See Marinus de Jonge, "The Earliest Christian Use of Christos: Some Suggestions," *New Testament Studies* 32 (1986): 321–43; also Cullmann, *Christology,* 125–27.

about them, Gamaliel stood up and gave his advice: " 'Men of Israel, consider carefully what you intend to do to these men. Some time ago Theudas appeared, claiming to be somebody, and about four hundred men rallied to him. He was killed, all his followers were dispersed, and it all came to nothing. After him, Judas[42] the Galilean appeared in the days of the census and led a band of people in revolt. He too was killed, and all his followers were scattered' " (Acts 5:35–37).

Josephus, in his record about Judas and other messiahs, says that crosses with the crucified bodies of insurrectionists lined some Roman roads in that part of the world. To everyone passing by, the crosses provided an object lesson in what could happen to those who followed a Jewish messiah. We can begin to understand, then, why Jesus was not eager to have the term "Messiah" applied to himself.[43]

Jesus in fact avoided the term "messiah."[44] This is one of the striking things about His messiahship. For example, He responded to Peter's confession, " 'You are *the Christ,* the Son of the living God,' " by saying, " 'Blessed are you, Simon son of Jonah, for this was not revealed to you by man, but by my Father in heaven' " (Matt. 16:16–17). But Jesus went on to warn "his disciples *not to tell anyone* that he was the Christ" (Matt. 15:20). Jesus wanted to avoid the term because it carried with it the connotation of political and military leadership, which were not a part of His kingdom activities in His first coming.

This approach to the term is also evident in Jesus' dealings with demons. Luke 4:41 reads,[45] "Moreover, demons came out of many people, shouting, 'You are the Son of God!' But he rebuked them and would not allow them to speak, because they knew he was the Christ." Jesus would not allow himself

---

[42]Judas was a name of great honor among the Jews of this time. Judas Maccabaeus, the heroic Jewish deliverer of the second century B.C., achieved a victory over the Seleucid kingdom, breaking the yoke of their domination over the nation of Israel (1 Macc. 3:1 through 5:28).

[43]Josephus, *Antiquities of the Jews,* 20.5.2; *Wars of the Jews,* 2.8.1. Another person who seems to have been a "messiah" is "the Egyptian" (Acts 21:37–38). Josephus, *Antiquities of the Jews,* 20.8.6, describes this person.

[44]Cullmann, *Christology,* 125–26.

[45]There is a textual question here. Some Bibles do not have the word "Christ" (Gk. *ho christos*) in the statement of the demons. Those that do include it are supported by the ancient manuscripts A, Q, Θ, Ψ, and others. For our point here, the absence or presence of *ho christos* does not matter, since it is definitely present in Luke's statement at the end of the verse.

to be swept into a messianic kingship that would avoid the cross.

Even at His trial Jesus exhibited reluctant acceptance of the title "messiah." In Mark 14:60–62 we read, "Then the high priest stood up before them and asked Jesus, 'Are you not going to answer? What is this testimony that these men are bringing against you?' But Jesus remained silent and gave no answer. Again the high priest asked him, 'Are you the Christ, the Son of the Blessed One?' 'I am,' said Jesus. 'And you will see the Son of Man sitting at the right hand of the Mighty One and coming on the clouds of heaven.' " The high priest understood and was so angry that he tore his clothes.

Jesus' reluctance can be seen especially when one looks at the context of how the question was asked and how long it took the high priest to get Jesus to confess to being the Messiah. Matthew 26:63 indicates even more reluctance, for the high priest eventually put Jesus under oath. Consequently, Jesus could not keep silent any longer. " 'Yes, it is as you say,' Jesus replied" (26:64). But He was not boasting about being the Messiah or trying to establish himself as the Messiah. He simply is the Messiah.

Finally, did Jesus ever really identify himself as the Messiah? The answer is rarely. In fact, Jesus does not designate himself as the Messiah in the Synoptic Gospels; He calls himself the Son of Man. He was not interested in calling himself the Messiah for the reasons given above. Yet, when the woman at the well in Samaria said, " 'I know that Messiah' (called Christ)[46] 'is coming,' " Jesus responded, " 'I who speak to you am He' " or "I am the One" (John 4:25–26). So Jesus did designate himself as the Messiah. But notice where He was when He did this: in Samaria, not Galilee, not Jerusalem.

The key expectation in Jesus' day was that the Messiah would be a political ruler. He would be King David's descendant. David was the prototype Messiah, the deliverer and conqueror. Then the Qumran community added the expectation of two Messiahs: the Messiah of Aaron, a priestly Messiah, and the Messiah of Israel, a kingly Messiah.[47] They apparently could not hold together the concepts of the political, kingly Messiah and the priestly, serving, ministering Messiah. So they divided the concept of the Messiah into two figures.

---

[46]John, writing in Ephesus, translates the Hebrew–Aramaic term for the benefit of Greek-speaking Gentile Christians.

[47]"Manual of Discipline," 9.11 in Theodor H. Gaster, ed., *The Dead Sea Scriptures* (Garden City: Anchor Press, 1976) 63–64.

Perhaps at the time this was the closest to an anticipation of Christianity in Judaism, because, in a much stronger way, that is actually what Jesus was to achieve: At His first coming, He was the serving, priestly Messiah; He will be the kingly Messiah in the power and glory of His second coming. However, the Qumran covenanters' viewpoint does not mean they were Christians or even incipient Christians. They were Jews. But they definitely had a very divergent approach to the whole question of the Messiah by proposing two figures as Messiahs.

Another aspect of the uniqueness of the title "Christ" is that it actually became a name for Jesus. And no other title for Jesus became a name for Him except Messiah, or Christ. Therefore, it is preeminent among all His titles. In the Acts and Epistles He is not called "Jesus Son of Man," or "Jesus Servant"; He is Jesus Christ (Jesus the Messiah). Also, God's unique Messiah, Jesus, *didn't cease being the Messiah* when He died on the cross, because there He perfected salvation. Then He rose from the dead and ascended into the Father's presence, where He is indeed still God's Messiah.

HERESIES CONCERNING THE NATURES OF JESUS CHRIST

The doctrine of Christ has undergone more heretical attempts to explain it than any other doctrine in Christianity. The stated and implied mystery in the New Testament of the incarnation of God the Son seems to draw to itself, like a magnet, variant explanations of the different aspects of this crucial doctrine. Heresy about Christ was already present in New Testament times, as 1 John 4:1–3 clearly shows:

Dear friends, do not believe every spirit, but test the spirits to see whether they are from God, because many false prophets have gone out into the world. This is how you can recognize the Spirit of God: Every spirit that acknowledges that Jesus Christ has come in the flesh is from God, but *every spirit that does not acknowledge Jesus is not from God.* This is the spirit of the antichrist, which you have heard is coming and even now is already in the world.

This denial of Jesus' fleshly existence was an early forerunner of the docetic heresy that plagued the Church in the second and third centuries.[48]

In the age of the church fathers, differences existed in the handling of Scripture in the two main branches of the Church.

---

[48]See below. See also chap. 5, p. 156.

The School of Alexandria emphasized the allegorical approach to interpreting Scripture. These Christians became adept at defending the deity of Christ, sometimes at the expense of His full humanity. The School of Antioch emphasized the literal approach to interpreting Scripture. They defended the doctrine of Christ's humanity well, but sometimes did so at the expense of His full deity.

We must point out that the trivializing of the concept of heresy, which is often done in our times, should not be read back into the ancient times we are studying. The church fathers took their controversies against heretics with utmost seriousness because they understood that Christianity's very foundations were at stake in these issues. Besides their concern for the correct understanding of Scripture, the fathers were also guided by a persuasion that the ultimate issue was salvation itself. Many times in these controversies the question became, Can the Christ presented here indeed be the sacrifice for the sin of the world?[49]

DOCETISM

Docetists denied the reality of Christ's humanity, saying He only seemed to suffer and die.[50] They erred by allowing Gnostic philosophy to dictate the meaning of the scriptural data.[51] In the final analysis, the Christ described by the Docetists could save no one, since His death in a human body was the condition of His destruction of the power of Satan's hold on humanity (Heb. 2:14).

EBIONISM

The Ebionite[52] heresy grew out of a branch of Jewish Christianity that attempted to explain Jesus Christ in terms of its Jewish preunderstandings of God.[53] For some of these early Christians, monotheism meant the Father alone was God. The

---

[49]For the development of these controversies see chap. 5, pp. 155–63.

[50]See chap. 5, p. 156.

[51]Millard J. Erickson, *Christian Theology* (Grand Rapids: Baker Book House, 1985), 714.

[52]*Ebion* means "poor." It may refer to their impoverished Christology.

[53]An unpublished thesis, "The Problem of the Expansion of Christianity as Faced by the Hebrew Christian in New Testament Times," by Stanley M. Horton (Gordon Divinity School, June 1944), shows that the majority of the Jewish believers scattered after A.D. 70 and 135 joined orthodox Christian churches.

Pharisees' presence among the believers is attested in Acts 15:1–2,5, and Pharisaic Ebionites began to teach that Jesus was just a man, begotten by Joseph and Mary. Some taught that Jesus was made to be the Son of God at His baptism by John. This teaching, called adoptionism, obviously did not agree with the New Testament statements of John and Paul[54] about Christ's origins.[55]

ARIANISM

Early in the fourth century, a man named Arius put forth his teachings with vigor, and they were believed by many people. The teachings are perhaps best understood as expressed in eight logically interlocking statements.

1. God's fundamental characteristic is solitude. He exists alone.
2. Two Powers dwell in God, Word and Wisdom.
3. Creation was accomplished by an independent substance that God created.
4. The Son's being is different from the Father's.
5. The Son is not truly God.
6. The Son is a Perfect Creation of the Father.
7. Christ's human soul was replaced by the Logos.
8. The Holy Spirit is a third created substance.

The core problem in Arius' teaching was his insistence that the Son was created by the Father. The Nicene Council dealt with this, and Athanasius successfully defended the orthodox position.[56] Although the doctrinal battle with the Arians raged for several decades, the Christology of Nicaea was established and remains a bulwark of orthodoxy to this day.

APOLLINARIANISM

Apollinaris of Laodicea lived through almost the entire fourth century and therefore saw firsthand the Arian controversy. He participated in the refutation of Arius and shared fellowship with the orthodox fathers of his day, including Athanasius. In his mature years, he gave himself to contemplation of the person of Christ under the philosophic premise that two perfect beings cannot become one. He believed the Nicene definition of the deity of Christ, but held that as a man,

---

[54]Specifically John 1:1; 8:58; Phil. 2:6–7; Col. 1:15–20.

[55]Erickson, *Christian Theology,* 731.

[56]See chap. 5, "Trinitarian Orthodoxy," pp. 164–66.

Jesus would have spirit, soul, and body. To add the Son's complete deity to this would result in a four-part being, which to Apollinaris would be a monstrosity. The solution to this problem for Apollinaris was that the *Logos,* representing the complete deity of the Son, replaced the human spirit in the man Jesus. By this means Apollinaris accomplished the union of the divine and human in Jesus.

But what about the human nature which now existed without a spirit? To understand the Christology of Apollinaris we must understand his view of human nature. He believed that the human being comprises a body (the fleshly corpse), a soul (the animating life-principle), and a spirit (the person's mind and will). According to his teaching, Jesus' mind was the divine mind, not a human mind. But is this the Jesus presented in the New Testament? How could such a Christ be truly tempted? The orthodox fathers took these questions and others to Apollinaris. When he would not change his position, the Council of Constantinople was convened in A.D. 381, and it refuted the teaching of Apollinaris.

Here we certainly have an important question about Jesus. Did He have a human mind? Several passages seem relevant to this issue. In Luke 23:46 we read that, at the point of death, "Jesus called out with a loud voice, 'Father, into your hands I commit my spirit.'" This indicates that the spirit was an aspect of Jesus' human existence and is mentioned here as that which returns to God at death. Hebrews 2:14,17 reads:

Since the children have flesh and blood, he too *shared in their humanity* so that by his death he might destroy him who holds the power of death—that is, the devil. ... For this reason *he had to be made like his brothers in every way,* in order that he might become a merciful and faithful high priest in service to God, and that he might make atonement for the sins of the people.

Here the humanity of Jesus is said to be the same as our humanity. He is made like us in every way, apparently including having a human mind, so that the Atonement could be completed. The doctrinal implications of the heresy of Apollinaris challenge the Atonement itself.[57]

MONARCHIANISM

Among the heresies concerning the nature of the Trinity that also misinterpreted Christ's nature is Monarchianism,

---

[57]Erickson, *Christian Theology,* 715–16.

which in both its dynamic and modalistic forms was deficient in its view of the person of Christ.[58]

NESTORIANISM

The teachings of Nestorius were popular in some areas of the world at the beginning of the fifth century. The controversy began as Nestorius found fault with the Church's teaching concerning Mary. Since the Council of Nicaea had asserted Jesus' full deity, it became necessary to explain Mary's status in bearing the Christ into the world. The Church of Nestorius' day was quite properly using the terminology *theotokos,* meaning "God-bearer," to describe Mary. Nestorius reacted against this terminology, teaching that Mary should be called *Christotokos,* meaning "Christ-bearer." He maintained that only Jesus should be called *theotokos.* This terminology was important to Nestorius because he wished to present Jesus as the God-bearing man.

Nestorius taught that the *Logos,* as the complete Deity, indwelt the human Jesus similarly to the way the Holy Spirit indwells the believer. In this manner, Nestorius kept the humanity and the deity at some logical distance from each other. What held them together was a moral link provided by the perfection of Jesus, according to Nestorius.

The teachings of Nestorius were examined and rejected by the Council of Ephesus, which convened in A.D. 431. The council found that the teaching of a God-bearing man drove a wedge between the divine and human natures which the moral link could not sufficiently rejoin. In the final analysis, Nestorius reduced the value of the divine nature by His denial of the personal union of the natures.

EUTYCHIANISM

The teaching of Eutyches was popular in some areas in the first half of the fifth century. Eutychianism began with the assertion that Jesus' body was not identical to ours, but was a special body brought into being for the messiahship of Jesus. This created the possibility, according to Eutyches, that the divine and the human were mingled together to create one nature instead of two. Therefore, in the Incarnation, Jesus was one Person with one nature, a deified humanity unlike any other humanity.

---

[58]See chap. 5, pp. 157–62.

CHAPTER
9

The Lord
Jesus
Christ

This teaching was examined by the Council of Chalcedon (A.D. 451). The human nature of Christ quickly was recognized to be the major issue in the teaching. The council creatively used the terminology coined at Nicea, that Christ was *homoousia* with the Father, to refute the teaching of Eutyches. The council asserted that Jesus is *homoousia hēmin,* which means He had in His humanity the same being or essence *as we.* This may seem to be a radical conclusion, but it is made necessary by several Scripture passages, not the least of which is Hebrews 2:14,17. This clear defense of Christ's humanity, alongside an equally clear affirmation of His deity, is an indication of the council members' willingness to maintain the tensions and paradox of the biblical revelation. In fact, the Chalcedonian Christology has remained in Christianity as the bulwark of orthodoxy for some fifteen centuries.

SYSTEMATIC CONSIDERATIONS IN CHRISTOLOGY

In the disciplined study of Jesus Christ, certain elements of teaching presented by the biblical text require analysis and theological synthesis beyond the exegesis of the text. Exegesis must be done first and must control the meanings we attach to the words of the Bible, but four elements in the doctrine of Jesus Christ need to be related to each other in a meaningful theological framework.

The first element is the Virgin Birth, as taught in the Gospels of Matthew and Luke. This doctrine shows us the initial phase of how Jesus could be both God and man.

The second doctrine is that Jesus, in His one Person, is fully divine and fully human. Although this element brings us to the limits of our human ability to understand, we must rigorously apply ourselves to investigating the terminology and meanings in this doctrine.

The third theological area is the place of Jesus in the Trinity. It is essential to a proper understanding that we know how Jesus is the Son in His relationship with the Father, and how He is the Giver of the Holy Spirit.[59] This has been well discussed in chapter 5.

When we come to the fourth element of this section, we find an area that has been somewhat neglected, at least in the realm of systematic theology. When we speak of Jesus as the Baptizer in the Holy Spirit, we must recognize that the prom-

---

[59]See chap. 5, pp. 145, 148–53.

ises of outpouring given in both Old and New Testaments have their fulfillment in the activity of Jesus Christ.

THE VIRGIN BIRTH

Probably no doctrine in Christianity has been scrutinized as extensively as the Virgin Birth, for two main reasons. First, the doctrine depends on the reality of the supernatural for its very existence. Many scholars in the past two centuries have had a bias against the supernatural; therefore, they have been biased in their handling of Jesus' birth. The second reason for criticism of the Virgin Birth is that the doctrine has had a history of development that takes us far beyond the simple data provided by the Bible. The term "virgin birth" itself reflects this issue. The Virgin Birth means that Jesus was conceived while Mary was a virgin, and that she was still a virgin when Jesus was born (not that the parts of Mary's body were supernaturally preserved from the course of events that take place in a human birth).[60]

One of the disputed aspects of the Virgin Birth is the origin of the concept itself. Some scholars have attempted to explain the origin by means of Hellenistic parallels.[61] The unions of gods and goddesses with humans in the Greek literature of antiquity are claimed to be the antecedents of the biblical idea. But this certainly ignores the use of Isaiah 7 in Matthew 1.

Isaiah 7, with its promise of a child to come, is the background for the concept of the Virgin Birth. Much controversy has swirled around the Hebrew term *'almah,* used in Isaiah 7:14. The word is usually translated "virgin," though some versions render it "maiden" or "young woman." In the Old Testament, when the context gives a clear indication, it is used of virgins of marriageable age.[62]

Then Isaiah said, "Hear now, you house of David! Is it not enough to try the patience of men? Will you try the patience of my God also? Therefore the Lord himself will give you [plural, the whole house of David] a sign: The virgin [*'almah*] will be with child and

---

[60]This is actually claimed in an apocryphal book called the *Protevangelion* 14:1–17.

[61]Morton Enslin, "The Christian Stories of the Nativity," *Journal of Biblical Literature* 59 (1940): 317–38. Eduard Norden, *Die Geburt des Kindes: Geschichte einer religiöser Idee* (Leipzig: B. G. Teubner, 1924).

[62]Edward J. Young, *The Book of Isaiah,* vol. 1 (Grand Rapids: Wm. B. Eerdmans, 1965), 287.

will give birth to a son, and will call him Immanuel" (Isa. 7:13–14).

It seems that, in the context of chapters 7 and 8 of Isaiah, the prophecy about the *'almah* had a meaning for the time of Isaiah that was quite important. To begin with, the prophecy was spoken not to King Ahaz, but to the whole house of David. King Ahaz was facing a military threat from the combined armies of the Northern Kingdom and the nation of Aram (7:1–9). In an attempt to assure him that the threat would not materialize, Isaiah challenged him to ask for any spiritual sign he wished—but Ahaz refused. Then the Lord promised a supernatural sign not for Ahaz, but for the whole house of David, a sign that would have significance right down through history.[63] Notice that the child's name would be Immanuel, "God with us."

The use of Isaiah 7:14 in Matthew 1:18–22 points out its great importance for understanding the birth of the Lord Jesus Christ. Here the virgin conception and birth of Jesus are treated with respect and dignity.

The Gospel of Matthew reports that the pregnancy of Mary was caused by the action of the Holy Spirit upon her as she conceived Jesus in her womb. Joseph, Mary's pledged husband, would not believe this until he was informed by the angel. Once the conception had occurred, it became clear that it was a divine fulfillment of the prophecy in Isaiah 7:14.

Another feature of the birth narratives of Jesus in the Gospels is the focus taken by each writer. Matthew focuses on Joseph's role in the story. He describes the angel's appearances and Joseph's righteous actions in obedience to the commands. Luke, on the other hand, seems to tell the story from Mary's perspective. From Luke we learn about the events surrounding Zechariah and Elizabeth and the kinship between Mary and Elizabeth. Luke also describes the appearance of the angel Gabriel to Mary (Luke 1:26–31) and Mary's beautiful response in the Magnificat (Luke 1:46–55).

Both Matthew and Luke use the Greek word *parthenos* to describe Mary as an unmarried and sexually pure young woman. In Matthew 1:23 this Greek word translates the Hebrew word *'almah,* from Isaiah 7:14. It conveys a clear con-

---

[63]The supernatural sign finds its complete fulfillment in the person of Jesus. However, a near fulfillment in Isaiah's time, such as the birth of a child to Isaiah's wife, that would foreshadow the fulfillment to come is proposed by some scholars.

textual meaning that indicates the bodily virginity of Mary, who then became the mother of our Lord Jesus.

THE HYPOSTATIC UNION

The hypostatic union is the description of the unity of the divine and human natures in Jesus' one Person. An adequate understanding of this doctrine is dependent on a complete understanding of each of the two natures and how they constitute the one Person.

The teaching of Scripture about the humanity of Jesus shows us that in the Incarnation He became fully human in every area of life except the actual commission of any sin.

One of the ways we know the completeness of Jesus' humanity is that the same terms that describe different aspects of humanity also describe Him. For example, the New Testament often uses the Greek word *pneuma,* "spirit," to describe the spirit of man; this word is also used of Jesus. And Jesus used it of himself, as on the cross He committed His spirit to His Father and breathed His last breath (Luke 23:46).

Contextually, the word "spirit" (Gk. *pneuma*) must mean the aspect of human existence that goes on in eternity after death. This point is quite important because it is as a human being that Jesus died. As God the Son, He lives eternally with the Father. In Jesus' experience of death we see one of the most powerful attestations to the completeness of His humanity. He was so human that He died a criminal's death.

The Incarnate Jesus also had a human soul. He used the Greek word *psuchē* to describe the workings of His inner self and emotions in Matthew 26:36–38.

Then Jesus went with his disciples to a place called Gethsemane, and he said to them, "Sit here while I go over there and pray." He took Peter and the two sons of Zebedee along with him, and he began to be sorrowful and troubled. Then he said to them, "My soul is overwhelmed with sorrow to the point of death. Stay here and keep watch with me."

Jesus was capable of the depths of human emotion. As we see in the Gospels, He felt pain, sorrow, joy, and hope. This was true because He shared with us the reality of being human souls.

Finally, Jesus had a human body just like ours. Blood ran through His veins as His heart pumped to sustain His human life in His body. This is clearly indicated in Hebrews 2:14–

18. In this powerful passage, Jesus' bodily existence on earth is said to provide the very possibility for our atonement. Because He was flesh and blood, His death could defeat death and bring us to God. Jesus' body[64] in the Incarnation was just like our bodies. His human body was placed in a tomb after His death (Mark 15:43–47).

Another witness to the completeness of Jesus' humanity is His participation in ordinary human weakness. Although He was God, He humbled himself, taking on human form. In John 4:6 we find the simple fact that Jesus became weary, as anyone would who traveled a long distance on foot. It is clear from Matthew 4:2 that Jesus was capable of hunger in the normal human way. "After fasting forty days and forty nights, *he was hungry.*" Jesus also clearly expressed a limitation of His knowledge. Speaking of the time of the Second Coming in Mark 13:32, He says, " 'No one knows about that day or hour, not even the angels in heaven, *nor the Son,* but only the Father.' " Certainly this limitation was allowed by himself under the conditions of the Incarnation, but it was a human limitation nevertheless.

The cumulative weight of these Scripture passages should cause us to conclude that Jesus was fully human. He was just like us in every respect but sin. His lowering of himself to servanthood as a man made it possible for Jesus to redeem us from sin and the curse of the Law.

The New Testament writers attribute deity to Jesus in several important passages. In John 1:1, Jesus as the Word existed as God himself. It is hard to imagine a clearer assertion of Jesus' deity. It is based on the language of Genesis 1:1[65] and places Jesus in the eternal order of existence with the Father.

In John 8:58 we have another powerful witness to Jesus' deity. Jesus is asserting of himself continuous existence, like that of the Father. "I AM" is the well-known self-revelation of God to Moses at the burning bush (Exod. 3:14). In saying "I am," Jesus was making available the knowledge of His deity to those who would believe.

Paul also gives us a clear witness to the deity of Jesus: "Your attitude should be the same as that of Christ Jesus: *Who, being in very nature God,* did not consider equality with God something to be grasped, but made himself nothing, taking the very nature of a servant, being made in human

---

[64]Gk. *sōma,* a real body of flesh, bone, blood, muscles, etc.
[65]Cullmann, *Christology,* 250.

likeness" (Phil. 2:5–7). The Greek uses very strong language here. The participle *huparchōn* is stronger than *eimi* and is a forceful statement of Christ's state of existence. The statement *hos en morphē theou huparchōn* (v. 6a) should be rendered "who, existing in the form of God." The statement *einai isa theō* (v. 6b) should be rendered "to be equal with God." The meaning Paul conveys here is that Jesus was in a state of existence in equality with God. However, He did not grasp, or cling, to this state, but rather released it and became a servant, dying on the cross for us.

When we use all the data of the New Testament on this subject, we realize that Jesus did not stop being God during the Incarnation. Rather, He gave up the independent exercise of the divine attributes.[66] He was still fully Deity in His very being, but He fulfilled what seems to have been a condition of the Incarnation, that His human limitations were real, not artificial.

In spite of these clear scriptural assertions of Jesus' deity, modern antisupernatural, critical scholarship has been very reluctant to accept the canonical view of Jesus' deity. Some scholars have claimed to detect a development of Christology in Early Church history, with the deity of the incarnational view standing at the end of a process of apostolic and churchly reflection on Jesus rather than at the beginning and all the way through.

John Knox's view is representative of a position held by some that Christology moved from a primitive adoptionism to kenoticism to incarnationalism.[67] Primitive adoptionism means that Jesus was taken up to be Son by the Father, without any considerations of preexistence or emptying of Jesus.[68] Kenoticism means, as Paul teaches in Philippians 2, that Jesus emptied himself of His heavenly glory for the purposes of salvation, not necessarily incarnationally.[69] The purported third stage of the development is incarnationalism, where the preexistent Son becomes a man by taking on human flesh.[70]

---

[66]Erickson, *Christian Theology,* 771.

[67]John Knox, *The Humanity and Divinity of Christ: A Study of Pattern in Christology* (London: Cambridge Univ. Press, 1967).

[68]This position is set forth by Dunn, *Christology in the Making,* 1–11, 33–46.

[69]The kenosis teaching is explained thoroughly by Donald Dawe, *The Form of a Servant: A Historical Analysis of the Kenotic Motif* (Philadelphia: Westminster, 1963).

[70]The view of incarnationalism as historically defensible is presented by Erickson, *The Word Became Flesh.*

C. F. D. Moule says, however, that incarnationalism is present throughout the New Testament, and that Jesus fulfilled His deity by humbling himself.[71] By saying this, Moule reduces the sharpness of the concepts drawn by Knox and others. But it seems appropriate in light of the Synoptic Gospels to observe that Jesus' deity is present in *all the strands* of the New Testament, though it is most pronounced in Paul's and John's writings.

Clearly, the Bible presents ample evidence of the scriptural affirmations of both Jesus' humanity and deity. It now remains to be established how these two natures can be together in one Person.

The Council of Chalcedon, which convened in A.D. 451, is usually viewed as a defining moment in the history of Christology. Standing at the culmination of a long line of Christological heresies the council defined the orthodox faith in the Lord Jesus Christ as being focused on His two natures, divine and human, united in His one person.

The Council of Chalcedon has a historical context. The separation of the natures advanced by Nestorius had been repudiated by the Council of Ephesus in A.D. 431. The blending of the two natures proposed by Eutyches came to be refuted by Chalcedon itself. In this climate of theological controversy, two writings had profound influence over the outcome of Chalcedon. The first was Cyril's letter to John of Antioch, which says:

Therefore we confess that our Lord Jesus Christ, the only-begotten Son of God, is complete God and complete human being with a rational soul and a body. He was born from the Father before the ages, as to his deity, but at the end of the days the same one was born, for our sake and the sake of our salvation, from Mary the Virgin, as to his humanity. This same one is coessential with the Father, as to his deity, and coessential with us, as to his humanity, for a union of two natures has occurred, as a consequence of which we confess one Christ, one Son, one Lord.[72]

The contribution of this statement to orthodox Christology is the concept that two complete natures were united in the

---

[71]C. F. D. Moule, "The Manhood of Jesus in the New Testament," *Christ, Faith, and History: Cambridge Studies in Christology,* S. W. Sykes and J. P. Clayton, eds. (Cambridge: Cambridge University Press, 1972), 95–110.

[72]Richard A. Norris, Jr., trans. and ed., *The Christological Controversy* (Philadelphia: Fortress Press, 1980) 141–42.

person of the Lord Jesus. The divine was identical with the divinity of the Father. The human was identical with us.

The other writing that heavily influenced Chalcedon was the letter of Leo I to Flavian of Constantinople, which states:

This birth in time in no way detracted from that divine and eternal birth and in no way added anything to it. Its entire meaning was worked out in the restoration of humanity, which had been led astray. It came about so that death might be conquered and that the devil, who once exercised death's sovereignty, might by its power be destroyed, for we would not be able to overcome the author of sin and of death unless he whom sin could not stain nor death hold took on our nature and made it his own.[73]

The emphasis here is on Jesus' humanity providing the possibility of the defeat of Satan, which Jesus did accomplish on the cross. Death could be defeated only by death, but the death was that of the perfect Lamb.

The actual findings of Chalcedon constitute a lengthy document. The Council of Nicea with its *homoousia* formulation on the relationship between the Father and the Son was affirmed, along with the findings of the Council of Constantinople. The essence of the Christology of Chalcedon may be seen in the following extract.

Following, therefore, the holy fathers, we confess one and the same Son, who is our Lord Jesus Christ, and we all agree in teaching that this very same Son is complete in his deity and complete—the very same—in his humanity, truly God and truly a human being, this very same one being composed of a rational soul and a body, coessential with the Father as to his deity and coessential with us—the very same one—as to his humanity, being like us in every respect apart from sin ... acknowledged to be unconfusedly, unalterably, undividedly, inseparably in two natures, since the difference of the natures is not destroyed because of the union, but on the contrary, the character of each nature is preserved and comes together in one person and one hypostasis, not divided or torn into two persons but one and the same Son.[74]

Therefore, the person of the Lord Jesus comprises two distinct realities, the divine and the human. Because Chal-

---

[73]Ibid., 146.
[74]Ibid., 159.

cedon located the union in the *person* of Christ, using the Greek word *hupostasis,* the doctrine is often called the hypostatic union.

We see that the divine nature and the human nature come together in the one person of Jesus Christ. When we speak of qualitatively different topics, such as a divine nature and a human nature existing in a union, we must inevitably take the issue of contradiction and paradox seriously. As normally understood, God is God and humanity is humanity and there is a qualitative distinction between them. When we say that Christ is the God-man, we are bringing together categories that normally negate each other. There are two responses to this dilemma. The first is to make adjustments to the human nature of Jesus, making it to fit logically in its union with the divine nature. The second is to assert that the union of the two natures is a paradox. Here the logical inconsistency of God's being a man is not resolved.

Two approaches to the problem of Christ's human nature have been taken in recent times. Both assume the veracity of the divine nature, so the issue becomes one of a clear delineation of the human nature.

Scripture passages that force this issue on us seem to be Hebrews 2:16–18 and Hebrews 4:15.

Surely it is not angels that he helps, but Abraham's descendants. For this reason he had to be made like his brothers *in every way,* in order that he might become a merciful and faithful high priest in service to God, and that he might make atonement for the sins of the people. Because he himself suffered when he was tempted, he is able to help those who are being tempted.

We do not have a high priest who is unable to sympathize with our weaknesses, but we have one who has been tempted *in every way, just as we are—yet without sin.*

These two passages insist on the identity of Jesus' temptations with our own. This insistence must be given its due in the understanding of Christ's humanity that we formulate.

Millard Erickson has brought forth a modern rendition of incarnational theology in which he attempts to solve the problem of Christ's human nature in the hypostatic union. He believes that the answer lies in seeing Jesus' humanity as ideal humanity, or humanity as it will be. In other words, methodologically, we do not begin with the acute difficulty of God's becoming a man with all the qualitative differences between the divine and human natures. Erickson wishes to begin instead with essential humanity (i.e., what God originally created), because, presumably, it is much more like God than the fallen humanity we observe today. "For the humanity of Jesus was not the humanity of sinful human beings, but the humanity possessed by Adam and Eve from their creation and before their fall."[75]

In perspective, it may seem that Erickson has offered a proper and orthodox viewpoint on Jesus' humanity. However, several questions may be asked:

First, why is it wrong to begin with the unlikeness of God and man? Even if we focused on the humanity of Adam and Eve before the Fall, where is the biblical data that would indicate that Adam could easily or ever become a God-man? Erickson himself (in dialogue with Davis) has pointed out that deity is necessary, eternal, omnipotent, omniscient, and incorporeal, while humanity is contingent, finite, nonomnipotent, nonomniscient, and corporeal. These differences exist whether we are discussing humanity before or after the Fall.[76]

Second, when Erickson says that we gain our understanding of human nature from "an inductive investigation of both ourselves and other humans as we find them about us," he indicates a part of the problem. Our view of humanity should come first from the Scriptures, then from our own observations. This point is more important than it may seem, as we consider the following. Erickson says that in our present condition we are "impaired, broken-down vestiges of essential humanity, and it is difficult to imagine this kind of humanity united with deity." But is this a correct picture of the humanity that Mary brought to the virgin conception of Jesus? In Luke 1:28–30 we read:

The angel went to her and said to her, "Greetings, *you who are highly favored! The Lord is with you.*" Mary was greatly troubled at his words and wondered what kind of greeting this might be. But the angel said, "Do not be afraid, *Mary, you have found favor with God.*"

The point of the birth narratives, as the angel declares to Mary in the verses that follow, is that Jesus will be the Son of God *and* the son of Mary.[77] So then, if we take a different

---

[75]Erickson, *Christian Theology,* 736.

[76]Erickson, *The Word Became Flesh,* 554–556.

[77]Williams, *Renewal Theology,* vol. 1, 347–50.

theological perspective on humanity and sin, methodologically we may wish to allow the contradictions in the Incarnation to stand, depending on God's revealing power to bring together that which logically may not seem to belong together. Ultimately, the truth of the Incarnation does not depend on our ability to logically process it as much as it depends on the fact that God supernaturally revealed it.[78]

Another issue that could be raised here is the extent of Jesus' participation in our human condition. The curse on Adam that resulted from his rebellion against God is recorded in Genesis 3:17–19. The curse seems to have three components: (1) a curse on the ground, (2) labor by human beings to provide food, and (3) physical death. Notice that Jesus participated in all of these in the days of His flesh. The curse on the ground was not lifted for Jesus; He worked as a carpenter; He ate food; and most significant, He died. In His humanity, Jesus participated in the nonmoral results of sin (Adam and Eve's) *without becoming sinful himself.* This understanding is in harmony with several important Scripture verses on the subject (e.g., 2 Cor. 5:21; 1 Pet. 2:22).

Finally, a few things need to be said on the issue of the differences between essential (or ideal) humanity as created by God and existential humanity (viewed as experienced by people in everyday life). Erickson says that it is incorrect for us to define Jesus' humanity from the standpoint of existential humanity, that only essential humanity will do. But our analysis of the Scripture verses above would seem to indicate that Jesus was in both aspects at the same time. He was in the linear, corporeal existence of a man who could, and did, die. In that sense He seemed to be in an existential humanity. He also was sinless—and there is no other human being who was—and He was raised by the Father to incorruption. Jesus' essential humanity seems to be present in these realities. The revelation of God the Son in the flesh may well challenge to the point of exhaustion our attempts to explain it. What is

---

[78] It has been suggested that the Holy Spirit in the Incarnation made it possible for Jesus to hold in the one Person a complete set of divine qualities and a complete set of sinless human qualities, but in such a way that they did not interfere with each other. Down through history, Christians as a whole have regarded the Incarnation as a mystery. See James Oliver Buswell, *A Systematic Theology of the Christian Religion,* vol. 2 (Grand Rapids: Zondervan Publishing House, 1963), 18.

crucial for us to believe is that Jesus was completely human and that He was like us.[79]

JESUS AND THE HOLY SPIRIT

Jesus is in a profound relationship with the Third Person of the Trinity. To begin with, the Holy Spirit accomplished the conception of Jesus in Mary's womb (Luke 1:34–35).

The Holy Spirit came upon Jesus at His baptism (Luke 3:21–22). There Jesus moved into a new aspect of His relationship to the Holy Spirit that could be possible only in the Incarnation. Luke 4:1 makes it clear that Jesus was prepared by this empowering to face Satan in the wilderness and to inaugurate His earthly ministry.

Jesus' baptism has played a key role in Christology, and we must examine it in some depth here. James Dunn argues at length that Jesus was adopted as the Son of God at His baptism. Therefore, its significance for Dunn is Jesus' initiation to divine sonship.[80] But does Luke 3:21–22—where a voice from heaven says, " 'You are my Son, whom I love' "—teach this?

That Psalm 2:7 is being used here is widely acknowledged. The question that must bear on our discussion is why the second part of the statement, "Today I have become your Father," found in that psalm has been left out. If the desired teaching (by the Voice from heaven and by Luke) is that Jesus became the Son of God at His baptism, it makes no sense that the second statement would be excluded, since it might seem to prove the point.[81] The statement of Jesus' sonship, then, is more likely an acknowledgment of what was already a fact. It is especially important here to notice that Luke 1:35 states, "The holy one to be born will be called the Son of God." Howard Ervin sums up the point well: "Jesus is the Son of God by nature. He never was, is not, and never will be other than the Son of God. ... There is no sense in which Jesus 'only becomes' Messiah and *Son* at Jordan."[82]

Finally, Jesus is the key player in the outpouring of the Holy

---

[79]J. Rodman Williams, however, describes the union of the divine and human in Jesus as the ultimate paradox. *Renewal Theology,* vol. 1, 342.

[80]James Dunn, *Baptism in the Holy Spirit* (London: SCM Press, 1970), 27–28. Dunn, *Christology in the Making,* 12–64.

[81]The Hebrew is rather a technical formula used by kings who brought out a son and declared him to be king, co-ruler with his father (as David did with Solomon).

[82]Howard M. Ervin, *Conversion-Initiation and the Baptism in the Holy Spirit* (Peabody, Mass.: Hendrickson Publishers, 1984), 12 (emphasis mine).

Spirit. After accomplishing redemption through the Cross and the Resurrection, Jesus ascended into heaven. From there, together with the Father, He poured out and continues to pour out the Holy Spirit in fulfillment of the prophetic promise of Joel 2:28–29 (Acts 2:33). This is one of the most important ways we know Jesus today, in His capacity as giver of the Spirit.

The cumulative force of the New Testament is quite significant. Christology is not just a doctrine for the past. Nor is Jesus' high-priestly work[83] the only aspect of His present reality. The ministry of Jesus, and no one else, is propagated by the Holy Spirit in the present. The key to the advance of the gospel in the present is the recognition that Jesus can be known, as the Holy Spirit empowers believers to disclose Him.

STUDY QUESTIONS

1. How is knowledge of Jesus Christ the same as knowledge of other subjects? How is it different?

2. How does ontological Christology differ from functional Christology?

3. What is the meaning of the phrase "hypostatic union" when it is applied to Christ?

4. What meaning was intended by the Nicene Fathers' use of the term *homoousia* for Christ?

5. How does the meaning of the title *Logos* in John 1 compare with its meaning in Greek philosophy?

6. What are the possible meanings for the title "Son of Man" as used in the Synoptic Gospels?

7. Why did Jesus avoid the title "Messiah" and command the disciples to silence when they used it of Him?

8. What is the uniqueness of Jesus as the Messiah?

9. What is meant by the terms "adoptionism," "kenoticism," and "incarnationalism"?

10. What is the significance of the Council of Chalcedon for the doctrine of Christ?

---

[83]See Heb. 6:19 through 10:39 for a scriptural description of Jesus' high-priestly work.

The Saving
Work of Christ

Daniel B. Pecota

The saving work of Christ stands as the central pillar in the structure of God's redemptive temple. It is the load-bearing support, without which the structure could never have been completed. We could also see it as the hub around which all of God's revelational activity revolves. It gives a head to the body, antitype to type, substance to shadow. These statements do not in the least diminish the importance of all God did for and with the Old Testament covenant people and the nations that surrounded them. That remains of incalculable significance to every student of the Scriptures. They reflect, rather, the thought of Hebrews 1:1–2: "In the past God spoke to our forefathers through the prophets at many times and in various ways, but in these last days he has spoken to us by his Son." God spoke infallibly and significantly in the past, but not finally. That had to wait for His Son's coming, the record and meaning of which appears infallibly and finally in the twenty-seven books of the New Testament canon.[1]

THE MEANING OF "SALVATION"

A study of the saving work of Christ must begin with the Old Testament. There we discover in divine action and word the redemptive nature of God. We discover types and specific predictions of the One who was to come and of what He was going to do. Part of what we find is in the Old Testament's use of terminology to describe both natural and spiritual salvation.

---

[1]See chap. 3, pp. 108–09, for a discussion of the reasonableness of affirming that the canon of Scripture is closed.

Anyone who has studied the Hebrew Old Testament knows the richness of its vocabulary. The writers use several words that refer to the general thought of "deliverance" or "salvation," whether natural, legal, or spiritual.[2] The focus here is on two verbs, *natsal* and *yasha'*. The former occurs 212 times,[3] most often with the meaning of "deliver" or "rescue." God told Moses that He had come down to "rescue" Israel from the hand of the Egyptians (Exod. 3:8). Sennacherib wrote to the king, "The god of Hezekiah will not rescue his people from my hand" (2 Chron. 32:17). Frequently the Psalmist pled for divine rescue (Pss. 22:21; 35:17; 69:14; 71:2; 140:1). These uses indicate that a physical, personal, or national "salvation" is in view.

But the word takes on connotations of spiritual salvation through the forgiveness of sins. David appealed to God to save him from all his transgressions (Ps. 39:8).[4] In Psalm 51:14 it appears that David had personal spiritual restoration and salvation in mind when he prayed: "Save me from bloodguilt, O God, the God who saves me, and my tongue will sing of your righteousness."

Although Psalm 79 is a lament because of the invasion of Israel and the desecration of the temple by their enemies, the Psalmist recognized that a deliverance would be possible only if it included the forgiveness of their sins (v. 9).

The root *yasha'* occurs 354 times, the largest concentration of occurrences being in the Psalms (136 times) and the Prophetic Books (100 times). It means "save," "deliver," "give victory," or "help." On occasion the word occurs free of any theological overtones (e.g., when Moses defended the daughters of Reuel and saved them from the oppressive action of the shepherds; Exod. 2:17). Most often, however, the word is used with God as the subject and God's people as the object. He delivered them from all kinds of distress, including such things as national or personal enemies (Exod. 14:30; Deut.

---

[2]See the following verbs in the appropriate stems: *ga'al*, "redeem," "set free"; *chayah*, "make alive," "revive"; *chalats*, "break away," "deliver," "set free"; *yathar*, "remain over," "save over" (i.e., "preserve alive"); *malat*, "slip away," "escape," "deliver"; *padhah*, "ransom"; *palat*, "escape," "deliver"; *shuv*, "turn back," "return." In all stems, and sometimes with many meanings, these verbs occur over 1750 times. The number of verbs that convey some idea of "rescue" or "salvation" and the frequency of their occurrence indicate the pervasiveness of these ideas in Hebrew thinking and culture.

[3]Primarily in the *hiphil* stem, which stresses causation.

[4]Although even here the emphasis is more on the effect of his sin in exposing him to the scorn of fools.

20:4; Judg. 3:9; Jer. 17:14–18) and from calamities (e.g., plague or famine; 2 Chron. 20:9). Therefore, *Yahweh* is "Savior" (Isa. 43:11–12), "my Savior" (Ps. 18:14), and "my salvation" (2 Sam. 22:3; Ps. 27:1).

God most often chose to use His appointed representatives to bring salvation, but "the obstacles surmounted were so spectacular that there unquestionably had to be special help from God himself."[5] In Ezekiel the word takes on moral qualities. God promises, " 'I will save you from all your uncleanness' " (36:29); " 'I will save them from all their sinful backsliding, and I will cleanse them' " (37:23).

When one reads the Old Testament and takes its message seriously and literally,[6] one can easily conclude that a dominant theme is salvation, God being the chief actor. The salvation theme appears as early as Genesis 3:15 in the promise that the offspring, or "seed," of the woman will crush the serpent's head. "This is the *protevangelium,* the first glimmer of a coming salvation through Him who will restore man to life."[7] Yahweh saved His people through judges (Judg. 2:16,18) and other leaders, such as Samuel (1 Sam. 7:8) and David (1 Sam. 19:5). Yahweh saved even Aram of Syria, the enemy of Israel, through Naaman (2 Kings 5:1). There is no savior apart from the Lord (Isa. 43:11; 45:21; Hos. 13:4).

The *locus classicus* for the theological usage of *yasha'* in the narrative texts is Exodus 14, where Yahweh "saved Israel from the hands of the Egyptians" (v. 30). That event became the prototype for what the Lord would do in the future in saving His people. All of this pointed to the time when God would bring salvation through the suffering Servant to all, not just to Israel. In Isaiah 49:6 He says to the Servant, " 'I will also make you a light for the Gentiles, that you may bring salvation to the ends of the earth.' " The "acts of salvation in the [Old Testament] build toward the final act of salvation which will include all people under its possible blessing."[8]

---

[5]John E. Hartley, *"Yasha','"* in R. Laird Harris, ed., *Theological Wordbook of the Old Testament,* vol. 1 (Chicago: Moody Press, 1980), 415.

[6]The literal approach looks for no hidden meanings known only to some spiritually elite "gnostic." It simply accepts at face value the literal, historical, and cultural meaning of the words, except when by reason of context, literary genre, figures of speech, etc., one cannot and should not do otherwise.

[7]J. Rodman Williams, *Renewal Theology,* vol. 1 (Grand Rapids: Zondervan Publishing House, 1988), 279.

[8]Hartley, *Theological Wordbook,* vol. 1, 416.

With regard to the concept of "save," "rescue," or "deliver," the lexical richness evident in the Old Testament does not occur in the New Testament.[9] It uses primarily the word *sōzō*—meaning "save," "preserve," or "rescue from danger"—and its derived forms.[10] In the Septuagint, *sōzō* occurs some three-fifths of the time for *yasha'*, and *sōtēria* is used mostly for derivatives of *yasha'*. The Hebrew term underlies the name the angel announced to Joseph: " 'You are to give him the name Jesus, because he will save his people from their sins' " (Matt. 1:21). "That the meaning of the name was thoroughly well known ... is attested by the Alexandrian Jewish exegete and philosopher ... Philo when he interprets Joshua's name as follows: *Iēsous sōtēria kyriou*, Jesus means salvation through the Lord."[11] Therefore, the word the New Testament employs when speaking of the saving work of Christ reflects Old Testament ideas.

Sōzō can refer to saving one from physical death (Matt. 8:25; Acts 27:20,31), from physical illness (Matt. 9:22; Mark 10:52; Luke 17:19; James 5:15), from demonic possession (Luke 8:36), or from a death that has already occurred (Luke 8:50). But by far the greatest number of uses refers to spiritual salvation, which God provided through Christ (1 Cor. 1:21; 1 Tim. 1:15) and which people experience by faith (Eph. 2:8).

Although the title "savior" (Gk. *sōtēr*) was attributed by the Greeks to their gods, political leaders, and others who brought honor or benefit to their people, in Christian literature it was applied only to God (1 Tim. 1:1) and to Christ (Acts 13:23; Phil. 3:20). The noun "salvation" *(Gk. sōtēria)* appears forty-five times and refers almost exclusively to spiritual salvation, which is the present and future possession of all true believers.[12] But even though the Greek words for "save" or "salvation" may be infrequent, Jesus himself pro-

---

[9]Many words and expressions relate to the nature and effect of Christ's work. They are part of the discussion later in this chapter.

[10]They appear about 180 times. The compound *diasōzō*, "bring safely through," "save," "rescue," is not used in a religious sense. Two others are *exaireō* and *hruomai*. Both words mean "rescue," "deliver," with emphasis on natural rescue (Acts 7:10; 12:11; 2 Tim. 4:17; 2 Pet. 2:7,9). Some uses have theological significance (Rom. 7:24; Gal. 1:4; Col. 1:13; 1 Thess. 1:10).

[11]Karl H. Rengstorf, "Jesus, Nazarene, Christian," in *The New International Dictionary of New Testament Theology*, Colin Brown, ed., vol. 2 (Grand Rapids: Zondervan Publishing House, 1976), 332. In the Old Testament, nine persons and one village bear the name "Joshua" (*yēhoshua'*), or its later form "Jeshua" (*yeshua'*).

[12]See Acts 7:25; 27:34; and Heb. 11:7 for exceptions.

claims the theme of the New Testament when He says, " 'The Son of Man came to seek and to save *[sōsai]* what was lost' " (Luke 19:10).

THE NATURES OF GOD AND OF HUMANKIND

The Bible, therefore, reveals a God who saves, a God who redeems. Two questions may arise: What makes spiritual salvation necessary? What makes it possible? The answers we give relate to how we view the natures of both God and humanity. What if God had not been the kind of God the Bible reveals to us, and what if we had not been created in the image of God and subsequently fallen? Salvation as the Bible describes it would be neither possible nor necessary. Therefore, the redemptive drama has as its backdrop the character of God and the nature of His human creation.

The Bible makes it abundantly clear that all people need a Savior and that they cannot save themselves. From the attempt of the first pair to cover themselves and in fear to hide from God (Gen. 3), and from the first angry rebellion and murder (Gen. 4) to the final rebellious attempt to thwart God's purposes (Rev. 20), the Bible is one long litany of the degraded attitude and willful sinning of the human race. Modern Enlightenment thinking, which most often reflects Pelagian ideas,[13] has committed itself to the belief in humanity's essential goodness. In spite of all that she had seen and experienced, Anne Frank in her diary concluded, "I still believe that people are really good at heart."[14] Much modern thinking appears to believe that what we need is educating, not saving; a campus, not a cross; a social planner, not a propitiating Savior. All such optimistic thinking stands in direct contradiction to the teaching of the Scriptures.

In the fiery cloud and pillar, in the thunder and darkness of Sinai, and in the establishment of the sacrificial system with all its prescriptions and proscriptions, God sought to make certain the people understood there was a gulf between himself and them that only He could bridge. At times we may tire when we read all the details of who and when and how and what God required and accepted. What can it mean to us who live in the era of the new covenant? Possibly that God says to all of us, "If you want to approach me, it must be on

---

[13]Including the denial of original sin.

[14]Anne Frank, *The Diary of a Young Girl*, trans. B. M. Mooyaart-Doubleday (New York: The Modern Library, Random House, 1952), 278.

my terms. You have no right to make up your own way." Nadab and Abihu learned that suddenly (Lev. 10:1–2; Num. 3:4), and all Israel with them. Could the experience of Ananias and Sapphira be a parallel example (Acts 5:1–11)? God will not allow any toying with what His holiness requires.

GOD'S HOLINESS AND LOVE

Since we are unholy and God is pure holiness, how can we even think of approaching Him? We can because He both chose and made the way: the cross of Christ. The New Testament has numerous references to "sins" or "sinners" linked with His death. Note a few: "He was delivered over to death for our sins" (Rom. 4:25). "While we were still sinners, Christ died for us" (Rom. 5:8). "Christ died for our sins according to the Scriptures" (1 Cor. 15:3). "Christ died for sins once for all" (1 Pet. 3:18). One cannot possibly take the New Testament statements seriously and deny they teach Jesus Christ died to bridge the gulf between a holy God and a sinful race that could not save itself.

When we consider the characteristics of God it is important to avoid any tendency to treat God's attributes in a way that essentially destroys the unity of His nature.[15] When the Bible says, "God is love," it uses the noun to describe Him, not the adjective "loving," the latter being a weaker characterization. Although the Bible does speak about the righteousness, holiness, justice, or goodness of God, it does not say God *is* righteousness, or God *is* goodness.[16] This has led some to affirm: "In the reality of God, love is more fundamental than, and prior to, justice or power." And: "If power, control, and sovereignty are the preeminent divine qualities according to Calvinism, then love, sensitivity, and openness, as well as reliability and authority, are the essential qualities of God for

---

[15]See Clark H. Pinnock, ed., *The Grace of God, The Will of Man* (Grand Rapids: Zondervan Publishing House, 1989), 34, 36, and 165, and Williams, *Renewal Theology,* vol. 1, 36, for examples of such a tendency. But note an appeal for balance in Louis Berkhof, *Systematic Theology* (Grand Rapids: Wm. B. Eerdmans, 1941), 368.

[16]We need to recall, however, that the Bible also says that "God is light" (1 John 1:5) and that He is "a consuming fire" (Heb. 12:29). Surely these metaphors are equivalent to saying "God is holiness" or "God is righteousness."

Arminians."[17] But in any discussion of God's nature we must not see it as one attribute superseding another, or keeping in check or balancing another. All the terms the Bible uses to describe the character of God are equally essential qualities of His nature. So in Him, holiness and love, righteousness and goodness do not stand in opposition to each other.

CHAPTER 10

The Saving Work of Christ

The Bible, both the Old and New Testaments, reveals God as a God of absolute holiness (Lev. 11:45; 19:2; Josh. 24:19; Isa. 6:3; Luke 1:49) and righteous justice (Ps. 119:142; Hos. 2:19; John 17:25; Rev. 16:5).[18] He cannot and will not tolerate or excuse unholiness or unrighteousness (Hab. 1:13).[19] We can see this in His judging Adam and Eve; in His destroying humankind by the Flood; in His commanding Israel to exterminate the Canaanites, whose iniquity had now "reached its full measure" (Gen. 15:16); in judging His own chosen people; in the final judgment of all who have spurned His Son; and, most important, in the Cross.[20]

---

[17]Pinnock, *Grace of God,* 35, 130. Has this tendency to elevate one divine attribute over another contributed to the great gulf that separates Calvinists from Arminians? This is not to suggest that attempting to see God holistically will eliminate all differences of opinion, but would it help? When the Bible says, " 'God so loved the world that he gave his one and only Son' " (John 3:16), does that mean His justice was inactive? Romans 3:25–26 gives the lie to that idea. Granted that when God acts in a particular way (e.g., in judgment) His justice and holiness are more evident. But does He cease to weep when He does judge? Luke records that Jesus wept over Jerusalem and then proceeded to prophesy its terrifying destruction (19:41–44).

See Williams, *Renewal Theology,* vol. 1, 379, the last three paragraphs of his excursus on theories of the Atonement, for an appeal to think of God holistically, especially in relation to the work of salvation. The biblical concept of love does not "embrace antithesis," says Helmut Thielicke, *The Evangelical Faith,* trans. and ed. Geoffrey W. Bromiley, vol. 2 (Grand Rapids: Wm. B. Eerdmans, 1977), 394. See David W. Diehl, "Righteousness," in Walter A. Elwell, ed., *Evangelical Dictionary of Theology* (Grand Rapids: Baker Book House, 1984), 952.

[18]"Even though there is no distinction between righteousness and justice in the biblical vocabulary, theologians often use the former to refer to the attribute of God in himself and the latter to refer to the actions of God with respect to his creation" (Diehl, *Evangelical Dictionary,* 953).

[19]That God's nature forbids His tolerating evil is a given to the prophet. That accounts for his bewilderment, because God appears to be doing so.

[20]Of course, God does not express His righteousness and justice only in judgment. In his farewell speech, Samuel alludes to the Exodus and the period of the judges and says, " 'I am going to confront you with evidence . . . as to all the righteous acts performed by the LORD for you and your fathers' " (1 Sam. 12:7). In the New Testament, 1 John 1:9 affirms that God will forgive because He is righteous.

At the same time, however, the Scriptures show that for a time God was willing to overlook humanity's ignorance in relation to idol worship, though now He commands all people everywhere to repent (Acts 17:29–30). In past generations He "let all nations go their own way" (Acts 14:16), though now He wants them "to turn from these worthless things" (14:15). Paul says that in the Cross God sought to demonstrate His justice "because in his forbearance he had left sins committed beforehand unpunished" (Rom. 3:25). He endured for four hundred years the gross iniquity of the Amorites (Gen. 15:13), though eventually His judgment fell with irresistible might. The Lord will "not acquit the guilty" (Exod. 23:7) and "accepts no bribes" (Deut. 10:17). "He will judge the world in righteousness and the peoples with equity" (Ps. 98:9). Proverbs 17:15 says, "Acquitting the guilty and condemning the innocent—the LORD detests them both." Those who test God's patience "are storing up wrath . . . for the day of God's wrath, when his righteous judgment will be revealed" (Rom. 2:5).

Attempts to weaken the meaning of these words that describe God and His actions, perhaps by seeing them as exaggerated expressions of God's displeasure at people's disobedience, lead to semantic nonsense. For if we refuse to understand them in their full strength, what can we say about those terms that describe His love and grace? To weaken one group is to weaken the other. The Cross and all it implies can have meaning only in view of a righteous and holy God who requires judgment. If it were not so, then Christ's agony in Gethsemane and His excruciating death become merely scenes in a passion play. Besides, they make a mockery of a loving God. If He really is not so angry with sin that He requires judgment, then the Cross becomes the most loveless act ever seen.

GOD'S GOODNESS, MERCY, AND GRACE

The Bible shows that we must take into account the divine nature as holy and righteous when considering its message of salvation. Yet, it just as equally reveals God's nature to be good in its very essence. The Old Testament continually affirms that the Lord is good (Heb. _tov_) and that He does only good things. The Psalmist invites us to "taste and see that the LORD is good" (Ps. 34:8). He declares, "The LORD is good" (100:5), and he says to the Lord, "You are good, and what you do is good" (119:68). One writer states, "The word 'good' is the most comprehensive term used when praising [the] excellence of something." When applied to God it implies the absolute perfection of this characteristic in Him. There is nothing in Him to make Him "nongood." Therefore, God's redemptive activity expresses His goodness, as is evident when the Bible says that He does not want (Gk. *boulomai*) "anyone to perish, but everyone to come to repentance" (2 Pet. 3:9).[21]

CHAPTER 10

The Saving Work of Christ

The goodness of God that moved Him to hold off judgment and to save lost humankind finds expression in several key ideas (although they do not appear the most frequently with reference to God's affective characteristics). The Bible clearly affirms His patience, long-suffering, and forbearance, the Old Testament writers expressing it most often by the phrase "slow to anger."[22] The primary word in the New Testament follows the pattern of the Hebrew. In 2 Peter we read that the Lord "is patient [Gk. *makrothumei*] with you, not wanting anyone to perish" (3:9). Peter says, "Our Lord's patience [Gk. *makrothumia*] means salvation" (2 Pet. 3:15). In Romans 2:4 Paul uses *anochē* (which means "restraint," "forbearance," or "patience"[23]) in warning those who judge others—while they do the same things themselves—against showing "contempt for the riches of his [God's] kindness, tolerance and patience." In some respects, God's patience reflects a reactive rather than a proactive reason[24] for providing salvation through Christ. But were it not for His forbearance would anyone be saved?

---

[21]Douglas Miller, "Good, the Good, Goodness," in *Evangelical Dictionary*, 470, 471.

This verse does not support the contention that *boulomai* reflects the willing of "determination" and *thelō* of "inclination." See the discussions in Joseph H. Thayer, *Greek-English Lexicon of the New Testament* (Grand Rapids: Baker Book House, 1977), for *thelō*, 285, 286, and Dietrich Muller, "Will, Purpose," in *New International Dictionary*, vol. 3, 1015–18 for *boulomai*.

[22]It appears nine times in the NIV (e.g., Exod. 34:6; Num. 14:18; Neh. 9:17). In Jer. 15:15 the NIV translates the same Hebrew phrase "long-suffering."

[23]There is no clear distinction between *makrothumia* and *anochē*. The former "is undoubtedly less active and vigorous. ... Furthermore, it has stronger eschatological overtones, looking forward to God's final judgment, whereas *anochē* denotes the period of God's gracious forbearance with particular reference in Rom. to Israel and the period up to the cross of Christ" (Ulrich Falkenroth and Colin Brown, "Patience, Steadfastness, Endurance," in *New International Dictionary*, vol. 2, 767). *Anochē* appears only twice in the New Testament—here and in Rom. 3:25.

[24]One should recall, however, that God's love, grace, mercy, and sovereign decision to redeem are all proactive.

The Bible reveals God's saving nature in its description of His mercy. Mercy is not so much a quality as it is an action. Patience requires no action; mercy does, though we must avoid seeing any kind of dichotomy between the two. The essential idea of mercy requires a condition in which the recipient of mercy has no claim of merit on the mercy giver. If merit is present, mercy ceases. The superior position of the mercy giver, however, does not lead to patronizing. Rather, God humbled himself and became one of us—the ultimate expression of mercy.

In the Old Testament, five important word groupings refer to God's mercy, compassion, or kindness.[25] When reflecting on what God had done in the past for the covenant people, Isaiah says, "In his love [Heb. *'ahavah*] and mercy [Heb. *chemlah*] he redeemed them" (63:9). David compares the compassion (Heb. *rachem*) of the Lord with the compassion of a father (Ps. 103:13). Psalm 116:5 says, "Our God is full of compassion" (Heb. *rachem*). The New Testament uses primarily *eleos* and its derived forms, found mostly in Paul's writings (twenty-six times) and in Luke and Acts (twenty times). In the Synoptics[26] the verb (Gk. *eleeō*) appears mostly in appeals for mercy to Jesus, "son of David" (Matt. 9:27; Mark 10:47), whereas in the Epistles the word refers primarily to God as He does or does not show mercy (Rom. 9:15–18; 1 Pet. 2:10). Mercy is both human (Matt. 23:23; James 3:17) and divine (Rom. 15:9; Heb. 4:16; 1 Pet. 1:3).

Four passages in the New Testament that bring mercy and salvation together call for special attention. First, in Luke 1, the great chapter that introduces God's final redemption, the word "mercy" occurs five times (vv. 50,54,58,72,78).[27] In the Magnificat, Mary rejoices in God for being "mindful of the humble estate of his servant" (v. 48), but she includes all "who fear him" (v. 50) and "his servant Israel" (v. 54) in the

---

[25]They are *chamal*, "spare" or "pity"; *racham*, "have compassion"; *chanan*, "be gracious"; *chus*, "look with pity"; and, probably the most important, *chesedh*, "love" or "kindness." These words also refer to the mercy humans express. The Hebrew concepts have a legal, covenantal background, differing from the predominantly psychological slant of the Greek. See Hans-Helmut Esser, "Mercy, Compassion," in *New International Dictionary,* vol. 2, 594.

[26]None of the words in this group appear in any of the Johannine writings, possibly because the notion of love predominates.

[27]Verse 58 has no redemptive slant. The word "love" is noticeable for its absence. Luke seeks to emphasize God's mercy in providing salvation, a thought that parallels the Old Testament with its stress on *chesedh*.

The Natures of God and of Humankind 335

CHAPTER
10

The Saving
Work of
Christ

mercy of God.[28] Zechariah's inspired prophecy especially shows the connection between mercy and salvation. In the first stanza he emphasizes a coming Exodus-like salvation "to show mercy to our fathers" (v. 72). But in the second he sings of "the knowledge of salvation through the forgiveness of their sins, because of the tender mercy of our God" (vv. 77–78).

Second, in Romans 11:28–32, as Paul concludes his discussion of Israel's place in God's plan, he refers to the bestowal of God's mercy on once-disobedient Gentiles in order that the now-disobedient Israelites may receive mercy. Paul says that God has imprisoned humankind as a whole[29] in disobedience so that all may see that salvation depends on mercy, not national identity.[30]

Third, in Ephesians 2:4–5 Paul shows the working of God's love, mercy, and grace in saving us. The Greek text reads more literally, "But God, being rich in mercy, because of His great love with which He loved us, made [us] alive with Christ." The richness of His mercy moved Him to save.

Fourth, in Titus 3:4–5 Paul joins mercy with two other tender words. God manifested His kindness[31] and love[32] when He saved us, "not because of righteous things we had done, but because of his mercy." The Parable of the Unmerciful Servant in Matthew 18:23–34 illustrates the New Testament teaching regarding God's mercy. Even though the first servant owed a debt that was impossible to pay, the master did not seek unmercifully to extract it from him. Rather, he graciously forgave him. In Christ, God has done that for us.

Another way in which God shows His goodness is in saving grace. The words for the idea of grace that the Old Testament uses most often are *chanan,* "show favor" or "be gracious," and its derived forms (especially *chēn*), and *chesedh,* "faithful lovingkindness" or "unfailing love." The former usually refers

---

[28]Often the prophetic person uses the past tense to refer to future events, for in God's eyes it is as good as done. See, e.g., Isa. 53.

[29]The Greek expression *tous pantas* emphasizes the collective unity of the race.

[30]Paul says essentially the same thing in Gal. 3:22, but in Gal. the Bible, as the expression of God's will, declares our being imprisoned (Gk. *sunekleisen*) due to sin. It emphasizes promise, faith, and believing, rather than mercy, but the promise "given through faith in Jesus Christ" refers to receiving life and righteousness (v. 22), i.e., salvation.

[31]Gk. *chrēstotēs,* "goodness," "kindness," "generosity."

[32]Gk. *philanthrōpia,* "lovingkindness for humankind;" "kindhearted benevolence."

to bestowing favor in redeeming one from enemies (2 Kings 13:23; Ps. 6:2,7) or in appeals for the forgiveness of sin (Pss. 41:4; 51:1). Isaiah says that the Lord longs to be gracious to His people (Isa. 30:18), but personal salvation is not in view in any of these instances. The noun *chēn* appears chiefly in the phrase "to find favor in someone's eyes" (of men: Gen. 30:27; 1 Sam. 20:29; of God: Exod. 34:9; 2 Sam. 15:25). *Chesedh* always contains an element of loyalty to covenants and promises expressed spontaneously in acts of mercy and love. In the Old Testament the emphasis is on favor shown to the covenant people, though the nations are also included.[33]

In the New Testament, "grace," as the undeserved gift by which people are saved, appears primarily in Paul's writings.[34] It is "a central concept that most clearly expresses his understanding of the salvation event . . . showing free unmerited grace. The element of freedom . . . is constitutive." Paul emphasizes God's action, not His nature. "He does not speak of the gracious God; he speaks of the grace that is actualised (sic) in the cross of Christ."[35] In Ephesians 1:7 Paul says, "In him we have redemption through his blood, the forgiveness of sins, in accordance with the riches of God's grace," for "it is by grace you have been saved" (Eph. 2:5,8).

GOD'S LOVE

Without minimizing His patience, mercy, and grace, the Bible most frequently associates God's desire to save us with His love. In the Old Testament the primary focus is on covenantal love, as in Deuteronomy 7:

The LORD did not set his affection [Heb. *chashaq*] on you and choose you because you were more numerous than other peoples. . . . But it was because the LORD loved [Heb. *'ahev*] you and kept the oath he swore to your forefathers that he . . . redeemed you from the land of slavery. . . . If you pay attention to these laws and are careful to follow them, then the LORD your God will keep his covenant of love [Heb. *chesedh*] with you, as he swore to your forefathers. He will love [Heb. *'ahev*] you and bless you (vv. 7–8,12–13).

---

[33]See Jer. 9:24. The verse stands in a passage that is universal in scope, i.e., vv. 23–26.

[34]For a notable exception, see Acts 15:11.

[35]Hans Conzelmann, "Charis," in *Theological Dictionary of the New Testament*, vol. 9 (Grand Rapids: Wm. B. Eerdmans, 1974), 393–94. Its freeness reflects the "element of spontaneous freedom" found in *chesedh*. See Gal. 2:21.

In a chapter of covenantal redemption the Lord says, " 'I have loved [Heb. *'ahev*] you with an everlasting love [Heb. *'ahavah*]; I have drawn you with loving-kindness [Heb. *chesedh*]' " (Jer. 31:3). In spite of Israel's backsliding and idolatry, God loved with an everlasting love.

The New Testament uses the words *agapaō* or *agapē* to refer to God's saving love. In prebiblical Greek the word had little power or strength. In the New Testament, however, its power and warmth are evident. "God is *agapē* " (1 John 4:16); therefore "he gave his one and only Son" (John 3:16) to save humankind. God has demonstrated His unmerited love in that while "we were still sinners, Christ died for us" (Rom. 5:8). The New Testament gives ample testimony to the fact that God's love impelled Him to save lost humankind. Therefore, all four of these attributes of God—patience, mercy, grace, and love—demonstrate His goodness in providing for our redemption.[36]

If the Bible teaches that God's goodness moved Him to save lost humankind, it also teaches that nothing external to himself compelled Him to do so. Redemption finds its source in His free and unfettered love and will. In Deuteronomy 7:7–8 Moses points this out when he says that the Lord did not choose Israel because of who they were, but because He loved them and was faithful to His promise. God's own character (i.e., His love and faithfulness) was expressed in choosing and redeeming them even though they were stiff-necked (Deut. 9:6; 10:16).[37]

In Galatians 1:4 Paul says that Christ "gave himself for our sins to rescue us from the present evil age, according to the will of our God and Father." On the Day of Pentecost Peter preached that Jesus was handed over to death "by God's set purpose and foreknowledge" (Acts 2:23). Although we must not compromise the infinitely impelling power of divine love, we may not, on the other hand, compromise His sovereignty.

The New Testament preserves both in that it offers no theory of the Atonement, though it does give "several indications of the principle on which atonement is effected."[38] In spite of the nontheoretical approach of the New Testament,

---

[36]One should notice the frequency with which the Old Testament brings together in God all four of these characteristics. See Exod. 34:6; Neh. 9:17; Pss. 86:15; 103:8; 145:8; Joel 2:13; and Jon. 4:2. See also Rom. 2:4 and Eph. 2:4–5,7.

[37]See also Deut. 4:37 and 10:15.

[38]Leon Morris, "Atonement" in *Evangelical Dictionary,* 97.

through the years church theologians have advanced several theories.[39] As it often happens when there are several theories to explain a biblical truth, each may contain a kernel of that truth.

THEORIES OF THE ATONEMENT

THE MORAL-INFLUENCE THEORY

The moral-influence theory (also called the love-of-God theory or exemplarism) is generally attributed to Peter Abelard.[40] In stressing God's love he rejected any idea that there was in God that which required satisfaction. God did not demand payment for sin, but in love He graciously forgave. In the Incarnation and the Cross we see a demonstration of God's overwhelming love. This vision moves us to gratitude and love and therefore incites repentance, faith, and a desire to change our behavior. The moral-influence theory sees no atoning purpose or effect in the Cross.

We should not reject the theory out-of-hand. It contains truth. Don't examples of bravery and kindness inspire us to change and to be brave and kind? One cannot look at the Cross and not be inspired. In singing the well-known hymn "When I Survey the Wondrous Cross," we give expression to this theory.

But though the theory correctly emphasizes God's love, it is woefully inadequate in explaining all the Bible says about the reason for the Cross. It fails to take fully into account God's holiness and righteousness as well as biblical statements to the effect that Christ's death accomplished a work of expiation, if not propitiation (Rom. 3:25–26; Heb. 2:17; 1 John 2:2). It also does not demonstrate that a mere stirring of the emotions will lead to repentance. It gives no satisfactory explanation of how the Old Testament saints came to be saved. Alister McGrath says, "Perhaps one of the most serious difficulties ... is the utter ambiguity of the cross. If the sole insight to be gained from the cross is that God loves us, why should he go about revealing it in so ambiguous a manner?"[41]

---

[39]That it happened becomes understandable when we realize that none of the early creeds (Nicea, A.D. 325; Constantinople, A.D. 381; Chalcedon, A.D. 451) formulated a theory of the Atonement. They were content simply to state that on the cross Christ effected salvation; they did not argue how.

[40]A French intellectual: philosopher, teacher, and theologian (1079–1142).

[41]Alister E. McGrath, *The Mystery of the Cross* (Grand Rapids: Zondervan Publishing House, 1988), 100.

If, in the Cross, Christ did nothing more than influence us, then His death is merely a performance for effect. The Bible asserts much more.

THE RANSOM THEORY

The theory that emphasizes Christ's victory over Satan is sometimes called the ransom theory, or the devil-ransom or dramatic theory. Because of our sin we are under Satan's domination. But because God loves us, He offered His Son to the devil as a ransom price to set us free. The evil one was more than glad to make the exchange, but he didn't know that he could not keep Christ in Hades, and with the Resurrection he lost both the ransom and his original prisoners. That this transaction involved God in deception, because He surely knew the outcome, did not trouble the church fathers. To them it merely meant that God was wiser and stronger than Satan. The humanity of Jesus was the bait that concealed the hook of His deity, and the devil took it.[42] The fault was his, not God's.

After Anselm this view disappeared, but in recent years a Swedish theologian, Gustaf Aulen (1879–1978), revived the positive aspects of the theory in his classic work *Christus Victor*. He emphasized the biblical truth that the death of Christ did defeat the devil (Heb. 2:14; Col. 2:15; Rev. 5:5). Death and hell have been conquered (1 Cor. 15:54–57; Rev. 1:18). The seed of the woman has crushed the serpent's head (Gen. 3:15). Seeing the Atonement as the victory over all the forces of evil must always be a vital part of our victorious proclamation of the gospel.[43] We must not discard that truth while rejecting the idea that God cunningly deceived Satan into his defeat.

---

[42]The idea of Gregory of Nyssa (ca. 330–ca. 395). For a very brief summary of the historical background of the various theories, see the article "Atonement," in *Baker's Dictionary of Theology,* Everett F. Harrison, ed. (Grand Rapids: Baker Book House, 1960), 71–75. For a fuller treatment of the first five centuries, see J. N. D. Kelley, *Early Christian Doctrines,* 2d ed. (New York: Harper & Row, Publishers, 1960), 375–400.

[43]Gustaf Aulen, *Christus Victor,* trans. A. G. Hebert (N.Y.: Macmillan, 1969). See Williams, *Renewal Theology,* vol. 1, 363, n.30, for a brief comment on teaching found among some Pentecostals that Christ's victory was won in Hades and not on the cross. See also D. R. McConnell, *A Different Gospel* (Peabody, Mass.: Hendrickson Publishers, 1988), 116–33.

THE SATISFACTION THEORY

Anselm (1033–1109)[44] propounded a theory that gave shape to nearly all Catholic and Protestant thought on the subject down to the present. In part aimed at Jews of his day who denied a true Incarnation, he wrote his treatise *Cur Deus Homo (Why God Became Man)*. In it he offered one of the first well thought-out theories of the Atonement, usually called the satisfaction theory.[45] He said that in their sinning, people insult the honor of the sovereign, infinite God. Insult to a sovereign head cannot go unpunished and demands satisfaction.[46] But how could that be achieved by us if the sovereign head is the infinite God? At the same time, God's love pleads for the sinner. How shall the apparent conflict in God find resolution? We commit the sin and therefore must render the satisfaction. But because only God could do so, and we alone must do so, only a God-man could satisfy the insult to God's honor and pay the infinite price for forgiveness.

The satisfaction theory has much to commend it. It focuses on what God requires in the Atonement and not on Satan. It takes a much more profound view of the seriousness of sin than do the moral-influence and ransom theories. It proposes a theory of satisfaction, an idea that is a more adequate explanation of the biblical materials.

But the satisfaction theory has weaknesses as well. God becomes a feudal lord whose vassals have gravely dishonored Him, and He cannot let that go unpunished if He is to preserve His position. What Anselm failed to take into account, however, is the possibility that a sovereign could be merciful without jeopardizing his superior station. The theory seems to imply a real conflict between the attributes of God, which the Bible disallows. Then it also takes on a quantitative dimension: Since sins are virtually infinite in number and infinite in nature—because they are against an infinite God, the sacrifice must also be quantitatively and qualitatively infinite. Although this explanation should not be totally rejected, the biblical emphasis is not on a commercial transaction but on the action of a loving and gracious God. We are not simply

---

[44]A medieval theologian and Archbishop of Canterbury.

[45]Sometimes called the commercial theory because it makes the sacrifice of Christ a transaction to satisfy God's honor. See Henry C. Thiessen *Introductory Lectures in Systematic Theology* (Grand Rapids: Wm. B. Eerdmans, 1949), 319.

[46]We must recall that Anselm lived in the days of knighthood and chivalry, a time when one's honor was prized above all else.

bystanders who receive indirect benefits from a transaction that takes place between God and His Son. We are the purpose of it all. Although Anselm's theory has weaknesses, they do not negate its underlying thrust, that is, an atonement that renders satisfaction.

THE GOVERNMENTAL THEORY

The governmental theory owes its origin to Hugo Grotius (1583–1645), a Dutch jurist, statesman, and theologian. He viewed God as a Lawgiver who both enacts and sustains law in the universe. Law is the result of God's will, and He is free to "alter or even abrogate it." The Law states unequivocally: "The soul that sins shall die." Strict justice requires the eternal death of sinners.

How could God maintain respect for the Law and at the same time show clemency to sinners? Simply forgiving them, which He could have done, would fail to uphold the Law. So He did it, not by appeasing a principle of judicial wrath in His nature, but by setting forth the death of Christ as "a public example of the depth of sin and the lengths to which God would go to uphold the moral order of the universe."[47] The effects of His death do not bear on us directly, only secondarily, in that Christ did not die in our place but only in our behalf. The primary focus was not saving sinners but upholding the Law. In the Cross, God showed He can abominate lawlessness and at the same time maintain the Law and forgive the lawless.

Although the governmental theory contains a kernel of truth in that "the penalty inflicted on Christ is also instrumental in securing the interests of divine government,"[48] it does not express the heart of biblical teaching, and in this we find the primary objection. It does a disservice to the many Scripture passages which, if taken at face value, indicate a substitutionary motif in Christ's death (e.g., Matt. 20:28; 26:28; John 10:14–15; 2 Cor. 5:21; Eph. 5:25). The theory fails to explain the reason for choosing a sinless person to demonstrate God's desire to uphold the Law. Why not put to death the worst of all sinners? Why Christ and not Barabbas? That would surely be a clearer example of the depth to which God felt the need to show how detestable lawlessness was

---

[47]Berkhof, *Systematic Theology,* 388. Leon Morris, "Theories of the Atonement" in *Evangelical Dictionary,* 102.

[48]Berkhof, *Systematic Theology,* 389.

to Him. In addition, the theory does not take fully into account the depravity of the race. Like the moral-influence theory it assumes that a mere example will be sufficient to enable us to carry on a law-abiding way of living. Nothing could be further from biblical truth.

THE PENAL-SUBSTITUTION THEORY

Reflecting the basic thought of the Reformers, evangelicalism affirms the idea of penal substitution to explain the meaning of Christ's death. It states that Christ bore in our place the full penalty of sin that was due us. That is, His death was vicarious, totally for others. This means that He suffered not merely for our benefit or advantage[49], but in our place, in our stead (Gk. *anti,* "instead of," as in Mark 10:45 and 2 Cor. 5:14).

The New Testament never uses the expression "penal substitution," but of all the various theories it appears to represent most adequately the teachings of the Bible. It takes the Bible seriously in its depictions of God's holiness and righteousness as they find expression in His judicial wrath. It takes fully into account what the Bible says about our depravity and consequent inability to save ourselves. It takes literally those statements that say typologically (in the sacrificial system), prophetically (in direct announcement), and historically (in the New Testament record) that Christ "took our place."[50]

We must express the view carefully, for not all agree with the penal-substitution theory. Some objections must be answered, such as the following.

1. Since sin is not something external, can it be transferred from one person to another? To do so would, in fact, be immoral.[51] Seeing it, however, not as a mechanical transfer

---

[49]The Greek preposition *huper,* which may be the meaning in Gal. 2:20 and Eph. 5:25, but cannot be the meaning in John 11:50; 2 Cor. 5:15; and Gal. 3:13.

[50]For the sacrificial system see Lev. 4:1 through 6:7; 6:24–30; 7:1–6; 8:14–17; and 10:3–20. Giving to God the firstborn of all clean animals was "in place of" a firstborn son (Exod. 13:1–16). The scapegoat was a substitute bearer of sins (Lev. 16:20–22). See Heb. 2:17; 7:27; 9:15,28; and 10:10 for the idea of substitution in sacrifices. See, e.g. of direct announcement, Isa. 53:4–6,8,12. For the New Testament record, see Mark 10:45; John 3:17; 10:11,15; Rom. 3:21–26; 2 Cor. 5:21; Gal. 3:13; 2 Pet. 2:24; etc. The references are many and varied.

[51]This reflects Pelagianism in its doctrine of original sin.

of sins but as Christ's identification with us, a sinful race, lessens the intensity of the objection. Other than in sinning, Christ became one with us. Could it, then, also be said that God's transferring to us the righteousness of Christ is immoral? We need to understand, as well, that God himself *is* the sacrifice. In Jesus, God assumed the guilt and bore the penalty.[52]

2. The penal-substitution theory implies a conflict in the Godhead. Christ becomes a loving Savior who must tear forgiveness from the closed fist of a wrathful Father. God's righteousness stands above His love. The fact remains, however, that the Scriptures clearly exclude this two-pronged objection. The Father loved the world so much that He sent the Son. John says, "This is love: not that we loved God, but that he loved us and sent his Son as an atoning sacrifice for our sins" (1 John 4:10). John 3:36 says, "Whoever believes in the Son has eternal life, but whoever rejects the Son will not see life, for God's wrath remains on him." Love and wrath appear together in relationship to God's sending Jesus. One is not above the other.

3. The penal-substitution theory minimizes God's free grace in implying He would not and, in fact, could not forgive unless appeased by a sacrifice. Although the objection touches a truth, it fails in that it does not recognize that Christ's atoning work *is* God's forgiveness. In it God shows that He *is* forgiving and *does* forgive. Those who object to the theory of penal substitution need to recognize the implications of such a decision. Who bears the penalty for sin, Christ or us? We cannot have it both ways. Is Christianity a redemptive religion? If not, where does our hope lie? If so, substitution is implicit.[53]

ASPECTS OF CHRIST'S SAVING WORK

SACRIFICE

Although some ideas have already been covered, we need to look more closely at several aspects of Christ's saving work. A number of biblical words characterize it. No one reading the Scriptures perceptively can escape the fact that sacrifice

---

[52]We must, of course, not construe this to imply any form of patripassianism, the idea that the Father suffered and died on the cross. See modalistic monarchianism or Sabellianism, chap. 3, pp. 161–62.

[53]See Thielecke, *The Evangelical Faith,* vol. 2, 405–6.

stands at the heart of redemption, both in the Old and New Testaments. The imagery of a lamb or a kid slain as part of the saving, redeeming drama goes back to the Passover (Exod. 12:1–13). God would see the sprinkled blood and "pass over" those whom the blood shielded. When the Old Testament believer placed his hands on the sacrifice it conveyed more than identification (i.e., this is "my" sacrifice); it was a sacrificial substitute (i.e., this I sacrifice in my place).

Although we must not press the comparisons too far, this imagery is clearly transferred to Christ in the New Testament.[54] John the Baptist introduced Him by announcing, " 'Look, the Lamb of God, who takes away the sin of the world' " (John 1:29). In Acts 8, Philip applies Isaiah's prophecy that the Servant would be "led like a lamb to the slaughter" (Isa. 53:7) to "the good news about Jesus" (Acts 8:35). Paul refers to Christ as "our Passover lamb" (1 Cor. 5:7). Peter says that we were redeemed "with the precious blood of Christ, a lamb without blemish or defect" (1 Pet. 1:19). Even those in the heavenlies praised and worshiped the Lion of the tribe of Judah as the slain Lamb (Rev. 5). Although some may cringe at the "blood and gore" associated with sacrifice, to remove it rips the heart out of the Bible.

Closely related to the concept of sacrifice are the terms "propitiation" and "expiation," which seek to answer the question, What effect does Christ's sacrifice have? In the Old Testament these words reflect the word group of *kipper* and in the New that of *hilaskomai.* Both word groups mean "to appease," "pacify," or "conciliate" (i.e., to propitiate), and "to cover over with a price" or "atone for" (so as to remove sin or offense from one's presence; i.e., to expiate). At times the decision to choose one meaning over the other relates more to a theological position than to basic word meaning. For example, one may make a theological decision concerning what the Bible means when it speaks of God's wrath or anger. Does it require appeasing?

Colin Brown refers to a "broad segment of biblical scholars who maintain that sacrifice in the Bible is concerned with expiation rather than propitiation." G. C. Berkouwer refers to Adolph Harnack's statement that orthodoxy confers on God the "horrible privilege" of not being in "a position to

---

[54]See Berkhof, *Systematic Theology,* 377. For example, some female animals were part of the sacrificial ritual, even when for sin (Lev. 4:28,32). The New Testament does not go into great detail concerning the Levitical sacrifices. It stresses the idea of sacrifice, not the specific kinds.

forgive out of love." Leon Morris expresses the general consensus of evangelicals in saying, "The consistent Bible view is that the sin of man has incurred the wrath of God. That wrath is averted by Christ's atoning offering. From this standpoint his saving work is properly called propitiation." Neither the Septuagint nor the New Testament emptied the force of *hilaskomai* as to its meaning of propitiation.[55]

The Bible abandons the crudeness often associated with the word in pagan ritual. The Lord is not a malevolent and capricious deity whose nature remains so inscrutable that one never knows how He will act. But His wrath is real. However, the Bible teaches that God in His love, mercy, and faithfulness to His promises provided the means by which to satisfy His wrath. In the case of New Testament teaching, God not only provided the means, He also became the means. First John 4:10 says, "This is love: not that we loved God, but that he loved us and sent his Son as an atoning sacrifice [Gk. *hilasmos*] for our sins."[56]

All the lexicons show that *kipper* and *hilaskomai* mean "propitiate" and "expiate." The difference lies in how one views their meaning in the biblical materials that deal with

---

[55]In the Old Testament, references to the wrath of God appear almost six hundred times. In the New Testament, they are less frequent but are still present.

"Hilaskomai," *New International Dictionary,* vol. 3, 145–76. See C. H. Dodd, *The Bible and the Greeks* (London: Hodder & Stoughton, 1935), 82–95, and Buschel "hilaskomai," *Theological Dictionary,* vol. 3, 310–23 for examples of this view. J. Rodman Williams says, "Although 'propitiation' conveys an important element of truth, it is less satisfactory [than expiation]" (Williams, *Renewal Theology,* vol. 1, 361, note 20). See Roger Nicole, "C. H. Dodd and the Doctrine of Propitiation," *Westminster Theological Journal,* 17:117–157, and Leon Morris, *The Apostolic Preaching of the Cross* (Grand Rapids: Wm. B. Eerdmans, 1956), chaps. 4–5, for a criticism of Dodd. See also H. C. Hahn, "Anger, Wrath" in *New International Dictionary,* vol. 1, 105–13.

G. C. Berkouwer, *The Work of Christ* (Grand Rapids: Wm. B. Eerdmans, 1975), 275–76.

Morris, "Propitiation," *Evangelical Dictionary,* 888.

Hilasmos and its cognates appear only eight times in the New Testament, but in the Septuagint they occur well over two hundred times, most often related to *kipper,* "cover over with a price," "pacify," or "propitiate." In the Septuagint, *exhilaskomai* and *hilasmos* are most frequent.

[56]The NIV translates *hilaskomai* and related forms as "atoning sacrifice," "make atonement" (Heb. 2:17), "atonement cover" (Heb. 9:5), and "sacrifice of atonement" (Rom. 3:25). It uses neither "propitiation" nor "expiation" anywhere in the translation. One can understand the reason for doing so: the terms have no common usage in today's English.

atonement. If one accepts what the Bible says about God's wrath, a possible solution presents itself. We could see the words as having a vertical and horizontal reference. When the context focuses on the Atonement in relation to God, the words speak of propitiation. But they mean expiation when the focus is on us and our sin. We do not choose either/or but both/and. The historical and literary context determines the appropriate meaning.[57]

The question may arise, If He bore the penalty of our guilt by taking the wrath of God on himself and covering our sin, did He suffer the exact same consequences and punishment in kind and degree that all for whom He died would cumulatively suffer? After all, He was only one; we are many. As with so many such questions there can be no final answer. The Bible makes no such attempt. One should, however, remember that in the Cross we do not deal with a mechanical event or commercial transaction. The work of salvation moves on a spiritual plane, and no tidy analogies exist to explain it all.

We need to keep in mind, first, that suffering by its very nature is not subject to mathematical calculation or to being weighed on a scale. In a sense, to suffer the severest broken arm possible is to suffer them all. To die one excruciating and agonizing death is to die all of them. Second, we have to recall the character and nature of the person suffering. Christ was perfect in holiness and therefore had no sense of personal blame or remorse, as we would have if we knew we were suffering justly for our sins. There is something heroic in the stinging rebuke the thief on the cross hurled at his companion in crime. " 'Don't you fear God, . . . since you are under the same sentence? We are punished justly, for we are getting what our deeds deserve. But this man has done nothing wrong' " (Luke 23:40–41). Christ's perfection did not detract from His suffering but may, in fact, have intensified it, because He knew His was undeserved. His prayer that He would not have to "drink the cup" was no ploy. He knew the suffering

---

[57]Not all will be satisfied with such a simple solution, of course. But it appears reasonable. Note 2 Kings 24:3–4; Ps. 78:38; and Rom. 3:25 for examples of God's anger or punishment joined with forgiveness or atoning sacrifice.

that lay before Him. That He suffered as God certainly has a bearing on the question.[58]

CHAPTER
10

The Saving Work of Christ

RECONCILIATION

Unlike some other biblical or theological terms, "reconciliation" appears as part of our common vocabulary. It is a term drawn from the social realm. Broken relationships of any kind cry out for reconciling. The New Testament is clear in its teaching that the saving work of Christ is a reconciling work. By His death He has removed all barriers between God and us. The word group the New Testament uses (Gk. *allassō*) occurs rarely in the Septuagint and uncommonly in the New, even in a religious sense.[59] The basic verb means "to change," "to cause one thing to cease and another to take its place." The New Testament uses it six times with no reference to the doctrine of reconciliation (e.g., Acts 6:14; 1 Cor. 15:51–52). Paul alone employs the word group with religious connotations. The verb *katallassō* and the noun *katallagē* properly convey the notion of "to exchange" or "to reconcile," as one would reconcile books in accounting practices. In the New Testament the application is primarily to God and us. The reconciling work of Christ restores us to God's favor because "the books have been balanced."

---

[58]Note the suffering in the messianic Pss. 22 and 69 and in the prophecy about the Servant in Isa. 53. For us who are Trinitarian, any hesitation to affirm that "God died" on the cross is misdirected. Of course, God cannot die. But Jesus was and is the God-Man, perfect God and perfect Man. God cannot be born either, but He was in Jesus. The best Greek texts of Acts 20:28 support the reading, "Be shepherds of the church of God, which he [God] bought with his own blood." Some translate the phrase *dia tou haimatos tou idiou* as "through the blood of His own," i.e., "His own Son." A study of the use of the adjective *idios* will show that the absolute use in the singular is rare, appearing at most four times if we exclude Acts 20:28 (i.e., John 15:19; Acts 4:32; Rom. 3:30; and possibly 1 Cor. 12:11). In each instance, the context makes explicitly clear what *idios* refers to. Heb. 9:12 and 13:12 have a different order, *dia tou idiou haimatos,* but that simply reflects a common position of the adjective when the writer wishes to stress the noun rather than the adjective. The difference does not demonstrate that the translation in Acts 20:28 must be "through the blood of his own Son."

[59]The word "reconcile" does not occur in any form in the NIV of the Old Testament. Its appearance in the KJV generally translates Heb. words having to do with "making atonement" (e.g., the *kipper* group, cf. Lev. 6:30 and 8:15). The NIV New Testament has sixteen uses, twelve of which have a religious sense. The double compound verb, *apokatallassō,* does not appear in any Greek literature before Paul. He coined it. See Eph. 2:16 and Col. 1:20,22.

The major relevant passages are Romans 5:9–11 and 2 Corinthians 5:16–21. In Romans, Paul places the emphasis on the assurance we can have regarding our salvation. In two "how much more" statements he asserts that Christ's work will save us from God's wrath (Rom. 5:9) and that even when we were enemies (Col. 1:21–22) His death reconciled us to God; therefore, His being alive assures our salvation (Rom. 5:10). We can rejoice in our reconciliation to God through Christ (5:11). If the stress in Romans is on what God did "for us" in Christ, in 2 Corinthians it is on God as the prime mover in reconciliation (cf. Col. 1:19–20).[60] Our being a new creation comes from God "who reconciled us to himself through Christ" (2 Cor. 5:18) and who "was reconciling the world to himself in Christ" (5:19). These verses emphasize what may be called active reconciliation, i.e., for reconciliation to take place the offended party takes the primary role. Unless the offended person shows a willingness to receive the offender, no reconciliation can take place.

Observe how reconciliation takes place in human relationships, say between husband and wife. If I were to sin against my wife, resulting in a break in our relationship, even if I were to take the initiative and earnestly appeal for reconciliation—with candy and flowers and on my knees begging— she must first forgive me in her heart for restoration to occur. She must take the initiative in that her attitude is the crucial factor. Through Christ, God assures us He has taken the initiative. He has already forgiven. Now we must respond and accept the fact that God has torn from top to bottom the veil separating us from Him and walk boldly into His forgiving presence. That is our part, accepting what God has done through Christ.[61] Unless both actions take place reconciliation will never happen.

───────

[60]The more literal translation of the first clause of 2 Cor. 5:19 is "God was in Christ [the] world reconciling to himself " *(theos ēn en Christō kosmon katallassōn heautō).* Does the phrase "in Christ" point back to *ēn,* "was," or forward to *katallassōn,* "reconciling"? In other words, does it affirm Christ's deity (i.e., "God was in Christ") or refer to the work God accomplished in Christ (i.e., "in Christ He was reconciling the world")? The position may appear to favor the former, but the latter is more in keeping with the context (i.e., the work of Christ is in view, not His character). See the NIV and the NRS.

[61]Except for 2 Cor. 5:19, the tense in each use is the aorist, expressing the decisiveness of God's work: It is done! Our response must be just as decisive: Be reconciled! (5:20).

REDEMPTION

The Bible also uses the metaphor of ransom or redemption[62] to describe the saving work of Christ. The motif appears much more frequently in the Old Testament than in the New. A large number of uses in the Old Testament refer to the rites of "redemption" in relation to persons or property (cf. Lev. 25; 27; Ruth 3 through 4, which use the Hebrew term *ga'al*). The "kinsman redeemer" functions as a go'el. Yahweh himself is the Redeemer (Heb. *go'el*) of His people (Isa. 41:14; 43:14), and they are the redeemed (Heb. *ge'ulim,* Isa. 35:9; 62:12).[63] The Lord made provision to redeem (Heb. *padhah*) the firstborn sons (Exod. 13:13-15). He has redeemed Israel from Egypt (Exod. 6:6; Deut. 7:8; 13:5) and will redeem them from exile (Jer. 31:11). At times God redeems an individual (Pss. 49:15; 71:23), or an individual prays that God will redeem him (Pss. 26:11; 69:18); however, God's redeeming work is primarily national in scope. In a few places redemption clearly relates to moral concerns. Psalm 130:8 says, "He himself will redeem Israel from all their sins." Isaiah says that only the "redeemed," the "ransomed," will walk on the highway called "the Way of Holiness" (35:8–10). He says, further, that the "Daughter of Zion" will be called "the Holy People, the Redeemed of the LORD" (62:11–12).

In the New Testament, Jesus is both the "Ransomer" and the "ransom"; lost sinners are the "ransomed." He declares that He has come "to give his life as a ransom [Gk. *lutron*] for many" (Matt. 20:28; Mark 10:45). It was a "deliverance [Gk. *apolutrōsis*] effected through the death of Christ from the retributive wrath of a holy God and the merited penalty of sin."[64] Paul joins our justification and the forgiveness of sins with the redemption Christ provided (Rom. 3:24; Col. 1:14, both *apolutrōsis*). He says that Christ "has become for us wisdom from God—that is, our righteousness, holiness and

---

[62]See above on Anselm's theory of the Atonement. The idea calls for amplification here. When God does the ransoming the Bible never puts the emphasis on the price paid but on the result (i.e., deliverance and freedom).

[63]The context of these references in Isaiah shows that he looks beyond the immediate future to the end times.

[64]Here the "many" stands in contrast with the death of the "one" person, Jesus, and therefore includes all, not merely some. See R. W. Lyon, "Ransom," *Evangelical Dictionary,* 908, and Pinnock, *The Grace of God,* 59–60 and 78. Thayer, *Greek-English Lexicon,* 65.

redemption" (1 Cor. 1:30). He says also that Christ "gave himself as a ransom [Gk. *antilutron*] for all men" (1 Tim. 2:6). The New Testament clearly shows that the redemption He provided was through His blood (Eph. 1:7; Heb. 9:12; 1 Pet. 1:18–19; Rev. 5:9), for the blood of bulls and goats could not take away sins (Heb. 10:4). Christ bought us (1 Cor. 6:20; 7:23; Gk. *agorazō*) back for God, and the purchase price was His blood (Rev. 5:9).

Since the words imply a deliverance from a state of bondage by payment of a price, from what have we been set free? The contemplation of these things should cause great joy! Christ has delivered us from the righteous judgment of God which we justly deserved because of our sins (Rom. 3:24–25). He has redeemed us from the inevitable consequences of breaking God's law, which subjected us to God's wrath. Even though we do not do everything the Law requires we no longer stand under a curse. Christ took that on himself (Gal. 3:10–13). His redemption secured the forgiveness of sins (Eph. 1:7) and set us free from them (Heb. 9:15). By giving himself for us, He redeemed "us from all wickedness [Gk. *anomia*]" (Titus 2:14), but not to use our "freedom to indulge the sinful nature" (Gal. 5:13) or "as a cover-up for evil" (1 Pet. 2:16). (*Anomia* is the same word Paul uses in 2 Thessalonians 2:3 in referring to "the man of lawlessness.") Christ's purpose in redeeming us is "to purify for himself a people that are his very own, eager to do what is good" (Titus 2:14).

Peter says that "you were redeemed from the empty way of life handed down to you from your forefathers" (1 Pet. 1:18). We cannot be certain whom he refers to by "forefathers." Is it to pagans or to Jews? Or to both? Probably to both in that the New Testament regarded pagan ways as futile (Acts 14:15; Rom. 1:21; Eph. 4:17) and also saw a kind of futility in the external practices of the Jewish religion (Acts 15:10; Gal. 2:16; 5:1; Heb. 9:10,25–26; 10:3–4). There will also be a final redemption from the groaning and pain of this present age when the resurrection takes place and we see the result of our being adopted as children of God through Christ's redeeming work (Rom. 8:22–23).

Evangelicals believe the New Testament teaches that Christ paid the full ransom price to set us free. His is "the" objective work of atonement, the benefits of which, when applied to us, leave nothing to be added by us. It is a final work and cannot be repeated. It is a unique work and can never be imitated or shared.[65]

THE EXTENT OF THE ATONING WORK OF CHRIST

A significant difference of opinion exists among Christians regarding the extent of Christ's atoning work. For whom did He die? Evangelicals as a whole have rejected the doctrine of absolute universalism (i.e., divine love will not permit any human being, and perhaps not even the devil and fallen angels,[66] to remain separated from it forever). Universalism posits that Christ's saving work embraced absolutely everyone. In addition to passages that show God's nature of infinite love and mercy, the key verse for universalism is Acts 3:21, where Peter says that Jesus "must remain in heaven until the time comes for God to restore everything." Some take the Greek expression *apokatastaseōs pantōn* ("restoration of all things")

---

[65]This differs from a basic idea in Roman Catholic theology, i.e., that the Atonement covers original sin and the eternal penalty of mortal postbaptismal sins. Catholicism teaches that the penalty for temporal (venial) sins must be satisfied by us in this world through penance and in the coming world in purgatory. See chap. 18, p. 612, for a discussion of purgatory.

If these things are so, how do we explain Col. 1:24? There Paul says, "Now I rejoice in what was suffered [Gk. *pathēmasin*] for you, and I fill up in my flesh what is still lacking in regard to Christ's afflictions [Gk. *ta husterēmata tōn thlipseōn*], for the sake of his body, which is the Church." Paul appears to be saying there was something deficient in Christ's atoning sacrifice. Of course, a single verse cannot affect everything the New Testament has to say about Christ's unique and final work. How impossible to suppose Paul in any way intended to say the work of Christ was not sufficient (cf. Col. 2:11–15)! But what does he mean? The word he uses for "afflictions" (Gk. *thlipsis,* from thlibō, "to press hard," "crowd," "afflict") refers to the ordinary burdens of life in a fallen world and not to Christ's atoning sufferings. The New Testament chooses *paschō* or *pathēma* to refer to that idea (cf. Acts 17:3; Heb. 13:12; 1 Pet. 2:21,23). The background of Paul's statement is the principle of our union with Christ. That union, by its very nature, implies suffering. Jesus said, "All men will hate you because of me" (Mark 13:13). In Acts 9:4 He says, " 'Saul, Saul, why do you persecute me?' " (See also Matt. 10:25; John 15:18–21; Acts 9:4–5; Rom. 6:6; 8:17; 2 Cor. 1:10; 4:10; Phil. 3:10; etc.) To persecute the Church is to persecute Jesus; in this way, He enters into the afflictions the Church experienced. Paul is not alone, however, in "making up what is lacking in Christ's afflictions." The whole Church, in solidarity with each other and in union with its Head, shares in that. Christ's "personal sufferings are over, but His sufferings in His people continue." See Frank E. Gaebelein, ed. *The Expositor's Bible Commentary,* vol. 11 (Grand Rapids: Zondervan Publishing House, 1976–92), 190.

[66]Such teaching goes back to Greek fathers such as Clement of Alexandria, Origen, and Gregory of Nyssa. Origen believed this to be a possibility.

to be absolute in intent, rather than simply "all things promised...through His holy prophets." Although the Scriptures
do refer to a future restoration (Rom. 8:18–25; 1 Cor. 15:24–
26; 2 Pet. 3:13), in light of all the Bible's teaching on the
eternal destiny of both human beings and angels, one cannot
use this verse to support universalism.[67] To do so would do
exegetical violence to what the Bible has to say in this regard.

Among evangelicals the difference lies in the choice between particularism, or limited atonement (i.e., Christ died
only for those whom God has sovereignly elected), and qualified universalism, or unlimited atonement (i.e., Christ died
for everyone, but His saving work is effected only in those
who repent and believe). That a clear-cut difference of opinion exists among equally devout, Bible-believing people should
steer us away from the extreme dogmatizing we have seen
in the past and do see yet today. Tied to a particular doctrine
of election, both views find their basis in the Bible and logic.
Both agree that the issue is not one of application. Not all
will be saved. Both agree that directly or indirectly all people
receive benefits from the atoning work of Christ. The point
of disagreement has to do with the divine intent. Was it to
make salvation possible for all, or for only the elect, and
thereby secure and guarantee their eternal salvation?

Particularists look to passages that say Christ died for the
sheep (John 10:11,15), for the Church (Eph. 5:25; Acts 20:28),
or for "many" (Mark 10:45). They also cite numerous passages
which, in context, clearly associate "believers" with Christ's
atoning work (John 17:9; Gal. 1:4; 3:13; 2 Tim. 1:9; Titus 2:3;
1 Pet. 2:24). Particularists argue: (1) If Christ died for all, then
God would be unjust if any perished for his or her own sins,
since Christ took on himself the full penalty for the sins of
all. God would not twice require the debt. (2) The doctrine
of unlimited atonement logically leads to universalism because to think otherwise calls into question the efficacy of
Christ's work, which was for "all." (3) Sound exegesis and
hermeneutics make evident that universal language is not
always absolute (cf. Luke 2:1, NRS; John 12:32; Rom. 5:18;
Col. 3:11).

Those who espouse qualified universalism argue: (1) It alone

---

[67]See Thielicke, *The Evangelical Faith,* vol. 3, 453–56. He says, "At this
point (even in a systematic theology) I can only express a personal conviction. In my view some theological truths and circumstances—in this
case the position of the lost—cannot be the theme of theological statements
but only of prayer" (456).

makes sense of the sincere offer of the gospel to all people. Opponents reply that the warrant for preaching the gospel to all is the Great Commission. Since the Bible teaches election, and since we don't know who the elect are (cf. Acts 18:10—"I have many people in this city," i.e., Corinth)—we must preach to all. But would it be a genuine offer from God who says, "Whosoever will," when He knows that that is not really possible? (2) Prior to the rise of Calvinism, qualified universalism had been the majority opinion from the beginning of the Church. "Among the Reformers the doctrine is found in Luther, Melanchthon, Bullinger, Latimer, Cranner, Coverdale, and even Calvin in some of his commentaries. For example Calvin says regarding . . . Mark 14:24, 'which is shed for many: By the word "many" he [Mark] means not a part of the world only, but the whole human race.' "[68] (3) The charges that if an unlimited atonement were true God would be unjust and that universalism is the logical outcome cannot be sustained. We have to bear in mind that one must believe to be saved, even the elect. The application of Christ's work is not automatic. Because a person chooses not to believe does not mean that Christ did not die for him or her, or that God's character becomes suspect.

The crux of the defense, however, is that one cannot easily dismiss the obvious intent of the many universalistic passages. Millard Erickson says, "The hypothesis of universal atonement is able to account for a larger segment of the biblical witness with less distortion than is the hypothesis of limited atonement."[69] For example, Hebrews 2:9 says that by the grace of God, Jesus tasted death for "everyone." It is rather easy to argue that the context (2:10–13) shows the writer does not mean everyone absolutely, but the "many sons" Jesus brings to glory. But such a conclusion stretches exegetical credibility. Besides, in the context there is a universal thrust (2:5–8,15).[70] When the Bible says that "God so loved the world" (John 3:16), or that Christ is "the Lamb of God, who takes away the sin of the world" (John 1:29), or that He is "the Savior of the world" (1 John 4:14), it means just that.

Certainly the Bible uses the word "world" in a qualitative

---

[68]Walter A. Elwell, "Extent of Atonement," *Evangelical Dictionary,* 99.

[69]Millard J. Erickson, *Christian Theology* (Grand Rapids: Baker Book House, 1985), 835.

[70]The reference to "Abraham's descendants" (Heb. 2:16) merely expresses the idea that Christ assumed human and not angelic nature. It does not support particularism in relation to Christ's work.

sense, referring to the evil world system that Satan dominates. But Christ did not die for a system; He died for the people who are part of it. No place in the New Testament does "world" refer to the Church or to the elect. Paul says that Jesus "gave himself as a ransom for all men" (1 Tim. 2:6) and that God "wants all men to be saved" (1 Tim. 2:4). In 1 John 2:1–2 we have an explicit separation between the believers and the world, and an affirmation that Jesus Christ, the Righteous One, "is the atoning sacrifice" (v. 2) for both. H. C. Thiessen reflects the thought of the Synod of Dort (1618–19) in saying, "We conclude that the atonement is unlimited in the sense that it is available for all; it is limited in that it is effective only for those who believe. It is available for all, but efficient only for the elect."[71]

THE ORDER OF SALVATION

Because of His infinite goodness and justice God sent His one and only Son to the cross to bear the full penalty of sin, so that He might freely and justly forgive all who come to Him. How does this take place in a person's life? Thinking about the application of Christ's work to us leads to a consideration of what has been called the *ordo salutis* ("order of salvation"), a term dating from about 1737 and attributed to Lutheran theologian Jakob Karpov, though the idea predates him. It asks the question, What is the logical (not the chronological) order in which we experience the process of going from a sinful state to one of full salvation? The Bible gives no order, though in embryo it can be found in Ephesians 1:11–14 and in Romans 8:28–30, where Paul lists foreknowledge, predestination, calling, justification, and glorification, each building on the prior idea.

Roman Catholicism has related the order to the sacraments, i.e., baptism, at which one experiences regeneration; confirmation, when one receives the Holy Spirit; the Eucharist, a participating in the physical presence of Christ; penance, the forgiveness of nonmortal sins, and extreme unction, when one receives assurance of entrance into God's eternal kingdom.[72]

---

[71]See also Isa. 53:6; Matt. 11:28; Rom. 5:18; 2 Cor. 5:14–15; 1 Tim. 4:10; 2 Pet. 3:9. Henry C. Thiessen, *Lectures in Systematic Theology* (Grand Rapids: Wm. B. Eerdmans, 1979), 242.

[72]Since Vatican II, Roman Catholics refer to extreme unction as "the anointing of the sick" and no longer limit it to the last rites.

Among Protestants the difference lies primarily in the Reformed and, in general, the Wesleyan approaches. The view one takes relates to one's doctrine of depravity. Does it imply a total inability that necessitates a regenerating work of the Holy Spirit to enable one to repent and believe, i.e., the Reformed position? The order would then be election, predestination, foreknowledge, calling, regeneration, repentance, faith, justification, adoption, sanctification, and glorification. Or does it imply that, because we continue to bear the image of God even in our fallen state, we are able to respond to God's drawing in repentance and faith? If this, the order is foreknowledge, election, predestination, calling, repentance, faith, regeneration, and the rest. The differences lie in the order of the first three, i.e., those that refer to God's activity in eternity, and in the placement of regeneration in the order. The latter order is the position of this chapter.

CHAPTER 10

The Saving Work of Christ

ELECTION

That the Bible teaches a divine choosing, a divine election, is evident. The Old Testament says that God chose Abraham (Neh. 9:7), the people of Israel (Deut. 7:6; 14:2; Acts 13:17), David (1 Kings 11:34), Jerusalem (2 Kings 23:27), and the Servant (Isa. 42:1; 43:10). In the New Testament God's choosing refers to angels (1 Tim. 5:21), Christ (Matt. 12:18; 1 Pet. 2:4,6), a remnant of Israel (Rom. 11:5), and believers, i.e., the elect, whether individually (Rom. 16:13; 2 John 1:1,13) or collectively (Rom. 8:33; 1 Pet. 2:9). Always the initiative is with God. He did not choose Israel because of their greatness (Deut. 7:7). Jesus tells His disciples, " 'You did not choose me, but I chose you' " (John 15:16).[73] Paul makes this very evident in Romans 9:6–24 in stating that God chose only the descendants of Isaac to be His children (vv. 7–8), and that even before they were born He chose Jacob, not his twin, Esau, "in order that God's purpose in election might stand" (v. 11).[74]

We need to note Paul's emphases. One is that being a child of God depends on the free and sovereign expression of His mercy and not on anything we are or do. Paul emphasizes a

---

[73]That is, they were chosen for a particular ministry. As in the case of Israel, the choice was for a work, not for salvation. But that work could be done only as they remained in relation to Him.

[74]One should observe here that in neither case is personal salvation in view.

divine mercy that includes Gentiles as well as Jews (Rom. 9:24–26; 10:12). Calvinism sees this passage as affirming the doctrine that God made an arbitrary choice that does not take into account human response or participation. However, that is not the only possibility. Even in this whole section (Rom. 9 through 11), evidence of participation and responsibility appears (cf. vv. 9:30–33; 10:3–6,9–11,13–14,16; 11:20,22–23). Paul says, "God has mercy on whom he wants to have mercy, and he hardens whom he wants to harden" (9:18). He also says that Israel has experienced "a hardening in part" (11:25), but the context seems to relate this to their disobedience, obstinacy, and unbelief (10:21; 11:20). In addition, Paul states that the reason "God has bound all men over to disobedience" is "that he may have mercy on them all" (11:32). Therefore, in seeing all that Paul stresses we are not forced to make only one conclusion, i.e., unconditional election.[75]

In any discussion of election we must always begin with Jesus. Any theological conclusion that has no reference to the heart and teaching of the Savior must be suspect. His nature reflects the God who elects, and in Jesus we find no particularism. In Him we find love. Therefore, it is significant that in four places Paul joins love with election or predestination. "We know, brothers loved by God, that he has chosen [Gk. *eklogēn*] you" (1 Thess. 1:4). "As God's chosen people [Gk. *eklektoi*],[76] holy and dearly loved..." (Col. 3:12)— in this context, loved by God. "For he chose [Gk. *exelexato*] us in him before the creation of the world. ... In love he

---

[75]The terms "elect" (verb or noun) and "election" always refer to those who are God's people, whether Israel (Rom. 11:28) or the Church (1 Pet. 1:1; 2 Pet. 1:10). They are not merely potentially God's people, they are. So the elect are the elected ones, i.e., believers. But the biblical teaching on election does not clearly demonstrate or prove the doctrine of unconditional election. Based on strong statements regarding the decrees of God (see various Calvinist theologians, e.g., Berkhof, Buswell, Hodge) the doctrine faces two difficulties. (1) It does not have a satisfactory idea of human freedom. Is freedom merely the ability to act according to one's nature or desires? Or does true freedom imply the real ability to choose between opposites? (2) If election is unconditional, how does one avoid the corollary doctrine of double predestination? If God unconditionally elected some, by that very decision He actively consigned the rest to damnation. To refer to this divine action as "preterition" (i.e., God's passing over the nonelect) makes the term a theological euphemism for double predestination.

[76]The emphasis is on an elect Body. See Robert Shank, *Elect in the Son* (Springfield, Mo.: Westcott Publishers, 1970).

predestined us to be adopted as his sons through Jesus Christ, in accordance with his pleasure and will" (Eph. 1:4–5). The last phrase is better translated "according to the good pleasure [Gk. *eudokia*] of his will" (NRS). Although divine intent is not absent from this word in the Greek, it has as well a sense of warmth not evident in *thelō* or *boulomai*. The verb form appears in Matthew 3:17, where the Father says, " 'This is my Son, whom I love; with him I am well pleased [Gk. *eudokēsa*].' "

Finally, Paul says, "We ought always to thank God for you, brothers loved by the Lord, because from the beginning God chose [Gk. *heilato*] you to be saved through the sanctifying work of the Spirit and through belief in the truth" (2 Thess. 2:13). The God who elects is the God who loves, and He loves the world. Can the notion of a God who arbitrarily chooses some and ignores the rest to their damnation stand under scrutiny in light of a God who loves the world?

In Jesus we also see foreknowledge. He knew that He would die on a cross (John 12:32), and He knew some of the details of that death (Mark 10:33–34). He knew that Judas would betray Him (John 13:18–27) and that Peter would deny Him (Mark 14:29–31). But we certainly cannot read causation into His foreknowledge. After the lame man was healed, Peter graciously said that the Jerusalem Jews had acted ignorantly in crucifying Jesus, but also that Christ's death fulfilled what God had spoken by the prophets (Acts 3:17–18). God did not *cause* them to crucify Jesus; they were yet to blame (Acts 4:27–28).[77] So when the Bible connects our election with foreknowledge (1 Pet. 1:2) we should not see causation in that. God does not have to predestine in order to foreknow. The statement in Romans 8:29 that those whom "God foreknew he also predestined" does not lend support to such a notion. Foreknowledge in such a case would be a meaningless term.

Could we not see foreknowledge and predestination as two sides of a coin? The top side, foreknowledge, looks up toward God and reflects what He knows. Now in relation to our part in being saved, the Bible gives no clue as to *what* God foreknew. However, if one holds to a doctrine of absolute omniscience, His foreknowledge could surely include our repentance and faith in response to His drawing. In stating this,

---

[77]The New Testament shows clear evidence of the concept that the plan of salvation stretches back into eternity (cf. 2 Tim. 1:9–11; Titus 1:2–3; 1 John 1:1–3; 1 Pet. 1:18–21).

we have not compromised God's sovereign action by making it dependent on something we do. But if the Bible does not say *what* God foreknew, it clearly refers to *whom* (Rom. 8:29). Predestination, the bottom side of the coin, looks toward human beings and shows the sovereign working out of God's will.[78]

Further, it has been said that the verb "to foreknow" (Gk. *proginōskō*) suggests more than mental cognition. Both the Old and New Testaments use the word "know" to refer to the intimacy of relationship between husband and wife (Gen. 4:1, NRS; Luke 1:34, KJV) and to knowing that goes beyond mere facts about someone. Through Amos, the Lord says to Israel, " 'You only have I known' " (3:2, NRS). Paul says, " 'I want to know Christ' " (Phil. 3:10). In addressing the "fathers" John says that they "have known him who is from the beginning" (1 John 2:13–14). These instances surely show that "knowing" in the Bible can include love and relationship. Can we, then, appropriately see in God's foreknowledge of us an expression of His love and concern? And God loves everyone in the world. He indeed foreknows cognitively all the thoughts and actions of all people. When, however, the Bible refers to those who believe in His Son, foreknowledge is applied to them and to them only. A loving Father presents a bride to His beloved Son.[79]

---

[78]Acts 13:48 says, "When the Gentiles heard this, they were glad and honored the word of the Lord; and all who were appointed for eternal life believed." The verse makes a strong statement about some being appointed to eternal life. Although it does not state it, God did the appointing. Those of us who are not of a strong Calvinist persuasion must not weaken the statement to make it more cordial to our theological position. A couple of things could be said. Luke gives no basis for the appointing, but perhaps it is similar to Lucan ideas elsewhere that see Christ's death and resurrection as the result of God's "purpose and foreknowledge" (Acts 2:23). Then, too, the possibility exists that the verb (Gk. *tetagmenoi,* from *tassō*) could be middle voice and not passive. In Acts 13:46, Paul says to the Jews, "Since you . . . do not consider yourselves worthy of eternal life, we now turn to the Gentiles." They did not put themselves into a position that brought them eternal life. The verb *tassō* basically means "to place" or "station in a fixed spot." If this were middle, it could then be translated, "They believed, i.e., those who placed themselves in a position to receive eternal life." The Jews refused to; the Gentiles did. In reference to Acts 13:48, Arndt and Gingrich say about this verb, as a passive, that it conveys the idea of "belong to, be classed among those possessing." That comes close to the idea of the middle voice.

[79]The idea that foreknowledge could have the meaning of "forelove" does not force one to take the position of unconditional election, no more than does a particular view of what the Bible means by election and pre-

Those whom God foreknew (Rom. 8:29; 1 Pet. 1:1) He elected in Christ[80] (Eph. 1:4) and predestined them "to be conformed to the likeness of his Son" (Rom. 8:29) and "for the praise of his glory" (Eph. 1:11–12). In keeping with His sovereign and loving purpose expressed in His "not wanting anyone to perish, but everyone to come to repentance" (2 Pet. 3:9), He calls people to himself (Isa. 55:1–8; Matt. 11:28). In the Old Testament God's calling had primarily to do with the people of Israel, beginning with their ancestor Abraham. In the New Testament the call became more universal and individualistic, primarily with saving purpose, though the emphasis differs. Sometimes the call refers to (1) a summons to follow Jesus (Matt. 4:21; Mark 2:14,17; cf. Luke 18:22); (2) an active, inward calling by God, when referring to believers (Rom. 8:30; Eph. 4:1; 2 Tim. 1:9); (3) a description of those who respond (i.e., they are the "called" [1 Cor. 1:24]); or (4) the purpose to which God has called them (e.g., to be "saints" [Rom. 1:7; 1 Cor. 1:2]).

In concluding the Parable of the King's Wedding Banquet (Matt. 22:1–14), Jesus said that "many are called [Gk. *klētoi*], but few are chosen [Gk. *eklektoi*]" (v. 13, NRS), in a context that certainly has eternal destiny in view (v. 13). "It shows that, at least from the standpoint of human response, the circle of the called and of the elect cannot be taken as necessarily coinciding."[81] The very word "call" implies a response, and if we respond to it we become God's elect. If God's eternal purpose is particularly in view (cf. Eph. 1:4), we show ourselves to be among the elect.

When God calls us to himself for salvation, it is always a call of grace, regardless of any distinction we may make between "prevenient" grace[82] and "efficacious" grace. Can we resist this gracious call? Calvinism teaches that we cannot because God's working always achieves its end. His grace is efficacious. Just as God irresistibly called creation into existence, so He irresistibly calls people to redemption. If one

---

destination. H. C. Thiessen says, "Foreknowledge, election, and predestination are simultaneous acts of God, though there is a logical sequence from one to the other" (Thiessen, *Lectures,* 259).

[80]Ephesians is talking about an elect Body. See Shank, *Elect.*

[81]Lothar Coenen, "Call," in *New International Dictionary,* vol. 1, 274–75.

[82]By "prevenient grace," Calvinists generally refer to God's gracious initiative in providing redemption for sinners. Based on what Christ did on the cross, Wesleyans see it as God's gracious initiative in drawing sinners to himself (John 6:44; 12:32), without which no one could come to Him.

accepts the *ordo salutis* Calvinists propose, in which regeneration follows the calling but precedes repentance and faith, then certainly grace is irresistible. One has already been born again. The idea of resisting in such a case becomes nonsense.

Can it be said, however, that the very expression "irresistible grace" is technically improper? It appears to be an oxymoron, like "cruel kindness," because the very nature of grace implies the offer of a free gift, and one can accept or reject a gift. That is true even if the gift is offered by a gracious, loving, and personal Sovereign who experiences no threat to, or diminishing of, His sovereignty if one refuses His gift. That is clearly evident in the Old Testament. The Lord says, " 'All day long I have held out my hands to an obstinate people' " (Isa. 65:2), and " 'I called but you did not answer, I spoke but you did not listen' " (Isa. 65:12). The prophets made clear that the people's refusal to receive God's gracious expressions did not in the least compromise His sovereignty. Stephen storms at his hearers, " 'You stiff-necked people, with uncircumcised hearts and ears! You are just like your fathers: You always resist the Holy Spirit' " (Acts 7:51). It appears evident that Stephen had in view their resistance to that Spirit that sought to draw them to God. That some later believed (e.g., Saul of Tarsus) is no evidence for the doctrine of irresistible grace.[83]

In addition, it needs to be said that if we cannot resist God's grace, then nonbelievers will perish, not because they would not respond but because they could not. God's grace would not be efficacious for them. God then looks more like a capricious sovereign who toys with His subjects than a God of love and grace. His "whosoever will" becomes a cruel game that has no equal, since God is the one who plays it. But the God and Father of our Lord Jesus Christ plays no games with us. When the arms of His Son stretched wide on the cross He embraced everyone, because God loves the world. God *is* love, and the very nature of love implies that it can be resisted or rejected. By its very nature love is vulnerable. It does no disservice to His magnificent greatness or His sovereignty to believe that we can refuse His love and grace which genuinely seek to draw all people to himself. Just the opposite is the case. A God whose love yearns for everyone

---

[83]In the story of the earnest young man who wanted to know what he had to do to inherit eternal life, yet who refused Jesus' conditions (Mark 10:17–22), do we have another example of one who resisted God's call of grace?

to come to Him but does not irresistibly compel them to come, and whose heart breaks over their refusal, has to be a God of greatness beyond our imagining.[84]

There can be only one appropriate response to such great love: to repent and believe. We cannot, of course, produce these actions apart from divine enabling, but neither are they produced within us apart from our willingness. We must avoid extreme expressions of both synergism, a "working together," and monergism, a "working alone." Monergism finds its roots in Augustinianism and affirms that to be saved a person cannot and does not do anything whatever to bring that about. Conversion is entirely a work that God does. If a sinner chooses to repent and believe, God alone is the active agent. If a sinner chooses not to repent and believe, the fault is entirely his.

Extreme forms of synergism go back to Pelagius, who denied humankind's essential depravity. But in its moderate evangelical expression it goes back to Arminius and, more important, to Wesley, both of whom emphasized our ability to freely choose, even in matters that affect our eternal destiny. We are depraved, but even the most depraved among us has not entirely lost the image of God. An evangelical synergist affirms that God alone saves, but he or she believes that universal exhortations to repent and believe make sense only if in fact we can accept or reject salvation. Salvation stems entirely from God's grace, but to state that that is so does not require us to diminish our responsibility when confronted by the gospel.

REPENTANCE AND FAITH

Repentance and faith constitute the two essential elements of conversion. They involve a turning from, i.e., repentance, and a turning to, i.e., faith. The primary words in the Old Testament for the idea of repentance are *shuv*, "to turn back," "return," and *nicham*, "to be sorry," "console." *Shuv* occurs over one hundred times in a theological sense, either to turn from God (1 Sam. 15:11; Jer. 3:19) or to turn back to God (Jer. 3:7; Hos. 6:1). One may also turn from good (Ezek. 18:24,26) or turn from evil (Isa. 59:20; Ezek. 3:19), i.e., repent. The verb *nicham* has an emotional aspect not evident in *shuv*, but both convey the idea of repentance.

---

[84]Let us remember too that God wants sons, not puppets. He could have programmed us to respond with political correctness, but that would not be love.

The New Testament uses *epistrephō* for the sense of "turning" to God (Acts 15:19; 2 Cor. 3:16) and *metanoeō/metanoia* for the idea of "repentance" (Acts 2:38; 17:30; 20:21; Rom. 2:4). The New Testament uses *metanoeō* to express the force of *shuv,* indicating an emphasis on the mind and will. But it is also true that in the New Testament *metanoia* is more than an intellectual change of mind. It stresses the fact that the whole person turns around and has a fundamental change of basic attitudes.

Although in itself repentance does not save, one cannot read the New Testament and be unaware of its emphasis on repentance. God "commands all people everywhere to repent" (Acts 17:30). The initial message of John the Baptist (Matt. 3:2), Jesus (Matt. 4:17), and the apostles (Acts 2:38) was "Repent!"[85] All must repent for all have sinned and fall short of God's glory (Rom. 3:23).

Although repentance involves the emotions and the intellect, a primary component is the will. One has only to think of two Herods. Mark's Gospel presents the enigma of Herod Antipas, an immoral despot who imprisoned John for denouncing Herod's marriage to his brother's wife, while at the same time he "feared John and protected him, knowing him to be a righteous and holy man" (Mark 6:20). Apparently Herod believed in a resurrection (6:16), so he had some theological insight. One can hardly imagine that John did not force him to grapple with the opportunity to repent.

Paul confronted Herod Agrippa II with the king's own belief in the prophetic statements about the Messiah, but he refused to be persuaded to become a Christian (Acts 26:28). He refused to repent even though he did not deny the truth of what Paul said about him. Like the Prodigal, all must say, " 'I *will* set out and go back to my father' " (Luke 15:18). Conversion implies a "turning away from," but it just as equally implies a "turning toward." Although we must not suggest an absolute dichotomy, for one must trust in order to make the move to repent, the distinction is not inappropriate. When we believe, put our trust in God, we turn toward Him.

At the head of all such biblical statements stands: "Abraham believed [Heb. *'aman*] the LORD, and he credited it to him

---

[85]The New Testament also suggests that repentance does not occur without divine aid. See Acts 11:18 and 2 Tim. 2:25.

as righteousness" (Gen. 15:6).[86] Moses connected Israel's rebellion and failure to obey God with their failure to trust the Lord (Deut. 9:23–24). The faithlessness of Israel (Jer. 3:6–14) stands in sharp contrast to the faithfulness of God (Deut. 7:9; Ps. 89:1–8; Hos. 2:2,5; cf. Hos. 2:20). Faith involves trusting. One can "trust" or "rely on" (Heb. *batach*) the Lord with confidence. The person who does is blessed (Jer. 17:7). We rejoice because we put our trust in His name (Ps. 33:21) and in His unfailing love (Ps. 13:5). We can also "take refuge in" Him (Heb. *chasah*), an idea that affirms faith (Ps. 18:30; see also Isa. 57:13).

In the New Testament the verb *pisteuō*, "I believe, trust," and the noun *pistis*, "faith," occur about 480 times.[87] Only a few times does the noun reflect the Old Testament idea of faithfulness (e.g., Matt. 23:23; Rom. 3:3; Gal. 5:22; Titus 2:10; Rev. 13:10). Rather, it functions as a technical term, used almost exclusively to refer to an unqualified trust in, obedience to, and dependence on God (Rom. 4:24), Christ (Acts 16:31), the gospel (Mark 1:15), or Christ's name (John 1:12). From this it is evident in the Bible that faith is no "leap into the dark."

We are saved by grace through faith (Eph. 2:8). Believing in the Son of God leads to eternal life (John 3:16). Without faith we cannot please God (Heb. 11:6). Faith, then, is the attitude of confident, obedient trust in God and in His faithfulness that characterizes every true child of God. It is our spiritual life-blood (Gal. 2:20).

One can argue that saving faith is a gift of God in such a way that the presence of religious yearnings, even among pagans, has no bearing on either faith's presence or its exercise. Yet most evangelicals affirm that such universally present yearnings constitute evidence for the existence of a God to whom they are directed. Have such yearnings no reality, no validity in and of themselves, apart from direct divine activity?

We cannot, of course, exercise saving faith apart from di-

---

[86]We must, of course, avoid any suggestion that Abraham's faith became a work that merited righteousness. The Bible never regards faith as meritorious.

[87]The noun appears nowhere in the Gospel of John, only twice in 1 John, and four times in Revelation, apparently indicating that John stresses the activity of obedient faith. The Greek commonly uses the preposition *eis* ("into," "unto") with the verb to emphasize that faith is not mere intellectual assent. Faith in the New Testament is not passive. Even the noun stresses the active sense of trustful obedience.

vine enabling, but does the Bible teach that when I believe I am simply giving God's gift back to Him? To protect the biblical teaching on salvation by grace through faith alone, must we insist that the faith is not really mine, but God's? Some cite certain verses as evidence for such an opinion. J. I. Packer says, "God is thus the author of all saving faith (Eph. 2:8; Phil. 1:29)." H. C. Thiessen states that there is "a divine and human side of faith," and then goes on to say, "Faith is a gift of God (Rom. 12:3; 2 Pet. 1:1), sovereignly given by the Spirit of God (1 Cor. 12:9; cf. Gal. 5:22). Paul speaks of the whole aspect of salvation as being a gift of God (Eph. 2:8), and surely that includes faith."[88]

But the question needs to be asked: Do all the references cited unequivocally refer to "saving" faith? That does not seem to be the case with Romans 12:3 and 1 Corinthians 12:9, and certainly not with Galatians 5:22. The faith in view in these verses refers to faith (or faithfulness) in the ongoing experience of believers. The verse in Ephesians is questionable, because the genders of "faith" and of the pronoun "this" are different. Ordinarily a pronoun will agree in gender with its antecedent. Paul means that the whole matter of our being saved is God's gift, as distinct from achieving it by works. The other two verses (Phil. 1:29 and 2 Pet. 1:1) come closest to suggesting that faith as a gift of God follows regeneration. Louis Berkhof says, "True saving faith is a faith that has its seat in the heart and is rooted in the regenerate life." Could we, however, look at these verses differently? For example, "Faith . . . is man's response. Faith is made possible by God, but the faith, the believing, is not God's but man's." Faith is not a work but an outstretched hand that reaches out to accept God's gift of salvation.[89]

REGENERATION

When we respond to God's call and the drawing of the Spirit and the Word, God performs sovereign acts that bring us into His kingdom family: He regenerates those who are dead in trespasses and sins; He justifies those who stand condemned before a holy God; and He adopts those who are children of the enemy. Although these occur simultaneously in the believing person, we can look at them separately.

———

[88]J. I. Packer, "Faith," in *Evangelical Dictionary,* 400. Thiessen, *Lectures,* 269.

[89]Berkhof, *Systematic Theology,* 503. Williams, *Renewal Theology,* vol. 2, 28–29. See chap. 12, pp. 401, 414, 417–18.

Regeneration is the decisive and instantaneous action of the Holy Spirit in which He re-creates the inner nature. The noun for "regeneration" (Gk. *palingenesia*) appears just twice in the New Testament. Matthew 19:28 uses it in reference to the end times. Only in Titus 3:5 does the word refer to the spiritual renewing of an individual. Although the Old Testament has national Israel primarily in view, the Bible uses different images to describe what takes place. The Lord will "remove from them their heart of stone and give them a heart of flesh" (Ezek. 11:19). God says, " 'I will sprinkle clean water on you, and you will be clean. . . . I will give you a new heart and put a new spirit in you. . . . And I will put my Spirit in you and move you to follow my decrees' " (Ezek. 36:25–27). God will put His law "in their minds and write it on their hearts" (Jer. 31:33). He will circumcise their hearts so that they may love Him (Deut. 30:6).

The New Testament has the image of being created anew (2 Cor. 5:17) and of renewal (Titus 3:5), but the most common image is that of "being born" (Gk. *gennaō*, "beget" or "bear"). Jesus said, " 'I tell you the truth, no one can see the kingdom of God unless he is born again' " (John 3:3). Peter states that through God's great mercy He "has given us new birth into a living hope" (1 Pet. 1:3). It is a work that God alone does. Being born again speaks of a radical transformation. But a maturing process is still needed. Regeneration initiates us into growing in our knowledge of God, in our experience of Christ and the Spirit, and in our moral character.[90]

JUSTIFICATION

If regeneration effects a change in our nature, justification effects a change in our status with God. The term refers to that act by which, on the basis of the infinitely righteous and satisfactory work of Christ on the cross, God declares condemned sinners to be free from all the guilt of sin and from its eternal consequences and declares them to be fully righteous in His sight. The God who detests "acquitting the guilty" (Prov. 17:15) maintains His own justice while justifying the guilty because Christ has already paid the full penalty for sin

---

[90]See also John 1:13; 3:5,7–8; 1 Pet. 1:23; 1 John 2:29; 3:9; 4:7; 5:1,18. See chap. 16, pp. 559–61, for a discussion of the relation of water baptism to regeneration. Billy Graham, *World Aflame* (Garden City, N.Y.: Doubleday & Co., Inc., 1965), 141. See chap. 12, pp. 415–16.

(Rom. 3:21–26). We, therefore, can and do stand before God fully acquitted.

To describe God's action of justifying us, the terms used by both the Old Testament (Heb. *tsaddiq:* Exod. 23:7; Deut. 25:1; 1 Kings 8:32; Prov. 17:15) and the New Testament (Gk. *dikaioō:* Matt. 12:37; Rom. 3:20; 8:33–34) suggest a judicial, forensic setting. We must not see it, however, as a legal fiction in which it is *as if* we are righteous when in fact we are not. Because we are in Him (Eph. 1:4,7,11), Jesus Christ has become our righteousness (1 Cor. 1:30). God credits, reckons, (Gk. *logizomai*) His righteousness to our account; it is imputed to us.

In Romans 4 Paul uses two Old Testament examples to argue for imputed righteousness. Of Abraham it was said that he "believed the LORD, and he credited [Heb. *chashav*] it to him as righteousness" (Gen. 15:6). This occurred before Abraham had obeyed God in relation to the covenant sign of circumcision. In perhaps an even more dramatic way, Paul quotes Psalm 32:2, in which David pronounces a blessing on "the man whose sin the LORD does not count against him" (4:8; see also 2 Cor. 5:19). To put to one's account the righteousness of another apart from any good a person may do is glorious enough. But to not hold the person accountable for his or her sins and evil acts is more glorious still. In justifying us God has graciously—and justly, because of Christ's sacrifice—done both.

How does justification take place with reference to the believer? The Bible makes two things abundantly clear. First, it is not because of any good work on our part. In fact, "Christ died for nothing" if righteousness comes by obedience to the Law (Gal. 2:21). Any person who seeks to be righteous by obeying the Law stands under a curse (Gal. 3:10), has been "alienated from Christ," and has "fallen away from grace" (Gal. 5:4). Anyone who believes he or she is more justified after serving the Lord for five or fifty-five years or who thinks good works gain merit with God fails to understand this biblical teaching.

Second, at the very heart of the gospel stands the truth that justification finds its source in the free grace of God (Rom. 3:24) and its provision in the blood Christ shed on the cross (Rom. 5:19), and we receive it through faith (Eph. 2:8). Very commonly, when the idea of justification occurs in the New Testament, faith (or believing) can be found joined to it (cf. Acts 13:39; Rom. 3:26,28,30; 4:3,5; 5:1; Gal. 2:16; 3:8). Faith is never the ground of justification. The New Testament never

says justification is *dia pistin,* "on account of faith," but always **CHAPTER**
dia pisteos, "through faith." The Bible does not regard faith **10**
as meritorious, but rather as merely a hand outstretched to
receive God's free gift. Faith has always been the means of The Saving
justification, even in the case of the Old Testament saints (cf. Work of
Gal. 3:6–9). Christ

Having been justified by grace through faith we do and will
experience great benefits. We "have peace with God" (Rom.
5:1) and preservation "from God's wrath" (Rom. 5:9). We
have the assurance of final glorification (Rom. 8:30) and present and future freedom from condemnation (Rom. 8:33–34;
see also 8:1). Justification leads to our becoming "heirs according to the hope of eternal life" (Titus 3:7, NRS). In praise
of justification, Charles Wesley wrote:

> No condemnation now I dread;
> I am my Lord's and He is mine;
> Alive in Him, my living Head,
> And clothed in righteousness divine.[91]

ADOPTION

God does more, however, than give us right standing with
himself. He also brings us into a new relationship; He adopts
us into His family. A legal term, "adoption" is that act of
sovereign grace by which God gives all the rights, privileges,
and obligations of being in His family to those who receive
Jesus Christ. Although the term does not appear in the Old
Testament, the idea does (Prov. 17:2). The Greek word
huiothesia, "adoption," appears five times in the New Testament, only in Paul's writings, and always with a religious
sense. In becoming the children of God we do not, of course,
become divine. Deity belongs only to the one true God.[92]

The New Testament teaching on adoption takes us from
eternity past, through the present, and to eternity future (if
such an expression is appropriate). Paul says that God "chose
us in him [Christ] before the creation of the world" and

---

[91]From the hymn, "And Can It Be?" in *Sing His Praise* (Springfield, Mo.:
Gospel Publishing House, 1991), 294.

[92]The teaching exists that, because of creation, all people are children
of God. Although there is a sense in which that is true, in the New Testament
only those who are "in Christ" are the adopted children of God, with the
full rights of being heirs of God and joint-heirs with Christ. See McConnell,
A Different Gospel. Especially chapter 7, "The Doctrine of Identification,"
116–33.

"predestined us to be adopted as his sons through Jesus Christ" (Eph. 1:4–5). He says about our present experience, "You did not receive a spirit that makes you a slave again to fear, but you received the Spirit[93] of sonship [*huiothesia*].[94] And by him we cry [in our own language], '*Abba* [Aramaic, Father], Father' [Gk. *ho patēr*]" (Rom. 8:15). We are fully sons though not yet fully mature. Then, in the future, when we lay aside mortality, we will receive "our adoption as sons, the redemption of our bodies" (Rom. 8:23). Adoption is a present reality, but it will be fully realized in the resurrection from the dead.[95] God gives us these family privileges through the redeeming work of His unique Son, the One who is not ashamed to call us brothers (Heb. 2:11).

PERSEVERANCE

If the doctrine of election raises the ire of nonbelievers, among believers the doctrine of perseverance does the same. The caricatures that the proponents of the differing views give of every other view most often have no basis in reality. Some among the Wesleyan-Arminian persuasion insist that Calvinists believe once they are saved they can do whatever sinful thing they please, as often as they please, and still be saved—as if they believe the sanctifying work of the Spirit and the Word does not affect them. Whereas some Calvinists might insist that Wesleyan-Arminians believe any sin they commit jeopardizes their salvation, so that they "fall in and out of" being saved each time they sin—as if they believe that God's love, patience, and grace are so fragile that they shatter at the slightest pressure. Any person who is biblically and theologically alert recognizes the lie in both of these caricatures. The presence of extremes has led to unfortunate generalizations.[96]

Of course, we must understand the impossibility of ac-

---

[93]English versions differ in how they translate *pneuma* here. The RSV, NRS, and NASB do not capitalize the word, though the NASB does in a footnote. The KJV, NIV, and NEB see it correctly as a reference to the Holy Spirit.

[94]As is so often the case when Christians are called sons or brothers, the meaning is generic and includes daughters and sisters.

[95]Paul suggests interesting contrasts in His use of the term. See Rom. 8:15,23; 9:4; Gal. 4:5,7; Eph. 1:3–7.

[96]Having been exposed by personal experience and in academic settings to the extremes, I have been frightened by the arrogant presumption some express and saddened by the terrorizing fear some experience.

cepting as equally true both the Calvinist and Wesleyan-Arminian positions. Either the Bible gives the assurance to a truly saved person that no matter how far at times the believer may depart from living out biblical Christianity he or she cannot and will not ultimately depart from the faith, or it does not. Both cannot be true.[97] But it is not impossible to seek a more balanced biblical orientation.

Biblically, perseverance does not mean that everyone who professes faith in Christ and becomes part of a community of believers is secure for eternity. In 1 John 2:18–19 we read that the rise of "antichrists" shows that "it is the last hour. They went out from us, but they did not really belong to us. For if they had belonged to us, they would have remained with us; but their going showed that none of them belonged to us." This is a favorite camping ground of Calvinists to argue that those who "depart" from the faith so as to be lost were believers in name only. Some argue that Simon the Sorcerer (Acts 8:9–24) is an example of such a person. Non-Calvinists do no service to their position by weakening the force of these statements. Not everyone in our churches, not everyone who gives apparent external evidence of faith, is a true believer. Jesus said to some who claimed extraordinary spiritual powers (which He did not deny), that He never knew them (Matt. 7:21–23). Such statements are not intended to strike fear in the heart of a genuine and simple-hearted believer, but to warn those who depend on external performance for assurance of salvation.

Biblically, perseverance refers to the ongoing operation of the Holy Spirit through which the work of God begun in our hearts will be carried on to completion (Phil. 1:6). It seems that no one, regardless of theological orientation, should object to such a statement. And one wishes it could be left at that. But in light of the necessity of seeking to exegete the Bible with integrity the wish proves impossible. What does the Bible say specifically in this matter?

Significant New Testament support exists for the Calvinist view. Jesus will lose nothing of all God has given Him (John 6:38–40). The sheep will never perish (10:27–30). God always hears Jesus' prayers (11:42), and He prayed that the Father would keep safe and protect His followers (17:11).

---

[97]Such is the case of most doctrines and truth statements, unless, of course, one holds to the relativistic notions of so-called New Age thinking. Either God exists or He does not; either Christ is divine or He is not; and so on.

We are kept by Christ (1 John 5:18). Nothing shall separate us from God's love (Rom. 8:35–39). The Holy Spirit in us is the seal and guarantee of our future redemption (2 Cor. 1:22; 5:5; Eph. 1:14). God will guard what we commit to Him (2 Tim. 1:12). He is able to save for all time those who believe (Heb. 7:24–25). His power guards us (1 Pet. 1:5). God in us is greater than anything outside of us (1 John 4:4). What grand assurances! No believer can or should live without them. And if that were all the New Testament had to say, the position of Calvinism would stand secure.

But there is more. Wesleyan-Arminians readily accept the strength and assurance of the above passages. But it appears that Calvinists sometimes resort to exegetical and hermeneutical twists and turns to avoid the implications of other passages in the New Testament.[98] Not merely formal but real apostasy is possible (Heb. 6:4–6; 10:26–31). The Greek word *apostasia,* "apostasy," "rebellion," comes from *aphistēmi,* "leave," "go away," conveying the idea of moving away from a place where one stands. Millard Erickson says, "The writer . . . is discussing a hypothetical situation. . . . Jesus [John 10:28] is telling us what *will* happen, namely His sheep will not perish. The Bible then can be understood as saying that we *could* fall away, but through the keeping power of Christ we *will* not."[99]

If it could happen, why is it only hypothetically possible? Erickson and most Calvinists refer to Hebrews 6:9 as evidence: "Even though we speak like this, dear friends, we are confident of better things in your case." Such a justification is tenuous in light of Hebrews 6:11–12: "We want each of you to show this same diligence to the very end, in order to make your hope sure. We do not want you to become lazy, but to imitate those who through faith and patience inherit what has been promised." Continuing in faith and practice makes sure a hope and an inheritance. Is it really possible to exegete Hebrews 10:26–31, even in spite of verse 39, in such a way as to conclude it refers merely to a logical but not a real possibility?[100]

---

[98]See the excellent treatment of the New Testament data in Robert Shank, *Life in the Son* (Springfield, Mo.: Westcott Publishers, 1961).

[99]Millard J. Erickson, *Does It Matter What I Believe?* (Grand Rapids: Baker Book House, 1992), 134.

[100]See Shank, *Life,* chap. 19, "Is Apostasy Without Remedy?" pp. 307–29, for a discussion of the impossibility of restoration. Millard J. Erickson, *Introducing Christian Doctrine* (Grand Rapids: Baker Book House, 1992), discusses Heb. 6 in relation to perseverance, but not this passage.

To state the case further, Jesus warns, " 'The love of most will grow cold, but he who stands firm to the end will be saved' " (Matt. 24:12–13). He says that looking back makes us unfit for the Kingdom (Luke 9:62) and tells us, " 'Remember Lot's wife!' " (Luke 17:32). He also says that if a person does not abide in Him, that person will be cut off (John 15:6; cf. Rom. 11:17–21; 1 Cor. 9:27). Paul says that we can be alienated from Christ and fall away from grace (Gal. 5:4); that some have shipwrecked their faith (1 Tim. 1:19); that some will abandon (Gk. *aphistēmi*) the faith (1 Tim. 4:1); and that if "we disown him, he will also disown us" (2 Tim. 2:12). The writer of Hebrews says that "we are His [God's] house, if we hold on to our courage and the hope of which we boast" (3:6); that we should see to it that none of us "has a sinful, unbelieving heart that turns away [Gk. *aphistamai*] from the living God" (3:12); and that we "have come to share in Christ if we hold firmly till the end the confidence we had at first" (3:14).

Peter speaks of those who "have escaped the corruption of the world by knowing our Lord and Savior Jesus Christ and are again entangled in it and overcome[;] they are worse off at the end than they were at the beginning. It would have been better for them not to have known the way of righteousness, than to have known[101] it and then to turn their backs on the sacred command that was passed on to them. Of them the proverbs are true: 'A dog returns to its vomit,' and 'A sow that is washed goes back to her wallowing in the mud' " (2 Pet. 2:20–22).

John says that eternal life is not the believer's possession independently of possessing Christ (1 John 5:11–12). The Father "has granted the Son to have life in himself" in the same sense as the Father has life by His own right and nature (John 5:26). He has not granted that to us. Eternal life is Christ's life in us, and we have it only as we are "in Christ."

In dealing with these warnings as essentially hypothetical for a true believer, Calvinists use various illustrations. Erickson refers to parents who fear their child may run into the

---

[101]In all three uses the word for "know" is the root *epiginōskō.* The compound word conveys a fullness of knowledge that goes beyond mere head knowledge. See 1 Cor. 13:12; Eph. 1:17; 4:13; Phil. 1:9; Col. 1:6,10; 3:10; 1 Tim. 2:4; 4:3; 2 Pet. 1:2. In commenting on these verses, the *NIV Study Bible* refers to those who say that the "person described here could not have been genuinely saved." In view of the meaning of *epiginōskō,* that appears an impossible position to take.

street and be struck by a car. They have two options. Build a fence so that it would be physically impossible for the child to leave the yard. But that restricts the child's freedom. Or warn the child of the danger of running into the street. In that case the child could run into the street, but he won't. However, if the cars, i.e., the dangers, do not really exist and the child knows that, can the warning really function as a deterrent?[102]

Allow another analogy. Let us say we were driving on a highway at night. Every few miles we came across warning signs. They warned of a sharp curve ahead, of a bridge that was out, of falling rocks, of a narrow, winding road, of a steep grade, of major construction, etc., but not one of the dangers materialized. What would we think? A prankster or a fool has been at work. In what way are they warnings if they do not correspond to reality?

Calvinists argue that they have assurance of salvation because of their position, whereas Wesleyan-Arminians don't. Is this really so? In view of passages like chapters 6 and 10 of Hebrews and the others above, how can Calvinists claim they have greater assurance than Arminians? How can they be sure they are one of the elect until they get to heaven? If one can be as close to the Kingdom as the letter to the Hebrews and 2 Peter and Matthew 7:22 describe and still not be "in" the Kingdom, where does their greater assurance come from? Actually, the assurance given to all true believers by the Holy Spirit who lives in us is that by grace through faith we are in Christ, who is our redemption and righteousness, and since we are in Him we are secure. This applies whether one is a Calvinist or a Wesleyan-Arminian. Both agree the Bible teaches that we dare not presume and that we need not fear.[103]

A fitting way to close this chapter is with worship in the words of the immortal hymn by Isaac Watts.

> When I survey the wondrous cross,
> On which the Prince of glory died,
> My richest gain I count but loss,
> And pour contempt on all my pride.

---

[102]Erickson, *Christian Doctrine,* 321–22.

[103]See William T. Abraham, "Predestination and Assurance" in Pinnock, *The Grace of God, The Will of Man,* 231–42, and R. E. O. White, "Perseverance," in *Evangelical Dictionary,* 844–45, for balanced, moderating, and helpful treatments.

Forbid it, Lord, that I should boast,
Save in the death of Christ, my God;
All the vain things that charm me most,
I sacrifice them to His blood.
See, from His head, His hands, His feet,
Sorrow and love flow mingled down;
Did e'er such love and sorrow meet,
Or thorns compose so rich a crown?
Were the whole realm of nature mine,
That were a present far too small;
Love so amazing, so divine,
Demands my soul, my life, my all.[104]

STUDY QUESTIONS

1. The Bible says that Christ is a Lamb "slain from the creation of the world" (Rev. 13:8); that He "was handed over . . . by God's set purpose and foreknowledge" (Acts 2:23); and that God "chose us in [Christ] before the creation of the world" (Eph. 1:4). What are the possibilities that God's eternal love embraces eternal suffering? Does God ever cease to grieve over people who are eternally separated from Him?

2. Based on 2 Corinthians 5:21 (and similar passages) some teach that Christ's nature changed and, after suffering in hell as a sinner, He had to be born again. Why is this teaching both unbiblical and heretical?

3. What is the biblical teaching on the relationship between the Old Testament and the New Testament?

4. What feeling response do you have to the Christian claim of exclusiveness in relation to eternal salvation? How can one help nonbelievers to understand?

5. We know and believe the Bible when it says we are not saved by works (Eph. 2:9), but how can we avoid falling into the trap of supposing that our good works are meritorious?

6. Discuss the teaching of some that in different dispensations God had different ways of effecting salvation for humankind.

7. The Bible teaches that Christ's death was a ransom for us. Why is it inappropriate even to ask to whom the ransom was paid?

8. Discuss the statement: Those who think lightly of the disease will loiter on the way to the physician.

---

[104]*Sing His Praise*, 455.

CHAPTER ELEVEN

The Holy Spirit

Mark D. McLean

The task given to the twentieth-century Church is to preach all the gospel. What is needed is not a different gospel but the fullness of the gospel as it is recorded in the New Testament. We emphasize this because the Holy Spirit has been neglected over the centuries. We have the task of understanding anew the person and work of the Holy Spirit as revealed in the Bible and experienced in the life of the Church today. The full-gospel message proclaims the centrality of the work of the Holy Spirit as the active agent of the Trinity in God's self-revelation to His creation. The full-gospel message says that God continues to speak and act today, just as He did in Old and New Testament times.

The full-gospel message is more than a simple declaration that speaking in tongues and the other gifts listed in the Bible are available to the believer today. Outbreaks of Pentecostal phenomena have occurred throughout the history of the church. Many of these outbreaks began within the church as reform or holiness movements. These movements fell by the wayside because they had no access to the Scriptures. Bibles were extremely expensive and were literally chained in the churches. Only the clergy were thought to have the training and access to spiritual truth that allowed handling the Sacred Writ. Without access to the Scriptures, people soon began to confuse their emotions with the Holy Spirit. Without the Bible to form the walls on the straight and narrow path, these groups soon lurched off the path and over the side.[1]

---

[1]Some extremes of the Montanists, the first major challenge to the Catholic church, can be seen in Stanley Burgess, *The Spirit and the Church: Antiquity* (Peabody, Mass.: Hendrickson Publishers, Inc., 1984), 49–53.

One reason for the longevity and success of the twentieth-century Pentecostal movement is the open access to the Bible, our infallible rule of faith and conduct. Admittedly, our interpretations of the Bible are all too often clearly fallible, even when done with much care and prayer. Yet without the Scriptures as our canonical guide to who God is and what His purposes are, we could easily lose our way.[2]

The task of proclaiming the full-gospel message is not an easy one. We live in a world in which secularists and theologically liberal academics of some of the most prestigious universities of our land have proclaimed that the traditional biblical belief in a personal God is dangerous to humanity's continued existence. They argue that there is no God who is actively involved with the redemption of the world or of individuals. Secularists call for an abolishment of all religion. Liberal theologians call for a deconstruction of the traditional elements of the Judeo-Christian faith: the Bible, God, and Jesus Christ. They want to replace or redefine them in the light of their belief that no one can save us from ourselves. They say the human race's continued existence is solely in the hands of human beings.[3]

One result of this liberal theological worldview appears in the text of Genesis 1:2. The NEB has translated the verse as "a *mighty wind* that swept over the surface of the waters" (see also NRS). In the footnote, one finds "others, the *Spirit of God.*" Having decided that the Old Testament contains no hint of the Holy Spirit as an agent in creation as found in the New Testament, the translators simply changed "spirit" to "wind," and "God" to "mighty." I have not been able to find any parallel translation in the canonical text that would suggest such a translation.[4]

---

[2]The same is true for anyone who would suggest that the living, dynamic word of the Holy Spirit must take precedence over the written word. See Mark D. McLean, "Toward a Pentecostal Hermeneutic," *Pneuma* 6:2 (Fall 1984): 36, n.9.

[3]Sallie McFague, *Models of God: Theology for an Ecological, Nuclear Age* (Philadelphia: Fortress, 1987), ix. Cf. Gordon Kaufman, "Nuclear Eschatology and the Study of Religion," *Harvard Divinity Bulletin* 13:3 (February/March 1993): 6–10.

[4]See *A New Concordance of the Old Testament,* ed. Abraham Even-Shoshan (Jerusalem: "Kiryat Sefer" Publ., 1989), 1063–66. *New Brown-Driver-Briggs Gensenius Hebrew and English Lexicon* (Peabody, Mass.: Hendrickson Publishers, 1979; hereafter BDB), says of the inquiries as to the original root and meaning of *'el* and *'elohim,* "the question is intricate and the conclusions dubious." Yet this is the basis for their translation "mighty wind." See also Stanley M. Horton, *What the Bible Says About the Holy Spirit* (Springfield, Mo.: Gospel Publishing House, 1976), 18–19.

The task has been further complicated by misunderstandings of the work and person of the Holy Spirit that have been consciously or unconsciously circulated through the Church at large. This includes misunderstandings of the Holy Spirit's role in the Old Testament, of the believer's relationship to the Holy Spirit before and after conversion and before and after the baptism in the Holy Spirit.

The chapter on the Trinity dealt with the issue of the Holy Spirit's place in the Godhead. Not too much more can be said. God has revealed himself as a Trinity. There is one God, yet three Persons—one God, not three, not one God with a multiple-personality disorder. To understand the doctrine of the Trinity we have to accept that we are forced by God's self-revelation in the Bible to ignore the ordinary laws of logic.[5] The doctrine of the Trinity proclaims God is one, yet three; He is three, yet one. This does not mean that Christianity has abandoned logic and reasoning. Instead, we accept the fact that the doctrine of the Trinity refers to an infinite Being who is beyond the complete comprehension of His finite creatures.

This brings us back to the function of the Holy Spirit as the active agent of the Godhead in His dealings with the creation. Without the ongoing activity of God through the Holy Spirit, knowledge of God would be impossible. Although many theologians have tried to describe God's attributes based on natural theology or scholastic theology,[6] they have been unable to describe correctly God's attributes or purposes. The only way any person can be known, including God, is by knowing what that person has said and done. The Bible tells us what God has said and done. And the Holy Spirit's ongoing work reveals to us what He continues to say and do today.

---

[5]This same problem occurs with the doctrines of Incarnation and Inspiration.

[6]I use the term "scholastic theology" to refer to traditional theologies that stress God's transcendence to the near exclusion of God's immanence. It depends much on Augustine, as does both Catholic and Protestant Scholasticism. In contrast, what I call "pulpit theology" refers to the concept of Immanuel, the indwelling of the Holy Spirit in each believer, the message that God cares for the individual and is active in history on behalf of his people. See Mark McLean, "Transcendence, Immanence and the Attributes of God," *Papers of the Twenty-second Annual Meeting of the Society of Pentecostal Studies,* 2 vols. (November 12–14, 1992), vol. 2, R1–34.

CHAPTER

11

The Holy
Spirit

THE HOLY SPIRIT IN SCRIPTURE

TITLES OF THE HOLY SPIRIT

For many in our society, names do not carry the significance they do in biblical literature. Parents name children after relatives, friends, or movie personalities without any real thought as to the name's meaning. A couple may name a son Michael without any knowledge of the name's original meaning ("Who is like God?").[7] Parents who have a favorite uncle named Samuel ("His name is God") may name their son after him. To an Israelite, the name Samuel proclaimed that the bearer of the name was a worshiper of God.

The names and titles of the Holy Spirit reveal much to us about who God the Holy Spirit is.[8] Although the name "Holy Spirit" does not occur in the Old Testament,[9] a number of equivalent titles are used. The theological problem of the personality of the Holy Spirit revolves around the issue of progressive revelation and understanding, as well as the reader's understanding of the nature of the Bible. The Holy Spirit as a member of the Trinity, as revealed in the New Testament, is not revealed in the Hebrew Bible. However, the fact that the doctrine of the Holy Spirit is not fully revealed in the Hebrew Bible does not change the reality of the Holy Spirit's existence and work in Old Testament times. The earth has never been the physical center of the universe. But until the observations of God's creation by Copernicus, Galileo, and others proved otherwise, both the theologians and scientists of their era believed the earth was the center of the universe.[10]

As noted above, there has yet to be an audience of God's

---

[7]Note that this is a question to which the answer is "no one." It is not a comparison.

[8]Some authors treat the names, titles, and symbols of the Holy Spirit during the discussion of the Trinity; others place this topic under the doctrine of the Holy Spirit. Cf. J. Rodman Williams, *Renewal Theology,* vol. 2 (Grand Rapids: Zondervan Publishing House, 1990), 139–48; Guy P. Duffield and Nathaniel M. Van Cleave, *Foundations of Pentecostal Theology* (Los Angeles: L.I.F.E. Bible College, 1983), 107–14; and Myer Pearlman, *Knowing the Doctrines of the Bible* (Springfield, Mo.: Gospel Publishing House, 1937), 281–90.

[9]Although "Holy Spirit" occurs in Ps. 51:11 and Isa. 63:10–11.

[10]See Timothy Ferris, *Coming of Age in the Milky Way* (New York: Wm. Marrow, 1988), 61–101, for an interesting summary of the discoveries of Copernicus and Galileo and the opposition they faced. We should note however that in the Bible "progressive revelation" is not a matter of replacing error with fact. Rather it is a matter of adding more truth and understanding to the truth already given.

self-revelation, both in the Bible and in creation, which has **CHAPTER 11**
fully comprehended all that God is saying or doing. The post-
Resurrection understanding of the suffering Servant, as epit- The Holy
omized in Philip's explanation of Isaiah 53:7–8 to the Ethi- Spirit
opian eunuch (Acts 8:26–40), was not a new revelation, but
a more accurate understanding of an old revelation.[11]

The most frequent title in the Old Testament is "the Spirit
of Yahweh" (Heb. *ruach YHWH [Yahweh]*), or as one generally finds in English translations, "the Spirit of the Lord." In
light of the attack on the Holy Spirit's presence in the Old
Testament, perhaps we should use the personal name of God,
"Yahweh," rather than the title "Lord" (which was substituted
by Jews after Old Testament times). The point is that one
meaning of *Yahweh* is "He who creates, or brings into being."[12]
Every use of the name *Yahweh* is a creation statement. The
"Lord of hosts" is better translated as "He who creates the
hosts." This refers to the hosts of heaven (both stars and
angels, depending on the context) and the hosts of the people
of God. The Spirit of Yahweh was active in creation, as is
revealed in Genesis 1:2, referring to the "Spirit of God" (Heb.
ruach 'elohim).

A rich cluster of titles of the Holy Spirit is found in John
14 through 16. In 14:16 Jesus said He would send another
Comforter (KJV), Helper (NKJV), or Counselor (NIV).[13] The
work of the Holy Spirit as Counselor includes His role as the
Spirit of Truth who indwells us (John 14:16; 15:26), as a
teacher of all things, as one who reminds us of all Christ has
said (14:26), as one who will bear witness of Christ (15:26),
and as one who will convict the world of sin, righteousness,
and judgment (16:8).

Several titles of the Holy Spirit are found in the Epistles:
"the Spirit of holiness" (Rom. 1:4); "the Spirit of life" (Rom.
8:2); "the Spirit of sonship" (Rom. 8:15; or "adoption," KJV);
the "Holy Spirit of promise" (Eph. 1:13, KJV; or "promised
Holy Spirit," NIV); "the eternal Spirit" (Heb. 9:14); "the Spirit
of grace" (Heb. 10:29); and "the Spirit of glory" (1 Pet. 4:14).

---

[11]This is a statement of faith of the Christian Church.

[12]The question of whether Yahweh should be seen as a Hiphil or Qal of
the verb *hyh* is still disputed. The scholastic theology tends toward the
Qal. This treats it as a statement of stative being, "He who is." The pulpit
theology tends toward the Hiphil or causative stem, a more dynamic "He
who creates." See *BDB*, 218.

[13]Gk. *paraklētos*, with the basic meaning of "Helper." See Stanley M.
Horton, "Paraclete," *Paraclete* 1:1 (Winter 1967): 5–8.

SYMBOLS OF THE HOLY SPIRIT

Symbols give us concrete images of things that are abstract, such as the Third Person of the Trinity. The symbols of the Holy Spirit are also archetypes. In literature, an archetype is a recurring character type, theme, or symbol that can be found in many cultures and times. Everywhere wind represents powerful, but unseen forces; flowing, clear water represents life-sustaining power and refreshment for those who are physically or spiritually thirsty; fire represents a purifying force (as in the purifying of metal ores) or a destroying force (often used in judgment). Such symbols stand for realities that are intangible yet real.[14]

Wind. The Hebrew word *ruach* has a wide semantic range. It can mean "breath," "spirit," or "wind." It is used in parallel with *nephesh*. The basic meaning of *nephesh* is "living being," that is, anything that has breath. Its semantic range develops from there to refer to just about every emotional and spiritual aspect of a living human being. *Ruach* takes on a part of the semantic range of *nephesh*. Therefore, in Ezekiel 37:5–10 we find *ruach* translated as "breath." In 37:14, Yahweh explains that He will put His Spirit on Israel.

The Greek word *pneuma* has a semantic range nearly identical to that of *ruach*. The symbol of wind carries with it the invisible nature of the Holy Spirit, as shown in John 3:8. We can see and feel the effects of the wind, but the wind itself is unseen. Acts 2:2 uses the image of wind forcefully to describe the coming of the Holy Spirit on the Day of Pentecost.

Water. Water, like breath, is necessary to sustain life. Jesus promised streams of living water. "By this he meant the Spirit" (John 7:39). Vital in the hierarchy of human physical needs, breath and water are just as vital in the realm of the Spirit. Without the life-giving breath and flowing waters of the Holy Spirit, our spirit life would soon suffocate and wither away. The person who delights in the Law (Heb. *torah*, "instruction") of Yahweh and meditates on it day and night "is like a tree planted by streams of water, ... whose leaf does not wither" (Ps. 1:3). The Spirit of Truth streams from the Word as living water that sustains, refreshes, and empowers the believer.

---

[14]Pentecostals reject the idea that religious symbols function only to provide substance to abstract ideas created by human beings. God, Jesus Christ, and Torah are more than human inventions to be deconstructed and reconstructed to fit the pleasure and presuppositions of any given human society. Cf. Kaufman, "Nuclear Eschatology," 7–8.

Fire. The purifying aspect of fire is clearly reflected in Acts 2. Whereas a coal taken from the altar purifies Isaiah's lips (6:6–7), on the Day of Pentecost "tongues of fire" signify the coming of the Spirit (Acts 2:3). This symbol is used but once in depicting the baptism in the Holy Spirit. The broader aspect of fire as a cleansing agent is found in the pronouncement or prophecy of John the Baptist: " 'He will baptize you with the Holy Spirit and with fire. His winnowing fork is in his hand, and he will clear his threshing floor, gathering his wheat into the barn and burning up the chaff with unquenchable fire' " (Matt. 3:11–12; see also Luke 3:16–17).

This applies most directly to the separation of God's people from those who have rejected God and His Messiah and will suffer the fire of judgment.[15] However, the purifying, fervent fire of the Spirit of Holiness is at work in the believer as well (1 Thess. 5:19).

Oil. In his sermon to Cornelius, Peter states, "God anointed Jesus of Nazareth with the Holy Spirit and power" (Acts 10:38). Quoting Isaiah 61:1–2, Jesus announced, " 'The Spirit of the Lord is on me, because he has anointed me to preach good news to the poor' " (Luke 4:18). Oil was used early on to anoint first the priests of Yahweh and then the kings and prophets. Oil is the symbol of God's consecrating the believer for service in the kingdom of God. In John's first letter he warns the believers about antichrists:

You have an anointing from the Holy One, and all of you know the truth. ... As for you, the anointing you received from him remains in you, and you do not need anyone to teach you. But as his anointing teaches you about all things and as that anointing is real, not counterfeit—just as it has taught you, remain in him (1 John 2:20,27).

The reception of the anointing of the Spirit of Truth who brings forth streams of living water from our innermost being empowers us to serve God. In the Holy Spirit, water and oil do mix.

Dove. The Holy Spirit descended upon Jesus in the form of a dove in all four Gospel accounts.[16] The dove is an archetype of gentleness and peace. The Holy Spirit indwells us. He does not possess us. He binds us to himself in love, in

---

[15]Horton, *What the Bible Says,* 84–89.

[16]It should be noted also that the dove was the poor person's substitute for a lamb and identified Jesus as the Lamb of God who by His sacrifice on Calvary takes away sin.

contrast to the chains of sinful habits. He is gentle. He provides peace in the storms of life. Even in dealing with sinners
He is gentle, as seen, for example, in His calling humanity to
life in that beautiful, but mournful cry found in Ezekiel 18:30–
32: "Repent! Turn away from all your offenses; then sin will
not be your downfall. Rid yourselves of all the offenses you
have committed, and get a new heart and a new spirit. Why
will you die? . . . For I take no pleasure in the death of anyone,
declares the Sovereign LORD. Repent and live!"

The titles and symbols of the Holy Spirit provide us with
the keys to understanding His work on our behalf. We will
use them as anchor points for the study of the work of the
Holy Spirit.

THE WORK OF THE HOLY SPIRIT

Several misconceptions about the work of the Holy Spirit
exist. Some of them have become rooted in the popular religion and popular doctrines of the Church at large. Popular
religion is the way we practice our daily lives in Christ. It is
an admixture of normative elements and nonnormative elements. Normative elements are correct biblical doctrines of
what one ought to believe and do. Nonnormative elements
are mistaken understandings of biblical doctrines and nonbiblical elements that creep in from the umbrella culture in
which the Christian lives.

No one fully comprehends the infinite God or His infinite
universe, or knows and understands perfectly every word of
the Bible. We are all still disciples (literally, "learners"). As
finite creatures, it should not surprise us to realize the utter
folly of claiming to have fully comprehended the infinite God.
God is still working on His church and on each individual,
transforming us into the image of Christ. The doctrine of
progressive sanctification speaks directly to this issue.[17] Christians need to avoid discouragement as they gladly embrace
the goal of knowing and experiencing God more fully every
day.

BEFORE THE DAY OF PENTECOST

"Let us put out of our minds completely the impression
that the Holy Spirit did not come into the world until the

---

[17]Chap. 12, pp. 416–18. See also William W. Menzies and Stanley M.
Horton, *Bible Doctrines: A Pentecostal Perspective* (Springfield, Mo.: Logion
Press, 1993), 145–54. Cf. Pearlman, *Knowing the Doctrines,* 249–67; Wil-
liams, *Renewal Theology,* 83–117; Duffield, *Foundations,* 236–45.

Day of Pentecost."[18] Consider Joel's prophecy in 2:28–29[19] and Peter's quotation of it in Acts 2:17–18.

Afterward, I will pour out my Spirit on all flesh. Your sons and your *daughters* will prophesy, your elders will dream dreams, your young men will see visions. Even on male *slaves* and *female slaves,* in those days I will pour out my Spirit (author's translation).

In the last days, God says, I will pour out my Spirit on all people. Your sons and daughters will prophesy, your young men will see visions, your old men will dream dreams. Even on my servants, both men and women, I will pour out my Spirit in those days, and they will prophesy.

Notice that the promise is not a change of activity or of the quality of the activity of the Spirit of God. A change in the quantity or scope of the activity is prophesied. The radical nature of the promise is clearly seen from the inclusion of daughters and male and female slaves. It is one thing for Yahweh to pour out His Spirit on the sons, young men, and elders of the free citizens of Israel. However, to pour out His Spirit on the chattel of the household is something quite different. In Joel we see one of the earliest overt statements of the principle, which Paul later expressed: "neither Jew nor Greek, slave nor free, male nor female" (Gal. 3:28).

The early faith of Israel was an inclusive faith. Yet Exodus 12:43–45 makes it clear that no foreigners were to eat of the Passover. What should the head of a household do if his foreign-born slave wanted to celebrate the Passover? The slave was to be circumcised. Any uncircumcised temporary workers or resident aliens staying in the household could not join the celebration unless they too submitted to circumcision. "An alien living among you who wants to celebrate the LORD's Passover must have all the males in his household circumcised; then he may take part like one born in the land. No uncircumcised male may eat of it. The same law applies to the native born and to the alien living among you" (Exod. 12:48–49).

Two prominent examples are Uriah the Hittite and Doeg the Edomite (2 Sam. 11:1–26; 21:7).[20] These men and their

---

[18]Ibid., 267.

[19]Joel 3:1–2 in the Masoretic Hebrew Text.

[20]Uriah means "My light is Yahweh."

families had become part of the covenant and the Children of Israel, though their non-Israelite lineage is plainly expressed. Circumcision and obedience to the Law were signs of their acceptance of Yahweh as their God and Yahweh's acceptance of them. Yet God makes it clear that outward circumcision is to be accompanied by the circumcision of one's heart (Deut. 10:16; 30:6; cf. Jer. 9:26). Deuteronomy 29:18–22 warns that if a decision is made to hide under the umbrella of the covenant, that individual and the community would suffer as a result of such high-handed disregard for Yahweh's covenant. The defeat at Ai and the subsequent destruction of Achan and his family bear vivid testimony of this (Josh. 7:1–26).

From the earliest chapters in Genesis through the New Testament, God's desire for a personal relationship with each individual, not just the covenant community, is clear. Samuel's encounter with God in 1 Samuel 3:1–21 indicates that the differences between being raised in the church and being born again are quite distinct in the Old Testament period as well as today.[21] Samuel "was ministering before the Lord," growing up "in the presence of the Lord" [and] "in stature and in favor with the Lord and with men." However, "Samuel did not yet know the Lord: The word of the Lord had not yet been revealed to him" (1 Sam. 2:18,21,26; 3:7).

The Hebrew word for "know" is *yada'.* This word often means to know by experience as opposed to knowing facts about history. Making known Yahweh by personal experience was the Holy Spirit's work in the lives of the Old Testament saints as well as in the lives of the New Testament saints. As Hebrews 11 makes clear, everyone who has ever been saved has been saved by faith, whether looking forward to promises yet unseen or backward to Jesus' resurrection.[22]

An important distinction must be noted. In the New Testament Church, God makes it clear that outward circumcision was no longer needed as a sign of inclusion in the Church. The account of Cornelius and Peter in Acts 10 illustrates the workings of Joel's prophecy and the work of the Holy Spirit. Cornelius and Peter both had a vision. The arrival of the messengers from Cornelius validated Peter's vision for him. However, this was not adequate validation for the Jerusalem

---

[21]I am not trying to be anachronistic. There is a clear parallel between what is referred to as "know the Lord" in the Old Testament and being "born again" in the New Testament.

[22]See chap. 10 for a discussion of salvation in the Old Testament.

Church. Cornelius' family was recognized as "devout and God-fearing" (Acts 10:2). Yet Peter is compelled to say, " 'You are well aware that it is against our law for a Jew to associate with a Gentile or visit him' " (Acts 10:28). Although this was a misinterpretation of the Law, it was a part of the popular doctrine of the predominantly Jewish Church by which Peter's vision was to be tested.

God acted in history by pouring out the Holy Spirit on the family of Cornelius. Before Peter could ask Cornelius, "Do you believe this gospel?" the Holy Spirit answered the question with an outpouring of himself. Many in the Church would have denied the family baptism in water until Cornelius and all the males were circumcised, but not the Holy Spirit.

The circumcised believers who came with Peter to test his vision were astonished at the outpouring of the Holy Spirit on this Gentile family. However, they had enough sense to accept the Holy Spirit's work as the only proper sign of inclusion in the Church. This work of the Holy Spirit includes the indwelling of the Holy Spirit at salvation and the subsequent baptism in the Holy Spirit.[23]

Joel's prophecy strikes at another conception prevalent in ancient Israel. The dynamic behavior associated with the true prophets of Yahweh was one of the signs of the prophetic office. This is sometimes referred to as ecstasy, but is totally unlike the ecstatic behavior of heathen prophets who worked themselves up into a frenzy that was beyond reason and self-control.[24] True prophets were empowered by the Holy Spirit and rose to a dynamic peak of joy in God's presence, or perhaps of deep concern for the lost. These deep emotional experiences at times led to laughter, singing, weeping, lying on the floor, dancing in the Spirit.[25]

In the Old Testament, this dynamic behavior is seen as a result of the Spirit of God resting upon a person (Num. 11:26) or coming upon a person with power (1 Sam. 10:6,11; 19:23–24). This type of behavior, while expected from a prophet, caused concern and became the stuff of sayings when exhibited by someone other than a prophet. Joshua implored

---

[23]Pearlman, *Knowing the Doctrines,* 306–7; Duffield, *Foundations,* 276–84; "The Holy Spirit bears witness to the believer's sonship"(277).

[24]Hobart E. Freeman, *An Introduction to Old Testament Prophets* (Chicago: Moody Press, 1969), 58–66.

[25]Early Pentecostals did not earn the nickname "Holy Rollers" as a compliment for their staid and formal worship services. But where there is "fire," there is always the danger of "wildfire."

Moses to stop Eldad and Medad from prophesying in the camp. Moses replied, " 'I wish that all the LORD's people were prophets and that the LORD would put his Spirit on them' " (Num. 11:28–29).

Saul had two ecstatic experiences. The first took place at Gibeah. When Saul met the band of prophets Samuel had said he would meet, Saul began to prophesy with them. This experience in the Spirit was accompanied by a change of heart. Saul became a different person. The astonished onlookers asked, "Is Saul also among the prophets?" (1 Sam. 10:6–12). Now Saul *knew* God. His second encounter at Naioth was of a different sort. It resulted from his resisting the Spirit so that he stripped off his royal robes and lay on the floor all day and all night before Samuel, reinforcing the saying "Is Saul also among the prophets?" (19:23–24).

This type of behavior by the prophets and their bands of followers was not a marathon foretelling of coming events. Much of the dynamic prophesying often accompanied by music seems to have been praise of Yahweh.

Unfortunately, this type of behavior had a dark side. Prophets from the surrounding religious culture of the ancient Near East exhibited ecstatic behavior. They also went so far as to participate in self-mutilation in frenzied attempts to produce a religious trance or to gain the attention of their gods. An example of this behavior by the prophets of Baal is found in 1 Kings 18:28–29. The same Hebrew word, *nava'* (prophesy), used for the activity of the prophets of Baal (v. 29) is used for prophets of Yahweh.[26] Naturally this caused great confusion for the Israelites.[27] Was self-mutilation an appropriate behavior for prophets of Yahweh?

If two prophets of Yahweh had different messages, which one should be believed? Upon whom was the Spirit of God resting? One must remember that the 400 prophets opposing Micaiah before Ahab and Jehoshaphat claimed to be prophets of Yahweh, not Baal (1 Kings 22)! Ecstatic behavior could not guarantee that a prophet had the "word of the Lord." The

---

[26]Note, however, the contrast with the dignity and simplicity of Elijah's prayer that brought down the fire from heaven (1 Kings 18:36–38). True prophets never imitated the ecstasy of the false prophets or the prophets of Baal.

[27]Second Kings 9:11–12 reflects the ambivalent attitude of the people to prophets. Jehu's officer asked, " 'Is everything all right? Why did this madman come to you?' " Jehu replies, " 'You know the man and the sort of things he says.' " But Jehu's men were quick enough to blow the trumpet and proclaim Jehu king when they heard what the "madman" had said.

prophet might have no more than the word of his own delusions or the word the audience wanted to hear. As a result, in Zechariah 13:2–6 we find a repudiation of such false prophets, of their attempts to identify themselves as prophets by distinctive dress, and of their ecstatic behavior, including self-mutilation.

In Joel's prophecy, then, we see an expansion of the activity of the Holy Spirit, not a change in the quality. From Eden to today, God has desired fellowship with humanity. The idea that the Holy Spirit was inactive in the laity of the Old Testament is unfounded. The Holy Spirit's activity in their lives parallels His involvement in the lives of those whom He has brought to salvation in the Church. The Spirit changes people's hearts and makes them different people. Another parallel exists between the Spirit's coming upon an individual, resulting in empowerment for an office or ministry, and the infilling of the Holy Spirit in the Church. Roger Stronstad has shown that one purpose of being "filled with the Holy Spirit" is to equip believers to fulfill the prophetic ministry of declaring God's will and purposes for the Church and the world.[28] This may involve unusual behavior. Even if it does not, being filled with the Spirit is a peak emotional, physical, and religious experience for a specific purpose. However, one cannot live continuously at that peak day after day. The Holy Spirit's indwelling at salvation is meant to keep one on an even keel day by day, moment by moment, particularly after experiences of the Holy Spirit's coming upon one "with power."

IN THE PENTECOSTAL MOVEMENT

The continuity of the Holy Spirit's work throughout the history of God's people was the focus of the previous section. Although the quantity of activity has increased as the Church has grown, the same Holy Spirit is at work in the world today as was at work in the world prior to the Day of Pentecost. However, by reason of progressive revelation and progressive understanding, our comprehension of the Spirit's work ought to be clearer. We have the entire canon of the Bible and two thousand years of history to draw upon. For this reason, the Church today has a distinct advantage over even the New Testament Church.

---

[28]Roger Stronstad, " 'Filled with the Holy Spirit' Terminology in Luke-Acts," in *The Holy Spirit in the Scriptures and the Church,* ed. Roger Stronstad and Laurence M. Van Kleek (Clayburn, B.C., Canada: Western Pentecostal Bible College, 1987), 1–13.

CHAPTER

11

The Holy
Spirit

During the early years of the Pentecostal movement, becoming Pentecostal generally resulted in being thrust out of one's original denomination into one of the Pentecostal fellowships. Even today some classical Pentecostals express consternation that a person could be baptized in the Holy Spirit, be identified as a charismatic Christian, yet remain in a traditional Protestant, Catholic, or Orthodox church. One does not earn the baptism in the Holy Spirit by membership in a certain denomination or by having a perfect theology. How else can we explain the baptism in the Holy Spirit enjoyed by both Unitarian and Trinitarian Pentecostals, let alone by those in the charismatic renewal? God takes us as we are, saves us, indwells us, and baptizes us. Then the Holy Spirit begins to transform us into the image of Christ.

Paul tells us that if we will confess with our mouth that Jesus is Lord, and truly believe that God raised Him from the dead, we will be saved. For when we believe in our heart, we are justified. When we confess that God raised Jesus from the dead, we are saved (Rom. 10:9–10). Paul goes on to assure us that no one can say, " 'Jesus is Lord,' except by the Holy Spirit" (1 Cor. 12:3). Paul is not saying that it is impossible for hypocrites or false teachers to mouth the words "Jesus is Lord." But to say Jesus is truly Lord (which means that we are committed to follow Him and to do His will instead of following our own plans and desires) requires the indwelling of the Holy Spirit, the new heart and new spirit called for in Ezekiel 18:31. Our very being confesses that Jesus is Lord as the Holy Spirit begins to transform us into the image of God. The inward transformation is a sign to the individual that he or she is a member of the body of Christ. The outward manifestation of the transformation, though it varies from person to person, is a sign to the Church.

A problem related to the activity of the Holy Spirit as a sign of inclusion in the body of Christ has been developing for a number of the third- and now fourth-generation young people of the traditional Pentecostal movement. In Pentecostal churches, positions of leadership are available only to those who can testify that they have been baptized in the Holy Spirit with the initial physical evidence of speaking in tongues. This is in line with the Bible (Acts 6:3,5) and is an important emphasis of the Pentecostal movement.[29] However, it has a

---

[29]Please see chapter 13 for a full discussion of the issues involved. It is sufficient to observe that where the baptism of the Holy Spirit becomes seen as nice but not necessary, there the baptism in the Holy Spirit ceases to exist.

serious side affect for some who know themselves to be saved. They experience the ongoing transforming power of the Holy Spirit in their lives, yet they feel like second-class citizens. For them, the baptism in the Holy Spirit becomes a social necessity to be achieved, instead of a desire for the deeper spiritual relationship that is inaugurated with the baptism in the Holy Spirit.[30]

This makes it all the more important to stress that the Holy Spirit's activity in believers, whether at salvation or at Baptism, is a sign to the individual, rather than to the congregation. Many people are saved in private prayer at times when they are alone. The same is true of those who are baptized in the Spirit in a private place of prayer. Even if we are saved and baptized in a public meeting, how many individuals in attendance at the meeting will remember what happened to us after a few weeks, or months, or years? If we move to where no one knows us, the believers there did not witness what happened to us. They must rely on our words and our lives to verify the Holy Spirit's activity in our lives.

AS COMFORTER

As noted in the discussion on the titles of the Holy Spirit, they provide us with keys to understanding His person and work. The Holy Spirit's work as Comforter includes His role as the Spirit of Truth indwelling us (John 14:16; 15:26), as a Teacher of all things, as One who reminds us of all Christ has said (14:26), as One who will bear witness of Christ (15:26), and as One who will convict the world of sin, righteousness, and judgment (16:8).[31] The importance of these tasks cannot be underestimated. The Holy Spirit in us begins to clear up the untidy, incomplete, erroneous beliefs concerning God, His work, His purposes, His Word, and the world, which we bring into our relationship with God. As Paul stated, it is a

---

[30]While I cannot agree with the doctrine that one is not saved until one has been baptized in the Holy Spirit with the initial physical evidence of speaking in tongues, this doctrine certainly removes an individual's ambiguity in respect to her or his place in the body of Christ.

[31]The word *paraklētos* is rendered "Comforter" in the KJV and "Counselor" in the NIV and RSV. In these verses, the meaning is one who helps or intercedes, rather than one who offers legal counsel or advocacy. See Walter Bauer, *A Greek-English Lexicon of the New Testament and Other Early Christian Literature,* 2d ed., trans. William F. Arndt and Wilbur Gingrich, rev. and augmented by F. Wilbur Gingrich and Frederick W. Danker (Chicago: University of Chicago Press, 1979), 623–24.

lifelong work that will never be completed on this side of
the veil (1 Cor. 13:12). Clearly, the Holy Spirit is more than
One who comforts us in our sorrow; He is also the One who
leads us into victory over sin and sorrow.[32] The Holy Spirit
indwells us to complete the transformation begun at salvation.
Jesus came to save us *from* our sins, not *in* them. He came
to save us from more than hell in the afterlife; He came to
save us from hell on earth in this life, the one we create by
our sins. Jesus works to accomplish this through the agency
of the Holy Spirit.

AS TEACHER

The Holy Spirit can and will help every believer to properly
interpret and understand the Word of God and His continuing
work in this world. He will lead us into all truth. However,
this promise requires work on our part as well. We must read
carefully and prayerfully. God never intended the Bible to be
a difficult book for His people to understand. But unless we
are willing to cooperate with the Holy Spirit by learning and
applying sound interpretive rules, our understanding of the
Bible, our infallible rule of faith and conduct, will be loaded
with error.[33] The Holy Spirit will lead us into all truth as we
carefully read and study the Bible under His guidance.

One of the truths the Holy Spirit teaches us is that one
cannot recite a magic formula of "I bind Satan; I bind my
mind; I bind my flesh. Now, Holy Spirit, I believe the thoughts
and words that follow are all from You." We cannot use
magical incantations to coerce God. John admonishes the
Church to "test the spirits to see whether they are from God"
(1 John 4:1). This means we are to allow the Spirit of Truth
to guide us in the task of interpreting God's Word and to test
all of our thoughts and those of others by the Scriptures.
There is real danger here. One author claims on the cover
of his book, "This book was written in the Spirit."[34] Another

---

[32]Duffield, *Foundations,* 285–86.

[33]Exod. 23:19; 34:26; and Deut. 14:21 admonish Israel, "You shall not
boil a kid in its mother's milk" (RSV). While teaching a Bible study to a
youth group at a church we were visiting in Southern California, I mentioned this law to help explain traditions related to Kosher foods. The eyes
of a fourteen-year-old boy turned into large saucers as he stammered in
surprise and horror, "You mean those mothers boiled their babies in their
own breast milk!" The only "kids" this young urbanite knew were human
children such as himself. He did not know a kid was a young goat.

[34]Heribert Mühlen, *A Charismatic Theology,* trans. by Edward Quinn
and Thomas Linton (New York: Paulist Press, 1978), back cover.

claims of his book, "100 Per Cent Correct Predictions of Things to Come."[35] The task of the reader with the help of the Holy Spirit is to follow the example of the Bereans who are commended by the Holy Spirit through Luke because they "examined the Scriptures every day to see if what Paul said was true" (Acts 17:11). Each believer is to read and test and understand God's Word and teachings about God's Word. The believer can do this with confidence, knowing that the Holy Spirit who indwells each of us will lead us into all truth.

There is yet another aspect of the work of the Holy Spirit as teacher. That work was preparing Jesus, the incarnate Son of God, for His task as King, Priest, and sacrificial Lamb. The Holy Spirit came upon Mary and overshadowed her, engendering Jesus, the Son of God. The Holy Spirit taught Jesus as a child, so that at age twelve he was able to amaze the teachers in the temple. "He was filled with wisdom, and the grace of God was upon him" (Luke 2:40). After His baptism in the Jordan, Jesus, described as full of the Holy Spirit, wrestled with the adversary for forty days (Luke 4:1–13). Jesus continued to walk full of the Holy Spirit. As a result, when the devil sought an "opportune time" to tempt Jesus further, the results were the same. Jesus "has been tempted in every way, just as we are—yet was without sin" (Heb. 4:15; see also 2:10–18). If we are full of the Holy Spirit when we wrestle with our flesh and the Adversary, through the Spirit we also can be victorious over temptation. Christ came to save us from our sins, not in them.

The Holy Spirit was active in the ministry of Jesus and the disciples. The Holy Spirit was at work in the preaching and miracles of the twelve disciples and then in that of the seventy-two that Jesus sent forth to preach the kingdom of God.[36]

---

[35]Finis Jennings Dake, *Revelation Expounded* (Atlanta: Bible Research Foundation, 1948), 10. This was written in 1926 when Dake was twenty-four years old. It was first published in 1931 and again in 1948. Dake promised the work would provide "100 Per Cent Correct Predictions of Things to Come. This book answers hundreds of questions on prophecy and brings out scores of new truths never before taught in the prophetical world—truths that we predict will completely revolutionize modern prophetical teaching. This book guarantees to prove from plain English Scriptures the following truths: . . . ."

[36]I have trouble agreeing with J. Rodman Williams' suggestion (172) that the Twelve and the Seventy were not "anointed" by the Holy Spirit as they preached, taught, healed, and cast out demons. Surely the anointing of these disciples would be no less than that of the prophets of the Old Testament when they proclaimed God's word and through the Spirit wrought miracles.

Another aspect of this task is the Spirit's help in remembering all that Jesus has said. One can remember only those things one has known and perhaps forgotten through disuse. This help from the Holy Spirit requires believers to study and memorize the Word, with the assurance that the Spirit will remind them of everything Jesus has said when they need it.[37] Those who delight in the Word of God and meditate upon it will find they are like trees planted by a stream (Ps. 1:2–3). In Luke 24:6–8, the disciples are asked why they are looking for the living among the dead? The words of the messengers were undoubtedly used by the Spirit to bring them to remembrance of Jesus' words. In John 2:19, Jesus said, " 'Destroy this temple, and I will raise it up again in three days.' " No one understood what Jesus meant until "after he was raised from the dead, his disciples recalled what he had said. Then they believed the Scripture and the words that Jesus had spoken" (2:22). John 12:16 is a similar example of this work of the Holy Spirit.

The Holy Spirit is also the teacher of the unbeliever. In this task, the Spirit (in the words of Jesus) convicts the world "of guilt in regard to sin and righteousness and judgment: in regard to sin, because men do not believe in me; in regard to righteousness, because I am going to the Father, where you can see me no longer; and in regard to judgment, because the prince of this world now stands condemned" (John 16:8–11). This ties into the work of the Holy Spirit in drawing every person to salvation. In John 14:6 Jesus stated that " 'no one comes to the Father except through me.' " John 6:44 states, " 'No one can come unto me unless the Father who sent me draws him.' " It is the Holy Spirit who draws every human being to God, although many refuse that drawing. He never relents from His ceaseless call, "But why will you die? Repent and live!"[38]

BEARING WITNESS TO CHRIST

The activity of the Holy Spirit as one who bears witness to Christ begins in the Old Testament and continues to this day. The Holy Spirit inspired the prophets of the Old Testament as they wrote the prophecies of the coming Messiah. This does not mean that the original human author or his imme-

---

[37]I begin every test for my students with the following short, but sincere prayer: "Lord, help these students to remember all that they have studied."

[38]See Ezek. 18:30–32 and the discussion above.

diate or extended audience always recognized or understood the full import of what was being written or read. Isaiah 11:1–2 is a good example of an easily recognizable messianic prophecy:

"A shoot will come up from the stump of Jesse; from his roots a Branch will bear fruit. The Spirit of the LORD will rest on him—the Spirit of wisdom and of understanding, the Spirit of Counsel and of power, the Spirit of knowledge and of the fear of the LORD."

Other passages such as Isaiah 53 and Psalm 110:1 require more help from the Holy Spirit and to some extent post-Resurrection hindsight. Clearly neither the disciples nor the Pharisees had recognized or were looking for a suffering Messiah.

Luke informs us that the Holy Spirit bore witness to the soon-coming Christ through John the Baptist, his parents, Mary, and through Simeon and Anna in Jerusalem (see Luke 1 through 3). In John 16:13–15, Jesus states that the work of the Holy Spirit is not to speak on His own, but only what the Father and Son direct Him to say.

AS A PROMISE

It is difficult to suggest that any one title or purpose of the Holy Spirit is more important than another. Everything the Spirit does is vital to the kingdom of God. Yet, there is a core purpose, a core function, of the Holy Spirit, without which everything that has been said of the Spirit up to this point is only so much wind: The Holy Spirit is the deposit guaranteeing our future inheritance in Christ.

"You also were included in Christ when you heard the word of truth, the gospel of your salvation. Having believed, you were marked in him with a seal, the promised Holy Spirit, who is a deposit guaranteeing our inheritance until the redemption of those who are God's possession—to the praise of his glory" (Eph. 1:13–14).

What is it that the working of the Holy Spirit in our lives and the life of the Church guarantees?

"Now we know that if the earthly tent we live in is destroyed, we have a building from God, an eternal house in heaven, not built by human hands. Meanwhile we groan, longing to be clothed with our heavenly dwelling, because when we are clothed, we will not be found naked. For while we are in this tent, we groan and are burdened, because we do not wish to be unclothed but to be clothed with our heavenly dwelling, so that what is mortal may be swallowed up by life. Now it is God who has made us for this very purpose and has given us the Spirit as a deposit, guaranteeing what is to come" (2 Cor. 5:1–5; see also 2 Cor. 1:22; Eph. 4:30).

Through the Holy Spirit we come to know God by experience, as in the Hebrew word *yada'*, "to know by experience." Our experience of the Holy Spirit is proof to us of the resurrection of Christ. As Paul stated in 1 Corinthians 15, if Christ has not been raised from the dead, there never will be a resurrection, and all our beliefs in God and salvation are lies. As we noted concerning Samuel, there is a difference between knowing about a person or God, and knowing a person or God by actually meeting and experiencing their presence.

An intellectual knowledge of the contents of the Bible is not *knowing God.* Many theologians and commentators on the Bible—some of whom I know personally, others only by their writings—know more about religion, the history of the Church, the contents of the Bible, and theology than many who call themselves Christians. Yet they have never yielded to or acknowledged the Holy Spirit's call on their lives. They have no experience of God in their life. They believe that if they have not experienced God, then no one has ever experienced God. Therefore, they deny the existence of God and denounce Christians for interpreting their subjective experiences as the activity of God in their lives. They declare there is no evidence of divine activity in the universe. Everything is natural cause and effect. Yet, all this is based on their exegesis of their subjective lack of divine activity.

Now we can begin to appreciate the importance of the work of the Holy Spirit as a sign of inclusion in the body of Christ for the believer, even more so than for the Church. The Holy Spirit not only verifies the Resurrection, but also, by extension, the veracity of the Scriptures. Without the earnest ("first installment") of the Holy Spirit to teach us, to lead us in truth, and to bear witness to Christ, there would be no Church today at all, because there would be no gospel to preach.

STUDY QUESTIONS

1. Why is it important for every Christian to know the elements of popular religion and the role popular religion plays in the daily life of the Christian?

2. What is the difference in the activity of the Holy Spirit

promised in Joel 2:28–29 and that promised in Acts 2:17–18?

3. What features of the promise of the Spirit would make it seem radical to the original audiences of this prophecy?

4. What are some of the differences and similarities between circumcision and the baptism in the Holy Spirit as signs of inclusion in the people of God?

5. Would you agree or disagree that the baptism in the Holy Spirit and the indwelling of the Holy Spirit is, most important, a sign for the individual, rather than for the Church? Why?

6. Why is the function of the work of the Holy Spirit as a guarantee of the resurrection so important? What are some of the results of this function of the Holy Spirit?

7. The role of the Holy Spirit as teacher of all things requires certain actions and attitudes on the part of the student. Name some of these requirements and discuss their importance to the proper understanding of the Bible and its doctrines.

8. Discuss the importance of the use of the Bible in testing claims about theology, prophecy, and the operation of the gifts of the Spirit. Will the Spirit ever give us directions that are contrary to clear teachings of the Scripture?

CHAPTER TWELVE

The Holy Spirit and Sanctification

Timothy P. Jenney

This chapter focuses on the Holy Spirit and sanctification, even though all three members of the Trinity are involved. The plan is God's. His desire is nothing less than the sanctification of the entire world and all its people. Jesus Christ died to make that plan possible, but His work on the Cross is finished (John 19:30; cf. Heb. 10:10–14). The active agent in sanctification today is the Spirit of God. His leading role in this process is indicated by His most common title, the *Holy* Spirit, and the cleansing symbols by which He is represented in Scripture: water and fire.[1]

The title "Holy Spirit" appears ninety-four times in the New Testament (including the single appearance of "Spirit of holiness" at Rom. 1:4). Alternate titles for the Spirit all appear far less often.[2] While some might argue that "Holy Spirit" is a simple shortening of the "Spirit of the Holy [One]," the title cannot be explained away so casually. God the Father has many unique attributes, any one of them—eternality, omnipotence, omniscience—could have served to identify the Spirit as well as holiness. The writers of the New Testament used the phrase "Holy Spirit" so often because they recognized the Spirit's significance for the sanctification of the world.

The symbols these writers used of the Spirit are also illuminating. The cleansing rituals of the Old Testament (about

---

[1]Wind is not merely a symbol of the Spirit of God. The tie is actually closer, for both the Hebrew and Greek terms for "spirit" also mean "wind" or "breath." The common link between the three possible translations is the idea of something invisible, but animate. This is certainly true of the Holy Spirit.

[2]See chap. 11, pp. 380–81.

which we will say more later) use blood, water, and fire. The first of them point to the ministry of Jesus; the second and (to some degree) the third, to the ministry of the Holy Spirit. The Spirit of God is often symbolized by water (Isa. 44:3–4; Ezek. 36:25–27; Joel 2:23; cf. 2:28; John 7:38–39; cf. 19:34) or spoken of in terms usually reserved for fluids: "pour out" (Zech. 12:10; Acts 2:17–18; 10:45), "filled" (Luke 1:15; Acts 2:4; Eph. 5:18), "anointed" (Isa. 61:1–2; cf. Luke 4:18), even "baptize" and "baptism" (John 1:33; Acts 1:5; 1 Cor. 12:13). Less often the Spirit is symbolized by fire (Acts 2:3; Rev. 4:5) or found in close association with it (Matt. 3:11; Luke 3:16). They were powerful symbols to Jewish audiences familiar with the baptisms and other purification rituals of first-century Judaism. Our misunderstandings about sanctification and the work of the Holy Spirit may be due, in part, to our lack of knowledge about those purification rituals.

Generally, when people today speak of the Spirit's work with regard to sanctification, they mean a spiritual process (or experience) through which one passes that makes one more holy. Some identify this experience with salvation, others identify it as a subsequent experience, still others identify it as a process that includes both previous experiences and more. But the sanctifying work of the Spirit is more comprehensive yet. It is an integral part of God's entire plan for humanity, His "salvation history."[3] As such, it includes His work with the converted and the unconverted.

Still, many are most concerned about how sanctification applies to them as individuals. That concern is appropriate. After all, God's plan for the world is achieved one person at a time. The practical questions about the sanctification of a person may be put quite simply:

What is sanctification?

Does it happen all at once or is it a process?

How does it relate to salvation?

What does it mean to be holy (or "sanctified")?

Who is responsible for making us holy and what can be done if we fall short of true holiness?

Does the believer ever reach a stage where it becomes impossible to sin, sometimes called Christian perfection?

Before we answer these questions, it will be helpful to

___

[3]Ger. *heilsgeschichte,* a concept developed by German theologians to distinguish the type of history found in the Bible from what they considered the "objective" study of history.

define terms, explain the limits of our study, and review the doctrine of sanctification throughout Church history.

DEFINITION OF SANCTIFICATION

It should be obvious from the preceding paragraphs that sanctification is presented here in its broadest sense. Sanctification is the process by which God is cleansing our world and its people. His ultimate goal is that everything—animate and inanimate—will be cleansed from any taint of sin or uncleanness. To this end He has provided the means of salvation through Jesus Christ. At the end of time He also intends to consign to the fire everything that cannot or will not be cleansed (Rev. 20:11 through 21:1; see also 2 Pet. 3:10–13), thus cleansing the earth of everything that is sinful.

The task of the Holy Spirit at this present stage in the history of salvation is fourfold: (1) to convict the world, (2) to cleanse the believer through the blood of Christ at the new birth, (3) to make real in the believer's life the legal pronouncement of righteousness that God has made, and (4) to empower the believer to assist in the sanctification process of others by (a) the proclamation of the gospel to the unbeliever and (b) the building up of the believer.

Typically, theologians use the term "sanctification" only to speak of the third one of these four tasks of the Holy Spirit. In this narrower sense, A. H. Strong defines sanctification as "that continuous operation of the Holy Spirit, by which the holy disposition imparted in regeneration is maintained and strengthened."[4] Charles Hodge agrees with the Westminster Catechism, which defines sanctification as "the work of God's free grace, whereby we are renewed in the whole man after the image of God, and are enabled more and more to die unto sin and live unto righteousness."[5] We have no quarrel with either of these explanations, but find Millard Erickson's definition of the term the clearest statement of our understanding of this part of the process. He says: "It is a continuation of what was begun in regeneration, when a newness of life was conferred upon and instilled within the believer.

---

[4]Augustus H. Strong, *Systematic Theology* (Old Tappan, N.J.: Fleming H. Revell, 1907; reprint: 1974), 869.

[5]Charles Hodge, *Systematic Theology,* vol. 3 (New York: Scribner, Armstrong, and Co., 1872), 213.

In particular, sanctification is the Holy Spirit's applying to the life of the believer the work done by Jesus Christ."[6]

SANCTIFICATION IN CHURCH HISTORY

Our purpose is not to make a comprehensive historical study of the theology of sanctification. Such a study would review all of the positions the Church has ever taken on the issue as well as the circumstances leading to those positions. Our intention is to explain what the Bible says about the sanctifying work of the Holy Spirit. This will help those who want to increasingly live more pleasing to God.

The Church has had theological strengths and weaknesses in every age, including our own. They can often be understood better by a look at the historical ebb and flow of various doctrines in the past. Due to limitations of space we cannot include a comprehensive study of the historical theology of sanctification. Our study can, however, serve as a guide to the development of the doctrine.[7] Whatever else one may learn from such a study, it is of some comfort to know that others in the Church have struggled with the practical implications of this doctrine.

The earliest followers of Jesus expected and preached His return at any moment (Acts 2; 7). So they placed a great deal of emphasis on salvation and evangelism (Matt. 28:18–20; Acts 1:7–8). As the years unfolded and the coming of Christ was delayed, the writings of the New Testament indicate that certain problems developed in the Church (1 Thess. 4:13–18; 1 Pet. 3:3–18). For example, some believers did not live holy lives, but used their freedom from the Jewish legal code as an excuse for licentious behavior (e.g., the churches at Corinth, Galatia, Colossae and those in Rev. 2 through 3). Others (the Judaizers) argued that the solution to the problem was for both Gentile and Jewish Christians to obey the Mosaic Law (Acts 15), a suggestion that threatened to diminish the importance of the sacrifice of Jesus (Heb. 6:4–6). Though the defeat of this suggestion was a milestone in keeping Christianity accessible to people of all races, it did not

---

[6]Millard J. Erickson, *Christian Theology,* (Grand Rapids: Baker Book House, 1985), 968.

[7]For a more detailed historical study of this doctrine, see Wilber T. Dayton, "Entire Sanctification: The Divine Purification and Perfection of Man," in *A Contemporary Wesleyan Theology,* ed. Charles W. Carter, vol. 1 (Grand Rapids: Zondervan Publishing House, 1983), 521–69, especially the extensive bibliography, 567–69.

solve the very real problem of how to maintain a holy life in a fallen world.

The post-New Testament Church rapidly retreated from the biblical doctrine of a sanctification of pure grace, one given and maintained solely by the power of God. Instead, it sought a compromise between the Pharisaic and legalistic interpretation of the Mosaic Law (Matt. 23) and the unlimited forgiveness taught by Jesus (Matt. 6:9–15; cf. 18:21–35) and expounded by Paul (Rom. 3:21–24). In short, despite all of Paul's letters and missionary efforts, many failed to learn the lessons of sanctification.

The way in which the Church compromised is illuminating. According to Louis Berkhof,[8] the early church fathers wrote little about the doctrine of sanctification. Ignatius of Antioch did teach that "having Jesus within you" brought moral renewal.[9]

The Early Church did, however, teach that salvation was dependent upon a combination of faith and good works. Specifically, they said that Christian baptism cleansed one from previous sins, but moral failure after Christian baptism required some form of counterbalancing of penance or good works.[10]

Augustine, whose writings shaped the Catholic Church to a great degree, thought of sanctification as a "deposit of God in man." Berkhof summarizes Augustine's doctrine, saying, "Since he believed in the total corruption of human nature by the fall, he thought of sanctification as a new supernatural impartation of divine life . . . operating exclusively within the confines of the Church and through the sacraments."[11]

Augustine's emphasis on the role of the sacraments in the process of sanctification had an important influence on the Church. Even more important though was his insistence that these sacraments were exclusively the property of the Church. At the height of the Middle Ages, Thomas Aquinas expanded

---

[8]Louis Berkhof, *Systematic Theology,* 4th ed. (Grand Rapids: Wm. B. Eerdmans, 1949), 529.

[9]Ignatius, *Magnesians,* 12.1.

[10]Robert R. Williams, *A Guide to the Teachings of the Early Church Fathers* (Grand Rapids: Wm. B. Eerdmans, 1960), 142.

[11]Berkhof, *Systematic Theology,* 529. In the *Enchiridion,* chap. 65, Augustine refused forgiveness to those outside the Church because the Church "alone has received the pledge of the Holy Spirit without whom is no forgiveness of sins." Cited in Geoffrey W. Bromiley, *Historical Theology* (Grand Rapids: Wm. B. Eerdmans, 1978), 114.

this doctrine, teaching that the Church controlled a "treasury of merit" which it might apportion to a believer in need of it. After Christian baptism, a believer's venial sins[12] could be offset by the sacrament of communion, while the more severe "mortal sins" required some form of penance.[13]

The leaders of the Reformation were distressed by the corruption they saw in the Catholic Church. Consequently, they de-emphasized the role of both the institutional church and the sacraments in sanctification. They argued that sanctification was the work of the Spirit "primarily through the Word and [only] secondarily through the sacraments." They also said that "justification provides the motive force in sanctification."[14]

Pietists and Methodists, in despair over the lack of spiritual vitality in their own ranks, removed the process even further from the control of the Church. They argued that the Holy Spirit achieved this work by means of the believer's love, devotion, and obedience to Christ along with a desire for practical holiness and a striving for perfection.[15] They emphasized an individual and personal spiritual *relationship*, rather than participation in an activity sponsored by the institutional church: the sacraments (Catholicism) or the preaching of the Word (Lutheranism).

John Wesley himself was even more extreme, teaching that those without spiritual vitality had been saved, but not sanctified. He believed that justification and sanctification were two separate works of grace. Salvation was the first; sanctification the second. He often called the latter work Christian perfection, saying that it precluded any *voluntary* transgression of the laws of God (he was willing to admit that involuntary transgressions might still occur). This perfection he defined as loving God and your neighbor, having the mind that was in Christ Jesus, having the undivided fruit of the Spirit united together in the soul of the believer, and having the moral image of God renewed in righteousness and true holiness. "This," he said, "is perfection." The solution to the spiritual problems of the Church in his day was this second work of grace, sanctification. Sanctification would provide a

---

[12]See chap. 8, p. 281.

[13]Berkhof, *Systematic Theology,* 529–30.

[14]Ibid., 530; Bromiley, *Historical Theology,* 238.

[15]R. Newton Flew, *The Idea of Perfection in Christian Theology: An Historical Study of the Christian Ideal for the Present Life* (New York: Humanities Press, 1968), 276.

greater personal spirituality and increased power for work in the harvest fields of the world.[16]

The Holiness movement of the mid-1800s to early 1900s, faced with the lackluster spirituality of their own (often what became "former") denominations, adopted many of the features of early Methodism. These features included the distinction between a first and a second work of grace and the emphasis on personal spirituality. In many instances, this second work of grace was identified as the baptism of the Holy Spirit. As in the teachings of John Wesley, this experience provided both increased spirituality (or "holiness") and more power for service.[17]

Other church leaders of the time agreed with the Holiness groups that the church was in need of renewal, but disagreed with their solution. One of them was Charles Finney, who took a more modest approach. He agreed with the Wesleyan teaching of a second (instantaneous) work of grace, but taught that it was not a work of sanctification; it was an enduement with power.[18]

Reuben A. Torrey was another important church leader in this area. Encouraged by evangelist Dwight L. Moody, he offered a different slant on this doctrine. He taught that sanctification was a process, but that power for service came from the baptism in the Spirit. In other words, he rejected the Holiness identification of the baptism of the Spirit as a "second work of grace" that provided holiness. He retained the term "baptism of the Spirit," agreed that it was subsequent to salvation, and taught it was solely a divine gift of spiritual power.[19]

---

[16]John Wesley, *Sermons on Several Occasions* (London: Epworth Press: 1977), 473–76. C. W. Conn, "Christian Perfection," in *Dictionary of Pentecostal and Charismatic Movements,* ed. Stanley M. Burgess, Gary B. McGee, and Patrick Alexander (Grand Rapids: Zondervan Publishing House, 1988), 169–80.

[17]Ibid., 170; Edith L. Blumhofer, *The Assemblies of God: A Chapter in the Story of American Pentecostalism,* vol. 1–To 1941 (Springfield, Mo.: Gospel Publishing House, 1989), 42. This terminology to describe the sanctification experience came from Wesley's friend, John Fletcher. However, because of the rise of the Pentecostal movement most Holiness groups now prefer the "altar terminology" of Phoebe Palmer, who said Christ is the Christian's altar and whoever touched the altar would be holy (Exod. 29:37); she connected sanctification with the "living sacrifice" of Rom. 12:1. See Melvin E. Dieter, "The Wesleyan Perspective" in Dieter, et al. *Five Views on Sanctification* (Grand Rapids: Zondervan Publishing House, 1987), 39. Blumhofer, *Assemblies of God,* vol. 1, 41–50.

[18]Ibid., 58.

[19]Ibid., 50–57.

The increasing emphasis on the work of the Holy Spirit in the late nineteenth century paved the way for the renewal of Pentecostalism in the early twentieth century. However, some early Pentecostals argued that baptism in the Holy Spirit was a *third* work of grace: (1) salvation, by which a person was cleansed from the sins of the unregenerate life; (2) sanctification, which provided victory over sin in this life in the Wesleyan sense; and (3) baptism of the Holy Spirit, which empowered the believer for service to God and people.[20] These latter two seemed to relegate the rest of the Church to a lower spiritual status, encouraging a Pentecostal spiritual elitism. Non-Pentecostals soon came to characterize all Pentecostals as elitist, even those that had not taken such extreme positions. Unfortunately, the doctrine of sanctification seems to have been lost in the heat of the battle.

At present a renewed emphasis on the doctrine of sanctification is sorely needed in Pentecostal circles. First, few Pentecostals would argue that they themselves are in need of spiritual renewal today. Despite the large numbers of believers baptized in the Holy Spirit, many Pentecostal churches lack the vitality and effectiveness evident in earlier years. Second, the Pentecostal emphasis on Spirit baptism and supernatural gifts of the Spirit have resulted in an underemphasis on the rest of the work of the Spirit, including that of sanctification. Third, wider acceptance of Pentecostals and charismatics appears to have threatened the traditional distinction between the Church and the world, calling many old holiness standards into question. Finally, modern Pentecostals relish their newfound popularity and are anxious to avoid any appearance of spiritual elitism, lest that popularity be lost.

SANCTIFICATION IN THE OLD TESTAMENT

TERMINOLOGY

Qadash and Its Cognates. The Hebrew *qadash,* often translated "be holy," carries the basic idea of separation or withdrawal from ordinary use in order to be dedicated to God and His service. It is found in the Bible both as a verb ("to be set apart," "consecrated") and as an adjective (Heb. *qa-*

---

[20]Stanley M. Horton, "The Pentecostal Perspective," in Melvin Dieter et al. *Five Views on Sanctification* (Grand Rapids: Academie Books,1987), 107.

dosh, "sacred," "holy," "dedicated" [thing, place, person, etc.]), whether that quality applies to God himself or places, things, persons, or times sanctified or set apart by (or to) God.[21] The New Testament typically uses the Greek *hagiazō* and its cognates (e.g., Gk. *hagios*) to communicate the same idea.

CHAPTER
12

The Holy
Spirit and
Sanctification

Perhaps the best way to define holiness is in terms of God's character. The Bible clearly teaches that God's fundamental characteristic is holiness. He says it of himself, " 'Be holy, because I am holy' " (Lev. 11:44; see also 1 Pet. 1:15–16); people proclaim it, " 'He is a holy God' " (Josh. 24:19); the seraphs worshiping God affirm it, " 'Holy, holy, holy is the LORD Almighty' " (Isa. 6:3; cf. Rev. 4:8); even Jesus, God's Son, calls him *"Holy Father"* (John 17:11).

The prophet Amos said, "The Sovereign LORD has sworn by his holiness" (4:2), later adding, He "has sworn by himself" (6:8), indicating that holiness is central to His innermost essence [cf. 6:8], which is different from anything He has created as well as being separated from all sin and evil. "God's holiness becomes an expression for his perfection of being, which transcends everything creaturely."[22]

Perhaps the best contemporary word to communicate this idea is "alienness," that is, if one can ignore its often negative connotation. Holiness, in its basic sense, is something neither human nor earthly; it is of another realm entirely. That is to say, a *holy* God is a God who is separate and distinct from his creation (the opposite of the teaching of pantheism).

We understand this quality of holiness to be the essential character of deity that He can impart. It is the manner in which God imparts this quality that is of most interest to us, particularly as it relates to individuals. The problem is that humankind, since the Fall, is living in a fallen world and is not holy. Yet God desires to have fellowship with us. Since He cannot become less holy in order to fellowship with us, we must become more holy.

God communicates this idea in the Old Testament in a variety of ways. First, He tells His people, " 'Be holy, because I am holy' " (Lev. 11:44). Then, He consecrates a variety of things to facilitate His fellowship with His people, His "holy

---

[21]Francis Brown, S. R. Driver, and Charles A. Briggs, eds. *The New Brown-Driver-Briggs-Gesenius Hebrew and English Lexicon* (Peabody, Mass.: Hendrickson Publishers, 1979), 872.

[22]O. Procksch and K. G. Kuhn, *"hagios",* in Gerhard Kittel, ed., *Theological Dictionary of the New Testament,* trans. G. W. Bromiley, vol. 1 (Grand Rapids: Wm. B. Eerdmans, 1964), 88–114.

nation" (Exod. 19:6): a holy priesthood to officiate (Exod. 29:1; 1 Sam. 7:1), with holy garments (Exod. 28:2–4; 29:29), a holy tabernacle (or temple) in which to dwell among His people (Exod. 29:31; Lev. 16:24; Pss. 46:4; 65:4), certain "holy days" on which they were to cease from everyday tasks and worship God (Exod. 16:23; Lev. 23:32; Jer. 17:21–27), even holy water for cleansing impure individuals (Num. 5:17).

Taher and Its Cognates. The Hebrew *taher* is not as common as *qadash* in the Old Testament, but it is at least as important for understanding sanctification. Its root meaning is "to be clean, pure." The cleanness may refer to ceremonial cleanness, moral purity, or even the relative purity of a metal.[23] In terms of its use, there does not seem to be any great distinction made between cleansing from physical impurity (contamination by contact with unclean substances) and cleansing from spiritual impurity (moral corruption). The former is much more common; the latter seems to be a logical extension of it.

Altogether the nouns of this group appear only nineteen times, but the adjective appears ninety times. In Genesis it is used only of "clean" animals (Gen. 7:2,8; 8:20) and in Exodus only of pure materials, most often of pure gold (Exod. 25:11–39; 30:3; 39:15; etc.). Leviticus tends to use it in terms of ceremonial cleanness (Lev. 4:12; 13:13,17,40–41), as does Numbers (Num. 5:28; 18:11,13; 19:9,18–19).

The shift from concrete to abstract use is instructive, for it illustrates the transition. The Lord's words are said to be pure (Ps. 12:6), His eyes "too pure to look on evil" (Hab. 1:13), that is, with approval. An individual's fear of the Lord is "pure" (Ps. 19:9). The Psalmist cries, "Create in me a pure heart, O God" (51:10; cf. Prov. 22:11). Ezekiel says God will "cleanse" His people from idolatry (Ezek. 36:25).

The verb is found eighty-nine times in various forms in the Old Testament, thirty-eight of which appear in a single book: Leviticus, which gives detailed instructions for the various rituals of cleansing.

THE CLEANSING RITUALS

The Old Testament teaches that something may be separated from God by either sin or uncleanness. One can obtain forgiveness from the sin by offering the appropriate sacrifice; cleansing from uncleanness requires that one go through the

---

[23] *BDB,* 372.

appropriate purification ritual. These rituals are important since they are visual presentations of spiritual truths.

There are a number of purification rituals described in the books of Leviticus and Numbers. They can be divided into two categories: (1) rituals for things that can be cleansed and (2) rituals for things that cannot be cleansed. All the rituals in the first category involve water. The simplest form of the rituals in this first category is that a person who had contracted uncleanness was to wash his clothes, and he would be unclean until evening (Lev. 11:38,40; 12:6; etc.). At that time, he would be considered clean and free to come and go as he pleased. A slightly greater amount of uncleanness, like coming into contact with another person's body fluids, could be cleansed by simply adding the requirement of bathing to the basic ritual (Lev. 15:1–32; Num. 19:11–13).

Greater amounts of uncleanness required more complicated ceremonies and powerful ingredients. Persons healed of a skin disease were sprinkled seven times with water mingled with blood. They were then to wash their clothes, shave off all body hair, bathe, and remain unclean for seven days (Lev. 14:1–9; cf. Num. 19:1–10,17–22). On the eighth day they would bring a sacrifice, and the priest would take some of the blood and oil from the sacrifice and anoint them with it. Then they would be clean (Lev. 14:10–32). Similar requirements were used for houses with simple mildew (14:48–53).

Under the right conditions, even water could be made unclean (Lev. 11:33–35). Later rabbis would go to great lengths to specify the amount of water and type of sprinkling or even baptism that each kind of uncleanness required for cleansing. Leviticus 11:36 does contain one more important detail: Water from a spring or underground cistern was always considered clean. The water of a spring, for instance, was literally "living water" (see NASB, margin): It moved and was therefore always being renewed from a hidden source. In effect, it could not become unclean.

Therein lies the significance of the phrase "living water." Grammatically, it simply means "water that moves or flows," but theologically it means "water that can never be made unclean." This is why so many of the purification rituals required "fresh," or "running" (KJV), water (Lev. 14:5–6,50–52; 15:13). This also explains why God describes himself to sinful Jerusalem as "a spring of living water" (Jer. 2:13; 17:13) and why commentators can say that the fountain and rivers in Zechariah are for cleansing (Zech. 13:1; 14:8).[24] Even more important, it explains why Jesus describes himself as the source of "living water" (John 4:10–11; 7:38); He provides unlimited cleansing from every kind of sin and uncleanness.

Other terms from these purification rituals make their way into the New Testament, forming part of the theology of sanctification. They include "sprinkling" (Heb. 9:13–28; 10:22; 11:28; 12:24; 1 Pet. 1:2), "washing" (Matt. 15:2; John 13:5–14; Acts 22:16; 1 Cor. 6:11; Rev. 1:5), and "baptism" (Rom. 6:4; Eph. 4:5; Col. 2:12; Heb. 6:2; 1 Pet. 3:21), as well as the more general terms for holiness and cleanness (which are covered in more detail below).

The second category of purification rituals is for things that could not be made clean. It included a variety of materials: clothing or leather with any kind of destructive mildew (Lev. 13:47–59) or a house from which mildew could not be cleansed (Lev. 14:33–53). Generally, such things were destroyed (Lev. 11:33,35; 14:40–41,45), often by fire (Lev. 13:52,55,57). God destroyed Sodom and Gomorrah by fire (Gen. 19:24; see also Luke 17:29–30), just as He did idolatrous Jerusalem later (Jer. 4:4; 17:27). Everything but the articles of metal from Jericho was to be burned (Josh. 6:17,24). When Achan stole such articles, he and his family and all their possessions were burned (7:12,25); so was the city of Hazor (11:11,13).

Since rituals are visual presentations of spiritual truths, what truths does God intend for us to learn from these rituals of purification? They certainly teach us that He is holy and requires holiness of His people. They also teach us something else: God desires that everything should be made holy. He provided a means of cleansing for every kind of material that could be cleansed, even if the procedure was expensive or extensive. That is, "washings" (e.g., Num. 11:19,21), or "baptisms" (e.g., Lev. 11:32, where "put it in water" is the Hebrew *taval,* "dip," "immerse"), removed the sin, but "saved" the material. Those materials that could not be cleansed, He destroyed (usually) by fire. This kept the camp and the people of God clean or holy.

This truth has a powerful spiritual application for those of us under the new covenant. God, through the sanctifying power of His Spirit, is still willing to cleanse people who will let go of their sin. He will remove the sin and save those

---

[24]See David Baron, *The Vision and Prophecies of Zechariah* (Grand Rapids: Kregel Publications, 1972 from 2d. ed. 1919), 459, 506.

people. Those who will not relinquish their sin, like the most contaminated materials in the Old Testament, must be destroyed along with their sin in exactly the same way: by fire.

THE PROPHETIC PROMISE

The Hebrew prophets looked forward to a time when God would cleanse all humankind and the world in which they lived. God revealed to them that He would accomplish this great work of cleansing by His Spirit: " 'Not by might nor by power, but by my Spirit,' says the LORD" (Zech. 4:6). Consequently, the prophets often used vocabulary borrowed from the purification rituals of the temple to describe this divine work. In Ezekiel, for example, God says to Israel, " 'I will sprinkle clean (Heb. *t^ehorim*) water on you, and you will be clean (Heb. *t^ehartem*); I will cleanse (Heb. *'ataher*) you from all your impurities and from all your idols. I will give you a new heart and put a new spirit in you; I will remove from you your heart of stone and give you a heart of flesh. And I will put my Spirit in you and move you to follow my decrees and be careful to keep my laws. ... I will save you from all your uncleanness' " (Ezek. 36:25–27,29).

God further promises that He will restore both Israel and Judah to the land and make them clean (Ezek. 37:21–23). The towns would be rebuilt and the land become "like the garden of Eden" (36:33–35).

This cleansing of the Spirit (as well as other aspects of His work) would be available to everyone in the future, male and female, Jew and Gentile, young and old (Joel 2:28–32). Sometimes the vision is one of a cleansing rain (Joel 2:23), at other times it is of a mighty river that would flow from the temple throughout the land, bringing cleansing and giving life (Ezek. 47:1–12).

Zechariah prophesied that this river of "living water" would split into four parts and water the land (Zech. 14:4,8), like the garden of Eden (Ezek. 36:35; cf. Gen. 2:10). On that day, the Lord will rule from Jerusalem and every nation will go up to worship Him there (Zech. 14:16). Jerusalem itself will be so holy that "HOLY TO THE LORD will be inscribed on the bells of the horses, and the cooking pots in the LORD's house will be like the sacred bowls in front of the altar. Every pot in Jerusalem and Judah will be holy to the LORD" (Zech. 14:20–21; cf. Jer. 31:40).

The passages from Ezekiel and Zechariah were read an-

nually at the Jewish Feast of Tabernacles.[25] Jesus attended
that feast at least once and "on the last and greatest day of
the Feast, Jesus stood and said in a loud voice, 'If anyone is
thirsty, let him come to me and drink. Whoever believes in
me, as the Scripture has said, streams of living water will flow
from within him' " (John 7:37–38).

"From within him" (Gk. *ek tēs koilias autou*) is literally
"out of his (or its) belly." This does not mean from the believer's belly, nor can it refer directly to the belly of the
Messiah, since neither concept is found in the Scripture of
the Old Testament. It refers to Jerusalem, where Jesus would
be crucified and where the Holy Spirit would be poured out
on the Day of Pentecost.[26]

The Jews understood Jerusalem (as the "navel of the
earth"[27]) and Jesus' words to refer to two of the liturgical
passages of the feast: Zechariah 14 and Ezekiel 36. They were
correct, but only in part. Jesus wanted them to know that
this mighty river of living water for cleansing, envisioned by
the prophets, was actually the Spirit of God. We know this
because John goes on to say "By this he meant the Spirit,
whom those who believed in him were later to receive" (John
7:39; cf. 4:13–14; 19:34). This is not Spirit baptism, or at least
Spirit baptism alone, but a reference to the mighty work of
sanctification that the Spirit would do among God's people
in the latter days.

SANCTIFICATION IN THE NEW TESTAMENT

TERMINOLOGY

The two critical Greek terms for the study of sanctification
in the New Testament are *hagiazō* (and its cognates) and
katharizō (and its cognates). *Hagiazō* is roughly equivalent
to the Hebrew *qadash* and almost always translates it in the

––––––––––––

[25]J. H. Hertz, ed. *The Pentateuch and Haftorahs,* 2d ed. (London: Soncino
Press, 1978), 973; also Jacob Neusner, trans., *The Talmud of Babylonia:
An American Translation, Tractate Sukkah,* Brown Judaic Studies, vol. 74
(Chico, Calif.: Scholars Press, 1984), 3:3–10.

[26]This view was held by Charles C. Torrey, *The Four Gospels* (New York:
Harper Brothers, 1933), 201. See also R. H. Lightfoot, *St. John's Gospel*
(Oxford: Clarendon Press, 1956), 183–84. However, many recent authors
do point to Jesus as the source.

[27]Joachim Jeremias, *Jerusalem in the Time of Jesus,* trans. by F. H. and
C. H. Cave (London: SCM Press, 1969), 51–52. See also Josephus, *Wars of
the Jews,* 3:3:5 where Jerusalem is called the navel of the country.

Septuagint. It means "to make holy, set apart, purify, dedicate, or consecrate," as well as "to treat as holy." The Greek *katharizō* almost always translates the Hebrew *taher* in the Septuagint. It means "to make clean or purify" and is used in both the ceremonial sense and the moral sense.

Though the Torah usually uses the two Hebrew terms rather precisely, the difference between them blurs when they are used in a figurative sense. This happens especially in the prophets and in the Psalms. The New Testament usually keeps the distinction between the Greek terms when speaking of the rituals of the old covenant or of the Pharisees, but also uses either term when speaking of Christ's work in the new covenant. Since our interest is in spiritual cleansing and the new covenant, we can fairly say that the New Testament uses *hagiazō* and *katharizō* interchangeably.

The most common word is *hagios* (derived from *hagiazō*). In the singular it is translated "holy" and often used as an adjective describing God, His Spirit, Jerusalem, etc. In the plural it is often used of the people of God. Then it is usually translated "holy ones" or "saints." This is a very common term in the New Testament (it appears sixty times) and solid evidence of the early Christians' understanding of their own distinctive quality: They had been made holy by God.

TWO THEOLOGIES OF SANCTIFICATION

The term "saints" is so familiar to us that we probably take it for granted. The Christians in New Testament times did not. They were well aware of the extensive Laws concerning kosher food, unclean substances, and purification rituals of the Mosaic Law. Many of the different sects of Judaism had elaborate rules and regulations about uncleanness. In general, the rule was that holiness could be maintained by avoiding uncleanness and isolating themselves from those who were unclean. If one contracted uncleanness, the solution was to remove it by baptisms of one kind or another (Heb. 6:2; 9:10). This is a fairly passive notion of holiness: it consists of avoiding uncleanness.

In addition, the Pharisees also had an interesting inconsistency in their own theology. Many of them understood that the kingdom of God was a spiritual one, one within, rather than an external (material), political one. Even so, they maintained that entrance into this inner kingdom was by *external* rituals that removed sin and uncleanness and brought holiness.

Yet God's holiness is active. Since He desires fellowship with people, God's active holiness consists of making the unclean clean and the unholy holy. Jesus' death made this kind of holiness possible. His followers gained access into the spiritual kingdom of God by a spiritual process, not an external one. Whether they were surrounded by unclean people or unclean things, they could still be holy. Consequently, "holy ones" or "saints" becomes their characteristic designation.

THE FULFILLMENT OF PROPHECY

Ultimately, the sanctification of the world takes place at an individual level. Each person must chose whether to accept God's rule and reign or reject it. Those people who have chosen not to give up their sin must be cleansed by fire. This process does not require their cooperation, but it is painful, destructive, and long-lasting. This is the eternal punishment the Bible calls "hell," "the lake of fire," and the "second death" (Isa. 66:24; Matt. 23:33; 25:30,41,46; Rev. 20:14–15). Although they will never be cleansed, the eternal fire guarantees that God's creation will never again be troubled by their uncleanness. In short, God has determined that He will sanctify the world. He will do it by water or fire (Matt. 3:11–12).

Christians choose to be sanctified by the Spirit, a process that requires each individual's continuing cooperation (1 John 3:3; Rev. 22:11)—much like the cleansing ceremonies using water that the Old Testament describes. This sanctification process removes the sin, but saves the individual. We have chosen to describe this process in four distinct stages below.

Convicting the World. The first stage of sanctification and the greatest work of the Holy Spirit is bringing people into a covenant relationship with God. The Spirit has three tasks among those who are unconverted: conviction of sin, testimony about Christ, and confirmation of the Word of God. They are His greatest tasks because they occur among the largest group of people—virtually everyone on earth who is not a Christian.

Salvation can begin only when an individual has been convicted of personal sin. By "conviction," we mean that a person is convinced of having done wrong, of standing truly guilty before God. The Holy Spirit is the one who brings conviction. This conviction of sin is the first stage in the sanctification of the individual and the *only* one that does not require one's consent. Jesus spoke of this ministry of the Spirit when He said: " 'When he comes, he will convict the world of guilt in regard to sin and righteousness and judgment: in regard to sin, because men do not believe in me; in regard to righteousness, because I am going to the Father, where you can see me no longer; and in regard to judgment, because the prince of this world now stands condemned' " (John 16:8–11).

Notice that Jesus says that the Spirit will convict "the world." In other words, the Holy Spirit has a ministry among the *unconverted.* It is one of conviction. He convicts them of three things: (1) that their sins, especially the sin of unbelief in God's Son, has made them guilty before God, (2) that righteousness is possible and desirable, and (3) that those who do not listen to the Spirit's prompting will face divine judgment.

The Spirit's attempt to bring conviction can be resisted (Acts 7:51), and often is, sometimes including an outright rejection that is reprobate (1 Tim. 4:2). This is also the reason blasphemy of the Spirit (Matt. 12:31–32; Mark 3:29) is potentially so serious: If the Spirit withdraws, there is no possibility of repentance or forgiveness because there is no conviction, no sense of guilt.[28]

The Spirit also testifies about Christ. Speaking of the world, Jesus said:

"If I had not done among them what no one else did, they would not be guilty of sin. But now they have seen these miracles, and yet they have hated both me and my Father. But this is to fulfill what is written in their Law: 'They hated me without reason.' When the Counselor comes, whom I will send to you from the Father, the Spirit of truth who goes out from the Father, he will testify about me. And you also must testify, for you have been with me from the beginning" (John 15:24–27).

Few people are willing to speak against Jesus, whether they are Christian or not. Why? We believe it is because of the Holy Spirit: He testifies about Christ, convicting men and women of the truth.

---

[28]Very often young Christians will feel tremendous remorse because they believe they have blasphemed the Spirit and cannot be forgiven. Remorse, in and of itself, is the best evidence that a person has not rejected the Spirit, since only the Spirit brings conviction. The truly reprobate person feels no remorse. In other words, those who desire forgiveness can always find it in God. See chap. 8, pp. 283, 288.

Christians can witness to the unconverted by sharing the truth of the gospel (John 15:27; cf. 3:3–4,16–21). God even promises the Spirit will guide us in what to say (Matt. 10:19; Acts 2; 7; etc.). Nevertheless, a faith response requires the action of the Holy Spirit (John 15:26; cf. 3:5–8).

In addition to internal conviction and testimony about Christ, the Spirit also confirms the Word of God. He does this by giving the supernatural signs and wonders that accompany its proclamation. Paul speaks of his own experience in this matter to the church at Corinth: "When I came to you, brothers, I did not come with eloquence or superior wisdom as I proclaimed to you the testimony about God. For I resolved to know nothing while I was with you except Jesus Christ and him crucified. I came to you in weakness and fear, and with much trembling. My message and my preaching were not with wise and persuasive words, but with a demonstration of the Spirit's power, so that your faith might not rest on men's wisdom, but on God's power" (1 Cor. 2:1–5; cf. 12:7–11).

Later, Paul wrote even more plainly of the way the Spirit enhanced his presentation of the gospel: "I will not venture to speak of anything except what Christ has accomplished through me in leading the Gentiles to obey God by what I have said and done—by the power of signs and miracles, through the power of the Spirit. So from Jerusalem all the way around to Illyricum, I have fully proclaimed the gospel of Christ" (Rom. 15:18–19).

This "power" Paul speaks of is the same kind of supernatural signs and wonders that accompanied the ministry of Jesus (Acts 2:22). In the same way, the Spirit continues to work powerfully through the believer today to confirm the preaching of the Word (Acts 4:8–12; 5:12; Rom. 12:4–8; 1 Cor. 12:27–28).

In summary, this means that the sinner's whole experience with the Spirit of God is negative! The unconverted experience conviction for sin, heightened by the fact that righteousness is now possible through Christ, increased still more because of the certainty of coming judgment. When the Spirit testifies about Christ, He reveals One who lived a righteous life. When the Word of God is preached, the Spirit confirms it with powerful signs and wonders. It is no wonder that the sinner hates to hear the Word of God preached. It brings feelings of guilt, inadequacy, anxiety, and conviction. Why? Because the Holy Spirit's work with the unconverted is directed toward a single goal: to bring that person to repentance!

Cleansing the Believer. The work of the Spirit does not cease when a person admits guilt before God; it increases, just as it does at each subsequent stage. The second stage in the Spirit's sanctification of an individual is conversion. Conversion is an instantaneous experience. It includes sanctification by the Spirit or, to put it in a more biblically correct fashion, the process of sanctification by the Spirit includes conversion.

We can easily demonstrate this from Scripture. Consider Paul's words, "We ought always to thank God for you, brothers loved by the Lord, because from the beginning God chose you to be saved through the sanctifying work of the Spirit and through belief in the truth" (2 Thess. 2:13). Notice that the word "saved" in this passage is qualified by two prepositional phrases, which describe how the believers of Thessalonica were saved. The second phrase, "through belief in the truth," describes the believer's role in salvation: to have faith in the gospel of Jesus Christ (v. 14). The first phrase, "through the sanctifying work of the Spirit," is more important for our purposes. It describes the Spirit's role in salvation: to sanctify the believer. The emphasis in this verse is not that God chose some people and not others (classic predestination[29]), but that God chose *the means* by which everyone would be saved: an individual's faith in the promises of God plus the cleansing power of the Spirit of God (see also Acts 10:15; 11:9; Rom. 15:16; 1 Pet. 1:1–2).

Another important example appears in Paul's first letter to the Corinthians. He chides the believers in Corinth for their immorality (5:1–8). After listing various kinds of sinful persons (6:9–10), he says, "And that is what some of you were. But you were washed, you were sanctified, you were justified in the name of the Lord Jesus Christ and by the Spirit of our God" (6:11). Paul says this work was accomplished by the Spirit (cf. 2 Thes. 2:13). The form of the Greek verbs "washed," "sanctified," and "justified" in this passage (aorist passive) gives no sense of any sort of process here. They all refer to the same instantaneous, completed experience: conversion.

There is simply no way that the Greek of these verses can be construed to mean that this sanctifying work of the Spirit is something distinct from salvation. It is not a second definite

---

[29]See chap. 10, pp. 355–61.

work of grace, as some would have it. Both passages describe the Spirit's sanctification as the means by which people are saved. The second passage, 1 Corinthians 6:11, represents this sanctification in a punctiliar way, occurring at the same time as washing and justifying.

The only way we can reconcile these passages with others that speak of sanctification as a process (see below) is to recognize that sanctification is not merely something that occurs after conversion but is identical to growing in the Lord. Sanctification includes all God's work in attempting to save men and women from the judgment to come.

At the moment of conversion we are born again, this time of the Spirit (John 3:5–8). Simultaneously, the Spirit baptizes us into the body of Jesus Christ, the Church (1 Cor. 12:13; Eph. 2:22).[30] Instantaneously, we are washed, sanctified, and justified, all through the power of the Spirit (1 Cor. 6:11; 2 Thess. 2:13; 1 Pet. 1:1–2). At that moment the Spirit of God begins to witness to our Spirit that we are now God's children (Rom. 8:15–16). The Spirit of Life sets us free from the law of sin and death (8:2; cf. John 6:63). We are new creations in God (2 Cor. 5:17).

The fundamental difference between a Christian and a non-Christian is not one of life-style, attitude, or even belief system. It is that the Christian has allowed God to sanctify him, the non-Christian has not. This difference is one of the reasons the New Testament often refers to believers as "saints" or "holy" ones (Matt. 27:52; Acts 9:13; Rom. 1:7; 1 Cor. 1:2; Eph. 1:1; Rev. 5:8; etc.), even if it goes on to describe their sins or shortcomings (as does Paul in 1 Cor.). So a Christian is not someone who is perfect, but someone who has repented of sin and submitted to the cleansing power of the Spirit of God.

Realizing Righteousness in the Believer. The Spirit of God does not abandon the believer after conversion (John 14:16). Just as in the transition from conviction to conversion, His role becomes greater after conversion. The believer's increased submission brings about a greater cooperation and intimacy with the Spirit, resulting in His ability to do an ever greater work in the individual after conversion. There are three additional ways the Spirit works with the believer: (a) He continually sanctifies the believer from sin, (b) He increas-

---

[30]This is often referred to as the "positional" aspect of sanctification—being "in Christ" the believer is instantaneously sanctified. See Horton, "Pentecostal Perspective," 116. This is augmented necessarily by the progressive aspect of sanctification noted below in points (a), (b), and (c).

ingly delivers the believer from sin in fact, and (c) He uses believers to assist in the work of sanctification.

No believer can ever truly say he is free from sin (1 John 1:8–9). We are guilty of sins of omission in that not one of us worships enough, loves enough, or serves God enough, totally apart from whatever sin we might commit from time to time. This is the reason the blood of Jesus *continually* purifies us from all sin (1:7 [the present tense of the Greek verb in this passage tells us this is a repeated, or ongoing, action]).

Jesus' role in sanctification is done (Heb. 10:12–13; cf. John 19:30). This continual application of the sacrifice of Jesus to our lives, about which 1 John speaks, is the work of the Spirit. This is the sense in which Jesus spoke of the Spirit as "streams of living water" (John 7:38–39), one sufficient to cleanse all our sinfulness. So, moment by moment, the Spirit cleanses the believer, who is thereby always holy before God.

As a result, believers enjoy many benefits. They are free from condemnation and guilt (Rom. 8:1–2). They have continual access to the Father (Eph. 2:18). They can worship now in the Spirit and truth (John 4:23–24). Finally, they have a deposit (the Spirit) of their future inheritance in the Lord (Eph. 1:14, cf. 5:5).

In addition to the Spirit's moment by moment cleansing, He also works to help us avoid sinning. Therefore we can speak of "a life process whereby His [God's] holiness is made actual in our lives."[31]

Paul uses many analogies in Romans 8 to speak of this work of the Spirit. Having the "mind of the Spirit" means living "in accordance with the Spirit" (Rom. 8:5) or being "controlled by the Spirit" (vv. 6–9). He used a common Pharisaic expression when he spoke of walking in the Spirit (Gk. *peripatousin,* "walk;" NIV, "live"). The body of laws which told the Pharisee how to apply the Mosaic law to everyday life were called the *halakah.* The word is derived from the Hebrew *halakh,* which means "to go" or "to walk."

The point is this: The Pharisee had a body of unwritten laws (the oral Torah, "instruction," or "tradition of the elders") which prescribed his conduct in every situation. This kept him from contracting uncleanness. The believer has the Holy Spirit, who does exactly the same thing. He gives guidance about how to act in order to avoid sin in every situation

CHAPTER

12

The Holy Spirit and Sanctification

---

[31]Horton, "Pentecostal Perspective," 114.

(Rom. 8:6–9). For the same reason, the Spirit opens the Word of God to believers (1 Cor. 2:9–16), often reminding them of what Jesus has said in the Word (John 14:26). This is how the Spirit helps in making the righteousness of the believer real, rather than just legal. This is an ongoing process and will last as long as the believer is on earth (1 Thess. 5:23).

Finally, the Spirit uses believers to assist in the work of sanctification. This goes far beyond requiring our continued cooperation in the process of our own sanctification (2 Cor. 6:16 through 7:1; Rev. 22:11): things like resisting the temptation of sin. It means assisting in the sanctification of others.

In this day when divorce abounds, it is of some comfort to know that believing husbands and wives, if they are willing to stay with their unbelieving spouse, can have a powerful ministry of assisting the Holy Spirit in bringing sanctification to that spouse and any children that live in the household (1 Cor. 7:14).

We will speak more of helping in the sanctification of the world in the next section, though much of it applies here equally well. Here we wish to focus on the way in which the believer is to assist the Spirit in the sanctification of other believers. The Spirit gives the believer "fellowship" with the rest of the saints (Phil. 2:1). Within this fellowship, God challenges us to confront one another with regard to sin (Matt. 18), to encourage one another (Heb. 10:24), to love one another (Rom. 13:8), to care for one another (1 Cor. 12:25), etc. All of these actions assist the Spirit as He works to shape us into the image of Christ, to sanctify us in reality.

God told the Israelites, "Sanctify yourselves." The New Testament picked up the theme, amplifying on it in a way that makes it especially relevant to today's sensual world: "It is God's will that you should be sanctified: that you should avoid sexual immorality; that each of you should learn to control his own body in a way that is holy and honorable, not in passionate lust like the heathen, who do not know God. . . . The Lord will punish men for such sins. . . . For God did not call us to be impure, but to live a holy life. Therefore, he who rejects this instruction does not reject man but God, who gives you his Holy Spirit" (1 Thess. 4:3–8).

Empowering the Believer. The baptism of the Holy Spirit opens up a new role for the believer in the sanctification of the world. Believers are better able to assist the Spirit in His work of sanctifying others once they are Spirit-baptized. Jesus commanded His disciples to wait for the baptism in the Spirit so that they would have power to witness (Acts 1:4–5,8).

That baptism came with a sign that signified the new covenant was available to everyone, everywhere; the sign was speaking in "other tongues" (2:4). Few people today recognize that "other tongues" was originally speaking of languages other than Hebrew or Aramaic. For virtually the first time, God spoke in other languages and called people who were not Jewish into a covenant relationship with Him.

This was a powerful sign that the universal sanctification, about which the prophets spoke, was now available to everyone. Peter, recognizing that the crowd included many different kinds of people, male and female, young and old, cited Joel 2:28–32 in support of the experience. God would shortly reveal to him that this included even the conversion of Gentiles (Acts 10 through 11). The Gentile mission would capture the imagination of the early Church. The gospel of Jesus Christ, in a matter of just a few short years, would spread across the known world.

Today's Spirit-baptized believer is called to that same task. Empowered by the Spirit, we can expect God to confirm His word with signs and wonders (Rom. 15:18–19). The Spirit continues speaking to believers to send forth specific people into special ministries (Acts 11:12; 13:2), sometimes even to special places (16:6–10). In this way, the Spirit-filled believer assists the Spirit in His task of sanctifying the world.

Spiritual gifts, available to those who are Spirit-baptized, can also aid in edifying the saints, another aspect of the Spirit's continuing work of sanctification. This may include a word of wisdom or knowledge, an exhortation, a prophecy, or tongues and interpretation (1 Cor. 12:7–10). Yet all such phenomena are "for the common good" (v. 7) and for the "strengthening of the church" (14:26).[32]

The Spirit also builds up the saints for effective ministry in another way: through His ministry of intercession. Paul says this: "In the same way, the Spirit helps us in our weakness. We do not know what we ought to pray for, but the Spirit himself intercedes for us with groans that words cannot express. And he who searches our hearts knows the mind of the Spirit, because the Spirit intercedes for the saints in accordance with God's will" (Rom. 8:26–27).

Notice that this kind of intercession is "for the saints" (v. 27) and specifically when "we do not know what we ought to pray" (v. 26). Some have argued that this relates to in-

---

[32]See chap. 14, pp. 465, 467, 471, 477.

tercession in tongues, though we can scarcely identify with any certainty the expression "groans that words cannot express" (v. 26) with "other tongues" (which are spoken), though praying in tongues may also include intercession.

We would like to encourage believers to be willing to allow the Spirit to use them in a ministry of intercession.[33] Perhaps interceding in tongues may have been behind the statements, made by early Pentecostals, about the relationship between Spirit baptism and cleansing. On the basis of Scripture, we cannot agree with those who want to identify Spirit baptism with a second, instantaneous work of grace called sanctification. Neither can we agree with those who want to make Spirit baptism a condition of salvation or a means by which some sort of special "status" in the kingdom of God is conveyed. Yet there are deep, very personal ways in which the Spirit is better able to work in those who have surrendered themselves to Him. We are convinced this even includes His work of sanctifying the believer in Christ.

The Holy Spirit will complete that work in us when Christ appears, but until then we have the responsibility of purifying ourselves (with the help of the Holy Spirit) (1 John 3:2–3).

Definitions and theologies of sanctification that relate to the believer only after salvation are inadequate. They do not fully represent the biblical view of sanctification, so they have difficulty making sense of the various ways in which the Bible speaks of it.

God's plan of sanctification includes the whole world—everything—animate and inanimate. What He could not achieve through the old covenant, the Holy Spirit is now achieving powerfully in the new covenant. What will not or cannot be cleansed this time will be destroyed by fire. We have the great privilege of being not only the objects of this sanctification process, but assistants in it, for the glory of God.

---

[33]We suggest that such a ministry of intercession by the Spirit may be even more profitable. During our years in the pastorate, we came across individuals who struggled with painful, sometimes bitter, memories. Some testified to a new freedom from these memories, or a feeling of cleanness, shortly after Spirit baptism. Their testimonies usually related to praying in the Spirit. The process often involved intercession, first in tongues, then with the interpretation. It lasted as long as a week or two. These believers were then able, for the first time, to surrender those experiences to the Lord. As a result, they experienced tremendous victory over them and great joy. After all, increasing intimacy with the Spirit and surrender to His prompting means He has greater cooperation in His work of sanctification, freeing us for more effective ministry.

STUDY QUESTIONS

CHAPTER

12

The Holy
Spirit and
Sanctification

1. What is the ultimate goal of God's plan of sanctification?

2. What is the fourfold task of the Holy Spirit in the process of sanctification?

3. Sanctification was an important doctrine to many early Pentecostals. Has it been largely ignored in recent years? If so, why?

4. What two words, grounded in the ritual of the Old Testament, are essential to a proper understanding of the biblical doctrine of sanctification?

5. How are the Old Testament rituals of cleansing that use water different from those that use fire?

6. What does the expression "living water" add to our understanding of sanctification?

7. Why does "saints" become the characteristic designation for Christians in the New Testament? How different was this from Pharisaism?

8. Is the cleansing work of the Holy Spirit more akin to the Old Testament cleansings by water or by fire? Why?

9. What role does the individual play in each of the four stages of the Spirit's work of sanctification?

10. In what way did (and does) the gift of tongues signify the beginning of God's fulfillment of the Old Testament prophecies of universal sanctification?

CHAPTER THIRTEEN

The Baptism in the Holy Spirit

John W. Wyckoff

Many systematic theology works do not include a chapter specifically on the subject of the baptism in the Holy Spirit. As a matter of fact, the entire area of the Person and the work of the Holy Spirit has been greatly neglected. William Barclay writes, "[T]he story of the Bible is the story of Spirit-filled men. And yet ... our thinking about the Spirit is vaguer and more undefined than our thinking about any other part of the Christian Faith." Carl F. H. Henry regretfully notes: "Theologians of the past ... left us no full delineation of the Holy Spirit's ministry."[1]

Fortunately for the whole Church, increased attention is finally being focused on the Holy Spirit.[2] Works like those by Frederick D. Bruner and James D. G. Dunn indicate a growing interest among non-Pentecostals in the subject. This increased interest is due largely to the persistence and growth of the Pentecostal movement. Church leaders now often speak of Pentecostalism as "a third force in Christendom," alongside Catholicism and Protestantism.[3]

---

[1]William Barclay, *The Promise of the Spirit* (Philadelphia: Westminster, 1960), 11. Carl F. H. Henry, *God, Revelation and Authority,* vol. 4 (Waco, Tex.: Word Books, 1979), 272.

[2]In the spring of 1984 I attended a graduate-level History of American Christianity course at Baylor University. In one class session the guest lecturer was the noted church historian Edwin Gaustad. During a discussion period a fellow classmate asked Gaustad a question. It went something like the following: When we get into the next century and church historians look back at our present century, what will they say was the most significant development in American Christianity during the twentieth century? Without hesitation, Gaustad's answer was the rise and growth of the Pentecostal movement.

[3]Frederick D. Bruner, *A Theology of the Holy Spirit: The Pentecostal*

Largely because of its worldwide visible presence, this "Third Force" is now also commanding the attention of theologians. That is, scholars are now recognizing that Pentecostalism is this third force in its presence because it is "a third force in its doctrine," specifically, the doctrine of the baptism in the Holy Spirit.[4] Dunn notes that Catholics emphasize the role of the Church and the sacraments, subordinating the Spirit to the Church. Protestants emphasize the role of preaching and faith, subordinating the Spirit to the Bible. Pentecostals react to both of these extremes— sacramentalism that can become mechanical and biblicist orthodoxy that can become spiritually dead—calling for a vital experience with God himself in the Holy Spirit.[5]

This chapter divides the subject of Holy Spirit baptism into five issues or subtopics: (1) the separability of baptism in the Holy Spirit from regeneration; (2) the evidences of the baptism in the Holy Spirit experience in the life of the believer; (3) the availability of the baptism in the Holy Spirit for believers today; (4) the purpose of the baptism in the Holy Spirit; and (5) reception of Spirit baptism. The focus of the material presented here is analytical and descriptive rather than either apologetic or polemic. =of or involving dispute.

SEPARABILITY AND EVIDENCES

Separability and evidences of the baptism in the Holy Spirit are discussed first because most positions on the other related issues are contingent upon both the idea of separability and the idea of evidential tongues. That is, positions on these two matters define and delineate the questions in other areas.

The question of the availability of the baptism in the Holy Spirit today is a case in point. On the one hand, many Bible scholars would answer that there is a Spirit baptism available to believers today, but they contend that it is simply a part of conversion-initiation.[6] On the other hand, when

---

Experience and the New Testament Witness (Grand Rapids: Wm. B. Eerdmans, 1970); and James D. G. Dunn, *Baptism in the Holy Spirit* (London: SCM Press, 1970). W. J. Hollenweger, *The Pentecostals* (Peabody, Mass.: Hendrickson Publishers, 1972), xix–xx. Henry P. Van Dusen, "The Third Force in Christendom," *Life* 44 (9 June 1958): 113–24; Gordon F. Atter, *The Third Force* (Peterborough, Ont.: The College Press, 1965), x–xi; and Dunn, *Baptism,* 2.

[4]See Bruner, *Theology,* 58–59.
[5]Dunn, *Baptism,* 224–25.
[6]This is the position of Dunn, *Baptism,* and Bruner, *Theology.*

Pentecostals say the Spirit is available, they are contending for an experience that is in some sense distinct from regeneration and also accompanied by the initial physical evidence of speaking in tongues.

Also, while separability and evidential tongues are quite closely related, they are distinct issues. Logically, there are four possible positions on separability and evidential tongues. One possible position is that the baptism in the Holy Spirit is a part of the conversion-initiation experience, with no special evidence such as speaking in tongues. This position is represented by Dunn and Bruner.[7] The second possible position is that the baptism in the Holy Spirit is a part of the conversion-initiation experience and it is always accompanied by the special evidence of speaking in tongues. This is the position of some Oneness Pentecostal groups.[8] The third possible position is that the baptism in the Holy Spirit usually follows regeneration, but the experience is not accompanied by speaking in tongues. This is the position of some Wesleyan Holiness groups such as the Church of the Nazarene.[9] The fourth possible position is that the baptism in the Holy Spirit usually follows regeneration and is always accompanied by the special evidence of speaking in tongues. This is the position of Pentecostals such as the Assemblies of God.[10]

THE TERMINOLOGY

The exact phrase "baptism in the Holy Spirit" is not found in the Bible. Nevertheless, it is biblical in that it originates from similar phraseology used by the biblical writers. All three of the Synoptic writers recount John the Baptist's comparison of his own activity of baptizing in water to that of Jesus' coming activity (Matt. 3:11; Mark 1:8; Luke 3:16). Speaking of Jesus, John says, "He will baptize you with [in] the Holy Spirit." Luke again picks up the terminology in Acts 1:5, where he writes of Jesus telling His followers that "in a few days" they would "be baptized with [in] the Holy Spirit." Luke uses

---

[7]Dunn, *Baptism,* 224–29; and Bruner, *Theology,* 163, 168–69, 280–82.

[8]T. M. Jackson, ed., *Bible Doctrines—Foundation of the Church* (Hazelwood, Mo.: Pentecostal Publishing House, 1984), 91. (An official publication of the United Pentecostal Church, International.)

[9]J. Kenneth Grider, *Entire Sanctification: The Distinctive Doctrine of Wesleyanism* (Kansas City, Mo.: Beacon Hill, 1980), 11, 24, 41, 141.

[10]See P. C. Nelson, *Bible Doctrines* (Springfield, Mo.: Gospel Publishing House, 1948, Revised Edition, 1971), 71, 85.

the terminology for the third time in Acts 11:16 where he recounts Peter's understanding of Cornelius' experience. When explaining Cornelius' reception of the Holy Spirit to the Jerusalem believers, Peter remembered the Lord's words: "You will be baptized with [in] the Holy Spirit." Apparently, Peter understood this terminology to be a description of Cornelius' experience when he spoke in tongues. Actually, the only difference between the phrase "baptism in the Holy Spirit" and the phrases in the above Scripture references is that the former uses the noun form, "baptism," rather than the verb forms.[11]

Another point to note is that this phrase "baptism in the Holy Spirit" is but one of several such biblical phrases that Pentecostals believe describe a unique event or experience of the Holy Spirit. Other terminology also derived from New Testament language, especially in the Book of Acts, includes "being filled with the Holy Spirit;" "receiving the Holy Spirit;" "the Holy Spirit being poured out;" "the Holy Spirit falling upon;" "the Holy Spirit coming on;" and variations of these phrases.[12]

Pentecostals generally hold that such phrases are synonymous terms for the same experience of the Holy Spirit. Howard M. Ervin notes that "in each instance, it is the Pentecostal experience that is described." Such variety of terminology is to be expected in light of the multifaceted nature and results of the experience. As Stanley Horton suggests: "Each term brings out some aspect of the Pentecostal experience, and no one term can bring out all the aspects of that experience."[13]

Consequently, the comparable nature of the phrases is both obvious and expected. Furthermore, the language is necessarily metaphorical, for these phrases speak of an experience in which the Spirit of the living God moves dynamically into the human situation. To use the words of J. Rodman Williams, "[W]hat these terms variously express—is the event/experi-

---

[11]J. Rodman Williams, *Renewal Theology,* vol. 2 (Grand Rapids: Zondervan Publishing House, 1988), 198, n. 68.

[12]Roger Stronstad, " 'Filled with the Spirit': Terminology in Luke-Acts" in *The Holy Spirit in the Scriptures and in the Church,* ed. Roger Stronstad and Laurence M. Van Kleek (Clayburn, B.C.: Western Pentecostal Bible College, 1987).

[13]Howard M. Ervin, *Spirit Baptism: A Biblical Investigation* (Peabody, Mass.: Hendrickson Publishers, 1987), 35. Stanley M. Horton, *The Book of Acts* (Springfield, Mo.: Gospel Publishing House, 1981), 32.

ence of the *dynamic presence* of God in the Holy Spirit." He correctly observes that such an experience is "far more than any words can contain."[14]

From among these comparable terms, Pentecostals seem to prefer "baptism in the Holy Spirit." Such a preference may be because the language is derived from Jesus' own statements, or it may be because of the profundity this particular metaphorical language carries. That is, the analogy intended here is baptism in water. As J. R. Williams notes, "[B]aptism in water means literally to be immersed in, plunged under, and even drenched or soaked with" water. In effect, to be *baptized* in the Holy Spirit is to be totally enveloped in and saturated with the dynamic Spirit of the living God.[15]

RELATIONSHIP TO REGENERATION

One of the major differences among theologians regarding this experience called baptism in the Holy Spirit has to do with its relationship to regeneration. As noted above, some argue that it is part of the conversion-initiation experience; others hold that it is an experience that is in some sense distinct from regeneration. This issue is stated as follows: Is there available to the believer today an experience commonly called the baptism in the Holy Spirit that is in some sense distinctive and unique in relationship to the conversion-initiation experience?

Usually, both those who deny and those who affirm that the baptism in the Holy Spirit is separable from regeneration recognize the importance of Scripture as the ultimate authority. On the one side, Bruner, who denies that the experiences are separable, sets out to consider "the New Testament Witness" and provide "exegesis of the major biblical sources" related to the subject. Dunn believes that a "complete re-examination of the N[ew] T[estament] teaching on the gift of the Spirit and its relation to belief and baptism" is necessary. He "hope[s] to show that for the writers of the N[ew] T[estament] the baptism in or gift of the Spirit was part of the event (or process) of becoming a Christian."[16]

On the other side, those who advocate a separable experience of the baptism in the Holy Spirit are similarly committed to showing that their position is taught in Scripture.

[14]J. R. Williams, *Renewal Theology*, vol. 2, 203.

[15]Ibid., vol. 2, 199–200.

[16]Bruner, *Theology*, 15, 153. Dunn, *Baptism*, 4.

Howard M. Ervin is representative of them. The full title of his work on the Spirit identifies it as "A Biblical Investigation." He notes that contemporary experience illustrates the Pentecostal perspective; nevertheless, for him, "only the biblical record adjudicates our conclusions." One other example will suffice: Stanley M. Horton, who writes *What the Bible Says About the Holy Spirit,* concludes that the baptism in the Holy Spirit is a subsequent experience.[17]

Much, though not all, of this discussion focuses on the Book of Acts.[18] Certainly, there are relevant passages in other areas of Scripture. However, scholars on both sides of the issue generally agree that the doctrine of separability depends largely on the Book of Acts. The Old Testament and the Gospels prophesy concerning it and look forward to it; the Epistles assume the experience and therefore only occasionally refer to it indirectly. Bruner is correct when he notes: "The major source of the Pentecostal doctrine of the subsequent baptism in the Holy Spirit is the Book of Acts." When the Assemblies of God Statement of Fundamental Truths says the experience of the baptism in the Holy Spirit "is distinct from and subsequent to the experience of the new birth," the Scripture references provided are found in the Book of Acts.[19]

Since the doctrine of separability is greatly dependent upon the Book of Acts, exegetical consideration of its relevant passages is crucial. Pentecostal scholars recognize this, as do also Bruner, Dunn, and others who deny the Pentecostal position.

The accounts usually considered to be especially relevant to the question of separability include the Day of Pentecost, Acts 2:1–13; the Samaritan revival, Acts 8:4–19; Paul's experience, Acts 9:1–19; Cornelius and other Gentiles, Acts 10:44–48 and 11:15–17; and the Ephesian believers, Acts 19:1–7. Conclusions from exegetical expositions of these passages come down on both sides of the issue. Those who believe that the baptism in the Holy Spirit is a distinctive

---

[17]Ervin, *Spirit-Baptism,* 3. See also Howard M. Ervin, *Conversion-Initiation and the Baptism in the Holy Spirit* (Peabody, Mass.: Hendrickson Publishers, 1984). Stanley M. Horton, *What the Bible Says About the Holy Spirit* (Springfield, Mo.: Gospel Publishing House, 1976), 159–61.

[18]This is true because the Epistles were written to people who had already received the baptism in the Holy Spirit.

[19]Bruner, *Baptism,* 61, 69. *Minutes of the 44th Session of the General Council of the Assemblies of God with Revised Constitution and Bylaws* (Springfield, Mo.: The General Council of the Assemblies of God, 1991), 129.

experience usually contend that in these cases the individuals were already believers who had experienced regeneration *before*—at least momentarily—their Holy Spirit baptism experience. Therefore, they say Luke shows that the baptism in the Holy Spirit is a distinct experience. Further, they hold that Luke intends to teach that a distinctive, separable baptism in the Holy Spirit experience is normative for Christian experience in all times. Those who deny separability contend that if the experience seems to be separable and distinct because it appears to be subsequent in these Acts cases, this is due to the unique historical situation during the initial stages of the Church. Luke, they say, is not intending to teach that a separate, distinct baptism in the Holy Spirit experience is normative for Christian experience during later stages of the Church.

Actually, there are two aspects to the contemporary debate concerning separability as seen in these Acts incidents. The first aspect of this debate has to do with the question, Do the Acts texts listed above show that, for the individuals in these incidents, the baptism in the Holy Spirit was a separable and distinct experience in relationship to their conversion, or regeneration, experience? Pentecostals answer yes.

The 120 on the Day of Pentecost were believers before the outpouring of the Spirit on that day. Prior to this event they had already repented and entered into a new life in Christ. The Samaritans had already come to faith in Jesus Christ and had been baptized in water by Philip before Peter and John prayed for them to receive the special gift of the Holy Spirit. Likewise, Paul's case was clearly subsequent. He had been converted and had become a new man in Christ at the time of his vision on the Damascus road. Three days later he received the Spirit in a new and special way when Ananias prayed for him. The case of Cornelius in Acts 10 is an unusual instance—experiencing the baptism in the Holy Spirit on the same occasion as experiencing regeneration by the Holy Spirit. Nevertheless, Pentecostals commonly contend that even in this case "there must be some distinction between their conversion and the gift of the Spirit here also."[20] The final case is the Ephesian "disciples" (Acts 19). Pentecostals maintain that they had either already received salvation before Paul arrived, or they were at least regenerated before the Holy Spirit came on them. Paul gave them some instructions and

---

[20]Horton, *What the Bible Says,* 157.

then baptized them in water. Following this, the Holy Spirit came on them when Paul laid his hands on them and prayed.

Therefore, Pentecostals conclude that in Acts, the baptism in the Holy Spirit is clearly subsequent in three cases (Pentecost, Samaria, and Paul) and logically separable in the remaining two cases (Cornelius and the Ephesians).[21]

Among those who do not believe that the fact of separability is as certain as Pentecostals contend are Dunn and Bruner. Both discuss the five Acts cases cited above. Dunn holds that the 120 on the Day of Pentecost were not "Christians in the New Testament sense" until that day, because prior to that "their response and commitment *was* defective." Cornelius' experience was a unity, according to Dunn. "Cornelius was saved, was baptized in the Spirit, ... was granted repentance unto life—all synonymous ways of saying: Cornelius became a Christian." Likewise, "Paul's three-day experience was a unity, ... a crisis experience extending over three days from the Damascus road to his baptism." Paul could not be called a Christian, Dunn says, until the series was completed at the hands of Ananias. Finally, in the Ephesians' case, Dunn believes Paul was not asking *Christians* if they had received the Spirit. Rather, he was asking *disciples,* who professed belief, whether they were Christians. Dunn concludes that they were not Christians until Paul rebaptized them and laid his hands upon them. Therefore, because of an apparent presumptive view of what Dunn calls conversion-initiation, he concludes that in no instance does Luke describe an incident where the baptism in the Holy Spirit is truly separable from conversion.[22]

Bruner maintains a position similar to that of Dunn's: Christian baptism is the baptism in the Holy Spirit. Yet, unlike Dunn, Bruner seems to allow that two cases in Acts are exceptional because of the historical situation. The first is the Day of Pentecost case. The 120 had to *wait* because of "that unusual period in the apostles' career between the ascension of Jesus and his gift of the Spirit to the church at Pentecost." After Pentecost, though, "baptism and the gift of the Holy Spirit belong indissolubly together." Yet, Bruner allows a second case, after Pentecost, as an exception. He calls the case of the Samaritans' believing and being baptized in water with-

---

[21]This paragraph is a summary of the Pentecostal view on this topic from such sources as Horton, *What the Bible Says,* 153–62; Ervin, *Spirit Baptism,* 14–20, 68–80; and J. R. Williams, *Renewal Theology,* vol. 2, 186–90, 206.

[22]Dunn, *Baptism,* 4, 52–53, 63, 68, 74, 77–78, 80–81, 83, 86, 88.

out being baptized in the Spirit a hiatus that occurred because "Samaria was the church's first decisive step out of and beyond Judaism." This one separation between Christian baptism and the gift of the Spirit was a "temporary suspension of the normal" allowed by God so that the apostles could witness and participate in this decisive step. According to Bruner, though, for the remaining cases in the Book of Acts, the baptism in the Holy Spirit is inseparable from and identical with Christian baptism in water.[23]

Dunn and Bruner are less than fully convincing in their arguments. There may be some sense—at least ideally—in which Luke understood all of the works of the Spirit in the individual to be a whole, a unity. Nevertheless, he does show that at least in some of the incidents there was indeed a lapse of time between the parts of the whole. As noted above, both Dunn and Bruner acknowledge this. And Gordon Fee contends that Luke clearly describes the Samaritans as Christian believers before the Spirit had fallen on them. The point is, there are incidents in Luke's accounts when time separates the parts of the Spirit's work in the lives of individuals.[24]

The fact that Luke clearly describes incidents in which the "parts" of Christian experience are separated by time is a point in favor of the Pentecostal position. Nevertheless, Pentecostals need not focus so intently upon *subsequence* to make their point for *separability* and *distinctiveness.* Subsequence puts the emphasis on following in time or order. Separability refers to the quality of being dissimilar in nature or identity. And distinctiveness has to do with being discrete in character and purpose or both. So subsequence is not absolutely essential to the concepts of separability and distinctiveness. Events may be simultaneous, yet separable and distinctive if they are dissimilar in nature or identity. They are also distinctive if they are discrete in character and/or purpose.

At least in theory, this could be the case with the Christian experiences of justification, regeneration, sanctification, and baptism in the Holy Spirit. Even if they all occurred at the same time, what theologian would argue that they are not distinctive in character and purpose and therefore not separable in nature and identity? In the same way, whatever its

---

[23]Bruner, *Theology,* 163, 168–69, 173–75, 178, 190–97, 207–14.

[24]Dunn, *Baptism,* 74, 77–78. Bruner, *Theology,* 173–74. Gordon D. Fee, *Gospel and Spirit: Issues in New Testament Hermeneutics* (Peabody, Mass.: Hendrickson Publishers, 1991), 97.

time relationship to these other works, the baptism in the Holy Spirit is a separable and distinctive work of the Spirit.

Certainly Pentecostals can acknowledge that in Cornelius' case he experienced regeneration and the baptism in the Holy Spirit on the same occasion.[25] Also, even if the 120 were not Christians in the New Testament sense until the Day of Pentecost[26] and even if the Ephesians were only disciples of John before Paul prayed for them—in all three cases the recipients received a distinctive experience of the baptism in the Holy Spirit.[27] This is true because, again, subsequence is not absolutely essential to separability and distinctiveness. However, Pentecostals can present a strong argument not only for separability and distinctiveness, but also for subsequence in the cases of the Samaritans and Paul. The important point to note is this: The fact Luke shows that the experience of the baptism in the Holy Spirit *can be* subsequent serves to underscore that it is a separable and distinctive experience. William Menzies notes, "[T]here is a logical distinction, if not always a temporal distinction, between new birth and baptism in the Spirit."[28]

The conclusion that in Acts the baptism in the Holy Spirit is a separable experience is only the first aspect of the issue. Whether separability or even subsequence is shown to be a pattern in Acts is one matter. Whether such a pattern should be viewed as normative for doctrine and practice today is yet another matter. Is Luke only describing what happened to be the case in that historical situation? Or does he intend to teach that the pattern and character of the baptism in the Holy Spirit in his historical narrative of Acts is normative for Christian doctrine and practice? Although this is not the place

---

[25]Cornelius already knew the facts of the gospel. He probably thought he would have to convert to Judaism to be saved and baptized in the Holy Spirit. Peter's words stimulated faith for both.

[26]Ervin makes a strong case for the position that the disciples were born again on the evening of Jesus' resurrection, according to John 20:19–23, *Spirit Baptism,* 14–20.

[27]I hold that the 120 on the Day of Pentecost had experienced New Testament regeneration prior to that day and the Ephesian disciples were full-fledged Christians before Paul arrived in Ephesus. Also, logically, Cornelius could have experienced regeneration momentarily before he experienced being baptized in the Holy Spirit. But none of these are absolutely essential to maintaining that the baptism in the Holy Spirit is always a separable, distinctive experience.

[28]William W. Menzies, "Synoptic Theology: An Essay on Pentecostal Hermeneutics," *Paraclete* 13 (Winter 1979): 20.

for a thorough consideration of this issue, its importance is such that there is need to consider it at least briefly.

The second aspect of the separability issue can then be stated as follows: Is the pattern and characteristic of the baptism in the Holy Spirit shown by Luke in Acts normative for the Church in all generations? Fee considers this second aspect of the issue a hermeneutical question. It focuses upon the practice of using biblical historical precedence to formulate Christian doctrine and establish normative Christian experience.[29] In this hermeneutical procedure, if one can show that the biblical writer describes a pattern of Christian experience that was typical, or normative, in the New Testament Church, then interpretatively it is expected to be normative in the Church today. Specifically, regarding the issue of separability, Pentecostal scholars believe Luke describes a pattern in Acts in which the baptism in the Holy Spirit is distinctive from the regeneration experience. Further, they contend that present-day Christians can expect the same pattern of experience.

THE THEOLOGICAL IMPORT OF HISTORICAL MATERIALS IN THE BIBLE

Scholars such as Anthony A. Hoekema and John R. W. Stott take a view that goes against this Pentecostal position. They distinguish between *historical* and *didactic* materials in the New Testament, regarding the purpose and use of each kind of material as different. They contend that historical materials are just that—historical; but didactic materials are designed and intended to teach. Historical narrative material, such as Luke's in the Book of Acts, does not have didactic and instructional purpose. Therefore, Hoekema says, "When we say . . . that we wish to be guided by Scripture in our understanding of the work of the Spirit, we must seek this guidance primarily in its *didactic* rather than in its *historical* parts." "More precisely," according to Stott, these didactic materials are found "in the teaching of Jesus, and in the sermons and writings of the apostles, and not in the purely narrative portions of the Acts."[30] Consequently, contrary to most Pentecostals, Hoekema and Stott contend that the historical materials in the Book of Acts cannot be used to formulate normative Christian doctrine and practice.

---

[29]Fee, *Gospel and Spirit,* 84–85.

[30]Anthony A. Hoekema, *Holy Spirit Baptism* (Grand Rapids: Wm. B. Eerdmans, 1972), 23–24. John R. W. Stott, *The Baptism and the Fullness of the Holy Spirit* (Downers Grove, Ill.: InterVarsity, 1964), 8.

Those who take the position of Hoekema and Stott assert that the procedure of formulating doctrine and practice from historical materials is improper hermeneutics. Fee also, though himself a Pentecostal, notes that this procedure is part of "a kind of pragmatic hermeneutics" that he believes Pentecostals often use in place of "scientific hermeneutics." He contends that this procedure is improper hermeneutics because it simply was not Luke's primary intention to teach that the baptism in the Holy Spirit is distinct from and subsequent to conversion. According to Fee, the fact that the reader of Acts can observe such a pattern of separability in Luke's account is "incidental" to Luke's primary intent of the narrative. Referring to the episode at Samaria—what he considers to be the Pentecostal's strongest case—Fee suggests that Luke probably was not therein "*intending to teach* 'distinct from and subsequent to'" conversion.[31]

This issue, then, focuses upon the question of the author's intention. On the one hand, scholars such as Hoekema, Stott, and Fee contend that when a New Testament author is writing historical material he is not intending to teach normative doctrine and practice for the church in all times. They say historical writings are "descriptive history of the primitive church" and as such "must not be translated into normative experience for the ongoing church." Accordingly, Fee says that what Luke the historian shows regarding the baptism in the Holy Spirit is what was the "normal" experience of the first-century Christians. Whatever "recurring pattern of the coming (or presence) of the Spirit" that Luke reveals is "repeatable." That is, the original model that Luke reveals is "something that we would do well to pattern our lives after." However, this pattern is not to be imposed as "normative"— enjoined as something that "must be adhered to by all Christians at all times and in all places." Fee's stance here is based upon his position that historical material does not have didactic value, i.e., historical material is not intended to be used for the formulation of Christian doctrine and experience.[32]

On the other hand, scholars such as Roger Stronstad and William W. Menzies make a strong case to the contrary. They consider the position of Hoekema, Stott, and Fee—that historical material does not have didactic value—rather arbitrary. Stronstad acknowledges that Luke's work is historical

---

[31]Fee, *Gospel and Spirit,* 86, 90–92, 97.
[32]Ibid., 85, 90–94, 98, 102.

narrative, but he denies the assumption that such material is without instructional intent. Menzies concurs: "The Genre of Acts is not merely historical, but also intentionally theological." By this he means that Luke intended to teach what is normative for Christian doctrine, practice, and experience.[33]

In making his case, Stronstad notes that "Luke and Acts are not two separate books. . . . Rather they are in fact two halves of one work and must be interpreted as a unit." The intent of one is shared by the other. Then he sets out to show that the way Luke developed his material, in both his Gospel and Acts, indicates he intended it to teach normative doctrine and practice. Luke used his sources and developed his material in a manner similar to Old Testament and intertestamental historians. He did this, Stronstad says, "specifically to introduce key theological themes" and "to establish, illustrate, and reinforce those themes through specific historical episodes." Stronstad continues to reinforce his point and finally concludes: "Luke had a didactic or catechetical or instructional rather than a merely informational purpose for his history of the origin and spread of Christianity."[34]

Closely related to the issue of the author's intent is the question of how present-day interpreters should understand the author's material in relationship to that intent. This is the issue of the relative place of scientific hermeneutics and pragmatic hermeneutics. Fee contends that the Pentecostal's pragmatic practice of basing normative doctrine and experience on biblical historical precedence is contrary to "scientific hermeneutics." However, most biblical interpreters recognize that good hermeneutics is not either/or—but both scientific and pragmatic. In his standard work, A. Berkeley Mickelsen writes: "The term 'hermeneutics' designates both the science and art of interpretation." He cautions against "a mechanical, rationalistic" approach, saying: "The mechanical rule approach to hermeneutics builds mistaken ideas from the start."[35] Scientific exegesis carries the interpreter only so far. There comes a point at which some degree of pragmatic hermeneutics must come into the process.

Certainly to the extent Fee raises a caution against those

---

[33]Roger Stronstad, "The Hermeneutics of Lucan Historiography," *Paraclete* 22 (Fall 1988): 6, 10–11. Menzies, "Synoptic Theology," 18–19.

[34]Stronstad, "Hermeneutics," 11, 15–16.

[35]A. Berkeley Mickelsen, *Interpreting the Bible* (Grand Rapids: Wm. B. Eerdmans, 1963), 3–4, 19.

pragmatics that ignore or reject the scientific approach, to that extent his caution must be received.

However, one should note that the relationship between scientific hermeneutics and pragmatic hermeneutics is only tensional and not antithetical. Therefore, the practice of translating biblical historical precedence into normative experience for the ongoing Church cannot be rejected out-of-hand simply because it includes an element of pragmatic hermeneutics. Stronstad believes this practice is, in fact, "reminiscent of the Pauline principle of interpreting historical narrative." When Paul says "All Scripture is God-breathed and is useful for teaching . . . and training in righteousness" (2 Tim. 3:16), he surely includes the narratives of Genesis as well as other historical portions. Based on this, most Pentecostals hold that the narrative of Acts as well as the teachings of Romans are just as God-breathed and just as profitable "for teaching . . . and training in righteousness."

Moreover, just as Paul believed that "whatever was written in earlier times [i.e., the Old Testament] was written for our instruction" (Rom. 15:4, NASB), so Pentecostals similarly believe that whatever was written in Acts, as well as in the Gospels or the Epistles, was written for our instruction.[36] There is sufficient reason, therefore, to conclude that Luke intended to teach Theophilus a model that he could consider normative for formulating Christian doctrine, practice, and experience.

Pentecostals are not alone in this position on historical narrative. I. Howard Marshall, a leading non-Pentecostal evangelical, sets forth the position that Luke was both a historian and a theologian. If Marshall's position is correct, then Luke's material, like that of any other New Testament theologian, is a valid source for understanding what is normative for Christian doctrine and practice. Menzies notes that there is "a growing body of substantial scholarship that points in the direction of a clear Lukan theology of the Spirit in Luke/Acts that supports the concept of 'normativity.'" Gary B. McGee cites additional scholars who hold a similar view regarding the theological nature of Luke's writings. He concludes: "Hermeneutically, therefore, Pentecostals stand in a respected and historic line of evangelical Christians who have legitimately

---

[36]Stronstad, "Hermeneutics," 8.

recognized the Acts of the Apostles to be a vital repository of theological truth."[37]

Taking this position, Pentecostals study the accounts in Acts where Luke relates historical incidents in which individuals evidently experience the baptism in the Holy Spirit. This study reveals Spirit baptism was a distinctive experience that was sometimes clearly subsequent and always logically separable from regeneration. Luke the theologian's material is acknowledged as a valid source for standard Christian doctrine and experience. The conclusion, then, is that a similar distinctive, separable baptism in the Holy Spirit experience is normative for contemporary Christian experience. Donald A. Johns states this position:

> The application of accepted principles ... will support the idea that being baptized in the Holy Spirit is something distinct from conversion. ... Conversion involves the establishing of relationship with God; being baptized in the Spirit involves initiation into powerful, charismatic ministry.[38]

EVIDENCES OF THE BAPTISM IN THE SPIRIT

Also central to contemporary discussion of this doctrine is the evidence(s) of the baptism in the Holy Spirit. Taken together, the position one takes on separability and evidence greatly determines or at least influences one's entire doctrine of the baptism in the Holy Spirit. This section addresses the issue of tongues[39] being the initial physical (or outward) evidence of the baptism in the Holy Spirit. It also considers other evidences of Spirit baptism in the lives of individuals.

TONGUES AS THE INITIAL PHYSICAL EVIDENCE

The current literature on the topic reveals considerable diversity of positions on speaking in tongues. Yet, with regard

---

[37]I. Howard Marshall, *Luke: Historian and Theologian,* enl. ed. (Grand Rapids: Zondervan Publishing House, 1970), 13–21. William W. Menzies, "Book Reviews," *Paraclete* (Winter 1993): 32. Gary B. McGee, "Early Pentecostal Hermeneutics: Tongues as Evidence in the Book of Acts," in *Initial Evidence: Historical and Biblical Perspectives on the Pentecostal Doctrine of Spirit Baptism,* ed. Gary B. McGee (Peabody Mass.: Hendrickson Publishers, 1991), 111.

[38]Donald A. Johns, "Some New Directions in the Hermeneutics of Classical Pentecostalism's Doctrine of Initial Evidence," in McGee, *Initial Evidence,* 162.

[39]See chap. 14, pp. 468, 471–75 for discussion of the nature of speaking in tongues.

to tongues being the initial evidence of the baptism in the Holy Spirit, these views can be categorized as follows: (1) speaking in tongues is not the evidence of the baptism in the Holy Spirit; (2) the baptism in the Holy Spirit is sometimes evidenced by speaking in tongues; (3) the baptism in the Holy Spirit is always accompanied by the initial evidence of speaking in tongues. Again, as with separability, in the tongues as initial evidence issue, the question of what the Book of Acts shows as a pattern and teaches as normative is most crucial.

The first view—which says that tongues is not the evidence of being baptized in the Holy Spirit—is the traditional evangelical view. Carl Henry articulates this position:

> The present controversy focuses largely on the charismatic claim that tongues evidence the baptism of the Spirit. ... This view has no support from such Christian stalwarts of the past as Luther, Calvin, Knox, Wesley, Whitefield, Edwards, Carey, Judson and others.[40]

Bruner, in keeping with his conviction that the baptism in the Holy Spirit and Christian conversion are one and the same, likewise denies that tongues is the evidence of the experience. He states that faith as expressed in the confession "Lord Jesus" is the only evidence of the Spirit's coming and presence.[41]

Those who take this first position on the issue of tongues as evidence often provide extensive discussion of the Acts materials on this subject. Hoekema acknowledges three incidents in Acts where tongues speaking occurred. On the Day of Pentecost, speaking in tongues was "one of three miraculous signs" of what he calls "the once-for-all, unrepeatable event of the outpouring of the Holy Spirit." "Cornelius's household did speak with tongues after the Spirit had fallen upon them," Hoekema admits, but "this fact does not demonstrate that tongues-speaking is proof of one's having received a post-conversion 'baptism in the Spirit.'" Likewise, in the case of the Ephesian disciples, "the fact that tongues-speaking occurred ... cannot be used to prove its value as evidence of a post-conversion 'baptism in the Spirit,'" according to Hoekema. Why? Because "the coming of the Spirit

---

[40]Henry, *God, Revelation,* vol. 4, 287.
[41]Bruner, *Theology,* 281.

upon the Ephesian disciples was not subsequent to but simultaneous with their conversion." He also notes: "There are nine instances in the Book of Acts where people are described as being filled with or full of the Holy Spirit where no mention is made of tongues-speaking." Therefore, he concludes that tongues-speaking is not evidence of receiving the baptism in the Holy Spirit.[42]

Following his discussion of the Acts cases, Bruner concurs with Hoekema. According to Bruner, faith, not tongues, is both the means and the evidence of being baptized in the Spirit.[43]

The second view concerning tongues as evidence says speaking in tongues is sometimes an evidence of the baptism in the Holy Spirit. This position is characteristic of some in the charismatic movement. Henry I. Lederle briefly summarizes the great variety of views among charismatics. He also succinctly states what he understands to be common to these views: "Most charismatics associate (renewal in or) being baptized in the Spirit with the manifestation of the charismata, which regularly include speaking in tongues. ... Few charismatics accept that glossolalia is the condition *sine qua non* [i.e., essential] for Spirit baptism."[44]

Lederle, thus, recognizes glossolalia (speaking in tongues) as being among the "legitimate aspects of our apostolic faith," but he rejects the doctrine of tongues as the sole evidence of Spirit baptism. He believes this doctrine lacks "explicit or conclusive support" in Scripture. Lederle agrees with a number of other charismatics that "there is no assertion anywhere in the New Testament claiming it [glossolalia] as the *only* evidence"[45]

The third view on tongues as the evidence of being baptized in the Holy Spirit is the traditional Pentecostal position. Pentecostals commonly contend that speaking in tongues is always the initial physical evidence of this special experience. In fact, as J. R. Williams notes: "Pentecostals have laid particular stress on speaking in tongues as 'initial evidence' of the baptism in the Spirit." The Assemblies of God Statement of

---

[42]Hoekema, *Holy Spirit Baptism,* 33, 40, 43, 44, 48, 53–54.

[43]Bruner, *Theology,* 281.

[44]Henry I. Lederle, "Initial Evidence and the Charismatic Movement: An Ecumenical Appraisal," in McGee, *Initial Evidence,* 136–37.

[45]Ibid. 132, 136. Lederle cites P. H. Wiebe, "The Pentecostal Initial Evidence Doctrine," *Journal of the Evangelical Theological Society* 27 (December 1984): 465–72.

Fundamental Truths states this position in point number 8: "The Baptism of believers in the Holy Ghost is witnessed by the initial physical sign of speaking with tongues as the Spirit of God gives them utterance (Acts 2:4)." Bruner is correct when he observes, "[I]t is in the understanding of the initial *evidence* of this subsequent experience that Pentecostals are unique, and it is this evidence which marks its advocates as Pentecostal."[46]

Pentecostals believe their conclusion about tongues being the initial physical evidence of the baptism in the Holy Spirit is based on Scripture, especially the Book of Acts. In three cases where Luke records details of individuals experiencing being baptized in the Holy Spirit, speaking in tongues is clearly evident. On the Day of Pentecost the 120 spoke in tongues—*glossolalia*—languages of which they had no command in normal circumstances (Acts 2:4). According to Ralph M. Riggs: "This speaking in other tongues then became the sign and evidence that the Holy Spirit had descended upon New Testament Christians." The next clear case of speaking in tongues in Acts is the incident of Cornelius (Acts 10:44–46). Horton observes: "The Spirit gave the evidence, and He gave only one. 'They spoke with tongues and magnified God' (exactly as in Acts 2:4,11)." The third and final clear case is the incident involving the disciples at Ephesus (Acts 19:1–6). Howard Ervin comments on this case: "The evidential nature of the glossolalia here is heavily underscored by the comment that 'the speaking with tongues and prophesying was external and *indubitable proof* that the Holy Spirit had come on these twelve uninformed disciples.' "

Competent exegetes then, including most non-Pentecostal scholars, quickly acknowledge that Luke was speaking of the supernatural manifestation of tongues in these three cases. Pentecostal scholars furthermore maintain that Luke revealed a *pattern* in these three cases—a distinctive experience of the Spirit evidenced by speaking in tongues. As J. R. Williams states, in these three cases, "speaking in tongues was clear evidence that the Holy Spirit had been given."[47]

---

[46]J. Rodman Williams, "Baptism in the Holy Spirit," in *Dictionary of Pentecostal and Charismatic Movements,* ed. Stanley M. Burgess, Gary B. McGee, and Patrick Alexander (Grand Rapids: Zondervan Publishing House, 1989), 44. *Minutes of the 44th Session of the General Council of the Assemblies of God,* 130. Bruner, *Theology,* 76.

[47]Ralph M. Riggs, *The Spirit Himself* (Springfield, Mo.: Gospel Publishing House, 1949), 87. Horton, *What the Bible Says,* 157. Ervin, *Spirit-Baptism,* 79. See F. F. Bruce, *Commentary on the Book of Acts* (Grand Rapids: Wm. B. Eerdmans, 1966), 57; Bruner, Theology, 163–64; and Hoekema, *Holy Spirit Baptism,* 33. J. R. Williams, *Renewal Theology,* vol. 2, 211.

Although Luke did not choose to state it, Pentecostals *also* believe tongues was likewise manifested in the other cases of initial baptism in the Holy Spirit in Acts. For example, Pentecostals maintain that the Samaritan believers (Acts 8:4–24) spoke in tongues like the 120 on the Day of Pentecost, the household of Cornelius, and the Ephesian disciples. Ervin states the obvious question: "What did Simon see that convinced him that these Samaritan disciples had received the Holy Spirit through the laying on of the hands of Peter and John?" Ervin cites several non-Pentecostal scholars who confirm his answer. "The context justifies the conclusion that these Samaritan converts received the baptism in the Holy Spirit after their conversion, with the probable evidence of speaking in tongues." F. F. Bruce seems to agree in his comments concerning the experience of the Samaritans: "The context leaves us in no doubt that their reception of the Spirit was attended by external manifestations such as had marked His descent on the earliest disciples at Pentecost." Others cited by Ervin include A. T. Robertson, who asserts that the text in this case "shows plainly that those who received the gift of the Holy Spirit spoke in tongues."[48]

Pentecostals contend that speaking in tongues was the normal, expected experience of all New Testament believers who were baptized in the Holy Spirit. That is, "the *primary activity* consequent to the reception of the Holy Spirit was that of speaking in tongues." Because of this, Luke felt no need to point out tongues speaking every time he discussed an instance of the experience. Luke's readers would have known that believers spoke in tongues when they were baptized in the Holy Spirit. Therefore, Pentecostals submit that not only the Samaritan converts but Paul and others whom Luke discusses also manifested the initial evidence of speaking in tongues. In the case of Paul they point out that he acknowledged speaking in tongues in his Corinthian correspondence (1 Cor. 14:18). On the basis of this, Ervin makes a strong case for affirming that "Paul also spoke in tongues when he received the Pentecostal gift of the Holy Spirit."[49]

---

[48]Ervin, *Spirit Baptism,* 74. Bruce, *Acts,* 181. A. T. Robertson, *Word Pictures in the New Testament,* vol. 3 (New York: Harper & Brothers, 1930), 107.

[49]J. R. Williams, *Renewal Theology,* vol. 2, 211. See Fee, *Gospel and Spirit,* 102. In the case of the Samaritan converts Luke clearly makes it known that there was some unusual, definitely observable manifestation when Peter and John laid their hands on them, an illustration of Luke's practice of discussing such things as being baptized in the Holy Spirit without always giving all of the details. See Ervin's complete argument for this in *Spirit Baptism,* 77.

In summary, Pentecostals then note that in some cases Luke describes in detail the manifestations attendant to believers' receiving the baptism in the Holy Spirit (Pentecost disciples, Cornelius, and Ephesians). In every one of these cases speaking in tongues is the clear evidence of the experience. In other cases where he did not specifically mention tongues (for example, the Samaritans and Paul), tongues were manifested but he simply did not need to reiterate the details every time. Pentecostals believe speaking in tongues was the initial evidence in every case; they hold that Luke revealed a consistent pattern in the New Testament period—a distinctive baptism in the Holy Spirit experience, separable from regeneration and evidenced initially by speaking in tongues.[50]

Further, Pentecostals hold that Luke's accounts not only reveal this pattern, but these accounts also teach that speaking in tongues is normative for Christian doctrine and practice. That is, speaking in tongues is always expected to be the initial evidence of being baptized in the Holy Spirit throughout the history of the Church. This is the way the Acts narratives are to be understood because, again, Luke was writing not only as a historian but also as a theologian. He was describing the work of the Holy Spirit in and through believers in the Church Age. True, these incidents occurred in a particular historical setting, but that is no reason to disallow this pattern as normative for all of the Church Age. After all, the Church Age is always a time when the presence of the Holy Spirit needs to be evident in the lives of believers. In the Church Age there is always the need for His presence and power to work through believers to bring Christ's saving grace to those who are without God. In conclusion, Pentecostals believe: (1) the baptism in the Holy Spirit is the coming of that special presence and power of the Spirit and (2) the initial evidence of this is, today as in the Book of Acts, speaking in tongues.

OTHER EVIDENCES OF THE BAPTISM

Special note now needs to be made that in Pentecostal understanding, speaking in tongues is only the initial evidence of the baptism in the Holy Spirit. Other evidences of His special presence follow in the lives of the recipients.

Some writers suggest that the "fruit of the Spirit" (Gal.

[50]Ibid., 84.

5:22), that is, Christian character qualities, is the continuing evidence of having been baptized in the Holy Spirit.

For example, in a chapter entitled "The Effects of the Coming of the Spirit," J. R. Williams identifies "fullness of joy," "great love," "sharing," and "continuing praise of God" as being among those effects.[51] An earlier well-known Pentecostal writer, Donald Gee, notes that the idea that the fruit of the Spirit is evidence of the baptism in the Holy Spirit is "a common and popular" teaching. But he cautions against this idea, saying: "The fruit of the Spirit . . . is proof of our walking in the Spirit . . . , not the proof of our being baptized in the Spirit." Nevertheless, in his next chapter, Gee discusses certain Christian character qualities as "marks," or evidences, of "being filled with the Spirit." These include "overflowing testimony," "brokenness and humility," "a teachable spirit" and "consecration."[52] Ervin's discussion on this idea is insightful: "Scripture does not coordinate the fruit of the Spirit with the charismata as evidence of the fullness of the Spirit." Yet he notes: "This does not deny that the practical consequences of the Holy Spirit's influence in the life of the Christian are reflected in holy impulses and aspirations conducive to spiritual growth."[53]

Therefore, Pentecostals generally hold that Christian character qualities, or the fruit of the Spirit, are not continuing evidences of Spirit baptism, but these qualities can be and should be enhanced in those who have this experience.

Another suggestion among Pentecostal writers is that various charismatic manifestations are continuing evidences of the baptism in the Holy Spirit. Referring to the spiritual gifts, Gee notes: "Since they are manifestations of the indwelling Spirit, it is fundamental that those who exercise them are filled with the Spirit at the time of their exercise."[54] Ervin sees "manifestations of the charismata" as "evidence of the Spirit's power" and "the continuing fullness of the Spirit." He writes: "The baptism in and fulness of the Spirit are synonymous terms, and a charismatic dimension to Christian experience is evidence of the Holy Spirit's fulness."[55] J. R. Wil-

---

[51]J. R. Williams, *Renewal Theology,* vol. 2, 309, 314, 319.

[52]Donald Gee, *Pentecost* (Springfield, Mo.: Gospel Publishing House, 1932), 27–39.

[53]Ervin, *Spirit Baptism,* 66.

[54]Donald Gee, *Spiritual Gifts in the Work of the Ministry Today* (Springfield, Mo.: Gospel Publishing House, 1963), 18.

[55]Ervin, *Spirit Baptism,* 67.

liams provides further elaboration on this idea in a discussion of the manifestation of the gifts in the Corinthian church. First he emphasizes that "the context for the gifts of the Spirit was the experience of the Spirit's outpouring." For the Corinthian Christians, "there was an abundant outpouring of the Spirit that all had shared." He then draws a parallel between the Corinthian situation and the contemporary charismatic renewal. Today, as in the Corinthian church, the operation of the gifts of the Spirit means those who manifest the gifts have experienced an outpouring of or a baptism in the Holy Spirit.[56]

The final suggestion for a continuing evidence of the baptism in the Holy Spirit is the reality of the dynamic power of the Holy Spirit in the life of the participant. J. R. Williams notes that "the central purpose of the giving of the Spirit is for that enabling power by which the witness of Jesus can be carried forward in both word and deed." In keeping with this observation, Ernest S. Williams identifies this power of the Spirit as "the foremost evidence" of the "Pentecostal experience."[57]

Availability of the Baptism in the Holy Spirit

Here the question is, Is the baptism in the Holy Spirit available to believers today, or was it available only in the Apostolic Age of the New Testament? Most contemporary Evangelicals—Pentecostals and non-Pentecostals alike—answer yes.[58] But by this answer each group means something different. On the one hand, scholars such as Hoekema, Bruner, and Dunn allow that being baptized in the Holy Spirit is a part of Christian reality; but is not a separate experience from regeneration. In the view of these scholars, the baptism in the Holy Spirit is simply part of the total event of becoming a Christian—termed conversion-initiation by Dunn.[59] On the other hand, when Pentecostal scholars say that the baptism in the Holy Spirit is available to believers today, they are insisting upon the contemporary availability of a separable, distinct experience that is evidenced by speaking in tongues.

---

[56]J. R. Williams, *Renewal Theology,* vol. 2, 325–27.

[57]Ibid., vol. 2, 311–12. Ernest S. Williams, *Systematic Theology,* vol. 3 (Springfield, Mo.: Gospel Publishing House, 1953) 47.

[58]Bruce, *Acts,* 76, states an earlier position that seems to be practically abandoned today: "The baptism of the Spirit ... was ... something that took place once for all on the day of Pentecost." See Hoekema's qualification of this position in *Holy Spirit Baptism,* 20.

[59]Dunn, *Baptism,* 7.

Sometimes the argument is set forth that, based on 1 Corinthians 13:8–12, the Pentecostal experience ceased at the end of the New Testament writing period. Some think that in these verses Paul teaches that prophecy, tongues, and knowledge ceased when the New Testament canon was completed. Paul says these charismata "will cease" (v.8) "when perfection (Gk. *teleion*) comes" (v.10)—when we see "face to face" (v. 12). On the basis of this, some deny that a Pentecostal type of Spirit baptism evidenced by tongues is available today. For example, Paul Enns writes: "With the completion of the Scriptures there was no longer any need for an authenticating sign. . . . Tongues were a sign gift belonging to the infancy stage of the church (1 Cor. 13:10–11; 14:20)."[60]

Pentecostal as well as many non-Pentecostal scholars refute the notion that Paul is saying anything like this here. W. Harold Mare shows why positions like Enns' are untenable. The idea of "the cessation of these gifts at the end of the first century A.D.," Mare says, "is completely extraneous to the context." "That these three charisms will come to an end is clearly affirmed by the text," Ervin acknowledges. "When they will cease can only be deduced from the context." Ervin cites various scholars who exegetically confirm his conclusion that here Paul is looking forward to the *Parousia*, or second coming of Christ, not the close of the canon.[61] Also, in these verses Paul is not even writing about the baptism in the Holy Spirit. His statements really have little if anything to do with the question of the availability of a distinctive baptism experience today.

The Pentecostal position on the availability of the baptism of the Holy Spirit evidenced by tongues begins with the Day of Pentecost. More specifically it begins with Peter's words: "The promise is for you and your children, and for all who are far off, as many as the Lord our God shall call to himself" (Acts 2:39, NASB). Horton comments on Peter's explanation of Joel's prophecy to the crowd who heard the 120 speaking in tongues. "The way Peter looked at Joel's prophecy shows he expected a continuing fulfillment of the prophecy to the

---

[60]Paul Enns, *The Moody Handbook of Theology* (Chicago: Moody Press, 1989), 273.

[61]Ervin, *Spirit Baptism*, 174–76. Also, see Gordon D. Fee, *The First Epistle to the Corinthians* (Grand Rapids: Wm. B. Eerdmans, 1987), 642–46; and Leon Morris, *The First Epistle to the Corinthians*, rev. ed. (Grand Rapids: Wm. B. Eerdmans, 1989), 182–83, who both agree with Mare and Ervin.

the last days to include the whole Church Age, from the ascension of Jesus forward. "Clearly, the fulfillment of Joel's prophecy cannot be limited to the Day of Pentecost or any one occasion." P. C. Nelson says simply: " 'To all that are afar off'—that includes us."[62]

Further, Pentecostals contend that indeed the experience of being baptized is repeated distinctively with the evidence of speaking in tongues following the Day of Pentecost. In the Book of Acts they point to the other four incidents (Samaritan converts, Paul, Cornelius, Ephesian disciples) discussed above, especially the latter two cases where tongues is clearly evident.[63] Also, since this is a question of the availability of the experience for today, Pentecostals point out that during the twentieth century the Acts type of distinctive experience, including speaking in tongues, has been repeated in the lives of millions of Christians around the world. After all, contends Menzies, "it should not be thought improper to include personal experience and historical accounts at some point in the process of doing theology." Biblical truth "ought to be demonstrable in life." For this reason, Ervin notes, "[I]t is axiomatic to Pentecostals, that the baptism in the Holy Spirit did not expire with Pentecost, nor even with the close of the apostolic age. They believe, and their experience confirms, that it is the birthright of every Christian."[64]

By insisting that a distinctive baptism in the Holy Spirit experience is available to believers today, Pentecostals are not implying that Christians who have not spoken in tongues do not have the Spirit. Baptism in the Holy Spirit is only one of His several works. Conviction, justification, regeneration, and sanctification are all works of the same Holy Spirit. Each of these works is distinctive, having a unique nature and purpose. If the individual responds positively to the Spirit's convicting work, then justification and regeneration occur. At that moment, the Holy Spirit dwells within the believer, and from that moment forward it is correct to say the individual has the Spirit. The baptism in the Holy Spirit with the initial evidence of speaking in tongues may occur on that same occasion, or it may occur at some later time—in keeping

---

[62]Horton, *What the Bible Says,* 147. Nelson, *Bible Doctrines,* 75. Actually, "far off" refers to the Gentiles. The following phrase, "As many as the Lord our God shall call," shows the promise applies to Christians today.

[63]See Ervin, *Spirit-Baptism,* 26–27; and Horton, *What the Bible Says,* 153–62.

[64]Menzies, "Synoptic Theology," 20. Ervin, *Spirit Baptism,* 26.

with the pattern revealed in the Book of Acts. In either case, the person has the Spirit dwelling within from the moment of regeneration.

Confusion concerning this matter of having or not having the Holy Spirit occurs because of a lack of understanding about how Luke uses certain terms. When Luke describes and discusses the baptism in the Holy Spirit, he uses terminology such as "being filled with the Holy Spirit," "receiving the Holy Spirit," "the Holy Spirit being poured out," "the Holy Spirit falling upon," and "the Holy Spirit coming on."[65] These terms are not so much terms of *contrast* as they are simply attempts to *describe* and *emphasize.* That is, in using these terms Luke is not contrasting the baptism in the Holy Spirit with regeneration, as if to say that in regeneration the Spirit does not come, is not received, or does not indwell. The Spirit does come, He is received, and He does indwell at regeneration (Rom. 8:9). But in using these terms for being baptized in the Holy Spirit, Luke is simply saying that this is a special experience of "being filled with" or "receiving" the Spirit, or of the Spirit's "falling upon" or "coming on" individuals.

Luke's terminology need not confuse the issue of the availability of a distinctive experience of baptism in the Holy Spirit. As Riggs says, Pentecostals insist that "all believers have the Holy Spirit, yet . . . all believers, in addition to having the Holy Spirit, may be filled with or baptized with the Holy Spirit."[66] The baptism in the Holy Spirit is a unique experience available to the converted, regenerated Christian for a special, specific purpose.

THE PURPOSE OF THE BAPTISM IN THE HOLY SPIRIT

The ultimate issue related to the idea of the baptism in the Holy Spirit has to do with the purpose of this experience. All other discussion of the baptism in the Holy Spirit should point to the reason for this special work and the need it is intended to fulfill.

Many Christians, in effect, see no special purpose related to being baptized in the Holy Spirit separate from the other aspects of conversion-initiation. Bruner writes: "The power of the baptism of the Holy Spirit is first and foremost a power which joins to Christ." According to Hoekema, *Baptism in the Spirit* simply "means the bestowal of the Spirit for sal-

---

[65] See pp. 425–27 for a brief discussion of these terms.
[66] Riggs, *The Spirit Himself,* 47.

vation upon people who were not believers in the Christian sense before this bestowal." There is no "Biblical proof for the contention that tongue-speaking is a special source of spiritual power," Hoekema concludes.[67]

Dunn reaches the same conclusion: "Baptism in the Spirit . . . is primarily initiatory." He allows that it is "only secondarily an empowering" experience. Apparently then for Dunn, and others who take his position, since the baptism in the Holy Spirit is in no sense distinctive in relationship to conversion, it therefore has no purpose that cannot be ascribed to each believer, since He is resident in all believers.[68]

Pentecostals have long recognized that the above position results in a subnormal Church in which the dynamic, experiential, empowering quality of Christian life is absent. J. R. Williams writes: "In addition to being born of the Spirit wherein new life begins, there is also the need for being baptized, or filled, with the Spirit for the outflow of the life in ministry to others."[69]

Fee makes a similar point and observes that "deep dissatisfaction with life in Christ without life in the Spirit" is precisely the background for the Pentecostal movement.[70] From the beginning of the twentieth century until the present, Pentecostals have believed that the full dynamic of the Spirit's empowerment comes *only* with the special, distinctive baptism in the Holy Spirit experience. When this special, distinctive experience is not normal in the Church, the Church lacks the reality of the empowering dimension of life in the Spirit.

Therefore, Pentecostals believe that a distinctive experience of the baptism in the Holy Spirit, such as Luke describes, is crucial to the contemporary Church. Stronstad says that the implications from Luke's theology are clear: "If the gift of the Spirit was charismatic or vocational for Jesus and the Early Church, so it ought to have a vocational dimension in the experience of God's people today."[71] Why? Because the Church today, like the Church in the Book of Acts, needs the dynamic power of the Spirit to enable it to evangelize the world effectively and build the Body of Christ. The Spirit

[67]Bruner, *Theology*, 160. Hoekema, *Holy Spirit Baptism*, 20, 54.

[68]Dunn, *Baptism*, 54.

[69]J. R. Williams, "Baptism in the Holy Spirit," 46.

[70]Fee, *Gospel and Spirit*, 118–19.

[71]Roger Stronstad, "The Holy Spirit in Luke-Acts," *Paraclete* 23 (Spring 1989): 26.

came on the Day of Pentecost because the followers of Jesus "needed a baptism in the Spirit that would empower their witness so that others might likewise enter into life and salvation."[72] And, because He came on the Day of Pentecost, the Spirit comes again and again for the same purpose.

According to Pentecostals, the purpose of this experience is the final and most important element that makes the baptism in the Holy Spirit separable and distinctive in relationship to regeneration. J. R. Williams notes: "[Pentecostals] urge that in addition—and for an entirely different reason than salvation—there is another action of the Holy Spirit that equips the believer for further service."

Conviction, justification, regeneration, and sanctification are all important works of the Spirit. But there is "another mode of operation, His energizing work," that is different and equally important, Myer Pearlman states. "The main feature of this promise is power for service and not regeneration for eternal life." Spirit baptism is "distinct from conversion," Robert Menzies says, in that it "unleashes a new dimension of the Spirit's power: It is an enduement of power for service."[73]

Pentecostals believe strongly in this point—the primary and foremost purpose of being baptized in the Holy Spirit is power for service. They look at Luke 24:49 and Acts 1:8 where Luke records Jesus' last instructions to His followers: "You shall receive power when the Holy Spirit has come upon you; and you shall be My witnesses" (Acts 1:8, NASB). They believe He was referring to the coming Day of Pentecost when the 120 would be baptized in the Holy Spirit. P.C. Nelson says Jesus' followers were given the Holy Spirit "as an enduement of power to fit them for bearing effective witness to the great soul-saving truths of the Gospel." Horton notes: "From the Day of Pentecost on we see the Holy Spirit active in the life of the Church . . . in the work of spreading the gospel and establishing the Church."[74] Pentecostals believe that this same unique baptism in the Holy Spirit is available to believers today for the same purpose of empowering them for service.

Because Pentecostals recognize the essential need of being baptized in the Holy Spirit and the importance of its purpose

---

[72]J. R. Williams, *Renewal Theology,* vol. 2, 179.

[73]J. R. Williams, "Baptism in the Holy Spirit," 46. Myer Pearlman, *Knowing the Doctrines of the Bible* (Springfield, Mo.: Gospel Publishing House, 1937), 309. Robert P. Menzies, "The Distinctive Character of Luke's Pneumatology," *Paraclete* 25 (Fall 1991): 18.

[74]Nelson, *Bible Doctrines,* 76. Horton, *What the Bible Says,* 148.

they sometimes overemphasize evidential tongues. Thoughtful Pentecostals, however, recognize the danger of such overemphasis. While insisting on a distinctive experience evidenced initially by tongues, they also insist that the ultimate and most important objective is the continuing evidence—a life dynamically empowered by the Spirit.

Non-Pentecostals and Pentecostals alike raise cautions concerning overemphasis on tongues and separability. J. Ramsey Michaels believes "there is a danger in the Pentecostal notion of 'initial evidence' of reducing the Spirit to tongues speaking." An early Pentecostal, E. S. Williams, indicates a similar concern when he writes: "We would do well to not overstress tongues." He correctly declares: "That which is of first importance is *'power from on high.'*" Likewise, Horton cautions:

> It should be recognized . . . that speaking in tongues is only the initial evidence of the baptism in the Holy Spirit. . . .
>
> In fact, it should always be kept in mind that the baptism in the Spirit is not a climactic experience. . . . [It] is only a door into a growing relationship with the Spirit.[75]

In the same spirit Fee expresses his concern about what he considers an undue focus on subsequence. He affirms that the Pentecostal experience itself is right for the Church today. He correctly notes that the most important quality of "mighty baptism in the Spirit" is "the empowering dimension of life in the Spirit," which he says Pentecostals have recaptured.[76]

The important point is that the initial experience, evidenced by speaking in tongues, is only an opening up into other dimensions of life in the Spirit. This initial, distinctive experience "leads to a life of service where the gifts of the Spirit provide power and wisdom for the spread of the gospel and the growth of the Church."[77]

Individuals baptized in and empowered by the Spirit affect the rest of the body of believers. Menzies says that "the baptism in the Spirit becomes the entrance into a mode of worship that blesses the assembled saints of God. The baptism is

---

[75]J. Ramsey Michaels, "Evidences of the Spirit, or the Spirit as Evidence? Some Non-Pentecostal Reflections," in McGee, *Initial Evidence,* 216. E. S. Williams, *Systematic Theology,* vol. 3, 47, 51. Horton, *What the Bible Says,* 261.

[76]Fee, *Gospel and Spirit,* 119.

[77]Horton, *What the Bible Says,* 261.

the gateway into the manifold ministries in the Spirit called gifts of the Spirit, including many spiritual ministries."[78]

In conclusion, the purpose of being baptized in the Holy Spirit—the ongoing dimension of the Spirit-empowered life—is what makes the experience itself important enough to know about, understand, and participate in. Speaking in tongues is not its ultimate purpose, nor is it the reason that the experience is to be desired. The need for supernatural power to witness and serve is the reason a distinctive experience of the baptism in the Holy Spirit is important. The ultimate need is for every member in the body of Christ to be thus empowered so the Church might operate in the full dimension of life in the Spirit.

RECEPTION OF THE BAPTISM IN THE HOLY SPIRIT

The final question in this discussion of the baptism in the Holy Spirit is, How does one receive this special experience? And these are some of the related issues: Are there certain conditions to receiving the baptism in the Holy Spirit? If so, what are they? Also, if such conditions are required *after* regeneration, do they amount to requirements in addition to faith?

There are various views regarding the conditions for receiving this experience. Simply stated, Pentecostals generally hold that the only prerequisite to being baptized in the Holy Spirit is conversion and the only condition is faith. "The Holy Spirit comes to those who believe in Jesus Christ," J. R. Williams says. Horton states that "the only condition for receiving the Promise of the Father is repentance and faith." Menzies notes: "The experience is described as a gift (Acts 10:45), and is therefore not in any way deserved or earned. It is received by faith—active, obedient faith."[79]

Note Menzies' qualifier at the end of this statement—"active, obedient faith." When closely considered, the condition of faith implies related conditions or attitudes. Here Menzies uses the terms "active" and "obedient." Pentecostals usually focus on prayer, obedience, yielding, and expectancy.

J. R. Williams says: "Prayer . . . in its many aspects of praise, thanksgiving, confession, supplication, and dedication . . . is

---

[78]William W. Menzies and Stanley M. Horton, *Bible Doctrines: A Pentecostal Perspective* (Springfield, Mo.: Logion Press, 1993), 126.

[79]J. R. Williams, *Renewal Theology,* vol. 2, 171. Horton, *Book of Acts,* 47. Menzies, *Bible Doctrines,* 130.

the context or atmosphere in which the Holy Spirit is given." He also explains that "obedience lies at the heart of faith, and it is by faith alone that the Holy Spirit is received." Obedience includes both a general attitude of obedience toward God as well as obedience to any and all particular commands of the Lord. Yielding is a special aspect of obedience. Pentecostals believe that the baptism in the Holy Spirit occurs in an atmosphere of total surrender, or yielding, to the lordship of Jesus Christ. Finally, J. R. Williams notes the importance of expecting to receive the Holy Spirit. He observes that those who expect little receive "little if anything. . . . But those who wait to receive everything God has to give . . ., those who stand on tiptoes of expectation—it is they whom God delights to bless."[80]

Pentecostals see nothing unusual about the idea that there are conditions to receiving the baptism in the Holy Spirit. Others, however, suggest that when coupled with the Pentecostal notion of separability and subsequence, the idea of conditions to Spirit baptism becomes a different issue. Bruner, for example, agrees that there are conditions to being baptized in the Holy Spirit, but that they are nothing different from or more than those for becoming a Christian. He believes that the Pentecostal position of separability implies conditions for being baptized in the Holy Spirit beyond those for salvation. If believers are not baptized in the Holy Spirit when they become Christians, then there must be requirements "in addition to the simple faith which apprehends Christ." Bruner submits that "the doctrine of the conditions for the baptism in the Holy Spirit" explains for the Pentecostal "why the spiritual baptism cannot usually accompany initial faith."[81]

At this point, Bruner declares, "the Protestant is compelled to enter not simply an analysis of the Pentecostal movement but a criticism as well." He objects to the Pentecostal notion that conditions for becoming a Christian are "followed by the fulfilling of the conditions for the baptism in the Spirit." To Bruner this means that after becoming a Christian there must be some "more than usual obedience and faith." To receive the baptism in the Holy Spirit some condition of *"absolute obedience and faith"* must be met. He rejects the idea that being baptized in the Holy Spirit requires something "in addition to the simple faith which apprehends Christ."[82]

---

[80]J. R. Williams, *Renewal Theology,* vol. 2, 295, 298–302, 305–6.

[81]Bruner, *Theology,* 88, 115.

[82]Ibid., 57, 115, 129, 262.

Pentecostals explain that although these conditions for being baptized in the Holy Spirit are necessary *after* regeneration, they are not *in addition to* conditions for salvation. Again, as cited above, Horton declares: "[T]he only condition for receiving the Promise of the Father is repentance and faith,"[83] the same as the condition for becoming a Christian. "Ideally, one should receive the enduement of power immediately after conversion," Pearlman writes.[84] This means that at the time of conversion the believer has met the conditions for being baptized in the Holy Spirit. J. R. Williams adds: "The conditions just mentioned are best understood not as requirements in addition to faith but as expressions of faith."[85] In another place he uses the terms "context" and "atmosphere" to convey the idea of "expressions of faith": the "atmosphere of prayer," the "context of obedience," an "atmosphere of surrender," and an "atmosphere of expectancy."[86]

So then these are not conditions or requirements added to those for salvation. Faith, prayer, obedience, surrender, and expectancy simply produce the context, or atmosphere, in which the baptism in the Holy Spirit is received. This may occur on the same occasion as regeneration, as in the case of Cornelius (Acts 10:44–48), or it may occur at some later time, as in the case of the Samaritans (Acts 8:14–19).

One final point needs to be made with regard to being baptized in the Holy Spirit. Since the only prerequisite is conversion and the only condition is faith, it is important to emphasize that every true Christian believer is a candidate for this experience. Pentecostals believe strongly that every believer should receive this special enduement of power for service. For example, the Assemblies of God doctrinal statement on the baptism in the Holy Spirit begins as follows: "All believers are entitled to and should ardently expect and earnestly seek the promise of the Father.... With it comes the enduement of power for life and service."[87] To read about the experience in the Book of Acts is not enough. Even to acknowledge its doctrinal soundness and to know that the experience is for Christians today is not enough. For the

---

[83]Horton, *Book of Acts,* 47.

[84]Pearlman, *Knowing the Doctrines,* 316–17.

[85]J. R. Williams, "Baptism in the Holy Spirit," 48.

[86]J. R. Williams, *Renewal Theology,* vol. 2, 295–305.

[87]*Minutes of the 44th Session of the General Council,* 129.

Church to have the dynamic dimension of life in the Spirit operating within it, individual believers must personally receive this baptism in the Holy Spirit.

CONCLUSION

The contemporary Church is taking a fresh look at the doctrine of the baptism in the Holy Spirit. The persistence and growth of the Pentecostal movement are largely responsible for the new interest in this doctrine. And whatever one's view of this movement, all agree that the focused attention on the person and work of the Holy Spirit is overdue. Carl Henry observes: "To neglect the doctrine of the Spirit's work . . . nurtures a confused and disabled church."[88]

Further developments in the discussion of the doctrine of the baptism in the Holy Spirit are crucial. Thus far the twentieth-century Pentecostal movement has succeeded in restoring the experiential dimension of the Spirit's dynamic presence to a significant segment of the Church. Pentecostals believe that recovery of the doctrine and experience of being baptized in the Holy Spirit is comparable to the Reformation's recovery of the doctrine of justification by faith. Even Dunn, who disagrees with much of Pentecostal doctrine, hopes that "the importance and value of the Pentecostal emphasis will not be lost sight of or ignored."[89]

New Testament scholars find it difficult to deny the validity of a unique, dynamic experience of being baptized in the Holy Spirit on biblical grounds. Dunn declares: "It goes without saying that in Acts the reception of the Spirit was a very vivid and 'concrete' experience."[90] Pentecostals see no reason why this should not be the same today. Further, they testify that indeed they do experience just such a vivid and concrete experience in being baptized in the Holy Spirit. Such a distinctive experience infuses the Church today with the dynamic, experiential quality of spiritual life that was normal for the New Testament Church.[91]

STUDY QUESTIONS

1. What are the chief beliefs and practices regarding the baptism in the Holy Spirit that have marked the Pentecostal movement?

---

[88]Henry, *God, Revelation,* vol. 4, 272.

[89]Dunn, *Baptism,* viii.

[90]Ibid., 102, n.24.

[91]Fee, *Gospel and Spirit,* 119.

2. What are the basic arguments for regarding the baptism in the Holy Spirit as an experience separate from conversion?

3. Why is it more important for us to focus on separability rather than subsequence?

4. What are the evidences that show that Luke and Acts are theological, not just historical, and are designed and intended to teach?

5. What are the biblical grounds for taking speaking in tongues as the initial physical evidence of the baptism in the Holy Spirit?

6. What is the relation of the baptism in the Spirit to the fruit of the Spirit and the gifts of the Spirit?

7. How would you answer those who say that the baptism in the Holy Spirit with its evidence of speaking in tongues is not available today?

8. What is the purpose of the baptism in the Holy Spirit and why is this important both theologically and practically?

9. What are the best ways to encourage believers to accept being baptized in the Holy Spirit?

CHAPTER FOURTEEN

Spiritual Gifts

David Lim

The revival and growth of Christianity around the world, especially in third world countries, is a powerful testimony that spiritual gifts are at work advancing God's kingdom. The Pentecostal-charismatic movement grew from 16 million in 1945 to 405 million by 1990.[1] The ten largest churches in the world belong to this movement.

Exegesis of all New Testament passages bearing on spiritual gifts is beyond the scope of this chapter.[2] Rather, my focus will be on Paul's main teachings on gifts in the Church and in the believer's daily life-style, how gifts and fruit interrelate, and how to exercise gifts. Biblical teaching without practice is disappointment, practice without solid teaching is dangerous. On the other hand, scholarship should lead to practice, and practice may enlighten scholarship.

The baptism in the Holy Spirit is covered in chapter 13. I must emphasize, however, three key purposes of the outpouring at Pentecost.

First, believers were equipped with power to do God's work, just as in Old Testament days. The anointing of the Spirit in the Old Testament was for every ministry God desired to raise up: priests, tabernacle craftsmen, military leaders, kings, prophets, musicians. The purpose of the anointing

---

[1]David B. Barrett, "Statistics, Global," *Dictionary of Pentecostal and Charismatic Movements,* ed. Stanley M. Burgess, Gary B. McGee, and Patrick Alexander (Grand Rapids: Zondervan Publishing House, 1988).

[2]For more detailed studies of the passages see David Lim, *Spiritual Gifts: A Fresh Look* (Springfield, Mo.: Gospel Publishing House, 1991); Stanley M. Horton, *What the Bible Says About the Holy Spirit* (Springfield, Mo.: Gospel Publishing House, 1976).

was to equip people for service. It is in this context that Luke and Acts discuss the Spirit's anointing. In Luke 1 through 2, an anointing rested upon two elderly priests, Zechariah and Simeon. Two women, Elizabeth and Mary, were anointed to miraculously bear and raise children. John the Baptist was filled with the Spirit from his mother's womb, not to be a priest like his father, but to be the prophet and forerunner of the Messiah. Likewise, in Acts, the focus is on an anointing that empowered the Church and changed the world.

Second, all are priests in this new community. From Israel's beginnings as a nation, God desired that all Israel would become a kingdom of priests and a holy nation (Exod. 19:5–6). The priestly role included worship, prayer, teaching, edifying, reconciling, counseling, loving, building relationships, and bringing hurting people to God. So believers, "like living stones, are being built into a spiritual house to be a holy priesthood, offering spiritual sacrifices acceptable to God through Jesus Christ" (1 Pet. 2:5).

Third, this community is a prophetic one. Moses told Joshua, " 'I wish that all the LORD's people were prophets and that the LORD would put his Spirit on them!' " (Num. 11:29). Joel spoke of the Spirit's coming upon all flesh to prophesy (Joel 2:28–29). Jesus identified His own ministry as prophetic (Isa. 61:1–3; Luke 4:18–19). Peter equated the experience at Pentecost with the fulfillment of Joel's prophecy (Acts 2:16–18). Paul said, "You can all prophesy in turn so that everyone may be instructed and encouraged" (1 Cor. 14:31). Clearly the Church serves in a prophetic role, bringing God's presence and powerful Word to sinners, to ethical issues, and to nations and individuals.

Paul moves beyond the Luke-Acts context. He focuses on activating the gifts, developing the fruit, walking in the Spirit, and building the believers in the local church to maturity. Paul saw the Church as an interdependent, interactive organism—with Christ as its head—walking righteously and powerfully in anticipation of the Lord's return. To grasp Paul's view of the Church, one must understand the gifts.

THE CHURCH THROUGH THE EXPRESSION OF GIFTS

Paul's greatest thinking on the Church was written to the churches at Rome, Corinth, and Ephesus. These churches were instrumental to Paul's missions strategy. Romans 12, 1 Corinthians 12 through 13, and Ephesians 4 were written from the same basic outline.[3] Although these were different churches, the same principles are emphasized. Each parallel passage serves as insightful commentary on the others. Paul discusses our part in exercising the gifts, the Trinity's modeling of unity and diversity,[4] unity and diversity in the body of Christ, our ethical relationships to each other—and all in light of Christ's ultimate judgment.

The context of these parallel passages is worship. After expounding on great doctrines of the faith (Rom. 1 through 11), Paul teaches that the fitting response is a life of worship (Rom. 12 through 16). First Corinthians 11 through 14 also has to do with worship.[5]

Chapters 1 through 3 in Ephesians present a rapturous worship of God. Ephesians 4 reveals the Church as a school of worship where we learn to reflect the master Teacher. Paul saw his converts as presented in living worship before God (Rom. 12:1–2; 2 Cor. 4:14; Eph. 5:27; Col. 1:22,28). Knowing doctrine or correcting falsehood is not enough; one's whole life must praise God. Worship is at the heart of church growth and revival.

Study the following chart.[6] Note the flow of the argument, the similarities, and the purposes Paul has in mind. Then, we shall examine key principles from these passages.[7]

---

[3]To go one step further, see Roger Stronstad, *The First Epistle of Peter,* (Vancouver, B.C.: CLM Educational Society, 1983), 52–53. He diagrams a parallel between 1 Pet. 4:7–11; Rom. 12:6–21; and 1 Cor. 12:1 to 13:13. Peter's teaching "closely parallels Paul's teaching, though it is briefer and reverses the Pauline order." For example, Peter's discussion on love in light of the coming of the Lord (1 Pet. 4:7–9) comes before his discussion on the exercise of gifts (4:10–11).

[4]Omitted in the Rom. 12 passage.

[5]Ralph Martin, *The Spirit and the Congregation: Studies in 1 Corinthians 12–15,* (Grand Rapids: Wm. B. Eerdmans, 1984), includes chapter 15 in the worship section, suggesting a problem at Corinth of overrealized eschatology. He feels some Corinthian teachers denied the need of resurrection because they felt the kingdom of God was fully available now for those who could reach that spiritual level.

[6]Lim, *Spiritual Gifts,* 186–87.

[7]Note Ernst Käsemann, *Commentary on Romans* (Grand Rapids: Wm. B. Eerdmans, 1980), 325–50; Markus Barth, *Ephesians: Translation and Commentary on Chapters 4–6,* Vol. 34A, The Anchor Bible Series (Garden City, N.Y.: Doubleday and Company, Inc., 1974), 451; Max M. B. Turner, "Spiritual Gifts Then and Now," *Vox Evangelica* 15 (1985): 28–29. These scholars see more than incidental similarities between these passages. Käsemann sees the whole of Rom. 12 related to the charismatic community. Barth sees in Eph. 4 the charismatic community (the church) involved in worship and action in light of the ultimate judgment of God. Turner shows the correlation between 1 Cor. 12 and Rom. 12. For too long scholars have missed the intimate interrelationships in these passages.

Main Points	Romans	1 Corinthians	Ephesians
Incarnational Nature	**12:1**	**12:1–2**	**4:1–3**
Exhortation	12:1	12:1	4:1
The Body	12:1	12:2	
The renewed mind	12:2	12:3; 13:1	4:2–3,17–24
Humility	12:3	13:4–5	4:2
Meekness or loss of control?	12:1–2	12:2–3; 13:4–7	4:2,14–15
Unity and Diversity in the Trinity		**12:4–6**	**4:4–6**
Spirit		12:4	4:4
Lord (Jesus)		12:5	4:5
Father		12:6	4:6
The Lists of Gifts—The Diversities of Ministries (see also 1 Pet. 4:9–11)	**12:6–8**	**12:7–11, 28–31** 13:1–3	**4:7–12**
Functional nature	12:6-8	12:11,29–30	4:7,11
Guidelines	12:6-8	12:7,12,19, 24–25; 13:1–31	4:11–12
One Body, Many Members	**12:4–5**	**12:12–27**	**4:15–16,25–29**
Edification	12:6–16	12:7; 14:3–6,12, 16–17,26	4:12–13,15–16,25–32
Empathy	12:10,15	12:25–26	4:16
Sincere Love	**12:9–21**	**13:1–13**	**4:25–5:2**
Hate evil, cling to good	12:9	13:6	4:25
Gentleness	12:10	13:4–5	4:32
Zeal	12:11	13:6	4:1,23–24
Rejoicing, steadfastness, prayer	12:12	13:7–8	
Fellowship with those in need	12:8,13	13:3	4:28

Main Points	Romans	1 Corinthians	Ephesians
No unwholesome talk	12:14	13:11	4:26–29
Humble mindset	12:16	12:25; 13:4	4:2,23
No revenge	12:17	13:5	4:31
Be at peace	12:18		4:3
Handling anger	12:17	13:5–6	4:26,31
Final Judgment	**12:19–21**	**13:10,12**	**4:13,15,30**

CHAPTER

14

Spiritual
Gifts

INCARNATIONAL NATURE OF GIFTS

Believers play a vital part in gift ministry. Note the parallels in these passages. Romans 12:1–3 tell us: Present your bodies and minds in spiritual worship. Test and approve what is the good, pleasing, and perfect will of God. Similarly, 1 Corinthians 12:1–3 says, Don't lose control of your bodies. Don't be deceived by false doctrine, but let Jesus be Lord. And Ephesians 4:1–3: Live worthy of God's calling. Have the right attitude. Keep the unity of the Spirit.

Our bodies are the temple of the Holy Spirit and therefore must be involved in our worship. Many pagan religions teach a dualism of body and spirit. For them the body is evil and is a prison, while the spirit is good and to be set free. This view was common in Greek thought.[8]

Paul urged the Corinthians not to let their pagan past influence them. They used to lose control; consequently, they might utter anything, claiming it was the Spirit of God. The biblical context of gifts does not indicate lack of control. Rather, as the Spirit works through us, we are more in control than ever. We yield our body and mind as instruments to God. We bring a transformed mind, placing it under the lordship of Christ, and come with a meek, disciplined spirit to allow God to work through us. Ephesians 4:1–3 tells us that right attitudes lead to effective ministry. Thus, body, mind, and attitudes become instruments for the glory of God.

There are various views on the nature of the gifts of the Spirit.[9] One view sees the gifts as natural abilities. For ex-

---

[8]See *Plato,* vol. 1, trans. Harold N. Fowler (Cambridge, Mass.: Harvard University Press, 1914), 485.

[9]Charles W. Carter, *1 Corinthians,* The Wesleyan Bible Commentary Series (Peabody, Mass.: Hendrickson Publishers, Inc., 1986), 200. Harold Horton, *The Gifts of the Spirit* (Springfield, Mo.: Gospel Publishing House, 1975), 27.

ample, a singer has the gift of music or a physician (via medical science) has the gift of healing. But human talent alone can never change the world.

Another view sees gifts as totally supernatural. This view denies human involvement, saying the Spirit bypasses the mind. It sees the flesh as being evil and capable of only distortion. A danger here is that few will have the courage to exercise the gifts. Most will feel unworthy, viewing the gifts as mystical or beyond their comprehension. They will fear making a mistake. However, sharing a gift is no proof of holiness or of spiritual attainment.

A third view is biblical: The gifts are incarnational. That is to say, God works through humans. Believers submit their minds, hearts, souls, and strength to God. They consciously, willingly surrender their all to Him. The Spirit supernaturally enables them to minister beyond their abilities, at the same time expressing each gift through their life experience, character, personality, and vocabulary. The gifts manifested need to be evaluated. That in no way lessens their effectiveness, but rather allows the congregation to test their biblical truth and edification value.

This incarnational principle is seen in God's revelation to humankind. Jesus is Immanuel, God with us (fully God and fully human). The Bible is both a divine book and a human book. It is divine, inspired by God, authoritative, and inerrant. It is human, reflecting the writers' backgrounds, life situations, personalities, and ministries. The Church is both a divine and a human institution. God established the Church or there would be no Church. Yet, we know how very human the Church is. God works through jars of clay (2 Cor. 4:7). The mystery hidden for ages and now revealed to the Gentiles is "Christ in you, the hope of glory" (Col. 1:27).

We need not fear. What God ministers through your life, ministry, and personality may be different from what He ministers through others. We should not feel that we are guaranteeing perfection when we share a gift. It can be lovingly evaluated by others. We need only to be a yielded vessel seeking to build the body of Christ. Rather than focusing on whether a gift is fully from God, we ask the more vital question, How can I best meet the needs of others and touch sinners for Christ? Understanding this principle alone can set the Church free to manifest gifts.

UNITY AND DIVERSITY IN THE TRINITY

CHAPTER

14

Spiritual
Gifts

To the superficial reader, the discussion of the Trinity at this point may seem not to add to the argument. But for Paul, it is foundational. Even the order in which Paul lists the Trinity in 1 Corinthians 12:4–6 and in Ephesians 4:4–6 is the same: Spirit, Lord, Father. Each Person of the Trinity plays a vital part in the manifestation of gifts. Sometimes the roles overlap, but essentially the Father superintends the plan of salvation and the expression of the gifts from beginning to end. Jesus redeems us and sets us in our place of ministry in His body, the Church. The Holy Spirit gives gifts.[10] The Persons of the Godhead have different roles, yet vitally work together, blending into a perfect unity of expression.

The Church must seek to reflect the nature of the Lord whom it serves. There is no schism, divisiveness, carnal pride, self-glorification, one-upmanship, or usurping of another's territory in the Trinity. We must not do what we want, but what we see God doing (John 5:19). What a difference this will make in the way we share the gifts! Ministered properly, the gifts reveal the coordination, the creative unity in diversity, and the wisdom and power the Spirit blends together. Everywhere we see diversity. The Church may face a variety of situations. But we can have this blending by the Spirit into a greater unity through falling before God, whose holiness, power, and purposes are awesome.

THE DIVERSITIES OF MINISTRIES

There are many gifts. No list is meant to be exhaustive. Twenty-one are listed in these passages. All are complementary; none is complete in and of itself. For example, every gift in Romans 12:6–8 can usefully be applied to a counseling situation. Some gifts in one list are easily related to gifts in other lists. The gift of giving may manifest itself in showing mercy, helps, exhorting, or even martyrdom. With this overlap we find that some gifts are easily identified by all, such as tongues and interpretation, healings, and miracles. Yet other gifts, such as a word of wisdom, a word of knowledge, discerning of spirits, and prophecy, may need evaluation to identify.

---

[10]Christ also gives gifts, but the gifts He gives are people taken captive by the ascended Christ and given as gifts "to prepare God's people for works of service, so that the body of Christ may be built up" (Eph. 4:12; see also 4:7–11).

*Synergy
the whole
is greater
than its
parts*

(Personal inadequacy leads to interdependence. Each believer is only one member of the body of Christ; each needs other members. Together they can do what one individual cannot do.) Even when people manifest the same gifts, they do it differently, with different results. No one person shares any gift in its total manifestation. Each needs the sharing of others as well.

Gifts must be shared in love because of the danger of miscommunication, even by those with the sincerest intentions. And every gift must be evaluated by others.

Paul is intensely practical. In the area of gifts he says nothing that is merely theoretical. Most writers have divided the gifts in 1 Corinthians 12:8–10 into the three categories of mind, power, and speech, with three gifts in each category. This is a convenient and logical division. However, based on 1 Corinthians 12:6–8 and 1 Corinthians 14:1–33, I believe Paul is making a functional division.[11]

From Paul's use of the Greek word *heteros* ("another of a different kind") twice in 1 Corinthians 12:6–8, we can see the gifts divided into three categories of two, five, and two gifts respectively.[12]

Teaching (and Preaching) Gifts:
The message of wisdom
The message of knowledge

Ministry Gifts (to the church and world):
Faith
Gifts of healings
Miraculous powers
Prophecy
Distinguishing between spirits

Worship Gifts:
Different kinds of tongues
Interpretation of tongues

---

[11]Lim, *Spiritual Gifts,* 65–86.

[12]Both Fee and Carson propose that if grouping is valid at all, it is based on the use of *heteros.* Carson gives no definite conclusions. Donald A. Carson, *Showing the Spirit: A Theological Exposition of 1 Corinthians 12–14* (Grand Rapids: Baker Book House, 1987), 37. Fee sees categories one and three as having to do with the problems at Corinth, while the middle category has to do with supernatural gifting. Gordon D. Fee, *The Epistle to the First Corinthians: The New International Commentary on the New Testament* (Grand Rapids: Wm. B. Eerdmans, 1987), 590–91. My view is that Paul is not only solving a Corinthian problem, but also teaching on the purposes and exercise of the gifts.

This threefold division may be confirmed by dividing 1 Corinthians 14 into paragraphs. In 1 Corinthians 14:1–5 the functional value of tongues and interpretation may be compared with prophecy in teaching (14:6–12), worship (14:13–19), evangelism (14:20–25), and ministry to the Body (14:26–33). Note that Paul adds the further category in 1 Corinthians 14:20–25 of "a sign . . . for unbelievers" (v. 22).

Teaching, ministry of the body of Christ to the Church and the world, and worship are three keys to a healthy local assembly. If we have only two of these categories without the third we have imbalance and open ourselves to difficulties. For example, if we have teaching and ministry without strong worship, we may lose much of the thrust of revival. We may readily burn out in our zeal in serving. If we have teaching and worship without practical ministry, our members will become lazy, ingrown, ineffective, critical, and divisive.

If we have ministry and worship without solid teaching, we open ourselves to extremes and wildfire that will damage the revival in both the short term and long term. Without the complement of all, the local assembly cannot reach its potential. Clearly Paul is interested in practical results, that which will set the body of Christ free for discipling, evangelism, unity, and Christlikeness.

The Message of Wisdom. Teaching, seeking divine guidance, counseling, and addressing practical needs in church government and administration may offer occasions for the gift of wisdom. It must not be limited to church worship or classroom experiences, however. It teaches people to grow spiritually as they apply their hearts to wisdom and make choices leading to maturity. The gift, however, is a message, proclamation, or declaration of wisdom and does not mean that those ministering the message are necessarily wiser than others.[13]

Our faith must not rest on human wisdom (1 Cor. 2:5). If we lack wisdom, we are exhorted to ask God for it (James 1:5). Jesus promised His disciples "words and wisdom that none of your adversaries will be able to resist or contradict" (Luke 21:15). That this promise referred to a supernatural gift is shown by His command "not to worry beforehand how you will defend yourselves" (Luke 21:14). The gift therefore goes beyond both human wisdom and human preparation.

The Message of Knowledge. This gift has to do with teaching

---

[13]For examples see Acts 4:8–14,19–21; 6:1–10; 10:47; 15:13–21; 16:35–40; 21:12–14.

the truths of the Word of God.[14] It is not the product of study as such. Donald Gee described it as "flashes of insight into truth that penetrated beyond the operation of . . . unaided intellect."[15] The gift may include such things as God's sharing of His secrets, as when He revealed to the Old Testament prophets a time of rain, an enemies' plans, or secret sins of kings and servants. It may also include Peter's knowledge of Ananias and Sapphira's deception and Paul's declaration of a judgment of blindness upon Elymas.[16]

Faith. Fervent prayer, extraordinary joy, and unusual boldness accompany the gift of faith. It is not saving faith, but rather a miraculous faith for a special situation or opportunity, such as Elijah's confrontation with the prophets of Baal (1 Kings 18:33–35). It can include special ability to inspire faith in others, as Paul did on board the ship in the storm (Acts 27:25).

Gifts of Healings. In Acts many responded to the gospel and were saved after being miraculously healed. In the Greek, both "gifts" and "healings" are plurals. Therefore, it seems that no one is given *the* gift of healing. Rather, many gifts are available to meet the needs of specific cases at specific times. Sometimes God heals sovereignly and sometimes He heals according to the faith of the sick person. The one who prays for the sick person is just the agent; the sick person (whether sick physically or emotionally) is the one who needs and actually receives the gift. In every case, God alone must receive the glory. We, however, can join our faith with that of the sick person, and together set the climate of love and acceptance so that gifts of healing may flow. In the body of Christ are power and strength to meet the needs of the struggling member. This is the incarnational aspect of healing.

Miraculous Powers. Here Paul combines two plurals, of *dunamis* (deeds of mighty supernatural power) and *ener-*

---

[14]Donald Gee, *Concerning Spiritual Gifts* (Springfield, Mo.: Gospel Publishing House, 1949), 27–34, 110–19; S. Horton, *What the Bible Says,* 271–72. Calvin, Alford, Morris, Pulpit, Hodge, Meyer, and a host of Pentecostal writers would agree with this definition. Hodge, Osiander, and MacGorman add the dimension of a special communication of truth given in such a way that believers may appropriate it readily.

[15]Donald Gee, *Spiritual Gifts in the Work of the Ministry Today* (Springfield, Mo.: Gospel Publishing House, 1963), 29.

[16]Howard Carter, *Spiritual Gifts and Their Operation* (Springfield, Mo.: Gospel Publishing House, 1968), 27–36; H. Horton *Gifts,* 51–64. L. Thomas Holdcroft, *The Holy Spirit: A Pentecostal Interpretation* (Springfield, Mo.: Gospel Publishing House, 1979), 148–50.

gēma (effectual results). This gift may have to do with providing protection, giving provision, casting out demons, altering circumstances, or passing judgment. The Gospels record
miracles in the context of the manifestation of the messianic
Kingdom (or rule), the defeat of Satan, the power of God,
and the presence and work of Jesus. The Greek word for
"miracle" (Gk. *sēmeion*) in John emphasizes its sign value to
encourage people to believe and keep on believing. The Book
of Acts emphasizes the continuation of that work in the Church,
showing that Jesus is Victor.

Prophecy. In 1 Corinthians 14 prophecy refers to a variety
of Spirit-inspired spontaneous messages in the speaker's known
language "for their strengthening [especially of faith], encouragement [especially to move ahead in faithfulness and
love], and comfort [that cheers and revives hope and expec-
tation]" (14:3).[17] By this gift the Spirit illumines the progress
of God's kingdom, reveals the secrets of peoples' hearts, and
puts the sinner under conviction (1 Cor. 14:24–25). A good
example is Acts 15:32, "Judas and Silas, who themselves were
prophets, said much to encourage and strengthen the brothers."

Those regularly used in the gift of prophecy were called
prophets. However, any believer may exercise this gift. But
it must be weighed carefully (and publicly) by "the others,"
that is, by the congregation (1 Cor. 14:29).[18] This evaluation
should include what God's purpose is, so that everyone may
learn and benefit.

Distinguishing between Spirits. "Distinguishing" and "spirits" are both plurals in the Greek. This indicates that there
are a variety of ways this gift may be manifested. Since it is
mentioned directly after prophecy, many scholars see it as a
companion gift involved in the "weighing" (1 Cor. 14:29).[19]
It involves a supernaturally given perception, differentiating
between spirits,[20] with an emphasis on protecting us from
the attacks of Satan and evil spirits (cf. 1 John 4:1). It allows
us to use all the gifts and the Word of God to work against

---

[17]See S. Horton, *What the Bible Says*, 225.

[18]Wayne Grudem, *The Gift of Prophecy in The New Testament and Today*
(Westchester, Ill.: Crossway Books, Good News Publishers, 1988), 71–74.

[19]Fee, *First Corinthians*, 596–97.

[20]This may include "a wide range of the human, the demonic, even the
angelic." J. Rodman Williams, *Renewal Theology*, vol. 2 (Grand Rapids:
Zondervan Publishing House, 1990), 389.

Satan in order to then make a full, free proclamation of the gospel.[21]

Like the other gifts, this one does not raise an individual to a new level of ability. Nor does it give anyone the power to go around looking at people and telling of what spirit they are. It is a specific gift for a specific occasion.[22]

Tongues and Interpretation. The gift of tongues needs interpretation to be effective in the congregation. Some say that because these two gifts are listed last they are the least in importance. Such a conclusion is insupportable. All five gift lists in the New Testament have the gifts in a different order.

In the gift of tongues the Holy Spirit touches our spirit. We find liberation to exalt God's goodness and we edify ourselves: We are built up spiritually as we speak. Then when the interpretation allows the congregation to understand what is being said, they are encouraged to worship. Praise more readily follows the gift of tongues and interpretation than it does the gift of prophecy. Prophetic utterances are more instructional.[23]

The basic difference between the phenomenon of tongues in Acts and in 1 Corinthians is purpose. The tongues in Acts were for self-edification, giving evidence that the disciples had indeed received the promised gift of the Holy Spirit, which was to clothe them "with power from on high" (Luke 24:49; Acts 1:4–5,8; 2:4). They did not need to be interpreted. In Corinth the purpose was to bless others in the congregation, making communication necessary.

The Holy Spirit distributes all these gifts according to His creative power and sovereignty. The word "determines" (1 Cor. 12:11 Gk. *bouletai*) is in the present tense and strongly implies His continually creative personality. We notice also that the Bible does not draw lines between the gifts. "Encouraging" is part of the gift of prophecy in 1 Corinthians 14:3, yet in Romans 12:8 it is treated as a separate gift. The categories of gifts given above are not mutually exclusive.

---

[21]Some examples may be found in Acts 5:3; 8:20–23; 13:10; 16:16–18.

[22]S. Horton, *What the Bible Says,* 277.

[23]Many take the latter part of 1 Cor. 14:5 to mean that interpreted tongues may have a message for the congregation. See S. Horton, *What the Bible Says,* 226.

Further, different personalities may express gifts differently in a variety of ministries.[24]

In 1 Corinthians 12:4–6 Paul taught that there are differing gifts (Gk. *charismatōn*), ministries (Gk. *diakoniōn*), and results (Gk. *energēmatōn*). That is to say, each gift may be exercised through different ministries and come up with different God-honoring results. By using the analogy of different members of the Body, by saying God sets members in the Body as He desires, giving us different ministries with various results, and by the outline of 1 Corinthians 14, we see Paul is talking about practical function. Incredible diversity, incredible practicality!

By looking at the parallel passages and adding 1 Peter 4:10–11 we see the following thirteen guidelines:[25]

1. We should exercise our ministry in proportion to our faith.[26]

2. We should concentrate on our known ministries and develop them.

3. We must maintain the right attitudes: give generously, lead diligently, show mercy cheerfully.

4. We all have different functions in the body of Christ and must understand the relationship to the whole body.

5. Gifts are to edify all, not just the individual.[27]

6. One must have no sense of superiority or inferiority, for every member is equally important.

7. The gifts are given to us, we do not attain them. God's will and sovereignty determine distribution. His specific action of placing these gifts in the Church is shown by the following verbs: given (Rom. 12:6), appointed (1 Cor. 12:28), and gave (Eph. 4:11). Paul further affirms in 1 Corinthians 12:28–31 that we should concentrate on the known ministries God has given us.

---

[24]For a discussion of other categories of gifts see S. Horton, *What the Bible Says,* 191–94, 263–70, 279–82.

[25]These guidelines come from Lim, *Spiritual Gifts,* 208–10.

[26]There are many different views on what the faith to prophesy is: our grasping hold of faith and exercising it; power given each Christian; an amount of faith given to each of us; gifts we receive as a result of our faith; or, simply, faithfulness. All these definitions have valid biblical foundation. The best definition is incarnational, involving both God and man: "Faith is the *pneuma* given to the individual and received by him. It is objective to the degree that none can establish or take it for himself and subjective because each must receive it for himself without being represented." Käsemann, *Romans,* 335.

[27]Uninterpreted tongues do edify the individual (1 Cor. 14:4). This is not wrong, for we need to be built up spiritually. However, messages in the public meeting need to be interpreted.

8. At the same time, these are God-given manifestations, not human talents. God continuously grants gifts as He wills.[28] We should be open to them all. If we know what part of the Body we are and what our ministries are, we can then channel the gifts effectively.

9. Though we may exercise a gift to its fullest, apart from love, such exercise is futile. Clearly, we have only partial knowledge; we can share only partial knowledge. Gifts are continually given according to one's measure of faith (not once for all). The gifts must be tested; they fall under the commands of our Lord. The focus is the maturation of the church, not the greatness of the gift. These truths should lead us to a humility, an appreciation for God and others, and an eagerness to obey Him.

10. Enabling ministries have a special function to set others free for their ministries and develop maturity in them. Apostles, prophets, evangelists, and pastor-teachers are gifts to the Church. They appear in historical order in the founding and establishing of the church, rather than some ranking of authority (1 Cor. 12:28).[29]

11. We are to minister God's grace in its various forms. First Peter 1:6 reveals the Christians had suffered grief through its various forms; God has a special grace to minister to each grief. A faithful minister will know how to minister to the need. We are to choose carefully when, where, and how to best minister the grace of God.[30]

12. We must minister confidently in the strength of the Lord. We must not be timid or do it in our own strength. This is similar to Romans 12 where we are to minister in proportion to our faith, but Peter goes on to say, speak as if you are speaking the "very words of God"! (1 Pet. 4:11).

13. Finally, God must have all the glory. All the gifts are graces with which God has blessed His Church.

––––––––

[28]1 Cor. 12:11 *diairoun* (giving, distributing) is present active participle, thus continuous action.

[29]Fee, *First Corinthians,* 619–20.

[30]*Poikilois* is used both in 1 Pet. 1:6 and 4:10. Eph. 3:10 describes the boundless variety of the wisdom of God that will be revealed to the rulers and authorities in the heavenlies through the Church (the stronger form, *polypoikilos* is used). Markus Barth, *Ephesians: Translation and Commentary on Chapters 1–3,* Vol 34, The Anchor Bible Series (Garden City, N.Y.: Doubleday and Company, Inc., 1974), 345, suggests the adjective "manifold," or "various," "probably denoted originally, the character of an intricately embroidered pattern, e.g., of a cloth or flowers.' What a picture of God's sovereign design! We may see the intricate pattern of trials; God sees the ultimate results.

ONE BODY, MANY MEMBERS

Unity in the body of Christ is based upon our common experience of salvation. We are all sinners, saved by the grace of God.

Paul's analogy of the Church to the physical body may have been too earthly for some of the spiritually minded Corinthians. They may have felt the flesh was evil. But God created the body. No better picture of the Church's interaction and interdependence has been developed. From the time of his conversion on the Damascus Road, Paul realized that to persecute the Church was to persecute Christ himself (Acts 9:4). The Church was nothing less than Christ's body! Paul held a very high view of the Church and its value to God. We have a calling and an obligation to build one another up, help each member find a personal ministry, work at clear communication, and commit our lives to one another.

The world tears down. Christians build up. But to do so, we ourselves must be built up first. Speaking in tongues edifies us personally (1 Cor. 14:4,14,17–18). If we are not built up, we will be ministering from empty vessels; the devotional life of many modern Christians is sadly lacking. Prayer and worship are our inner strengths. But if we seek only personal edification we become like spiritual sponges. We must seek to build others up.

"Do not let any unwholesome talk come out of your mouths, but only what is helpful for building others up" (Eph. 4:29). A healthy body builds itself up, being able to heal its own injuries. Edification should be the Church's highest goal in its use of the gifts. Love builds up. The purpose of gifts is to build up. God's people must be supportive, open, forgiving, reaching out. What an example such action would be to the world!

True fellowship is built on empathy. We are to rejoice with those who rejoice, mourn with those who mourn (Rom. 12:15). We are to have equal concern for each other. If one part suffers, every part suffers with it; if one part is honored, every part rejoices with it (1 Cor. 12:25–26). This is the opposite of the way the world thinks. It is easier to rejoice over those who weep, and weep over those who rejoice; human nature prefers to be judgmental. But believers belong to one another. My victory is your cause for rejoicing because the kingdom of God is advanced. Your victory lifts me up as well. Ephesians 4:16 gives us the culminating point of empathy: The Body builds itself up in love, as each supporting ligament receives from Christ and does its work.

The word for "supporting" is *epichorēgias.* It is used in Greek literature to describe a choir leader bearing responsibility for abundantly supplying his group's needs, or a leader supplying amply his army's needs, or a husband caring amply for his wife, giving her abundant support. If each one fulfills his or her responsibility, health and vitality will result. What release of power can happen in this kind of fellowship! Miracles and healings can readily take place in such an atmosphere. If we can truly be supportive and open to one another, we will set Christians free to reach out to God for solutions.

We all have different personalities, temperaments, and ministries. We must have a commitment to understand one another and set each other free to minister. This takes time. As we learn about others, we begin to appreciate them, honor them, and grow in fellowship.

SINCERE LOVE

After each of Paul's expositions on gifts, he beautifully crafts three messages from one outline on love (Rom. 12:9–21; 1 Cor. 13; Eph. 4:17–32). Each passage is creatively different, yet the same essential points are there.

Anders Nygren says of Romans 12, "One needs only to make 'love' the subject throughout 12:9–21 to see how close the contents of this section are to 1 Corinthians 13."[31] The whole of Romans 12 is a unit. Paul is not speaking of two separate topics, gifts and ethics (love).[32] The context of Romans 12 is the urgency of the hour, how good must triumph over evil, and living in light of Christ's return. The people of God must live in right relationships. Neither may 1 Corinthians 12 and 13 be divided: The context for exercising gifts is love. Ephesians 4 emphasizes the dramatic difference between our former life as pagans and our new life in Christ. That is why we must speak the truth in love. Love is practical when we build one another up.[33] The three passages develop separate themes. Yet, good over evil, love in the exercise of gifts, and truth in love are three dynamic expressions of love—Mes-

---

[31]Anders Nygren, *Commentary on Romans* (Philadelphia: Fortress Press, 1972), 425. See also Lim, *Spiritual Gifts,* chap. 3.

[32]Käsemann, *Romans,* 344.

[33]All three passages on love have hymnic elements. Barth, *Ephesians 4–6,* 429, 435, 473, 557.

siah's army marches with a different methodology! Our life-style is key to effective utilization of gifts. (We will discuss this more in the section on "The Relation Between Gifts and Fruit.")

ULTIMATE JUDGMENT

Leave room for God's wrath, for it is written: "It is mine to avenge; I will repay," says the Lord. On the contrary: "If your enemy is hungry, feed him; if he is thirsty, give him something to drink. In doing this, you will heap burning coals on his head." Do not be overcome by evil, but overcome evil with good (Rom. 12:19–21).

When perfection comes, the imperfect disappears. ... Now we see but a poor reflection; ... then we shall see face to face. Now I know in part; then I shall know fully, even as I am fully known (1 Cor. 13:10,12).

Reach unity in the faith ... become mature, attaining to the whole measure of the fullness of Christ.... In all things grow up into him who is the Head, that is, Christ.... Do not grieve the Holy Spirit of God, with whom you were sealed for the day of redemption (Eph. 4:13,15,30).

By examining these verses we see that all three passages on love are written in the context of Christian conduct in light of Christ's coming. We do not build our ethics around philosophy, culture, or convenience, but around the righteousness of God and in view of His final judgment. Theologians call it eschatological conduct.[34]

The quotation in Romans 12:20 is from the wisdom literature of the Old Testament (Prov. 25:21–22). In these pas-

---

[34]From the Greek *eschatos,* "last"; thus, conduct in view of the prophesied last things. In the early 1900s, men like Albert Schweitzer spoke of Paul's theology as "interim ethics." They said both Jesus and Paul were mistaken about the timing of the Second Coming. Therefore, Paul and others wrote about a radically demanding life-style, an interim ethic, assuming the Lord's return was very near. This supposedly explained some of the strong statements on holiness, marriage, loving enemies, and doing good to those who hurt us. But such explanation was based on mistaken assumptions about the authority and inspiration of the Word. The principles articulated by Paul are valid for the whole Church Age; the Church is *meant* to live as if Jesus could come at any moment, expressing a faithful witness whether Christ should come in two days or two centuries. God is Judge, His righteousness will be vindicated, the Church will be victorious, and Satan will be vanquished. Our lives, empowered by the Spirit, should express that.

sages on love, Paul has quoted Jesus, the Law, the wisdom literature, and shared a prophetic concern for the poor and needy. This is God's wisdom. To "heap burning coals on his head" may picture an Egyptian practice of placing a pan of burning charcoal on one's head, indicating penitence. If so, Paul is saying that through love we may lead the person to repentance. Let the enemy realize it is God he is fighting, not us. We do not want to defeat our human enemies; we wish to win them to the Lord! We must not succumb to Satan's pressures. The warfare is between the evil and the good. We can conquer evil only with the good.

First Corinthians points to a time of total clarity when we shall see face-to-face and know fully as we are fully known. It is the day of the coming of the Lord; it is Judgment Day. All our actions will be judged by His standards (Rom. 2:6,16).

In Ephesians, references to the prophesied last things are plentiful. Paul speaks of the future point of full maturity and the day of redemption. We are sealed by the Spirit until that day (Eph. 4:13,15,30). But until then, the gifts are God's empowerment to accomplish the task of building up each other and touching the world. Paul's commands throughout Ephesians require radical, dramatic, urgent change. We must make the most of every opportunity (Eph. 5:16). Christ seeks to present to himself a radiant Church (Eph. 5:27). Slaves and masters have a Master in heaven to answer to (Eph. 6:9). And lastly the word "finally" (Eph. 6:10) may be a reference to the final days when the day of evil comes (Eph. 6:13).

The parallel passages of Romans 12, 1 Corinthians 12 through 13, and Ephesians 4 focus on the life-style of the Spirit-filled believer—finding a place in the body of Christ, exercising gifts in love, witnessing and serving in anticipation of the coming of the Lord.[35] This is the Church's purpose and calling. The Church is a school. As believers gather, they learn how to minister spiritual gifts and be disciples of Christ. As they go forth, they apply God's power to life's situations. We must be open to the Spirit's speaking through us at any time.

THE FUNCTIONS OF GIFTS

Paul contrasts the value of tongues and prophecy in four different functions in 1 Corinthians 14: teaching (verses 6–12), worship (verses 13–19), signs for the unbeliever (verses

---

[35]Käsemann, *Romans,* 349; and Barth, *Ephesians 4–6,* 526, speak of eschatological conduct.

19–25), and **ministry to the local church** (verses 26–33). He cautions against abuse of gifts and gives positive guidelines for their exercise. I have summarized key instructions below.

First, the key test of effectiveness of function is clear communication. Communication is complex. Clear communication strengthens (14:3). It is easy to misunderstand intentions, attitudes, and words. We are imperfect. That is why gifts must be exercised in love. Because of Corinthian selfishness, superspirituality, and abuse of tongues, many problems arose. Paul reemphasizes the need for clarity of direction and instruction. Thus he uses prophecy to represent all gifts exercised in the known tongue. Tongues when interpreted encourage the congregation to worship (1 Cor. 14:2,5,14–15) and is a gift as valid as prophecy. There is no biblical basis for calling some gifts superior and some inferior. Each gift does its unique work if communicated properly. Paul gives the analogy of flute, harp, or trumpet when played without a clear sound: There is no benefit to anyone else. In the local assembly we need to be clear on God's direction and what He says to all of us.

Paul valued the gift of tongues for worship (1 Cor. 14:2), for self-edification (14:4), for praying (14:14), for giving thanks (14:17), and as a sign to the unbeliever (14:22). Paul prayed, sang, praised, and spoke in tongues (14:13–16). In fact, he spoke in tongues more than the exuberant Corinthians. He speaks of the value of praising and praying in the Spirit and in the understanding.

The Corinthians had abused the gift: Some may have believed they were speaking in angelic languages (1 Cor. 13:1), services may have been dominated by tongues (14:23), and speakers apparently interrupted each other to give their utterance in tongues, disregarding interpretation (14:27–28).

A key question of this passage is, Does Paul encourage or discourage periods of corporate worship where all speak in tongues? Two views are held on 1 Corinthians 14:23–24. One is that Paul was minimizing the use of tongues, and only two or three people at most should ever speak in tongues in a service for any reason. This rules out corporate worship in tongues. From this point of view, Paul is making a minimal concession to the tongues speakers at Corinth.[36]

---

[36]This question arises not only among some charismatics, but also among Pentecostals, especially in the western world. William Richardson, "Liturgical Order and Glossolalia in 1 Corinthians 14:26c–33a," *New Testament Studies* 32 (January 1986): 148, says, "[I]n an era when great stress is placed on a more cerebral approach to religion, it is conceivable that Paul's counsel might easily stress the need for more 'praying with the Spirit' rather than less."

A second view sees 1 Corinthians 14:23–24 as two parallel statements: everyone speaks in tongues; everyone prophesies. If 14:23 means everyone speaks in tongues "at the same time," then 14:24 also refers to everyone prophesying "at the same time." Obviously 14:24 cannot mean that. Everyone prophesying "at the same time" would be seen as confusion, if not lunacy. Paul does allow prophesying "one at a time" in ministry to the congregation (1 Cor. 14:31). Since prophecy represents all the gifts in the understood language, other gifts may be ministered prophetically.

The only limitation on prophetic messages is that which is "fitting and orderly." The Corinthians were not to dominate the whole ministry time with tongues by speaking in tongues "one at a time." A limit is placed on two or at the most three utterances in tongues and interpretations (14:27). The basic purpose of tongues and interpretation is worship and encouraging others to worship God. If a congregation is ready to worship, it should need only two or three exhortations to move freely into this area.

In Acts 2:4; 10:44–46; and 19:6, all spoke in tongues in corporate worship. No interpretation is mentioned. Everyone worshiping in tongues at the same time cannot be denied from a biased interpretation of 1 Corinthians 14:2,22–25. Paul and Luke do not contradict each other.

If the primary purpose of tongues is to praise God, tongues with interpretation will encourage others to worship. To then deny people the opportunity to respond by worshiping God in tongues would seem to be a contradiction. Paul would then be saying "You may worship with understanding in the assembly, but not in Spirit. Only two or three are allowed that experience." What about meetings where prayer is the primary agenda? Or meetings to encourage others to receive the infilling of the Spirit? Or times of sheer celebration? When God touches us in any public gathering, we respond; however, our response must not draw undue attention to ourselves.

The Pentecostal-charismatic revival around the world has not apologized for genuine celebration. It has encouraged wholehearted worship. The individual spirit is not suppressed for the corporate Body. Rather, it is fully utilized and controlled for that Body. Tongues have not been relegated to the prayer closet. Indeed, we learn through the model of corporate worship how to worship in private. If all understand that there are mutual times to praise God, no confusion exists.

All gifts have sign value and content value. The gift of tongues focuses on the sign aspect: It arouses attention.

Prophecy focuses on content, though in some instances it has great sign value. It confronts people with God's Word and invites repentance. Palmer Robertson points out: " 'Tongues' serve as an indicator; 'prophecy' serves as a communicator. 'Tongues' call attention to the mighty acts of God; 'prophecy' calls to repentance and faith in response to the mighty acts of God."[37]

Healings have sign value for those observing and content value for those healed. Words of wisdom and knowledge focus more on content value, though at times may have great sign value. The issue is pragmatic: What is God doing and what is needed in the situation?

Although nothing can surpass or take the place of God's Word,[38] God continually speaks to churches and individual needs. We gather together to hear from God afresh; He speaks to our present situation through His Word and through the body of Christ. If we all come with a readiness to minister gifts and the opportunity is given, then ministry can flow. An ideal place for such ministry is the small setting, such as a cell group. Tight schedules, large crowds, and shy members militate against such sharing in a Sunday worship service (14:26).

Paul's hand was steady as he guided the Corinthian church. Many were united against him. Some Corinthians thought they were superspiritual, feeling the Kingdom had arrived, that there was no need for resurrection if they truly had faith. They alone had the fullest manifestation of gifts.[39] Yet Paul does not react against them. He gives positive guidelines. First, prophecy must be clearly communicated so that it strengthens, encourages, and comforts (14:3).

Second, the needs of believers, unbelievers, and inquiring seekers must be considered. Believers need to be instructed and edified (14:1–12), to give thanks along with other believers (14:17), to mature in thinking (14:20), to minister a variety of gifts (14:26–33), to evaluate gifts (14:29), and to be discipled (14:31). Unbelievers need to understand what

---

[37]O. Palmer Robertson, "Tongues: Sign of Covenantal Curse and Blessing," *Westminster Theological Journal* 38 (Fall 1975), 52.

[38]See chap. 3, pp. 63–64, 68, 82, 112.

[39]This is the thrust of present scholarly understanding of the Corinthian situation. See Fee, *First Corinthians;* Carson, *Showing the Spirit;* and Martin, *The Spirit and the Congregation.*

is happening in a service (14:16),[40] to awaken to the fact that God is speaking (14:22), and to have the secrets of the heart laid bare before God (14:25) so that they may believe. Inquiring seekers need to understand what is happening in a service (14:16), to not be confused (14:23), and to know that God is truly among us (14:25).

Third, it is important not to react. Paul says to the Corinthians, "eagerly desire spiritual gifts" (14:1), be zealous for them and channel the zeal to build the Church (14:12), and don't forbid speaking in tongues (14:39). Fear of extremes often causes churches to shrink from a complete gift ministry. The baby is thrown out with the bath water, the fire is feared because of possible wildfire, or, as the Chinese proverb puts it, we trim the toe to fit the shoe. On the other hand, to zealously follow an untested position that has little biblical base is to ask for problems that will hinder the very revival we all seek.

Sometimes we judge mercilessly and legalistically those who make mistakes. Then we dampen the will of others to begin ministry in gifts. Extreme fear of error may cut us off from God's blessing. We must build on solid theology. But we must also teach in love, test revelations by what other mature believers in the Body sense from the Spirit, and develop, not deny, what may be a genuine gifting from the Spirit (14:39–40).

Fourth, accountability must be demanded. Throughout this chapter, Paul reveals that the corrections to excess are a healthy exercise of gifts, evaluation, and accountability. We are responsible to others.

In the worship service the highest priority is to build others up. Our lives, our methodology, and our utterances all have to be exercised in the context of what God is doing in the Church and must be willingly subject to the evaluation of the Body of believers. Excesses come when people exercise gifts or make statements that are accountable to no one.

THE RELATIONSHIP OF THE GIFTS AND THE FRUIT

What is the relationship between the Spirit's gifts and the Spirit's fruit? Fruit has to do with growth and character; life-

---

[40]Although the Greek word in 1 Cor. 14:16 is *idiōtēs,* and refers to the inquiring seeker, I see this verse applying to the unbeliever also. We must assume that all who come have a hunger in their hearts to encounter the living God, whether they are aware of it or not. Therefore even unbelievers, *apistos* (14:22), should have a basic understanding of what is happening in the service, even though they do not understand everything.

style is the key test of genuineness. The fruit in Galatians 5:22–23 are the "nine graces which make up the fruit of the Spirit—the life-style of those who are indwelt and energized by the Spirit."[41] Jesus said, "By their fruit you will recognize them" (Matt. 7:16–20; see also Luke 6:43–45). These aspects of fruit are intricately interwoven in the three gift passages. In the gift passages and in Galatians the fruit qualities flow horizontally in ministry to one another (1 Cor. 13; Rom. 12:9–10; Eph. 4:2). The prime theme of Galatians is not justification by faith, though this seems dominant. Rather, the purpose of justification by faith is the walk in the Spirit.[42]

The same emphasis on the walk, or life, in the Spirit prevails in lessons to the churches in Asia Minor (Ephesus), Achaia (Corinth), and Italy (Rome).

Let us look at the fruit qualities in Galatians 5:22–23 and see how they are interwoven with the exercise of gifts in Paul's gift passages.

LOVE

The Greek *agapē* is most frequently used of a loyal love and is seen in its highest degree as a revelation of the very nature of God. It is a steadfast, freely given love. Love is central to each passage (Rom. 12:9–21; 1 Cor. 13; Eph. 4:25 to 5:2). In fact, it is the ethical principle, the motivating force, and the proper methodology for all ministry.[43] Without love there is little benefit to others and none to the person exercising the gift. Misunderstandings arise and the Church is divided; people are hurt. Love is the foundation from which gifts can

---

[41]F. F. Bruce, *Commentary on Galatians,* The New International Greek Commentary Series (Grand Rapids: Wm. B. Eerdmans, 1982), 251.

[42]The common view, from Martin Luther to F. F. Bruce and Roland Fung in their excellent commentaries on Galatians, is that the key theme is justification by faith. Gordon Fee (while teaching Galatians at Asia Pacific Theological Seminary, Baguio, Philippians, in January 1988) suggested in conversation that the thrust of Galatians was walking in the Spirit: Gal. 3:3—after beginning with the Spirit; 5:16—live by the Spirit; 5:18—led by the Spirit; 5:22—the fruit of the Spirit; 5:25—live by the Spirit, let us keep in step with the Spirit; 6:1—you who are spiritual, restore him gently; 6:8—sow to please the Spirit; there is no law in this realm. Just as the climax of Romans is chapter 8 on the dynamic walk in the Spirit so this is the focal point of Galatians. The Holy Spirit is referred to thirteen times.

[43]See Jack V. Rozell, *Christian Counseling: Agape Therapy,* Belgium: International Correspondence Institute, 1988, for a developed discussion on how love affects the whole life-style of the believer.

be ministered and the context in which the gifts are to be received and understood.

JOY

The Greek *chara*, which we translate "joy," includes the idea of an active delight. Paul speaks of rejoicing in truth (1 Cor. 13:6). The word is also closely connected to hope. Paul speaks of being joyful in hope (Rom. 12:12). It is the positive expectation that God is at work in the lives of fellow believers, a celebration of our ultimate victory in Christ. Joy is the heart of worship: It turns drudgery into delight, lifts ministry to a higher plane, and puts sparkle in the ministry of the gifts.

PEACE

The Greek *eirēnē* includes the ideas of harmony, health, wholeness, and well-being. In relationships, we are to live at peace with all men (Rom. 12:18); in exercise of gifts, God is not a God of disorder but of peace (1 Cor. 14:33); and in the assembly, we are to strive to keep the unity of the Spirit through the bond of peace (Eph. 4:3). Peace is foundational to moving ahead in unity, to receiving the ministries of others, and to learning even through failure. The exercise of gifts should lead to greater unity and peace. Because we realize the need for each other and that God's blessings flow through others, because no gift is exercised in perfect manifestation, and because we all make mistakes, it teaches us to be tender to one another and seek the greater good of all.

PATIENCE

The Greek word *makrothumia* means patience with people. It includes long-suffering and forbearance that endures the misconduct of others and never seeks revenge. The Roman Christians were soon to face persecution. During stress and suffering Christians may have less patience with each other, so Paul urges them to be "patient in affliction" (Rom. 12:12). In sharing gifts Paul starts with patience with people and ends with patience with circumstances (1 Cor. 13:4,7). It takes time for us as the Church to mature through all our differences, differences stemming from culture, education, even personality. Therefore, Paul urges us to be completely humble and gentle; be patient (Eph. 4:2).

For full ministry in the Spirit, we need to learn together,

make mistakes, grow, forgive, and confront in love without having a critical spirit. This takes patience. Whenever God's power is manifested, it is important that we look to Him instead of looking at our inadequacies. Then we will not do the hasty thing or go to extremes that will hurt the Church.

KINDNESS

The Greek word *chrēstotēs* reminds us of Christ, the supreme example of kindness. Patience and kindness are coupled together in line one of Paul's description of God's love (1 Cor. 13:4). Paul urges us to follow Christ's example, to be kind and compassionate to one another, forgiving (Eph. 4:32). Harshness is not the way of the body of Christ. Mutual esteem and respect are. Kindness is a healing balm that unites us as we learn to appreciate each other. Even the gifts are the result of God's kindness to us. We do not deserve the gifts, nor do we deserve each other's kindness. We receive both with grateful hearts and then share both unconditionally.

GOODNESS

The essential meaning of *agathōsunē,* translated "goodness," is generosity that flows out of a holy righteousness given by God.[44] Paul says, "Share with God's people who are in need. Practice hospitality" (Rom. 12:13). "Share with those in need" (Eph. 4:28).

The basic reason for all the gifts is to bless others. Goodness, or generosity, brings a practical, down-to-earth caring about people where they are. The Early Church knew how to care for one another. If anything, it erred on the side of generosity.

Although careless generosity is not good stewardship, our motive is to show generosity. A danger is that we show generosity in order to boast. In all our giving, we must have love, or it is of no benefit (1 Cor. 13:3).

FAITHFULNESS

The Greek term *pistis* often means trust expressed in a life of faith. In this context it has the meaning "faithfulness." This reflects the nature of our Heavenly Father. He is dependable.

---

[44]Walter Bauer, *A Greek-English Lexicon of the New Testament and Other Early Christian Literature,* 2d edition. Translated by F. Wilbur Gingrich and Frederick W. Danber (Chicago: University of Chicago Press, 1979), 3. Also Bruce, *Commentary on Galatians,* 252.

He is patient toward us no matter how often we fail Him. He is committed to us: true to His great plan of redemption! We are to reflect God's image to others. We must be dependable. If we are committed to one another, God can truly pour forth the Spirit's blessings. Faith, hope, and love (1 Cor. 13:13) are qualities by which we build relationships with each other. Through unity of faith we can attain to the whole measure of the fullness of Christ (Eph. 4:13). Growth in this fruit builds confidence in God. It can be a stepping-stone to the gift of faith.

The gift of faith heads the category of five powerful gifts in 1 Corinthians 12:8–10 that have to do with the ministry of the body of Christ to one another.

GENTLENESS

The Greek word *prautēs* has the idea of a humble gentleness that is more concerned about others than oneself. Jesus said, "Blessed are the meek for they will inherit the earth" (Matt. 5:5). The cognate word *praus* means "meek," "humble," or "gentle." Aristotle described the word as the mean between excessive proneness to anger and incapacity for anger.[45] A meek person has a disciplined spirit. Potentially, all spiritual blessings are available to this person. While the word itself is not used in Romans, this gentle spirit is described in Romans 12:12–14 as able to persevere in affliction and persecution, faithfully serving in prayer and practical care. It is a gentleness that knows God is in control and does not take revenge (Rom. 12:17–21; Eph. 4:26). Instead of being rude, self-seeking, and easily angered, we show gentleness, protect others, and persevere (1 Cor. 13:5,7). Our attitude toward each other is to be completely humble, gentle, free from arrogance (2 Cor. 10:1; Eph. 4:2).

Too often spiritual manifestations have been expressed in harsh, manipulative, and authoritarian ways. Rather than encouraging others in gift ministry, such a manner actually stifles it, especially ministry from the whole Body. How important that we learn to guard each other's dignity and save each other's pride. Be gentle!

SELF-CONTROL

The word *egkrateia* means "self-control," including control of sensual passions; thus it includes chastity.[46] This emphasis

---

[45]Aristotle, *Ethic. Nicomachaen*, 2.1108a.
[46]Bauer, *Greek-English Lexicon*, 216.

is not in the gift passages of Romans 12 and 1 Corinthians 12 through 14. Earlier treatment of this subject is thorough, however. The new life is contrasted sharply with the old life in Ephesians 4:17–22. Immorality has no place in a person who seeks to be used of God. Without holy living accompanying the gifts, the name of Christ is shamed. Truly effective ministry is blunted. Miracles may continue for a while but God receives no glory. Miracles do not guarantee holiness, but holiness is vital to true spiritual ministry.

Gifts and fruit are carefully interspersed. When gifts are emphasized at the expense of fruit, a terrible price is paid. Christian character, holy living, and relationships with fellow believers are pushed aside with the rationale that God blesses us with power. Thus the work of the Holy Spirit is diluted. We must not divorce power from holiness. God purifies us to use us. Christians whose lives are consistent and unfettered by carnality will be free from condemnation. They will have a good reputation. They will be powerful.

Although neither age nor experience can guarantee spiritual maturity, the fruit of the Spirit produces it. Spiritual maturity means a greater understanding of the Spirit of God and the needs of people. Then we can best exercise gifts. Maturity develops sensitivity to the Spirit, so one might understand how the gifts operate and when they are needed. We will see the balance and not move to extremes. We will look to long-term results, not just short-term blessing. We will seek a revival that lasts until Jesus comes.

Spiritual maturity helps us relate to people. We understand people better and realize how to best minister to them. We must strive for unity. As people watch our character and conduct, they will develop trust in us; the Early Church chose its first seven deacons on the basis of how they were "known" (Acts 6:3). A good reputation and affirmation by others are crucial to a full release of the Spirit in ministy to one another and for the Church to grow.

The fruit becomes the method of exercising the gifts. All the fruit is wrapped up in love, and any gift, even in its fullest manifestation, apart from love is nothing. "On the other hand, a genuine fullness of the Holy Spirit is bound to produce fruit also because of the quickened and enriched life of communion with Christ."[47] Knowing the awesome, love, power and grace of God should make us tender vessels. We do not de-

---

[47]Donald Gee, *The Fruit of the Spirit* (Springfield, Mo.: Gospel Publishing House, 1975), 15.

serve the gifts. God empowers us anyway. We will become Kingdom people, ready to bring in the harvest. We rise to a new realm.

THE EXERCISE OF GIFTS

Leadership plays the vital role in bringing a congregation to the point of exercising gifts. The following suggestions may prove helpful:

1. Provide opportunities. At board meetings, staff meetings, and staff retreats, give time for all to listen to the Spirit and share impressions God makes on their hearts. See if God is saying similar things to several people and if what is said relates to where the assembly is at that point. Pray for the sick, exercise ongoing concern, and if they are not healed immediately, pray again.

2. Create awareness. Share how God speaks to you and guides you. Testify to miracles that take place among your people. Allow gifts to be manifested naturally; don't force or demand them. We are not here for the short term, but the long term. The Spirit may minister in a service, a cell-group meeting, or in personal conversation.

3. Develop a readiness to share. Gifts are manifested when people expect to hear from God, whether by Scripture, song, or a gentle whisper. Teach about hearing God's voice. Give practical application from your life and others. When worship leaders give time to share gifts, they themselves should be prepared to share. Don't allow long periods of silence to be characterized as "nobody heard from God." Rather we should say, "Let us wait in the presence of an awesome God, and if anyone has something to share, do so." Then positively conclude by sharing impressions God made on you. As leader, be ready to share. Model that expectancy.

4. Create a spirit of acceptance. Your people must not feel self-conscious or that others are judging them. Start in small groups. Use a natural tone of voice. Do not worry about mistakes, but teach gently, in love. The church is a school, and we are learners.

5. Evaluate. Comment after three or four share, whether choruses, Scripture, exhortations, or even testimonies. Does it fit the local assembly? Teach your people to be sensitive to what God may be saying in the whole service and what God is doing in your fellowship. Relate Scripture to what is said. Your positive reinforcement is crucial. To say nothing is to cause confusion or dampen further exercise of gifts.

Affirm what can be affirmed, set aside as tentative whatever needs evaluation. Try not to criticize, but evaluate in love. Evaluation gives people a sense of security, a framework within which they can minister gifts.

6. Spend time in prayer. Build a church on prayer. There is no substitute for waiting on God. Practice the presence of God all day. God will speak to you and through you. Your people will pray only if we as leaders pray.

7. Understand cultural differences. The church I pastor is multicultural. The way I preach to the Chinese-educated and English-educated is different, even if the basic content is the same. In recent years we have seen many differences in worship style and in people's expectations as we talk to them before praying for them. In worship, some like hymns, some like choruses, some like music reflecting their culture and heritage. Some use complex interviews before prayer, some just pray over a large group of people. Be simple. Gifts shared in a natural tone of voice encourage others to share. We also encourage more dynamic sharing. We need not force each assembly into the same worship style or the same way of manifesting gifts as another.

8. Strong worship releases gifts. Worship leads to an expectancy of encountering our awesome God. That is where the miraculous can readily happen. Build to one or two peaks of worship. If people know there is a best time to share gifts, they will do so. But if you wait after every chorus, this is not as effective and may cause an uncertainty of whether or not to share. Worship should follow similar patterns. It gives people a sense of security and a freedom to worship in that context. To change the pattern every week is not so effective. Incorporate psalms, hymns, and spiritual songs. Make room for the whole congregation to feel they can touch God in worship.

9. Often I will hear from God first, give opportunity for others to share, then affirm what God has already said to me. This encourages others. I may say, "God has touched my heart with three thoughts, but before I share, I want to give you opportunity to minister to one another." Then, when people who have never exercised the gifts before realize that they are in tune with the Lord, just as the leadership is, it will encourage them to share more.

10. The channel for spiritual gifts is ministry. Mark 16:17 points to signs that follow those who believe. As we are active in reaching a world, ministering where God places us, we become usable vessels. Many miracles in Acts happened in

the course of everyday life. The Christians were on their way to a temple, to witness, to suffer for Christ's sake. If we care to reach out to people in need, we become bearers of God's gifts, even at unusual times and in unusual situations. The gifts happen when Christians are "on the way" in service for the Lord.

11. Focus on the whole process. Gifts flow through people. What is God doing in their lives? Also, the words are important. What is actually being said? The context is vital. Do the messages shared relate to the life of the church or the flow of that service? The response is important. How are we to receive what has been shared? Always remember: The goal is to build the Church and to win the lost for Christ. The mission of the Church is the number one priority. The gifts are to be seen in the light of the total work God is doing among His people.

When we do not understand the nature and purpose of gifts, we focus on the wrong issues. The question is not primarily what my gifts are, but how to exercise gifts to build the Church. Rather than equate gift manifestation with spirituality, we value and seek the contribution of all, strong or weak. Rather than assuming the gifts are totally supernatural and, therefore, infallible, we must recognize that the gifts are ministered through fallible humans and need to be tested. We grow as we learn how to exercise them. Rather than whether women have a place in public ministry, the question should be proper methodologies of ministry.

Rather than debating which is the greatest or least gift, we need to share God-given gifts in love. A church that ignores the dynamic of Spirit-led ministry misses what God is doing in the world. Providing and modeling the healthy flow of gifts is the biblical alternative to fear of extremes.

If gifts are exercised only in a Sunday service, then they are not essential to the growth of a church. If we focus only on the more spectacular gifts, they are seen as spiritual extras. On the other hand, if we view gifts as an essential element of everyday life, crucial to effective ministry, we can develop a sensitivity to the Spirit that frees us to minister all the gifts. None are spiritual extras that make us superior to others.

The Gospels do not formally conclude. Matthew records the great commission that the Church must yet fulfill under the authority given to Jesus. Mark abruptly concludes, leaving the reader in silent awe and expectation of the powerful, all-sufficient Lord who could interrupt any situation, no matter how desperate. Luke-Acts is really "one integrated whole."[48] Luke 24 is not the conclusion. The Early Church carried on the mission and work that Christ performed on earth. And Acts does not conclude. John, by including the personal post-Resurrection commission to Peter in John 21, clearly implies the Church will carry on until Jesus returns.

All of Paul's epistles were written to proclaim the Lord's death "until He comes." The gifts of the Spirit were given as a deposit, "a first installment," in anticipation of the full inheritance that the Church shall receive. Hebrews encourages us to "run with perseverance the race marked out for us" (Heb. 12:1). Revelation concludes with "Amen. Come, Lord Jesus" (Rev. 22:20). As has been pointed out, there can be no new revelations given that will supersede or bypass the Bible; at the same time, God continues to speak to and through His Spirit-empowered believers.

Every pastor needs to listen to the Spirit about developing the local assembly in gift ministry. Each assembly must aggressively press into the area of spiritual gifts. Everything that Christians do is their worship to God. He is the audience and our lives are the stage of redemption on which our worship is expressed. The preacher does not labor in the Word to impress his congregation, but to present it as an offering to the Lord. We do not act Christianly toward one another or work in the assembly to impress others with our spirituality and churchmanship; we do it all as an act of worship to God.

This liberates our ministries. We are no longer bound by the fear of human opinions but seek only to be faithful to our calling in Christ. From the overflow of worship we find God's supernatural enabling. Burnout will be precluded by rest from the Lord and encouragement from other believers. Saints will come alive and get excited. The gifts will flow as part of the normal life-style of the assembly to edify and evangelize.

The individuals of such an *ekklēsia* will each be a powerful witness (Acts 1:8), possessed of a deep filial affection for the Lord, fearing lest they should hurt or grieve Him. The demonstration of God's power will be the normal function of their community (Acts 4:33), who will be held in favor and respect by all and to whose company will come a daily increase as souls are saved (Acts 2:47).[49]

---

[48]F. F. Bruce, *Commentary on the Book of Acts* (Grand Rapids: Wm. B. Eerdmans, 1975), 18.

[49]R. B. Chapman, "The Purpose and Value of Spiritual Gifts," *Paraclete* 2:4 (Fall 1968): 28.

Amen! May it be so. May the Church fulfill its potential and touch the world.

STUDY QUESTIONS

1. The Corinthian church went to excess. Ultimately it could have torn itself apart or quenched the ongoing exercise of gifts. Discuss the problems of the Corinthian church's views that would have caused this.

2. What prejudices or past experiences keep churches from moving into spiritual gifts more freely?

3. Paul did not react to Corinthian extremism. Instead, he balanced it and guided it. He wanted a dynamic, free-flowing, Spirit-led church. Discuss how he did this.

4. With every new teaching has come a reaction to that teaching. How can a leader keep people from being so gullible that they accept such teachings? How can one take the best of such teaching rather than simply being reactionary about it?

5. Is your local church clear on its vision, calling, unique direction, and mission? What is it? Be as specific as you can. Are the energies of the members of the assembly focused in that direction? Can you see how the gifts would move your church in that direction.

6. Can any part of your church program function well apart from the Holy Spirit? Do careful soul-searching in this area. If gifts are optional, they will soon become unnecessary.

7. Develop a step-by-step approach for moving your church toward a balanced gift ministry. Then evaluate. For example, why do some steps seem to fail or to lead to a dead end? What is a realistic timetable for achieving an ideal worship and a free flow of gifts?

8. Gifts and fruit of the Spirit must flow together. Discuss what happens when fruit is missing. Discuss how exciting it is when each quality of fruit is manifest along with the gifts.

9. Can you think of times when God moved through you and you perhaps did not realize it was a gift of the Spirit? Describe this experience.

10. Is holiness a prerequisite to exercising the gifts? Why or why not?

11. Discuss whether a person possesses a gift or it is given as the need arises.

CHAPTER FIFTEEN

Divine Healing

Vernon L. Purdy

Divine healing has received a renewed emphasis in the preaching, teaching, and practice of many churches today. It has been an essential element in the current success in evangelism and missions. Like the Early Church, many have prayed that God would confirm the gospel through healings wrought in Jesus' name (see Acts 4:24–31).[1]

There are at least four major reasons for believing that God heals today. First it is found in the Bible, and the Bible, inspired as it is by the Holy Spirit, is for us today. The same Jesus Christ revealed in the Scriptures as Healer is the same Lord we serve today. Hebrews 13:8, "Jesus Christ is the same yesterday and today and forever," fits in well with the overall message of Hebrews. There is a great continuity in the person, character, and work of Christ after His death, resurrection, and ascension.

The second reason for believing in divine healing is the fact that it is in the atoning work of Christ. The Bible's teaching of healing parallels its teaching of salvation.[2] Salvation includes the healing of our lives in all aspects, and it all "issues from [the] atonement."[3] All the "good and perfect gifts" from above are the result of the cross of Christ. As will be pointed out later, Matthew understood the Suffering Servant passage

---

[1]Howard Clark Kee, *Good News to the Ends of the Earth: The Theology of Acts* (Philadelphia: Trinity Press International, 1990), 9.

[2]Hans-Ruedi Weber, *The Cross: Tradition and Interpretation,* trans. Elke Jessett (Grand Rapids: Wm B. Eerdmans, 1979), 55.

[3]Paul S. Fiddes, *Past Event and Present Salvation: The Christian Idea of Atonement* (Louisville: Westminster/John Knox, 1989), 4.

(Isaiah 53) in terms of Jesus' healing ministry being part of His atoning work.

The third reason for believing in divine healing is found in the convergence of the Bible's teaching on salvation and on the nature of humankind. If a human being is not a disjointed association of body, soul, and spirit, and is in a very real way a unity, then salvation will apply to all the facets of human existence. This is a truly biblical theme which needs renewed emphasis—the whole gospel is for the whole person.

The last reason for commitment to the teaching of divine healing is the belief that salvation is ultimately to be understood as a restoration of the fallen world. God is against human suffering, for suffering is the result not of the will of God but a consequence of the Fall. Redemption ought to be understood as God's plan for restoring all of creation, especially humankind.

THE ORIGIN AND NATURE OF SICKNESS

Where did human suffering originate? Was it part of God's plan or was it an effect of something that contradicted the divine intention for creation? The Bible as a whole teaches the latter position. This is not to say that suffering was unanticipated by God. Quite the contrary. Scripture is very clear on this point. Jesus Christ is the Lamb "slain from the creation of the world" (Rev. 13:8). It did not take God by surprise.

The issue before us, and it is a very important issue, is whether or not God himself is the one who willed human suffering. The Bible makes it clear that He is not. Human suffering is the consequence of the Adamic Fall, not the will of God. God judges human evil. Adam as our representative in the Garden brought judgment upon all of us. This act did not spring from the volition of God but of Adam. God's desire is clearly to bless His creation, not to harm it (Gen. 12:3; James 1:17).

This points us to the source of human suffering: our fallenness. It is Adam and his progeny who are to blame, not God. James Crenshaw points out that in the Old Testament the issue was not theodicy, or how we can justify God, but "anthropodicy," or how can we justify human beings.[4]

The Adamic Fall was the result of rebellion, a rebellion that was catastrophic in its results and cosmic in its proportions.

---

[4]James L. Crenshaw, ed., *Theodicy in the Old Testament* (Philadelphia: Fortress Press, 1983), 1–12.

The world in its Edenic state was a stranger to human suffering, and in God's New Heaven and Earth suffering will again be a stranger. It is fundamentally contrary to God's will.

Some might respond that suffering would not exist if it were not God's will. Two answers should suffice in response. First, it exists under the auspices of God's righteous reign, so it is tolerated by God, but it is not of His making or desire. Second, there are many things in this world, like sin itself, that are quite contrary to the will of God, but are nonetheless tolerated for the time by God.

But just as the Bible informs us that there will be a time when sin is vanquished, so too it informs us of a time when human suffering will be no more (Rev. 21:4). The fact sin and suffering exist is no indication that they are God's will. God has chosen to allow sin and sickness, but both are fundamental contradictions of God's intention for His creation. The world and all that was in it was, according to the earliest testimony of Scripture, "very good" (Gen. 1:31). There is no biblical basis for supposing it was God's desire that the creation be racked with the pain of the Fall. This was a human doing that God went to extremes to correct by His plan of redemption.

The dominion of the powers of darkness also affects the present reality of suffering. Herman Ridderbos says that "not only sin, but also suffering, oppression, anxiety, and adversity belong to the dominion of Satan" (see 1 Cor. 5:5; 2 Cor. 12:7; 1 Thess. 2:18; 1 Tim. 1:20).[5] The present experience of the created universe is due, not to the will of God, but "to the fact that the cosmos is the world turned away from God."[6]

Though we should not construe nonbiblical sources as doctrinally authoritative, some of them demonstrate very clearly that Judaism itself held that human suffering was a consequence of human rebellion, not the divine will: "Although things were created in their fulness, when the first man sinned they were corrupted, and they will not come back to their order before Ben Perez (the Messiah) comes."[7] This text shows clearly the messianic expectations of the Jewish people in the time of Jesus. No wonder His miracles elicited such excitement and wonder. They were the signs of the Messiah

---

[5]Herman Ridderbos, *Paul: An Outline of His Theology,* trans. J. R. DeWitt (Grand Rapids: Wm. B. Eerdmans, 1975), 92.

[6]Ibid.

[7]Genesis Rabbah 12.6 in *Midrash Rabbah,* Rabbi H. Freedman, trans. (New York: The Soncino Press, 1983), 92.

who would restore the fallen world and its inhabitants. Jesus' miracles of healing speak of the desire of God to restore broken humanity physically as well as spiritually.

SICKNESS IN THE OLD AND NEW TESTAMENTS

In Jewish thought, physical suffering and sin were always associated to some degree.[8] It is worth noticing that in the account of the Fall in Genesis 3, human suffering made its first appearance in the form of physical hardship and the pain of childbirth. The judgment is that God would "greatly increase . . . pains in childbearing" (Gen. 3:16). These words, however, do not imply that there already was suffering, only that suffering itself would be intense.[9] The Hebrew word used is *'itsts^{e}bōn* which comes from the word *'ātsav:* "to find fault with," "hurt," "trouble," "grieve." It carries with it the idea of pain, both physical and emotional. The same word is used of the judgment on both the woman and the man. As soon as the disobedience was committed, the beauty and harmony of existence was shattered. Anyone who takes the Bible as the Word of God must recognize the direct causal connection at this point between human transgression and suffering. Walther Eichrodt writes that the event of the Fall is a "falling out of the line of development willed by God"; the will of God for humanity is here contradicted.[10] At the Fall it is not just that Adam and Eve are confronted with their own eventual demise, but that the creation is now enslaved to the hostile powers of death.

Israel tended to link disease to both human sin and divine anger. There are many biblical passages that link sin and sickness and, consequently, forgiveness and healing (Pss. 6; 13; 22; 31; etc.). Most often the Old Testament presents affliction and sickness as the "consequences of human sin."[11]

---

[8]R. T. France, *Matthew* (Grand Rapids: Wm. B. Eerdmans, 1985), 158; David Hill, *The Gospel of Matthew* (Grand Rapids: Wm. B. Eerdmans, 1972), 161.

[9]Henri Blocher, *In the Beginning: The Opening Chapters of Genesis* (Downers Grove, Ill.: InterVarsity Press, 1984), 180.

[10]Allen P. Ross, *Creation and Blessing: A Guide to the Study and Exposition of Genesis* (Grand Rapids: Baker Book House, 1988), 137, 146–47. Walther Eichrodt, *Theology of the Old Testament,* vol. 2, trans. J. A. Baker, (Philadelphia: The Westminster Press, 1967), 406.

[11]Christoph Barth, *God with Us: A Theological Introduction to the Old Testament* (Grand Rapids: Wm. B. Eerdmans, 1991), 35. Howard Clark Kee, *Medicine, Miracle and Magic in New Testament Times* (New York: Cambridge University Press, 1986), 15.

Peter Craigie points out that in Psalm 38:3, "The link between sin and punishment is expressed most forcefully in the parallelism of verse 4, where divine indignation and human sin are linked as a primarily spiritual diagnosis of a physical complaint." Another example of this phenomenon is found in Psalm 107:17, "Some . . . suffered affliction because of their iniquities." "Affliction" here means "sickness" and demonstrates that "this verse emphasizes the connection between illness and sin."[12]

There are many more examples that could be mentioned from the Old Testament. Uzziah the King of Judah was afflicted with leprosy due to a sacrilegious act (2 Chron. 26:16–19). We also have the case study of Asa in 2 Chronicles 16:11–12. Asa was rebuked not for going to physicians, but for not trusting Yahweh. The text declares that he "did not seek help from the LORD, but only from the physicians." This should not be understood as a prohibition against physicians. Rather it highlights the importance of trusting the Lord and demonstrating that when one is ill, one ought to look to Him.[13]

Though Jesus denied a mechanical dogma of retribution there are numerous indications within the New Testament that sickness and sin were sometimes connected. Ulrich B. Mueller in his studies of sickness and sin in the Scriptures is persuaded that sickness may indicate a "disturbed relationship with God."[14] William Lane notes that in Mark chapter 2 Jesus implies a cause and effect relationship between sickness and sin when He tells the man that his sins are forgiven and commands him to rise up and walk. This saying is only intelligible, according to Lane, if it is seen against the Old Testament background where "sin and disease, forgiveness and healing are frequently interrelated concepts."[15] In John 5:14 Jesus instructs someone He has healed to stop sinning lest something worse befall him. It appears fairly clear that the command 'stop sinning' presupposes that the man's sickness

[12]Peter C. Craigie, *Word Biblical Commentary: Psalms 1–50,* vol. 19 (Waco, Tex.: Word Books, 1983), 303. A. A. Anderson, *Psalms,* vol. 2 (Grand Rapids: Wm. B. Eerdmans, 1977), 753.

[13]J. Barton Payne, "1 and 2 Chronicles," in *Expositor's Bible Commentary,* ed. Frank E. Gaebelein, vol. 4 (Grand Rapids: Zondervan Publishing House, 1988), 491.

[14]Klaus Seybold and Ulrich B. Mueller, *Sickness and Healing* (Nashville: Abingdon Press, 1981), 166.

[15]William L. Lane, *The Gospel According to Mark* (Grand Rapids: Wm. B. Eerdmans, 1974), 94.

was caused by his own sin, otherwise Jesus' command would make no sense.

Certainly, there is a relationship between sickness and sin in some cases. This was the opinion of the Church as well as Judaism.[16] However, the exact nature of the relationship between sickness and sin is not easy to determine in individual cases. What is important is the recognition that such a relationship existed in the thought of Judaism and the Early Church. Because sin leads to human suffering, it was only natural for the Early Church to understand the ministry of Christ as the alleviation of human suffering, since He was God's answer to sin. Those who teach that divine healing is in the Atonement recover a holistic conception of persons and of the atoning work of Christ. T. F. Torrance suggests that "miraculous healing" demonstrates the power of the "word of forgiveness," disclosing at the same time "that forgiveness reached its full reality in the healing and creative work of God upon the whole man."[17] The restoration of fellowship with God is the most important thing, but this restoration not only results in spiritual healing but many times in physical healing as well.

Another area that we must pay heed to is the relationship between the demonic and sickness. There is a great deal of evidence from the Scriptures, especially in the Gospels, that point to the reality of some sicknesses being demonic in origin. In Luke 13:11–17 a woman is said to have been bound by Satan. In verse 11 the text states that she had "been crippled by a spirit." The text literally says "a woman having a spirit of illness" (Gk. *gunē pneuma echousa astheneias*). This does not mean, however, that all "illnesses, like possession, were ascribed to spirits, expressing the sense of a superior power that holds the upper hand." Jesus asked rhetorically, "Should not this woman ... be set free?" Thus He implied clearly that God's will for her was her healing. Verse 16 may be translated, "She should not remain bound for a moment longer, for, look she has already suffered 18 years."[18] Clearly,

---

[16]Bo Reicke, *The Epistles of James, Peter and Jude* (New York: Doubleday, 1982), 59; see also J. Christian Becker, *Paul's Apocalyptic Gospel* (Philadelphia: Fortress Press, 1982), 42.

[17]Thomas F. Torrance, *Space, Time and Resurrection* (Grand Rapids: Wm. B. Eerdmans, 1976), 62.

[18]Eduard Schweizer, *The Good News According to Luke* (Atlanta: John Knox Press, 1984), 222. I. Howard Marshall, *Commentary on Luke: A Commentary on the Greek Text* (Grand Rapids: Wm. B. Eerdmans, 1978), 561.

in this case Satan was the cause of the woman's illness and Jesus placed himself against such physical suffering.

On another occasion a man who could not talk was brought to Jesus (Matt. 9:32–34). In this text no mention is made of faith or of touching the afflicted. Jesus simply drove out the demon. This "indicates that this case was regarded as primarily one of possession, with the dumbness [being mute] as a 'by-product.'" There are other examples in the Gospels, but this should suffice to show that illness can be the result of demonic possession or attack.[19]

We must disagree, however, with those who assume that the "Christian interpretation of healings proceeds on the common assumption that illness results from the possession by demons."[20] This is an oversimplified position. There are many examples of demons causing illness, but there are also many cases where there is no connection made or even suggested. The idea that all sickness is caused by demons is clearly not the position of Jesus as recorded in the Gospels, nor is it the position of any New Testament writer.

There are examples of God's allowing Satan to inflict sickness upon God's servants as a form of disciplinary action or instruction, as with Job and Paul. Even so, such cases should not be construed as a form of demonization,[21] for all the enemy can do is touch the body, not the soul. Therefore, the development of some doctrine of demonization from the experience of Job is unwarranted. Nor is it warranted in 1 Corinthians 11:30 where believers are sick as a disciplinary action of the Lord. "Probably the rash of illnesses and deaths that had recently overtaken them is here being viewed as an expression of divine judgment on the whole community."[22]

The Bible does not indicate that in any way a sick believer can be "possessed by demons." Some do suggest that 2 Corinthians 12:7 is an example of a believer being stricken with some physical malady through the activity of demonic

CHAPTER

15

Divine
Healing

---

[19]France, *Matthew*, 173. For more examples of sicknesses related to demonic possession see Johann Michel, "Demon," in *Encyclopedia of Biblical Theology*, ed. Johannes B. Bauer (New York: Crossroad Pub. Co., 1981), 191–94.

[20]Lloyd G. Patterson, "Healings," in Everett Ferguson, *Encyclopedia of Early Christianity* (New York: Garland Publishing Co., 1990), 413.

[21]Murray J. Harris, "2 Corinthians," in *The Expositor's Bible Commentary* (Grand Rapids: Zondervan Publishing House, 1976), 396.

[22]Gordon D. Fee, *The First Epistle to the Corinthians* (Grand Rapids: Wm. B. Eerdmans, 1987), 565.

forces. But clearly in this case it did not involve demon possession nor was it the result of sin. Rather it was what may be called "a part of God's providential means of insuring his servant's dependence upon him."[23]

It is significant that the Greek word *daimonizomai* is used thirteen times in the New Testament but never to describe the condition of a believer. The word "designates a condition of sickness that is explained by a demon dwelling in the person ('possession')."[24] There are most certainly instances of demonic oppression and believers engaged in warfare against the spiritual powers of darkness, but the language of demonization is reserved exclusively for the unregenerate.

HEALING IN THE OLD AND NEW TESTAMENTS

One scholar has written that "in all three sections of the Jewish Scriptures . . . the image of Yahweh as healer is present as a central aspect of God's relationship to the covenant people."[25] The Old Testament conveys an understanding of sickness and healing as a manifestation of what may be called God's "control of history and human destiny."[26]

Some suffering, like that of the Egyptians, was the result of disobedience—which implies obedience brings health. Herodotus, the fifth century B.C. Greek historian, declared that "the Egyptians were the healthiest of the nations of antiquity, [until] their defiance of God made their diseases and plagues

---

[23]Clinton E. Arnold, *Powers of Darkness: Principalities & Powers in Paul's Letters* (Downers Grove, Ill.: InterVarsity Press, 1992), 133; Ralph Martin, *2 Corinthians* (Waco, Tex.: Word Books, 1986), 415. For an extended discussion of the issues brought up by the so-called Third Wave Charismatic movement from a Classical Pentecostal perspective see Opal L. Reddin, ed., *Power Encounters: A Pentecostal Perspective* (Springfield, Mo.: Central Bible College Press, 1989). The article by Douglas Oss on "The Hermeneutics of Power Encounter" (21-40) is especially helpful. Oss demonstrates that the chief sources of authority for those who articulate the position that Christians can be demonized is primarily experience and human reason, sources that are at best inadequate and very misleading.

[24]Horst Balz and Gerhard Schneider, eds., *"daimonizomai," Exegetical Dictionary of the New Testament,* vol. 1 (Grand Rapids: Wm. B. Eerdmans, 1990), 274.

[25]Howard Clark Kee, "Medicine and Healing," in *The Anchor Bible Dictionary,* David Noel Freedman, ed., vol. 4 (New York: Doubleday, 1992), 659.

[26]Kee, *Medicine, Miracle and Magic,* 10.

legendary."[27] **This is the point of Exodus 15:26.** God portrays himself as the supporter of His people by using the name *Yahweh-Roph'eka,* "the LORD your Physician." Since the names of God reveal the very essence of His nature,[28] this name shows Exodus 15:26 is not just a temporal promise to Israel, but let's us know He wants to be our Physician as well. The verb "heal" (Heb. *rapha'*) in the Old Testament is used initially and primarily of physical healing; only later, in the prophets, does it begin to be used in a spiritual sense. Even so, the extension into the second sense is based on the first, that of God as healer of the body.

The Old Testament reveals the world as open to God's supernatural intervention. Therefore, "since God was His people's physician, health . . . could be expected as the result of implicit obedience to the divine commands."[29]

The first healing mentioned in the Old Testament resulted from Abraham's intercession for Abimelech's families' infertility (Gen. 20:17). Of course, the Book of Job is very important for our understanding of divine healing, for it clearly indicates that sickness is not necessarily the result of sin.[30] A person's illness may have absolutely nothing to do with what he or she did or did not do. In Job's case, the origin of his suffering was the animus of Satan toward both him and God. Another thing that the Book of Job teaches us is that there is in Scripture what may be called a "correctional role of God."[31] God can use sickness, as He can other not so pleasant experiences, in our lives. Finally, the Book of Job points to the restorative powers of God and His desire to heal: "For he wounds, but he also binds up; he injures, but his hands also heal" (Job 5:17–18).

Throughout the Psalms we find numerous associations between sin and sickness, forgiveness and healing (see Pss. 30:2; 41:4; 103:3; 107:19–20; etc.). The ministry of both Elijah and

CHAPTER

15

Divine
Healing

---

[27]Walter Kaiser, "Exodus" in *Expositor's Bible Commentary,* Frank E. Gabelein, ed., vol. 2 (Grand Rapids: Zondervan Publishing House, 1990), 399.

[28]Otto Weber, *Foundations of Dogmatics,* trans. Darrell L. Guder, vol. 1 (Grand Rapids: Wm. B. Eerdmans, 1981), 415; Herman Bavinck, *The Doctrine of God* (Grand Rapids: Baker Book House, 1951), 84.

[29]R. K. Harrison, "Heal," *The International Standard Bible Encyclopedia,* ed. Geoffrey W. Bromiley, vol. 2 (Grand Rapids: Wm. B. Eerdmans, 1982), 644.

[30]Ibid.

[31]Kee, "Medicine and Healing," 659.

Elisha saw people raised from the dead. Elisha was used in the healing of Naaman (2 Kings 5:3–14). Healing also resulted from Hezekiah's deepening spirituality (2 Kings 20:1–21).

The last book of the Old Testament concludes with a messianic prophecy that presents the hope of One who would reveal God's righteousness through a victory over "all the arrogant and every evil doer" and whose divine presence would be known as the "sun of righteousness [that] will rise with healing in its wings [rays, NCV]" (Mal. 4:1–2). This text undoubtedly refers to the healing that will be the "consequence of the vicarious suffering of the Servant of the Lord." The Old Testament was pointing to a time when "[t]he evils of physical weakness, sickness, and death will be swallowed up in the life of the Kingdom of God." That would be revealed in the New Testament; the presence of this messianic kingdom would be seen in Jesus' miracles of healing.[32]

The New Testament presupposes the Old Testament revelation that affirms the reality of divine healing. Ignoring this, some scholars have placed an exaggerated emphasis on the sociological context and the influence of the Greco-Roman world on the development of the New Testament. In contrast to that we would emphasize that the essential and primary influence upon the writers of the New Testament was not the pagan world of Gentile magicians and occult practices, but the divine preparation given in the Old Testament.

The place to begin a study of healing in the New Testament is the ministry of Jesus. Rene Latourelle suggests that we understand Jesus' healing miracles as "signs of the Kingdom." Through these signs Jesus introduces us to the kingdom of God's deliverance and rectification of the broken world that effects the "whole person." What they imply is that the "transformation to come" finds its source in the person of Christ.[33]

Jesus further emphasized that "these deliverances were evidences of the presence of the messianic salvation (Matt. 11:4–5)."[34] They were signs and assurance that God will carry out His plan and ultimately bring in the prophesied restoration,

[32]Pieter A. Verhoef, *The Books of Haggai and Malachi* (Grand Rapids: Wm. B. Eerdmans, 1987), 330. George Eldon Ladd, *A Theology of the New Testament* (Grand Rapids: Wm. B. Eerdmans, 1974), 74.

[33]Rene Latourelle, *The Miracles of Jesus and the Theology of Miracles* (New York: Paulist Press, 1988), 19–21.

[34]Ladd, *A Theology of the New Testament,* 76. H. van der Loos, *The Miracles of Jesus.* Supplements to Novum Testamentum, vol. 8 (Leiden: E. J. Brill, 1965).

which includes our resurrection and our new bodies. We have the first installment now, but the full consummation has not yet come. Divine healing, therefore, is not only a part of the gospel, it is also an important witness to the truth of the gospel.

Jesus' miracles of healing fall into one of three classifications: healings, exorcisms, or resurrections (or raisings, in order not to equate them with that of Jesus).[35] This understanding of healing may lie behind Paul's use of the plurals in describing the "gifts of healing[s]" (1 Cor. 12:9). All of them speak of God's power over forces that contradict God's will for human beings. They are expressions of Jesus' triumph over Satan and destruction of his works (see 1 John 3:8). The emphasis placed on miracles of healing is substantial just in terms of the space devoted to them in the Gospels. For example, in Mark's Gospel over thirty-one percent of the verses are about Jesus' miracles of healing.[36]

Space forbids going into detail about Jesus' miracles of healing. Suffice it to say that each of the gospel writers makes use of the healings, not just to impress us but to teach us about Jesus and the character of God, for it is His very nature to heal. In Matthew they are intended to help identify Jesus as the Messiah. For Luke they demonstrate that Jesus is Savior. He pictures Jesus as "embroiled in . . . battle with Satan, whose power he is decisively vanquishing as he ushers in the age of the new covenant."[37] John's Gospel is structured around "signs," most of which are healing miracles, recorded to help people continue to believe in Jesus as the Messiah and the Son of God.

If anything stands out about Jesus' view of sickness, it is that He is against it. It contradicts His will. And since He is God incarnate, it is thus a contradiction of God's will.

It can be demonstrated from an attentive reading of the Gospels that Jesus understood His healing ministry as the subjugation of the powers of death. In the Gospel of John we read that Jesus declares that though Satan has come "to steal and kill and destroy," He has come to bring life "to the full"

---

[35]Craig L. Blomberg, "Healing," in *Dictionary of Jesus and the Gospels,* Joel B. Green and Scot McKnight, eds. (Downers Grove, Ill.: InterVarsity Press, 1992), 300.

[36]Michael Harper, *The Healings of Jesus,* The Jesus Library, Michael Green, ed. (Downers Grove, Ill.: InterVarsity Press, 1986), 15.

[37]Blomberg, "Healing," 303.

(see John 10:10).[38] Verses 9–10 are explanations of what Jesus meant when He called himself the gate of the sheep. He is the One that brings fullness of life. The Lord here is declaring that He "desires and promotes their well-being: He is not content that they should eke out a bare miserable existence; he wants them to live life to the full, to have plenty of good pasturage and enjoy health."[39]

Both the Old and New Testament present God as Healer. Both demonstrate a connection between God as Lord and as Healer. The analogies between the Exodus narratives and New Testament teachings are obvious. Yet, the differences between the Old and New Testament are also significant. In the Old Testament God laid down the condition of keeping the Law to experience the benefits of healing (see Exod. 15:26). In contrast, the New Testament shows that healing benefits are available to all who turn to God through Jesus Christ in faith.

HEALING AS PART OF SALVATION

It is abundantly clear on the basis of the Bible's view of the nature of human beings that there is coherency and logic in the doctrine of divine healing. If humankind was created by God intentionally for wholeness, then it is reasonable on the basis of the biblical evidence to conclude that healing is, at least in a limited sense, part of God's salvific work in Christ. The idea that God cares just for souls and not whole persons is foreign to the Scriptures. "The whole gospel for the whole person" is rightly a prominent theme for today's preaching and teaching.

In the past under the influence of Hellenistic philosophy, human beings were understood primarily in nonmaterial terms. The dualism of the Hellenist philosophers made an impact upon some of the Church fathers. The denigration of the body and material world was prominent within many of

---

[38]There is some debate about who the thief is that Jesus is referring to in this passage. Some suggest that it is the false teachers, but the suggestion by Raymond Brown is probably correct. He writes, "In the Tabernacles discourse in 8.44 we heard that the devil is a murderer, so that opposition between the thief and the shepherd is a reflection of the opposition between Satan and Jesus." *The Gospel According to John I-XII.* (New York: Doubleday, 1966), 394.

[39]F. F. Bruce, *The Gospel of John* (Grand Rapids: Wm. B. Eerdmans, 1983), 226.

the early Greek philosophers. Plato considered the body (Gk. *sōma*) a tomb or grave (Gk. *sema*).[40]

Unfortunately, Augustine's thinking on this topic has also had an inordinate influence. That is to say, his view of the nature of humankind was influenced by Neoplatonic constructs that for all practical purposes belittled the importance of the physical dimensions of human existence.[41] This emphasis upon radically separating human beings into component parts is not based on the Scriptures.

There has developed in this century a scholarly consensus that the biblical understanding of the nature of humankind is holistic. H. Wheeler Robinson has suggested that we have tended to interpret the Bible in the light of the "interpretation natural to Augustine or a Calvin."[42]

Just two examples from Augustine's writing should suffice in making this point about him. In his work *On Free Will* Augustine wrote that the "body occupies by nature a lower rank in the scale of being than does soul." In another place Augustine declares that the "Soul is universally superior to body. No soul can fall so far in sinfulness as to be changed into a body ... *the worst soul is superior to corporeal ... things*" (italics mine). This disdain for the physical is not biblical. However, Augustine later changed his mind about a number of things and became as much "anti-Platonic" as Platonic. Nonetheless, his contribution to a tradition within Christian theology that demeans the concern of God for whole persons is still with us.[43]

As for Calvin, even some Reformed theologians admit that he was not able to extricate himself from the stranglehold of nonbiblical conceptions of humankind. "Plato was too much part of his thought world."[44]

One reason so many theologians today show such reticence about including divine healing in the Atonement is this un-

---

[40]Andrew Louth, *The Origins of the Christian Mystical Tradition* (New York: Oxford University Press, 1981), xiii.

[41]J. Patout Burns, S. J. *Theological Anthropology* (Philadelphia: Fortress Press, 1981), 7.

[42]H. Wheeler Robinson, *The Christian Doctrine of Man* (Edinburgh: T. T. Clark, 1958), 5.

[43]J. H. S. Burleigh, ed., *Augustine: Earlier Writings* (Philadelphia: The Westminster Press, 1953), 165, 180. Angelo Di Berardino ed., *Patrology,* vol. 4 (Westminster, Md.: Christian Classics, 1986), 405.

[44]Gordon J. Spykman, *Reformational Theology: A New Paradigm for Doing Dogmatics* (Grand Rapids: Wm. B. Eerdmans, 1992), 234.

fortunate inheritance of inadequate views of the nature of human beings. That is, many seem unaware that their view of human nature owes as much to a Hellenistic worldview as to the Bible's, perhaps more. The concepts and classifications that they use were essentially the same ones that the Roman Catholic theologians used,[45] ones drawn from the Neoplatonism and Aristotelianism of the medieval scholastics.

Yet we have seen even in non-Pentecostal circles a greater appreciation for what George Eldon Ladd calls the "whole man." Anthony A. Hoekema declares that "man must be understood as a unitary being." Francis Schaeffer in one of his great apologetic works wrote that "even in this present life we are to have a substantial reality of redemption of the whole man. God made man and is interested in the whole man." G. C. Berkouwer points out that in the Scriptures "the whole man comes to the fore."[46] We believe that there is no way to get around the fact that the Bible portrays human nature as a unity. Pentecostals have in practice and preaching recognized this truth.

We affirm, in fact, that there is a duality, a material and immaterial aspect, to human persons, as well as a unity. "Holism need not entail the denial that wholes contain distinguishable parts."[47] Nor does it mean that we should consider biblical holism as a form of monism. Rather, Biblical holism consists of a recognition of the human person as a total person, with all parts integrated and operating properly for the benefit of the whole. What does this mean? Everything we do is an act of the whole person. It is not the soul, but the person that sins. It is the whole person, "body and soul[,] that is redeemed in Christ." The picture of human beings set before us in Scripture is that of "a unitary being" rarely addressed spiritually apart from bodily existence.[48]

---

[45]Spykman, *Reformational Theology,* 235; for a completely different perspective on this issue see Richard A. Muller, *Post-Reformation Dogmatics* (Grand Rapids: Baker Book House, 1987), 17–22. Muller basically argues that scholasticism is a method not necessarily a specific content.

[46]Ladd, *Theology of the New Testament,* 457. Anthony A. Hoekema, *Created in God's Image* (Grand Rapids: Eerdmans, 1986), 216. Francis A. Schaeffer, *The Complete Works of Francis Schaeffer,* vol. 1 (Westchester: Crossway Books, 1982), 224. G. C. Berkouwer, *Man the Image of God* (Grand Rapids: Wm. B. Eerdmans, 1962), 203.

[47]John Cooper, *Body, Soul & Life Everlasting: Biblical Anthropology and the Monism-Dualism Debate* (Grand Rapids: Wm. B. Eerdmans, 1989), 49–50.

[48]Louis Berkhof, *Systematic Theology* (Grand Rapids: Baker Book House, 1941), 192. Millard J. Erickson, *Christian Theology* (Grand Rapids: Baker Book House, 1985), 536.

Why is it so important to point out that dualistic anthropology is an alien addition to the gospel? Because dualism with its understanding of human existence has been the presupposition of those who would sever from the body the salvific implications of Christ's atonement. The reduction or diminishing of Christ's atonement to the spiritual sphere alone is the result not of the teachings of Scripture but of the influence of a pagan philosophy. Denigration of the physical and material realm is absent from Scripture, both Old and New Testament. God created whole persons and it is His will, as revealed in Scripture, to restore whole persons.

As Stuart Fowler rightly says, this view of the nature of human beings is a "corrupting intrusion of pagan philosophy into Christian thought and a serious hindrance to experiencing the richness of the gospel." Texts like 1 Thessalonians 5:23, "May God himself, the God of peace, sanctify you through and through. May your whole spirit, soul and body be kept blameless," speak of God's concern for the whole person. Charles Wannamaker suggests that Paul is communicating his [and God's] desire for them as "complete human beings." Robert L. Thomas says that Paul here is referring to the "wholeness" of human persons when he uses this tripartite language.[49]

"[H]ealing should not be thought of as something extraneous and entirely apart from our salvation."[50] The Scriptures know nothing of a concept of salvation that excludes all aspects of a physical nature. Such a concept is a Western philosophical accretion, not a biblical definition of salvation. To say that Isaiah 53:5 and 1 Peter 2:24 speak exclusively of spiritual healing or salvation of the soul and not physical healing is to establish an alien dichotomy between the spiritual and physical dimensions of human existence that is not warranted from the Scriptures.[51]

---

[49]Stuart Fowler, *On Being Human* (Blackburn, Australia: Foundation for Christian Scholarship, 1980), 3–4. Charles A. Wannamaker, *The Epistles to the Thessalonians: A Commentary on the Greek Text* (Grand Rapids: Wm. B. Eerdmans, 1990), 207. Robert L. Thomas, "1, 2 Thessalonians," in *The Expository Bible Commentary* (Grand Rapids: Zondervan Publishing House, 1978), 294–95.

[50]Hugh Jeter, *By His Stripes* (Springfield, Mo.: Gospel Publishing House, 1977), 11.

[51]It is apparent that as Matthew has physical healing primarily in mind (Matt. 8:17), Peter has spiritual healing in mind (1 Pet. 2:24). Yet by taking advantage of the same image to define Jesus' work of spiritual restoration, he is not ruling out Matthew's recognition of physical healing. Both are in the Atonement.

CHAPTER
15

Divine
Healing

Salvation (Gk. *sōtēria*) refers to both salvation and healing. Quite often the only clue to its meaning is the particular context within which it is found. The correlative of the doctrine of reconciliation is "restoration and healing." Thus, a person who has been saved and sanctified inwardly, made spiritually and emotionally whole by the Holy Spirit, "has no less need or right to be physically whole."[52]

It is clear from the Gospels that many times Jesus was pointing out, at least in a general way, that there is a correlation between sin and sickness and forgiveness and healing. An example of this is Mark 2:5, where Jesus says to the paralytic, " 'Son your sins are forgiven.' " It does not appear strange in light of all of this to see why we must affirm healing as a part of God's plan of salvation. Ray Anderson writes, "He is the source of health because he himself has been made health for us even as he was made sin for us."[53]

No one should misunderstand this, however, as teaching that there is always a necessary correlation between sickness and sin on an individual level. Jesus dismissed this wrongheaded assumption, which was apparently current among the rabbis of His day (see John 9:1–3). What the Bible does affirm is the fact that when sin entered the picture humanity began to suffer, so ultimately human suffering and sickness are the result of sin. Thus the Atonement provided by Christ is much more than the reconciliation of the "religious aspects of the self." On the basis of Christ's work as Savior there is redemption for the whole person.[54]

H. D. MacDonald writes, "In the Old Testament 'to be saved' has the general primary sense of being delivered or preserved from a danger of disease; the result is the experience of safety or health."[55] It is true that the later prophets in the Old Testament focus more on the spiritual and moral aspects of salvation but even then they have the promise of restoration of the physical and material benefits of salvation (see Isa. 58:13–14; 60:10–22; Jer. 30:10–24). Yet to establish a hard dichotomy between the spiritual and the physical on the basis of Scripture is to do an injustice to the worldview represented

---

[52]Ray S. Anderson, *On Being Human: Essays in Theological Anthropology* (Grand Rapids: Wm. B. Eerdmans, 1982), 31, 172.

[53]Ibid., 173.

[54]Leon Morris, *The Gospel According to John* (Grand Rapids: Wm. B. Eerdmans, 1971), 477–78. Ray Anderson, *On Being Human,* 174.

[55]H. D. McDonald, *Salvation* (Westchester, Ill.: Crossway Books, 1982), 13.

in Scripture. Ladd speaks of salvation, as defined in the New Testament, as consisting of "restoration of communion between God and man" and "the redemption of the body."[56] The full realization of this salvation will happen in connection with the resurrection and rapture of believers when Jesus returns, but even now the reality of God's kingdom has broken in, bringing us this promised salvation in the present. The Early Church Father Irenaeus believed that salvation was a "salvation of the body, not from the body."[57] In this century the Pentecostal Movement has consistently upheld this biblical view of salvation.

One of the arguments for healing's being in the Atonement is the promise of the resurrection of our bodies. The empty tomb implies a "whole Christ died for us and that it is a whole Christ who lives forevermore; that He came to redeem us as whole men, not just a part of us."[58]

The belief that healing is in the Atonement stands upon solid exegetical ground. Probably two of the most important texts for understanding the relationship of Jesus' atoning work and healing are Isaiah 53:4–5 and Matthew 8:17. In the Early Church the text "by his wounds we are healed" (Isa. 53:5) was the basis of what has been called a "tradition of healing."[59] But it is more than a tradition. The hermeneutical model we should work with assumes that a New Testament interpretation of an Old Testament passage is authoritative. This means that the intentionality of an Old Testament text is defined theologically not only by its historical context, but also by its usage in the New Testament. There exists in the Scriptures what is identified frequently as a *sensus plenior* interpretation, that is, a deeper meaning intended by God, and in Christian theology the emphasis is placed on the New Testament understanding.

Does Isaiah 53:4 refer to physical healing? Herbert Wolf in his work on Isaiah says, " 'Infirmities' is primarily a reference to sins, though this term may also refer to physical diseases."[60] Wolf has it turned around. This word primarily refers to physical disease and secondarily to sin. The word translated "in-

---

[56]Ladd, *Theology of the New Testament,* 74.

[57]Maurice Wiles, *The Christian Fathers* (London: SCM Press Ltd., 1966), 92.

[58]Torrance, *Space, Time and Resurrection,* 66.

[59]Weber, *The Cross,* 55.

[60]Herbert M. Wolf, *Interpreting Isaiah: The Suffering and Glory of the Messiah* (Grand Rapids: Zondervan Publishing House, 1985), 216.

firmities" is the Hebrew word *choli*. This word is translated a number of ways in the Old Testament, all of which have some connotation of physical illness. The other word in this text translated "sorrows" is *makh'ov*, literally "pain." This word is also used of the suffering caused by slave drivers in Egypt (Exod. 3:7). Therefore, Isaiah 53:4 cannot be limited to spiritual healing.

The words used in verse 4 and "peace" and "healed" in verse 5 of Isaiah 53 speak of the physical and psychological devastation of sin that Jesus bore in our stead. Prior to the Fall the situation in the Garden was one of peace (Heb. *shalom*). It is an experience of health and well-being devoid of suffering as well as of peace with God. God's desire to restore this experience of shalom is seen in the Suffering Servant passage (Isa. 53:5). The work of Christ on the Cross is first and foremost the restoration of spiritual *shalom*, but it is not God's intention that it stop there. Rather, the entire existence of human beings is to be inundated with *shalom*.

The typical greeting in Pauline letters reflects not merely a Greek form for letter writing, but a genuine Christian salutation and prayer that believers would experience the grace and *shalom* that is found in Christ. C. K. Barrett says that "It is unthinkable . . . that he [Paul] did not enrich the word with its specific Christian content."[61] This *shalom* that Jesus suffered for is not to be understood as many believers understand it: merely psychological or emotional peace alone. The *shalom* that Jesus Christ suffered, died, and rose again for is *shalom* for the whole person—body, soul, and spirit.

R. K. Harrison writes, "The evangelist [Matthew] interpreted the prophetic oracle more accurately than many modern English versions." The Hebrew text of Isaiah 53:4 "employs the simple words for 'disease' and 'pains' which relate the healing of sickness directly to the work of the servant." Harrison summarizes the issue that is set forth in Isaiah 53 when he declares "that the incarnate Lord dealt also with disease and sickness on the cross as well as with human sin— i.e., his atonement avails for the whole personality, body as well as soul." Nor is the belief that Isaiah 53:4 speaks of physical as well as spiritual healing a Christian invention. Even

---

[61]C. K. Barrett, *The First Epistle to the Romans* (San Francisco: Harper & Row Pub., 1968), 22.

within Rabbinic tradition there are witnesses to a similar interpretation.[62]

Some modern evangelicals like John Stott would deny categorically that there is healing in the Atonement. Stott says the very idea of Jesus bearing our sickness is "not an intelligible notion."

Maybe it is unintelligible to Stott but it was not to Matthew. Leon Morris, commenting on the passage before us, observes, "There may be the thought that Jesus in some way took on himself the ailments he cured; healing is at a cost." Herman Hendrickx describes Matthew's very literal rendering of Isaiah 53:4 (in contrast to the Septuagint and the Targum) as a "very correct" rendering of the Hebrew.[63] Matthew's rendering of "took up" and "carried" are "exact renderings of the Hebrew" and they do speak of Jesus bearing in a vicarious fashion our suffering. D. A. Carson, who is not a Pentecostal, writes concerning Matthew 8:17, "This text and others clearly teach that there is healing in the atonement." Carson rightly points out that the Atonement is the basis of "all benefits that accrue to believers." This does not mean we necessarily enjoy all of them now (e.g., the resurrection body), but because of Christ's atoning work, we will.[64]

Does Carson stand alone as an evangelical biblical scholar in affirming that divine healing is in the Atonement? Not at all. B. B. Warfield also affirmed that divine healing is in the Atonement. In his attack on the "Faith Healers" of his day he admitted that their error was not "in the supposition that redemption is for the body as well as the soul. This is true. Nor does it lie in the supposition that provision is made in the atonement for the relief of men from disease and suffering, which are fruits of sin. This too is true." Warfield becomes eloquent at this point, "This is the teaching of the Bible; and this is what Christ illustrated when He healed the sick in His ministry on earth that men might see, as an object-lesson, that provision was made in His substitutionary work for the

---

[62]R. K. Harrison, "Healing," in *Interpreter's Dictionary of the Bible,* George Buttrick, ed., vol. 2 (New York: Abingdon Press, 1962), 547. H. L. Strack and Paul Billerbeck, *Kommentar zum Neuen Testament aus Talmud und Midrasch,* vol. 1 (Munich: Beck, 1961), 481–83.

[63]John R. W. Stott, *The Cross of Christ* (Downers Grove, Ill.: InterVarsity Press, 1986), 245. Leon Morris, *The Gospel According to Matthew* (Grand Rapids: Wm. B. Eerdmans, 1992), 198. Herman Hendrickx, *The Miracle Stories* (San Francisco: Harper & Row, 1987), 78.

[64]D. A. Carson, "Matthew," in *The Expositor's Bible Commentary* (Grand Rapids: Zondervan Publishing House, 1984), 207.

relief of every human ill."[65] Warfield's problem was with those who felt that they could command and manipulate God to bring about healings as they wished, as a consequence of the Atonement.

Craig Blomberg, commenting on Matthew 8:17, writes, "There is physical healing in the atonement for this age, but it is up to God in Christ to choose when and how to dispense it."[66] Yes, and He has chosen to heal in answer to believing prayer.

Millard Erickson, an evangelical, states that Isaiah 53:4 allows for a number of interpretations, the best of which, as far as they line up with the linguistic data, is the one that states "the prophet is referring to actual physical and mental illnesses and distresses."[67] Erickson suggests, however, that Jesus did not actually vicariously bear our sufferings in himself but that He sympathized with us. Erickson's interpretation clearly does not do justice to the text before us. We would have to go along with J. B. Torrance when he writes that in Jesus' incarnation He was "bone of our bone, flesh of our flesh, in solidarity with all men, all races, all colours [sic], bearing on His divine heart the names, the needs, the sorrows, the injustices of all nations."[68]

Critics of the biblical doctrine of divine healing do not understand the full extent and significance of Christ's atoning work. Jesus' suffering was for us, in our stead and on our behalf. In Isaiah 53, the Servant of Yahweh experiences rejection and suffering, "not as a consequence of his own disobedience, but on the behalf of others."[69] What is the result? It effects the healing of God's people through "his stripes." The affirmation that the sufferings of Jesus bring healing to those who suffer stands on firm theological ground.

The fact that God has healed the sick in the past and that He heals the sick today is evidence of His promised redemption of our bodies (Romans 8:23). When we observe a manifestation of God's power to heal it reminds us that some day, when Christ returns, His people will be delivered completely

---

[65]B. B. Warfield, *Counterfeit Miracles* (London: The Banner of Truth Trust, 1918), 176–77.

[66]Craig Blomberg, *Matthew* (Nashville: Broadman Books, 1992), 145.

[67]Erickson, *Christian Theology,* 840.

[68]J. B. Torrance, "The Vicarious Humanity of Christ," in *The Incarnation: Ecumenical Studies in the Nicene-Constantinopolitan Creed,* ed. Thomas F. Torrance (Edinburgh: The Handsel Press, 1981), 138.

[69]Kee, *Medicine, Miracle and Magic,* 15.

from the pangs of a fallen world. Even when we are not healed ourselves in the present, the healing of another need not serve as an irresolvable quandary but rather as a divine testimony that we too—if not now, then—shall be made whole.

Divine healing is actually an inbreaking of the power of the coming ages. This is how the author of the epistle to the Hebrews understood the signs and wonders that he beheld. They were confirmations of the salvation promised (see Heb. 2:3–4), signs of the "powers of the coming age" (Heb. 6:5). The passage just prior to the verse quoted refers to the "heavenly gift," which most likely is a "general image for the gracious bestowal of salvation with all that it entails." And the reason that it is called "heavenly" is because of its "source and goal."[70]

At the same time, divine healing is temporary in this age (this is what might be called "the limitation of . . . physical deliverances"[71]), serving notice of the impending judgment of God on the kingdoms of this world as well as the establishment in this world of God's righteous rule. That is, healing is a very tangible expression of God's enduring love for His creation.

The healings that Christ performed in the power of the Spirit were signs that the kingdom of God was near (see Matt. 10:7–8). The healing of the sick was understood by Christ and the gospel writers to be an expression of God's future victory, to be consummated when Jesus comes back to earth again. It was the "already" of God's kingdom verifying the promised "not yet." Robert Mounce writes, "The long awaited reign of God is about to break into human history. That is why the sick are being healed."[72] Every time a sick person is healed through prayer and faith in Christ a witness is proclaimed concerning His promised return. It is a testimony of God's faithfulness. Thus, the healings that we experience today are just a first installment of the future redemption of our bodies.

CHALLENGES TO THE DOCTRINE OF DIVINE HEALING

CHALLENGES BY THE SECULAR WORLD

No doubt the first challenge placed before the believer from the secularist is an outright denial of the supernatural. A num-

---

[70]Harold W. Attridge, *Hebrews* (Philadelphia: Fortress Press, 1989), 170.

[71]Ladd, *Theology of the New Testament,* 76.

[72]Robert H. Mounce, *Matthew* (San Francisco: Harper & Row, 1985), 91.

ber of philosophers, both Christian and non-Christian, have demonstrated recently that the modern disposition against the supernatural is not necessarily the result of superior rational argumentation. Two secular philosophers of science, Thomas Kuhn and Paul Feyerabend, among others, have shown that many of the beliefs of our age, scientific or otherwise, are dogmatic affirmations—not science, but scientism.[73] There are just as many reasons to believe in the supernatural as to discount it. And for the Christian, there is no reason not to believe in the miracles of the New Testament, since the experience of regeneration itself ranks as a miracle in the thinking of the New Testament (John 3:5–8; 2 Cor. 5:17). Brown retells the C. S. Lewis story of a determined agnostic who found himself in the lake of fire at the end of the world. "He doggedly continued to regard his experiences there as an illusion, looking for explanations from psychoanalysis and cerebral pathology."[74] Brown points out that Lewis was telling us that many persons will not change their worldview no matter what the evidence indicates (cf. Luke 16:19–31).

The second challenge set forth by the secularist is often the reductionistic comparisons made between the miracles of the New Testament and the pagan magic of the first century. According to Colin Brown, Celsus, the great antagonist of Origen, defined Jesus as a magician who had picked up "the tricks of his trade in Egypt." In recent times a number of scholars have set forth similar ideas. A well-known scholar who espouses such a view is Morton Smith. Smith views Matthew's story of the flight to Egypt as a thin cover-up designed to answer accusations about Jesus' ability to do miracles.[75]

There are a number of scholars who have shown that this is a total misrepresentation of Jesus. Howard Clark Kee has published a number of significant works in the area of miracles and healing in the first century. He points out that the healings

---

[73]Thomas Kuhn, *The Structure of Scientific Revolutions* (Chicago: University of Chicago Press, 1970); Paul Feyerabend, *Farewell to Reason* (New York: Verso, 1987). For a discussion of the issue of scientific rationality and its implications for theology see Nancey Murphy, *Theology in an Age of Scientific Reasoning* (Ithaca: Cornell University Press, 1990) and Philip Clayton, *Explanation from Physics to Theology: A Essay in Rationality and Religion* (New Haven: Yale University Press, 1989).

[74]Colin Brown, *That You May Believe: Miracles and Faith Then and Now* (Grand Rapids: Wm. B. Eerdmans, Pub. Co., 1985), 35.

[75]Colin Brown, *Miracles and the Critical Mind* (Grand Rapids: Wm. B. Eerdmans, 1984), 5. Morton Smith, *Jesus the Magician* (San Francisco: Harper & Row, 1978).

we find in the New Testament stand in "sharp contrast to magic." The biblical records of the healings wrought by Jesus and the Early Church have "no trace of the elaborate multi-named invocations of the gods." A. E. Harvey of Oxford writes, "In general, one can say that the miracle stories in the gospels are unlike anything else in ancient literature in that they avoid . . . the tendencies which we find in any comparable ac-counts." And the reason for such comparisons is simply pre-supposition, bias—which Blomberg pinpoints: "Once anti-supernatural bias is removed, the Gospel healing miracles actually satisfy the various historical criteria of authentic-ity."[76]

CHALLENGES BY CHRISTIANS

Now let us consider the challenges within Christendom, beginning with that of liberal Protestantism. Many of these liberals rule out divine healing, based on a philosophical po-sition they have espoused. Theologians like Rudolf Bultmann deny all miracles because of a faulty worldview. John Mac-quarrie speaks of what he calls the "grave dangers" inherent in philosophical theologizing, which is the chief method of today's liberal Protestantism. He mentions three perils. First, there is what he calls the "preoccupation with secular phi-losophy" that leads to a "distortion of Christian teaching" through an overemphasis on the specific areas of convergence between philosophy and Christian doctrine. Second, he points out that it is very common for ideas foreign to Christianity to be slipped in and later on masquerade as traditional Chris-tianity. Third, the worst danger is a complete accommodation to whatever the prevailing philosophy may be.[77] All of these perils are present within liberal Protestantism.

The utilization of the category of "myth" from form criti-cism, and now the more popular category of "story," also tends to obscure and confuse if not outright deny the reality of the supernatural. There are those like Ernst and Marie-Luise Keller and Rudolf Bultmann who suggest that we either demythologize the supernatural or recognize once and for all that these miracle stories are unnecessary. The Kellers

---

[76]Kee, *Medicine, Miracle and Magic,* 126. A. E. Harvey, *Jesus and the Constraints of History* (Philadelphia: The Westminster Press, 1982), 110. Blomberg, "Healing," 304.

[77]John MacQuarrie, *An Existential Theology* (London: SCM Press Ltd., 1955), 4.

mistakenly call up the apostle Paul as a witness for their position. According to them Paul was "not interested in physical miracles; they do not fit into the picture which he gives us of the earthly Jesus and they are meaningless for the Christology that he preaches."[78]

It is hard to imagine a position that is further from the truth than that of the Kellers. Paul's conversion experience is rooted firmly in the supernatural. The miracle of the Resurrection is foundational to Paul's Christology (see Rom. 1:4; 1 Cor. 15:3–9,12–19). Paul's Jesus was very much a historical figure who did miracles, suffered and died and was resurrected miraculously in real history, and now sits exalted at the Father's side (see Phil. 2:6–11). As Wolfhart Pannenberg said, "The story of Jesus Christ has to be history . . . if the Christian faith is to continue."[79] Macquarrie calls this reticence to deal with the miraculous in the New Testament a hangover from liberal modernism. He points out that many scholars, like Bultmann, have without serious consideration of the evidence "decided in advance that in this scientific age we cannot believe in miracles." Macquarrie explicitly pegs this as "fallacious" reasoning and we must do no less. Those who want to maintain the name Christian yet deny the reality of the supernatural are Christian in name only.[80]

Another example of erroneous thinking in liberal Protestant circles is the denial of the demonic. There has been a rash of publications by nominal Christian theologians who deny the reality of a personal Satan and demons. "For many years now Christian liberalism has undermined the church's acceptance of the reality of Satan."[81]

Next we ought to look at the errors of some evangelicals in reference to divine healing. One of their most significant errors in regard to the doctrine of divine healing is the belief in the cessation of the *charismata*. This is an error that recently has been repudiated by many evangelical scholars, but is still strongly held by most dispensationalists and by the Reformed Evangelicalism that was heavily influenced by Princeton Theological Seminary in the last century. Basically the Cessationist view is that the gifts were simply tempo-

---

[78]Ernst and Marie-Luise Keller, *Miracles in Dispute: A Continuing Debate* (Philadelphia: Fortress Press, 1969), 190.

[79]Wolfhart Pannenberg, *An Introduction to Systematic Theology* (Grand Rapids: Wm. B. Eerdmans, 1991), 5.

[80]MacQuarrie, *An Existential Theology,* 186.

[81]Harper, *The Healings of Jesus,* 30.

rary—until the formation of the New Testament canon, after
which they either were done away with by the Holy Spirit
or disappeared with the apostles. Warfield is a proponent of
this view. He writes, "These gifts ... were distinctively the
authentication of the apostles. They were part of the credentials of the apostles as the authoritative agents of God in
founding the church."[82]

A number of recent studies have pointed out that the gifts
of the Holy Spirit did not cease at the end of the Apostolic
age. Ronald A. N. Kydd demonstrated in a University of St.
Andrews dissertation that the gifts of the Spirit continued into
the third century. The apparent loss of the gifts after this
stemmed from a diminishing regard for them: "they no longer
fitted into the highly organized, well-educated, wealthy and
socially-powerful Christian communities."[83] It was not that
the gifts were removed from the church by the Holy Spirit,
rather they were given up along with many other things during what has been called the Constantinization of the Church.
Constantine as the initiator of the age of the Church's pros-
perity has become "the symbol of the epoch of the great
reversal."[84]

Besides the unknown author of the Apocryphal Acts, some
of the church fathers that mention the gifts of the Spirit in
their day are Justin Martyr, Irenaeus, Theodotus, Hippolytus,
Novatian, and even Augustine. Justin Martyr defends the gifts
of healings in the church of his day from the criticisms of a
certain Trypho. Ireneaus bears witness to the presence of the
gifts of healings toward the end of the second century.[85]

Augustine bears special mention, for his understanding of
the cessation of the gifts undergirds much of Calvin and Warfield's thinking on this matter. Much is made of Augustine's
comments about the age of miracles having passed. Sullivan
points out that after these remarks were written Augustine
retracted them. What changed Augustine's mind? The same
thing that had convinced him to some extent of his previous
views: pastoral experience. Sullivan writes that after several
years of pastoral experience as Bishop of Hippo Augustine

[82]Warfield, *Counterfeit Miracles,* 6.

[83]Ronald Kydd, *Charismatic Gifts in the Early Church* (Peabody, Mass.:
Hendrickson Publishers, 1987), 87.

[84]John Howard Yoder, *The Priestly Kingdom: Social Ethics as Gospel*
(Notre Dame: University of Notre Dame Press, 1984), 135–47, 209.

[85]Francis A. Sullivan, S. J., *Charisms and Charismatic Renewal: A Biblical
Theological Study* (Ann Arbor: Servant Books, 1982), 112.

could testify that in his own diocese in a two-year period there were nearly seventy well-attested miracles of healing.[86] In Augustine's own words he declares, "If I kept merely to miracles of healing and omitted all others . . . and if I limited myself to those that happened at Hippo and Calama, I should have to fill several volumes, and even then I could do no more than tell those cases that have been officially recorded and attested." He goes on to say, "This . . . I took care to have done, once I realized how many miracles were occurring in our own day and which were so like the miracles of old."[87]

So all the way down to the fifth century we have Augustine as a witness to God's healing the sick. Apparently the gifts of healings did not pass away with the apostles, the opinions of Warfield and others notwithstanding. Patterson tells us that the continuation of the gifts of healings were understood by some to be "evidence of the continuation of the saving work of Christ."[88]

Ken Blue points out a number of errors in evangelical circles that corrupt the biblical doctrine of divine healing. He speaks of them as theological hindrances to healing.[89] First, there is what he calls the "Sanctification through sickness" view. Second, there is the Calvinistic divine determinism that states that God has willed everything, even the physical suffering of His obedient children. There are problems with these views. They make prayer for the sick absurd; if God controls everything directly, then one need not pray. God will heal if He desires us to be well and if He doesn't it won't do any good to pray anyway. Many times this point of view is betrayed when there is an extremely heavy emphasis on "If it be your will, Lord." Often these prayers are not prayers of submission to the will of God but rather confessions of doubt that God would really intervene in the sick person's

---

[86]Ibid., 155.

[87]See *Retractaiones* 12, 7; 13, 5 (in the translation *The Fathers of the Church,* 60:55, 61f); *De Civitate Dei* 22, 8 (in the translation *The Fathers of the Church,* 8:445).

[88]See Patterson, "Healings"; Justin, 2 Apol. 13; Dial. 17; 30; Irenaeus, Haer, 3.18.4; 4.20.2; 5.3.1ff; Origen, Cels. 7.32; Cyprian, Ep., 74.2; 76.2); of the goodness of the body (Justin 1 Apol. 18ff; Tatian Orat. 6; 16; 20; Theophilus, Autol. 1.7; 2.26; Irenaeus, Haer, 5.12.16; Origen, Cels. 5.19); the possibility of the resurrection (Tertullian, Resurr. 12; Gregory of Nyssa, Hom. opif. 25.6ff; Augustine, civ. Dei. 22.5, 8ff.) For further discussion of the cessation of the charismata, see chap. 13, p. 445.

[89]Ken Blue, *Authority to Heal* (Downers Grove, Ill.: InterVarsity Press, 1987), 21–51.

life in a supernatural way and restore health. Most certainly God's will is primary. Yet as we have mentioned, there is little evidence, if any, that God chooses deliberately an experience of suffering for His children. The only exception may be the believer who is walking in disobedience or possibly one like Job or Paul who needs to learn a specific truth. It is worth mentioning at this juncture that Job did finally come to a proper understanding (Job 42:1–6).

The will of God, normally, is that the believer be healthy. This does not mean believers don't get sick. We live in a fallen world. Sickness does not mean we are poor excuses for Christians. The believer can trust God for basic needs being met, health being one of them. Can God use sickness in our lives? Absolutely, but He revealed himself in the ministry of Jesus Christ as a God of healing and restoration.

Another hindrance to biblical healing is what Blue calls the faith formula that focuses not on the divine power and desire to heal but on human faith and confession. He points out that "[c]an-do American optimism has fused with Christian fundamentalism to spawn a triumphalistic theological hybrid, both attractive and dangerous."[90] It defines faith as if it were a technique by which one may manipulate the power of God. It promotes the sovereignty of human beings, rather than the sovereignty of God. The issue that runs the faith formula's ship aground is the absolute connection they claim to establish between faith as a cause and healing as an effect. Such a causal relationship between the two leaves little (if any) room for what might be called mitigating circumstances, such as God's timing or chastisement. We deplore such reductionism.[91]

There are a number of problems with this movement's understanding of divine healing: first, the cultic nature of these proponents' doctrine of the Atonement, the so-called "born-again" Jesus theory in which the devil is atoned and Jesus gains victory through His Gnostic-like knowledge. The Scriptures teach that Christ's sufferings and death provide atonement for sins and deliverance from sickness. In contrast

---

[90]Ibid., 41.

[91]There have been a number of books in the last few years, such as Gordon Fee, *The Disease of the Health and Wealth Gospels* (Beverly, Mass.: Frontline Publishing, 1985); and D. R. McConnell, *A Different Gospel: A Historical and Biblical Analysis of the Modern Faith Movement* (Peabody, Mass.: Hendrickson Publishers, 1988), that deal in some detail with the errors of this so-called faith movement.

to this orthodox Christian position, the faith movement, as represented by Kenneth Hagin and Kenneth Copeland, teach that "diseases are healed by Christ's spiritual atonement in hell, not by His physical death on the cross."[92] This is in clear violation of Scripture.

A second problem with their view of healing is the contribution made by New Thought and other metaphysical cults to their view of the nature of human beings.[93]

A third problem is that they teach that a sick believer is a reproach. E. W. Kenyon writes that "it is wrong for us to have sickness and disease."[94] The difference between this position and the biblical position is clear. The Bible attaches no moral qualifications to either sickness or health. Being physically healthy or sick may have little to do with our faith or spirituality. The believer, according to the proponents of the faith movement, is made completely responsible for personal illness. The inscrutable will of God or the mere consequences of living in a fallen world may play absolutely no part.

A fourth problem is the practice of positive confession itself. It is a denial of obvious realities under the guise of exercising one's faith. It has more in common with Christian Science than with biblical faith. This error is related to another one that D. R. McConnell identifies as "denying the symptoms." Nowhere in Scripture are we encouraged to deny symptoms. This view is bolstered by a New Thought philosophy that denies the reality of the physical world. Other errors espoused by the faith movement include the necessity of enduring pain, outgrowing the need for medical science, the conviction that believers should never die of disease, and that believers should never die before they are seventy years old.[95]

The faith movement teaches that believers can be totally delivered from bodily suffering in this life. This is in contradiction to the teaching of Scripture. In Romans 8 Paul refers to the sufferings of this life that will not be removed completely until the future redemption of our bodies when we

---

[92]McConnell, *A Different Gospel,* 150.

[93]The views of E. W. Kenyon, Kenneth E. Hagin, and Kenneth Copeland are basically New Thought with its denial of the reality of the physical world. They deny that disease has any "physical or organic causes," rather everything is defined in spiritual terms.

[94]Essek W. Kenyon, *Jesus the Healer* 19th ed. (Seattle: Kenyon Gospel Publishing Society, 1968), 44 (cf. 32).

[95]McConnell, *A Different Gospel,* 149–50.

are changed and become like the risen Christ (Rom. 8:18– 25; see also 1 Cor. 15:42; 1 John 3:2). McConnell is absolutely right when he says, "The error of the Faith theology is that it ascribes power to faith healing that will only be manifest at the end of the age."[96]

Can sin make us physically sick? Yes, but that is not the same as saying that whenever you are sick it is the direct result of sin. Can faith be used by God to bring healing to our bodies? Yes, but it does not follow that if we are not healed the problem is necessarily a lack of faith. We whole-heartedly agree with McConnell when he writes, "We must neither deny healing, nor simplify it into 'steps' or 'principles' or 'formulas' to which God must respond."[97]

COMMON QUESTIONS ABOUT DIVINE HEALING

1. Why are some healed and others not?

The answer to this question lies within the sovereign wisdom of God, but a few remarks can be made.[98] Some are sick because of sin's effect. An example of this in the New Testament can be found in 1 Corinthians 11:27–30. This is why we should always ask the Holy Spirit to search our hearts and show us possibly hidden areas of sin that are keeping us from receiving healing.

Another possibility is that the Lord is trying to teach us something, as He did Paul (2 Cor. 12:7) or Job. In those cases we need to seek the Lord for understanding.

Then there is the issue of timing. Many do not receive healing immediately. In such a case we need to remember the words of the Lord when He admonished us that we ought always to pray and faint not (Luke 18:1). God has His time. The word *kairos* in the Greek language of the New Testament implies "a distinct point in time," "a time for decision," or it can mean "favorable moment," as in Acts 24:25. The believer should not give up hope, for God has a time of healing for His sons and daughters.

Lack of faith can also impede the reception of healing. The author of the Epistle to the Hebrews, in a number of places, admonishes us to keep up our faith in God. The First Epistle

---

[96]Ibid., 160.

[97]Ibid., 159.

[98]See Steve D. Eutsler, "Why Are Not All Christians Healed?" *Paraclete* 27 (Spring 1993): 15–23; John Katter, "Divine Healing" *Paraclete* 27 (Spring 1993): 24–29.

of John reminds us that the victory of the believer is tied to personal faith (1 John 5:4–5). Ladd points out that not all who came in contact with Jesus were healed. Why? According to Ladd, "[T]his physical salvation required the response of faith." No wonder James wrote in his epistle, "The prayer offered in faith will make the sick person well; the Lord will raise him up" (James 5:15). After we have examined our heart and there seems to be no indication of a reason for not being healed we must rest in God. There are times when healing does not come. Many times from our perspective there is no penetrating the inscrutable will of God. As Ladd has written, "In the present working of the Kingdom ... [n]ot all the sick and crippled were saved. ... The saving power of the Kingdom was not yet universally operative."[99]

2. If healing is in the Atonement why can't we be as assured of our healing as we are of our salvation?

There are those who argue that although God has promised to save all who call upon him, He has nowhere promised to heal all that come to him.[100] Healing does not have the same place in the Atonement that salvation has, though healing is inherent in salvation. Virgil Warren provides some significant insight into this matter. He addresses three types of healing. First, there is psychological and emotional healing. Many times psychological and emotional problems are the result of guilt. With the expurgation of guilt through regeneration, the believer is free to experience God's healing grace in the emotions. Warren mentions second that psychosomatic healing must be allowed, since, in Warren's words, "organic disorders" may be the result of psychological causes. Third, there is also the issue of physical healing. Warren believes that this will come with less certainty since it requires a "special divine providence to enter the picture." Warren calls divine physical healing a "non-uniform" result of salvation.[101] What is meant by this term is that we cannot assume there will necessarily be a manifestation of God's healing every time we pray for it. There is always the issue of God's wisdom and will, among other things, to be considered.

---

[99]Ladd, *New Testament Theology*, 76.

[100]J. Sidlow Baxter, *Divine Healing of the Body* (Grand Rapids: Zondervan Publishing House, 1979), 116, 269.

[101]Virgil Warren, *What the Bible Says about Salvation* (Joplin, Mo.: College Press Publishing Co., 1982), 545–46.

On the other hand, it appears from Scripture that when we are sick we should be prayed for, and as we shall see later in this chapter, it appears that God's normal will is to heal. Instead of expecting that it is not God's will to heal us, we should pray with faith, trusting that God cares for us and that the provision He has made in Christ for our healing is sufficient. If He does not heal us, we will continue to trust Him. The victory many times will be procured in faith (see Heb. 10:35–36; 1 John 5:4–5).

CHAPTER
15

Divine
Healing

3. Why were all New Testament believers healed, but not all today's believers healed?

First, though some passages in the Gospels speak of Jesus healing all of the sick, other passages imply not all were healed. An example is found in John 5. This text tells us in verse 3 that "a great number" were "disabled," but Jesus healed only, as John puts it, "one who was there [who] had been an invalid for thirty-eight years" (v. 5). Later, John refers to "the man who was healed" (v. 13), as if in this particular setting only one was healed.

Second, we know from 2 Corinthians 12:7–10 and Galatians 4:13 that Paul also struggled with some infirmity, possibly a recurring infirmity, that did not go away for some time, if ever. Hans Dieter Betz, commenting on Galatians 4:13, writes that "[t]he term *astheneia tēs sarkos* ... in all probability points to a real illness of Paul." It is true that *astheneia* refers to human weaknesses as well, but here it has the sense of illness.[102] It is worth noting that one of the answers to why God allows us to be sick might be in this text. Paul says that it was through (Gk. *di'*) this sickness that he came to preach to the Galatians. For Paul "everything became a *kairos* ('good opportunity') when the gospel was to be proclaimed."[103] So in this context, an illness was used by God to get His servant to a specific place, to a specific people, for the specific purpose of sharing the gospel.

There is also the case of Epaphroditus who was deathly ill (Phil. 2:25–27). Paul describes Epaphroditus' illness in very poignant terms. The phrase *paraplēsion thanatō* literally

---

[102]Hans Dieter Betz, *Galatians* (Philadelphia: Fortress Press, 1979), 224. Frank J. Matera, *Galatians* (Collegeville: Michael Glazier Books, 1992), 159.

[103]Betz, *Galatians,* 224.

means "a near neighbor to death."[104] He did recover, but only after he nearly died.

And, finally, mention ought to be made of Paul's young associate in ministry, Timothy. Paul recommends in 1 Timothy 5:23 that Timothy take a little wine for a stomach problem. This was obviously an ongoing health problem that Timothy struggled with. Certainly Timothy must have been prayed for, but at the time Paul wrote, there had been no healing. What is Paul's advice? Use what you have at your disposal to help in the situation. J. N. D. Kelly points out that the "beneficial effects of wine as a remedy against dyspeptic complaints, as a tonic, and as counteracting the effects of impure water, were widely recognized in antiquity."[105] In the modern vernacular Paul was telling Timothy to take the medicine he needed. This is what might be called a historical narrative as illustration and pattern.[106] That is, this text functions as a historical precedent to justify the use of medicines during times of illness, when we have not experienced a divine healing. It does not give grounds for indulging in alcoholic beverages.

4. Shouldn't divine healing be considered the exception rather than the rule?

The Bible shows that God does not leave us to our own devices in facing life's trials and struggles. We are to be acutely aware of both God's concern for His children and His desire to be involved in our lives in a supernatural way. What this has meant, in practice, is an expectation that God would be involved in things like sickness by healing the afflicted. Take, for instance, James 5:14–16. It is probable that the healing mentioned in James 5:14–16 is not the charismatic gift of healing, but rather the result of community and elder prayers for the sick. This passage is inclusive in its call for the sick to be healed. James writes, "Is any one of you sick? He should call the elders of the church to pray over him and anoint him with oil in the name of the Lord. And the prayer offered in

---

[104]Gerald F. Hawthorne, *Philippians,* vol. 43 (Waco, Tex.: Word Books, 1983), 118.

[105]J. N. D. Kelly, *The Pastoral Epistles* (San Francisco: Harper & Row Pub. Co., 1960), 129. See Athenaseus, *Banquet,* 2, 24; Pliny, *Natural History* 14.18; cf. "Wine in New Testament Times," *The Full Life Study Bible* (Grand Rapids: Zondervan Publishing House, 1992), 1538, 1594.

[106]Gordon D. Fee, *Gospel and Spirit: Issues in New Testament Hermeneutics* (Peabody, Mass.: Hendrickson Publishers, 1991), 95.

faith will make the sick person well; the Lord will raise him
up. If he has sinned, he will be forgiven." It is clear that prayer
brings the healing, not the anointing with oil or the laying
on of hands.[107]

Some today speak of divine healing as something "exceptional and unexpected."[108] But the Early Church did not believe that divine healing was "an altogether unexpected act
of God." On the contrary, they prayed for the sick in anticipation of their recovery. The language of James 5:14–15
doesn't hedge at this point. It plainly states that "the prayer
offered in faith will make the sick person well." Obviously,
God can and does say no at times. In His wisdom He may
withhold healing, but that is not what the Scriptures point to
as normative. God's normative will is to heal the sick on the
basis of Christ's work, through the believer's faith in Him.

How was the prayer to be made? James says *"tēs pisteōs,"*
that is, "in faith." Faith will make whole (Gk. *sōzō*), "save,"
which includes the meanings "keep safe," "preserve," "rescue,"
and "make well."[109] James goes on to say in 5:16 that we
ought to pray for one another so that we might be healed
(Gk. *iathēte*—subjunctive passive of *iaomai*). The subjunctive implies healing might be ours if we pray and have others
pray for us. There is a definite indication of expectancy. The
text is very positive about healing. If you are sick, get believers, not just elders (see 5:16), to pray for you so you can
be healed. "The expectation of healing is related to the efficacy of prayer." "The promised result, which must have been
normally the case, ... is that the power in the prayer will
heal." A scholar who belongs solidly to evangelical ranks,
though not normally associated with beliefs in divine healing,
D. Edmond Hiebert writes, "James' statement does not contemplate failure."[110]

Divine healing is more than an exceptionality. It is definitely

[107]M. Dennis Ham, "Gifts of Healing," in *The Anchor Bible Dictionary,*
ed. David Noel Freedman, vol. 3 (New York: Doubleday, 1992), 89. Peter
Davids, *James* (San Francisco: Harper & Row, 1983), 94.

[108]C. Samuel Storms, *Healing & Holiness: A Biblical Response to the
Faith-Healing Phenomenon* (Phillipsburg: Presbyterian and Reformed Pub.
Co., 1990), ix.

[109]See chap. 10, p. 328.

[110]Sophie Laws, *The Epistle of James* (San Francisco: Harper & Row,
1980), 232. Peter H. Davids, *The Epistle of James: A Commentary on the
Greek Text* (Grand Rapids: Wm. B. Eerdmans, 1982), 194. D. Edmond
Hiebert, *The Epistle of James: Tests of a Living Faith* (Chicago: Moody
Press, 1979), 322.

something with which God would like to bless us more than we experience it. P. T. Forsyth put it well when he said, "It is His will—His will of Grace—that prayer should prevail with Him and *extract* blessings."[111] What is the problem? Why don't we experience it more often? As indicated above, the answer is found in James 5:14–16.

Concluding Remarks

The doctrine of divine healing is a natural outgrowth of this search for biblical Christianity. It is not a minor doctrine, but rather an integral part of the message of the entire Bible. The Anglican theologian James Packer points out that the issue of whether or not God heals directly has been debated for the last century among evangelical Protestants. The problem with this debate is that it "regularly isolates the healing of the body from the healing of the person, as if the body-soul dualism of ancient and modern philosophies were true, and the biblical view of man as a psycho-physical unity were false. . . ."[112]

In contrast to some dispensational fundamentalists and liberal Protestants, Pentecostals do not find the idea strange that God would heal the sick today, but comforting and most of all biblical. It is part of the ongoing work of Jesus in His Church as we anticipate His return, when that which is "perfect comes" and "the partial will be done away" (1 Cor. 13:10, NASB). We wholeheartedly agree with Friedrich Graber and Dietrich Muller when they declare, "When human well-being and good health are impaired, God is actively involved in the work of restoration, and Christians have the responsibility of sharing in this ministry."[113] Until Jesus comes again, it is the call of the Master to preach the whole gospel to the whole person. This includes the supernatural healing of the body as well as the soul.

Study Questions

1. What part should the ministry of divine healing have in evangelism?

---

[111]P. T. Forsyth, *The Soul of Prayer* (London: Independent Press, 1966), 90.

[112]C. Samuel Storms *Healing and Holiness: A Biblical Response to the Faith-Healing Phenomenon* (Phillipsburg, Penn.: Presbyterian and Reformed Publishing, 1990), ix.

[113]Friedrich Graber and Dietrich Muller, "Heal," in *The New International Dictionary of New Testament Theology,* Colin Brown, ed. vol. 2 (Grand Rapids: Zondervan Publishing House, 1976), 163.

2. Why is sickness so prevalent in the world?

3. What is the relation between individual sickness and sin?

4. To what extent are demons responsible for sickness?

5. What part did healing the sick have in the ministry of Jesus?

6. What is the relation of divine healing to salvation?

7. What do we mean when we say healing is in the Atonement?

8. How are healings a manifestation of the kingdom of God?

9. What are the problems with the so-called faith formula teaching?

10. What are some of the ways we can encourage the faith of those who are not yet healed? those in the final stages of a serious illness?

CHAPTER SIXTEEN

The New Testament Church

Michael L. Dusing

An area of Christian theology often minimized and taken for granted is the doctrine of the Church. In part, this is due to the common assumption that some areas of theological study are more essential to salvation and the Christian life (e.g., the doctrines of Christ and salvation) and others are simply more exciting (e.g., manifestations of the Holy Spirit or the doctrine of last things). The Church, on the other hand, is a subject that many Christians consider themselves familiar with; after all, it has been a regular part of their lives. What more could be gained by an extensive study of something so common and routine in the experience of most believers? The answer, of course, is plenty.

The Scriptures, along with the history of the development and expansion of Christianity, offer a wealth of insight into the nature and purpose of the Church. Acquiring a better theological understanding of the Church is not only a worthy academic exercise, but also essential to a well-rounded and balanced perspective of how theology is to be applied and lived out in everyday life. The Church is God's creation and design; it is His method of providing spiritual nurture for the believer and a community of faith through which the gospel is proclaimed and His will advanced in every generation. Therefore, the doctrine of the Church addresses issues of fundamental importance to one's individual Christian walk and proper understanding of the corporate dimension of Christian life and ministry.

THE ORIGIN AND DEVELOPMENT OF THE CHURCH

THE CHURCH DEFINED

Jesus asserted in Matthew 16:18, "I will build my church." This is the first of more than one hundred New Testament

CHAPTER
16

The New
Testament
Church

references that employ the primary Greek term for church, *ekklēsia.* The word is compounded from the preposition ek, "out," and the verb *kaleō,* "to call." Hence *ekklēsia* originally denoted a group of citizens called out and assembled for a specific purpose. The term is found from the fifth century B.C. forward in the writings of Herodotus, Xenophon, Plato, and Euripides. This concept of *ekklēsia* was especially prevalent in the capital city of Athens, where the political leaders were called together as a constitutional assembly as often as forty times a year.[1] This more secular usage of the term can also be seen in the New Testament. For example, in Acts 19:32,41 *ekklēsia* refers to the angry mob of citizens that assembled in Ephesus to protest the effects of Paul's ministry.[2] The majority of New Testament uses of *ekklēsia,* however, have a more sacred application, referring to those whom God has called out of sin into the fellowship of His Son, Jesus Christ, and who have become "fellow citizens with God's people" (Eph. 2:19). The word is always used of people and also identifies their gathering to worship and serve the Lord.

The Septuagint, a Greek translation of the Old Testament, also uses *ekklēsia* nearly one hundred times, usually as a translation for the Hebrew term *qahal* ("assembly," "convocation," "congregation"). The Old Testament usage of this term, like the New, sometimes refers to a religious assembly (e.g., Num. 16:3; Deut. 9:10) and at other times to a gathering for more secular, even evil, purposes (e.g., Gen. 49:6; Judg. 20:2; 1 Kings 12:3). A Hebrew term with a meaning similar to *qahal* is *'edah* ("congregation," "company," "assemblage," "gathering"). It is significant to note that *ekklēsia* is frequently used in the Septuagint to render *qahal,* but never *'edah.* Rather, this latter term is most often rendered *sunagōgē* ("synagogue"). For example, the phrase "community of Israel" (Exod. 12:3) could be translated the "synagogue of Israel" if one were to follow the Septuagint's rendition (see also Exod. 16:1ff.; Num. 14:1ff., 20:1ff.).[3]

[1]Karl L. Schmidt, *"ekklēsia,"* in *Theological Dictionary of the New Testament,* Gerhard Kittel and Gerhard Friedrich, eds., trans. Geoffrey W. Bromiley, vol. 3 (Grand Rapids: Wm. B. Eerdmans, 1965), 513. Cf. Lothar Coenen, "Church," in *The New International Dictionary of New Testament Theology,* ed. Colin Brown, vol. 1 (Grand Rapids: Zondervan, 1967), 291.

[2]This indicates that by New Testament times the word no longer had the meaning "called out," but simply meant an "assembly of citizens" whether called out or not.

[3]Thoralf Gilbrant, ed., *The Complete Biblical Library,* vol. 12 (Springfield, Mo.: The Complete Biblical Library), s.v. "Ecclesia," 334–35. William L.

The Greek term *sunagōgē,* like its frequent Hebrew counterpart *'edah,* has the essential meaning of people assembled together.[4] When hearing the word "synagogue" today, one usually pictures an assembly of Jewish persons gathered to pray and to listen to the reading and exposition of the Old Testament. Such a meaning of the word is also in the New Testament (e.g., Luke 12:11; Acts 13:42). And although early Christians normally avoided this word to describe themselves,[5] James did not (using the term [James 2:2] to refer to believers who met for worship perhaps because most of his readers were Jewish converts).

Consequently, whether one refers to the common Hebrew terms *qahal* and *'edah* or the Greek words *sunagōgē* and *ekklēsia,* the essential meaning is still the same: The "Church" comprises those who have been called out of the world, out of sin and isolation from God, and through the redemptive work of Christ have been gathered as a community of faith that shares in the blessings and the responsibilities of serving the Lord.

The English word "church" and its related cognate terms in other languages (e.g., the German *kirche* and the Scottish *kirk*) originated from the Greek word *kuriakos,* "belonging to the Lord." This term is found only twice in the New Testament (1 Cor. 11:20; Rev. 1:10). It was significant in early Christianity, however, in that it became a designation for the place where the Church, or *ekklēsia,* gathered. This place of assembly, regardless of its normal usage or surroundings, was considered "holy," or belonging to the Lord, because God's people assembled there to worship and serve Him.

Today the word "church" is used in a variety of ways. It often refers to a building where believers meet (e.g., "we are going to the church"). It can refer to one's local fellowship or denomination (e.g., "my church teaches baptism by immersion"). In some areas, it can refer to a regional or national religious group (e.g., "the Church of England"). The word is frequently used in reference to all born-again believers, regardless of their geographical or cultural differences (e.g.,

Holladay, *A Concise Hebrew and Aramaic Lexicon of the Old Testament* (Grand Rapids: Wm. B. Eerdmans, 1971), 265. Millard J. Erickson, *Christian Theology* (Grand Rapids: Baker Book House, 1985), 1032.

[4]Joseph Henry Thayer, *The Greek-English Lexicon of the New Testament* (Grand Rapids: Zondervan Publishing House, 1962), 600.

[5]Emil Schürer, *The History of the Jewish People in the Age of Jesus Christ,* vol. 2 (Edinburgh: T. & T. Clark, rev. ed. 1979), 429, note 12.

"the Church of the Lord Jesus Christ"). Be that as it may, the biblical meaning of "church" refers primarily, not to institutions or structures, but rather to the people who have been reconciled to God through the saving work of Christ and now belong to Him.

POSSIBILITIES OF ORIGIN

Precisely when the New Testament Church began has been a matter of some debate in theological circles. Some have taken a very broad approach, suggesting the Church has existed since the conception of humanity and includes all persons who have ever exercised faith in God's promises, starting with Adam and Eve (Gen. 3:15). Others endorse an Old Testament beginning for the Church, specifically with the covenantal relationships of God with His people, beginning with the patriarchs and continuing with the Mosaic period. Many scholars prefer a New Testament origin for the Church, but in this context there are also differences of opinion. For example, some believe the Church was founded when Christ began His public ministry and called His twelve disciples.[6] Other viewpoints abound, including some ultradispensationalists who think the Church did not truly begin until the ministry and missions trips of the apostle Paul.[7]

The majority of scholars, whether from Pentecostal, evangelical, or liberal backgrounds, believe that the scriptural evidence for the inauguration of the Church favors the Day of Pentecost in Acts 2. Some, however, recognize that Christ's death put the New Covenant into effect (Heb. 9:15–16). Therefore they take John 20:21–23 to be the inauguration of the Church as a new covenant body (cf. John 20:29 which shows that the disciples were already believers and thus were already the Church before they were empowered by the baptism in the Holy Spirit).

There are several reasons for the belief that the Church originated, or at least was first publicly recognized, on the Day of Pentecost. Although in the pre-Christian era God cer-

---

[6]R. B. Kuiper, *The Glorious Body of Christ* (Grand Rapids: Wm. B. Eerdmans, n.d.), 21–22. Charles Hodge, *Systematic Theology,* vol. 3 (N.Y.: Scribner Armstrong & Co., 1877), 549. See also Louis Berkhof, *Systematic Theology* (Grand Rapids: Wm. B. Eerdmans, 1941), 570. Cf. Raymond M. Pruitt, *Fundamentals of the Faith* (Cleveland, Tenn.: White Wing Publishing House and Press, 1981), 350.

[7]Representatives of this view include Ethelbert Bullinger and J. C. O'Hair. Cited in Robert L. Saucy, *The Church in God's Program* (Chicago: Moody, 1972), 57.

tainly had association with a covenant community of righteous believers, there is no clear evidence that the concept of the Church existed in the Old Testament period. When Jesus expressed the first direct statement concerning the *ekklēsia* (Matt. 16:18), He was speaking about something that He would initiate in the future ("I will build" [Gk. *oikodomēsō*] is simple future—not an expression of disposition or determination).

By its very nature as the body of Christ, the Church is integrally dependent on the finished work of Christ on earth (His death, resurrection, and ascension) and the coming of the Holy Spirit (John 16:7; Acts 20:28; 1 Cor. 12:13). In connection with this, Millard J. Erickson notes that Luke never uses *ekklēsia* in his Gospel, but employs it twenty-four times in the Book of Acts. This would suggest that Luke did not think of the Church as being present until the period covered in Acts.[8] Following that great day when the Holy Spirit was outpoured upon the gathered believers, the Church began powerfully to propagate the gospel as predicted by the risen Lord in Acts 1:8. From that day forward, the Church has continued to develop and expand throughout the world in the power, and by the direction, of that same Holy Spirit.

A BRIEF HISTORY

As the Church developed in the centuries following the New Testament Era, its character was altered in many different ways, some far astray from the teachings and patterns of the first-century Church. Many good volumes on the history of Christianity are available that would help one gain a broader and enhanced perspective on this subject. For the purposes of this chapter, several brief observations are in order.

During the Patristic Era (the ancient period of the church fathers and apologists of the faith), the Church experienced both external and internal difficulties. Externally it faced severe persecution by the Roman Empire, especially the first three hundred years. At the same time, within the Church numerous heresies were developing—which in the long run proved to be more calamitous than the persecutions.

The Church, by God's sovereign grace, survived these arduous times and continued to grow, yet not without some changes with negative consequences. In an effort to unite and withstand the onslaught of persecutions and heresies, the

---

[8]Erickson, *Christian Theology*, 1048.

Church increasingly rallied around and elevated the authority of its leadership. Especially after political peace and harmony were achieved with the Roman government in the fourth century, the religious hierarchy escalated. As the authority and control of the clergy (particularly the bishops) increased, the importance and participation of the laity decreased. In this way, the Church became more institutionalized and less dependent on the empowerment and direction of the Holy Spirit. The status of the bishop of Rome and the church under his control grew, so that by the end of the Ancient Era the position of "Pope" and the authority of what was becoming known as the Roman Catholic Church were secure in Western Europe. The Eastern Church, however, broke away and remained under the direction of chief bishops whom they termed "patriarchs."[9]

In the Middle Ages the Church continued in the direction of formality and institutionalism. The papacy attempted to exercise its authority not only in spiritual matters but in temporal affairs as well. Many popes and bishops sought to "spiritualize" this period of history, in which they envisioned the kingdom of God (or the Roman Catholic Church) spreading its influence and regulation throughout the earth. This created a continuous tension between the secular rulers and the Popes about who had control. Nevertheless, with few exceptions the papacy held supremacy in nearly every area of life.

Certainly, not everyone accepted this increased secularization of the Church and its aspiration to Christianize the world. There were some notable medieval attempts to reform the Church and to return it to a path of true spirituality. Several monastic movements (e.g., the Cluniacs of the tenth century and the Franciscans of the thirteenth century) and even lay movements (e.g., the Albigenses and the Waldensians, both of the twelfth century) made such efforts. Prominent individuals, such as the mystics Bernard of Clairvaux (twelfth century) and Catherine of Siena (fourteenth century), and Catholic clerics, such as John Wycliffe (fourteenth century) and John Hus (late fourteenth, early fifteenth century), sought to rid the Catholic Church of its vice and corruption and return it to the pattern and principles of the New Testament Church. The Church of Rome, however, largely

---

[9]The Eastern Church is not treated in this volume beyond mentions such as this because it had little effect on the history and development of the western and American churches.

rejected these reform efforts, instead becoming more crystallized in its doctrine and institutionalized in its tradition. Such an attitude made the Protestant Reformation nearly inevitable.

The sixteenth century saw the emergence of great Reformers who led the way in revolutionizing the Church, men such as Martin Luther, Huldreich Zwingli, John Calvin, and John Knox. These men and their followers shared many of the same ideas of earlier Reformers. They saw Christ, not the Pope, as the true Head of the Church; Scripture, not the tradition of the Church, as the true basis of spiritual authority; and faith alone, not works, as essential for salvation. The Renaissance had helped pave the way for the introduction and acceptance of such ideas, ideas once familiar to the Church in the first century but now radical to the Church of the sixteenth. Reformers differed among themselves on many of the specific doctrines and practices of Christianity (e.g., their views on the ordinances and government of the Church, which will be addressed in later sections of this chapter), but they shared a passion for the return to biblical faith and practice.

In the centuries since the Reformation (commonly known as the post-Reformation era), individuals and organizations have taken many and varied directions as they have tried to apply their interpretation of New Testament Christianity. Unfortunately, some have repeated mistakes of the past, emphasizing the rituals and formalism of the institutional Church to the neglect of the biblical emphases on salvation by grace through faith and on life in the Spirit.

The rationalism of the eighteenth century helped prepare the stage for many of the liberal and sometimes antisupernatural teachings of the nineteenth and twentieth centuries. Louis Berkhof aptly states that such movements have led to the "modern liberal conception of the Church as a mere social center, a human institution rather than a planting of God."[10] From a more positive perspective, however, the post-Reformation Era has also witnessed reactions to these stifling and liberalizing tendencies through movements that have once more yearned for and received a genuine experience with God. The Pietist movement (seventeenth century), the Moravian and Methodist movements (eighteenth century), and the Great Awakenings, Holiness movement, and Pentecostal movement (eighteenth-twentieth centuries) are all examples

---

[10]Berkhof, *Systematic Theology*, 561.

that the Church founded by Jesus Christ (cf. Matt. 16:18) is still alive and well, and shall continue to progress until He comes.

THE NATURE OF THE CHURCH

BIBLICAL TERMS APPLIED TO THE CHURCH

The Church has previously been defined by examining primary biblical terms, such as *ekklēsia* (a group of citizens assembled together for a specific purpose) and *kuriakos* (a group which belongs to the Lord). The nature of the Church, however, is far too extensive to be encompassed in a few simple definitions. The Bible uses numerous metaphorical descriptions for the Church, each of which portrays a different aspect of what the Church is and what it is called to do. Paul Minear indicates that as many as eighty New Testament terms delineate the meaning and purpose of the Church.[11] An exploration of each of them would make a fascinating study, but for the present chapter several of the more significant designations will be examined.

People of God. The apostle Paul borrowed from the Old Testament description of Israel and applied it to the New Testament Church when he declared, "As God has said: 'I will live with them and walk among them, and I will be their God, and they will be my people' " (2 Cor. 6:16; cf. Lev. 26:12). Throughout the Scriptures, the Church is depicted as God's people. Just as in the Old Testament God created Israel to be a people for himself, so the New Testament Church is God's creation, "a people belonging to God" (1 Pet. 2:9–10; cf. Deut. 10:15; Hos. 1:10). From the Church's beginning and throughout its history, it is clear the Church's destiny is founded upon the divine initiative and calling of God. As Robert L. Saucy notes, the Church is "a people called forth by God, incorporated into Christ, and indwelt by the Spirit."[12]

As the people of God, the Church is described by many very meaningful terms. The Church is an "elect" body. This does not mean that God has arbitrarily selected some for salvation and others for eternal condemnation. The people of God are called "elect" in the New Testament because God has "chosen" that the Church should do His work in this age

---

[11]Paul S. Minear, *Images of the Church in the New Testament* (Philadelphia, Pa.: Westminster, 1960), 173.

[12]Saucy, *The Church,* 19.

by the Holy Spirit, who is actively at work to sanctify and conform believers to the image of Christ (Rom. 8:28–29).

Over one hundred times in the New Testament, the people of God are referred to as the "saints," or "holy ones," (Gk. *hagiois*) of God. This does not imply that those so designated have achieved a superior spiritual status or that their behavior could be depicted as perfect or "saintly." (The many references to the Church in Corinth as "saints of God" should serve as a sufficient indication of this.) Rather, this again draws attention to the fact that the Church is God's creation and that by His divine initiative believers are "called to be holy" (1 Cor. 1:2). The people of God are frequently designated as those who are "in Christ," which suggests that they are the recipients of Christ's atoning work, and they share corporately in the privileges and responsibilities of being called Christians (Gk. *Christianous*).[13]

The people of God are referred to in other ways. Three are worthy of brief mention: "believers," "brethren," and "disciples." "Believers" is from the Greek term *pistoi*, "the faithful ones." This term intimates that the people of God have not simply believed, that is, given mental assent at some point in the past to the saving work of Christ, but rather that they live continuously in the attitude of faith, obedient trust, and commitment to their Savior. (This is further highlighted by the fact that *pistoi* is normally found in the present tense in the New Testament, denoting ongoing action.) "Brethren" (Gk. *adelphoi*) is a generic term, referring to both men and women, frequently used by the New Testament writers to express the fact that Christians are called to love not only the Lord, but also one another (1 John 3:16). Such a mutual love and fellowship are inherent among the people of God and help to remind them that regardless of individual callings or offices of ministry, all the brethren have equal standing in the presence of the Lord (Matt. 23:8).

The word "disciples" (Gk. *mathētai*) means "learners" or "pupils." Being such a student in biblical times meant more than listening to and mentally assimilating information given by a teacher. It also denoted that one would emulate the

---

[13]Although the term "Christian" has been widely used through the years to identify those who follow the teaching and way of Christ, it is found only three times in the New Testament: in Acts 11:26 (coined by the pagans in Antioch to refer to Christ's followers); Acts 26:28 (used by King Agrippa in conversation with Paul); and in 1 Pet. 4:16 (used by Peter in reference to those who suffer for the name of Christ).

teacher's character and conduct. The people of God are indeed called to be such disciples of their Teacher, Christ. As Jesus said, "If you hold to my teaching [literally, 'if you remain or continue in my word'], you are really my disciples" (John 8:31). Jesus did not falsely present the life of being His disciple as something easy or glamorous (see Luke 14:26–33), but He did indicate that it is no less than essential for those who desire to follow Him. The German theologian Dietrich Bonhoeffer has aptly noted that true Christian discipleship requires a willingness to die to self and to give all to Christ. Such authentic discipleship is possible only through what Bonhoeffer termed "costly grace" as, "Such grace is *costly* because it calls us to follow, and it is *grace* because it calls us to follow *Jesus Christ.* It is costly because it costs a man his life, and it is grace because it gives a man the only true life."[14]

Body of Christ. A very meaningful biblical image for the Church is the "body of Christ." This expression was a favorite of the apostle Paul, who often compared the parts of the human body to the interrelationships and functions of the members of the Church. Paul's writings emphasize the true unity that is essential in the Church. For example, "The body is a unit, though it is made up of many parts. . . . So it is with Christ" (1 Cor. 12:12). Just as the body of Christ is designed to function effectively as one, so the gifts of the Holy Spirit are given to equip the body by "the same Spirit . . . the same Lord . . . the same God [who] works all of them in all men . . . for the common good" (1 Cor. 12:4–7). Because of this, members of Christ's body are to exercise great caution that "there should be no division [Gk. *schisma*] in the body, but that its parts should have equal concern for each other" (1 Cor. 12:25; cf. Rom. 12:5). Christians can have this unity and mutual concern because they are "all baptized by one Spirit into one body" (1 Cor. 12:13). The Holy Spirit's indwelling each member of the body of Christ allows for the legitimate manifestation of this unity. Gordon D. Fee correctly states, "Our desperate need is for a sovereign work of the Spirit to do among us what all our 'programmed unity' cannot."[15]

While there must be unity within the body of Christ, it is not antithetical to emphasize that there is a necessary diver-

---

[14]Dietrich Bonhoeffer, *The Cost of Discipleship,* 2d ed. (New York: The Macmillan Company, 1959), 47.

[15]Gordon D. Fee, *The First Epistle to the Corinthians* (Grand Rapids: Wm. B. Eerdmans, 1987), 607.

sity if the body of Christ is to function properly. In the same context in which Paul emphasizes unity, he states, "Now the body is not made up of one part, but of many" (1 Cor. 12:14). Referring to the same analogy in a different Epistle, Paul declares, "Each of us has one body with many members, and these members do not all have the same function" (Rom. 12:4). Fee observes that unity "does not mean uniformity. . . . there is no such thing as true unity without diversity."[16]

The significance and beauty of this diversity are stressed throughout 1 Corinthians 12, especially in connection with the spiritual gifts that are so essential for the ministry of the Church (see 1 Cor. 12:7–11,27–33; cf. Rom. 12:4–8). God has not cast each member of the Church in the same mold, and He does not call all the members to the same ministry or equip them with the same gift. Rather, just as with the human body, God has so composed the Church that it functions most effectively when each part (or member) is efficiently fulfilling the role (or calling) for which it was designed.

In this way, there is "unity in diversity" within the body of Christ. In other words, inherent in this metaphor is the idea of mutuality, of each believer working with and striving for the edification of other believers. For example, this may involve suffering with those in pain or rejoicing with those being honored (1 Cor. 12:26); bearing the burdens of a brother or sister in the Lord (Gal. 6:2) or helping to restore one who has fallen into sin (Gal. 6:1). There are countless other practical ways in which this mutuality is exemplified in Scripture. The main point here is that a member of the body of Christ cannot have an exclusive, individualistic relationship with the Lord—each "individual" is in fact a necessary component of the corporate structure of the Church. As Claude Welch asserts, "There is no purely private Christianity, for to be in Christ is to be in the church, and to be in the church is to be in Christ, and any attempt to separate relation to Christ in faith from membership in the church is a perversion of the New Testament understanding."[17]

A final aspect that is integral to the image of the body of Christ is the Body's relation to its Head, Jesus Christ (Eph.

---

[16]Ibid., 602.

[17]Claude Welch, *The Reality of the Church* (New York: Charles Scribner's Sons, 1958), 165.

1:22–23; 5:23)[18] As the Head of the Body, Christ is both the source and the sustenance of life for the Church. As its members are arranged under Christ's headship and function as He desires, the body of Christ will be nourished and sustained and will grow "as God causes it to grow" (Col. 2:19). The unity, diversity, and mutuality that are indispensable for the body of Christ are attainable as the Church "will in all things grow up into him who is the Head, that is, Christ. From him the whole body . . . grows and builds itself up in love, as each part does its work" (Eph. 4:15–16).

Temple of the Spirit. Another very meaningful New Testament image for the Church is its depiction as the "temple of the Holy Spirit." The biblical writers make use of several symbols for the building components of this Temple, which correspond to the materials necessary for the construction of an earthly structure. For instance, any building needs a solid foundation. Paul clearly indicates that the primary foundation of the Church is the historical person and work of Christ: "For no one can lay any foundation other than the one already laid, which is Jesus Christ" (1 Cor. 3:11). Yet in another letter Paul suggests that there is a sense in which the Church is "built on the foundation of the apostles and prophets" (Eph. 2:20). Perhaps this means that these early leaders were uniquely used by the Lord to establish and undergird the temple of the Spirit with the teachings and practices they had learned from Christ, which continue to be communicated to believers today through Scripture.

Another important component of this building imagery, closely associated with the foundation, is the cornerstone. In modern buildings a cornerstone is usually more symbolic than integral, perhaps giving the date of its being laid and the names of key benefactors. In the biblical era, however, the cornerstone was very significant: It was typically larger than the other stones and helped to control the proper design for the rest of the building, bringing symmetry to the remainder of the edifice.[19] Christ is described as the "chief cornerstone" through whom "the whole building is joined together and

---

[18]Jesus here is compared to the head. Note that Paul also compares the head and parts of the head (e.g., eye, ear) to members of the body (1 Cor. 12:16–21). The language of comparison (simile, metaphor, etc.) usually emphasizes just one aspect of whatever is used in the comparison and must not be pressed too far.

[19]E. Mack, "Cornerstone," in *The International Standard Bible Encyclopedia,* G. Bromiley, ed. (Grand Rapids: Wm. B. Eerdmans, 1979), 784.

rises to become a holy temple in the Lord" (Eph. 2:20–21; cf. 1 Pet. 2:6–7).

Connected to the cornerstone were the normal stones necessary to complete the structure. The apostle Peter depicts believers in this role, describing them as "living stones, [who] are being built into a spiritual house to be a holy priesthood" (1 Pet. 2:5). The term used here by Peter is *lithos,* a common Greek word for stone. However, unlike the more familiar synonyms *petros* (a loose stone or small pebble) and *petra* (a solid rock sufficient to build on), the "living stones" (Gk. *lithoi zōntes*) in this context suggest "worked stones," that is, those that have been hewn and shaped by the master builder (i.e., Christ) for a proper fitting.[20] In both Ephesians 2 and 1 Peter 2, the verbs which describe the building of this Temple are usually found in the present tense, conveying a sense of continuous action. Perhaps it could be inferred from this that Christians are, as the saying goes, "still under construction." The purpose, of course, is to emphasize that the sanctifying work of the Spirit is a progressive, ongoing venture to accomplish God's purposes within the lives of believers. They are being "joined together . . . to become a holy temple in the Lord. . . . in him . . . *being built* together *to become* a dwelling in which God lives by his Spirit" (Eph. 2:21–22).

The metaphor of the temple of the Holy Spirit adds further surety that the Church is indwelt by God's Spirit, whether individually or collectively. For example, Paul queried the Corinthian believers, "Don't you know that you yourselves are God's temple and that God's Spirit lives in you? . . . God's temple is sacred, and you are that temple" (1 Cor. 3:16–17). In this particular passage, Paul is addressing the Church corporately ("you" is plural in the Greek). In 1 Corinthians 6:19, however, Paul poses a similar question to individual believers ("you" is singular): "Do you not know that your body is a temple of the Holy Spirit, who is in you, whom you have received from God?" In both 1 Corinthians 3 and 6, as well as in a similar passage in 2 Corinthians 6:16ff., the word used by Paul for "temple" is *naos.* Unlike the more general term *hieron,* which refers to the whole temple, including its courts, *naos* signifies the inner sanctuary, the Holy of Holies where the Lord manifests His presence in a special way. Paul is in effect saying that believers, as the temple of the Holy Spirit, are nothing less than the habitation of God.

---

[20]Cf. Edward G. Selwyn, *The First Epistle of St. Peter* (London: Macmillan, 1961), 158.

The Spirit of God not only conveys power to the Church for service (Acts 1:8), but also by dwelling within He imparts His life to it.[21] Consequently, there is a true sense in which those qualities that exemplify His nature (e.g., the "fruit of the Spirit," Gal. 5:22–23) are to be found in the Church, evidencing the reality that the Church is "keep[ing] in step with the Spirit" (Gal. 5:25).

Other Images. In addition to the somewhat Trinitarian pattern of images of the Church mentioned above (people of God, body of Christ, temple of the Holy Spirit), many other biblical metaphors help to broaden one's perspective of the nature of the Church. Portrayals of the Church as the priesthood of believers (1 Pet. 2:5,9), the Bride of Christ (Eph. 5:23–32), the flock of the Good Shepherd (John 10:1–18), and the branches of the True Vine (John 15:1–8) are a sampling of the diverse ways in which Scripture represents the makeup and distinct features of the one true Church, composed, as it is, of the redeemed. In different ways, these biblical images illustrate the Church's identity and purpose, which Jesus expressed so beautifully in His High Priestly Prayer:

My prayer is . . . that all of them may be one, Father, just as you are in me and I am in you. May they also be in us so that the world may believe that you have sent me. . . . May they be brought to complete unity to let the world know that you sent me and have loved them even as you have loved me (John 17:21,23).

THE CHARACTER OF THE CHURCH

In addition to the metaphors describing the nature of the Church, Scripture suggests other concepts by which theologians have described the character of the Church. One common method of doing this is to depict the Church as being both local and universal. There are many New Testament references to the universal Church (e.g., Jesus' proclamation in Matthew 16:18, "I will build my church"; also Paul's statement in Eph. 5:25, "Christ loved the church and gave himself up for her"). The universal Church incorporates all true believers regardless of geographical, cultural, or denominational differences. They are those who have responded in faith and obedience to Christ and are now "members of Christ" and consequently "members of one another" (see Rom. 12:5).

The phrase "universal Church" is used in some circles in-

---

[21]Cf. Erickson, *Christian Theology,* 1039.

terchangeably with phrases such as "ecumenical church" and "catholic church." Although the simple meaning of the terms "ecumenical" and "catholic" is "universal," the manner in which these words have been historically used implies substantial differences. For instance, when one today speaks of the "ecumenical" church, one is normally referring to an organization that is composed of several denominations that join together around common beliefs or practices, or both. The term "catholic" has essentially become synonymous with the Roman Catholic Church. While there are certainly true believers within the ranks of these organizations, it would be a mistake to confuse earthly associations as such with the universal body of believers.

Ideally the local church should be a small replica of the Church universal; that is, it should be composed of persons from all backgrounds, racial or ethnic cultures, and different socioeconomic levels who have been born again and share in common the commitment of their lives to the lordship of Jesus Christ. Unfortunately, such spiritual ideals are seldom realized among humans who are somewhat less than glorified. Just as in New Testament times, some local Christian assemblies likely have insincere or even false sheep among the flock. And so in spite of the best intentions, the local church often falls short of the character and nature of the true universal Church.

In a similar fashion, the Church is sometimes perceived as the visible and the invisible Church. This distinction appeared in Christian literature as early as Augustine and was frequently found in the writings of Reformers such as Luther and Calvin.[22] Some opponents of Luther charged that he was in fact suggesting that there were two different Churches, partly because Luther spoke of an invisible *ekklēsiola* within the visible *ekklēsia.* Luther's intention, however, was not to differentiate between two distinct Churches, but to speak of the two aspects of the one church of Jesus Christ. This simply indicates that the Church is invisible because it is essentially spiritual in nature: believers are invisibly united to Christ by the Holy Spirit, the blessings of salvation are not discernible by the natural eye, etc. This invisible Church, however, assumes a visible form in the external organization of the earthly Church. The Church is visibly exhibited through Christian testimony and practical conduct, through the tangible min-

---

[22]Cf. Augustine, *On Christian Doctrine,* 3.34; Martin Luther, "Preface to Revelation"; John Calvin, *Institutes of the Christian Religion,* 4.1.7.

istry of believers corporately and individually. The visible Church, like the local church, should be a smaller version of the invisible (or universal) Church; yet, as noted previously, such is not always the case. One may profess faith in Christ yet not truly know Him as Savior, and while being associated with the Church as an external institution, one may not really belong to the invisible Church.[23]

The tendency throughout church history has been to swing from one extreme to another. For example, some traditions, such as the Roman Catholics, Eastern Orthodox, and Anglicans, place great emphasis on the priority of the institutional or visible Church. Others, such as the Quakers and Plymouth Brethren, stressing a more internalized and subjective faith, have minimized and often reproached any type of formal organization and structure, seeking for the true, invisible Church. As Millard Erickson notes, Scripture definitely looks on the individual's spiritual condition and standing in the invisible Church as a priority, but not to the neglect or debasement of the importance of the visible Church organization. He suggests that while there are distinctions between the visible and the invisible Church, it is important to have a "both-and" approach so that one seeks to make the two as identical as possible. "Just as no true believer should be outside the fellowship, so also there should be diligence to assure that only true believers are within."[24]

It would be impossible to properly understand the true nature and character of the Church (local or universal, visible or invisible) without acknowledging the fact that from its inception, the Church has been empowered and directed by the Holy Spirit. This is certainly shown in Luke's account in Acts of the Church's beginning and development through its first three decades. The later epistles of the New Testament, as well as the ongoing history of the Church, give added emphasis to the Holy Spirit's vital role in the life of the Church. Just before His ascension, Jesus declared to His disciples, "You will receive power when the Holy Spirit comes on you; and you will be my witnesses in Jerusalem, and in all Judea and Samaria, and to the ends of the earth" (Acts 1:8). In reference to the imminent coming and enabling ministry of the Spirit, Jesus had earlier told His followers that they would do even greater things than they had seen Him do (John 14:12). This

---

[23]Cf. Berkhof, *Systematic Theology,* 565–66.
[24]Erickson, *Christian Theology,* 1047–48.

pledge was confirmed following the unique outpouring of the Spirit at Pentecost.

The reader of Acts marvels not only at the initial response to the first Spirit-filled gift of prophecy and exhortation uttered by the apostle Peter, when nearly three thousand persons were saved, but also at the continued responsiveness of those who encountered the ministry of a Church that was energized and equipped by the Holy Spirit (see Acts 2:47; 4:4,29–33; 5:12–16, etc.). In regard to Peter's message on the Day of Pentecost, one evangelical (but non-Pentecostal) scholar states, "One simply cannot account for the results of Peter's sermon on the basis of the skill with which it was prepared and delivered. The reason for its success lies in the power of the Holy Spirit." In a similar fashion, the same scholar states that the continued effectiveness of the early believers in Acts could not be accounted for on the basis of their own abilities and efforts. "They were not unusual persons. The results were a consequence of the ministry of the Holy Spirit."[25]

The Holy Spirit continued to provide strength and direction for the Church following the New Testament Era. Contrary to popular opinion in some non-Pentecostal camps, the gifts and manifestations of the Spirit did not cease with the Apostolic Era, but continued in the centuries following the New Testament period.[26] As mentioned in a previous section which reviewed the history of the Church, there is little question that as the Church expanded, gained legal status and acceptance, and became increasingly formal and institutionalized, its sense of immediate dependency upon the Spirit's leading and empowerment began to wane. Various revivalistic movements, however, provide historic evidence that the prominence of the Spirit was not totally forgotten or ignored by all.

The modern Church, especially those who consider themselves among the hundreds of millions of Pentecostal and charismatic believers worldwide, must never lose sight of the biblical and theological importance of continued attention and obedience to the sovereign working of the Spirit of God. His actions are manifested not only in unusual exhibitions of miraculous power, but also in more normative and at times

---

[25]Ibid., 1040.

[26]Many fine works substantiate this claim. Two of the better ones include Ronald A. N. Kydd, *Charismatic Gifts in the Early Church* (Peabody, Mass.: Hendrickson, 1984), and Stanley M. Burgess, *The Spirit and the Church: Antiquity* (Peabody, Mass.: Hendrickson, 1984).

almost unnoticed ways of providing direction and assistance (cf. 1 Kings 19:11–12). May the modern Church always remain sensitive and submissive to the Holy Spirit's direction and gentle guidance. Only then can contemporary Christianity claim affinity with the New Testament Church.

Another means of understanding the character of the New Testament Church is to examine its relation to the kingdom of God (Gk. *basileia tou theou*). The Kingdom was a major teaching of Jesus during His earthly ministry. In fact, while the Gospels relate only three specific mentions of the church, *ekklēsia* (all in statements of Jesus, recorded in Matt. 16 and 18), they are replete with emphasis on the Kingdom.

The term *basileia*, "kingdom," is usually defined as the rule or realm of God, the universal sphere of His influence. Following this understanding, some differentiate between the Kingdom and the Church. They see the Kingdom as including all unfallen heavenly creatures (angels) and the redeemed of humanity (before and after the time of Christ).[27] In contrast, the Church consists more specifically of those humans who have been regenerated by the atoning work of Christ. Those who accept this distinction also believe the kingdom of God transcends time and is concurrent with the universe, whereas the Church has a definite beginning point and will have a definite culminating point, at the second advent of Christ. Therefore, from this perspective the Kingdom comprises the redeemed of all ages (Old Testament saints and New Testament saints), and the Church comprises those who have been redeemed since the finished work of Christ (His crucifixion and resurrection). Following this reasoning, one may be a member of the kingdom of God without being a member of the Church (e.g., the patriarchs, Moses, David), but one who is a member of the Church is simultaneously a member of the Kingdom. As more individuals are converted to Christ and become members of His church, they are brought into the Kingdom and it is enlarged.

Others interpret the distinction between the Kingdom and the Church differently. George E. Ladd saw the Kingdom as the reign of God, but by contrast felt the Church to be the realm of God, those who are under God's rule. Similar to those who differentiate between the Kingdom and the Church, Ladd felt the two should not be equated. Rather, the Kingdom creates the Church and the Church bears witness to the King-

---

[27]Emery H. Bancroft, *Christian Theology*, 2d rev. ed. (Grand Rapids: Zondervan, 1976), 286.

dom. Further, the Church is the instrument and custodian of the Kingdom, being the form that the Kingdom or reign of God takes on earth as a concrete manifestation among humanity of God's sovereign rule.[28]

Others distinguish between the kingdom of God and the Church in that they believe the Kingdom is primarily an eschatological concept and the Church has a more temporal and present identity. Louis Berkhof sees the primary scriptural idea of the Kingdom as the rule of God "acknowledged in the hearts of sinners by the powerful regenerating influence of the Holy Spirit." This rule is now realized on earth in principle ("the present realization of it is spiritual and invisible"), but will not be fully achieved until Christ's visible return. In other words, Berkhof sees an "already-not yet" aspect at work in the relation of the Kingdom and the Church. For instance, Jesus emphasized the present reality and universal character of the Kingdom, which was realized in a new way through His own ministry. Yet He also held out a future hope of the Kingdom which would come in glory. In this regard, Berkhof is not far from the previously stated positions, in that he describes the Kingdom in broader terms than the Church. In his words, the Kingdom "aims at nothing less than the complete control of all manifestations of life. It represents the dominion of God in every sphere of human endeavor."[29]

THE PURPOSE OF THE CHURCH

Chapter 17 deals with the mission of the Church. However, before leaving this section on the nature of the Church a few observations are in order concerning the purpose for which the Church was called into being. It was not the Lord's intention for the Church to simply exist as an end in itself, to become, for example, simply another social unit formed of like-minded members. Rather, the Church is a community created by Christ for the world. Christ gave himself for the Church and then empowered it with the gift of the Holy Spirit so that it could fulfill God's plan and purpose. Many possible items could be included in a discussion of the Church's mission. However, this brief discussion will examine four: evangelization, worship, edification, and social responsibility.

Central to Jesus' last instructions to His disciples before

---

[28]George E. Ladd, *Jesus and the Kingdom* (New York: Harper and Row, 1964), 259–60.

[29]Berkhof, *Systematic Theology,* 568, 570.

His ascension was the command (not suggestion) to evangelize the world and make new disciples (Matt. 28:19; Acts 1:8). Christ did not abandon these evangelists to their own abilities or techniques. He commissioned them to go under His authority (Matt. 28:18) and in the power of the Holy Spirit (Acts 1:8). The Spirit would do the convicting of sin (John 16:8–11); the disciples were to proclaim the gospel. This task of evangelization is still an imperative part of the Church's mission: The Church is called to be an evangelizing community. This command has no restrictions or boundaries, geographically, racially, or socially. Erickson declares, "[L]ocal evangelism, church extension or church planting, and world missions are all the same thing. The only difference lies in the length of the radius."[30] Modern believers should not fail to remember that while they are the instruments of proclaiming the gospel, it is still the Lord of the harvest who "brings forth the increase." Believers are not accountable for their "success rate" (according to the world's standards), but for their commitment and faithfulness in service.

The Church is also called to be a worshiping community. The term "worship" is derived from an old English word that means "worth-ship," denoting the worthiness of the one who receives special honor in accordance with that worth.[31] Genuine worship is characterized by the Church's focusing its attention on the Lord, and not on itself.[32] In turn, as God alone is worshiped, believers invariably are blessed and spiritually strengthened. Worship need not take place only in a regularly scheduled church service. In fact, every aspect of one's life as a believer should be characterized by the desire to exalt and glorify the Lord. This seems to be Paul's point in saying, "So whether you eat or drink or whatever you do, do it all for the glory of God" (1 Cor. 10:31).

A third purpose of the Church is to be an edifying community. In evangelization the Church focuses on the world, in worship the Church focuses on God, and in edification the Church (correctly) focuses on itself. Believers are repeatedly

---

[30]Erickson, *Christian Theology*, 1054.

[31]E. F. Harrison, "Worship," in *Evangelical Dictionary of Theology*, ed. Walter A. Elwell (Grand Rapids: Baker, 1984), 1192.

[32]The common Greek word for "worship," *proskuneō*, originally meant "kiss toward" and may have been used of kissing the feet of a superior. It came to mean "bowing down in reverence and humility"; in the New Testament it is used of worship and praise to God, ascribing Him worth (e.g., Rev 11:16–17).

admonished in Scripture to build up one another into a mature community of believers (e.g. Eph. 4:12–16). Edification can be accomplished in many practical ways: For example, teaching and instructing others in the ways of God certainly enrich the household of faith (Matt. 28:20; Eph. 4:11–12). Administering spiritual correction in an attitude of love is essential if one desires to help a wayward brother or sister continue on the path of faith (Eph. 4:15; Gal. 6:1). Sharing with those in need (2 Cor. 9), bearing one another's burdens (Gal. 6:2), providing opportunities for wholesome Christian fellowship and social interaction are all meaningful ways of edifying the body of Christ.

The Church is also called to be a community with social concern and responsibility. Unfortunately this calling is minimized or neglected among many evangelicals and Pentecostals. Many sincere believers are perhaps afraid of becoming liberal or going in the direction of the so-called social gospel if they become involved in socially oriented ministries. Taken to an unhealthy extreme, and overlooking eternal verities for the sake of temporal relief, this could become true. This neglect of social concern, however, overlooks a vast number of scriptural admonitions for God's people to fulfill such obligations. Jesus' ministry was characterized by a loving compassion for the suffering and destitute individuals of this world (Matt. 25:31–46; Luke 10:25–37). This same concern is shown both in the prophetic writings of the Old Testament (Isa. 1:15–17; Mic. 6:8) and in the epistles of the New Testament (James 1:27; 1 John 3:17–18). Expressing the love of Christ in a tangible way can be a vital means of the Church fulfilling its God-given mission. As with all aspects of the Church's mission, or purpose, it is essential that one's motives and methods be directed to doing all for the glory of God.

THE ORGANIZATION OF THE CHURCH

ORGANISM OR ORGANIZATION?

Is the Church properly understood as an organism, something that has and generates life, or an organization, something characterized by structure and form? This question has been asked in various ways and with various motives throughout the history of Christianity. Every generation of believers (including some of the early-twentieth-century Pentecostals) has included some who feel the Church can be understood correctly only as an organism. Such persons emphasize the spiritual nature of the Church and tend to feel that any attempt to organize the body of believers will result in the erosion and ultimate death of the spontaneity and life that characterize true spirituality.[33] Others believe firmly in the necessity of organizational structure for the church. Such people sometimes go to the extreme of teaching that the Bible gives specific details for church order and regulation. (Unfortunately, they undermine their own argument by disagreeing on precisely which details are mandated.)

Perhaps the best approach to this sometimes controversial issue is not to pose the problem as an "either-or" question, but as a "both-and" solution. An inspection of the New Testament Church will reveal that it certainly had aspects that favor the "organism" view. The Church was dynamic and enjoyed the liberty and enthusiasm of being led by the Spirit. However, such an inspection will also reveal that from its beginning the Church operated with a degree of organizational structure. The two sides (organism and organization) do not have to be in tension, but can be perceived as having a complementary nature. Each of the biblical descriptions of the Church addressed earlier—people of God, body of Christ, temple of the Holy Spirit—suggest an organic unity in the Church. After all, Christians derive their spiritual life from their relationship with Christ, and in turn His life flows through them as they become channels of nutrition for the strengthening of the community of faith (Eph. 4:15–16). For this organism to survive, however, it must have structure. To carry the gospel throughout the world and to make disciples of all nations, the Church needs some type of organizational system for the most efficient use of its resources.

The desire to have a New Testament church is in many ways a worthy and noble aspiration. Believers should still pattern their theology after apostolic teachings and should still seek the Holy Spirit's direction in their lives. However, the New Testament indicates a variety of organization to meet the need. For example, the church did not have deacons until deacons were needed. Later, women deacons were added. There is room in the New Testament for variety to meet the needs of vastly different geographical and cultural situations. One must remember that the New Testament message is

---

[33]Note that science today shows that nothing is more highly organized than a living organism, even a living cell. When a living cell loses its organization it is dead.

eternal and cannot be compromised; for that message to be made effective, however, it needs to be applied to the contemporary environment.

MAJOR FORMS OF CHURCH GOVERNMENT

It has been suggested that the question of church organization, that is, church government, or polity, is, in the last analysis, a question of authority—where does the authority of the Church reside, and who has the right to exercise it?[34] While most believers would quickly answer that God is the final authority of the Church, they still must determine how and through whom God desires to administer His authority for the Church on earth. Throughout Christian history, there have been several major forms of church polity. Some of them give a great degree of authority to the clergy. Others stress that the laity should wield greater control in the church. Still others attempt to find a mediating position between those extremes. With few exceptions, most types of organizational structure can be categorized as one of three forms: episcopal, presbyterian, or congregational.

Episcopal is normally regarded as the oldest form of church government. The term itself is taken from the Greek word *episkopos,* meaning one who oversees. The most frequent English translation of this term is "bishop." Those who adhere to this form of polity believe that Christ, as the Head of the Church, has ordained that the control of His church on earth be entrusted to an order of officers known as bishops, who would be considered the successors to the apostles. Christ has further constituted these bishops to be a "separate, independent, and self-perpetuating order,"[35] meaning that they have final control in matters of church government and that they select their own successors.

Church history gives evidence of the gradual exaltation of the bishop's position over that of other positions of church leadership. In the second century, Ignatius of Antioch (himself a bishop) gave some of the rationale for apostolic succession when he wrote, "For Jesus Christ—that life from which we can't be torn—is the Father's mind, as the bishops too, appointed the world over, reflect the mind of Jesus Christ."[36]

[34]Cf. Erickson, *Christian Theology,* 1069.

[35]Berkhof, *Systematic Theology,* 579.

[36]Ignatius, "To the Ephesians," in *Early Christian Fathers,* ed. Cyril C. Richardson, vol. 1 (New York: Macmillan, 1970), 88.

In another letter, Ignatius gave credence to other church officers as well, including presbyters and deacons, noting that "[y]ou cannot have a church without these"; however, he emphasized that the bishop alone "has the role of the Father."[37]

The third-century church father Cyprian even further elevated the significance of the bishop and the episcopal form of government by declaring, "The bishop is in the church and the church in the bishop, and where the bishop is not there is no church."[38] The extreme version of the episcopal system is exhibited in the organization of the Roman Catholic Church, dating back to at least the fifth century. In the Catholic tradition, the Pope ("exalted father") has served as the only recognized successor to the apostle Peter, who is regarded by the Catholic Church as the one upon whom Christ established the Church (Matt. 16:17–19) and who became the first bishop of Rome.[39]

In Catholicism, there are many bishops, but all are regarded as under the authority of the Pope, who in his role as "vicar of Christ" rules as the supreme, or monarchical, bishop of the Roman Church. Other churches that adhere to the episcopal system of government take a less exclusive approach and have several (often many) leaders who exercise equal authority and oversight of the church in their role as bishops. Such groups would include the Anglican Church (or the Episcopal Church in America), the United Methodist Church, and several Pentecostal groups, including the Church of God (Cleveland, Tennessee) and the Pentecostal Holiness Church. Often the specific details of church government are modified greatly within these various groups, but they have in common the comprehensive format of the episcopal system.

The presbyterian form of church polity derives its name from the biblical office and function of the *presbuteros* ("presbyter," or "elder"). This system of government is less centrally controlled than the episcopal model and depends instead on representational leadership. Christ is perceived to be the ultimate Head of the Church, and those who are chosen (usually by election) to be His representatives to the church provide

---

[37]Ignatius, "To the Trallians," in *Early Christian Fathers*, 99.

[38]Cyprian, "On the Unity of the Church," in Justo L. Gonzalez, *A History of Christian Thought,* vol. 1 (Nashville: Abingdon, 1970), 249.

[39]Although there is strong tradition that Peter was martyred in Rome there is no real evidence that he was "bishop" there.

leadership in the normal affairs of Christian life (worship, doctrine, administration, etc.).

Once again, the specific application of the presbyterian system will vary from denomination to denomination, but typically the pattern will consist of at least four levels. First is the local church, governed by the "session," consisting of "ruling elders" (or deacons) and "teaching elder(s)" (ministers). The second level of authority is the presbytery, consisting of representative ruling and teaching elders from a given geographical district. On still a higher level is the synod, and finally at the top position of authority is the general assembly. Again, these levels are directed by representative leaders, both clergy and laity, elected by the people to provide spiritual and pragmatic direction. Although there is no strong centralized authority, such as typically is seen in the episcopal system, the churches that compose the presbyterian system have a strong bond of fellowship and a common tradition of doctrine and practice. Churches that have adopted this form of polity include the Presbyterian and Reformed Churches, and some Pentecostal groups, including to a large degree the Assemblies of God (more will be said concerning this later).

The third form of church government is the congregational system. As the name suggests, its focus of authority is on the local body of believers. Out of the three major types of church polity, the congregational system places the most control in the hands of the laity and comes closest to exemplifying a pure democracy. The local assembly is considered autonomous in its decision-making processes, with no person or agency having authority over it except Christ, the true Head of the Church. This is not to suggest that congregational churches act in total isolation from or indifference to the beliefs and customs of sister churches. Congregational churches of the same theological persuasion typically share a bond of fellowship and unity and often genuinely try to cooperate on larger-scale programs, such as missions or education (as shown, for example, within the Southern Baptist Convention). At the same time, although such churches have a sense of unity and cohesiveness about their denomination's overall purpose and ministry, their association is voluntary, not mandated, and is more loosely structured than in either the presbyterian or, particularly, the episcopal systems. Churches that operate with a congregational format include most Baptist associations, the Congregational Church, and

CHAPTER

16

The New
Testament
Church

many within the broad spectrum of the free church, or independent, ecclesiastical movements.

Those who endorse any of the three major types of church
government believe the New Testament supports their system of polity. For example, a casual reading of the New Testament epistles will reveal that both the titles *episkopos*
("bishop," "overseer," "superintendent") and *presbuteros*
("presbyter," "elder") are frequently used in reference to the
leaders of the Early Church. In 1 Timothy 3:1–7, Paul gives
instructions about the office of bishop (*episkopos*) and re-
peats some of the same instructions in Titus 1:5–9. In Titus,
however, Paul apparently uses the terms *episkopos* (v. 7) and
presbuteros (v. 5) interchangeably. In other places, the two
offices seem to stand alone (cf. Acts 15:4,22; Phil. 1:1). Consequently, depending on the emphasis given to certain passages, one could interpret the structure of the Early Church
in either episcopalian or presbyterian terms.

One selection of Scripture that is often used by both groups
to illustrate their system is Acts 15, concerning the Jerusalem
Church Council. James, the brother of Jesus, seems to preside
over the council.[40] This fact, along with other references to
James as an "apostle" and a "pillar of the church" (Gal. 1:19;
2:9), has convinced some that James is exercising the authority of a bishop. On the other hand, proponents of the
presbyterian system point out that James appears to be more
of a moderator than a figure of authority and that the others
seem to be functioning as representative leaders from their
various churches. In favor of the congregational system are
New Testament references which suggest that the Early
Church elected their own leaders and delegates (e.g., Acts
6:2–4; 11:22; 14:23[41]) and that the local congregation was
charged with the responsibility of maintaining sound doctrine
and exercising discipline (e.g., Matt. 18:15–17; 1 Cor. 5:4–5;
1 Thess. 5:21–22; 1 John 4:1).

Obviously no complete pattern of church government is

---

[40]However, rather than being a moderator, James simply gave a word of
wisdom from the Holy Spirit. The letter sent out said, "It seemed good to
the Holy Spirit and to us," not "to James and to us" (Acts 15:28). The
decision was made by "the apostles and elders, *with the whole church*"
(15:22).

[41]The word translated "appointed" (Gk. *cheirotonēsantes*) means con-
ducting an election by the show of hands. Paul and Barnabas undoubtedly
told the people what the qualifications were (as in 1 Tim. 3:1–10) and
encouraged the people to consider the character, spiritual gifts, reputation,
and fruit of the Spirit in those they elected.

specified in the New Testament. Actually, variety met the need, in effect establishing principles for exercising authority and providing examples that possibly lend support to any of the three historic types of church government. Today, most churches essentially are patterned after one of these three, yet not without modifications designed to adapt to each group's unique understanding and style of ministry. And although no one system is inherently right or wrong, each may be seen to have both positive and negative aspects.

Whichever type of ecclesiastical government one chooses, several biblical principles stand out that should undergird any governing structure. Christ must always be recognized and honored as the supreme Head of the Church. If Christians lose sight of this absolute truth, no form of government will succeed. W. D. Davies has well stated, "The ultimate New Testament criterion of any Church order ... is that it does not usurp the Crown Rights of the Redeemer within His Church."[42] Another underlying principle should be the recognition of the basic unity of the Church. Certainly, there is much diversity among the beliefs and practices of different denominations (indeed, within a single denomination). Cultural and traditional values vary widely. However, with all the differences, the body of Christ is still a "oneness in multiplicity,"[43] and great care should be exercised to maintain harmony and unity of purpose among the people of God.

Before moving from this section on church government, a word is in order concerning the organizational structure of the Assemblies of God. Many of the pioneers of this Fellowship, from its inception, reacted against a strong central governing authority, which in some cases had "disfellowshipped" those who were being filled with the Holy Spirit as (among other things) threats to the status quo. Some early Pentecostals wanted nothing more to do with what they identified as "organized" religion. Within time, however, many of the early Pentecostal leaders saw the need for some type of structure through which the modern message of Pentecost could be advanced. Consequently, the Assemblies of God was organized as a "fellowship" or "movement" (many were still shy of the term "denomination") with an emphasis on having the freedom to be directed by the Spirit. As the Assemblies of God has grown and matured through the twentieth century,

---

[42]W. D. Davies, *A Normative Pattern of Church Life in the New Testament: Fact or Fancy?* (London: Clark, n.d.), 21.

[43]Saucy, *The Church*, 119.

the need for increased organization to keep up with the demands placed on ministry has been realized.

Opinions differ about which of the three types of church government is accepted by the Assemblies of God. Perhaps it could be suggested that in some ways all three are. The overall organizational structure of the Assemblies of God most closely resembles presbyterian polity (as was alluded to earlier). From the local church to the district and General Council levels, a key emphasis is placed on elected, representational leadership. The clergy are often represented by "presbyters," and the laity are given representation by duly chosen delegates. On the other hand, the congregational system of government can be readily observed at the level of the local church. Although many Assemblies of God churches are considered "dependent" in that they look to district leadership for direction and support, many others have advanced to "sovereign" status. They have a great deal of autonomy in decision making (choosing their own pastors, buying or selling property, etc.), while maintaining a bond of unity in matters of doctrine and practice with the other churches in the section, district, or in the General Council. The episcopal format, according to some, is also present to a degree in the Assemblies of God. For example, some of the national or General Council agencies (Division of Foreign Missions, Division of Home Missions, Department of Chaplaincy) have valid reason to appoint individuals to key areas of ministry, based on their call and aptitude for such ministry.

The Ministry of the Church

PRIESTHOOD OF BELIEVERS

One of the most important doctrines to receive emphasis during the Protestant Reformation was the priesthood of all believers: each person having access to God through the High Priesthood of Jesus Christ himself. Such an idea, after centuries of the Roman Catholic hierarchy's controlling the ministry of the church, impassioned many. In turn they realized that Christ has given all believers ministries to perform for the good of the entire Body of faith.

This concept of the priesthood of all believers is certainly scripturally based. Referring to believers, Peter describes them as a "holy priesthood" (1 Pet. 2:5) and borrows from the Old Testament the analogy that the Church is a "royal priesthood"

(1 Pet. 2:9). Believers are described by John as having been made into "a kingdom [kings having royal power] and priests" to serve God (Rev. 1:6; see also 5:10). Regardless of one's position or vocation in life, one may enjoy the privileges and responsibilities of serving the Lord as a member of His church. Paul Minear refers to the New Testament concept of Christians as being "shareholders (Gk. *koinōnoi*) in the Spirit [and] . . . shareholders in the manifold vocation that the Spirit assigns."[44] This understanding emphasizes that ministry is both a divine and a universal calling. Saucy suggests, "In reality, the ministry of the church is the ministry of the Spirit which is divided among the various members, each contributing his gift to the total work of the church."[45] Believers are dependent on the Spirit to equip and work through them, but the Spirit's work is available to every believer.

The Church through the centuries has tended to divide itself into two broad categories: clergy (Gk. *klēros,* "lot," i.e., God's lot or separated ones) and laity (Gk. *laos,* "people"). The New Testament, however, does not make such a marked distinction. Rather, God's "lot," or *klēros*, His own possession, refers to all born-again believers, not just to a selected group (cf. 1 Pet. 2:9). Alan Cole aptly states that "all clergy are laymen, and all laymen are also clergy, in the biblical sense of these words."[46]

OFFICES AND FUNCTIONS OF MINISTRY

Although the New Testament emphasizes the universal nature of ministry within the body of Christ, it also indicates that some believers are uniquely set apart for specific functions of ministry. Reference is often made to Ephesians 4:11— "It was he who gave some to be apostles, some to be prophets, some to be evangelists, and some to be pastors and teachers"—for a list of what occasionally are called the "charismatic offices" (rather "ministries") of the Early Church. Differentiated from these are the "administrative offices" (bishop, elder, deacon) especially addressed in the later epistles of the New Testament. Many other ways have been suggested to classify the various offices, or categories, of New Testament ministry. For example, H. Orton Wiley refers to "Extraordi-

---

[44]Minear, *Images of the Church,* 262.

[45]Saucy, *The Church,* 128.

[46]Alan Cole, *The Body of Christ* (London: Hodder & Stoughton, 1964), 40.

nary and Transitional Ministry" and "Regular and Permanent Ministry"; Louis Berkhof prefers "Extraordinary Officers" and "Ordinary Officers"; and Saucy rightly uses the simpler designations "General Ministries" and "Local Officers."[47] The significant role of the apostles, prophets, and evangelists for the ministry of the Early Church is well attested in the New Testament. For the purposes of the present discussion, those offices that are normally considered more ordinary in the life of the local church will be examined.

The modern position of "pastor" seems to coincide with the biblical position of bishop (Gk. *episkopos*) or elder (Gk. *presbuteros*) or both. These terms appear to be used interchangeably in the overall context of the New Testament. Berkhof suggests that the word "elder" or "presbyter" was borrowed by the Church from the concept of elders who were the rulers in the Jewish synagogue.[48] As the name implies, "elder" often referred literally to those who were older and respected for their dignity and wisdom. As time passed, the term "bishop" became more prominently used for this office, for it highlighted the "overseeing" function of the elder.

The term "pastor" is more widely used today for the one who has the spiritual responsibility and oversight of the local church. Interestingly, the Greek term *poimēn* ("shepherd") is used only once in the New Testament in direct reference to the ministry of pastor (Eph. 4:11). The concept or function of pastor, however, is found throughout Scripture. As the name suggests, the pastor is one who tends to the sheep. (Cf. Jesus' depiction of himself as the "good shepherd," *ho poimēn ho kalos,* in John 10:11ff.) The connection between the three terms "bishop," "presbyter," and "pastor" is made clear in Acts 20. In verse 17, Paul calls for the elders (Gk. *presbuterous*) from the church in Ephesus. Later in that context, Paul admonishes the elders, "Keep watch over yourselves and all the flock of which the Holy Spirit has made you overseers [Gk. *episkopous*]" (v. 28). In his very next statement, Paul exhorts those who have just been called bishops or overseers to "be shepherds [Gk. *poimainein*] of the church of God" (v. 28).

The responsibilities and functions of modern-day pastors, like those of New Testament pastors, are many and varied.

---

[47]H. Orton Wiley, *Christian Theology,* vol. 3 (Kansas City, Mo.: Beacon Hill Press, 1943), 129–35. Berkhof, *Systematic Theology,* 585–87. Saucy, *The Church,* 137–40.

[48]Berkhof, *Systematic Theology,* 585.

Three major areas to which pastors must devote themselves are administration (cf. 1 Pet. 5:1–4), pastoral care (cf. 1 Tim. 3:5; Heb. 13:17), and instruction (cf. 1 Tim. 3:2; 5:17; Titus 1:9). Concerning this last area of responsibility, it is often noted that the roles of pastor and teacher seem to have much in common in the New Testament. In fact, when Paul mentions both of these divine gifts to the Church in Ephesians 4:11, the Greek wording of the phrase "pastors and teachers" (*pomenas kai didaskalous*) could be indicative of one who fills both functions: a "pastor-teacher." Although "teacher" is mentioned elsewhere separately from "pastor" (e.g., James 3:1), indicating that they may not always be considered synonymous roles, any genuine shepherd will take seriously the obligation of teaching the flock of God. Much could be stated concerning each of these three areas of responsibility, but suffice it to say that shepherds of God's flock must lead by example, never forgetting that they are serving as undershepherds to the One who is the true Shepherd and Overseer of their souls (1 Pet. 2:25). He set the example for servant-leadership (Mark 9:42–44; Luke 22:27).

Another ministry office, or function, associated with the local church is that of deacon (Gk. *diakonos*). This term is related to *diakonia*, the most commonly used New Testament word describing normal Christian service. Used broadly in Scripture, it describes the ministry of God's people in general (Eph. 4:12), as well as the ministry of the apostles (Acts 1:17,25). It was even used by Jesus himself to describe His primary purpose: "The Son of Man did not come to be served *[diakonēthēnai]*, but to serve *[diakonēsai]*, and to give his life as a ransom for many" (Mark 10:45). Put simply, deacons are servants, or "ministers," in the most authentic sense of the word. This is accented in Paul's list of qualifications for the role of deacon in 1 Timothy 3:8–13. Many of the stipulations here are the same as those of the office of bishop (or pastor) mentioned in the preceding verses (1 Tim. 3:1–7).

In the 1 Timothy 3 passage concerning deacons, Paul's statement in verse 11 about women (literally, "women similarly should be grave," *gunaikas hōsautōs semnas*) has been the subject of different interpretations. Some versions (e.g., NIV, KJV) prefer to translate this as though it refers to the wives of deacons, which could be an acceptable translation. Others (e.g., NASB, RSV), however, prefer to translate *gunaikas* simply as "women," leaving open the possibility of women deacons, or deaconesses. As always, the translation of a term depends on its contextual usage; here, unfortunately, the context is not clear enough to provide a dogmatic so-lution. Many compare this to Paul's reference to Phoebe as a "servant [Gk. *diakonon*][49] of the church" (Rom. 16:1). Once more, the context of Romans 16 does not provide enough evidence to determine whether Paul was calling Phoebe a deaconess, or if he was simply saying that she had a valuable ministry to the church, but not one that was qualitatively different from that performed by other Christian servants.

Concerning both the Romans 16 and 1 Timothy 3 verses, scholars are somewhat divided in their opinions on the proper translation. In any regard, church history provides evidence that women functioned in the capacity of deaconesses from as early as the second century onward.[50] As one scholar notes, "The gospel of Christ brought a new dignity to women in ancient times, not only giving them personal equality before God, but a share in the ministry."[51]

THE ORDINANCES OF THE CHURCH

The final section of this chapter will explore an area that has been the focus of considerable controversy in the history of Christian doctrine. Most Protestant groups agree that Christ left the Church two observances, or rites, to be incorporated into Christian worship: water baptism and the Lord's Supper.[52] (Protestantism, following the Reformers, has rejected the sacramental nature of all rites but the original two.) Since the time of Augustine, many have followed his view that both baptism and the Lord's Supper serve as "an outward and vis-

---

[49]Since *diakonon* is masculine, it may very well refer to the office of deacon.

[50]For an interesting pro-deaconess argument, see Homer A. Kent, Jr., *The Pastoral Epistles* (Chicago: Moody, 1958), 140–42. For a representative anti-deaconess argument, see John Murray, *The Epistle to the Romans,* vol. 2 (Grand Rapids: Wm. B. Eerdmans, 1965), 226–27.
For example, Pliny the Younger wrote to the Emperor Trajan in A.D. 112 of torturing two Christian handmaidens who are called deaconesses. The third-century Syrian *Didascalia* summarizes the functions of a deaconess, including assisting at the baptism of women, ministering to those who are sick and in need of personal care, etc. See M. H. Shepherd, Jr., *"Deaconess; KJV Servant,"* in *The Interpreter's Dictionary of the Bible,* ed. George A. Buttrick, vol. 1 (Nashville, Tenn.: Abingdon, 1962), 786–87.

[51]Saucy, *The Church,* 161.

[52]The Roman Catholic Church, at the sixteenth-century Council of Trent, reaffirmed its adherence to seven sacraments: baptism and the Lord's Supper, plus ordination, confirmation, marriage, penance, and extreme unction. (Since Vatican II "extreme unction" has been called "anointing of the sick.")

ible sign of an inward and spiritual grace." The problem is not whether these two rites are to be practiced, but how to interpret their meaning (e.g., what does "an inward and spiritual grace" imply?). These historic rites of the Christian faith are normally called either sacraments or ordinances. But again, some use these terms interchangeably, while others point out that a correct understanding of the differences between these concepts is important for an accurate theological application.

The term "sacrament" (from the Latin *sacramentum*) is older, and seemingly more widely used, than the term "ordinance." In the ancient world, a *sacramentum* originally referred to a sum of money deposited in a sacred place by two parties engaged in civil litigation. When the decision of the court was rendered, the winning party's money was returned, and the loser's was forfeited as an obligatory "sacrament," considered sacred because it was now offered to the pagan gods. As time passed, the term "sacrament" was also applied to the oath of allegiance taken by new recruits into the Roman army. By the second century, Christians had adopted this term and began associating it with their vow of obedience and consecration unto the Lord. The Latin Vulgate (ca. A.D. 400) used the term *sacramentum* as a translation for the Greek term *mustērion* ("mystery"), which added a rather secretive or mysterious connotation to those things considered "sacred."[53] Indeed, sacramentalists through the years, to varying degrees, have tended to see the sacraments as rituals that convey spiritual grace (often "saving grace") to those who participate in them.

The term "ordinance" is also derived from the Latin (*ordo*, "a row, or an order"). Relating to the rites of water baptism and Communion, the word "ordinance" suggests that these sacred ceremonies have been instituted by the command, or "order," of Christ. He ordained that they be observed in the Church, not because any mystical power or saving grace is attached to them, but rather because they symbolize what has already taken place in the life of the one who has accepted the saving work of Christ.[54]

Largely due to the somewhat magical connotation accompanying the use of the word "sacrament," most Pentecostals and evangelicals prefer the term "ordinance" to express their understanding of baptism and the Lord's Supper. Even as early

---

[53]Cf. Wiley, *Christian Theology*, vol. 3, 155. Cf. Saucy, *The Church,* 191.
[54]Ibid.

as the Reformation Era, some objected to the word "sacraments," preferring to speak of "signs" or "seals" of grace. Luther and Calvin both used the term "sacrament," but called attention to the fact that their usage was in a different theological sense than the word's original implication. Luther's associate Philipp Melanchthon preferred to use the term *signi* ("sign").[55] Today some who do not regard themselves as "sacramentalists" (i.e., they do not feel that saving grace is bestowed through the sacraments) still use the terms "sacrament" and "ordinance" synonymously. One should carefully interpret the term's meaning according to significance and implications that are attached to the ceremony by those participating. As something ordained by Christ and participated in both because of His command and example, the ordinances are not perceived by most Pentecostals and evangelicals as producing a spiritual change by themselves, but rather they serve as symbols or forms of proclamation of what Christ has already spiritually effected in the believer's life.

WATER BAPTISM

The ordinance of water baptism has been a part of Christian practice from the beginning of the Church. This practice was such a common part of the Early Church's life that F. F. Bruce comments, "The idea of an unbaptized Christian is simply not entertained in the New Testament."[56] Actually, other somewhat similar baptismal rituals pre-date Christianity, including those among some pagan religions and among the Jewish community (for Gentile "proselytes" or converts to Judaism). Preceding Christ's public ministry, John "the Baptist" emphasized a "baptism of repentance" for those who wished to enter the promised kingdom of God. Despite some similarities with these various baptisms, the meaning and purpose of Christian baptism supersede them all.

Christ set the pattern for Christian baptism when He himself was baptized by John at the beginning of His public ministry (Matt. 3:13–17). Then He later commanded His followers to go into all the world and make disciples, "baptizing them in [Gk. *eis,* 'into'] the name of the Father and of the Son and of the Holy Spirit" (Matt. 28:19). Therefore, Christ in-

---

[55]Berkhof, *Systematic Theology,* 617.

[56]F. F. Bruce, *The Book of Acts,* The New International Commentary on the New Testament (Grand Rapids: Wm. B. Eerdmans, 1954), 77.

stituted the ordinance of baptism by both His example and command.

A major purpose of believers' being baptized in water is that it signifies their identification with Christ. New Testament believers were baptized "into" (Gk. *eis*) the name of the Lord Jesus (Acts 8:16), indicating that they were entering the realm of Christ's sovereign lordship and authority. In baptism, the new believer "testifies that he was in Christ when Christ was judged for sin, that he was buried with him, and that he has arisen to new life in him." Baptism indicates that the believer has died to the old way of life and entered "newness of life" through redemption in Christ. The act of water baptism does not effect this identification with Christ, "but presupposes and symbolizes it." Baptism thus symbolizes the time when the one who previously had been the enemy of Christ makes "his final surrender."[57]

Water baptism also signifies that believers have identified with the body of Christ, the Church. Baptized believers are initiated into the community of faith, and in so doing they give public testimony to the world of their allegiance with the people of God. This seems to be a major reason New Testament believers were baptized almost immediately upon conversion. In a world that was hostile to the Christian faith, it was important that new believers take their stand with the disciples of Christ and become immediately involved in the total life of the Christian community. Perhaps one of the reasons water baptism does not enjoy the place of prominence in many modern churches that it once did is that the act of baptism is so often separated from the act of conversion. Baptism is more than being obedient to Christ's command; it is related to the act of becoming His disciple.[58]

Historically, the three major methods of baptism have been immersion, affusion (pouring), and sprinkling. Most New Testament scholars agree that the essential meaning of the verb *baptizō* is "to immerse, or submerge." One of the earliest Christian documents outside of the New Testament, the *Didachē*, gives the first known instructions that allow baptism by some method other than immersion. After giving detailed prescriptions for baptism—it must be in "running water," but if that is not available cold water (and as a last alternative,

---

[57]Henry C. Thiessen, *Lectures in Systematic Theology*, rev. ed. (Grand Rapids: Wm. B. Eerdmans, 1979), 324. G. R. Beasley-Murray, *Baptism Today and Tomorrow* (New York: St. Martin's, 1966), 43.

[58]Cf. Saucy, *The Church*, 196.

warm water) must be used; it must employ the Trinitarian formula, etc.—the *Didachē* advises that if there is not sufficient water for immersion, then one is to "pour water on the head three times 'in the name of the Father, Son, and Holy Spirit.' "[59] Sprinkling came into use as early as the third century, particularly in cases of clinical baptisms (for those near death and desirous of Christian baptism). While immersion is the generally accepted mode among evangelicals (including Pentecostals), there may be unusual and rare occasions when it is appropriate to use another method, for example, when baptizing an elderly or physically disabled person. The mode should never become more important than the spiritual identification with Christ in His death and resurrection, which baptism symbolizes.

An issue that has caused considerable controversy in Christian history concerns the appropriate candidates of baptism. Should the Church baptize the infants and small children of its members or only believers, that is, those who can consciously and rationally make a decision to accept Christ? This has been a complex issue, which largely stems from one's understanding of baptism as either a sacrament or an ordinance. Does the act itself convey grace (sacrament), or does it symbolize the grace that has already been conveyed (ordinance)? Arguments have been used from the early church fathers both for and against the baptism of infants. For example, in the third century Origen asserted that "the Church received a tradition to administer baptism even to infants." At the same time, however, Tertullian argued against baptizing infants and children: "[W]hy does the age of innocence hasten to secure remission of sins?" Tertullian further stated, "So let them come when they are bigger, when they [can] learn, when they [can] be taught when to come; let them become Christians when they are able to know Christ."[60] Most of the statements made by the church fathers in regard to this issue are not explicit enough to determine with certainty the attitudes of the ancient Church on this subject. Many arguments that have been used by both sides are arguments from silence and conjecture, and could be used either way.

Since medieval times, many Christians have practiced infant

---

[59]"The Teaching of the Twelve Apostles, Commonly Called the Didache," in *Early Christian Fathers,* 174.

[60]Cited in W. F. Flemington, *The New Testament Doctrine of Baptism* (London: S. P. C. K., 1964), 132–33. Joachim Jeremias, *The Origins of Infant Baptism* (London: SCM Press, 1963), 49.

baptism. It has usually been supported by three major contentions. The first is the suggestion that infant baptism is the new covenant counterpart to circumcision in the Old Testament. As such, it is seen as a rite of initiation into the covenant community of believers, granting to the baptized all the rights and blessings of the covenant promises.[61] Although this seemingly makes a nice parallel, it lacks solid scriptural support. The Bible clearly does not substitute baptism for circumcision in Galatians 6:12–18.

The second argument supporting infant baptism is an appeal to "household" baptisms in the Bible, what Joachim Jeremias calls the *oikos* formula. For instance, passages such as Acts 16:15 (household of Lydia), Acts 16:33 (household of the Philippian jailer), and 1 Corinthians 1:16 (household of Stephanas) are inferred to mean that at least some of these homes included infants or small children among the number being baptized.[62] Again, this is largely an argument from silence, based on what is conjectured rather than what is stated. It could be equally inferred that the biblical readers would have understood that such household baptisms included only those who had personally accepted Christ as Savior, for all "believed" and all "rejoiced" (Acts 16:34).

A third often-used argument is that the infant is born with the guilt of original sin and is in need of forgiveness, which comes by means of baptism. This idea, however, is based largely on the notion that humans biologically inherit sin (as opposed to it being imputed representatively) and that baptism has the power to perform a type of sacramental regeneration. Concerning the baptismal remission of original sin, Oliver Quick makes an amusing observation: "So far as experience can show, the sinful tendencies or spiritual defects of a baptized and an unbaptized child are very much the same."[63]

As earlier suggested, most who hold to baptism as an ordinance, rather than as a sacrament, feel that baptism was intended only for born-again believers. And it should be noted

[61]Flemington, *The New Testament Doctrine,* 131.

[62]Joachim Jeremias, *Infant Baptism in the First Four Centuries* (London: SCM Press, 1960), 21, 23.

[63]For a discussion on whether infants or small children need baptism to be saved, and on the destiny of infants who die, see John Sanders, *No Other Name: An Investigation into the Destiny of the Unevangelized* (Grand Rapids: Wm. B. Eerdmans, 1992), 287–305. Flemington, *The New Testament Doctrine,* 139.

that even some of the more prominent non-evangelical theologians of modern time, who generally hold to a sacramen-
talist theology, have also rejected the practice of infant baptism.[64] Baptism symbolizes a great spiritual reality (salvation)
which has revolutionized the life of a believer; nevertheless,
the symbol itself should never be elevated to the level of that
higher reality.

THE LORD'S SUPPER

The second ordinance of the Church is the Lord's Supper,
or Holy Communion. Like baptism, this ordinance has been
an integral part of Christian worship since Christ's earthly
ministry, when Jesus instituted this rite on the night of His
betrayal at the Passover meal. The Lord's Supper has some
comparable counterparts in other religious traditions (such
as the Jewish Passover, and other ancient religions which had
a type of sacramental meal to identify with their deities), but
it goes far beyond them in meaning and importance.

Following the instructions set forth by Jesus, Christians
partake of Communion in "remembrance" of Him (Luke
22:19–20; 1 Cor. 11:24–25). The term translated "remembrance" (Gk. *anamnēsis*) may not mean quite what you think.
Whereas today to remember something is to think back to
some past occasion, the New Testament understanding of
anamnēsis is just the opposite. Such a remembrance was
meant to "transport an action which is buried in the past in
such a way that its original potency and vitality are not lost,
but are carried over into the present."[65] Such a concept is
even reflected in the Old Testament (cf. Deut. 16:3; 1 Kings
17:18).

In the Lord's Supper, perhaps it could be suggested that
there is a threefold sense of remembrance: past, present, and
future. The Church gathers as a body at the Lord's table,

---

[64]This would include Karl Barth, who rejected baptism as a means of
grace, declaring that the saving event was completed and perfected in
Christ; Emil Brunner, who felt that infant baptism lacked a genuine "I-
Thou" relationship to God; and Jurgen Moltmann, who believes that a
responsible church will baptize only responsible persons, i.e., those who
freely respond to the call of discipleship. See Jurgen Moltmann, *The Church
in the Power of the Spirit* (New York: Harper, 1977), 232–39. Also see
Dale Moody, *Baptism: Foundation for Christian Unity* (Philadelphia, Pa.:
Westminster, 1967), 51–65.

[65]Ralph P. Martin, *Worship in the Early Church* (Grand Rapids: Wm. B.
Eerdmans, 1964), 126.

remembering His death. The very elements typically used in Communion are representative of Christ's ultimate sacrifice: giving His body and blood for the sins of the world. There is also a present sense of fellowship with Christ at His table. The Church comes to proclaim not a dead hero, but a risen and conquering Savior. The phrase the "Lord's table" suggests that He is in charge as the true host of the meal, connoting the sense that believers are secure and have peace in Him (see Ps. 23:5). Finally, there is a future sense of remembrance in that the believer's present fellowship with the Lord is not final. In this way the Lord's Supper has an eschatological dimension, being taken in anticipation of His return and the Church's eternal reunion with Him (cf. Mark 14:25; 1 Cor. 11:26).

Fellowship with Christ also denotes fellowship with His body, the Church. The vertical relationship that believers have with the Lord is complemented by their horizontal relationship with one another; loving God is vitally associated with loving one's neighbor (see Matt. 22:37–39). Such a true fellowship with one's brothers and sisters in Christ necessitates the overcoming of all barriers (social, economic, cultural, etc.) and the correction of anything that would destroy true unity. Only then can the Church genuinely participate (or have *koinōnia*) in the Lord's body and blood and be truly one body (1 Cor. 10:16–17). This truth is brought out vividly by Paul in 1 Corinthians 11:17–34. A major emphasis of the apostle in this passage is that believers should examine their spiritual conduct and motives before participating in the Lord's Supper—not only with respect to the Lord himself, but also with respect to fellow members of Christ's body.

Because the Lord's Supper is a true fellowship of believers, most churches in the Pentecostal and evangelical traditions practice open Communion. This means that all born-again believers, regardless of their less significant differences, are invited to join with the saints in fellowship with the Lord at His table.

While most Christians would agree that the Lord is present at His table, this is interpreted in many different ways. Most Christians align their thinking on this subject with one of four traditions: Roman Catholic, Lutheran, Zwinglian, or Calvinist (Reformed). Each of these will be briefly considered.

The Roman Catholic doctrine officially adopted at the Fourth Lateran Council (1215) and reaffirmed at the Council of Trent (1551) is known as transubstantiation. This view teaches that when the priest blesses and consecrates the elements of bread and wine, a transforming, metaphysical change occurs so that the bread is changed into Christ's body and the wine into His blood. The term "metaphysical" is used because the Catholic Church teaches that the appearance, taste, etc., of the elements (or "accidents") remain the same, but the inner essence, or metaphysical substance, has been changed. Taking a very literal interpretation of Jesus' words, "This is my body. . . . This is my blood" (Mark 14:22–24), Catholics believe that the whole of Christ is fully present within the substance of the elements. Consequently, the one who partakes of the consecrated host is receiving atonement from venial, that is, pardonable, sins (as opposed to mortal sins).

A second view stems from the teachings of Martin Luther. Celebrating his first mass as a young Catholic priest, Luther came to the words that announced a new sacrifice of Christ was being presented—"We offer unto thee, the living, the true, the eternal God." Luther was, in his own words,

utterly stupefied and terror-stricken. . . . Who am I, that I should lift up mine eyes or raise my hands to the divine Majesty? . . . shall I, a miserable little pygmy, say 'I want this, I ask for that'? For I am dust and ashes and full of sin and I am speaking to the living, eternal and the true God.[66]

Realizing that no human has the priestly power to effect change from bread and wine to the body and blood of Christ, Luther was on his way to an eventual break with the Roman Catholic Church, along with its doctrine of transubstantiation. Although Luther rejected other facets of the Catholic doctrine concerning the Lord's Supper, he did not totally reject the idea that Christ's body and blood are present. Luther taught that the body and blood of the Lord are "with, in, and under" the elements of bread and wine, a doctrine that would later become known as consubstantiation. Perhaps it could be said that this view, like the Catholic concept of transubstantiation, is still highly sacramental, still taking too literally Christ's figurative words about His body and blood.

A contemporary of Luther's who differed extensively with him on his understanding of Christ's presence in Communion was Huldreich Zwingli. The Zwinglian position is better known today as the memorial view. Its emphasis is that the Lord's

---

[66]Roland H. Bainton, *Here I Stand: A Life of Martin Luther* (New York: New American Library, 1950), 30.

Supper is a rite that commemorates the Lord's death and its efficacy for the believer. It is in this sense a sign, pointing back to Calvary. Zwingli rejected any notion of Christ's physical presence at His table (whether transformed in the elements or joined with the elements) and taught instead that Christ was spiritually present to those of faith. Many of Zwingli's followers so fervently rejected the idea of Christ's physical presence that they in effect rebuffed even the concept of Christ's being spiritually present in the Communion service. For that reason, most who follow this concept tend to stress only that the Lord's Supper is a commemorative ceremony in which the believer recalls the atoning work of Christ.

The fourth major view concerning the Lord's Supper is the Calvinistic, or Reformed, view. Like Zwingli, John Calvin rejected any notion of Christ's being physically present in or with the elements. More than Zwingli, however, Calvin greatly emphasized the spiritual presence of Christ at His table. This was understood to be a dynamic presence (similar to the meaning of the Greek term *anamnēsis*) through the power of the Holy Spirit. The Reformed view stresses that the efficacy of Christ's sacrificial death is applied and made meaningful to the believer who participates in Communion with an attitude of faith and trust in Christ.

In addition to these four major views of the Lord's Supper, many modifications and combinations of the above are held by contemporary Christians. This is especially evident within the Pentecostal and charismatic movements; the theological understanding of many of their members has been greatly influenced by their former association with more traditional or liturgical church bodies. Probably most Pentecostals are more theologically comfortable with the positions expressed by the Zwinglian or the Reformed views. In any case, all Christians today should take seriously the biblical emphasis and instruction on both of the ordinances, water baptism and the Lord's Supper, and should rejoice that their meaning is still as significant and applicable as it was for the New Testament Church.

STUDY QUESTIONS

1. Define the significance of the term *ekklēsia.* Do you think that the meaning of this term accurately describes the modern Church? Why or why not?

2. Explain the similarities and the differences between the local, visible church, and the universal, invisible Church.

When describing the universal Church, why is it important to distinguish the term "universal" from the related terms "ecumenical" and "catholic"?

3. In what ways is the Church similar to, and different from, the kingdom of God?

4. Give a brief synopsis of the history of the Church, from the time of the New Testament through the Patristic period, the Middle Ages, and the Reformation and post-Reformation periods. In what significant ways has the Church changed or remained the same during its history?

5. The biblical imagery of the Church as the body of Christ suggests that the Church is a "unity in diversity." What does this mean? Give some examples of how this can be seen in your own local church.

6. Explain the significance of these terms by which the people of God are called in the New Testament: elect, saints, believers, brethren, disciples.

7. Briefly describe the major facets of the three basic types of church government. Describe at least one positive and one negative aspect of each type. Which form of government do you prefer, and why?

8. Four primary aspects of the mission, or purpose, of the Church were discussed in this chapter. From your own experience, do you feel that your local church adequately involves itself in these four areas of mission? Are there other areas that you think need to be added to these four?

9. Is it acceptable for infants and very young children to be baptized in water? Should local church leadership withhold the elements of the Lord's Supper from those who are not saved? Give reasons for your position on both these issues.

CHAPTER SEVENTEEN

The Mission of the Church

Byron D. Klaus

Any discussion of the mission of the Church leads participants to consider the very foundations on which they build their identity. Pentecostals have certainly been noted for the fervor of their obedient response to the redemptive mission given to all Christians. However, each generation must attain a fresh appreciation for the mission and purposes around which they center their identity.[1]

Our perspective on the Church and its mission is deeply rooted in our experience with Christ and the Holy Spirit. To suggest that we can step back from the influence of this spiritual encounter and simply theorize about the Church and its mission is to remove an essential part of our calling. Although other religious traditions may still view the Pentecostal Movement as primarily experience-centered, we should not allow this to cast shadows on God's sovereign work reintroduced in the twentieth century. The Spirit has graciously enabled our Movement to stand as a testimony of the empowerment necessary for the Church to be a vehicle of God's redemptive mission.[2]

A BIBLICAL UNDERSTANDING OF THE MISSION

Although the themes of Pentecost and mission are impor-

---

[1]Ray S. Anderson, "A Theology for Ministry," in *Theological Foundations for Ministry,* Ray Anderson, ed. (Grand Rapids: Wm. B. Eerdmans, 1979), 6–7.

[2]Vinson Synan, *In the Latter Days* (Ann Arbor, Mich.: Servant Books, 1984), 7.

tant to our reflection on the Church, a truly biblical understanding of mission must build its foundation on the entirety
of Scripture. From creation to consummation the Bible records reconciliation as central to God's character. The mission
of God to reconcile humanity, authoritatively recorded in
Scripture, reveals the source of our prime motivation for
Church mission.

OLD TESTAMENT FOUNDATIONS

The Old Testament gives us the initial images of God's
seeking to redeem a people to reflect His glory. The early
history of the people of God is set in the context of "the
nations" (Gen. 12:3; 22:17). This has profound significance
for the unfolding of God's redemptive intent for humanity.[3]

Genesis 1:26–28 reveals that that humanity has been created in the image of God. Although this fact requires considerable explanation, for our purposes two key elements are
obvious: (1) We have been created for fellowship with God.
(2) We have a responsibility—evident from the fact that we
are made in His image—to maintain the relationship with
God. The whole human race shares a common origin and
dignity because of common roots. We can never view the
world without seeing God as the God of all humanity. We
are subject to God and we live in the sphere of His redemptive
activity.[4]

The Book of Genesis (chapters 1 through 11) records history's beginnings; the Book of Revelation reveals its culmination. God's redemptive character permeates the salvation
theme, a theme that cuts a path through the complexity of
history and will climax in a countless number of people, from
every "tribe and tongue," gathering around the throne of God
(Rev. 5:9–10; 7:9–17).

In the account of the family of Abraham, we see the beginning of redemption's worldwide scope (Gen. 12:1–3). God
did not choose one man or one people to the exclusion of
the rest of humanity. On the contrary, Abraham and Israel
were chosen to serve as a means of bringing blessing to all

---

[3]Roger E. Hedlund, *The Mission of the Church in the World* (Grand
Rapids: Baker Book House, 1991), 33.

[4]Ibid., 22–23.

the peoples of the earth (Gen. 12:3).[5] God dealt with Abraham and Israel to express His redemptive claim on all nations.[6]

Israel, as the Old Testament people of God, had a history of forgetting why God had chosen them. Their pride became a source of much tragedy. God continually used Spirit-inspired, prophetic leadership to remind them of their identity as a "light for all nations" (Isa. 49:6, NCV). Exodus 19:4–6 portrays God's rescue of Israel from Egypt as an eagle's overseeing its offspring as they learn to fly. Israel was a "treasured possession." The whole earth is the Lord's, but Israel was to be "a kingdom of priests and a holy nation," holy in the sense of being separated to God to carry out His purpose of blessing all nations.

In a parallel passage (Deut. 7:6–8) God reminded His people that they did not merit this status because of their greatness, either qualitatively or quantitatively. They were His treasured possession by His choice and grace and because He is love. As the holy people of God, they were to show His love. Therefore, His love made them a "kingdom of priests." In this passage God was reminding them of their mission. The people of God were to function on behalf of God in a mediatorial role to the nations. As a "holy nation" they were to be given completely to the purposes for which they had been chosen and placed. Their identity had no other source than God's love, and their purpose had no other origin than that which was defined by the Lord.[7]

Another Old Testament passage gives us a clear perspective on God's intent for His people. Psalm 67 is a missionary psalm, a prayer that God may be pleased to bless His people. God's blessings would demonstrate to the nations that He is gracious. His salvation would become known and all the nations of the earth would join in joyful praise. This psalm was probably sung regularly in connection with the high priestly benediction (see Num. 6:24–26). We see here a message to the Old Testament people of God and to the Church today: God

---

[5]Someone has compared them to the commandos of World War II. The commandos were a chosen group who went into enemy-held territory to make a beachhead so others could follow.

[6]Johannes Verkuyl, "The Biblical Foundation for the Worldwide Mission Mandate," in *Perspectives on the World Christian Movement,* Steven C. Hawthorne and Ralph D. Winter, eds. (Pasadena, Calif.: Institute of International Studies, 1981), 36.

[7]Walter C. Kaiser, Jr., "Israel's Missionary Call," in *Perspectives on the World Christian Movement,* 26–27.

gives His people the central role in the mediatorial task of proclaiming and demonstrating His name (that is, His character) and His salvation to the nations.

The people of God are called (1) to proclaim His plan to the nations (Gen. 12:3; see above); (2) to participate in His priesthood as agents of blessing to the nations (Exod. 19; Deut. 7); and (3) to demonstrate His purpose to the nations (Ps. 67).[8]

THE SERVANT OF THE LORD

God's redemptive mission, seen most clearly in Jesus Christ, must be viewed against the backdrop of what God had already been doing throughout the Old Testament period of preparation and expectation. This is brought out forcefully in Isaiah 49:3–6. In verse 3 the Servant is called Israel; however, national Israel cannot be meant because God's purpose is to use the Servant to bring restoration *to* Israel (v. 5).[9] God also declares to Him, "I will also make you a light for the Gentiles, that you may bring my salvation to the ends of the earth" (v. 6). The Holy Spirit was on Simeon when he took the baby Jesus in his arms and praised God for Him as the fulfillment of Isaiah 49:6 (Luke 2:25–32). Jesus passed the commission on to His followers in Luke 24:47–48 and Acts 1:8, with the additional command to wait for the Father's promise of power from on high. The same verse (i.e. Isa. 49:6) gave further grounds for God's salvation being sent to the Gentiles (Acts 28:28).

The incarnation of Christ, therefore, displayed in human flesh the reconciling character of God. In sovereign grace God seeks to restore His creation to himself. The Church's identity and mission are rooted in who Jesus Christ is and what God has accomplished through Him. In seeking to understand the Church and its mission, we must always return to the redemptive mission so clearly articulated and modeled by God's only Son, Jesus Christ.[10]

In Jesus Christ we see the most fundamental testimony to the kingdom of God. God's reign was personified in Jesus, as seen in His ministry and miracles. His life, death, and resur-

---

[8]Ibid., 26.

[9]Edward J. Young. *The Book of Isaiah,* vol. 3 (Grand Rapids: Wm. B. Eerdmans, 1972), 274.

[10]Darrell Guder, *Be My Witnesses* (Grand Rapids: Wm. B. Eerdmans, 1985), 14–15.

rection assure us that when He comes again He will shatter the pride and autonomy that has destroyed relationships between nations as well as people. In Jesus we see the power of God that will someday neutralize the rule of human kingdoms and fill the world with a reign of righteousness.[11] The kingdom, or rule, of God—through the life and ministry of Jesus—revealed the power to destroy every stranglehold of sin on humanity. This is the foundation of the Church's global mission in the present age.[12]

Jesus' proclamation of the good news of the Kingdom must be understood in terms of the covenant to Abraham, terms that declared God's purpose to bless all the peoples of the earth (Gen. 12:3).[13] Jesus left no doubt that the reign of God (the Kingdom) has entered history, even though its consummation is yet to come (Matt. 24:14). Because that reign is now manifest at the right hand of the Father's throne, where Jesus is exalted and is interceding for us (Acts 2:33–34; Eph. 1:20–22; Heb. 7:25; 1 John 2:1) and from where He "has poured out the promised Holy Spirit" (Acts 2:33), the Church can go forward with confidence. The authoritative testimony to Christ's earthly ministry recorded in the Gospels helps us to understand where we will find our purpose and how we are to offer our service in Christ's mission.

Essential to any understanding of the Church and its mission is the awareness that any ministry attempt in Christ's name must replicate His ministry, its purpose, character, and empowerment. Our ministry is legitimate only if it is a true representative of Christ's ministry. Any effort presented as His ministry must reflect His eternal redemptive concerns. Christ walks among us intent on ministering to the lost, broken, captive, and oppressed peoples of the world. To be Christian is to ask where Christ is at work among us and how we may join His work. That eternal purpose is the only cause worth joining and leading God's people toward.[14]

---

[11]George E. Ladd, *The Gospel of the Kingdom* (Grand Rapids: Wm. B. Eerdmans, 1973), 31.

[12]Gordon Fee, "The Kingdom of God and the Church's Global Mission," in *Called and Empowered: Global Mission in Pentecostal Perspective,* ed. Murray A. Dempster, Byron D. Klaus, Douglas Petersen (Peabody, Mass.: Hendrickson Publishers, 1991), 14.

[13]Ibid., 7.

[14]This is the point of 2 Tim. 4:7. Paul had fought "the good fight," the only fight worth fighting.

CHAPTER

17

The Mission
of the
Church

NEW TESTAMENT FOUNDATIONS

The New Testament records the testimony of not only Christ's earthly ministry, but also the Church's emergence as the fullest expression of God's people. Themes found in Scripture are numerous and easily provide adequate underpinnings for any serious attempt at theological reflection on the Church's mission. Several key texts provide a place to start.

The mandate for mission is found in each gospel and in the Book of Acts. Because all authority in heaven and earth was given to Jesus, He said, "Therefore go and make disciples of all nations, baptizing them in the name of the Father and of the Son and of the Holy Spirit, and teaching them to obey everything I have commanded you. And surely I am with you always, to the very end of the age" (Matt. 28:18–20).

"Go" (Gk. *poreuthentes*) is not a command. It literally means "having gone." Jesus assumes believers will go, whether because of vocation or leisure or persecution. The only command in the passage is "make disciples" (Gk. *mathēteusate*), which involves baptizing them and continually teaching them.

Mark 16:15 records the command also, "Having gone into all the world, proclaim [announce, declare, and demonstrate] the good news to all creation" (literal translation).

Luke 24:45 tells how Jesus opened the minds of His followers "so they could understand the Scriptures." Then "He told them, 'This is what is written: The Christ will suffer and rise from the dead on the third day, and repentance and forgiveness of sins will be preached in his name to all nations, beginning at Jerusalem' " (Luke 24:46–47). They must wait, however, until Jesus would send what the Father had promised so that they would be "clothed with power from on high" (Luke 24:49).

Jesus also said that one reason He would send the Spirit was because " 'he will convict the world of guilt in regard to sin and righteousness and judgment' " (John 16:8). Then when the disciples saw the risen Lord, He commissioned them by saying " 'As the Father has sent me, I am sending you' " (John 20:21). But they would not have to go in their own strength. Jesus' final words before His ascension confirmed that the mandate must be carried out in the power of the Spirit (Acts 1:8). The Spirit, through them, would do the work of convicting and convincing the world.

Later, the apostle Paul gave a picture of how the Church is to understand itself and its mission (2 Cor. 5:17–20). Verse 17 declares that Christ's rule has come in great power, that the new era of reconciliation victory has dawned. Verses 18–20 make it quite clear that Christ's victory is now to be made tangible by believers, who are called "Christ's ambassadors." Paul depicts a Church whose members by their actions portray to the world what it means to be reconciled to God. Paul calls for a Church that by its corporate life demonstrates to the world the character of God, a God of reconciliation. Confidently and aggressively, as Christ's ambassadors, we are to appeal to humanity to be reconciled to God. Our mission as the Church finds its significance in sharing with a dying world a God whose purpose is to have "a people out of every people."[15]

Ephesians pictures the Church as being mission-centered. It puts to rest any attempt by Christians to conceive of the Church and its mission as merely a program, that is, foreign and home missions that may be treated with only a token emphasis, having no priority over countless other programs. Ephesians portrays a vibrant new community of people who reflect the rule of their victorious King in every aspect of their relationships. This community of believers is not left to wonder what its members have been called and empowered to do. Believers are intimately related to the God they give witness to (Eph. 1:9–10). They are unified in the identity given to the community by the Lord Jesus himself. Their chief concern is the one great purpose: continuation of Christ's reconciliatory mission, which the Church is now energized to extend.[16]

Paul highlights the fact that all our considerations about the Church and mission are not mere abstractions, simply subjects to be discussed or argued about. The Church is a visible community that reflects the mission of a reconciling God. The Church should be the "hermeneutic of the Gospel," the place where people can see the gospel portrayed in living color (2 Cor. 3:3). One might ask how the gospel can be credible and powerful enough that people would actually believe that a man who hung on a cross really has the last word in human affairs. Undoubtedly, the only answer, the only hermeneutic of the gospel, is a congregation of people who believe it and live by it (Phil. 2:15–16). That is to say, only a Church in mission can give an adequate answer to the

---

[15]Stanley A. Ellisen, "Everyone's Question: What Is God Trying to Do?" in *Perspectives on the World Christian Movement,* 23.

[16]Charles Van Engen, *God's Missionary People: Rethinking the Purpose of the Local Church* (Grand Rapids: Baker Book House, 1991), 52–55.

need for reconciliation, which the world unwittingly cries out for.[17]

First Peter makes the Church a prominent theme. In the second chapter Peter borrows freely from Old Testament themes and applies them to the Church. In verses 9 and 10 he refers to Old Testament passages in Deuteronomy and Exodus (briefly touched on earlier in this chapter). The Church is to be a corporate display of reconciliation, that is, a royal priesthood. The Church is a holy people set apart for a well-defined mission. Believers declare the good news that God has redeemed them out of the darkness of self-destruction and Satan's rule. They now find themselves in divine light that reveals their identity and purpose as God's people. Peter in these verses synthesizes his view of the Church and mission. The mission of the Church rests on the mission of God to reconcile humanity to himself. The Church declares among all peoples what God has done in Jesus Christ. Peter seems almost to be recalling the admonition in Psalm 96:3—"Declare his glory among the nations, his marvelous works among all the peoples!"[18]

Clearly, the New Testament portrays a community empowered by the Spirit to continue God's mission of reconciliation. With Christ and the Spirit, the Church has already begun its existence as the people of God having not only roots in the past, but also, and more importantly, a focus on the future. This latter dimension places a sense of confidence and boldness in God's people as they live out the *koinōnia* ("fellowship," "partnership") of the Spirit and bear powerful witness globally to the good news of Jesus Christ.[19]

POWER FOR THE MISSION

Central to a self-understanding of being Christian is the deep-seated affirmation that the mission of reconciliation empowered by the Holy Spirit supplies the essence of our identity: We are a people called and empowered (Acts 1:8) to be fellow workers with Christ in His redemptive mission. Then, what it means to be Pentecostal is at least partially embodied

---

[17]Lesslie Newbigin, *Sign of the Kingdom* (Grand Rapids: Wm. B. Eerdmans, 1980), 61, 63. Id., *The Household of God* (New York: Friendship Press, 1953), 169–70.

[18]Hedlund, *Mission of the Church,* 256–57.

[19]Gordon D. Fee, *Gospel and Spirit* (Peabody: Hendrickson Publishers, 1991), 137–38.

in an evaluation of the nature and result of the Pentecostal baptism as recorded in Acts 2. Pentecostals have historically affirmed that this Pentecostal gift, promised to all believers, is a gift of power for mission.[20] Pentecostals are so called, said Pentecostal missiologist Melvin Hodges, because they believe that the Holy Spirit will come to believers in the present just as He did to disciples on the Day of Pentecost. Such an encounter yields the Spirit's leadership and empowering presence. The result also includes evident manifestation of His power to redeem and to carry forth the mission of God.[21]

THE SIGNIFICANCE OF PENTECOST

The Day of Pentecost brought Jesus' gift of the Spirit's power to the disciples. This promised pouring out of the Spirit's power on the waiting people made it possible for them to continue to do and to teach those things "that Jesus began to do and to teach" (Acts 1:1–2). The gift of the Spirit suggests the believers were empowered on the Day of Pentecost with the same anointing Jesus had received for His mission. This empowerment bred confidence in the 120 and in those who were added daily to the Church. They would not be left to carry out the task on their own. Therefore, Pentecost was central to the Early Church's self-understanding of its purpose. Two thousand years later, Pentecost is still vital to the self-understanding of the Church. We must continually seek and gain further clarity concerning it.[22]

At Pentecost a charismatic community emerged as the primary residence of God's rule. The believers could go forward in their declaration of the Kingdom because the ruling Christ had come upon all of them by the Spirit. They were now to witness to the rule of Christ, calling attention in word and deed to the character and authoritative power of the King. "Pentecost is God's offer of himself in total adequacy to His children, made possible by the redeeming work of His Son Jesus Christ. Pentecost is God's call to His children to be

---

[20]Robert P. Menzies, ed., "The Essence of Pentecostalism," *Paraclete* 26 (Summer 1992): 4–5.

[21]Melvin Hodges, "A Pentecostal's View of Mission Strategy," *The Conciliar-Evangelical Debate: The Crucial Documents, 1964–76,* 2d ed., Donald McGavran, ed. (South Pasadena, Calif.: William Carey Library, 1977), 142.

[22]Roger Stronstad, *Charismatic Theology of St. Luke* (Peabody, Mass.: Hendrickson Publishers, 1984), 49–53.

purified inwardly and to be empowered for witness." The
coming of the Spirit was the first installment of the Kingdom
and a witness to its reality. It was also a witness to the continuation of God's redemptive mission, which is driven forward to the "regions beyond" with relentless fervor and sustained by the deployment of the gifts.[23]

As was stated earlier, Pentecost is crucial to the self-
understanding of Pentecostals. Not only is it an event of significance in salvation-history, but the Pentecostal gift itself
provides deep implications for a discussion of the Church
and its mission: It is linked both to the formation of the
Church's mission of proclamation of the good news and its
mission to create redeemed patterns of living that would
testify to changed lives.[24]

LUKE'S UNDERSTANDING OF THE MISSION

Luke's development of this crucial connection between
Spirit baptism and effective Church mission can be seen in
the interrelatedness of at least three texts in Luke and Acts.
Luke 24:49 yields a mission perspective in its focus on the
need of empowerment for the task that lies ahead: " 'I am
going to send you what my Father has promised; but stay in
the city until you have been clothed with power from on
high.' " This theme of empowerment for mission is picked up
again in Acts 1:8, when Jesus, about to ascend to the Father,
reaffirms to His disciples, " 'You will receive power when the
Holy Spirit comes on you; and you will be my witnesses in
Jerusalem, and in all Judea and Samaria, and to the ends of
the earth.' " The promise was fulfilled on the Day of Pentecost
and is recorded in Acts 2. Spirit baptism with its outward
evidence of speaking in other tongues is vital to the fulfillment
of the promise we see traced through all three texts.

Peter's inspired words following the Pentecostal outpouring show that he received a significant clarification of the
mission Christ came to introduce. Speaking by the Spirit, Peter
identified the apostolic implications in the prophecy of the
ancient prophet Joel. Peter clearly saw the coming of the
Spirit on the Day of Pentecost as a confirmation that the "last
days" had arrived (Acts 2:14–21). That is, the Church Age,

---

[23]Frank B. Stanger, *The Church Empowered* (Grand Rapids: Francis As-
bury Press, 1989), 33. Newbigin, *Sign of the Kingdom,* 41.

[24]Murray W. Dempster, "The Church's Moral Witness," *Paraclete* 23
(Winter 1989): 2.

the age of the Spirit, is the last age before the return of Christ to establish His kingdom on earth. There will be no other age before the Millennium. Peter further explained that the coming of the Spirit made it clear that Christ's work was victorious and His place as Lord and Christ assured (Acts 2:34–36).[25]

Peter then experienced a most important result of empowerment through Spirit baptism: He became the mouthpiece of the Holy Spirit to proclaim the good news of forgiveness through Jesus Christ and issued an appeal for people to be reconciled to God. He was empowered to announce the good news of reconciliation with God. At the same time, Peter led people to understand that an obedient response to the message of reconciliation results in their becoming the community of people who vividly display, through a new redemptive order of humanity, what it means to be reconciled to God (Acts 2:37–40). The remainder of chapter two gives a small glimpse into the first church. We see how believers attempted to embody the Spirit baptism's call to be a community born of the Spirit, commissioned to bear witness by the Spirit to Christ's ongoing ministry.

A Pentecostal theology of Church mission must take seriously that Spirit baptism is a promise fulfilled. Luke's line of argument throughout the Book of Acts shows the nature of the Spirit's role in God's redemptive plan. The structure in Acts shows the intent of this empowerment to move God's people across geographical and cultural landscapes with the good news of the gospel. The Church breaks out of the myopia of the Old Testament people of God and begins to reflect the universal nature of God's eternal redemptive plan.[26]

Pentecostal empowerment makes possible the varied expressions of ministry that appear in Acts. The Holy Spirit is the director of mission. Not only does the Spirit enable people to witness, He also directs when and where that witness is to take place.

Vast cultural boundaries were crossed as the gospel went beyond Jerusalem (Acts 8). The Christians who left Jerusalem

---

[25]What Peter said was not a sermon in the ordinary sense of the word but a manifestation of the gift of prophecy. "Addressed" (Gk. *apephthen-xato,* Acts 2:14) is a form of the same verb translated "enabled" (Gk. *apophthengesthai*), when they spoke in other tongues as the Spirit "enabled" them. A. T. Lincoln, "Theology and History in the Interpretation of Luke's Pentecost," *Expository Times* 96 (April 1985): 204–9.

[26]Dempster, "Moral Witness," 3. Donald Senior and Carroll Stuhlmueller, *The Biblical Foundations for Mission* (Maryknoll, N.Y.: Orbis Books, 1983), 259.

proclaimed the gospel "wherever they went" (v. 4). Verses 5–8 record Philip's announcement of the gospel to the Samaritans and the resultant powerful encounters in which the gospel triumphed and brought "great joy."

Acts 10 shows how the Church was made to realize that the Gentiles were to be included in the kingdom of God. The Church must include all peoples and actively bear witness to the fact that the gospel is for all nations. The angelic visitation and dreams also seem to indicate that the supernatural may in fact have been quite the norm in this redemptive plan of God as He made it known to the Gentiles.

Acts 11:19–26 reveals the gathering of numerous Gentiles into the church at Antioch. Barnabas was sent to help them and evaluated this growing church as truly legitimate. The result was a genuine multicultural church that embodied both the fact that the gospel should be preached in power to the "ends of the earth," and that those who have heard should respond with genuine change in the way they lived and in their relationships to one another. The fact that "the disciples were called Christians at Antioch" first (v. 26) shows others recognized the change.

This unique testimony to the powerful movement of the gospel across cultural and geographical boundaries bore great fruit when Antioch became an international, multicultural, missionary-sending church. Acts 13:2–3 records its selection and confirmation process, as it sent out its first missionaries, Paul and Barnabas. Acts 13:4 shows that the Holy Spirit, besides prompting the church at Antioch to send out these missionaries, also sent them to specific destinations. Such missionary activity, guided by the Holy Spirit, continued to move in ever-enlarging circles, surmounting cultural barriers. Acts 15 recounts the guidance of the Holy Spirit to affirm that the gospel of Christ is all-inclusive and not exclusively Jewish. The Spirit-guided decision of the Jerusalem conference caused Paul, Barnabas, and others to achieve even greater barrier crossings.

In the subsequent chapters of the Book of Acts, Luke continues his charting of the redemptive plan of God superintended by the Holy Spirit through Spirit-empowered servants. Clearly Luke emphasizes the point that these apostles and believers in the Book of Acts received empowerment and direction from the Spirit in much the same way that Jesus did in His earthly ministry.[27]

---

[27]James B. Shelton, *Mighty in Word and Deed* (Peabody, Mass.: Hendrickson Publishers, 1991), 125–26.

Luke's alignment of Spirit baptism with the empowerment **CHAPTER** for Church mission may be succinctly summarized: "Glossolalia[,] as an indigenous part of the experience of Spirit baptism in Acts 2, represented a verbal participation in the Spirit's empowerment and ... the Spirit's creative power to initiate Christ's redemptive order of life."[28]

In Acts 10 and Acts 19 this experience is also explicitly mentioned and in several other cases implied (Acts 4 and Acts 8). It is a crucial part of the theology of Acts to link speaking in tongues with the Spirit's power to initiate a person and a group as witnesses, taking part both individually and corporately in the redemptive mission of Jesus Christ.

In both Acts 11:17 and 15:8, Peter relates the fact that inclusion of Gentiles in the redemptive community is connected to a common experience in Spirit baptism. When he says that God " 'showed that he accepted them by giving the Holy Spirit to them, just as he did to us' " (15:8), he categorically aligns Spirit baptism with the intent of the outpouring on the Day of Pentecost. He essentially says to all those listening to his recounting of that significant day at the house of Cornelius that Spirit baptism with the evidence of speaking in tongues is an indigenous part of that spiritual encounter with God. This encounter with God clearly signals the lordship of Christ: He is in charge. He is giving evidence of His authority by creating in us a new language, thereby demonstrating He is not only the Creator but also the re-Creator. He is the God who is incorporating some from every tribe and language and people and nation into His kingdom, and the gates of Hades cannot prevail against such an endeavor (Matt. 16:18; Rev. 5:9). The same encounter with Jesus Christ today empowers us to bear witness to the Kingdom's message and to creatively participate in a redemptive community that shouts to the world "be reconciled to God" (2 Cor. 5:20).[29]

In conclusion, several issues must be reiterated concerning the importance of Pentecost for the development of a theology of Church and mission. The connection between Spirit baptism given on the Day of Pentecost and our understanding and implementation of Church mission are intrinsically bound together. "Pentecost means that God's own eternal and su-

---

[28]"Speaking in tongues," from the Greek *glōssa*, "tongue," and *lalia*, "speaking," "speech." Dempster, "Moral Witness," 3.

[29]Howard M. Ervin, *Conversion-Initiation and the Baptism in the Holy Spirit* (Peabody, Mass.: Hendrickson Publishers, 1984), 41–42.

pernatural life overflowed upon the Church and that God himself, in His own divine being and power, was present in its midst."[30]

The empowerment that is present in Spirit baptism is meant to move God's people across geographical and cultural landscapes with the good news of the gospel. "The mission of the Church is the continuation of the mission of Jesus Christ": Just as the Holy Spirit was given to Jesus for the fulfillment of His mission (Luke 3:22), so the Spirit is given to His disciples (Acts 1:8; 2:4) to continue that same mission (of reconciliation)—and that in a charismatic fashion.[31]

THE GLOBAL CONNECTION

"Worldview" is a term anthropologists use to describe what lies at the heart of every culture. Worldview is a network of interrelating perceptions that guide every facet of one's life. It is the manner in which the human universe is perceived and understood by members of a given society. It provides guidelines for our use of time and our assumptions about the material world. Worldview asks such questions as What causes things? What power lies behind this action? What forces are at work in the universe? What results do they bring, and are these forces personal, impersonal, or both?

The Pentecostal worldview reflects an understanding that embraces the reality of all aspects of life—natural and supernatural. Prophecy, divine guidance, visions and dreams, healings, and other miracles are seen not as static examples of what Christ did, but as anticipated present-day realities that allow God's greatness and glory to be displayed. The fact that the Holy Spirit wants to be powerfully at work in and through the life of every believer can make each day new and exciting. This empowerment opens the door for the Spirit to give the Christian a sense of what must be done and the capacity to do it. Pentecostal believers not only affirm that Christians are entitled to experience the supernatural involvement of God's Spirit, but they also expect God's power to permeate their lives.

We cannot understand the essence of Pentecostalism with-

---

[30]T. F. Torrance, "The Mission of the Church," *Scottish Journal of Theology,* 19 (June 1966): 132.

[31]Arnold Bittlinger, "The Significance of Charismatic Experiences for the Mission of the Church," *International Review of Mission,* 75 (April 1986): 120.

out acknowledging that our dynamic view of causality shapes our understanding of the Church's mission and the consequent expression of our ministries for Christ. The lens through which Pentecostals see so that they may act is labeled with the ancient prophet Zechariah's declaration, " 'Not by might nor by power, but by my Spirit' " (Zech. 4:6). Pentecostals take part in the mission of the Church with the affirmation that God is as good as His word. His reconciliatory purposes are unswerving and His power to bring those purposes to pass are resident in Christ's resurrection. We also affirm that Pentecost is the guarantee that Christ's redemptive mission continues intact through the ministry of the Holy Spirit. The doorway to such a Pentecostal worldview is Spirit baptism as described in Acts 1:8 and 2:4.[32]

While all Christians must look to the Bible as their final authoritative source, encounters with a living God certainly impact our view of the Church's mission and even our interpretation of biblical texts. Although responsible Pentecostalism will never advocate spiritual experience as an end in itself, we do affirm that a genuine encounter with the living God will leave an emotional impact. This is what may be called "Christ-centered experience-certified theology."[33] The worldview, and therefore the presuppositions Pentecostals have as they reflect on the Church and its mission, cannot be removed from this encounter with God, for it is central to our identity. At no time is this more evident than when we attempt to express conceptually what we are to actualize through Church mission.[34]

THE VISION OF THE MISSION

EARLY THEOLOGICAL REFLECTION

The history of Pentecostalism cannot be properly understood apart from its missionary vision. The emergence of the

---

[32]These concepts were originally part of a group writing project, a part of graduate course work offered in the summer of 1990 by the Costa Rica Study Center, in San Jose, Costa Rica. This center is part of masters level course work offered on-site in Costa Rica by Southern California College, an Assemblies of God college in Costa Mesa, California. The participants in this project were Bob Abair, Kathleen Jingling, and Denise Johnson-Ryan. Faculty supervisors were Byron D. Klaus and Douglas Petersen.

[33]William MacDonald, "A Classical Viewpoint," in *Perspectives on the New Pentecostalism,* Russell P. Spittler, ed. (Grand Rapids: Baker Book House, 1976), 6.

[34]Roger Stronstad, "Pentecostal Experience and Hermeneutics," *Paraclete* 26 (Winter 1992): 16–17.

Pentecostal movement at the beginning of the twentieth century brought a surge in missions efforts. Even a cursory evaluation of the early records of the Pentecostal revival leads to the observation that a very close relationship was forged between speaking in tongues as the evidence of being clothed with power for Christian witness, a fervent hope in the soon return of Christ, and His command to evangelize the uttermost parts of the earth. Spirit baptism, viewed as the fulfillment of Joel's prophecy of the "last days," served to energize early Pentecostals' commitment to aggressive evangelistic efforts across both cultural and geographical barriers.[35]

William J. Seymour, the black Holiness leader at the Azusa Street revival, affirmed:

[The] one that is baptized with the Holy Ghost has the power of God on his soul and has power with God and men, power over all the kingdoms of Satan and over all his emissaries.

When the Holy Ghost comes and takes us as His instruments, this is the power that convicts men and women and causes them to see that there is a reality in serving Jesus Christ.

The Holy Spirit is power with God and man.[36]

The Apostolic Faith, a publication of the Azusa Street Mission, repeatedly shows that early Pentecostal leaders viewed the outpouring of God's Spirit as a fulfillment of Joel's prophecy and consequently a greater reason for involvement in global mission efforts. They wrote: "Pentecost has surely come and with it the Bible evidences are following. ... The real revival is only started, ... laying the foundation for a mighty wave of salvation among the unconverted."[37]

It is noteworthy that while the baptism in the Holy Spirit with the evidence of speaking in tongues was the experience of countless people in the sovereign move of God in the early part of the century, and while many critics have labeled Pentecostalism as the "tongues movement," early leaders like William Seymour were quite clear about understanding some-

---

[35]Gary B. McGee, "Early Pentecostal Missionaries—They Went Everywhere Preaching the Gospel," in *Azusa Street and Beyond,* ed., L. Grant McClung, Jr. (South Plainfield, N.J.: Bridge Publishing, Inc.), 33.

[36]L. Grant McClung, Jr., "Truth on Fire: Pentecostals and an Urgent Missiology," in *Azusa Street and Beyond,* 50.

[37]*The Apostolic Faith* (September 1906), 1; quoted in Gary B. McGee, *This Gospel Shall Be Preached,* vol. 1 (Springfield, Mo.: Gospel Publishing House, 1986), 44.

thing more significant in this gracious move of God. Seymour admonished people to "not go from this meeting and talk about tongues, but try to get people saved."[38]

Although excesses were certainly present, Seymour and other leaders focused much more on the Christological impact of the baptism in the Spirit. To exalt Christ was essential to receiving the experience. This Christocentricity must be seen as a key reason for the revival's fervent evangelism. The impact of Spirit baptism heightened this awareness. These early Pentecostals believed that the biblical evidence of tongues accompanying the baptism in the Spirit was a signal that "Bible days were here again." They looked at the Book of Acts and saw the Spirit's empowerment to be part of the ongoing ministry of Jesus Christ across cultural landscapes. Their logic was simply to follow that biblical pattern, because they too had encountered the risen Lord through the baptism in the Spirit. This brought an ever-growing awareness that Christ's reconciliatory mission and ministry were something they had now been commissioned into. Their eyes were open to the Spirit's direction and these early Pentecostals were empowered to obey His bidding.

Stanley Frodsham, Azusa Street revival participant and Pentecostal historian, insisted that the essence of this early Pentecostal movement was not tongues, but magnifying the person of the Lord Jesus Christ.[39] This "experience-certified theology" led to fervent missionary effort both domestically and cross-culturally. The motive clearly originated in a deep and overwhelming encounter with Jesus Christ, compelling the participant to serve.

J. Roswell Flower, writing in 1908, summarized the meaning of Spirit baptism and its impact on the Church and its mission:

> The baptism in the Holy Ghost does not consist in simply speaking in tongues. No. It has a much more grand and deeper meaning than that. It fills our souls with the love of God for lost humanity.
>
> When the Holy Spirit comes into our hearts, the missionary spirit comes in with it; they are inseparable. . . . Carrying the gospel to hungry souls in this and other lands is but a natural result [of being baptized in the Holy Spirit].[40]

---

[38]McClung, "Truth on Fire," 50.

[39]Ibid., 51.

[40]J. Roswell Flower, *The Pentecost*, editorial (August 1908), 4; quoted in McGee, *This Gospel Shall Be Preached*, vol. 1, 45–46.

Another key component of the reflection of early Pentecostals concerning the Church's mission was their intense attention to the truth of Christ's second coming. This certainty forged the missionary fervor of the early Pentecostal movement. Pentecostals affirmed that the promises of the prophet Joel were for their day. They reviewed biblical discussions of the "former" and the "latter rain" (2:23, KJV) and surmised that they were in the last days' outpouring of the Spirit that would occur just before Christ's return.[41] A "last days" mentality was present.

Although many may view Pentecostalism as merely a "tongues movement," the early Pentecostals had a theological self-understanding that cannot be simply written off as merely an experience-based, emotional Movement. Early Pentecostals showed that they had the experiential dimensions of their spirituality in perspective, particularly when they tied their obedient participation in Church mission efforts to the empowerment of the baptism in the Holy Spirit.

APPROACHING THE TWENTY-FIRST CENTURY

A Pentecostal perspective on the Church and its mission cannot be separated from its early twentieth-century roots. As we enter the twenty-first century we can gain crucial self-understanding by seeing how the pioneers of this Movement understood the baptism in the Holy Spirit. Living in a world where theological understanding all too often mirrors the surrounding popular culture, we would do well to contemplate the fervor of early Pentecostals as they entered "the harvest" (see John 4:35). Just as the Book of Acts records for us the event of Pentecost as the guarantee that Christ's redemptive mission continued intact, so let us gain perspective from the early pioneers of the Pentecostal movement. They affirmed that the "Comforter had come" and hence heralded a last-days harvest that Spirit baptized-empowered believers should joyfully participate in.

The Pentecostal movement stands as a testimony to all Christians who are hungry for God to break through the status quo, replacing empty religious forms with spiritual vitality and self-centered church life with the dynamic of a Church in mission to the world. The God who graciously moved on hungry hearts at the turn of the twentieth century is the redemptive God whose mission has not changed. He still is

---

[41]McClung, "Truth on Fire," 51–52.

seeking to empower the Church with the power of Pentecost that sustains and sends forth His people to display His mission of reconciliation.

The Church's mission is really a continuance of God's mission of reconciliation. God's mission has always been to have a people who reflect His glory (including His character and presence). God's revelation of himself always involves His efforts to reconcile humanity to himself. Jesus is the clearest picture of God and His mission the world has ever seen. With His life, death, and resurrection we see the victorious completion of all the factors necessary to redeem humanity and to restore fellowship with the Father. The declaration of this good news is launched in the proclamation and ministry of Jesus Christ. Pentecost assures us that the mission of Christ continues intact.[42]

Melvin Hodges stated that the Church's mission is facilitated by three interrelated aspects of ministry, each of which is equally important and each of which is equally necessary for the effectiveness of the other two. First, the Church is called to minister to God through worship. Second, it is called to minister to the members of the Church itself. Members of the Church are to exercise the gifts and the *koinōnia* of the Spirit in a relationship of edification with one another. Third, the Church is to minister to the world, to proclaim the good news of the gospel of Jesus Christ. These three interrelated aspects of ministry should ever be embodied by the local church. They are all necessary for effective church mission.[43]

---

[42]Tom Bohnert, "A Pentecostal Theology of Church Mission and Its Implications for Ministry," (M.A. paper, May 1992). I am indebted to the work of Tom Bohnert, who has explored aspects of Pentecostal theological reflection on the Church and its mission.

[43]Melvin L. Hodges, *A Theology of the Church and Its Ministry: A Pentecostal Perspective* (Springfield, Mo.: Gospel Publishing House, 1977), 77. The Assemblies of God in Article V, 10, of its Constitution's Statement of Fundamental Truths states this in terms of priority: "Since God's purpose concerning man is to seek and to save that which is lost, to be worshiped by man, and to build a body of believers in the image of His Son, the priority reason for being the Assemblies of God as part of the Church is:

"a. To be an agency of God for evangelizing the world (Matt. 28:19–20; Mark 16:15–16; Acts 1:8).

"b. To be a corporate body in which man may worship God (1 Cor. 12:13).

"c. To be a channel of God's purpose to build a body of saints being perfected in the image of His Son (1 Cor. 12:28; 14:12; Eph. 4:11–16)."

Worship and Bible study contribute to and prepare one for evangelism. Preparation for evangelism is an important part of the edification of believers.

Ministry to God. Any discussion of what the Church is to be or do in the world necessarily must begin with its foremost ministry to God: worship. Christians gain an awareness of who they are as the people of God and the degree to which they are bound together as they encounter a living God through the ministry of worship. Ministry to the world that reflects the standards of Christ's ministry should find its moorings in fervent ministry to God, who alone is worthy of our honor.

Worship moves us beyond the barriers of time and space and allows us to actualize our earthly experience in an eternal realm where God's will is done. Out of this encounter with the eternal we position ourselves among a rebellious creation. We do so with eagerness because through worshiping the God who redeems we see more clearly our role in reflecting God's purposes of reconciliation with a needy humanity.[44]

Worship should be marked by the varied ministries of the Spirit that build up the worshipers spiritually and give honor to God. Speaking in tongues is a vital part of the worship encounter, relating us directly to God (1 Cor. 14:2,14). It transcends the ordinary limitations of speech and enters a level of encounter with God that goes beyond mere lip service. It allows a person to act in accordance with new and previously unimagined possibilities not drawn out of already existing perceptions of reality. This growing awareness is given an authentic new character. Spirit-empowered ministry to God through worship produces a community of believers who have tasted the "new wine." Now they are not only Kingdom people who hunger and thirst after God and His righteousness, but also people who desire to act under the motivation and empowerment of the Spirit to be part of Christ's continuing ministry.[45]

Pentecostal worship means more than reveling in the joyful experience of God's power. It is full of awe and wonder as it contemplates the majesty of God, which often overwhelms us with a sense of how much we fall short (Isa. 6:5). It brings

---

[44]Byron D. Klaus, "A Theology of Ministry: Pentecostal Perspectives," *Paraclete* 23 (Summer 1989): 1–10. Thoughts and concepts shared in this section appeared in initial form in the summer 1989 issues of *Paraclete.* These concepts in an updated form will be developed throughout these sections.

[45]Klaus, "A Theology of Ministry," 1–10. Also see Murray Dempster, "Soundings in the Moral Significance of Glossolalia," paper presented to the Society of Pentecostal Studies, 1983 Annual Meeting, Cleveland, Tenn., November 1983.

a maturity that is empowered to bear witness to the good news throughout the world. So the Spirit's activity in the worship encounter must be balanced by allowing the Spirit to compel the Church to go out into a needy world. God has not called us to be comfortable but to be partakers of His holiness and fellow workers in His harvest field. The Church is not the Church unless lives are changed and become different from the life-style and values of nonbelievers.

In Pentecostal worship, particularly through the manifestation of all the gifts of the Spirit, we transcend the routinization that so easily occurs in our lives. Our tendencies toward rationalization need to be balanced by genuine encounters with God that allow us to minister in the Spirit. In this arena of "lived transcendence" we know and develop intimacy with the Good Shepherd, whose very nature is to interact with His creation and to lead us toward His purposes in reconciliatory ministry.[46]

The Pentecostal community in worship is really involving itself in a ministry to God that acknowledges His rule over the universe. Through the baptism in the Spirit and a continuing involvement in praying in tongues and other gifts of the Spirit, Pentecostals participate in worshipful activity that builds the foundations of a Christocentric ministry. To worship God is to encounter Jesus, who is the Savior, Baptizer, Healer, and soon-coming King. Therefore, such worship compels us to participate in ministry rooted in the historicity of Christ's ministry on earth, ministry that has been transposed into a form that fits the present context.

As believing communities encounter Christ in the dynamic of spiritual worship, they also learn that worshiping God can never be fully understood unless it takes place in the context of fellow believers. This is because all true encounters with God through worship will build communities that mature together. Through their corporate development as a vehicle of God's grace they are to move forward in sacrificial witness, called and empowered by the same power that raised Jesus Christ from the dead.

Ministry to the Church. The Church is a signpost to the

---

[46]The concept of lived transcendence is developed by Ray Anderson in *Historical Transcendence and the Reality of God* (Grand Rapids: Wm. B. Eerdmans, 1975). Although this concept is postulated through the Reformed tradition, it certainly holds promise for Pentecostals who wish to describe the impact on communities of believers in response to the reality of the presence of God as encountered in worship.

reconciliation of humanity to God and one another. It is "the community of justified sinners, . . . who experience salvation and live in thanksgiving. . . . With its eyes fixed on Christ, it lives in the Holy Spirit."[47] Ministry that extends itself to the Church affirms that what binds us together cannot be summarized in dogma, but has much to do with being enfolded into a community that reflects communion with God and subsequently the fellowship of a redeemed humanity.

The apostle John's writings (especially John 17 and 1 John 4) suggest a parallel between the communion within the Trinity and the potential communion within the Church. John 17 records Jesus' prayer in which He explicitly parallels the communion He has known with the Father with what He prays can be made manifest among believers on earth. Ministry of fellow believers to each other should involve activity that will provide a supernatural expression of the fellowship between the Persons within the Godhead and the people of God on earth, thereby linking vertical and horizontal relationships. Therefore we should respond to our fellow members of the Church with the same communion-fellowship attitude God offers us. Communion with God without communion with our brothers and sisters in the Lord is relationally and biblically off-center.[48]

Ministry to the Church includes sharing in divine life. We have the dynamic of that life only as we remain in Him and as we continue passing on His life to each other within the Body. This process of edification is described by Paul as relationships of interreliance: We belong to each other, we need each other, we affect each other (Eph. 4:13–16).[49] This includes sacrifice to help meet each others' needs. We are not a social club but an army that demands cooperation and concern for each other as we encounter the world, deny the flesh, and resist the devil.

God does not consult us about the people He brings into the Church. Galatians 3:26–29 makes it clear that all humanly devised barriers between God and humanity, as well as between human beings, have been made meaningless by Christ. The Spirit has transcended human ties and boundaries and placed us in a union where we live out the implications of

---

[47]Jurgen Moltmann, *The Church in the Power of the Spirit* (London: SCM Press Ltd., 1977), 33.

[48]Klaus, "A Theology of Ministry," 6–7.

[49]Greg Ogden, *The New Reformation: Returning the Ministry to the People of God* (Grand Rapids: Zondervan Publishing House, 1990), 36.

belonging to each other because of our common bond in Christ. Whether poor or rich, educated or uneducated, talented or unskilled, and regardless of our ethnicity, we must not despise one another or think we have a special status above others before God. There is no favoritism with God (Eph. 6:8; James 2:1–9).

Paul's usage of the metaphor of the body of Christ recognizes that all parts of the Body "are interdependent and necessary for the Body's health."[50] The dynamic of relationship is not merely a convenient option. We have been made in the image of God (Gen. 1:26–28), and the Church is meant to be a corporate restoration of the broken image. The Church is not simply a good idea, it is essential to God's redemptive plan (Eph. 3:10–11). God manifests His presence to the world through an interreliant people who are servants of one another.[51]

Because ministry to the Church reflects a biblical image of the Church as an organism, we can see how the relational dimension of life in the Church is dynamic, not static. We do have an effect on each other. Ministry to the Church counteracts the tendency of Western society to emphasize the individual over the community. The Church's ministry includes equipping a group of people who live in community with one another so that they will grow into a loving, well-balanced, mature entity. Paul clearly says in Ephesians 4:11–16 that the equipping of saints for compassionate service in Christ's name must happen in community. Spiritual growth and the context it most effectively occurs in do not come by mere coincidence. Maturing as a believer cannot happen outside of the community of faith. Discipleship has no context other than that of the church of Jesus Christ, because the faithful following of Jesus cannot be maintained apart from an ever-maturing participation with other believers in Christ's life and ministry.[52]

Koinōnia ("fellowship," "sharing," "partnership," "participation") is a biblical theme that offers an enriching perspective for understanding ministry to the Church. It is cre-

---

[50]Ibid., 38.

[51]Ibid., 40.

[52]Christian books, study Bibles, tapes, radio, and television have their place, but they must not be used as an excuse for neglecting the fellowship and ministry of the local church (Heb. 10:25). Howard A. Snyder, *The Community of the King* (Downers Grove, Ill.: InterVarsity Press, 1977), 75.

ated by the Holy Spirit's energizing of believers' common affirmation that Jesus is Lord over the Church. The fellowshipping community ideally stands as an ever-present reminder to the world of what life looks like where God's reign is present.[53] Permeating this *koinōnia* is the character of Christ, which has a teaching and building effect on the Christian community.[54] Although teaching the truth of God's Word is certainly vital to ministry to the Church, disciples are built not only by teaching truth, but also by being in an affirming, loving, giving community of people who together are being conformed to the image of Christ.[55]

Believers are maturing into a community that demonstrates Christ's character and authoritative power. Therefore, the structures and processes we set up for our corporate maturing and equipping in Christ must facilitate the cultivation and demonstration of the fruit and gifts of the Spirit. Churches that do not allow the *koinōnia* of the Spirit to create their ministry to one another lose fellowship with Christ. He placed the promise "I am with you always" alongside the command to "go and make disciples."[56]

Ministry to the World. That the Church's identity is bound up in ministry to the world is a principal premise. Therefore, we must seriously consider the activities with which we involve ourselves in Christ's name and how those activities replicate Christ's ministry on earth. His ministry sets the standard by which we evaluate our ministry. Such a process is critical in light of Matthew 7:21–23, for it indicates that we are not to assume our ministry is representative. Only if it truly takes on His character and purpose and is energized by divine power can we hope to align ourselves with His continuing ministry. That we can do so is guaranteed by Pentecost and the empowerment of the Holy Spirit.

One of the earliest Christian creedal statements is simply "Jesus is Lord." This affirmation was the Early Church's declaration of Christ's rule not only over the Church but also

---

[53]Murray W. Dempster, "Evangelism, Social Concern, and the Kingdom of God," in *Called and Empowered,* 30–31.

[54]The local church will always have shortcomings and frailties; the weeds will remain among the wheat until the end. The Bible does not teach that they are to be purged in preparation for Christ's second coming (Matt. 13:29).

[55]Bohnert, "Pentecostal Theology," 17.

[56]Ibid., 19. Van Engen, *God's Missionary People,* 92.

over the universe and its purposes.[57] The declaration of who Jesus Christ is and what He has done and will do is the essence of the biblical proclamation. The Church cannot escape the fact that making the confession that Jesus is Lord moves believers into proclamation of this divine fact to the world. We cannot confess Jesus is Lord without at the same time proclaiming His lordship over all nations.[58]

Ministry to the world is certainly given content by this biblical theme. The declaration that Jesus is Lord calls every human being to accountability to God. All ministry must carry with it a drive to declare a message of divine consequences; the gospel of "the good news" (Mark 1:14) is a word of judgment, as well as a way of repentance and the promise of a new way of life.[59]

The proclamation of Christ and His offer of salvation is not just an affirmation to ponder and dialogue about—it requires a decision (Matt. 18:3). It is a demand as well as an invitation to join the people of God, who now enjoy "his glorious riches in Christ Jesus" (Phil. 4:19). It is also a demand to be totally committed to God and to humanity. There must be an urgency about proclaiming this gospel and a willingness by the Church to call for repentance and obedience to God's Word.[60]

Diakonia ("service," "ministry") can be described as efforts in serving Christ that continue the incarnational ministry He carried out and enables us to carry out. The character of that ministry is servanthood; it does not imitate this world's model of authority or purpose. The essence of ministry has been once and for all modeled in Christ (Mark 10:45), and consequently we serve Christ by serving the creation that is under His lordship.[61]

The service dimension of ministry moves us from boldly spreading the good news to participating in God's desire to reach out to the nonperson of society in a practical way. People who have no one to plead their cause and who have been ignored and abandoned have also been created in the image of God. The Spirit-empowered Church, to see God's

---

[57]Harry R. Boer, *Pentecost and Missions* (Grand Rapids: Wm. B. Eerdmans, 1961), 153–55.

[58]Van Engen, *God's Missionary People,* 93.

[59]Orlando E. Costas, *The Integrity of Mission* (San Francisco: Harper and Row, 1979), 3–6.

[60]The message and worship must not be modified to make people feel comfortable.

[61]Guder, *Be My Witnesses,* 206.

purposes realized, must move beyond words to deeds. There can be no escaping the fact that if we are to truly serve in the continuing ministry of Jesus Christ, such service must follow the example of Christ's ministry.

Luke 4:18–21 gives emphasis to servant ministry. The rule of the Lord Jesus sends us forward to be something more than a Christian version of the Red Cross. The evil that is perpetrated on victims the world over has been overcome by Christ. How will servant ministry display this victory through compassion in the midst of evil? Physical disabilities are no hindrances to the reign of God. In the midst of sickness and physical tragedy we have the privilege now to say, "Rise and be healed!" To those bound by the chains of the demonic, captives to the destructive power of the evil one, we can proclaim that deliverance is at hand and God's "new" rule sets the captive free.[62] To those multiplied masses whom society has abandoned on the roadside of life, we can authoritatively demonstrate by our tangible acts of mercy and compassion that the kingdom of God brings dignity and human value to "the least of these" (Matt. 25:40).[63]

As Pentecostals we must realize that our explosive growth worldwide among the most destitute of humanity requires us to seriously consider how we may more powerfully and clearly participate in servant ministry. That we are growing in an unprecedented manner in non-Western parts of the world is no accident. In these same places the population is largely oppressed and without dignity.[64]

The Church, full of God's Spirit, can creatively develop and compassionately act through service (moved by the reconciling heart of God) to the "least of these." God's transforming power, which changes us at conversion, gathers us into communities that reflect corporately the reconciliation of God (1 Cor. 12:13; 2 Cor. 5:17–20). These empowered communities must not restrict themselves in the kind of people they

---

[62]Douglas Petersen, "The Kingdom of God and the Hermeneutical Circle: Pentecostal Praxis in the Third World," in *Called and Empowered,* 52–53.

[63]Wealthy believers have a responsibility to give generously. Instead of indulging in luxury, lavish homes, expensive cars, etc., they should sacrifice for promoting the gospel and helping the poor. So should wealthy churches—and so should we all.

[64]Larry Pate, a leading Pentecostal missiologist, defines the "two-thirds world" as representing two-thirds of the world's land mass and two-thirds of the world's population. See Larry D. Pate, *From Every People* (Monrovia, Calif.: MARC, 1989).

will serve, because they are under the rule of the One who has clearly identified the object of His love (Luke 4:18–19). We can do nothing less than reflect our Commander-in-chief, who seeks those still bound by sin, held captive by the devil. The Spirit desires to empower His people to enter boldly the arenas of hopelessness and destruction, lest we become a Church like the people the prophet Amos censured—a people with a ritualized religion without pity or ethical content.[65] For the sake of our witness, we must forget our rights, be humble and forgiving in the midst of persecution, and "always be prepared to give an answer to everyone who asks you to give the reason for the hope that you have. But do this with gentleness and respect, keeping a clear conscience" (1 Pet. 3:15–16).

We must repeat that Pentecostal self-identity should be rooted in Acts 1:8. These words state clearly that the Church's existence is one of being a witness globally. The *koinōnia* created by the Spirit, the proclamation that Jesus is Lord and Savior, and the compassionate servant ministry together yield a powerful witness to the ongoing ministry of Jesus Christ.[66]

The witness to the world is the practical outworking of our participation in God's mission of reconciliation with the world. We proclaim and demonstrate the compassionate character and authoritative power of Christ that has broken into the present age. Through word and deed we witness to the good news that Jesus loves the poor, the sick, the hungry, the demon-possessed, the physically tortured, the emotionally wounded, the unloved, the unlovely, and even the self-sufficient. Then we continue to love and care for them, to make them disciples that are no longer "infants, tossed back and forth by the waves, and blown here and there by every wind of teaching and by the cunning and craftiness of men in their deceitful scheming" (Eph. 4:14).[67]

A prime motivation of Pentecostal ministry in the world has been the belief that we minister as a witness to Christ's authoritative power. Demonstrations of the power of the Spirit then are an essential element of that witness (Mark 16:15–20), for Christ's ministry continues intact by the power of the Holy Spirit (Matt. 28:19–20). Supernatural demonstration of God's presence and power overcomes humanity's resis-

---

[65]Dempster, "Evangelism, Social Concern," 32.

[66]Van Engen, *God's Missionary People,* 97.

[67]It is not enough to get people to repeat the sinner's prayer. They must be made a vital part of the local church in its worship and ministry.

tance to the gospel. Such demonstrations are actually the presence of the risen Christ who has broken Satan's rule and is now making a public spectacle of the inadequacy of any power that questions Christ's divine authority (Col. 2:15). When people come in contact with this witness to Christ's authority they are encountering the reality of God and the community of God's power that gives authoritative witness to Christ's lordship over the world, the flesh, and the devil.[68]

This authoritative power in word and deed has received a contemporary renewal. The Pentecostal experience testifies to the fact that God has reminded all who claim Jesus as Lord that He has not left them as orphans (John 14:18), but has commissioned them with power for the continuing of His redemptive mission. Pentecost testifies to the "latter rain" (Hos. 6:1–3; Joel 2:23–27) just prior to Christ's soon return. It sends us forth in ministry to the world with a divinely inspired compassion and passion. We enter into this battle with expectancy and anticipation. Stanley Frodsham summed it up well when he wrote:

> The time is short; the coming of the Lord is near; the present opportunities of evangelism will not last long.
> . . .
> Thank God, He is mightily pouring out His Spirit in the last days.
> The fire still blazes, . . . it will blaze until that glad day when the Lord Jesus Christ shall descend from heaven and take His church to be with Him forevermore.[69]

STUDY QUESTIONS

1. Why is the Pentecostal experience crucial to a Pentecostal perspective on the Church and its mission?

2. What does a study of the Old Testament people of God add to our understanding of the contemporary Church and its mission in the world?

3. How does the Book of Ephesians help us to see the Church in mission as more than a budgeted program among other programs?

4. What is unique about Luke's understanding of Pentecost and mission?

---

[68]Don Williams, *Signs and Wonders and the Kingdom of God,* (Ann Arbor: Vine Books, 1989), 137.

[69]Stanley H. Frodsham, *With Signs Following* (Springfield, Mo.: Gospel Publishing House, 1946), 275–79.

5. How are the baptism in the Holy Spirit and our understanding of Church mission intrinsically bound together?

6. How did early Pentecostals understand the connection between the outpouring of the Spirit that began in A.D. 1900 and the development of a vision for Church mission?

7. How does a Pentecostal understanding of worship fuel our fervency for mission?

8. How might the word "mission" and the threefold ministry of the Church be seen as an integrated whole?

9. How does the Spirit create biblical *koinōnia?*

10. What are some ways we can expect to see Christ's power demonstrated in our ministry?

11. Review Stanley Frodsham's summary statement at the end of this chapter. How does it give a good synthesis of a Pentecostal worldview and understanding of the Church and its mission?

CHAPTER

17

The Mission
of the
Church

CHAPTER EIGHTEEN

The Last Things

Stanley M. Horton

What the Bible says about the last events of life and history is not a mere afterthought.[1] Genesis 1 shows that God created according to a plan, a plan that included sequence, balance, correspondence, and a climax.[2] Such things do not happen by chance. Then when Adam and Eve sinned, God gave a promise that the offspring of the woman would crush the head of the very serpent that tempted Eve (Gen. 3:15; cf. Rev. 12:9). From that point on the Bible gradually unfolds a plan of redemption with promises given to Abraham (Gen. 12:3), to David (2 Sam. 7:11,16), and to the Old Testament prophets, promises that point ahead to the coming of Jesus and to His ultimate triumph. The gospel assures us further "that he who began a good work in you will carry it on to completion until the day of Christ Jesus" (Phil. 1:6). That is, the whole Bible focuses on the future, a future that is assured by the very nature of God himself.

THE BELIEVER'S HOPE

God is revealed in the Bible as the God of hope who gives us peace and joy as we trust in Him (Rom. 15:13). The assurance of the believer's hope is twofold: God's love that sent Jesus to the cross for us (Rom. 5:5–10) and the Holy Spirit's acts of power that cause us to "overflow with hope by the

---

[1]Theologians often refer to this as "eschatology" (Gk. *eschatos*, "last"), "the study of last things."

[2]See chap. 7, pp. 209, 220.

597

power of the Holy Spirit" (Rom. 15:13).[3] In this way, the Holy Spirit who baptizes and fills us "is a deposit [a first installment] guaranteeing our inheritance" (Eph. 1:14). Paul shows us also that our hope is not uncertain; it is as sure as anything that we already have. The only reason the promise of our resurrection, our new bodies, our reigning with Christ, and our eternal future are called a hope is that we do not have them yet (Rom. 8:24–25).[4] But this hope will never disappoint us or cause us to be ashamed for having held to it, for it is kept alive and shown to be true by the love of God which the Holy Spirit has poured out into our hearts (Rom. 5:5).[5] The fact He sent His Son to die for us is the supreme demonstration of that love and assures us that the same love will provide everything necessary to see us all the way through to eternal glory (John 3:16; Rom. 5:8–10; 8:18–19).

Paul emphatically states that apart from Christ people do not have hope (Eph. 2:12); that is, they do not have the kind of hope the Bible talks about. Many other ancient religions have a cyclical view of history, everything recurring again and again, so they do not offer any future goal in history. Hinduism only wants to stop any desires for life in order to get off the wheel of birth, death, and reincarnation. Some Greeks and Romans looked to the past to try to find laws that governed what they considered an eternal repetition of history—the results were usually pessimistic. Their cyclical view of history gave no hope of a glorious destiny. So when people were interested in the future, in most cases it was the immediate future—which they sought to influence or avoid through astrology, fortune-telling, and various occultic practices or pagan worship. Many of those who turn away from the Bible today are doing the same. Or else, they hold to empty hopes in evolutionary progress or communist dreams.[6]

---

[3]Neill Quinn Hamilton, *The Holy Spirit and Eschatology in Paul: Scottish Journal of Theology Occasional Papers,* No. 6 (Edinburgh: Oliver and Boyd Ltd., 1957.), 35.

[4]"Hope" (Gk. *elpis*) in the New Testament includes not only the ideas of "hope," "expectation," and "prospect," it also refers to a Christian hope that is absolutely certain and has no sense of contingency. Someone has called it a "know-so" hope.

[5]Ewert, David, *And Then Comes the End* (Scottdale, Pa.: Herald Press, 1980), 176–78.

[6]The Old Testament does see the cycle of the seasons and of human life, but it has a strong emphasis on the chronological presentation of history. See James Barr, *Biblical Words for Time,* 2d. rev. ed. (Naperville, Ill.: Alec R. Allenson, Inc., 1969), 28–32, 147. Hans Schwarz, *On the Way to the*

The Bible rejects all those expectations as false: empty, meaningless, degrading, defiling. Believers have a better hope in and through Christ, who himself is our hope (Col. 1:27; 1 Tim. 1:1). The Bible presents what is basically a linear view of history that expects—for those who trust Him—God's help and blessing in the present and a glorious future. The Book of Hebrews urges us who have taken "hold of the hope offered" to be greatly encouraged and to "hold unswervingly to the hope we profess, for he who promised is faithful" (Heb. 6:18; 10:23). As Paul Minear says, this hope is no "vague, future possibility."[7] From the beginning God had the last things in mind. It is true that the Bible centers its attention around the first coming of Christ, which accomplished salvation and caused the future to break in on the present in a promissory way. Yet the second coming of Christ, which will bring in the consummation of God's plan and the glory we shall share, is also always in view.

Old Testament prophets looked ahead to the last days without indicating just when they would be. Their purpose was not to satisfy people's curiosity, but to focus on God's purpose and to use the prophecies as an incentive for obeying God's will in the present. For example, Isaiah told of a time when God's house will be exalted "and all nations will stream to it. Many peoples will come and say, 'Come, let us go up to the mountain of the LORD, ... He will teach us his ways, so that we may walk in his paths' " (Isa. 2:2–3). Then God would bring judgment and peace. This truth brought the call, "Come, O house of Jacob, let us walk in the light of the LORD" (Isa.

Future: A Christian View of Eschatology in the Light of Current Trends in Religion, Philosophy, and Science, rev. ed. (Minneapolis: Augsburg Publishing House, 1979), 17–18. Louis Berkhof, *Systematic Theology,* 4th ed. rev. (Grand Rapids: Wm. B. Eerdmans, 1941), 661, mentions that the Stoics "spoke of successive world-cycles." Bultmann points out that the Greek idea of a sequence of worlds coming to be and passing away arose because they were looking at nature. Rudolf Bultmann, *The Presence of Eternity: History and Eschatology* (Westport, Conn.: Greenwood Press, 1957), 5, 24. For a good discussion on Marxist communism as a "pseudoreligious movement" see Hans Schwarz, "Eschatology," in *Christian Dogmatics,* Carl E. Braaten and Robert W. Jenson, eds., vol. 2 (Philadelphia: Fortress Press, 1984), 545–50.

[7]Claus Westermann, *A Thousand Years and a Day: Our Time in the Old Testament,* trans. Stanley Rudman (Philadelphia: Muhlenberg Press, 1962), 21, points out that "history means growth," and "God's dealing with the whole world is, from the call of Abraham onwards, a *progressive* work." Paul S. Minear, *Christian Hope and the Second Coming* (Philadelphia: The Westminster Press, 1954), 26.

2:5). Zephaniah also used future judgment to provide incentive for right attitudes in the present when he said, "Seek the LORD. . . . Seek righteousness, seek humility; perhaps you will be sheltered on the day of the LORD's anger" (Zeph. 2:3).

In a similar way the New Testament uses the hope of Christ's return as motivation. "We know that when he appears, we shall be like him, for we shall see him as he is. Everyone who has *this hope* in him purifies himself, just as he is pure" (1 John 3:2–3).

Because His disciples thought the future Kingdom would immediately appear, Jesus had to let them know there would be delay—yet at the same time they would have to be on the alert, ready whenever He might come. In a parable Jesus compared himself to a man of noble birth who went to a "distant" country to have himself appointed king and then to return (Luke 19:11–27). Later, the disciples understood that Jesus meant He must ascend to heaven and be enthroned there before He could return as King. The comparison to a journey to a distant country also emphasized that He would be gone a long time.

Just how long He would be gone, Jesus did not say; the time of His return only the Father in heaven knows (Matt. 24:30,36; Mark 13:32–33). Perhaps God withheld this information in order to minimize the dangers of delay. Many will be tempted to follow the example of the wicked servant in Matthew 24:45–51, who "says to himself, 'My master is staying away a long time,' and he then begins to beat his fellow servants and to eat and drink with drunkards. The master of that servant will come on a day when he does not expect him and at an hour he is not aware of. He will cut him to pieces and assign him a place with the hypocrites, where there will be weeping and gnashing of teeth" (vv. 48–51). It is better that we do not know the time of Christ's coming. God wants us to do His work. We are more likely to be faithful if we know we must always be alert, ready at any time for His coming (Matt. 24:42; 25:13).

Though Jesus again indicated that it would be a long time (Matt. 25:19), He repeatedly emphasized that His coming would be both sudden and unexpected. Faithful believers will not be taken by surprise because they will be waiting, working, no matter how long the Lord's coming is delayed (Luke 12:35–38). Christians can be taken by surprise only if they let their hearts "be weighed down with dissipation, drunkenness and the anxieties of life." Then "that day will close on" them "unexpectedly like a trap" (Luke 21:34). Jesus warned,

" 'Be always on the watch, and pray that you may be able to escape all that is about to happen, and that you may be able to stand before the Son of Man' " (Luke 21:36).

Among the last words of Jesus recorded in the New Testament is His declaration, " 'Behold, I am coming soon!' " (Rev. 22:7,12). Scoffers may say " 'Where is this "coming" he promised?' " (2 Pet. 3:4). But we have to remember that God does not look at time the way we do: "With the Lord a day is like a thousand years, and a thousand years are like a day" (2 Pet. 3:8). He is also concerned about more coming to repentance, allowing us to continue to carry forward the Great Commission (2 Pet. 3:9). It is good for us, therefore, to live in the tension between "soon" but "not yet," doing His business, carrying out the tasks He gives us to do, until He comes back (Mark 13:33–34; Luke 19:13).

Jesus also compared the world at the time of His coming to the world of Noah's day. In spite of the warnings, the preaching, the building of the ark, the gathering of the animals, the people were unheeding and unprepared. They did not really believe God's judgment would come. To them, the day of the Flood dawned like any other day: They had their meals planned, their work planned, their parties and weddings planned. But that day brought an end to the world as they knew it. In the same way the present world will go blindly on, making its own plans. But one day Jesus will come back (Matt. 24:37–39).

To emphasize that it will be like any other day, Jesus said, " 'Two men will be in the field; one will be taken and the other left. Two women will be grinding with a hand mill; one will be taken and the other left' " (Matt. 24:40–41). That is, people will be going about their normal, everyday tasks and suddenly there will come a separation. "Taken" (Gk. *paralambanetai*) means "taken along or received." Jesus "took Peter and the two sons of Zebedee *along* with him" (Matt. 26:37). He promised, " 'I will come back and *take* you to be with me' " (John 14:3). So the one who is taken is received into Jesus' presence to be with Him forever (1 Thess. 4:17). "Left" (Gk. *aphietai*) means "left behind," as in Mark 1:18,20— left behind to face the wrath and judgments of God. In other words, there will be no prior warning and no opportunity to get ready at the last minute. The same truth is brought out in the Parable of the Ten Virgins (Matt. 25:1–13). All this reminds us that in spite of the delay, we must always consider Christ's return imminent.

To sharpen the exhortation to be constantly ready Jesus

also repeated the fact that no one knows the time of His return except the Father (Matt. 24:36,42,44; Mark 13:32–37). This was hard for the disciples to understand, and just before Jesus ascended to heaven they asked, " 'Are you at this *time* going to restore the kingdom to Israel?' " (Acts 1:6). Jesus replied, " 'It is not for you to know the *times* or *dates* the Father has set by his own authority' " (v. 7). In other words they are none of our business.[8] Our business is Acts 1:8, " 'You will receive power when the Holy Spirit comes on you; and you will be my witnesses . . . to the ends of the earth.' " This rules out all date setting, including all suggestions about the time and even the season of the year when Christ might return.[9] The attention of believers is to be on Jesus (Heb. 12:2–3) and on faithfully fulfilling the Great Commission (Matt. 24:45–46; 25:21,23).

Paul reinforces the warnings of Jesus by recognizing that the "day of the Lord will come like a thief in the night" (1 Thess. 5:2). However, believers will not be taken by surprise—not because they know the time, but because they are "day persons," living in the light of God's Word (not night persons who belong to the darkness of evil). Consequently, they are alert, self-controlled, protected by faith and love as a breastplate, and the hope of salvation as a helmet (1 Thess. 5:4–9). Like the apostle Paul, they maintain an intense longing

---

[8]Throughout Church history, people have speculated about the time of Christ's return. There was a rash of date setting just preceding A.D. 1000. William Miller set dates in the 1840s and deceived many. We can expect more speculation about dates, some from people who may be sincere but who misinterpret Scripture, some from deceivers who use people's fears and curiosity to get them to send money. It should be noted also that "generation" (Gk. *genea,* Matt. 24:34) can also mean "race" and may refer to the fact that the Jewish people would not pass away or be destroyed utterly. Even if it is taken to mean "generation," it could refer to a length of thirty, forty, a hundred years, or even an indefinite time, since "all these things" are probably meant to include the destruction of Jerusalem as well as the consummation and the *parousia.* See Henry B. Swete, *Commentary on Mark* (Grand Rapids: Kregel Publications, 1977 reprint from Macmillan, London, 1913), 315. See also R. C. H. Lenski, *The Interpretation of Matthew's Gospel* (Minneapolis: Augsburg Publishing House, 1943, 1964), 952–53, which points out that already in Matt. 24:14 we are referred to "the end" and that, like the Hebrew *dor,* translated *genea* in the LXX, the word can refer to a kind of people "that reproduces and succeeds itself in many physical generations."

[9]See William M. Alnor, *Soothsayers of the Second Advent* (Old Tappan, N.J.: Power Books, Fleming H. Revell Co., 1989), 194–95, where he refers to David Lewis' "Manifesto on Date Setting." Lewis takes Mark 13:33 as a key verse against all forms of date setting.

for His appearing (2 Tim. 4:8) because they love and trust Him so much. Paul's hope was never "bound to a fixed date but to the gospel that pronounced the fulfillment of the Old Testament promises and called for trusting existence."[10]

Jesus also warned against giving too much attention to signs. False christs (messiahs, "anointed ones," including people who claim to have a special anointing beyond the rest of us) will use signs to deceive (Matt. 24:4–5). Jesus explained that wars and rumors of wars are *not* signs. Such things must happen, for they—along with famines, earthquakes, persecution, apostasy, false prophets, and increasing wickedness—are simply characteristics of the entire age between Christ's first and second comings, the age in which we have the responsibility of preaching the gospel in the whole world (Matt. 24:6–14). Instead of focusing on signs, we are to take our stand for Jesus and lift up our heads; that is, we must keep our attention on Jesus, because our redemption is drawing near (Luke 21:28).

God's saving grace "teaches us to say 'No' to ungodliness and worldly passions, and to live self-controlled, upright and godly lives in this present age, while we wait for the *blessed hope*—the glorious appearing of our great God and Savior, Jesus Christ" (Titus 2:12–14). "Blessed" (Gk. *makarian*) implies a fullness of blessing, happiness, and joy through the gracious, unmerited favor of God. Though we, as believers, are blessed now, there is much more to come.

Most theologians recognize that "in the New Testament the future is seen as the unfolding of what is given in the resurrection of Christ."[11] His resurrection was a key theme in the preaching of the Early Church. On the Day of Pentecost Peter centered attention on Jesus. Paul proclaimed that "Christ has indeed been raised from the dead, the firstfruits of those who have fallen asleep" (1 Cor. 15:20). "And if the Spirit of him who raised Jesus from the dead is living in you, he who raised Christ from the dead will also give life to your mortal bodies through the Spirit, who lives in you" (Rom. 8:11). Peter also spoke of "a living hope through the resurrection of Jesus Christ from the dead, and into an inheritance that can never perish, spoil or fade" (1 Pet. 1:3–4).

Christ's resurrection by the Spirit is thus the guarantee that we shall be raised and changed, so that our resurrection bod-

---

[10]Schwarz, "Eschatology," vol. 2, 498.

[11]Hendrikus Berkhof, *Well-Founded Hope* (Richmond, Va.: John Knox Press, 1969), 18.

ies will be immortal and incorruptible (1 Cor. 15:42–44,47–48,50–54). As Ralph Riggs put it:

> This resurrection and translation of the saints has an extent of glory which we cannot comprehend. . . . The time is coming when the Spirit will envelop us with His power, transform our bodies by His might, and transport us to glory. . . . This will be the manifestation of the sons of God, the glorious liberty of the children of God. . . . the triumphant climax to the work of the Holy Spirit.[12]

Our resurrection bodies will be like His (Phil. 3:21; 1 John 3:2). Though God created mankind in His likeness, and the image was still there after the Fall (Gen. 9:6), we are told that Adam "had a son in his own likeness, in his own image" (Gen. 5:3). Therefore, Paul says, "Just as we have borne the likeness of the earthly man, so shall we bear the likeness of the man from heaven" (1 Cor. 15:49). Our new bodies will be as much different from our present bodies as the plant is from the seed (1 Cor. 15:37).

The believers' resurrection bodies are also described as "spiritual" in contrast to our present "natural" bodies. It is generally agreed that "spiritual" (Gk. *pneumatikon*) does not mean "consisting of spirit;" nor is the body immaterial, ethereal, or lacking in physical density. The disciples knew from experience that Christ's resurrection body was real, touchable—not ghostly, yet somehow of a different order suited for both earth and heaven, though not limited to the conditions of our present "space-time dimensions."[13] So our resurrection bodies are described as "of heaven" (Gk. *epouranios*).

So even though our present bodies are earthly, natural (Gk.

---

[12]Ralph M. Riggs, *The Spirit Himself* (Springfield, Mo.: Gospel Publishing House, 1949), 188–89. Riggs was general superintendent of the Assemblies of God, 1953–59.

[13]"Spiritual" (Gk. *pneumatikos*) is used of the manna as "spiritual bread," bread from heaven (1 Cor. 10:3), of "spiritual songs" (Eph. 5:19; Col. 3:16), "spiritual wisdom and understanding," wisdom and understanding given by the Spirit (Col. 1:9), "spiritual gifts" given and empowered by the Spirit (1 Cor. 12:1), and of people who are filled with and used by the Holy Spirit (1 Cor. 14:37; Gal. 6:1). See Geerhardus Vos, *The Pauline Eschatology* (Grand Rapids: Wm. B. Eerdmans, 1972), 166–67; id., *Redemptive History and Biblical Interpretation: The Shorter Writings of Geerhardus Vos,* Richard B. Gaffin, Jr., ed. (Phillipsburg, N.J.: Presbyterian and Reformed Pub. Co., 1980), 49–50. For "space-time dimensions," see Henry Blamires, "The Eternal Weight of Glory" *Christianity Today* 35 (27 May 1991): 30–34.

psuchikon), with the same limits Adam had after the Fall, our resurrection bodies will take on supernatural qualities and glory. Though we shall still be finite beings, dependent wholly on God, our bodies will be the perfect instruments to enable us to respond to the Holy Spirit in new and marvelous ways.[14]

When Jewish believers cry, *Abba!* or Gentile believers cry out, "Father!" the Holy Spirit "testifies with our spirit" that what we are saying is not mere words, confirming to us that God really is our Father. Our relation to God as His children, however, is not limited to this life. It makes us heirs of God and coheirs with Christ (Rom. 8:17). Now we have "the first-fruits of the Spirit" (v. 23). The fullness will come with the fullness of the adoption ("the placing of sons") and with the redemption of our bodies (v. 23), that is, at the time of the Resurrection.

In the meantime the Spirit prepares us for the fulfillment of our hope of glory in many ways. He helps us pray (Rom. 8:26–27) as "by faith we eagerly await through the Spirit the righteousness for which we hope" (Gal. 5:5). The gift of the Holy Spirit is a seal and a "first installment" of what we shall receive in greater fullness in our future inheritance as the children of God (Eph. 1:13–14). It is also a "pledge" that we shall indeed receive it if we keep our faith in Jesus and continue to sow "to please the Spirit" rather than our sinful nature (Gal. 6:7–10; see also Rom. 2:10).[15]

In Paul's writings the work of the Spirit in preparing for the coming age is very much in view. The point of Romans 14:17 is that righteousness, peace, and joy in the Holy Spirit are what show that we are under the rule of God—that God is really King in our lives. Yet Paul is not limiting the Kingdom to these present blessings. They are, in fact, blessings of the future Kingdom. But through the Spirit, they are ours now as well. Paul goes on to show that they prepare us for the future and increase our anticipation of our future hope (Rom. 15:13). This hope was behind the cry *"Marana tha,"* that is, "Come, O [our] Lord!" (1 Cor. 16:22).

Along with these first installments of the blessings of the age to come we can have special times of refreshing from the

---

[14]Henry Barclay Swete, *The Holy Spirit in the New Testament* (Grand Rapids: Baker Book House, 1976), 190–91.

[15]Charles Webb Carter, *The Person and Ministry of the Holy Spirit: A Wesleyan Perspective* (Grand Rapids: Baker Book House, 1974), 300–302. Cf. Dale Moody, *The Hope of Glory* (Grand Rapids: Wm. B. Eerdmans, 1964), 46.

Lord whenever there is repentance or a change of attitude toward the Lord (Acts 3:19). But, as has been emphasized, the warnings of Jesus must not be taken lightly. Again and again He emphasized the importance of being ready and living in the light of His return (Matt. 24:42,44,50; 25:13; Luke 12:35,40; 21:34–36).[16]

THE INTERMEDIATE STATE OF DEATH

Death will not bring an end to our hope, for we have the assurance that when Christ returns "the dead in Christ will rise first" (1 Thess. 4:16). They will not miss any of the glory of the Rapture and that promised meeting in the air (4:17). The Bible, however, does not tell us all we would like to know about the state of our existence between death and the resurrection. It is more concerned that we look ahead to the inheritance and fulfillment that will be ours when Jesus comes again.

OLD TESTAMENT TEACHING

The Old Testament makes it very clear that God is the source of all life and that death is in the world as the result of sin (Gen. 1:20–27; 2:7,22; 3:22–23). Most Israelites, however, looked on life with a positive attitude (Ps. 128:5–6).[17] Suicide was extremely rare, and long life was considered a blessing from God (Ps. 91:16). Death brought sorrow, usually expressed in loud wailing and deep mourning (Matt. 9:23; Luke 8:52).

Israelite burial customs differed from those of the surrounding peoples. The tombs of Egyptian pharaohs were filled with furniture and many other things intended to help them maintain their station in the afterlife. Canaanites included a lamp, a jar of oil, and a jar of food with every burial.[18] Israelites did not normally do this. The body, wrapped in linen, usually

---

[16]Schwarz suggests that "[i]mmediate readiness does not necessarily express belief in the chronologically near return of the Lord, but shows that our present attitude is expressive of our ultimate future. . . . Christians are asked to live their lives in active anticipation, as if each moment were their last." Schwarz, "Eschatology," vol. 2, 583.

[17]Cf. Robert Martyn-Achard, *From Death to Life: a Study of the Development of the Doctrine of the Resurrection in the Old Testament* (Edinburgh: Oliver and Boyd, 1960), 3–8.

[18]I observed this in 1962 when excavating Canaanite family, or clan, tombs in Dothan. Some had five levels of burials from a period of over two hundred years.

anointed with spices, was simply laid in a tomb or buried in a grave. This did not mean, however, that they did not believe in an afterlife. They spoke of the spirit going to a place called in the Hebrew *Sheʼol* or, sometimes, of going into the presence of God.

Because the terms *Sheʼol,* "death" (Heb. *maweth*), "grave" (Heb. *qever*), "pit" (Heb. *bor*), and "destruction" (Heb. *'araddon,* or "Abaddon") are sometimes parallel (e.g., Ps. 30:3), some say both *Sheʼol* and "pit" always mean the grave.[19] However, the Bible pictures people as still having some kind of existence in *Sheʼol* (Isa. 14:9–10). Others take *Sheʼol* to mean the place of the afterlife and say it never means the grave.[20]

Three passages are often cited to prove *Sheʼol* is the grave. Psalm 6:5 reads, "No one remembers you when he is dead. Who praises you from the grave [Heb. *Sheʼol*]?" The remembering, however, is parallel to the praising. The same word ("remembering") is used of a solemn naming of God among the people (Exod. 3:15). It speaks of an active reminding here on earth, which ends when a person dies. Therefore, when the spirit goes to *Sheʼol,* that person's praise and testimony to the people on earth ceases.[21] From the point of view of people on earth, death is thought of as silence (Ps. 115:17). However, the Psalmist goes on to say, "It is we who extol the LORD, both now and forevermore" (Ps. 115:18), which implies a better hope and certainly does not rule out praising the Lord in the afterlife.

Hezekiah in his prayer stated, "In your love you kept me from the pit of destruction; you have put all my sins behind your back. For the grave [Heb. *Sheʼol*] cannot praise you; death cannot sing your praise; those who go down to the pit cannot hope for your faithfulness" (Isa. 38:17–18). Again, Hezekiah is concerned about his testimony and the results of it among the people. God's forgiveness of his sins kept him from going down to the place of punishment. Now that he was healed, he would see God's faithfulness—and he did, for fifteen added years (Isa. 38:5).

---

[19]The KJV translated *Sheʼol* sometimes as "hell," sometimes as "the grave," sometimes as "the pit." The NIV usually translates it as "the grave," sometimes as "death."

[20]Ernest Swing Williams, *Systematic Theology,* vol. 3 (Springfield, Mo.: Gospel Publishing House, 1953), 178. See also George Eldon Ladd, *The Last Things: An Eschatology for Laymen* (Grand Rapids: Wm. B. Eerdmans, 1978), 32.

[21]James Buswell, Jr., *A Systematic Theology of the Christian Religion,* vol. 2 (Grand Rapids: Zondervan Publishing House, 1962), 317.

Actually, *Sheʼol* is often described as a depth that contrasts with the height of heaven (Job 11:8; Ps. 139:8; Amos 9:2). Often the context refers to the anger or wrath of God (Job 14:13; Pss. 6:1,5; 88:3,7; 89:46,48), and sometimes to both wrath and fire (Deut. 32:22). In some cases the references are brief and it seems it is treated simply as the place or the state of the dead. In it the dead are called *rephaim*, what we might call "ghosts" (Isa. 14:9; 26:14). Other passages refer to some of the dead as *ʼelohim*, in the sense of "powerful spirit beings" (1 Sam. 28:13).[22] But very often it is clear that *Sheʼol* is the place for the wicked and all "the nations that forget God" (Ps. 9:17; cf. Pss. 39:12–13; 55:15; 88:11–12; Prov. 7:27; 9:18; Isa. 38:18).[23] Where the New Testament quotes Old Testament passages referring to *Sheʼol*, it translates the word by *Hadēs*, which it sees, not as the vague place pagan Greeks talked about, but as a place of punishment.[24]

In view of this it is important to note that the Old Testament does not teach that everyone goes to *Sheʼol*. It is true that Job spoke of death as a *beth moʻēd*, a "meeting house" for all living (Job 30:23), but he was referring simply to the fact that all die; he was not implying that all go to the same place after death.

Some Old Testament saints, at least, had a better hope. Enoch and Elijah were taken directly to heaven (Gen. 5:24; 2 Kings 2:11). When David felt the wrath of God because of his sin, he cried out for mercy in order to escape *Sheʼol*. But when his faith rose, his hope was to "dwell in the house of the LORD forever" (Ps. 23:6; cf. Pss. 16:11; 17:15). Psalm 49:15 in contrast to the wicked who are headed for *Sheʼol*, says, "God, however, will redeem my soul from the hand of *Sheʼol*, for He will take me [to himself]" (author's translation). That is, *Sheʼol* is personified as trying to grab him and take him down to the place of punishment, but God redeems and rescues him so that he escapes from having to go to *Sheʼol* at all. The psalmist Asaph wrote, "You guide me with your counsel," that is, while on earth, "and afterward you will take me

---

[22]*Elohim* is used of the one true God, of pagan gods, of angels, and of departed heroes, depending on the context.

[23]See R. H. Charles, *A Critical History of the Doctrine of a Future Life: In Israel, in Judaism, and in Christianity* 2d ed. (London: Adam and Charles Black, 1913), 33–35. He accounts for this by referring to "the biblical doctrine that death is the issue of sin."

[24]See Acts 2:27 where Peter quotes Ps. 16:10, clearly understanding *Sheʼol* as *Hadēs*.

into glory," that is, into heaven (Ps. 73:24).[25] Solomon also declared that "the path of life leads upward [to the place above] for the wise [that is, for those who fear the Lord] in order to avoid *She'ol* beneath" (author's translation). God's message to Balaam made him recognize that the death of the righteous is better than the death of the wicked (Num. 23:10).

Possibly because Jacob spoke of going down to *She'ol* to his son (Joseph) mourning, later Jews considered Jacob and Joseph righteous; so some came up with the idea of divisions in *She'ol:* a place for the righteous as well as for the wicked (Enoch 22:1–14).[26] However, Jacob at that time refused to be comforted, no doubt thinking that both he and Joseph were somehow under God's judgment. There is no record of Jacob seeking the Lord again until after he received the news that Joseph was alive (Gen. 45:28 through 46:1); Jacob probably considered *She'ol* a place of punishment. Actually, no passage in the Old Testament clearly necessitates dividing *She'ol* into two compartments, one for punishment, one for blessing.

Another phrase seems to indicate the Old Testament saints expected an afterlife. God told Moses that after he went up the mountain and looked across to the Promised Land, " 'You too will be gathered to your people, as your brother Aaron was' " (Num. 27:13). Aaron, however, was buried at Mount Hor and no one knows where God buried Moses (Deut. 34:5–6). Therefore, being "gathered to one's people" can hardly refer to the grave.

NEW TESTAMENT TEACHING

The New Testament emphasis is on the resurrection of the body rather than on what happens immediately after death. Death is still an enemy,[27] but is no longer to be feared (1 Cor. 15:55–57; Heb. 2:15). For the believer, to live is Christ and to die is gain; that is, to die means more Christ (Phil. 1:21). Thus, to die and go to be with Christ is far better than remaining in the present body, though we must remain as long

---

[25]The majority of Bible scholars hold that Ps. 73:24 means that at death "the righteous will be received to the presence of Yahweh and will dwell in His glory." Martin-Achard, *From Death to Life,* 163.

[26]Some rabbis said the compartments of the righteous were separated from the compartments of the wicked by only a handbreadth; others said by only a fingerbreadth.

[27]Erickson says that death is not natural to mankind. Millard J. Erickson, *Christian Theology* (Grand Rapids: Baker Book House, 1985), 1170–71.

as God sees that it is necessary (Phil. 1:23–24). Then death will bring a rest from (that is, a ceasing of) our earthly labors and sufferings and an entrance into glory (2 Cor. 4:17; cf. 2 Pet. 1:10–11; Rev. 14:13).

Jesus in Luke 16 describes an unnamed rich man[28] who dressed like a king and every day enjoyed a banquet complete with entertainment. At his gate was laid a beggar named Lazarus, covered with sores, who wanted the scraps of food that would be swept out the door for the street dogs. These scavengers, unclean animals under the Law, licked his sores, making him unclean. Lazarus had only one thing in his favor—his name,[29] which means "God is my help," and indicates that in spite of everything, he kept his faith in God. At death the angels carried him away to Abraham's side,[30] which was certainly a place of blessing, for he received comfort there. The rich man after death found himself in agony in the fires of Hades. When he looked up, that is, to heaven (cf. Luke 18:13), he saw Abraham and Lazarus "far away." But it was too late for him to receive help, for Abraham said "between us and you a great chasm has been fixed, so that those who want to go from here to you cannot, nor can anyone cross over from there to us." In other words, the destinies of both the wicked and the godly cannot be changed after death.[31] Some treat this account as a parable, since it follows a series of parables, but even in His parables Jesus never said anything that was contrary to the truth.[32]

The apostle Paul's desire was to be not with Abraham, but with the Lord. He indicated that as soon as he was away from the body (at death), he would be present with the Lord (2 Cor. 5:6–9; Phil. 1:23). This was the promise of Jesus to the dying thief on the cross, "[T]oday you will be with me

---

[28]"Dives" (KJV) is simply transliterated from the Latin (Vulgate), meaning "a rich man," and is not a proper name.

[29]A Greek form of "Eliezer."

[30]"Bosom" (KJV) was used of eating together on the same couch (cf. John 13:23). It implies close communion and probably a place of honor.

[31]Origen, a few mystics, some Anabaptists, Schliermacher, and Jehovah's Witnesses are among those who hold to a second chance for salvation after death. Boettner points out that this "depreciates the importance of the present life and ... extinguishes missionary zeal." Loraine Boettner, *Immortality* (Philadelphia: The Presbyterian and Reformed Publishing Co, 1956), 104–8.

[32]In addition to Hades as a place of punishment 2 Pet. 2:4 speaks of Tartarus as a place of punishment for fallen angels. (See Charles B. Williams, *New Testament in the Language of the People.*)

in paradise" (Luke 23:43).[33] In a vision Paul was caught up to the third heaven, which he also calls paradise (2 Cor. 12:1–5).[34] Jesus speaks of it as a prepared place where there is plenty of room (John 14:2). It is a place of joy, of fellowship with Christ and other believers, and resounds with worship and singing (Rev. 4:10–11; 5:8–14; 14:2–3; 15:2–4).[35]

Because Paul longed for the resurrection body that will be immortal, not subject to death or decay, and because he seems to withdraw from the idea of being a naked spirit (2 Cor. 5:3–4), some teach that in the intermediate state between death and resurrection believers will be disembodied spirits who, however, will be comforted by being with Christ. Others teach that at death believers receive a temporary "heavenly" body, noting that Moses and Elijah appeared on the Mount of Transfiguration with some kind of a body and that white robes were given to the souls of martyrs in heaven (Luke 9:30–32; Rev. 6:9–11). However, the resurrection of the body is clearly at the time of Christ's coming for His church (Phil. 3:20–21; 1 Thess. 4:16–17).[36]

OTHER VIEWS OF THE AFTERLIFE

Because Jesus spoke of Lazarus and the daughter of Jairus as "sleeping" and because Paul referred to death as sleep (1 Cor. 15:6,18,20; 1 Thess. 4:13–15), some have developed a theory of "soul sleep." By this, they mean that the soul or spirit is not simply in a state of stupor after death, but that the total person is dead and the soul or spirit goes out of existence until re-created at the resurrection. Moses and Elijah at the Mount of Transfiguration, however, knew what was going on and talked to Jesus "about his departure [Gk. *exodos,* including His death, resurrection, and ascension], which he was about to bring to fulfillment at Jerusalem" (Luke 9:31). They understood this would mean something to them as well.

---

[33]This is very emphatic. The Greek word order is "Today, with me, you will be in Paradise!"

[34]Paul seems to have thought of the first heaven as the atmosphere surrounding the earth, the second heaven as that of the stars, the third heaven as the place where the throne of God and paradise are.

[35]Boettner, *Immortality,* 92, points out that "rest" (Rev. 14:13) does not mean idleness or inactivity but "carries with it the idea of *satisfaction in labor or joy in accomplishment."*

[36]Moody, *The Hope of Glory,* 65; William W. Stevens, *Doctrines of the Christian Religion* (Nashville: Broadman Press, 1967), 379. Ladd, *The Last Things,* 35–36.

Paul understood that he would be able to feel whether he was a naked spirit or not. "Sleep," therefore, can apply only to the body.[37]

Others suppose that after death the person is not out of existence, but is in a state of stupor. Certainly neither Lazarus, Abraham, nor the rich man were unconscious or in a state of stupor. They knew what was going on, and Lazarus was being "comforted" (Luke 16:25).

Roman Catholics teach that all except special saints and martyrs[38] must go through purgatory (a condition rather than a place) to prepare them for entrance to heaven.[39] Augustine introduced the idea in the fourth century, but the word "purgatory" was not used until the twelfth century, and the doctrine was not fully worked out until the Council of Trent in the sixteenth century.[40]

Some Roman Catholics also conjectured that there is a condition called Limbo for unbaptized babies and another for Old Testament saints, where they suffered temporary punishment until Jesus died. Then the soul of Jesus descended into the latter Limbo "to introduce them to the beatific vision of God" and since His ascension they have been in heaven. Limbo (for infants) is "now generally rejected" in favor of the idea that infants and the severely retarded will, after death,

---

[37]See Boettner, *Immortality,* 109–16, for a good discussion of the doctrine of "soul sleep." See also Thomas R. Edgar, "The Meaning of 'Sleep' in 1 Thessalonians 5:10," *Journal of the Evangelical Theological Society* 22:4 (December 1979), 345–49; Wilbur M. Smith, *The Biblical Doctrine of Heaven* (Chicago: Moody Press, 1968), 156; Stevens, *Doctrines.* 381. Passages used as proof texts for soul sleep (Pss. 6:5; 13:3; 115:17; 146:3–4; Eccles. 9:5–6; Matt. 9:24; John 11:11–14; Acts 7:60; 1 Cor. 15:51; 1 Thess. 4:13–14) all deal with the dead body as it appears from the standpoint of the ordinary person who is still living. They do not deal with what happens to the person who goes to hell or who goes to be with the Lord after death.

[38]Alois Winklhofer, *The Coming of His Kingdom: A Theology of the Last Things,* trans. A. V. Littledale (Herder, Montreal: Palm Publishers, 1962), 114.

[39]Some Roman Catholics will admit there is no scriptural support for purgatory, but they say there is nothing in the Bible contrary to the doctrine. Zachary Hayes, "The Purgatorial View" in *Four Views on Hell,* William Crockett, ed. (Grand Rapids: Zondervan Publishing House, 1992), 107.

[40]Jacques Le Goff, *Birth of Purgatory,* trans. Arthur Goldhammer (Chicago: University of Chicago Press, 1984), 3, 41, 61. The Council of Trent said nothing about the nature of the fire, the location of purgatory, or even that it is a place. Hayes, "The Purgatorial View," 113.

be presented with God's offer of eternal life and allowed to accept or reject it.[41]

Spiritism (spiritualism) teaches that mediums can communicate with the dead and that the spirits of the dead remain in the vicinity of the earth. G. W. Butterworth explains, "There is an almost universal insistence that the supraterrestrial world is composed of seven or eight spheres, each a little higher than its predecessor."[42] This is contrary to the assurance that at death the believer is "present with the Lord."

A number of Eastern religions, because of their cyclic view of history, teach reincarnation: At death the person is given a new identity and is born into another life as an animal, a human being, or even a god. They hold that a person's actions generate a force, *karma*, that demands transmigration and determines the destiny of the person in the next existence.[43] The Bible, however, makes it clear that now is the day of salvation (2 Cor. 6:2). We cannot save ourselves by our good works. God has provided a full salvation through Jesus Christ that atones for our sin and cancels our guilt. We do not need another life to try to take care of sins and mistakes of this or any supposed former existences. Furthermore, "Man is destined to die once, and after that to face judgment, so Christ was sacrificed once to take away the sins of many people; and he will appear a second time, not to bear sin, but to bring salvation [including the full blessings of our inheritance] to those who are waiting for him" (Heb. 9:27–28).

It is clear also that when Moses and Elijah appeared on the Mount of Transfiguration they were still Moses and Elijah. Jesus Christ also retained His identity after His death and resurrection, and "this same Jesus," not some reincarnation, will come back to earth again (Acts 1:11).

---

[41]Joseph Pohle, *Eschatology or the Catholic Doctrine of the Last Things: A Dogmatic Treatise,* English version by Arthur Preuss (Westport, Conn.: Greenwood Press, Publishers, 1971 reprint from 1917), 26–27. Francis X. Cleary, "Roman Catholicism" in *How Different Religions View Death and Afterlife,* Christopher J. Johnson and Marsha G. McGee, eds. (Philadelphia: The Chrales Press Publishers, 1991), 271.

[42]"There is no satisfactory proof that the mediums actually do contact those spirits. . . . Even the most famous mediums have been detected in fraud." Also, the witch at Endor was very surprised at Samuel's appearance. God took over and used this occasion to pronounce judgment upon King Saul (1 Sam. 28:12). Boettner, *Immortality,* 138, 149. G. W. Butterworth, *Spiritualism and Religion* (London: Society for Promoting Christian Knowledge, 1944), 129.

[43]See Anne C. Klein, "Buddhism," and Swami Adiswarananda, "Hinduism" in *How Different Religions View Death,* 85–108, 157–84.

The End Times

The followers of Jesus who saw Him ascend had the assurance of His return (Acts 1:11). Then when the gospel came to the Gentiles "with power, with the Holy Spirit and with deep conviction," great numbers "turned to God from idols to serve the living and true God, and to wait for his Son from heaven, whom he raised from the dead—Jesus, who rescues us from the coming wrath" (1 Thess. 1:5,9–10). Though many suffered persecution they believed that "if we endure, we will also reign with him" (2 Tim. 2:12). Then John's visions on the Isle of Patmos (recorded in the Book of Revelation) gave a picture of Christ's ultimate victory and added the assurance of a millennial reign before the last judgment and the new heavens and new earth prophesied by Isaiah (65:17; 66:22). From Asia Minor, then, premillennial concepts quickly spread.[44]

Until the middle of the second century most Christians held to the hope that Christ would return and they would reign with Him for a thousand years. Then concern over Christology turned attention away from the future hope. Origen (ca. 185–ca. 254), influenced by Greek philosophy, popularized an allegorical method that led to spiritualizing the future Kingdom. By the fifth century the kingdom of God and the hierarchical church were identified with each other, with the church giving out the judgments; as a result, the future Kingdom and the final judgments were no longer emphasized. Then in the later part of the Middle Ages, the Roman church believed it was building the eternal city of God here on earth. Most closed their eyes to the evil that was rampant and gave no evidence of believing that God has a plan or that He will establish the future Kingdom by His own act. Only occasionally did the belief in a future Millennium flare-up, usually in protest against hierarchical authority.[45]

---

[44]Larry V. Crutchfield, "The Apostle John and Asia Minor as a Source of Premillennialism in the Early Church Fathers" *Journal of the Evangelical Theological Society* 31 (December 1988): 412, 427.

[45]For a turning away from future hope, see Schwarz, *On The Way,* 175. Berkhof, *Systematic Theology,* 663. There was a brief flare-up of an expectation of the end of the world just before A.D. 1000 due to the teaching of some church fathers that the earth was created about 5000 B.C. and to the idea in Barnabas (15:4) that at the end of six thousand years after creation there would be a final sabbath rest. Cf. William Manson, G. W. H. Lampe, T. F. Torrance, W. A. Whitehouse, *Eschatology* (Edinburgh: Oliver and Boyd Ltd, 1953), 31. For the Middle Ages, see R. P. C. Hanson, *The Attractiveness of God: Essays in Christian Doctrine* (Richmond, Va.: John

The Reformation brought a new emphasis on the authority of the Bible and the activity of God in history. However, with respect to the last things, the attention was given to the glorification of believers, and there was little mention of the consummation of the age and the final state.[46]

In seventeenth-century England, belief in a millennium became more popular, especially among Puritans trained by Joseph Meade, even though many still believed the Millennium was already fulfilled in the history of the Church. Those who did preach the second coming of Christ to bring in the Millennium, however, hurt their cause by making computations that put His return between 1640 and 1660.[47]

By the beginning of the eighteenth century Daniel Whitby popularized the view that Christ would not return until after a millennium of progress brought the world under the authority of the gospel.[48] This view became dominant in nineteenth-century America and fitted in with the then current philosophies of automatic progress. By the end of the century, however, summer Bible conferences were spreading the hope of a future millennium again. With this came the spread of dispensationalism, whose literal interpretation of prophecy is in extreme contrast to the figurative interpretations of postmillennialists and amillennialists, as well as those of liberals and existentialists.[49]

Liberals, who were really antisupernaturalists, under the

Knox Press, 1973), 194. Manson; Lampe; Torrance; Whitehouse, *Eschatology,* 37. Stephen Travis, *The Jesus Hope* (Downers Grove, Ill.: Inter-Varsity Press, 1974), 54. Berkhof, *Systematic Theology,* 663. An important example of a future Millennium is that of Joachin of Floris in Calabria (died 1202). See Le Goff, *The Birth of Purgatory,* 83.

[46]Manson, *Eschatology,* 38; Berkhof, *Systematic Theology,* 663.

[47]Wilber B. Wallis, "Eschatology and Social Concern" *Journal of the Evangelical Theological Society* 24 (March 1981): 5. Bryan W. Ball, *A Great Expectation: Eschatological Thought in English Protestantism to 1660,* vol. 12 in *Studies in the History of Christian Thought,* ed. Heiko A. Oberman (Leiden: E. J. Brill, 1975), 1–4, 19–23.

[48]Wallis, *Eschatology,* 4,5.

[49]Craig A. Blaising, "Introduction" 13–36 in *Dispensationalism, Israel and the Church: The Search for Definition,* Craig A. Blaising and Darrell L. Bock, eds. (Grand Rapids: Zondervan Publishing House, 1992), 16–22. Thomas N. Finger, *Christian Theology: An Eschatological Approach,* vol. 1 (Nashville: Thomas Nelson Publishers, 1985), 110.

influence of the philosophers Kant, Ritchl, Hegel, and Schlier-macher, deleted any future divine intervention from the social gospel they preached.[50] To them the kingdom of God was something human beings could create by their own wisdom without any help from above.

This antisupernaturalism reached a climax with Albert Schweitzer and Rudolf Bultmann. Schweitzer stripped the biblical presentation of Jesus down to make Him a mere man who mistakenly thought the end would come in His own lifetime. Schweitzer took "astonishing liberties with the historical evidence." So did Bultmann when he excised miracles from the Bible, was concerned only with the present existence, rejected the Bible's linear view of history, and treated the biblical hope as mere human speculation.[51]

Also in Europe existentialism, by its focus on the human, ignored "the cosmic dimensions of Scripture" and provided an escape from any concern over the past or future. Among them the neoorthodox attempted to reclaim orthodox doctrines while at the same time treating the Bible as a merely human record. In England C. H. Dodd popularized the idea that the kingdom of God had fully come "once and for all" in the ministry of Jesus, and that the writers of the New Testament misunderstood His teachings and developed an expectation that He would return. A modification, called "inaugurated eschatology" by R. P. Fuller, taught that Jesus looked back to the coming of the Kingdom, in effect explaining away the New Testament record that shows He looked forward to a future Kingdom.[52]

---

[50]Helmut Thielicke, *The Evangelical Faith,* trans. G. W. Bromiley, vol. 1 (Grand Rapids: Wm. B. Eerdmans, 1974), 125.

[51]J. H. Leckie, *The World to Come and Final Destiny,* 2d ed. (Edinburgh: T. & T Clark, 1922), 42. Against Bultmann see the defense of linear history in Oscar Cullmann, *Christ and Time: The Primitive Christian Conception of Time and History,* trans. Floyd V. Filson (Philadelphia: Westminster Press, 1964), 96, 105. See also James Barr, *Biblical Words for Time,* 2d rev. ed. (Naperville, Ill.: Alec R. Allenson, 1969), 12–180 for criticisms of Cullmann's overstatements. Bultmann treated eschatology as "mythological" and considered the miraculous obsolete and unacceptable. See comments by Emil Brunner, *Eternal Hope,* trans. Harold Knight (Philadelphia: The Westminster Press, 1954), 214. See also Erickson, *Christian Theology,* 1159.

[52]Zachary Hayes, *What Are They Saying About the End of the World?* (New York: Paulist Press, 1983), 7. Carl E. Braaten, *Eschatology and Ethics* (Minneapolis: Augsburg Publishing House, 1974), 15–16. Hendrikus Berkhof, *Well-Founded Hope* (Richmond: John Knox Press, 1969), 12. Finger observes that "Israel's 'ingrafting' is another indication that the existential

There have been several reactions to Bultmann. One of the most prominent has been Jurgen Moltmann's theology of hope. He emphasized that "Christianity . . . is hope, forward looking and forward moving, and therefore also revolutionizing and transforming the present."[53] This, along with the political theology of the Roman Catholic John Baptist Metz, inspired the development of liberation theology, which sees the kingdom of God as a metaphor and seeks to make radical political and social change in the present.[54] Though Christians have a responsibility to do what they can for others in a sacrificial way, there is, however, no scriptural basis for New Testament believers to become involved in political change by means of armed revolution. No political utopia is possible by such means. The millennial Kingdom will not come through human effort. The Bible shows that our only hope is that God will intervene, bring judgment on the present world system, and send Jesus back to earth again to establish His rule and make David's throne eternal.

---

view of our future hope is not biblical. Finger, *Christian Theology,* vol. 1, 170. In a letter to Dr. George Beasley-Murray, Dodd admitted Jesus may have used apocalyptic language, but "certainly in a symbolic sense." George Raymond Beasley-Murray, *Jesus and the Future: An Examination of the Criticism of the Eschatological Discourse, Mark 13 with Special Reference to the Little Apocalypse Theory* (London: Macmillan & Co. Ltd., 1954), 100. I. H. Marshall, *Eschatology and the Parables* (London: Theological Students' Fellowship, 1973), 13. J. E. Fison, *The Christian Hope: The Presence and the Parousia* (London: Longmans, Green and Co., 1954), ix-x. Dodd dismisses the *parousia,* disposes of the apocalyptic elements in the New Testament as Jewish influence, and imports "a Platonic conception of time" that has no place for God, Christ, or the Holy Spirit acting in a future age. For critical evaluation of Dodd's theology see Hamilton, *The Holy Spirit and Eschatology,* 54–60, and Clayton Sullivan, *Rethinking Realized Eschatology* (Macon, Ga.: Mercer University Press, 1988), vii,4,34–70. See also Marshall, *Eschatology and the Parables,* 13–14; Hanson, *The Attractiveness of God,* 190.

[53]Jurgen Moltmann, *Theology of Hope: On the Ground and the Implications of a Christian Eschatology,* trans. James W. Leitch (New York: Harper & Row Publishers, 1967), 16. Koch points out that Moltmann separates this hope from history and "in the end tears salvation and creation apart." Klaus Koch, *The Rediscovery of Apocalyptic* trans. Margaret Kohl (Naperville, Ill.: Alec R. Allenson, Inc., [1972?]), 107–8. Randall E. Otto, "God and History in Jurgen Moltmann" *Journal of the Evangelical Theological Society* 35:3, (September 1992): 375–88, also points out that Moltmann denies the supernatural, does not view the Bible's history as real history, and denies the Bible's view of the fulfillment of the hope it presents. He also imposes on the Bible "a view of history derived from revisionist Marxism" (379, 384).

[54]Finger, *Christian Theology,* vol. 1, 74–77; Hayes, *What Are They Saying,* 10–11; Schwarz, *On the Way to the Future,* 107.

CHAPTER 18

The Last Things

The fact that Jesus is coming back to earth again is clear in the Scriptures. Evangelicals in general accept Acts 1:11 as assuring His personal, visible return. Various theories have arisen, however, to try to explain it away. Some say Christ returned in the person of the Holy Spirit on the Day of Pentecost. However, it was the exalted Christ who poured out the Spirit at that time (Acts 2:32–33). Others say that Christ's second coming occurs when He enters the believer's heart at conversion (Rev. 3:20 is usually cited), but the Scriptures teach that those who receive Him wait for His coming (Phil. 3:20; 1 Thess. 1:10).[55] Still others say His coming is fulfilled when He comes for the believer at death. However, both the dead and the living will be "caught up together" at His appearing (1 Thess. 4:17). Jehovah's Witnesses say He returned invisibly in 1874. Others say He returned invisibly in judgment when Jerusalem was destroyed in A.D. 70.

Still others take "the manifestation of the sons of God" (Rom. 8:19, KJV) out of context and claim they are the manifested sons. They say that Christ's second coming is fulfilled in them as His matured sons, who are maturing the Church to take over the kingdoms of this world. They reject the Rapture[56] and claim they are fulfilling it by being "caught up" into spiritual maturity. They also claim they are already the New Jerusalem and they are as well the "clouds" of power and glory in whom Christ is now appearing and through whom Christ will reign on the earth.[57] A similar group call themselves theonomists and want to bring in the Kingdom by bringing the whole world under God's law, specifically, some or all of the law of Moses, even if it takes twenty thousand years. These groups take great liberties in spiritualizing plain biblical statements and forget that we do not have our hope yet, but "we wait for it patiently" (Rom. 8:25). The personal return of Jesus Christ to earth is the only way we will receive the fullness of the hope we are waiting for.

---

[55]"Heb. 9:28 is decisively against" the idea that the *parousia* can "be spiritualized away into the mere continued presence of Jesus with His beloved at all times." Bernard Ramm, "A Philosophy of Christian Eschatology," in *Last Things*, H. Leo Eddleman, ed. (Grand Rapids: Zondervan Publishing House, 1969), 20–42.

[56]See p. 623.

[57]Hobart E. Freeman, *Exploring Biblical Theology* (Warsaw, Ind.: Faith Ministries and Publications, n.d.), 298–99.

VIEWS OF THE BOOK OF REVELATION

There is considerable variety in the interpretation of the sequence of end-time events among Bible believers. Part of the variety comes from the interpretation of the Book of Revelation as a whole, part from the interpretation of Revelation 20, and part from whether the hermeneutics employed tend to interpret the Bible more literally or more figuratively.

The historicist view of the Book of Revelation tries to match the events in the book with church history from the first century to the present, drawing attention to such things as the rise of the Papacy and the Moslem invasions. This avoids the idea of a great tribulation at the end of the age. A weakness in this view is the tendency for each generation to rework the whole interpretation to try to make it come out in their own day.

The preterist[58] view of the book tries to tie everything but the very end to events in the first century, with Rome and its early emperors the only principals. Identifications are very subjective and precarious, however, and the events of the book are definitely tied to the end times and the return of Christ in glory.

The idealist[59] view of the book makes no identification with anything historical. It takes the symbols and figures in the book as simply representing the ongoing struggle between good and evil. However, though the book does have many symbolic figures, they all represent realities. The Antichrist is called a beast, but he will be a real person and will fulfill plain statements given in other prophecies (such as 2 Thess. 2:3–12). Jesus must personally come to bring about the final triumph.

The futurist view of the book looks for everything, or almost everything, after chapter 4 to be fulfilled in a short period at the end of the Church Age, a period of great tribulation, wrath, and judgment that will climax with Christ's return in glory to destroy the armies of the Antichrist and establish His millennial kingdom.[60]

Most premillennialists, including both dispensationalists and nondispensationalists, identify the Tribulation with the seventieth week (period of seven years) of Daniel 9:27. After

---

[58]From Lat. *praeter,* "past."

[59]From Lat. *idea,* referring not to values (i.e., ideals) but mental images.

[60]Stanley M. Horton, *The Ultimate Victory* (Springfield, Mo.: Gospel Publishing House, 1991), 18–19.

the Messiah, "the Anointed One," is "cut off" (Dan. 9:26), the "people of a ruler who will come" would destroy the city of Jerusalem and the temple. This was fulfilled in A.D. 70 where the people were the Romans. Then it speaks of a ruler who will come and make a covenant with Israel—which he will break after three and one-half years, declaring himself to be God and forbidding the worship of the Lord (cf. 2 Thess. 2:4).

Some suppose the seventieth week followed immediately upon the death of Jesus. But the Romans made no covenant with Israel at that time. Neither did Titus in A.D. 70. Nor were all the signs Jesus gave fulfilled in the destruction of A.D. 70. The Old Testament often jumps over the entire Church Age in prophecy. (Compare Zech. 9:9–10 where verse 9 deals with Christ's first coming, but the end of verse 10 jumps ahead to His second coming without showing the time between.) Therefore, it is not contrary to sound exegesis to see the seventieth week of Daniel as still future.[61]

Revelation 20:1–7 repeatedly mentions a thousand-year period, the Millennium.[62] Amillennialists[63] teach that there will be no Millennium, at least not on earth. Some take an idealist view and say there will be no literal Millennium at all. Others take the thousand years as going on in heaven during the Church Age.[64] Most take the number "one thousand" as an ideal number representing an indefinite period. They expect the Church Age to end with a general resurrection and a general judgment of both the righteous and wicked at the same time, followed immediately by the eternal Kingdom of the new heavens and the new earth. With respect to the Book of Revelation as a whole, many are preterists. Since they have no room in their system for a literal restoration of Israel or the reign of Christ on earth, they take the prophecies of the Old Testament that relate to Israel, spiritualize them, and apply them to the Church. However, it is very clear, for example, in Ezekiel 36, that God will restore Israel for His own holy name's sake in spite of what they have done.[65]

---

[61]Michael Kalafian, *The Prophecy of the Seventy Weeks of the Book of Daniel* (Lanham, Md.: University Press of America, Inc., 1991), 227. See the entire book for detailed explanation of premillennial, amillennial, and higher critical interpretations of this prophecy.

[62]From the Latin *mille*, "thousand," and *annus*, "year."

[63]The "a" means "no."

[64]Anthony A. Hoekema, *The Bible and the Future* (Grand Rapids: Wm. B. Eerdmans, 1979), 235.

[65]Williams, *Systematic Theology*, vol. 3, 224, 233.

Postmillennialists treat the thousand years of the Millennium as an extension of the Church Age when, by the power of the gospel, the world as a whole will be won to Christ.[66] Like amillennialists, many postmillennialists are preterists and they all teach a general judgment of both the righteous and the wicked, followed by the eternal Kingdom of the new heavens and the new earth.[67] They also spiritualize Old Testament prophecies and have no room in their system for a restoration of national Israel or a literal reign of Christ on earth. Though some will allow for a resurgence of evil just before Christ returns in a "cataclysmic" way,[68] most look for a great spread of the gospel that will bring the return of Christ nearer. They disregard, however, the fact that the Old Testament prophets (and Jesus himself) show that the Kingdom must be brought in through judgment (Zeph. 3:8–9; Matt. 24:29–30). For example, the statue in Daniel 2 represents the present world system. The rock that represents Christ's kingdom does not penetrate the statue and transform it. It hits the statue in the feet (representing the world system at the end of this age) and shatters it to powder in one blow. Only then does God set up His kingdom so that it fills the earth (Dan. 2:44).

A group of modern variants of postmillennialism are referred to by such terms as "kingdom now" and "dominion theology." They teach that this present age is the kingdom of God and Christians must use God's power to bring it to completion by becoming a mature Church, something that "could have happened thousands of years ago, had the Church of that day achieved the necessary maturity." They believe that Christ will return to a world where the Church has taken dominion "over every aspect of the societal framework." The Church must regain control over all the kingdoms of this world. Some say the Church must put down all rule opposed to God. Even death must be "totally conquered before Jesus's

---

[66]Most postmillennialists (as well as amillennialists) take the binding of Satan (Rev. 20:3) to mean he is unable to prevent the gospel from being proclaimed with power. However, Satan is shut in the abyss and locked in, powerless, not just against Christians, but against the nations—all the people of the world. See Donald G. Bloesch, *Essentials of Evangelical Theology,* vol. 2 (New York: Harper & Row, Publishers, 1979), 195.

[67]Those who are not preterists are historicists and say that the Church is and has always been in the Tribulation. See John F. Walvoord, *The Rapture Question* (Grand Rapids: Zondervan Publishing House, 1972), 41.

[68]This was proclaimed in a sermon by Dr. E. Stanley Jones at Gordon College, in 1944, at which I was present.

return."[69] They forget that the wheat and the weeds will exist together throughout this age until God sends His angels to bring in the harvest (Matt. 13:36–43). Many do not believe in the doctrine of the Rapture, looking instead for victory and dominion as they establish the kingdom of God on earth. Most are preterists and believe the Great Tribulation took place in the first century. They also believe that "[e]thnic Israel was excommunicated for its apostasy" and "Christ transferred the blessings of the kingdom from Israel to a new people, the church." They ignore the many Scripture passages that show God still has a purpose for national Israel in His plan.[70]

Premillennialists take the prophecies of the Old Testament, as well as those of Jesus and the New Testament, as literally as their contexts allow. They recognize that the simplest way to interpret these prophecies is to place the return of Christ, the resurrection of the believers, and the judgment seat of Christ before the Millennium, after which there will be a temporary release of Satan followed by his final defeat. Then will come the Great White Throne Judgment of the rest of the dead, and finally the eternal Kingdom of the new heavens and the new earth.

With respect to the Book of Revelation as a whole, many premillennialists in the 1800s were historicists. Most today are futurists. They do not see the world getting better in this age and feel the importance of calling the world to flee from the wrath to come by accepting Christ as Savior and Lord.[71] Yet they are not pessimists. They look with joyous anticipation for the blessed hope, the return of our Lord.

---

[69]Earl Paulk, *Satan Unmasked* (Atlanta: K Dimension Publishers, 1984), 254, 264. Michael G. Moriarty, *The New Charismatics* (Grand Rapids: Zondervan Publishing House, 1992), 93. See also Earl Paulk, *The Wounded Body of Christ* (Decatur, Ga.: K Dimension Publishers, 1985), 140.

[70]Pauline G. MacPherson, *Can the Elect Be Deceived?* (Denver: Bold Truth Press, 1986), 46. See also David Chilton, *Paradise Restored: A Biblical Theology of Dominion* (Fort Worth: Dominion Press, 1985), 53; Earl Paulk, *The Great Escape Theory* (Decatur, Ga.: Chapel Hill Harvester Church, n.d). David Chilton, *Paradise Restored: A Biblical Theology of Dominion* (Tyler, Tex.: Reconstruction Press, 1985), 224. Gary DeMar and Peter Leithart, *The Reduction of Christianity* (Fort Worth: Dominion Press, 1988), 213. For God's purpose for Israel, see Deut. 4:27–31; Isa. 2:2–3; 14:1–3; Jer. 23:5–6; 32:37–42; Ezek. 36:22–32; 39:25–29; Amos 9:11–15; Zeph. 3:14–15; Zech. 8:7–8,13–15; Rom. 11:15,25–27.

[71]Wayne House and Thomas Ice, *Dominion Theology: Blessing or Curse?* (Portland, Oreg.: Multnomah Press, 1988), 390.

TWO ASPECTS OF CHRIST'S SECOND COMING

The Bible indicates two aspects of Christ's coming. On one hand, He will come as the Preserver, Deliverer, or Rescuer "from the coming wrath" (1 Thess. 1:10). "Since we have now been justified by his blood, how much more shall we be saved from God's wrath through him!" (Rom. 5:9). We are to keep awake spiritually, live sober, well-balanced, self-controlled lives, and wear the gospel armor of faith, love, and the hope of salvation—"God did not appoint us to suffer wrath but to receive salvation through our Lord Jesus Christ. He died for us so that, whether we are awake or asleep, we may live together with Him. Therefore encourage one another" (1 Thess. 5:9–11).

These verses of encouragement refer back to the promise that "the Lord himself will come down from heaven, with a loud command, with the voice of the archangel and with the trumpet call of God, and the dead in Christ will rise first. After that, we who are still alive and are left will be caught up together with them in the clouds to meet the Lord in the air. And so we will be with the Lord forever. Therefore encourage each other" (1 Thess. 4:16–18).

Only the resurrection of those who died "in Christ" is in view here. They are changed, clothed with immortality, "in a flash, in the twinkling of an eye" (1 Cor. 15:52; see also vv. 53–54), transformed "so that they will be like his glorious body" (Phil. 3:21). Then those believers who are still alive will be changed and caught up together with them, in one Body. The one requirement for both the dead and obviously the living believers is to be "in Christ," that is, in a relationship of faith in Him and faithfulness to Him.

"Caught up" (Gk. *harpagēsometha*)[72] refers to what is often called "the Rapture."[73] "To meet the Lord" (Gk. *eis apantēsin*

---

[72]The same verb is used of the male child who was "snatched up" to God and His throne (Rev. 12:5). It is also used of Paul being "caught up" to the third heaven, to paradise (2 Cor. 12:2,4), and of the Spirit when He "suddenly took Philip away" (Acts 8:39). In addition to being used of supernatural transfer, the verb is used of a wolf seizing the sheep (John 10:12), the evil one snatching away the Word (Matt. 13:19), and the instruction by the Roman officer that his soldiers "snatch away" Paul from the Jews (Acts 23:10). Its usages taken altogether, the word involves the idea of a powerful "snatching away."

[73]"Rapture" is from the Latin *raptus*, the past participle of *rapere*, "to seize," and has the original meaning of being snatched up and carried away. Therefore, "the Rapture" is a proper designation of our "being caught up together . . . to meet the Lord in the air."

tou kuriou) can be translated "for a meeting with the Lord." "Meeting" was often used as a technical term for people of a city meeting kings or generals some distance outside a city and escorting them into the city.[74] This is parallel to the use of *parousia,* "presence," "coming," of the Lord (1 Thess. 4:15), which has a technical status when it refers to Christ's return, and is most often used of the Rapture.[75]

On the other hand, God's justice will be vindicated "when the Lord Jesus is revealed from heaven in blazing fire with his powerful angels. He will punish those who do not know God and do not obey the gospel of our Lord Jesus. ... On the day he comes to be glorified in his holy people and to be marveled at among all those who have believed" (2 Thess. 1:7–8,10). This fits with other passages which show that the Kingdom must be brought in through judgment (Dan. 2:34–35,44–45; Rev. 19:11–16).

Most amillennialists and postmillennialists, if they deal with the Second Coming, see these two aspects occurring in connection with one descent of Christ followed by a general judgment.[76] Premillennialists who are historicists agree, for they do not see a special period of great tribulation at the end of the Church Age.[77] Premillennialists who are futurists do recognize a "Great Tribulation" at the end of this age, but are divided into pre-, mid-, and posttribulationists.

Most posttribulationists interpret the wrath we are to escape (1 Thess. 5:9) to be the final state of the wicked, the lake of fire. The context, however, is that of the Rapture. They expect that all living believers will go through the Great

---

[74]See the usage of the word in the Parable of the Ten Virgins (Matt. 25:1–10) and in the case of Paul being met by Christians from Rome who escorted him into the city (Acts 28:15). See also Polybius, 18,48,4 (second century B.C.) ed. Th. Buttner-Wobst, 1882–1904.

[75]Thoralf Gilbrant, ed., *The Complete Biblical Library,* vol. 15 (Springfield, Mo.: The Complete Biblical Library, 1991), 101–2. *Epiphaneia,* "appearing," and *apokalupsis,* "revelation," "disclosure," are also used of Christ's return. The three words can be used interchangeably for Christ's coming for His waiting saints (cf. 1 Cor. 1:7; 1 Thess. 2:19; 1 Tim. 6:14) as well as for His coming in flaming fire at the end of the Tribulation (cf. 1 Thess. 3:13; 2 Thess. 1:7; 2:8; 1 Pet. 1:7).

[76]For an amillennial view see Anthony A. Hoekema, *Bible and the Future,* 255, and Philip E. Hughes, *The Book of the Revelation* (Grand Rapids: Wm. B. Eerdmans, 1990), 204, 219. For a postmillennial view see Augustus H. Strong, *Outlines of Systematic Theology* (Philadelphia: The Judson Press, 1908), 263,267.

[77]Henry Alford, "prolegomena" in *The Greek Testament,* 3d ed., vol. 4 (London: Rivingtons, 1866), 246–47.

Tribulation, some supposing many of them will become martyrs, others supposing that God will protect them in some
special way, perhaps as God protected the Israelites from the
plagues of Egypt.[78] They argue that the New Testament does
not promise that believers will escape tribulation and suffering. The point they miss is that the Bible uses the word
"tribulation" to talk about two different things. Sometimes
the word refers to the distress, persecution, trouble, pressure,
and anguish of heart that outward circumstances may bring
upon a Christian as he serves the Lord in a Christ-rejecting
world. The same word is translated "troubles" when Paul talks
about "our light and momentary *troubles* . . . achieving for us
an eternal glory that far outweighs them all" (2 Cor. 4:17).
But the judgments of the Great Tribulation are not in the
same class. They are God's wrath (Rev. 6:16; 15:1,7; 16:1).

Midtribulationists usually take the first part of the Tribulation to be peaceful, while the Antichrist is establishing his
rule. Most believe the Rapture will take place at the sounding
of the seventh trumpet of the Book of Revelation (Rev. 11:15),
which they identify with the last trumpet of 1 Corinthians
15:52. They sometimes speak of a "prewrath Rapture" and
take the last three and one-half years of the Antichrist's rule
as the period of wrath. However, the vision of the sixth seal
would indicate wrath extends throughout the entire seven
years (Rev. 6:17).[79]

Some teach a partial Rapture with part of the Church going
through the Tribulation. Others teach multiple Raptures.[80]
Many of these divide the Church into various companies, such
as the Bride, the Friends of the Bridegroom, the Servants, and
the Guests. However, the parables of Jesus do not actually
treat these as separate divisions. Each is an aspect of the true
Church. Paul makes it clear that all the dead in Christ and all
the believers who remain are caught up "together" in one
Body in the Rapture (1 Thess. 4:16–17).[81]

Pretribulationists recognize that the apostle Paul still had
the Rapture in mind when he said, "God did not appoint us

---

[78]J. Rodman Williams, *Renewal Theology,* vol. 3 (Grand Rapids: Zondervan Publishing House, 1992), 378.

[79]Cf. Buswell, *A Systematic Theology,* vol. 2, 398, 431, 444, 450, 456,
458–59. Martin J. Rosenthal, *The Prewrath Rapture of the Church* (Orlando,
Fla.: Zions Hope, 1989), and Horton, *Ultimate Victory,* 104–7.

[80]Glen Menzies and Gordon L. Anderson, "D. W. Kerr and Eschatological
Diversity in the Assemblies of God," *Paraclete* 27 (Winter 1993), 8–16.

[81]See Walvoord, *The Rapture Question,* 105–25, for a discussion of this.

to suffer wrath but to receive salvation through our Lord Jesus Christ" (1 Thess. 5:9). Christ's sacrificial death guarantees that whether we die before the Rapture or are alive at that time, we shall "live together with him" (1 Thess. 5:10), for He will "rescue us from the coming wrath" (1 Thess. 1:10). The same verb (Gk. *rhuomai*) is used of the rescue of Lot "before" God's judgment fell on Sodom (2 Pet. 2:7). Some see this contradicted in Matthew 24:30–31; however, "at that time" (Gk. *tote*) is very general. Jesus, in dealing with His coming, deals with a period of time which includes both His coming for His elect or chosen (that is, for true believers) and a coming that the whole world will see. But Jesus does not deal with this period in chronological fashion. Like the Old Testament prophets, He moves back and forth, dealing with one aspect of His coming and then another, not always in order, and without indicating the time interval between. But the time interval is there.[82]

The pretribulational view fits in best with the future hope the Bible presents.[83] Believers, who are told repeatedly to be watchful and to wait for God's Son from heaven (1 Thess. 1:10), are never told "to watch for the Great Tribulation or the appearance of the Antichrist. To expect that such things must happen before the Rapture destroys the teaching of imminence with which the New Testament is replete."[84] The fact that passages dealing with the Rapture speak of Christ's coming to snatch up believers to be with Him (1 Thess. 4:17), while other passages speak of believers being with Him at His coming (Col. 3:4; Jude 14), show it is scriptural to recognize two phases of Christ's coming. The fact we are not appointed to wrath indicates that the Great Tribulation occurs between these two phases of His coming.[85]

THE TRIBULATION

After Jesus declared that the gospel of the Kingdom, the gospel of God's power and rule, must be preached to all

---

[82]Stanley M. Horton, *Welcome Back Jesus* (Springfield, Mo.: Gospel Publishing House, 1967), 33.

[83]See p. 629.

[84]Assemblies of God, *Where We Stand* (Springfield, Mo.: Gospel Publishing House, 1990), 129.

[85]Some accuse pretribulationists of being escapists. However, it is a practical doctrine and its emphasis on imminence keeps the thought of the Lord's return before us and encourages witnessing and missions as well as godly living. Cf. James Montgomery Boice, *Foundations of the Christian Faith* (Downers Grove, Ill.: InterVarsity Press, 1986), 707–8.

nations before the consummation of this age (Matt. 24:14), He went on to talk about " 'the abomination that causes desolation, spoken of through the prophet Daniel' " (Matt. 24:15). The initial fulfillment of this prophecy took place in December, 167 B.C., when Antiochus Epiphanes set a pagan altar on the altar of burnt offering and dedicated the Jerusalem temple to the Greek god Zeus.[86] But both Daniel and Jesus saw a greater fulfillment. Daniel 12:1 jumps ahead to the time of the Tribulation and identifies it as "a time of distress such as has not happened from the beginning of nations until then." Jesus also identified the time as "great distress" (Matt. 24:21). In the present world many believers are already suffering distress, but the Great Tribulation will be marked by the wrath of God beyond anything the world has ever known, as Revelation 6 to 18 indicate. It will also see the rise of a world dictator, the Antichrist.

THE ANTICHRIST

The apostle Paul had to deal with false teachers who were saying that the Day of the Lord had "already come" (2 Thess. 2:2). The Thessalonians were unsettled and alarmed because these teachers apparently denied the literal return of the Lord and "our being gathered to Him" in the Rapture (2:1). Obviously, they were no longer encouraging one another as Paul had commanded them (1 Thess. 4:18; 5:11). So Paul declared that "that day will not come until the rebellion[87] occurs and the man of lawlessness[88] is revealed, the man doomed to destruction" (2 Thess. 2:3). That is, the rebellion and the revelation of the Antichrist would be the first things to take place on the Day of the Lord. This would not happen until "the secret power of lawlessness" is no longer held back (2 Thess. 2:7). Since these things had not taken place, they were not in the Day of the Lord, and they could still encourage each other with the sure hope of being snatched up to meet the Lord in the air.

The name Antichrist comes from John's letters where John

---

[86]1 Maccabees 1:47,54,59; 2 Maccabees 6:2.

[87]Gk. *apostasia*, which may mean a spiritual rebellion but more commonly refers to a military rebellion, possibly a world war or a fulfillment of Ezekiel 38 and 39.

[88]Many early manuscripts as well as church fathers, such as Tertullian, have "the man [Gk. *anthrōpos*, a human being] of sin," but this does not essentially change the meaning. He will put himself above law and make his will supreme as an absolute dictator.

implies that the Antichrist will indeed come. His readers, however, needed to be concerned over the many antichrists (who falsely claimed to be "anointed ones") as well as the spirit of antichrist that was already at work (1 John 2:18–19,22; 4:2; 2 John 7). On the other hand, the final Antichrist is doomed to destruction, and his time will be comparatively short.[89]

Since he "will oppose and will exalt himself over everything that is called God or is worshiped" we can take the "anti" to mean against. However, the Greek *anti* most often means "instead of" or "in place of,"[90] and he will set himself up "in God's temple, proclaiming himself to be God" (2 Thess. 2:4). That is, the Antichrist will not call himself the Antichrist. He will be the ultimate of all the counterfeit christs and will probably claim to be the real Christ as well as the true God. (Cf. Matt. 24:4,23–24.)

His coming "will be in accordance with the work of Satan displayed in all kinds of counterfeit miracles, signs and wonders, and in every sort of evil that deceives those who are perishing" (2 Thess. 2:9–10).[91] This description fits that of the world ruler who makes the covenant with Israel and later breaks it (Dan. 9:27), as well as that of the beast, the blasphemous world ruler, who is energized and indwelt by Satan and whose false prophet does counterfeit miracles (Rev. 13:1–17).[92] By the middle of the Tribulation he requires everyone to receive a mark on the right hand or forehead, a mark "which is the name of the beast or the number of his name."

This number is identified as 666, a number that has given rise to all kinds of speculation, but "it is a man's [a human being's] number," thus somehow identified with the fact that the Antichrist claims to be God but is really just a man.[93] By this means he will gain economic control and become the

---

[89]Cf. Matt. 24:22, where in God's plan those days have been cut short (but not shorter than the three and one-half years of the second half of the Tribulation).

[90]Cf. Matt. 20:28 where Jesus came "to give his life as a ransom *anti* [instead of] many."

[91]Posttribulationists usually say that those who have been taught a preTribulation Rapture will be so disillusioned when they have to face the Antichrist that they will fall away and be deceived by him. See Williams, *Renewal Theology,* vol. 3, 381. However, it is only those who refuse "to love the truth and so be saved" that the Antichrist will deceive (2 Thess. 2:10). No saved person will be deceived by the Antichrist.

[92]Horton, *Ultimate Victory,* 183–94.

[93]Ibid., 196–97.

dictator of the whole world. But he will not be able to prevent the fall of the Babylonian world system and total economic collapse (Rev. 18:1–24). Then at the end of the Tribulation he will lead the armies of many nations, armies gathered by Satan, at Armageddon. It is then that Jesus will "overthrow [him] with the breath of his mouth and destroy [him] by the splendor of his coming" (2 Thess. 2:8). This is pictured powerfully in Daniel 2:34–35, 44–45 and Revelation 19:11–21. His final destiny is "the fiery lake of burning sulfur" (Rev. 19:20).

THE WEDDING SUPPER OF THE LAMB

When Jesus appears to destroy the Antichrist and his armies, the armies of heaven follow Jesus, riding on white horses (symbolizing triumph) "and dressed in fine linen, white and clean" (Rev. 19:14). This identifies them with the Lamb's bride (the Church)[94] who take part in the wedding supper of the Lamb (Rev. 19:7–9). That is, they have already been in heaven, they are already fully clothed with "the righteous acts of the saints" (v. 8). This implies also that those acts are complete and the believers have been resurrected, changed, and taken to heaven. This would imply also that they have already appeared before the judgment seat of Christ (2 Cor. 5:10).[95] What a time of joy and delight that wedding supper will be!

THE MILLENNIUM

Revelation 20:1–3 and verses 7–10 deal with the judgment of Satan. He will be imprisoned in the abyss for a thousand years. The abyss will be locked and sealed over him, so that he will have no possibility of any activity on earth during that period. Then he will be released for a short time, before his eternal judgment in the lake of fire.

In between, in Revelation 20:4–6 the Bible speaks of those who are priests of God and of Christ and who reign with Him for a thousand years. This reign will bring the fulfillment of many prophecies.[96]

---

[94]Ibid., 277–79. See also p. 625.

[95]See p. 632.

[96]The sixfold repetition of the thousand years gives emphasis and suggests that it should be taken literally. Pss. 2:8; 24:7–8; Isa. 9:7; 11:6–10; 35:1–2; 61:3; Jer. 23:5–6; Ezek. 40 to 48; Dan. 2:44; Hos. 1:10; 3:5; Amos 9:11–15; Mic. 4:1–8; Zech. 8:1–9; Matt. 19:28; Acts 15:16–18; Rev. 2:25–28; 11:15.

Revelation 20:4 deals with two groups of people. The first sits on thrones to judge (that is "rule," as the word so often means in the Old Testament). The message to all the churches (Rev. 3:21–22) indicates they are all the believers from the Church Age who remain faithful, being overcomers, that is, conquerors, winners (Rev. 2:26–27; 3:21; see also 1 John 5:4). Among them, as Jesus promised, are the twelve apostles judging (ruling) the twelve tribes of Israel (Luke 22:30); for Israel, restored, cleansed, filled with God's Holy Spirit, will undoubtedly occupy all the land promised to Abraham (Gen. 15:18).[97]

In addition to the overcomers from the Church Age, John saw "souls," that is, living individuals who will have been martyred during the Tribulation (Rev. 6:9–11; 12:15). These two groups are joined to reign with Christ for the thousand years. It will be a time of peace and blessing, with righteousness prevailing (Isa. 2:2–4; Mic. 4:3–5; Zech. 9:10). The Holy Spirit will do a work of restoration. Even the natural world will reflect the order, perfection, and beauty God intended His creation to have.[98] The animal world will be changed (Isa. 11:6–8; 35:25; Ezek. 34:25). Nevertheless, there will still be cause for punishment and death (Isa. 65:17–25). This implies that those born during the millennial reign of Christ on earth to unbelievers who survived the Tribulation will still find it necessary to make their choice to follow Christ in faith and obedience.

Revelation 20:5 makes a plain (but parenthetical) statement about "the rest of the dead." These include all who are not in the two groups mentioned in verse 4. That is, they include all who died in their sins apart from the saving grace of God. They will not be resurrected until after Christ's millennial reign.

"This is the first resurrection" (v. 5) means that those mentioned in verse 4 complete the first resurrection. Jesus spoke of two resurrections (John 5:29): the first, the resurrection of life for those who have done the good God meant for them to do in accepting Christ and living for Him; the second, the resurrection of judgment for those who have done evil,

---

[97]In the Millenium, as Bruce Ware puts it, "Israel and the church are in fact one people of God . . . one by faith in Christ and common partaking of the Spirit, and yet distinct insofar as God will yet restore Israel as a nation to its land. . . .[under] One new covenant." "The New Covenant and the People(s) of God," 68–97 in Blaising, *Dispensationalism*, 97.

[98]Pss. 96:11–13; 98:7–9; Isa. 14:7–8; 35:1–2,6–7; 51:3; 55:12–13; Rom. 8:18–23.

through unbelief. But just as the Old Testament prophets did not show the time difference between Jesus' first and second comings, so Jesus in John 5:29 did not show the time difference between the two resurrections. His purpose was to encourage people to live for God, so the time difference between the two was not relevant to what He was teaching.

First Corinthians 15:20,23 gives us more insight as Paul compares the first resurrection to a harvest. The resurrected Christ is the "firstfruits of the harvest." The main body of the harvest comes "in [its] own order" at the time of His coming to meet us in the air.[99] Then the gleanings of the harvest will be those martyred during the Tribulation; the first resurrection to life will then be complete. The first resurrection is also called "the resurrection of the righteous" (Luke 14:14). They are identified as blessed (Rev. 20:6) for they will enjoy the fullness of God's blessing. They are "holy," that is, dedicated to God and His will. Because their resurrection is like Christ's resurrection they rise to die no more. The "second death" (the lake of fire) will therefore have no power over them.

SATAN RELEASED

The Book of Revelation gives no details of the Millennium, probably because previous prophecies are sufficient. After the thousand years Satan will be released, possibly to bring a final vindication of the justice of God. That is, although people will have experienced the wonderful rule of Christ, they will apparently follow Satan at their first opportunity.[100] This shows that with or without the knowledge of what Christ's reign is like, unsaved people rebel. In justice God can do nothing but separate them from His blessings forever. Satan, the great deceiver, also deceives himself into believing he can yet defeat God. But his final attempt will fail. There will never be any further rebellion against God and His love.

THE JUDGMENTS

Throughout the Bible God is seen as a righteous Judge. He brought judgment on both Israel and the nations in ancient

---

[99]The Old Testament saints will be included in the main body of the harvest (Isa. 26:19–21; Ezek. 37:12–14; Dan. 12:2–3).

[100]The nations are here identified as "Gog and Magog." The battle here is quite different from that in Ezekiel 38 and 39, however. It may be that a comparison is being made, meaning that these people are acting like Gog and Magog, not that they actually are Gog and Magog.

times. At the end of the age He will still be the righteous Judge, but will mediate that judgment through the Son, for "the Father judges no one, but has entrusted all judgment to the Son, that all may honor the Son just as they honor the Father" (John 5:22–23; cf. 2 Tim. 4:8).

The Rapture is no mere "escape." Believers will forever be with the Lord. But all without exception will be subject to judgment when brought into His presence (Rom. 14:10–12; 1 Cor. 3:12–15; 2 Cor. 5:10). God's judgment seat, or throne (Gk. *bēma*, Rom. 14:10), is also called the judgment seat of Christ (2 Cor. 5:10). There each one will "receive what is due him for the things done while in the body, whether good [Gk. *agathon*, "spiritually and morally good or useful in God's sight"] or bad [Gk. *phaulos*, "worthless, evil; including selfishness, envy, and laziness"]" (2 Cor. 5:10).[101] No secret thing can be hidden (Rom. 2:16). Everything will be judged: our words, our acts, our motives, our attitudes, and our character (Matt. 5:22; 12:36–37; Mark 4:22; Rom. 2:5–11,16; Eph. 6:8; 1 Cor. 3:13; 4:5; 13:3). Of these, our motives (especially love) and our faithfulness seem to be the most important (Matt. 25:21,23; Luke 12:43; 1 Cor. 13:3; Col. 3:23–24; Heb. 6:10). They can make the difference between whether our deeds are judged as "gold, silver, costly stones" or "wood, hay or straw" (1 Cor. 3:12).

The judgment includes the possibility of either "loss" (1 Cor. 3:15) or "reward" (Rom. 2:10; 1 Cor. 3:12–14; Phil. 3:14; 2 Tim. 4:8; 2 John 8). We must continue "in him [Christ], so that when he appears we may be confident and unashamed before him at his coming" (1 John 2:28). Otherwise, there is the danger of having all our works burned up (1 Cor. 3:13–15). Only those who respond in love and faith to the grace, abilities, and responsibilities God gives them will hear Jesus say, " 'Well done, good and faithful servant! You have been faithful with a few things; I will put you in charge of many things. Come and share your master's happiness!' " (Matt. 25:21,23). Though we are not saved by our works, we are "created in Christ Jesus to do good works" (Eph. 2:10). As Romans 2:7 tells us, the righteous judgment of God will give eternal life to those who "by persistence in doing good seek glory, honor and immortality."

After Satan is cast into the lake of fire, a huge white throne

---

[101]Some ancient Greek manuscripts have *kakos*, a more general word for "bad," "evil," "lack," "harm," "wrong," instead of *phaulos*.

appears, white because it radiates the holiness, majesty, and glory of God (Rev. 20:11). Standing before it are all the dead, "great and small," that is, regardless of their station in life on earth. (This number does not include those mentioned in Rev. 20:4, for they are already resurrected with new immortal bodies that cannot die or even decay.) They have been resurrected to judgment. Since resurrection is bodily, they will have some sort of body, and they will be judged by their works (from divinely kept records that undoubtedly include their rejecting Christ and following Satan, as well as all their other sins, public and private). The Book of Life will also be open there, probably as evidence that their names are not in it.

The Bible speaks of other judgments, but without giving details of the time or place. Paul mentioned that the saints (all true believers, for they are dedicated to the worship and service of the Lord) will judge the world and will judge angels and contrasts it to judging in this life (1 Cor. 6:2–3). This may take place during the Millennium.

Some take Matthew 25:31–46, the separation of the people "one from another as a shepherd separates the sheep from the goats" (v. 32), to be a special judgment of the nations at the beginning of the Millennium. It is a judgment of works, recognizing that whatever is done or fails to be done for others is done or fails to be done for Christ. Whatever we do, we are to do as unto the Lord. The word "nations"[102] means peoples, not national states. The acts are acts done by individuals who have care for Christ's brothers [and sisters] or who neglect them.[103] The results are an inheritance for those who are the blessed and an eternal fire for the rest, fire prepared for the devil and his angels. That is, the final state, not the Millennium, is in view in this picture. James Oliver Buswell makes an interesting suggestion. Since the scene is "of vast cosmic perspective" it may be that Jesus put both the judgment seat of Christ and the Great White Throne in

---

[102]Gk. *ethnos, ethnē* (pl.), has a broad meaning covering any group of people. God's people are a holy *ethnos* (1 Pet. 2:9). *Ethnē* was often used to mean "Gentiles."

[103]Some hold that "these brothers of mine" (v. 40) refer to the Jewish people. However, Jesus consistently called His own followers His brothers (Matt. 12:46–50; 28:10; Mark 3:31–35; Luke 8:19–21; John 20:17; Rom. 8:29; Heb. 2:11). They are the "least of these," the "little flock," to whom He is pleased to give the Kingdom (Luke 12:32).

the one picture for the sake of the lesson, without indicating the time difference between them.[104]

THE FINAL STATE OF THE WICKED

The Bible describes the final destiny of the lost as terrible beyond imagination. It is "outer darkness," where there will be weeping and gnashing of teeth from frustration and remorse as they continually suffer the wrath of God (Matt. 22:13; 25:30; Rom. 2:8–9; Jude 13). It is a "fiery furnace" (Matt. 13:42,50), where the fire by its very nature is unquenchable and never goes out (Mark 9:43; Jude 7). It causes eternal loss, or everlasting destruction (2 Thess. 1:9), and "the smoke of their torment rises for ever and ever" (Rev. 14:11; cf. 20:10).[105] Jesus used the word *Gehenna* as the term for it.

Gehenna is an Aramaic name for the Valley of Hinnom, a narrow ravine to the west and south of Jerusalem. During the decline of Judah's kingdom, apostate Jews offered their children there in a fiery sacrifice to the Ammonite God Molech (2 Kings 23:10; Jer. 7:31). Therefore, Jews in New Testament times made it a city dump, and a fire was always burning there, so Jesus used it figuratively for the place of final judgment, the lake of fire.[106] There the flames of burning sulfur

---

[104]Buswell, *A Systematic Theology*, vol.2, 422–23.

[105]Unbelievers do not like the idea of endless torment. Most cults also discard the idea. See Bloesch, *Essentials of Evangelical Theology*, vol. 2, 219. Universalists say a good God would not send anyone to hell. Unitarians say there is too much good in every person for God to send anyone to hell. Both ignore the holiness and justice of God. A good earthly father would not give a glass of milk with an ounce of strychnine in it to his children saying, "There is too much good in this milk to throw it out." So our Heavenly Father must cast out those who have refused the only antidote for sin, the blood of Jesus. See Harry Buis, *The Doctrine of Eternal Punishment* (Philadelphia: Presbyterian and Reformed Publishing Co., 1957), 112–22, for a discussion of this. Universalism is dangerous because in effect it denies "the existence of any ultimate risk in the moral life." Leckie, *The World to Come*, 286. There will be gradations in the intensity of the punishment (Luke 12:47–48), according to their works (Rev. 20:12–13), but no limits as to the time. It will be eternal. Some take eternal to mean "age lasting," but the usage in the New Testament shows it to mean "without end." The same word is used of eternal life (Matt. 25:46; John 3:16) and "the eternal God" (Rom. 16:26).

[106]A heresy spread in the 1920s by Charles H. Pridgeon, *Is Hell Eternal or Will God's Plan Fail?* (Pittsburgh: The Evangelization Society of the Pittsburgh Bible Institute, 1920), identified the fire of 1 Cor. 3:15 with the lake of fire. It suggests that believers who are not holy enough will need

tell us how disagreeable the fire will be. The darkness also indicates they are shut out of the light of God. The faith, hope, and love that remain for us (1 Cor. 13:13) will be forever lacking in that environment.[107] The "rest" we shall enjoy will never be available to them, nor will the joy and peace our Lord gives to those who believe. It will also be a lonely place, shut off from fellowship with God, and the bitterness and gnashing of teeth as well as their unchanged fallen nature will prevent fellowship with each other.[108]

. After the final judgment, death and Hades are thrown into it (Rev. 20:14), for the lake of fire, which is outside the entire new heavens and earth (cf. Rev. 22:15), will be the only place where death will exist.[109] Then will Christ's victory over death as the wages of sin be finally and fully consummated (1 Cor. 15:26), and in the new heavens and earth there will be no more death (Rev. 21:4).

THE FINAL STATE OF THE RIGHTEOUS

Abraham was willing to live in the Promised Land like a stranger, for "he was looking forward to the city with foundations, whose architect and builder is God" (Heb. 11:9–10), a city that already exists in heaven (Gal. 4:26; Heb. 11:16). This city, the final home of the redeemed and the dwelling of God, is the New Jerusalem that John saw in a vision coming down out of heaven to the new earth. No longer will we be on earth and God in heaven, but God's headquarters and

---

to spend some time in the lake of fire. It suggests further that the purpose of the fire is purification and that through it all will be saved, including the devil and his demons. They take the phrase "restitution of all things" (Acts 3:21) out of context, not recognizing that the "all things" include only those things spoken by God's holy prophets. It is hard to see why the Cross would be necessary if the lake of fire could provide another means of salvation.

[107]A person lacking faith cannot enjoy eternal life in Christ any more than a fish lacking lungs can live on dry land. See T. A. Kantonen, *The Christian Hope* (Philadelphia: Muhlenberg Press, 1954), 107. Consequently, there is no hope of final universal salvation.

[108]Erickson, *Christian Theology,* 1235.

[109]Annihilationists teach that after a brief period God will cause a total cessation of their being. Some say man was created mortal and immortality is gained only as a reward from God. Others say man was created immortal but God by His act deprives them of it. There would be little reason for the fire to be "unquenchable" if either were the case. Boettner, *Immortality,* 117–19; Clark H. Pinnock, "The Conditional View" in *Four Views on Hell,* 135–66. See also Stephen H. Travis, *I Believe in the Second Coming of Christ* (Grand Rapids: Wm. B. Eerdmans, 1982), 198.

God's throne will be with His people on the earth (Rev. 21:3,22; 22:3). The city will have no temple, "because the Lord God Almighty and the Lamb are its temple"[110] (Rev. 21:22). That is, the presence and glory of God and Christ will fill the city so that those who dwell in it will always be enveloped in an atmosphere of worship and praise.[111]

Inscribed on its twelve gates are the names of the twelve tribes of Israel. Its foundations bear the names of the twelve apostles. Clearly, the true people of God of all ages from both Israel and the Church will be united in one body of people in Christ as the ultimate fulfillment of Galatians 3:28 (cf. Eph. 2:11–22).[112] Most important, John saw that "it shone with the glory of God" (Rev. 21:11). "Though it is an actual literal city, its glory will far surpass the language that John uses to portray it."[113]

Though the New Jerusalem is described, the new heavens and earth are not.[114] Some consider them to be the present heavens and earth renovated by fire, pointing to passages that speak of the earth remaining forever (Eccles. 1:4). But this probably means there will always be an earth even though the present earth may be replaced by a new one.

When the Great White Throne is set up, the earth and heavens will flee from God's presence, for there will be "no place for them" (Rev. 20:11). This suggests they go out of existence. The Psalmist contrasts their existence to God's eternal existence: "They will perish, but you remain; they will

---

[110]Gk. *naos,* "sanctuary."

[111]David L. Turner, "The New Jerusalem in Revelation 21:1–22:5: Consummation of a Biblical Continuum," in Blaising, *Dispensationalism,* 273. Some conservatives such "as Joseph Seiss, William Kelly, Walter Scott, J. N. Darby, A. C. Gaeblein, and even G. R. Beasley-Murray" hold that "Rev. 21:1–8 refers to the eternal state while 21:9 through 22:5" refers to the Millennium. However, it is better to take the entire passage to refer to the eternal state. Wilbur M. Smith, *The Biblical Doctrine of Heaven,* 258–59. Because the city is identified with "the bride, the wife of the Lamb" (Rev. 21:9–10), some believe it is symbolic of the Church and not a literal city. However, in the Bible a city is often identified with its inhabitants, as Jesus did when He wept over Jerusalem (Matt. 23:37).

[112]Horton, *Ultimate Victory,* 313–17. See also Carl B. Hoch, Jr. "The New Man of Ephesians 2," in Blaising, *Dispensationalism,* 113.

[113]Turner, "The New Jerusalem," in Blaising, *Dispensationalism,* 276.

[114]Isa. 65:17 prophesies that God will create new heavens and a new earth. Then v. 18 makes a strong contrast and draws attention to the fact that the present Jerusalem will also have its fulfillment (that is, in the Millennium), then vv. 19–25 go on to describe millennial conditions that do not fit the New Jerusalem as described in Revelation at all.

all wear out like a garment. Like clothing you will change them and they will be discarded. But you remain the same" (Ps. 102:25–27; Heb. 1:10–12). Changing clothes means taking off an old set and putting on a new one. This suggests something brand-new, not mere renovation. Similarly, Isaiah saw that "all the stars of the heavens will be dissolved" (Isa. 34:4), that "the heavens will vanish like smoke, the earth . . . wear out like a garment" (Isa. 51:6). Jesus also recognized the present heaven and earth will pass away (Mark 13:31), as did Peter (2 Pet. 3:10–12).[115] "New" (Gk. *kainos*) usually means brand-new and has the connotation of "marvelous," "unheard of."[116] God will create a wonderful new heavens and earth that will be free of all taint of sin and a joy forever.[117]

Our salvation brings us into a new relationship that is better than what Adam and Eve enjoyed before the Fall. The description of the New Jerusalem shows God has a better place than the Garden of Eden for us, with all the blessings of Eden intensified. God is so good: He always restores us to something better than what we lost. We enjoy fellowship with Him now, but the future holds "intensified fellowship with the Father, Son, and Holy Spirit and with the whole company of the saints."[118] Life in the New Jerusalem will be exciting. Our infinite God will never run out of new joys and blessings for the redeemed, and since the gates of the city are always open (Rev. 21:25; cf. Isa. 60:11), who knows what the new heavens and earth will have for us to explore!

Study Questions

1. How is the Christian's hope different from any hopes held by unbelievers?

---

[115]Some take the word "melt" (Gk. *luthēsetai;* 2 Pet. 3:10, KJV) to mean be "untied," "loosed," "broken up" and refer it to a renovation of the surface of the earth. However, 2 Pet. 3:12 uses a different word, *tēketai,* for "melt," which can only mean "melt" or "dissolve," which is also a meaning of *luthēsetai.*

[116]Walter Bauer, *A Greek-English Lexicon of the New Testament and Other Early Christian Literature,* 2d ed., trans. William F. Arndt and Wilbur Gingrich, rev. and augmented by F. Wilbur Gingrich and Frederick W. Danker (Chicago: University of Chicago Press, 1979), 394.

[117]Those who hold to a purification of the present earth compare the fire to Noah's flood, which "purified" the old earth. Turner, "The New Jerusalem," 274.

[118]Bloesch, *Essentials of Evangelical Theology,* vol. 2, 228. See Heb. 12:22–24.

2. What is the importance of recognizing the imminence of Christ's second coming?

3. In what ways is the resurrection of believers related to the resurrection of Jesus?

4. What are the biblical grounds for preaching that there is "a heaven to gain and a hell to shun"?

5. How have various groups interpreted Acts 1:11?

6. What are the weaknesses of amillennialism and post-millennialism?

7. What are the chief grounds for believing the Rapture will take place before the Tribulation?

8. What will the Millennium be like?

9. Both the judgment seat of Christ and the Great White Throne Judgment will be judgments of works. How will they differ from each other?

10. What does the Bible emphasize most about the New Jerusalem? (Include all passages that deal with it.)

Glossary

Abba. An Aramaic word for "the father" or "O Father."

Abomination of desolation. Refers to that which causes pollution of what is holy (Dan. 9:27; 11:31; 12:11; Matt. 24:15; Mark 13:14). May refer to the destruction of both the temple (A.D. 70) and the image of the Antichrist (Rev. 13:14–15; 19:11–21).

Adoptionism. An eighth century A.D. false teaching that said Jesus was adopted (possibly at His baptism) by the Father and (by this) incorporated into the Godhead, thus denying Christ's eternal existence and incarnation.

Age of Enlightenment. The era beginning in the eighteenth century when philosophers began saying truth could be found only through reason, observation, and experiment. They rejected supernatural revelation and encouraged secularism.

Agnosticism. "Not knowing." T. H. Huxley (1825–95) used this term to express his opinion that it was impossible to know whether or not God exists.

Albigensians. A medieval French sect that claimed the baptism in the Holy Spirit through the laying on of hands and lived by strict rules. They wanted to see the spiritual life of ordinary people deepened. They were suppressed by the Roman Church.

Allegory. A way of interpreting Scripture by looking for some deeper or "spiritual" meaning behind the literal sense.

Amillennialism. The view that there will be no future reign of Christ on earth. Some spiritualize the Millennium and make it represent Christ's present reign in heaven during the entire Church Age. They deny that Revelation 20 refers to a literal period of one thousand years.

639

Ancient of Days. A title of God the Father indicating His wisdom (Dan. 7:9,13,22).

Angelology. The study of the nature and work of angels.

Animism. A pagan belief that spirits inhabit trees, stones, and other natural objects.

Anthropodicy. The "justification of humanity." The attempt to vindicate humanity in connection with the problem of evil.

Anthropology. In theology, used of the Bible's view of human beings, including creation, sin, and our relation to God.

Antichrist. A false Christ who will appear at the end of this age, become a world dictator, and demand worship.

Antisupernaturalism. Denies the existence and reality of the supernatural. Tries to explain everything in terms of natural law.

Apocalyptic. (Gk. *apocalupsis,* "revelation," "disclosure.") The literature that uses rich symbolism to describe the coming kingdom of God and the events leading up to it. The visions of Daniel and Revelation are examples.

Apollinarianism. Apollinarius (died, ca. A.D. 390) taught that Jesus had a human body and soul, but deity, or the Logos ("Word," John 1:1), took the place of the spirit or mind in Him. Apollinarius did not consider Jesus either fully human or fully divine.

Apologetics. The defense of Christian faith, usually on intellectual principles.

Apostle. A "messenger." Two groups are mentioned in the New Testament. The Twelve: especially trained and commissioned by Jesus to be primary witnesses to His resurrection and His teachings, and to spread the gospel. They will judge (rule) the twelve tribes of Israel in the millennial kingdom (Luke 22:30). Also used of others directly commissioned by Christ, including Paul, Barnabas, Andronicus, Junia, and James, the Lord's brother.

Apostles' Creed. A statement of faith, not actually from the apostles, but from the Roman church. It deals with the Father, Son, and Holy Spirit.

Archaeology. The scientific study of the remains of a culture and a people. It involves digging up these remains.

Arianism. Arius about A.D. 319 began teaching that Jesus Christ is a spirit created by God before He created the universe, and that Christ does not share the essence, or substance, of God, but has a similar essence.

Arminianism. Jacobus Arminius (1560–1609) taught in the "Remonstrance" (1610) that all who will believe in Christ are eternally elected by God, that Christ died for everyone, that each believer is regenerated by the Holy Spirit, and that it is possible to fall away from grace and be eternally lost.

Articles of Remonstrance. See "Arminianism."

Atheism. The denial that any god or God exists.

Atonement. (Heb. *kippurim.*) "The act of reconciliation" to God by covering with a price, the blood of a substitute, so that no punishment is necessary. (Gk. *katallagē,* "reconciliation.")

Autographs. The original (handwritten) manuscripts produced by the human authors of Scripture. These were probably circulated and copied so many times that they wore out. None of them are now known to exist. However, copies made in ancient times do exist.

Biblical criticism. The analysis of the literary qualities and the history found in the Bible, not criticism in the ordinary sense of the word.

Biblical theology. The study of the teachings of the Bible, book by book or writer by writer, usually with an emphasis on progressive revelation.

Blasphemy. Slander, abusive speech that reviles or injures the reputation of persons, or especially such speech directed against God, Christ, or the Holy Spirit.

Calvinism. The teachings of John Calvin (1509–64), especially as developed by the Synod of Dort (1618–19), emphasizing total depravity, unconditional divine election, limitation of the Atonement to the elect, irresistible grace, and perseverance in grace. Reformed churches are Calvinistic.

Canon. (Gk. *kanōn,* "a straight rod.") It came to mean a rule, or standard, and then the list of books accepted by the Church as a whole as Scripture inspired by the Holy Spirit, that is, the sixty-six books of the Bible.

Charismata. A Greek word meaning "freely bestowed gracious gifts." Used of the gifts of the Holy Spirit (Rom. 12:6; 1 Cor. 12:4,9,28,30,31).

Charismatic. Related to or possessing one or more of the gifts of the Holy Spirit. Often used of all who put emphasis on the person and work of the Spirit and the availability and usefulness of the gifts today.

Cherubim. Plural of "cherub" (i.e., "cherubs"), beings first mentioned in the Garden of Eden (Gen. 3:24) and described in Ezekiel 1:5–14; 10:14.

Christology. (From the Gk. *Christos,* "Anointed One," and *logos,* "word," "teaching," "message.") The study of what the Bible teaches about the person, ministry, and work of Jesus Christ.

Church Age. The period between Christ's resurrection and His second coming.

Closed canon. The fact that no books can be added to the sixty-six books of the Bible.

Closed Communion. The teaching that only members of a particular local church may share in the Lord's Supper.

Cluniacs. Members of a reform movement of the tenth to twelfth centuries, centered at the Abbey of Cluny in the Rhone Valley of France. They also included about ten thousand monks in England.

Commercial theory. Another name for the satisfaction theory, which treats the Cross as a commercial transaction satisfying God's honor and paying the infinite price for forgiveness.

Congregational government. Government of the church by the members, who regard themselves as having equal rights.

Consecrated. Set apart for the Lord's use or service. Also used of a richer, deeper Christian life, wholly committed to God.

Consubstantiality. The sharing of the one divine being or substance by the Father, Son, and Holy Spirit.

Consubstantiation. The teaching that the body of Christ is spiritually united with the bread, and the blood of Christ is spiritually united with the wine, of the Lord's Supper.

Cosmogony. Any theory of the origins of the physical universe.

Creed (confession). A statement summarizing the chief teachings of the Bible that Christians are to believe.

Daniel's seventieth week. A final "seven" or week of years which most premillennialists identify with the Great Tribulation at the end of the Church Age.

Deity. Being God, having the nature of God.

Diaspora. The scattering of the Jews into various nations that began as God's judgment on Israel and Judah. Now used of Jews living outside Palestine.

Dichotomism. The view that the human person is composed of two basic aspects, body and soul.

Didache. A Greek word meaning "teaching." The Didache or *Teaching of the Twelve Apostles* (written about A.D. 100) was a manual on Christian life and church practice which claimed to have the authority of the apostles.

Disciple. "Learner," "student." Includes all who seek to learn from Jesus and obey His teachings.

Dispensationalism. A view first popularized by J. N. Darby (1800–1882) and spread by the *Scofield Reference Bible.* It divides God's activity in history into seven dispensations, emphasizes a literal interpretation of prophecy, and holds that God has two plans, one for Israel and one for the Church.

Ditheism. The teaching that there are two gods or Gods.

Docetism. (From Gk. *dokeō,* "seem," "have the appearance.") The teaching that Jesus was God but only appeared to be a man and did not actually die on the cross. A form of Gnosticism.

Dominicans. A Roman Catholic order founded by Dominic in 1215. They emphasized both study and converting others to the Catholic Church.

Dualism. The teaching that good and evil are fundamental realities in the universe. Also the teaching that human beings are composed of two totally distinct elements that are not unified.

Dynamic Monarchianism. A teaching spread in the second and third centuries that God is sole sovereign and that Jesus was an ordinary man who at baptism began to be inspired by the Spirit, though not indwelt by the Spirit.

Ebionism. The Ebionites (from Heb. for "poor men") taught that Jesus was the son of Joseph and Mary and became the Son of God when the Holy Spirit descended on Him. They also emphasized keeping the Law.

Ecclesiology. The study of the biblical teachings concerning the church and its practices.

Ecumenical. (From Gk. *oikoumenē,* "the inhabited earth.") Refers to modern attempts to unite various denominations.

Eisegesis. A Greek word meaning "lead into," "introduce into." The reading of one's own ideas into the biblical text.

El Elyon. A Hebrew term meaning "God Most High" (Gen. 14:18–22).

El Olam. A Hebrew term meaning "The God of All Time," "The Eternal God."

El Shaddai. A Hebrew term meaning "God Almighty."

Elohim. The plural form of the Hebrew word *'Eloah,* "God." Used of heathen gods, angels, powerful spirit beings, and used of the one true God to show that all that is God is only in Him.

Episcopal government. Rule by bishops.

Epistemology. The study of human knowledge or how the mind attains and uses knowledge to determine truth.

Eschatology. (Gk. *eschatos*, "last.") The study of what happens in the afterlife and what happens at the end of the age and in the final state of both the righteous and the wicked.

Eunuch. A physically castrated man.

Eutychianism. The teaching of Eutyches (ca. A.D. 375–ca. 454) that the human nature of Jesus was absorbed into the divine so that He had only one nature.

Evangelicalism. Affirms the inspiration and authority of the Bible and the truth of its teachings, with emphasis on the need for personal conversion and regeneration by the Holy Spirit.

Ex nihilo. A Latin term meaning "out of nothing." It refers to God's work at creation.

Exegesis. (Gk. *exēgēsis*, "explanation," "interpretation.") The process of explaining a Bible text using rules supplied by hermeneutics.

Exegetical theology. Theology derived from form, structure, grammatical data, and historical and literary contexts of the books of the Bible.

Existential revelation. Revelation sought through the human person's own experience of and participation in reality.

Existentialism. Based on the teaching of Søren Kierkegaard (1813–55). Emphasizes subjectivity, seeking truth through one's own experience (especially of anxiety, guilt, dread, anguish) rather than by scientific objectivity.

Expiation. The making of full Atonement by the Blood.

Faith. Belief in God and Christ expressed in wholehearted, trustful obedience. Biblical faith is always more than believing something is true. It always has God and Christ as its object.

False prophet. Many false prophets appeared in Bible times and their number will increase in the last days. The final false prophet will accompany the Antichrist (Rev. 16:13; cf. 13:12).

Federalism. Covenant theology or mature Calvinism as developed in the seventeenth century.

Fiat creationism. Creation by God's direct command.

Filiation. (Lat. *filius*, "a son.") The relation of God the Father and God the Son within the eternal Godhead.

Foreknowledge. The knowledge God has of things and events before they occur. Calvinism identifies this with predestination. Process theology makes it God's knowledge of all the possibilities of what may take place.

Franciscans. A Roman Catholic order founded by Francis of Assisi in 1209. They started as street preachers.

Futurist view. The view that everything in the Book of Revelation after chapter 4 takes place in a short period at the end of the Church Age.

Gap theory. The theory that Genesis 1:1 represents an original creation that was ruined. Thus Genesis 1:2 is supposed to describe a gap between the original creation and a later six-day creation.

General revelation. What God has made known of himself and His will in nature and in the human conscience (Rom. 1:18–20; 2:14–15).

Genre. A type, or form, of literature, such as prose, poetry, narrative, speech, lament, hymn, vision, wisdom saying, etc.

Glossolalia. (Gk. *glōssa,* "tongue," "language," and *lalia,* "speech," "speaking.") The Spirit's gift of speaking in tongues.

Gnosticism. A teaching, beginning in the second century, that salvation comes through special superior knowledge. Some taught that physical matter is evil; most denied the humanity of Christ.

Governmental theory. The proposal by Hugo Grotius (1583–1645) that Christ's death was not in our place but was a substitute for the penalty we deserve and a demonstration of what a just God will require if we continue to sin. *If* we repent, we will be forgiven, and this preserves God's moral government.

Grace. "Unmerited favor." God's Riches At Christ's Expense; His generosity to humanity.

Great Awakening. The American revival of 1725–60.

Hades. Greek mythology used it as the name of a grim god as well as a shadowy underworld of departed spirits. In the New Testament it translates the Hebrew *Sheʿol* and is always a place of agony (Luke 16:23–24).

Hamartiology. (Gk. *hamartia,* "sin.") The study of the cause, nature, and results of sin.

Hellenistic. Related to the ideas and practices of Greek culture as it developed in the Roman Empire.

Henotheism. The worship of one god without denying the existence of other gods.

Heresy. An opinion or way of thinking that contradicts the teachings of the Bible.

Hermeneutics. (Gk. *hermēneuō,* "explain," "interpret.") The theory of understanding the meaning of a passage, including analysis of the text, its intentionality, its context, and the customs and culture of the human author.

Higher criticism. Literary and historical analysis of the books of the Bible.

Historical narrative. A narrative recognized as fact.

Historical theology. The study of the teachings of the various theologians in their context down through church history.

Historicist view. The view that the events in the Book of Revelation have been gradually fulfilled during the course of church history.

Homoousia hemin. A Greek term meaning "of the same nature or essence as us."

Hypostasis. A Greek term meaning "actual being," "real being." Used to mean persons in the one being or essence of the Triune God.

Idealist view. The view that the figures and symbols in the Book of Revelation represent only the ongoing struggle between good and evil, with the ultimate triumph of righteousness.

Illumination. The Holy Spirit's work in bringing understanding of the truths of the Bible.

Incarnation. The act by which the eternal Son of God became a human being without giving up His deity.

Indigenous church principle. The principle that churches once established should be under the control of the local believers.

Inerrancy. Truth without error of any kind.

Infallibility. The Bible's incapability of error.

Intertestamental period. The period between Malachi (about 430 B.C.) and the birth of Jesus.

Judaism. The religion and culture that developed from Phariseeism among the Jews after the temple was destroyed (A.D. 70). It exists in a variety of forms today.

Judeo-Christian. Referring to the values held by both Jews and Christians.

Justification. God's act of declaring and accepting a person as righteous in His sight. God pardons sinners who accept Christ and treats them as not guilty—just as if they had never sinned.

Karma. In Hinduism and Buddhism, the force resulting from a person's actions that determines the destiny of the soul in the next life.

Kenosis. A Greek term meaning "emptying." The self-emptying of Christ (Phil. 2:7) when He became man and emptied himself of the outward expressions of His glory.

Keswick. Referring to evangelical gatherings originating in Keswick, England, for Bible study, for seeking deeper spiritual life or victorious living.

Kingdom now theology. A form of postmillennialism that emphasizes making the kingdoms of this world the kingdom of Christ now.

Koran. The sacred book of Islam.

Liberalism. A movement that denies the supernatural and redefines Christian teachings and practices in terms of current human philosophies.

Liberation theology. A reactionary theology that interprets the Bible in such a way as to allow a Marxist type of revolution to liberate the poor.

Limbo. (Lat. *limbus,* "border.") According to Roman Catholic theology, the permanent state of babies who die unbaptized. They are not personally guilty so they do not go to hell, but because of original sin they cannot go to heaven.

Literary-historical criticism. See "higher criticism."

Lower criticism. The analysis of the texts and manuscripts of the Bible with a view to determine what is the true reading.

Macroevolution. The theory of the evolution of all living things from an original living cell.

Manuscripts. Handwritten books. Before A.D. 100 these were scrolls, or rolls. After that they were bound books.

Maranatha. An Aramaic word meaning "Our Lord Come!" (1 Cor. 16:22).

Mass. The Roman Catholic name for the Lord's Supper.

Messiah. From the Hebrew *Mashiach,* "Anointed One."

Microevolution. Small changes within the development of the kinds created by God. Provision for these changes was undoubtedly made by God in His creation. Most, however, have produced deterioration due to the Fall.

Midrash. A Hebrew word meaning "explanation." A Jewish type of explanation of the meaning supposed to underlie biblical texts.

Mid-Tribulation theory. The theory that the rapture of the Church will occur in the middle of the seven years of the Great Tribulation at the end of the Church Age.

Millennium. A Latin term meaning "thousand years." Used to refer to the future reign of Christ on earth.

Modalism. The teaching that God is one Person who manifests himself sometimes as Father, sometimes as Son, sometimes as Holy Spirit.

Monarchianism. A second- and third-century movement that stressed the unity and oneness of God. Some made Jesus just a man. Others taught a form of Modalism.

Monasticism. Seclusion from the secular world in order to live a life of self-denial, service, prayer, and obedience.

Monism. Views the human person as a radical unity, a self not composed of separable parts such as body, soul, and spirit.

Monotheism. The worship of one God.

Moral influence theory. The theory that God graciously forgives and that the purpose of the Cross was simply to influence people toward good.

Moravians. Members of a church that resulted from a revival beginning in 1722 at Herrnhut, the estate of Count Zinzendorf in Saxony.

Mortal sin. According to Roman Catholic theology, a mortal sin causes a person to lose the state of grace and will cause eternal damnation if death occurs before penance is made.

Narrative. An account of events, especially as it advances action. Some look for a plot with a buildup and release of tension.

Neoorthodoxy. A type of theology associated especially with Karl Barth (1886–1968). It accepts the destructive critical methods of the liberals for the interpretation of the Bible, but teaches the major doctrines of the Reformation and believes that God speaks to people through Scripture (even while holding that Scripture is not inerrant).

Neoplatonism. The teachings of Plato as modified by Plotinus (205–70) and others. It conceived of the world as an emanation from deity and thought the soul could be reunited with deity in ecstatic experiences.

Neouniversalism. A trend among some Evangelicals to see the possibility of the ultimate salvation of all human beings due to the extravagant love and grace of God.

Nestorianism. The teaching of Nestorius, bishop of Constantinople (428–), that Jesus had within himself two persons as well as two natures. The Nestorians now call themselves Assyrian Christians.

Nicene Creed. The Council of Nicea (A.D. 325) produced a creed that was revised at the Council of Constantinople (A.D. 381). The revised version is still recited in many churches as a confession of faith.

Omnipotent. "All powerful."

Omnipresent. "Everywhere present."

Omniscient. "Having all knowledge."

Oneness Pentecostalism. The movement beginning in 1913 that views God in a modalistic manner and demands rebaptism in the name of Jesus only.

Ontological. Related to being, or to existence.

Open Communion. The willingness to serve the Lord's Supper to all believers who may be present whether or not they are members of the church.

Ordinance. A practice commanded by Jesus and continued as a memorial in obedience to Him. The two specific ordinances are water baptism and the Lord's Supper.

Orthodox. (From the Gk. *orthōs,* "upright," "straight," "correct," "true," and *dokeō,* "think," "believe.") Refers to correct teachings and practices as established by the Church. Used by Evangelicals of correct biblical teachings. The eastern churches took the name "orthodox" when the western (Roman Catholic) church split off from them.

Palestine. (From the Hebrew *Pᵉlishtim,* "Philistines.") A term used by the Greek historian Herodotus (5th century B.C.) for southern Syria and then for Canaan by the Romans (in the Latin form, *Palaestina*). It includes the land west of the Jordan, called "the Holy Land" in the Middle Ages, and has several regions including coastal plains stretching for about 120 miles along the Mediterranean Sea from Lebanon to Gaza, the *Shᵉphelah* ("foothills" ["low plains" or "low country," KJV]), the central hill country, and the Jordan-Dead Sea valley (part of the great Rift valley that stretches on through the Red Sea into central Mozambique in Africa).

Pantheism. The belief that God and nature, or the universe, are identical: "God is all, all is God."

Parousia. A Greek word meaning "presence," "coming," "arrival." Used in theology to describe the coming of Christ at the end of this age.

Patriarch. A Greek term meaning "father of a nation." Used of Abraham (Heb. 7:4) and the twelve sons of Jacob (Acts 7:8–9).

Patripassianism. The teaching that God the Father suffered on the cross.

Patristic era. (Lat. *patres,* "fathers.") The first seven centuries of church history.

Pelagianism. Pelagius (ca. A.D. 354–420) taught that the human will is the key to achieving salvation. He also denied original sin and said people are free to do right or wrong, are responsible for their deeds, and receive grace according to their merits.

Penal substitution theory. Jesus on the cross took the place of sinners and suffered the punishment due them.

Pentateuch. The five books of Moses (Genesis through Deuteronomy), called in Hebrew the *Torah,* "Instruction."

Pentecostal. The movement that began in 1901 and emphasizes the restoration of the baptism in the Holy Spirit with the evidence of speaking in other tongues and the restoration of the gifts of the Holy Spirit.

Perseverance. Steadfastly continuing in a life of faith and obedience throughout life.

Pharisee. "A separatist." A member of a strict party that came into existence a century or more before Christ. The Pharisees observed the letter of the written law of Moses and added oral tradition that they claimed had been given to Moses.

Philology. The study of language as used in literature and as a medium of culture.

Pietists. Members of a movement that began in the seventeenth century among German Lutherans. They emphasized religious experience, communion with God, and missions.

Pluralism. The idea that various religious groups should be free to function in society, or that various interpretations of the faith should be accepted and encouraged within the Church.

Pneumatology. The study of who the Holy Spirit is, what He does, and the gifts He gives.

Polemics. The vigorous defense of Christian truth against false teachings, such as those promoted by cults.

Polytheism. The worship of many gods.

Postmillennialism. The teaching that the Millennium is the Church Age or an extension of the Church Age, with Christ ruling but not personally present.

Post-Tribulation theory. The theory that Christian believers will go through the seven-year Great Tribulation at the end of the age. The Rapture is considered identical with Christ's return in glory to destroy the Antichrist and establish the millennial kingdom.

Practical theology. The study of the administration, function, work, and life of the Church.

Predestination. The teaching that God chooses something in advance. He predestined that Jesus would be the Head of the Church and that the Church would be a chosen Body that He will glorify when Jesus returns. Calvinists believe God predestines individuals to be saved. This comes from Calvin's philosophy, not from the Bible.

Premillennialism. The teaching that Jesus will personally return at the end of the Church Age and will establish His kingdom on earth for a thousand years. Emphasizes the literal interpretation of the Bible.

Presbyterian government. Church government directed by elders (presbyters), including preaching elders (pastors) and ruling elders (assisting the pastor).

Presupposition. A supposition held before investigating the facts.

Preterist view. The view that the majority of the events in the Book of Revelation refer to the first century and are already fulfilled.

Pre-Tribulation theory. The theory that the rapture of the Church takes place at the beginning of the Great Tribulation and that the Judgment Seat of Christ and the Marriage Supper of the Lamb take place in heaven before the Church returns with Christ to destroy the Antichrist and establish the millennial kingdom.

Progressive creationism. The idea that God created by distinct creative acts that either had time in between or that overlapped during a considerable period of time.

Propitiation. The making of atonement by satisfying God's wrath against human sin by Christ's sacrifice on the cross.

Propositional revelation. Revelation stated in a clear objective, definite way, usually in sentence form, and therefore to be believed.

Proselyte. A Greek term meaning "one who has come over." A convert from paganism to Judaism.

Providence. God's care and guidance.

Pseudepigrapha. A Greek term meaning "falsely entitled writings." Jewish writings from near the time of Christ not included in the Septuagint. They were attributed to people like Moses and Solomon, who were not their true authors.

Purgatory. (Lat. *purgatus,* "cleansing.") The sphere where Roman Catholics believe the souls of the faithful are purified before entering heaven.

Qumran. A place overlooking the northwest corner of the Dead Sea where a Jewish religious community lived from about 150 B.C. to about A.D. 70. Books of the Old Testament that they copied have been found (the Dead Sea Scrolls).

Ransom theory. The theory that Jesus' death on the cross was a payment to Satan to release people from Satan's bondage.

Rationalism. A system of thought that depends totally on human reason and denies the need for divine revelation.

Reconciliation. The bringing of people to God in a restored fellowship.

Redaction criticism. Treats the writers of the Gospels as authors and theologians (rather than mere collectors of traditions as in form criticism), and seeks to determine why and how the writers used the information available to them.

Redemption. Restoration to fellowship with God through Christ's payment of the penalty for our sins by His death on the cross and the shedding of His blood.

Regeneration. The Holy Spirit's work of giving new life to the sinner who repents and believes in Jesus.

Reincarnation. The belief that when a person dies the soul leaves the body and enters into another body (a baby, an animal, an insect, or even a god, according to Hinduism).

Religion. A system of belief and a way of worship. The term is also used of human attempts to please God or gods.

Repentance. (Gk. *metanoia,* "a change of mind.") A change of the basic attitudes toward God and Christ, which involves a turning away from sin and a seeking of God's rule and righteousness.

Restorationism. Teaches a second chance for salvation after death.

Revelation. God's disclosure of himself and His will.

Sabellianism. The teaching of Sabellius (third century A.D.) that God is one Person who revealed himself in three forms, modes, or manifestations, in succession.

Sacerdotal. Referring to the domination of church life by the clergy, or the powers of the priesthood as mediators between God and human beings, often in special relation to the mass.

Sacrament. A religious rite. Roman Catholics believe grace is dispensed through these rites.

Sadducees. They rejected the traditions of the Pharisees and gave their attention to the written Law and the temple. During the time of Jesus, the Jewish high priest and his friends were Sadducees (cf. Matt. 16:1–2; 23:23–34; Acts 23:7–8).

Salvation. Includes all that God has done and will do for the believer in delivering from the power of sin and death and restoring to fellowship, as well as assuring future resurrection and the full inheritance He has promised.

Sanctification. The work of the Holy Spirit that separates believers from sin and evil and dedicates them to the worship and service of the Lord. There is an initial act of sanctification at conversion and a continuing process of sanctification as we cooperate with the Holy Spirit in putting to death wrong desires.

Sanctify. "Separate to God," "make holy."

Semipelagianism. The teaching that sinful human beings can take the first step toward God and then God helps them repent and exercise saving faith.

Sensus plenior. A Latin term meaning "fuller sense."

Septuagint. The translation of the Old Testament from Hebrew to Greek made during the two hundred years before Christ. A later tradition said it was done by seventy (or seventy-two) men. As a consequence, it is often referred to by the Roman numerals for seventy, LXX.

Seraphim. Plural of "seraph" (i.e., seraphs), "burning ones." They so reflected the glory of God that they seemed to be on fire (Isa. 6:2).

Sheol. The Hebrew word for the place of the wicked dead, translated *Hadēs* in the New Testament.

Soteriology. (Gk. *sōtēria*, "deliverance," "salvation.") The study of the saving work of Christ.

Special revelation. God's revelation in the written Word (the Bible) and in the person of Jesus.

Syncretism. The fusing of pagan ideas and pagan ways of worship with Christianity.

Targumim. Plural of "targum" (i.e., targums), "translations," "interpretations." Aramaic paraphrases of portions of the Old Testament.

Tenet. A belief or teaching held to be true.

Textual criticism. The analysis of variations in the wordings of the Hebrew, Aramaic, and Greek manuscripts of the Bible to determine what the original wording must have been. Most of these variations are minor differences in spelling and word order.

Theodicy. "The justification of God." The vindication of God's love and providence in view of the sin, evil, and suffering in the world.

Theology. "The study of God." Also used as a general term for the study of all the teachings of the Bible.

Theonomism. The teaching that God's will and law are the ultimate moral authority. Others use the term to refer to a principle that fulfills a person's being by uniting it with God.

Torah. "Instruction," usually translated "Law"; usually refers to the Pentateuch, sometimes the whole Old Testament.

Traducianism. (Lat. *tradux*, "offshoot.") The theory that when human fertilization takes place the soul is transmitted from the parents along with the genes.

Transubstantiation. The Roman Catholic teaching that the bread and the wine of the Lord's Supper are changed into the real body and blood of Christ when the priest consecrates them. The fact that they still look and taste like bread and wine is termed an "accident," i.e., merely incidental.

Tribulation. (Gk. *thlipsis*, "pressure," "oppression," "affliction," "distress caused by circumstances.") Also used of the Great Tribulation at the end of the age when God's wrath is outpoured just preceding Christ's return in glory.

Trichotomism. The teaching that the human person consists of body, soul, and spirit.

Tritheism. The idea that the Father, Son, and Holy Spirit are three separate Gods or beings.

Types, figures, and shadows. Old Testament persons, events, or objects that foreshadow or anticipate New Testament truth, especially as relating to Jesus Christ.

Typology. The study of types.

Universalism. The teaching that all human beings, angels, and Satan himself will eventually be saved and enjoy God's love and presence forever.

Venial sin. In Roman Catholic theology, sin that is minor or that is committed without full reflection or intent and does not remove the person from God's grace and favor.

Verbal plenary inspiration. Full inspiration of the Scriptures right down to the words (of the autographs).

Waldensians. Peter Waldo started a religious movement (flourished 1170–76) that stressed poverty and simplicity, rejected purgatory and prayers for the dead, and refused to take civil oaths. They are still prominent in Italy.

Wesleyan. Refers to followers of the original teachings of John and Charles Wesley.

Xenolalia. The speaking in tongues in a known language that is unknown to the speaker.

Yahweh (Jehovah). The Hebrew personal name of God formed from the consonants YHWH, also written as JHVH. By putting the vowels for the Hebrew title "Lord" with these four consonants (after the eighth century A.D.), Jews were reminded to read "Lord" instead of attempting to pronounce the personal name of God. Thus the vowels put with JHVH become "JeHoVaH," in effect a word coined by translators from a personal name and a title.

Yahweh Nissi. A Hebrew term meaning "The Lord is my Banner [Flag]" (Exod. 17:15).

Yahweh Ropheka. A Hebrew term meaning "The Lord your [personal] Physician" (Exod. 15:26). Sometimes wrongly called Jehovah Rapha.

Yahweh Sabaoth. A Hebrew term meaning "The Lord of Hosts [Armies, including angels and stars]" (Rom. 9:29; James 5:4).

Yahweh Yireh. A Hebrew term meaning "The Lord will see and provide" (Gen. 22:14).

Zionist. A member of the movement attempting to return Jews to the land God promised them. Political Zionists were instrumental in helping to establish the modern state of Israel.

Selected Bibliography

GENERAL WORKS

Althaus, Paul. *The Theology of Martin Luther.* Translated by Robert C. Schultz. Philadelphia: Fortress Press, 1966.

Anchor Bible Dictionary. New York: Doubleday Pub. Co., 1992.

Balz, Horst, and Gerhard Schneider, eds. *Exegetical Dictionary of the New Testament.* Grand Rapids: Wm. B. Eerdmans, 1990.

Bancroft, Emery H. *Christian Theology.* Rev. Ed. Grand Rapids: Zondervan Publishing House, 1987.

Barth, Christoph. *God with Us.* Grand Rapids: Wm. B. Eerdmans, 1991.

Barth, Karl. *Church Dogmatics: Doctrines of Creation.* T. F. Torrance and Geoffrey W. Bromiley, eds. 4 Vols. Edingburgh: T. & T. Clark, 1960.

Bauer, Walter. *Greek-English Lexicon of the New Testament, and Other Early Christian Literature.* Translated by W. F. Arndt and F. W. Gingrich. Chicago: University of Chicago Press, 1979.

Berkhof, Louis. *Systematic Theology.* 4th Ed. Grand Rapids: Wm. B. Eerdmans, 1941.

Bloesch, Donald G. *Essentials of Evangelical Theology.* New York: Harper & Row, Publishers, 1978.

Botterweck, G. Johannes, and Helmer Ringgren, eds. *Theological Dictionary of the Old Testament.* 6 Vols. Grand Rapids: Wm. B. Eerdmans, 1974–90.

Braaten, Carl, and Robert W. Jensen, eds. *Christian Dogmatics.* Philadelphia: Fortress Press, 1984.

Bromiley, Geoffrey W. *Historical Theology.* Grand Rapids: Wm. B. Eerdmans, 1978.

―――――, ed. *The International Standard Bible Encyclopedia,* 4 Vols. Grand Rapids: Wm. B. Eerdmans, 1979–1988.

Brown, Colin, ed. *New International Dictionary of New Testament Theology.* 4 Vols. Grand Rapids: Zondervan Publishing House, 1975–86.

Brown, Francis, S. R. Driver, and Charles A. Briggs. *A Hebrew and English Lexicon to the Old Testament,* based on the lexicon of William Gesenius. Translated by Edward Robinson. Oxford: Oxford University, 1907.

Bultmann, Rudolf. *Theology of the New Testament.* Translated by Kendrick Grobel. New York: Charles Scribner's Sons, 1951.

Burgess, Stanley. M., Gary B. McGee, and Patrick Alexander, eds. *Dictionary of Pentecostal and Charismatic Movements.* Grand Rapids: Zondervan Publishing House, 1988.

Buswell, J. Oliver. *A Systematic Theology of the Christian Religion.* Grand Rapids: Zondervan Publishing House, 1972.

Buttrick, G. A., et al., eds. *Interpreter's Dictionary of the Bible.* Nashville: Abingdon Press, 1962.

Calvin, John. *Institutes of the Christian Religion.* John T. McNeill, ed. Philadelphia: The Westminster Press, 1973.

Carlson, G. Raymond. *Our Faith and Fellowship.* Springfield, Mo.: Gospel Publishing House, 1977.

Carter, Charles W., ed. *A Contemporary Wesleyan Theology.* 2 Vols. Grand Rapids: Zondervan Publishing House, 1983.

Chafer, Lewis. *Sperry Systematic Theology.* 8 Vols. Dallas: Dallas Theological Seminary, 1947.

Davis, John Jefferson. *Foundations of Evangelical Theology.* Grand Rapids: Baker Book House, 1984.

Dayton, Donald W. *Theological Roots of Pentecostalism.* Grand Rapids: Zondervan Publishing House, 1987.

Douglas, J. D., ed. *The New International Dictionary of the Christian Church.* Rev. Ed. Grand Rapids: Zondervan Publishing House, 1978.

Duffield, Guy P., and Nathaniel M. Van Cleave. *Foundations of Pentecostal Theology.* Los Angeles: Life Bible College, 1983.

Edwards, David L., and John Stott. *Evangelical Essentials.* Downers Grove, Ill.: InterVarsity Press, 1988.

Eichrodt, Walther. *Theology of the Old Testament.* Philadelphia: The Westminster Press, 1967.

Elwell, Walter A., ed. *Evangelical Dictionary of Theology.* Grand Rapids: Baker Book House, 1984.

Erickson, Millard J. *Christian Theology.* Grand Rapids: Baker Book House, 1985.

————. *Does It Matter What I Believe?* Grand Rapids: Baker Book House, 1992.

Ferguson, Everett. *Encyclopedia of Early Christianity.* New York: Garland Publishing Co., 1990.

Ferguson, Sinclair B., and David F. Wright, eds. *New Dictionary of Theology.* Downers Grove, Ill.: InterVarsity Press, 1988.

Gaster, Theodor H. *The Dead Sea Scriptures.* Garden City, N.Y.: Anchor Press, 1976.

Gilbrant, Thoralf, ed. *Complete Biblical Library.* 16 Vols. Springfield, Mo.: Complete Biblical Library, 1986–1991.

Girdlestone, Robert Baker. *Synonyms of the Old Testament.* Grand Rapids: Wm. B. Eerdmans, 1948.

Gonzalez, Justo L. *A History of Christian Thought.* 3 Vols. Nashville: Abingdon Press, 1970.

Green, J. B., and Scot McKnight, eds. *Dictionary of Jesus and the Gospels.* Downers Grove, Ill.: InterVarsity Press, 1992.

Harris, R. Laird, Gleason L. Archer, and Bruce K. Waltke, eds. *Theological Wordbook of the Old Testament.* 2 Vols. Chicago: Moody Press, 1980.

Harrison, Everett F., ed. *Baker's Dictionary of Theology.* Grand Rapids: Baker Book House, 1960.

Henry, Carl F. H. *Christian Faith and Modern Theology.* New York: Channel Press, 1964.

————. *God, Revelation, and Authority: God Who Speaks and Shows.* Waco, Tex.: Word Books, 1976–1983.

Hodge, Charles. *Systematic Theology.* 3 Vols. New York: Scribner's Sons, 1871–1872.

Jeremias, Joachim. *New Testament Theology: The Proclamation of Jesus.* Translated by J. Bowden. New York: Charles Scribner's Sons, 1971.

Kaiser, Walter C., Jr. *Toward an Old Testament Theology.* Grand Rapids: Zondervan Publishing House, 1978.

Kelly, J. N. *Early Christian Doctrines.* 2d. Ed. New York: Harper and Row Publishers, 1960.

Kittel, Gerhard, ed. *Theological Dictionary of the New Testament.* Translated by G. W. Bromiley. Grand Rapids: Wm. B. Eerdmans, 1964.

Ladd, George E. *A Theology of the New Testament.* Grand Rapids: Wm. B. Eerdmans, 1974.

Lightfoot, J. B. *The Apostolic Fathers.* Grand Rapids: Baker Book House, 1956.

Lightner, Robert P. *Evangelical Theology: A Survey and Review.* Grand Rapids: Baker Book House, 1986.

Louw, Johannes P., and Eugene A. Nida, eds. *Greek-English Lexicon of the New Testament based on Semantic Domains.* 2 Vols. New York: United Bible Societies, 1988.

McConnell, Dan R. *A Different Gospel.* Peabody, Mass.: Hendrickson Publishers, 1988.

Martens, Elmer A. *God's Design: A Focus on Old Testament Theology.* Grand Rapids: Baker Book House, 1981.

Menzies, William W., and Stanley M. Horton. *Bible Doctrines: A Pentecostal Perspective.* Springfield, Mo.: Logion Press, 1993.

Miley, John. *Systematic Theology.* 2 Vols. Peabody, Mass.: Hendrickson Publishers, 1989.

Muller, Richard A. *Post-Reformation Reformed Dogmatics.* Grand Rapids: Baker Book House, 1987.

Oden, Thomas C. *The Living God.* San Francisco: Harper & Row, 1987.

Pannenberg, Wolfhart. *An Introduction to Systematic Theology.* Grand Rapids: Wm. B. Eerdmans, 1991.

Pearlman, Myer. *Knowing the Doctrines of the Bible.* Springfield, Mo.: Gospel Publishing House, 1937.

Ridderbos, Herman. *Paul: An Outline of His Theology.* Grand Rapids: Wm. B. Eerdmans, 1975.

Schaeffer, Francis A. *The Complete Works of Francis Schaeffer.* 5 Vols. Wheaton, Ill.: Crossway Books, 1982.

Schaff, Phillip. *The Creeds of Christendom.* 3 Vols. New York: Harper, 1931.

Shedd, William G. T. *Dogmatic Theology.* 3 Vols. Grand Rapids: Zondervan Publishing House, 1992.

Spykman, Gordon J. *Reformational Theology.* Grand Rapids: Wm B. Eerdmans, 1992.

Stamps, Donald, ed. *The Full Life Study Bible.* Grand Rapids: Zondervan Publishing House, 1992.

Strong, Augustus H. *Systematic Theology.* Philadelphia: Judson Press, 1947.

Thayer, Joseph Henry. *Greek-English Lexicon of the New Testament.* Grand Rapids: Zondervan Publishing House, 1976.

Thielicke, Helmut. *The Evangelical Faith.* 3 Vols. Translated by Geoffrey W. Bromiley, Grand Rapids: Wm. B. Eerdmans, 1974.

Thiessen, Henry C. *Lectures in Systematic Theology.* Grand Rapids: Wm. B. Eerdmans, 1979.

Trench, Richard C. *Synonyms of the New Testament.* Grand Rapids: Wm. B. Eerdmans, 1983.

Van Til, Cornelius. *An Introduction to Systematic Theology.* Phillipsburg, N.J.: Presbyterian and Reformed Publishing Co., 1978.

Vine, W. E., Merrill F. Unger, and William White, eds. *An Expository Dictionary of Biblical Words.* Nashville: Thomas Nelson, 1984.

Warfield, Benjamin B. *The Inspiration and Authority of the Bible.* Philadelphia: The Presbyterian and Reformed Publishing Co., 1970.

Wenham, John W. *Christ and the Bible.* Downers Grove, Ill.: InterVarsity Press, 1973.

Where We Stand. Springfield, Mo.: Gospel Publishing House, 1990.

Wiley, H. Orton. *Christian Theology.* 3 Vols. Kansas City, Mo.: Beacon Hill Press, 1940.

Williams, Ernest S. *Systematic Theology.* 3 Vols. Springfield, Mo.: Gospel Publishing House, 1953.

Williams, J. Rodman. *Renewal Theology.* 3 Vols. Grand Rapids: Zondervan Publishing House, 1988–92.

Williams, Robert R. *A Guide to the Teachings of the Early Church Fathers.* Grand Rapids: Wm. B. Eerdmans, 1960.

Wynkoop, Mildred Bangs. *A Theology of Love.* Kansas City, Mo.: Beacon Hill Press, 1972.

CHAPTER 1

Dayton, Donald W. *Theological Roots of Pentecostalism.* Metuchen, N.J.: Scarecrow Press, 1987.

Goff, James R., Jr. *Fields White Unto Harvest: Charles F. Parham and the Missionary Origins of Pentecostalism.* Fayetteville, Ark.: University of Arkansas Press, 1988.

McDonnell, Killian, and George T. Montague. *Christian Initiation and Baptism in the Holy Spirit.* Collegeville, Minn.: Liturgical Press, 1991.

McGee, Gary B., ed. *Initial Evidence: Historical and Biblical Perspectives on the Pentecostal Doctrine of Spirit Baptism.* Peabody, Mass.: Hendrickson Publishers, 1991.

————. *This Gospel Shall Be Preached.* 2 Vols. Springfield, Mo.: Gospel Publishing House, 1986, 1989.

Nienkirchen, Charles W. *A. B. Simpson and the Pentecostal Movement.* Peabody, Mass.: Hendrickson Publishers, 1992.

Woodbridge, John D., and Thomas E. McComiskey, eds. *Doing*

Theology in Today's World. Grand Rapids: Zondervan Publishing House, 1991.

CHAPTER 2

Barr, James. "Biblical Theology." In Supplementary Volume. *The Interpreter's Dictionary of the Bible.* New York: Abingdon Press, 1976, 104–111.

Carson, D. C. "Unity and Diversity in the New Testament: The Possibility of Systematic Theology." In *Scripture and Truth.* Grand Rapids: Zondervan Publishing House, 1983, 65–95.

Fee, Gordon. *Gospel and Spirit: Issues in New Testament Hermeneutics.* Peabody, Mass.: Hendrickson Publishers, 1991.

Hasel, Gerhard. *New Testament Theology: Basic Issues in the Current Debate.* Grand Rapids: Wm. B. Eerdmans, 1978.

Kee, Howard C. *Knowing the Truth: A Sociological Approach to New Testament Interpretation.* Minneapolis: Fortress Press, 1989.

Malina, Bruce. *The Social World of Luke Acts.* ed. Jerome H. Neyreys. Peabody, Mass.: Hendrickson Publishers, 1991.

McKnight, Scot. *Interpreting the Synoptic Gospels.* Grand Rapids: Baker Book House, 1988.

———. *Introduction to New Testament Interpretation.* Grand Rapids: Baker Book House, 1989.

Menzies, William. "Review of *Gospel and Spirit: Issues in New Testament Hermeneutics,* by Gordon Fee." *Paraclete* 27 (Winter 1993): 29–32.

Ollenburger, Ben C., Elmer A. Martens, and Gerhard F. Hasel, eds. *The Flowering of Old Testament Theology.* Winona Lake, Ind.: Eisenbrauns, 1992.

Osborne, Grant R. *The Hermeneutical Spiral: A Comprehensive Introduction to Biblical Interpretation.* Downers Grove, Ill.: InterVarsity Press, 1991.

Parsons, Mikeal C. "Canonical Criticism." In *New Testament Criticism & Interpretation,* eds. David Alan Black and David S. Dockery. Grand Rapids: Zondervan Publishing House, 1991, 255–294.

Stendahl, Krister. "Contemporary Biblical Theology." In *The Interpreter's Dictionary of the Bible.* Vol. 1. George A. Buttrick, ed. New York: Abingdon Press, 1962, 418–32.

Stronstad, Roger. *The Charismatic Theology of St. Luke.* Peabody, Mass.: Hendrickson Publishers, 1984.

Tate, W. R. *Biblical Interpretation: An Integrated Approach.* Peabody, Mass.: Hendrickson Publishers, 1991.

Thiselton, Anthony C. *New Horizons in Hermeneutics.* Grand Rapids: Zondervan Publishing House, 1992.

CHAPTER 3

Boice, James M. *The Foundations of Biblical Authority.* Grand Rapids: Zondervan Publishing House, 1978.

Bright, John. *The Authority of the Old Testament.* Nashville: Abingdon Press, 1967.

Bromiley, Geoffrey W. "The Inspiration and Authority of Scripture." *Eternity* (August 1970): 18.

Bruce, F. F. *The Books and the Parchments.* Rev. Ed. West-wood, N.J.: Fleming H. Revell, 1963.

Demarest, Bruce A. *General Revelation: Historical Views and Contemporary Issues.* Grand Rapids: Zondervan Publishing House, 1982.

Geisler, Norman, ed. *Inerrancy.* Grand Rapids: Zondervan Publishing House, 1979.

Henry, Carl F. H. *God, Revelation, and Authority.* Waco, Tex.: Word Books, 1976.

Ladd, George. *The New Testament and Criticism.* Grand Rapids: Wm. B. Eerdmans, 1967.

Lloyd-Jones, Martyn. *Authority.* London: InterVarsity Fellowship, 1958.

McDonald, Lee Martin. *The Formation of the Christian Biblical Canon.* Nashville: Abingdon Press, 1988.

McKim, Donald K., ed. *The Authoritative Word.* Grand Rapids: Wm. B. Eerdmans, 1983.

Metzger, Bruce M. *The Canon of the New Testament.* Oxford: Clarendon Press, 1987.

Montgomery, John Warwick, ed. *God's Inerrant Word.* Minneapolis, Minn.: Bethany Fellowship, 1974.

Noll, Mark A., ed. *The Princeton Theology 1812–1921.* Grand Rapids: Baker Book House, 1983.

Pinnock, Clark H. *Biblical Revelation—The Foundation of Christian Theology.* Chicago: Moody Press, 1971.

CHAPTER 4

Albright, W. F., "El and Yahweh," *Journal of Semitic Studies,* 1:25–37.

Bavinck, Herman. *The Doctrine of God.* Carlisle, Pa.: Banner of Truth Trust, 1951.

Gruenler, Royce Gordon. *The Inexhaustible God: Biblical*

Faith and the Challenge of Process Theism. Grand Rapids: Baker Book House, 1983.

Kaiser, Christopher B. *The Doctrine of God: An Historical Survey.* Westchester, Ill.: Crossway Books, 1982.

Packer, J. I. *Knowing God.* Downers Grove, Ill.: InterVarsity Press, 1973.

CHAPTER 5

Brown, Harold O. J. *Heresies: The Image of Christ in the Mirror of Heresy and Orthodoxy from the Apostles to the Present.* Garden City, N.Y.: Doubleday & Co., Inc., 1984.

Christian Research Institute. *The "Jesus Only" or "Oneness" Pentecostal Movement.* San Juan Capistrano, Calif.: The Christian Research Institute, 1970.

Kelly, J. N. D. *Early Christian Creeds.* London: Longmans, 1950.

Lewis, C. S. *God in the Dock: Essays on Theology and Ethics.* Grand Rapids: Wm. B. Eerdmans, 1970.

Montgomery, John Warwick. *How Do We Know There Is a God?* Minneapolis: Bethany House Publishers, 1973.

_____. *Principalities and Powers: The World of the Occult.* Minneapolis: Pyramid Publication for Bethany Fellowship, Inc., 1975.

_____. *The Suicide of Christian Theology.* Minneapolis: Bethany Fellowship Inc., 1970.

Sproul, R. C. *The Holiness of God.* Wheaton, Ill.: Tyndale House Publishers, 1985.

Wood, Nathan R. *The Trinity in the Universe.* Grand Rapids: Kregel Publications, 1978 reprint from 1955.

CHAPTER 6

Blumhardt's Battle: A Conflict with Satan. Translated by F. S. Boshold. New York: Thomas E. Lowe, 1970.

Bundrick, David R. *"TA STOICHEIA TOU COSMOU (GAL 4:3)."* *Journal of the Evangelical Theological Society* (September 1991): 353–64.

Caird, G. B. *Principalities and Powers, a Study in Pauline Theology.* Oxford: Clarendon Press, 1956.

Davidson, Gustav. *The Dictionary of Angels: Including the Fallen.* New York: Free Press, 1972.

Dickason, C. Fred. *Angels: Elect and Evil.* Chicago: Moody Press, 1975.

Godwin, Malcolm. *Angels: Endangered Species.* New York: Simon & Schuster, 1990.

Guelich, Robert A. "Spiritual Warfare: Jesus, Paul, and Peretti." *Pneuma* (Spring 1991): 33–64.

Montgomery, J. W., ed. *Demon Possession, a Medical, Historical, Anthropological, and Theological Symposium.* Minneapolis: Bethany Fellowship, 1976.

Reddin, Opal, ed. *Power Encounter: A Pentecostal Perspective.* Springfield, Mo.: Central Bible College Press, 1989.

Russell, Jeffrey B. *Satan, the Early Christian Tradition.* Ithaca, N.Y.: Cornell University Press, 1981.

Ward, Theodora. *Men & Angels.* New York: Viking Press, 1969.

CHAPTER 7

Custance, Arthur C. *Without Form and Void: A Study of the Meaning of Genesis 1:2.* Brockville, Ontario: Doorway Papers, 1970.

Davis, P., and D. H. Kenyon. *Of Pandas and People: The Central Question of Biological Origins.* Dallas: Haughton Publishing Co., 1989.

Dillow, J. C. *The Waters Above: Earth's Pre-Flood Vapor Canopy.* 2d. Ed. Chicago: Moody Press, 1982.

Fields, W. W. *Unformed and Unfilled: A Critique of the Gap Theory.* Phillipsburg, N.J.: Presbyterian and Reformed Publishing Co., 1976.

Gentry, R. V. *Creation's Tiny Mystery.* Knoxville, Tenn.: Earth Science Associates, 1986.

Harris, R. L. *Man—God's Eternal Creation: Old Testament Teaching on Man and His Culture.* Chicago: Moody Press, 1971.

House, H. Wayne. "Creation and Redemption: A Study of Kingdom Interplay." *Journal of the Evangelical Theological Society* 35 (March 1992), 3–17.

Moreland, J. P. *Christianity and the Nature of Science.* Grand Rapids: Baker Book House, 1989.

Morris, H. M. *The Biblical Basis of Modern Science.* Grand Rapids: Baker Book House, 1984.

Morris, Henry M., and Gary E. Parker. *What Is Creation Science?* Rev. Ed. San Diego: Creation-Life Publishers, Inc., 1982.

Muller, R. A. *God, Creation, and Providence in the Thought of Jacob Arminius.* Grand Rapids: Baker Book House, 1991.

Newman, R. C., and Eckelmann, H. J., Jr. *Genesis One and the Origin of the Earth.* Grand Rapids: Baker Book House, 1981.

Pun, P. P. T. *Evolution: Nature & Scripture in Conflict?* Grand Rapids: Zondervan Publishing House, 1982.

Ramm, Bernard. *The Christian View of Science and Scripture.* Grand Rapids: Wm. B. Eerdmans, 1954.

Van Til, Howard J., Davis A. Young, and Clarence Menninga. *Science Held Hostage: What's Wrong with Creation Science AND Evolutionism.* Downer's Grove, Ill.: InterVarsity Press, 1988.

Waltke, Bruce K. "The Literary Genre of Genesis, Chapter One." *Crux* (December 1991), 3–5.

Whitcomb, J. C., and H. M. Morris. *The Genesis Flood: The Biblical Record and Its Scientific Implications.* Phillipsburg, N.J.: Presbyterian and Reformed Publishing Company, 1961.

Wonderly, Dan. *God's Time-Records in Ancient Sediments: Evidence of Long Time Spans in Earth's History.* Flint, Mich.: Crystal Press, 1977.

CHAPTER 8

Berkouwer, G.C. *Sin.* Translated by Philip C. Holtrop.Grand Rapids: Wm. B. Eerdmans, 1971.

Brunner, Emil. *Man in Revolt, A Christian Anthropology.* Translated by Olive Wyon. London: Lutterworth, 1939.

Ramm, Bernard. *Offense to Reason.* San Francisco: Harper & Row, 1985.

CHAPTER 9

Beasley-Murray, George R., *Baptism in the New Testament.* London: MacMillan, 1963.

_____*Jesus and the Kingdom of God.* Grand Rapids: Wm. B. Eerdmans, 1986.

Bornkamm, Günther, *Jesus of Nazareth.* Translated by F. Mcluskey with J. M. Robinson. New York: Harper, 1960.

Collins, John J. "The Son of Man and the Saints of the Most High in the Book of Daniel." *Journal of Biblical Literature* 93 (1974): 50–66.

Cullmann, Oscar. *The Christology of the New Testament.* Translated by S. Guthrie and C. Hall. Philadelphia: Westminster Press, 1959.

Dahl, Nils Alstrup. "The Problem of the Historical Jesus." In *The Crucified Messiah and Other Essays.* Minneapolis: Augsburg Publishing, 1974, 48–49.

Dawe, Donald G. *The Form of a Servant: A Historical Analysis of the Kenotic Motif.* Philadelphia: Westminster Press, 1963.

Dodd, Charles H. *The Founder of Christianity.* New York: Macmillan Publishing, 1970.

Dunn, James. *Christology in the Making: A New Testament Inquiry into the Origins of the Doctrine of the Incarnation.* Philadelphia: Westminster Press, 1980.

Erickson, Millard J. *The Word Became Flesh.* Grand Rapids: Baker Book House, 1991.

Fuller, Reginald. *The Foundations of New Testament Christology.* New York: Collins, 1965.

Knox, John. *The Humanity and Divinity of Christ: A Study of Pattern in Christology.* Cambridge: Cambridge University Press, 1967.

Ladd, George, "The Christology of Acts," *Foundations* 11 (1968): 27–41.

Lafferty, O. J., "Acts 2,14–36: A Study in Christology," *Dunwoodie Review* 6 (1966): 235–53.

Moltmann, Jürgen, *The Crucified God.* Translated by R. A. Wilson. New York: Harper & Row, 1973.

Moule, C. F. D., "The Manhood of Jesus in the New Testament." In *Christ, Faith, and History.* Cambridge: Cambridge University Press, 1972.

Norris, Richard, Jr., ed. *The Christological Controversy.* Philadelphia: Fortress Press, 1980.

Ramsey, William. *The Christ of the Earliest Christians.* Richmond: John Knox Press, 1959.

Stott, John, R. W. *The Cross of Christ.* Downers Grove, Ill.: InterVarsity Press, 1986.

CHAPTER 10

Berkouwer, G. C. *The Work of Christ.* Grand Rapids: Wm. B. Eerdmans, 1975.

Hill, D. *Greek Words and Hebrew Meanings: Studies in the Semantics of Soteriological Terms.* Society for New Testament Studies Monograph Series, 1967.

Klein, William W. *The New Chosen People: A Corporate View of Election.* Grand Rapids: Zondervan Publishing House, 1990.

McGrath, Alister E. *The Mystery of the Cross.* Grand Rapids: Zondervan Publishing House, 1988.

Marshall, I. Howard. *Kept by the Power of God: A Study of Perseverance and Falling Away.* Minneapolis: Bethany Fellowship, Inc., 1969.

Pinnock, Clark H., ed. *The Grace of God, The Will of Man.* Grand Rapids: Zondervan Publishing House, 1989.

Shank, Robert. *Elect in the Son.* Springfield, Mo.: Westcott

Publishers, 1970; Reprint, Minneapolis: Bethany House Publishers, 1989.

_____. *Life in the Son.* 2d. ed. Springfield, Mo.: Westcott Publishers, 1961.

Stohlmacher, Peter. "Reconciliation in the Preaching and Work of Jesus." *Theology News and Notes* 32 (March 1985): 4–8.

CHAPTER 11

Burgess, Stanley. *The Spirit and the Church: Antiquity.* Peabody, Mass.: Hendrickson Publishers, Inc., 1984.

Horton, Stanley M. *What the Bible Says About the Holy Spirit.* Springfield, Mo.: Gospel Publishing House, 1976.

McLean, Mark D. "Toward a Pentecostal Hermeneutic." *Pneuma* 6 (Fall 1984), 35–56.

Muhlen, Heribert. *A Charismatic Theology.* New York: Paulist Press, 1978.

Stronstad, Roger, and Lawrence Van Kleek, eds. *The Holy Spirit in the Scriptures and the Church.* Clayburn, B.C., Canada: Western Pentecostal Bible College, 1987.

CHAPTER 12

Blumhofer, Edith L. *The Assemblies of God: A Chapter in the Story of American Pentecostalism.* 2 Vols. Springfield, Mo.: Gospel Publishing House, 1989.

Dieter, Melvin E., et al. *Five Views on Sanctification.* Grand Rapids: Zondervan Publishing House, 1987.

Flew, R. Newton. *The Idea of Perfection in Christian Theology: An Historical Study of the Christian Ideal for the Present Life.* New York: Humanities Press, 1968.

Procksch, O., and K. G. Kuhn. *"hagios,"* etc. *Theological Dictionary of the New Testament.* Grand Rapids: Wm. B. Eerdmans, 1974, 88–114.

CHAPTER 13

Atter, Gordon F. *The Third Force.* Peterborough, Ont.: The College Press, 1965.

Barclay, William. *The Promise of the Spirit.* Philadelphia: Westminster Press, 1960.

Bruce, F. F. *Commentary on the Book of Acts.* Grand Rapids: Wm. B. Eerdmans, 1966.

Bruner, Frederick D. *A Theology of the Holy Spirit: The*

Pentecostal Experience and the New Testament Witness. Grand Rapids: Wm. B. Eerdmans, 1970.

Dunn, James D. G. *Baptism in the Holy Spirit.* London: SCM Press, 1970.

Ervin, Howard M. *Conversion-Initiation and the Baptism in the Holy Spirit.* Peabody, Mass.: Hendrickson Publishers, 1984.

————. *Spirit Baptism: A Biblical Investigation.* Peabody, Mass.: Hendrickson Publishers, 1987.

Fee, Gordon D. *Gospel and Spirit: Issues in New Testament Hermeneutics.* Peabody, Mass.: Hendrickson Publishers, 1991.

Gee, Donald. *Pentecost.* Springfield, Mo.: Gospel Publishing House, 1932).

————. *Spiritual Gifts in the Work of the Ministry Today.* Springfield, Mo.: Gospel Publishing House, 1963.

Hoekema, Anthony A. *Holy Spirit Baptism.* Grand Rapids: Wm. B. Eerdmans, 1972.

Hollenweger, W. J. *The Pentecostals.* Peabody, Mass.: Hendrickson Publishers, 1972.

Horton, Stanley M. *The Book of Acts.* Springfield, Mo.: Gospel Publishing House, 1981.

————. *What the Bible Says About the Holy Spirit.* Springfield, Mo.: Gospel Publishing House, 1976.

McGee, Gary B., ed. *Initial Evidence: Historical and Biblical Perspectives on the Pentecostal Doctrine of Spirit Baptism.* Peabody, Mass.: Hendrickson Publishers, 1991.

Marshall, I. Howard. *Luke: Historian and Theologian.* Enl. Ed. Grand Rapids: Zondervan Publishing House, 1970.

Menzies, Robert P. "The Distinctive Character of Luke's Pneumatology." *Paraclete* 25 (Fall 1991): 17–30.

Stott, John R. W. *The Baptism and the Fullness of the Holy Spirit.* Downers Grove, Ill.: InterVarsity, 1964.

Stronstad, Roger. *The Charismatic Theology of St. Luke.* Peabody, Mass.: Hendrickson Publishers, 1984.

————. "The Hermeneutics of Lucan Historiography." *Paraclete* 22 (Fall 1988): 5–17.

————. "The Holy Spirit in Luke-Acts." *Paraclete* 23 (Spring 1989): 18–26.

Womack, David A., ed. *Pentecostal Experience: The Writings of Donald Gee.* Springfield, Mo.: Gospel Publishing House, 1993.

CHAPTER 14

Carson, Donald A. *Showing the Spirit: A Theological Exposition of 1 Corinthians 12–14.* Grand Rapids: Baker Book House, 1987.

Carter, Charles W. *1 Corinthians.* The Wesleyan Bible Commentary Series. Peabody, Mass.: Hendrickson Publishers, 1986.

Carter, Howard. *Spiritual Gifts and Their Operation.* Springfield, Mo.: Gospel Publishing House, 1968.

Chapman, R. B. "The Purpose and Value of Spiritual Gifts." *Paraclete* 2 (Fall 1968): 24–28.

Fee, Gordon D. *The Epistle to the First Corinthians.* The New International Commentary on the New Testament. Grand Rapids: Wm. B. Eerdmans, 1987.

Gee, Donald. *Concerning Spiritual Gifts.* Springfield, Mo.: Gospel Publishing House, 1949.

_____. *Spiritual Gifts in the Work of the Ministry Today.* Springfield, Mo.: Gospel Publishing House, 1963.

Grudem, Wayne. *The Gift of Prophecy in the New Testament and Today.* Westchester, Ill.: Crossway Books, Good News Publishers, 1988.

Holdcroft. L. Thomas. *The Holy Spirit: A Pentecostal Interpretation.* Springfield, Mo.: Gospel Publishing House, 1979.

Horton, Harold. *The Gifts of the Spirit.* Springfield, Mo.: Gospel Publishing House, 1975.

Horton, Stanley M. *What the Bible Says About the Holy Spirit.* Springfield, Mo.: Gospel Publishing House, 1976.

Lim, David. *Spiritual Gifts: A Fresh Look.* Springfield, Mo.: Gospel Publishing House, 1991.

Martin, Walter. *The Spirit and the Congregation: Studies in 1 Corinthians 12–15.* Grand Rapids: Wm. B. Eerdmans, 1984.

Richardson, William. "Liturgical Order and Glossolalia in 1 Corinthians 14:26c–33a." *New Testament Studies* 32 (January 1986): 144–53.

Stronstad, Roger. *The First Epistle of Peter.* Vancouver, B.C.: CLM Educational Society, 1983.

Turner, Max M. B. "Spiritual Gifts Then and Now." *Vox Evangelica* 15 (1985): 7–64.

Womack, David A., ed. *Pentecostal Experience: The Writings of Donald Gee.* Springfield, Mo.: Gospel Publishing House, 1993.

CHAPTER 15

Baxter, J. Sidlow. *Divine Healing of the Body.* Grand Rapids: Zondervan Publishing House, 1979.

Blue, Ken. *Authority to Heal,* Downers Grove, Ill.: InterVarsity Press, 1987.

Brown, Colin. *Miracles and the Critical Mind.* Grand Rapids: Wm. B. Eerdmans, 1984.

―――――. *That You May Believe: Miracles and Faith Then and Now.* Grand Rapids: Wm. B. Eerdmans, 1985.

Carson, D. A. *How Long, O Lord? Reflections on Suffering and Evil.* Grand Rapids: Baker Book House, 1990.

Fee, Gordon. *The Disease of the Health and Wealth Gospels.* Beverly, Mass.: Frontline Publishing, 1985.

Hall, Douglas John. *God and Human Suffering.* Minneapolis: Augsburg Publishing House, 1986.

Harper, Michael. *The Healings of Jesus.* Downers Grove, Ill.: InterVarsity Press, 1986.

Hendrickx, Herman. *The Miracle Stories.* San Francisco: Harper & Row, 1987.

Jeter, Hugh. *By His Stripes.* Springfield, Mo.: Gospel Publishing House, 1977.

Kee, Howard Clark. *Medicine, Miracle and Magic in New Testament Times.* New York: Cambridge University Press, 1986.

Kydd, Ronald. *Charismatic Gifts in the Early Church.* Peabody, Mass.: Hendrickson Publishers, 1987.

Latourelle, Rene. *The Miracles of Jesus and the Theology of Miracles.* New York: Paulist Press, 1988.

McConnell, D. R. *A Different Gospel: A Historical and Biblical Analysis of the Modern Faith Movement.* Peabody, Mass.: Hendrickson Publishers, 1988.

Mayhue, Richard. *Divine Healing Today.* Chicago: Moody Press, 1983.

Reddin, Opal L., ed. *Power Encounters: A Pentecostal Perspective.* Springfield, Mo.: Central Bible College Press, 1989.

Seybold, Klaus, and Ulrich B. Mueller. *Sickness and Healing.* Nashville: Abingdon Press, 1981.

Warfield, B. B. *Counterfeit Miracles.* London: The Banner of Truth Trust, 1918.

CHAPTER 16

Beasley-Murray, G. R. *Baptism Today and Tomorrow.* New York: St. Martin's, 1966.

Bonhoeffer, Dietrich. *The Cost of Discipleship.* 2d Ed. New York: The Macmillan Company, 1959.

Burgess, Stanley M. *The Spirit and the Church: Antiquity.* Peabody, Mass.: Hendrickson Publishers, 1984.

Cole, Alan. *The Body of Christ.* London: Hodder & Stoughton, 1964.

Flemington, W. F. *The New Testament Doctrine of Baptism.* London: S. P. C. K., 1964.

Jeremias, Joachim. *Infant Baptism in the First Four Centuries.* London: SCM Press, 1960.

Kuiper, R. B. *The Glorious Body of Christ.* Grand Rapids: Wm. B. Eerdmans, n.d.

Ladd, George E. *Jesus and the Kingdom.* New York: Harper & Row, 1964.

Martin, Ralph P. *Worship in the Early Church.* Grand Rapids: Wm. B. Eerdmans, 1964.

Minear, Paul S. *Images of the Church in the New Testament.* Philadelphia: Westminster, 1960.

Moltmann, Jürgen. *The Church in the Power of the Spirit.* London: SCM Press, 1977.

Moody, Dale. *Baptism: Foundation for Christian Unity.* Philadelphia: Westminster, 1967.

Sanders, John. *No Other Name: An Investigation into the Destiny of the Unevangelized.* Grand Rapids: Wm. B. Eerdmans, 1992.

Saucy, Robert L. *The Church in God's Program.* Chicago: Moody Press, 1972.

Welch, Claude. *The Reality of the Church.* New York: Charles Scribner's Sons, 1958.

CHAPTER 17

Anderson, Ray S. "A Theology for Ministry." In *Theological Foundations for Ministry.* ed. Ray Anderson. Grand Rapids: Wm. B. Eerdmans, 1979, 6–7.

Bittlinger, Arnold. "The Significance of Charismatic Experiences for the Mission of the Church" *International Review of Mission* 75 (1986): 117–122.

Boer, Harry R. *Pentecostals and Missions.* Grand Rapids: Wm. B. Eerdmans, 1961.

Costas, Orlando E. *The Integrity of Mission.* San Francisco: Harper and Row, 1979.

Dempster, Murray W. "Evangelism, Social Concern and the Kingdom of God." In *Called and Empowered,* ed. Murray

Dempster, Byron Klaus, and Douglas Petersen. Peabody, Mass.: Hendrickson Publishers, 1991, 30–31.

Fee, Gordon D. *Gospel and Spirit: Issues in New Testament Hermeneutics.* Peabody, Mass.: Hendrickson Publishers, 1991.

Frodsham, Stanley H. *With Signs Following.* Springfield, Mo.: Gospel Publishing House, 1946.

Hedlund, Roger E. *The Mission of the Church in the World.* Grand Rapids: Baker Book House, 1991.

Hodges, Melvin L. "A Pentecostal's View of Mission Strategy," *The Conciliar-Evangelical Debate: The Crucial Documents, 1964–76.* 2d ed. Donald McGavran, ed. South Pasadena, Calif.: William Carey Library, 1977, 142–49.

————. *A Theology of the Church and Its Ministry: A Pentecostal Perspective.* Springfield, Mo.: Gospel Publishing House, 1977.

Klaus, Byron D. "A Theology of Ministry: Pentecostal Perspectives." *Paraclete* 23 (Summer 1989): 1–10.

MacDonald, William. "Pentecostal Theology: A Classical Viewpoint." In *Perspectives on the New Pentecostalism,* ed. Russell P. Spittler. Grand Rapids: Baker Book House, 1976, 59–74.

McClung, L. Grant, Jr. "Truth on Fire: Pentecostals and an Urgent Missiology." In *Azusa Street and Beyond,* ed. L. Grant McClung, Jr. South Plainfield, N.J.: Bridge Publishing, Inc., 1986, 47–61.

McGee, Gary B. *This Gospel Shall Be Preached.* Vol. 1, Springfield, Mo.: Gospel Publishing House, 1986.

Moltmann, Jürgen. *The Church in the Power of the Spirit.* London: SCM Press Ltd., 1977.

Ogden, Greg. *The New Reformation: Returning the Ministry to the People of God.* Grand Rapids: Zondervan Publishing House, 1990.

Pate, Larry. *From Every People.* Monrovia, Calif.: MARC, 1989.

Senior, Donald, and Carroll Stuhlmueller. *The Biblical Foundation for Mission.* Maryknoll, N.Y.: Orbis Books, 1983.

Shelton, James S. *Mighty in Word and Deed.* Peabody, Mass.: Hendrickson Publishers, 1991.

Torrance, T. F. "The Mission of the Church" *Scottish Journal of Theology* 19 (June 1966): 129–43.

Van Engen, Charles. *God's Missionary People: Rethinking the Purpose of the Local Church.* Grand Rapids: Baker Book House, 1991.

Verkuyl, Johannes. "The Biblical Foundation for the Worldwide Missions Mandate." In *Perspectives on the World*

Christian Movement, Steven C. Hawthorne and Ralph D. Winter, eds. Pasadena: Institute of International Studies, 1981, 35–50.

CHAPTER 18

Beasley-Murray, George Raymond. *Jesus and the Future: An Examination of the Criticism of the Eschatological Discourse.* London: Macmillan & Co. Ltd., 1954.

Berkhof, Hendrikus. *Well-Founded Hope.* Richmond, Va.: John Knox Press, 1969.

Blaising, Craig A., and Darrell L. Bock, eds. *Dispensationalism, Israel and the Church: The Search for Definition.* Grand Rapids: Zondervan Publishing House, 1992.

Blamires, Henry. "The Eternal Weight of Glory." *Christianity Today* 35 (27 May 1991), 30–34.

Boettner, Loraine. *Immortality.* Philadelphia: The Presbyterian and Reformed Publishing Co. 1956.

Buis, Harry. *The Doctrine of Eternal Punishment.* Philadelphia: Presbyterian and Reformed Publishing Co., 1957.

Charles, R. H. *A Critical History of the Doctrine of a Future Life: In Israel, in Judaism, and in Christianity.* 2d Ed. London: Adam and Charles Black, 1913.

Clouse, Robert G. *The Meaning of the Millennium: Four Views.* Downers Grove, Ill.: InterVarsity Press, 1977.

Crockett, William, ed. *Four Views on Hell.* Grand Rapids: Zondervan Publishing House, 1992.

Finger, Thomas N. *Christian Theology: An Eschatological Approach.* Vol. 1. Nashville: Thomas Nelson Publishers, 1985.

Hamilton, Neill Quinn. *The Holy Spirit and Eschatology in Paul: Scottish Journal of Theology Occasional Papers No. 6.* Edinburgh: Oliver and Boyd Ltd., 1957.

Horton, Stanley M. *The Ultimate Victory.* Springfield, Mo.: Gospel Publishing House, 1991.

————. *Welcome Back Jesus.* Springfield, Mo.: Gospel Publishing House, 1967.

Johnson, Christopher J., and Marsha G. McGee, eds. *How Different Religions View Death and Afterlife.* Philadelphia: The Charles Press, Publishers, 1991.

Ladd, George Eldon. *The Last Things: An Eschatology for Laymen.* Grand Rapids: Wm. B. Eerdmans, 1978.

Marshall, I. H. *Eschatology and the Parables.* London: Theological Students' Fellowship, 1973.

Moltmann, Jürgen. *Theology of Hope: On the Ground and*

the Implications of a Christian Eschatology. Translated by James W. Leitch. New York: Harper & Row, 1967.

Moody, Dale. *The Hope of Glory.* Grand Rapids: Wm. B. Eerdmans, 1964.

Pentecost, J. Dwight. *Things to Come.* Grand Rapids: Zondervan Publishing House, 1958.

Smith, Wilbur M. *The Biblical Doctrine of Heaven.* Chicago: Moody Press, 1968.

Travis, Stephen. *I Believe in the Second Coming of Christ.* Grand Rapids: Wm. B. Eerdmans, 1982.

_____. *The Jesus Hope.* Downers Grove, Ill.: InterVarsity Press, 1976.

Vos, Geerhardus. *The Pauline Eschatology.* Grand Rapids: Wm. B. Eerdmans, 1972.

Wallis, Wilber B. "Eschatology and Social Concern" *Journal of the Evangelical Theological Society* 24 (March 1981): 3–9.

Walvoord, John F. *The Rapture Question.* Grand Rapids: Zondervan Publishing House, 1972.

Scripture Index

NEW TESTAMENT

Subject Index